Recently, I have begun reading the published accounts of the JFK medical evidence taken from numerous interviews given by me over the last thirty plus years. I have always felt that the information in these interviews was published with somewhat of a slant to support the supposition of the publishing author. This is not to say that the published facts were all wrong, but that the presentation of these facts was directed toward conclusions that were not the intended of my given interviews.

After reading *IN THE EYE OF HISTORY*, I find that the interview I gave to this author was presented without bias to support personal suppositions or conclusions.

I also found the remainder of this book to be informative and interesting. The book seems to treat the interviews as intended by those interviewed.

I would like to thank the author for his efforts to present the material as it was related to him and to leave any suppositions and conclusions to the reader.

James C. Jenkins
– Navy medical corpsman who assisted with
the JFK autopsy at Bethesda, 11/22/63

IN THE EYE OF HISTORY

Disclosures in the
JFK Assassination
Medical Evidence

WILLIAM MATSON LAW

Published by:
Trine Day LLC
PO Box 577
Walterville, OR 97489
1-800-556-2012
www.TrineDay.com
publisher@TrineDay.net

Library of Congress Control Number: 2015953663

Law, William Matson.
In The Eye of History: Disclosures in the JFK Assassination Medical Evidence –
1st ed.
p. cm.

Epud (ISBN-13) 978-1-63424-047-5
Mobi (ISBN-13) 978-1-63424-048-2
Print (ISBN-13) 978-1-63424-046-8
1. Kennedy, John F. -- (John Fitzgerald), -- 1917-1963 -- Assassination. 2. Autopsy. 3. Death -- Causes. 4. Medical jurisprudence. I. Law, William Matson. II. Title

Second Edition
10 9 8 7 6 5 4 3 2 1

Printed in the USA
Distribution to the Trade by:
Independent Publishers Group (IPG)
814 North Franklin Street
Chicago, Illinois 60610
312.337.0747
www.ipgbook.com

To the family

I Have A Rendezvous With Death

At some disputed barricade,
When Spring comes back with rustling shade
And apple-blossoms fill the air –
I have a rendezvous with Death
When Spring brings back blue days and fair.
It may be he shall take my hand
And lead me into his dark land
And close my eyes and quench my breath –
It may be I shall pass him still.
I have a rendezvous with Death
On some scarred slope of battered hill,
When Spring comes round again this year
And the first meadow-flowers appear.
God knows 'twere better to be deep
Pillowed in silk and scented down,
Where love throbs out in blissful sleep,
Pulse nigh to pulse, and breath to breath,
Where hushed awakenings are dear …
But I've a rendezvous with Death
At midnight in some flaming town,
When Spring trips north again this year,
And I to my pledged word am true,
I shall not fail that rendezvous.

– Alan Seeger (1888-1916)

"The great enemy of truth is very often not the lie--deliberate, contrived and dishonest--but the myth--persistent, persuasive and unrealistic. Too often we hold fast to the cliches of our forebears. We subject all facts to a prefabricated set of interpretations. We enjoy the comfort of opinion without the discomfort of thought.

–John F. Kennedy
Commencement Address at Yale University,
June 11 1962

CONTENTS

ACKNOWLEDGMENTS

I am indebted to the people who have helped this expanded edition come into being. First and foremost, my wife Lori Michelle, without her kindness, love and understanding this book would not have been possible.

My friend Matthew Smith, author of several books on the JFK assassination, has an encyclopedic knowledge of the case, and has put his knowledge at my disposal for the last several years. I value his counsel and friendship.

My friend Phil Singer, started out as a fan of my work, which has led to friendship over the years. Phil was responsible for members of the Kennedy Honor Guard, attending the gathering in Westmont, Illinois, and as a result, new breakthroughs have been made in the case. Phil also did double duty reading early drafts of the new chapters, giving me his suggestions and correcting my spelling and punctuation errors.

Thanks are due to Dr. David Mantik, who also read early drafts of chapters, and helped with editing. Dr. Mantik's efforts have brought us all closer to the truth of John Kennedy's murder. He is nothing short of brilliant.

The same can be said of Douglas P. Horne, late of the Assassination Records Review Board. His master work inside the Assassination Records Review Board, stands as a direct counterpoint to Vincent Bugliosi's lawyer's brief *Reclaiming History*. Horne's insight into the character of Dr. James Humes, "J." Thornton Boswell and Pierre Finck, is outstanding, and brings us closer to how Kennedy's autopsy was managed.

Colin McSween is due special thanks for his being there for me and my film partner, Mark Sobel, when we called upon his talents in making a replica of JFK's head as seen in the "so-called" Kennedy autopsy photos for Mark's movie, *The Commission*, and sharing his knowledge with me about what he learned about JFK's wounds while making the wax bust.

I would also like to thank Scott Baumann, of Air Park at The Museum of Flight in Seattle, Washington. Scott allowed Colin and me to tour SAM 86970 a.k.a. 970 a.k.a. "Queenie." It was Air Force Two on the Texas trip on November 21, and 22, 1963. I can't speak for Colin, but I could feel the history, as we walked through the plane.

I thank the man known in this book as "The White House Witness" and his daughter-in-law – hereby known as "The Princess," the woman who led me to him. I conducted the interview with "The White House Witness" some years ago now, and since that time, I have seen pictures of him with President Kennedy, and found his name in official records, so the "witness" is indeed who he claims to be.

I first interviewed members of the Kennedy autopsy team, over seventeen years ago. I felt these men could take me closer to the answers I sought in Kennedy's murder, and they did just that. They all gave me gifts of their time and knowledge of the events of that tragic time in November of 1963, what I wasn't expecting was the gift of friendship. Dennis David, Paul O'Connor, James Jenkins and Jim Metzler have over the years, given that to me in abundance.[1]

The men who were members of the Kennedy Honor Guard have my sincere thanks for attending the conference held in Westmont, Illinois. The presence of the three men who were able to attend: Hubert Clark, Tim Cheek and James Felder, made it a truly historic event. My thanks as well, to the members of the Honor Guard who were unable to attend, but took the time to talk to Phil Singer and me by phone and answered questions. They are George A. Barnum, U.S. Coast Guard; Specialist IV Douglas A. Mayfield, Army; S/Sargeant Richard E. Gaudreau, Air Force. Two more military men were added to the Honor Guard due to the extreme weight of the mahogany casket: PFC Larry J. Diamond, Marine Corp, and SA Larry B. Smith, Navy. They are now deceased. A special mention must be made of First Lieutenant Samuel R. Bird, Officer in Charge, 3rd Infantry. Every member of the Honor Guard Phil Singer and I met or talked to by phone, had nothing but the highest praise for the late Commander Bird. He sustained terrible injuries while he was in Vietnam and spent the remainder of his days confined to a wheelchair. By all accounts, he was the finest of men. Also to the finest of men: my thanks to Hugh Clark for his forward to this new edition of *In the Eye of History*. I know Hugh feels betrayed by what he learned at the gathering in Westmont, Illinois, but he needn't feel bad, he and his Honor Guard comrades gave and did their best for President Kennedy and America during those four dark days. *Those who took President Kennedy's life betrayed us all.*

---

1. As a result of the response Jim Jenkins received at the 50th anniversary conference of John F. Kennedy's assassination held in Dallas, Texas, Jim has decided to write his own memoir of the events at Bethesda Naval Hospital. History will be served well.

My thanks to Noel Twyman, for his introduction to this new edition and his kindness to me over the years.

My thanks as well to: Robert Groden, Glenn Bybee, Mark Young, Debra Conway, David Lifton, Skip Rydberg, the late Saundra Spencer, the late Jerrol Custer, the late James Sibert, the late Frank O'Neill and my publisher Kris Millegan.

My love and thanks to my children: Trevit, Ryan, Shawn and Haylee (Sissy). In the decade that has passed since the books first publication, my sons and their significant others have presented me with five more grandchildren, bringing the total at this point to eight. They are the reasons I continue to chase the truth of John Kennedy's murder: Tristan (August 22, 1995 – August 31, 1996), Christian, Trey, Tylar, Mary Jane, Sienna, Vanessa (Nessie) and Mykah.

Thanks also to my mother-in-law Dodi Reinoehl, for keeping me on the straight and narrow, my step-sons Tre' and Josh Leckbee, my sister-in-law Melissa Smith, and her children Tyler and Eric Bracken.

My thanks to my sister Elizabeth Ann White, my brother-in-law Robert Dale White, Bobbi and David Dunne, Cari Elizabeth and Sonny Saeid, Wesley White, Ralph and Linda Wilson, Jason Wilson, Kevin and Amber Wilson, Corey Wilson, Christopher Wilson, Teresa Ashpole, Adam Ashpole, Aric Ashpole, Ayrana Ashpole, Aiden Ashpole, Natasha Dunne Bjornsen, Jesse Bjornsen, Garrett Dunne, David Bjornsen, Gabriella Bjornsen, Kayerra Bjornsen, Quinnton Bjornsen, Garrett Dunne Bjornsen, Nasreen Sanaee, Nabby Sanaee, Sayan Sanaee, Jesse White, Katelyn White, Colby Wilson, Jesse Wilson.

INTRODUCTION

W illiam Law's excellent work in this book concentrates on the autopsy evidence in the JFK assassination. It is a remarkable example of persistent and courageous effort over a period of years to interview FBI agents who were key witnesses to the autopsy and others who were finally willing to talk, including very important new witnesses. He is to be congratulated and thanked for his gift to America. He has shown to all who will open their minds, and apply simple logic, that the murder of the president on November 22, 1963 was a conspiracy of unprecedented, historical proportions. I say this not just because a president was assassinated but because the conspiracy was covered up by direct actions of U.S. Government officials aided by those who took their orders. There is no other scandal or single event in our history that even approaches this.

In brief, the heinous acts that this evidence reveals, and proves, with eyewitness testimony, scientific data and documents, is this:

At some time between when the president's body was transported from the Parkland Hospital in Dallas, Texas and delivered to the autopsy room at the Naval Hospital in Bethesda, Maryland, it was intercepted by conspirators and taken to a secret location where they enlarged the bullet exit wound in the rear of the skull to make the wound extend to the top and right side of the skull, and crudely excised a major portion of the brain to remove incriminating bullet fragments. They also grossly enlarged a small tracheotomy incision that had been made by a doctor in Dallas; by so doing, a bullet entry wound in the throat was made less obvious. By performing these operations, the conspirators obscured the direction from which the fatal head shot occurred. They then delivered the body to the morgue at the rear of Bethesda Naval Hospital.

The Navy doctors and technicians then proceeded with the autopsy while taking photos and X-rays. But unfortunately for the conspirators, the alteration of the wounds was so hastily botched that they were compelled to alter the X-rays of the head and brain, and substitute a drawing of the brain in the autopsy report that clearly was not Kennedy's brain.[1] They then ordered personnel who were engaged in the autopsy to remain silent, talk to no one, under penalty of imprisonment.

The conspirators were also compelled to hastily edit the famous Zapruder film of the assassination by cutting out frames that showed debris from an exit wound in the back of the head; evidence of a shot from the front. Again, it proved to be impossible to conceal the film alterations because it resulted in jumpy or impossibly rapid movements of people and objects in the film.

All of the above, standing alone, fits into a body of evidence proving the conclusions herein. There is much more evidence that further reinforces the conclusion, including eye witness testimony of dozens of people in Dealey Plaza, and at Parkland Hospital, and statements of secret service agents directly witnessing the events.

After fifty-two years, many questions remain before we can fully gain perspective of the mystery and its broad ramifications. We need to know why our government tried so desperately to cover up the murder; that is who, or what government secret, was being protected? Why did otherwise good people, such as medical professionals and military personnel, allow themselves to be brought into the cover-up? Were any of those in the cover-up involved in the assassination itself? Why did Congress, the U.S. Supreme Court and all government agencies including the CIA and the FBI roll over? And what government officials were in charge, directing the action?

This story boggles the mind. It is unbelievable but true. It makes us shrink and hide and want to withdraw into denial. If someone should provide a comprehensive answer to these questions, it would give insight into how our system of government actually works. I suspect that governments act in a nationally collective survival instinct, following the leader to conceal family sins and secrets. I think that we would find that nations hide their secrets similarly to individuals, and that the United States is no exception.

Noel Twyman
September 22, 2015,
San Diego California

---

1. Noel Twyman's belief as to where Kennedy's body was altered differs from my own.

FOREWORD

On November 22nd, 1963 – the day John F. Kennedy died – I was nineteen years old. I'd been in the Navy a little over fifteen months. I was born in New Jersey and grew up in New York. I had eleven brothers and sisters. And I played a lot of sports growing up. I loved Jackie Robinson, Willie Mays and the Boston Celtics. And I loved doo wop, R. & B. and soul music. In high school, I wanted to be a designer. I went to a special high school for the fashion industries on 24th Street: H.S.F.I. – the High School of Fashion Industries. And I made my own suits! I had an internship as a senior at Saks Fifth Avenue in New York City. When I saw my two brothers in their Marine Corps uniforms and my other brother in his Air Force clothes, it really excited me. I wanted to join the Navy and see the world. I wanted to get out of New York. I begged my dad to let me enter the military. He was a pastor. I pleaded with him and the recruiter too. I was still only seventeen. But I had graduated high school and really wanted to be in the Navy. In August of 1962, I signed up. Eventually, three of my brothers, myself and one of my sisters ended up in the military. So I have to thank my dad for allowing me to join.

I loved marching. At the end of boot camp, my superior convinced me to join the honor guard. I was in awe the first time I went to Arlington National Cemetery. When I got into it, I really got into it. I knew all the routines. I practiced and practiced. And then I practiced some more. I learned everything I could. I loved it. Having caught on very well, I soon got promoted to be the head of the Navy Honor Guard. I was responsible for the training and teaching for military funerals for the Navy. My title was Acting Petty Officer for the Navy Honor Guard. And so I taught them all kinds of stuff. At the time Kennedy died, I had done hundreds of funerals for the U.S. Navy Honor Guard.

Upon hearing the news that the President had died, I thought it was Herbert Hoover. He was 89 years old and had been ill. In fact, we had practiced, in preparation, for his funeral. But it wasn't Hoover. It was Kennedy.

[Hoover did die in 1964, less than a year later.] We were stunned. We were ordered to report to Andrews Air Force Base. At around 6 p.m., Air Force One landed at Andrews and we attempted to assist in loading the bronze Dallas casket containing the body of President Kennedy into the gray Navy ambulance. The casket did not have a flag over it. And it almost got dropped. Too many people were involved. Too many inexperienced people were trying to help out. We weren't allowed to do our job and handle the casket. Brigadier General Godfrey McHugh said, "That's my Commander In Chief!" I almost got shoved into the ambulance by accident. There's a picture of it. Shortly thereafter, the gray Navy ambulance took off with the bronze Dallas casket. Jackie and Bobby Kennedy also rode in this ambulance. The autopsy was going to be performed at the Bethesda Naval Hospital in Bethesda, Maryland.

The Honor Guard, including myself, General Philip Wehle, Lt. Sam Bird and Lt. Richard Lipsey got into a helicopter and also headed to Bethesda. We essentially shadowed the ambulance and the motorcade on the way to Bethesda. It was scary. I had never been in a helicopter before. Lt. Bird conferred with General Wehle and informed him of how the casket almost got dropped on the tarmac at Andrews due to the intrusion of too many people trying to help out. Wehle assured Bird that there would be no interference from any others going forward. We got there prior to the motorcade's arrival at the front of Bethesda so that we could be prepared to handle the casket from this point on.

When the ambulance arrived from Andrews, it seemed like hundreds of photographers and reporters came out of nowhere. They rushed us. Flashbulbs. Confusion. It was crazy. And the ambulance took off. We got into the back of a Navy pick-up truck and chased the ambulance around the grounds. It was cold and we're in the back of this pick-up truck in the dark flying around the grounds of Bethesda. It was scary. We couldn't tell where we were going. There were no points of reference for us. It was hard to tell how long it was that we were out there.

Eventually, we carried the casket into the back of the hospital. We put the casket onto a dolly and left. I was in the hallway during the autopsy, guarding one of the doors to the morgue. At one point, I was asked if I wanted to go in and I said, "No." However, people were coming and going throughout the night. At one point when the door was opened, I looked in. And I saw the President lying on his back. It looked like he was asleep. This was early in the evening. His body hadn't been cut open yet. And his neck was on a chock. I didn't know what it was called right then, but I was later told that that device was called a chock or a chock block. Years later, I was a New York City policeman and detective and I became familiar with this device as I had been in the morgue numerous times and had witnessed autopsies on occasion. I did not see any wounds on the President when I looked into the morgue. It was just for maybe five to ten seconds. But his neck was on a chock block. No doubt about it. None at all. I know what I saw.

In the early morning hours of the next day – Saturday, the 23rd – the autopsy was done and the embalmers had finished their job. We carried the casket out of the morgue, this time with a flag on it. The original bronze Dallas casket had incurred some damage – it was beat up a bit and at least one of the handles was loose. Now the President's body was in a mahogany casket from the Gawler's Funeral Home. This casket was much, much heavier than the previous one. It was obvious to us right away. We drove to the White House and carried this mahogany casket into the East Room. Due to the weight of this casket, two men were later added to the team to ensure that we didn't drop it. We went from six to eight guys, and Lt. Bird helped out as well, making it nine of us in all. And it was still a monster. By far, the heaviest casket we had ever dealt with. It wasn't even close. I was so worried about messing up. You just didn't want to mess up and trip or stumble or fall. On Saturday evening, we were at Arlington National Cemetery practicing with a rehearsal casket on the steps to the Tomb of the Unknown Soldier to prepare ourselves for carrying the extremely heavy mahogany casket up the steps of the Capital to the Rotunda.

We weighted down this practice casket to simulate what we would be doing the next several days. Up and down the steps we went. Our big concern was keeping the casket level – front to back and side to side. We had to take short steps and be synchronized together. There were four, instead of three, guys on each side of the casket. Spacing was pretty tight. We did this over and over and over until we felt comfortable with the task of going up and down the steps. It was now past midnight. We were exhausted. Over the weekend and extending into Monday, the 25th, we carried the casket into the Capital and into St. Matthew's Cathedral and then finally into Arlington National Cemetery. While still inside St. Matthew's Cathedral, the smell of incense lingered heavily in the air. I started to tear up a bit. And a lady said, "Look! The sailor's crying!" We finally made it to Arlington National Cemetery. We folded the flag into a triangle. It was an excellent fold – perfect. We had buried our President. And then it was over. We were totally exhausted – both mentally and physically. Over the weekend, we had maybe gotten nine or ten hours of sleep. It was the last funeral I ever did for the military. And the next day I was transferred out. I left the military in 1966, having spent a little over four years in the service.

I never got a chance to talk with my family on the phone that weekend. There were no calls coming in or going out. And we were so busy. Every-thing was so tense. We were constantly on standby. Later, my family members told me that my dad had seen me on TV during the various events of those four days – Friday through Monday. He had spotted me. Gathered around the television set, my siblings said, "No, dad, that isn't Hubert." But my dad was insistent. He said, "That's Hubert. That's him. That's my boy. There he is. That's my boy!" He had recognized me by my small ears. In the days after the funeral of President Kennedy, I went back to my high school, in uniform, and gave a talk about my experiences to the students. In fact, I gave a few talks about the events of that weekend. One of them was at my elementary school.

Over the years, I would get calls and do interviews about being part of President Kennedy's Honor Guard. Sometimes I would get people sending me photographs of us carrying the casket and wanting me to autograph the picture. In December of 2014, I got a call from a man. He had some questions for me. And he told me that he was helping to put together an event – a reunion and a conference of some of the men that were at Bethesda that night. It was Phil Singer, a long-time JFK researcher from Illinois. At this time, I hadn't seen or spoken to the other Honor Guard guys since the day that we had buried the President. Over 51 years had elapsed. We had all gone our separate ways. Well, Phil and I spoke on the phone several times a week from that day forward. I had some questions for him. And he had some for me. Phil helped me connect with the other Honor Guard guys. We spoke on the phone and reconnected after all of these years. I was excited about the opportunity to see some of these guys again. And having our story documented for history. Phil mailed me a photograph of a young Navy guy standing in the hallway of Bethesda that night. I had never seen it. But it was me alright. I was standing right outside of the morgue.

At first, I thought that I'd just drive from Georgia to Illinois for the February 2015 event. But I decided to fly instead. The Chicago area got hit hard with about two feet of snow on February 1st – Super Bowl Sunday, in fact. But I was able to make my flight into Chicago on the 3rd. Phil made arrangements for me to be picked up at the airport and get driven to the Clubhouse Inn in Westmont, a suburb just west of Chicago. I got to meet Phil and his partner in the project, William Law. We sat down pretty much right away and started talking. The cameras were recording everything. I told the guys my story and participation in the Honor Guard involving JFK's caskets – the bronze Dallas one and the bigger, heavier mahogany one from Gawler's Funeral Home. I showed everyone my scrapbook, including a couple of items that I personally received from Jackie Kennedy several years later. My nephew James Clark III from Naperville, Illinois even was able to come out the next day and visit me at the hotel during one of the breaks in the sessions. It was great to see him. Everyone was very friendly.

As the afternoon progressed, Tim Cheek and James Felder arrived at the hotel. These were two of the other Honor Guard men. Several other people that were at Bethesda that day, arrived. Soon there were seven of us. We were all young military men back then. And now, after 51-plus years, we were all in our seventies. We went out to dinner that evening at Giordano's Pizza and had some fun reminiscing. The next day – Wednesday, the 4th – we all got together and discussed our recollections of the events related to the autopsy of the President, along with other related topics. I went into this event with hardly any questions about what had happened. I left the next day with a lot of questions. A whole lot of them. The detective in me – from my years as a New York City cop – sort of kicked in. I learned from Dennis David that another casket, a gray lightweight shipping casket, had arrived in a black unmarked hearse just before we had even arrived from Andrews in the helicopter. James Metzler, who was standing outside on the loading dock to the morgue, recalled seeing a pick-up truck driving around the grounds and someone yelling out, "Have you seen the ambulance?" It was probably Lt. Bird in the front passenger seat of the vehicle. Metzler yelled back, "No." I was in the back of that pick-up truck, along with the rest of the Honor Guard casket team. Jim Jenkins told us about the wounds that he observed on the President's body. He was in the morgue during the autopsy, assisting the doctors. So I learned what happened inside the morgue while I was in the hallway guarding the door that evening. Jenkins described seeing what appeared to be a small round entrance wound near Kennedy's right ear. And a bigger hole in the back of the head. Phil had the guys draw on white Styrofoam heads, with a black magic marker pen, the wounds that they saw on President Kennedy's body that night. Jenkins also described how the back wound to the President was probed by the doctors. And it didn't go through the body. It never came out the front of JFK at all. And he said that if it had exited the front of JFK – which it didn't do – that it would have come out below his right nipple, based upon the location of the back wound and the steep downward trajectory. Jenkins told us that when he left the morgue the following morning, he was absolutely convinced that the

President had been shot from two different directions. There was no doubt in his mind about that.

I heard about logs books missing and official records being falsified upon orders from superiors. In the military you take orders. Or you get in trouble. Big-time. Richard Lipsey described, and demonstrated for the group how Kennedy's left arm was bent at about a ninety-degree angle at the elbow at the beginning of the autopsy and that they had to virtually get up on top of him and straighten it out. Felder described seeing a huge hole in the rear of Kennedy's head that was devoid of hair, scalp and bone. Essentially, a massive blowout. And Jenkins also described how he was told not to open one of the caskets that night, that it was an Air Force major or colonel. What was that about? A lot of stuff just didn't seem to make sense. But all of these guys were sincere and credible.

One of the things that was brought to the event was a chock block. It's all on the film that they took. They showed it to us. We handled it. I told the group that that was what I saw under Kennedy's neck that night. Others present agreed with me. That's what some of the others saw too. None of them saw a curved metal stirrup that is present in some of the "official" autopsy pictures. It led us to seriously question the validity – the authenticity – of these "official" autopsy pictures. Several other issues were brought up about these pictures too. It wasn't just the chock block issue. Dennis David told us about the four bullet fragments that he held in his hand a bit later that evening. And how he typed up a memorandum about this for some agent in a suit. And then the guy took the piece of paper out of the typewriter and took the ribbon too and reminded Dennis that he wasn't allowed to discuss this incident with anyone. Period. It was classified information. But Jenkins said that they couldn't find any bullets or bullet fragments during the autopsy. And that this was a major issue causing a lot of tension in the morgue that night among the doctors and other military officials. It seemed like a lot of strange things were going on at the Bethesda Naval Hospital.

The more that I listened, the more that my eyes were opened. Having been a detective in New York City for a number of years, it really made me wonder about what was going on that night. For years, I have wondered about Lee Harvey Oswald being shot while in custody in the Dallas Police Department by Jack Ruby. It just seemed too convenient. I had told Phil this over the phone before we ever met. But the things that I learned at this Westmont, Illinois event in February of 2015 really have me wondering what was going on at Bethesda that night. Quite frankly, I feel betrayed. At no time were any of the members of the Honor Guard called to testify before any commission or investigative committee. In fact, I found out that not one of the seven of us that were at the Westmont, Illinois event were called to testify before the Warren Commission. I can only hope that we can learn the full truth about the assassination of President Kennedy in my lifetime. And that this information gets out to as many people as possible. I am looking forward to seeing the documentary of this JFK event of the seven of us that were at Bethesda that night and got thrown into history. I want my children and grandchildren to know what I did. And what we all participated in. That's why I'm so excited – it's all documented for history.

Lastly, I wish that the other members of the Honor Guard casket team could've been there at this JFK event in Illinois, along with Tim Cheek and James Felder. Sam Bird – our great, diligent, steady and inspirational leader – died some years ago. More recently, Larry Smith and Jerry Diamond passed away too. They were good, decent men. Bud Barnum and Doug Mayfield couldn't attend. But I did get to talk with them on the phone after more than half a century. That was nice. And unfortunately, Richard Gaudreau was not tracked down and contacted until just after the event had taken place. But I got to talk with him as well. For four days back in November of 1963, we were the Honor Guard for President John F. Kennedy and we laid him to rest. It's sometimes hard to believe that I'm that skinny nineteen-year-old kid in all of those pictures and films and that we buried JFK But we did. And we did it proudly. And with honor. We got thrown into history. And did our job. We came through under the pressure. The whole world was watching. And we didn't mess up. We didn't trip, stumble, fall or drop the heaviest casket, by far, that any of us had ever dealt with. And we kept it level. Many special thanks to Phil Singer and William Law, for making me a part of the JFK event in Westmont, Illinois in February of 2015. I can only hope that everyone got as much out of it as I did. Which was a whole lot. Being at the Westmont conference, left me with more questions than answers, but I am forever grateful. I appreciated it immensely.

Hubert Clark
July 17, 2015
Georgia

RECLAIMING HISTORY

—

The Assassination of President John F. Kennedy

—

VINCENT BUGLIOSI

AUTHOR OF
HELTER SKELTER

PREFACE

Vincent Bugliosi is dead. His obituary reported that he died from cancer on June 6, 2015, at 80 years old. Some readers, I am sure, will ask why I would take on the deceased Bugliosi's work on the Kennedy assassination almost eight years after his magnum opus: *Reclaiming History*. I did write a piece on Bugliosi's massive work, shortly after it was first published. I trudged my way through its pages, trying to control the anger I felt just over how he treated my work. I sent the lengthy piece I had written to a few writers whose work on the Kennedy assassination I respected. All gave me the same advice: "Don't waste your time giving Bugliosi more publicity. All of us have real work to do concerning Kennedy's death. Leave it alone."

Bugliosi was the prosecutor in the Tate-LaBianca murders in the late 1960's and wrote the bestselling book *Helter Skelter*. He ran for office of the Los Angeles District Attorney in 1972, hoping, I would guess, that his successful prosecution of Charles Manson would propel him into office, it did not. In 1974 he ran for the office of State Attorney General, but failed to secure the Democratic nomination. Bugliosi then ran for D.A. in 1976, once again losing to his opponent.

Vincent Bugliosi would go into private practice, continuing to write books, mainly based off criminal cases he was involved in. His best book, he said, was *Reclaiming History,* a book which took the ex-prosecutor 1,632 pages, including a CD-rom containing 958 end notes and 170 pages of source notes. All to "prove" Lee Harvey Oswald acting alone killed John F. Kennedy. One reviewer for the *New York Times* wrote: "*Reclaiming History* should be applauded, I am not sure it should be read." I disagree with the reviewer; *Reclaiming History* should be neither applauded nor read. And if one decides to take the plunge and read the massive diatribe, one should not take it as the truth of who killed JFK, but rather a lawyer's brief, giving a rather lopsided case for Lee Harvey Oswald's guilt in the killing of Kennedy.

The years passed and I decided to publish a new edition of *In the Eye of History* with new material and include a DVD of film footage I had never shown to the public. It would be my answer to the "Oswald did it alone" crowd. But in re-reading my original piece and going back through reviews of Bugliosi's book and the mainstream media's response to Bugliosi's work, I decided to use Bugliosi as a metaphorical surrogate for all the persistent nay-sayers that still exist, who still believe the Warren Commission, never mind all the unanswered questions about Kennedy's death. I am old enough to have lived through Kennedy's assassination, watched on TV as men first walked on the moon, bringing President Kennedy's dream of "landing a man on the moon before this decade is out," saw the era of Vietnam ushered in and out, the Watergate affair that put an end to Richard Milhous Nixon's presidency, not to mention Ronald Reagan's Iran Contra scandal and the scandals of the elections of 2000 and 2004. (In about 2005, I did a mind blowing interview with Gene Wheaton, the whistleblower for the Iran Contra scandal.) And let's not forget the furor that has been raised around the world by Wikileaks. I am, to say the least, less than inclined to believe anything as the whole and full truth coming from the United States government.

A Short overview of the life of Lee Harvey Oswald

Tracing the past of Lee Harvey Oswald is, of course, a large part of the tangled skein of the Kennedy assassination. Whole books have been, and will continue to be, written about the 24 year old ex-marine. Oswald was born October 18, 1939, in New Orleans, Louisiana, to Robert Oswald Sr. and Marguerite Frances Clavert. Oswald's father, Robert Lee, died of a heart attack two months before Lee Oswald's birth. Marguerite moved Oswald and his two older brothers, Robert Oswald and half- brother John Pic, to Dallas, Texas in 1944 where Lee attended different schools in Dallas/Fort Worth through the 6th grade. It is known that the Oswald brothers lived for a time in an orphanage, Lee being all of four years old. In the 4th grade Oswald was given an I.Q. test where he scored 103 according to the Warren report. By the age of 12, Lee and his mother went to live in New York City in a small apartment in the Bronx. Marguerite Oswald worked days in a dress shop and Lee spent his hours alone at the public library, or at the zoo, or riding the New York subway system. Although enrolled in the 8th grade, Oswald wasn't attending school, and a truant officer discovered him and he was taken to court, where he was sent to a youth detention center for a few weeks evaluation. In the report (May 7, 1953) by case worker Evelyn Siegel, Oswald had a "pleasant appealing quality – although laconic and taciturn." At the end of the report Ms. Siegel concludes Lee Oswald "is a seriously withdrawn, detached and emotionally isolated boy of 13." By the age of 15, Lee filled out a personal history in school indicating he wanted to be in the military. Later that same year, he joined the New Orleans Civil Air Patrol. At 16 years of age Oswald dropped out of school. At about this point in time, Lee Harvey Oswald is said to have begun to study Marxism. On October 26, 1956 Oswald reported for duty at the Marine Corp Recruit Depot in San Diego, California. He was trained in the use of the M-1 rifle. His practice scores "were not very good," according to the Warren Commission report, but when his company fired for the record on December 21st, Oswald scored 212, two points above the score necessary to qualify as a "sharp shooter." He did not do nearly as well when he fired for record again shortly before he left the Marines, but no scores were recorded. His closest friend at the time, Nelson Delgado, told the Warren Commission that Oswald ... "didn't show no particular aspects of being a sharp shooter at all." Asked by Warren Commission lawyer Wesley J. Liebeler, if Oswald kept his rifle in good shape, Delgado replied "he kept it mediocre. He always got gigged for his rifle." Delgado told writer Mark Lane that Oswald frequently got "Maggie's drawers" (a red flag) for missing the target. It's worth noting that Delgado moved to England for three years after he gave his testimony to the Warren Commission, for fear that he would be killed.

After Basic Training, Oswald qualified as an aviation electronics operator and in 1957, he was stationed at Atsugi Air Force Base. His life at Atsugi began to change for him, as noted by writer and historian, Matthew Smith. *"Some of his fellow Marines found him easy to get along with and a well-informed individual with whom it was comfortable to get into conversation. Those around him rated him a good egg, good natured and likable."* Others found him just the opposite.

Mysteries about Oswald abound. He accidentally shot himself in the arm with a small caliber pistol he kept in his locker. It has been written that Oswald was keeping company with a group of Communists on visits to Tokyo, and that he was involved in a government mission and was trying to keep himself at Atsugi to continue his relationship with this group. For those who scoff at this idea, it needs to be pointed out that his Marine records indicate that Oswald's wound was "incurred in the line of duty."

There is a laundry list of things that make Oswald's life while in the Marines puzzling. Oswald was often called comrade by his fellow Marines and spoke Russian, and although it was brought to the attention of Oswald's superiors, they did not appear to be concerned. Oswald, it was found out by no other than L.J. Rankin, counsel to the Warren Commission, that Oswald took a course in Russian at the Monterey Language Institute in Monterey, California. It came to light in a release of top secret documents due to a FOIA request in 1979. Oswald was granted early release from the Marines due to a hardship application, saying his mother was in poor health. There is no evidence of this, and had anyone of Oswald's superiors bothered to check this story, he would have been denied. After Oswald received his early release from the Marines, he went home for a few days, and then traveled to France and England, and on to Helsinki, Finland, and then to Moscow. It is there that Oswald goes to the U.S. Embassy and declares that he wishes to renounce his American citizenship and become a Soviet citizen and remain in Russia. The Russians however, are skeptical of Oswald and deny him his request.

It is reported that Oswald cut his wrist requiring hospital treatment. He was then given permission to stay in the Soviet Union, and was sent to Minsk where he was given a job at a radio factory. He meets and marries a Russian woman, Marina Nikolayevna Prusakova, has a child with her, stays two years, decides he wants to come back to the Unites States, bringing with him his Russian wife and child, and is granted visas in an expedited manner. When Oswald does return to the United States, he is not met by anyone, except Spas T. Raikin, a case worker with the Traveler's Aid Society.[1]

Oswald then lives in Dallas/Fort Worth for ten months. During this time the Oswalds become acquainted with a number of anticommunist Russian immigrants. Lee is befriended by George de Mohrenschildt, a 51 year old geologist, and Marina is befriended by Ruth Paine, a woman who is trying to learn the Russian language. While living in Dallas, Oswald orders a .38 caliber Smith and Wesson pistol via mail. Oswald orders a rifle also via mail – when he could have bought a rifle and pistol anywhere in Dallas. In March of 1962, Marina takes pictures of Lee in their back yard. He is holding the rifle, pistol strapped on his hip, and holding communist newspapers. Many researchers claim that these pictures have been faked to implicate Oswald in Kennedy's assassination. (I don't know if the pictures were faked or not, but in a conversation I had over the phone with Marina Oswald Porter nearly two decades ago, I asked her about the photographs. Marina admitted she had taken the photographs "but" she told me, "Lee was holding something else.") Regardless, the back yard photographs do the job – Oswald is linked to the rifle and pistol.

Oswald is accused of shooting at General Edwin A. Walker around this time, but Dallas police records contain information that Walker's neighbors see two men at the scene of the crime running to a car and speeding away.

1. Some researchers find it strange that while Oswald is still in Russia, there is a memo sent to the State department by director of the FBI, J. Edgar Hoover, dated June 3, 1960 indicating that someone was using Lee Harvey Oswald's identity for some purpose, a full two years before John F. Kennedy was assassinated in Dallas.

The bullet from the rifle was so damaged it could not be linked to the so-called Oswald rifle.

In April of 1963 Lee Oswald decides to move to New Orleans. (Marina is living with Ruth Paine.) He finds work there and by May 11th Ruth Paine drives Marina and the baby June to live with him at his apartment. In that same month Oswald orders a thousand hand bills with the words HANDS OFF CUBA. Some of these hand bills (that Oswald hands out on the street) are stamped with the address of 544 Camp Street. He visits a store managed by Carlos Bringuier, a Cuban refugee, and an avid opponent of Castro. Oswald tells Bringuier that he is interested in joining the struggle against Fidel Castro, and that he is an ex-Marine trained in guerrilla warfare. A few days later, Oswald is seen on Canal Street handing out pro-Castro leaflets. Bringuier and a few friends show up and, although no real fight breaks out, Oswald and Bringuier and the other Cubans are arrested and taken to jail. Oswald is fined $10 and released, but before he is released, he requests to see John Quigley from the FBI. Quigley spends an hour with Oswald but Quigley destroys his notes of the meeting, so no one knows what Oswald said. Some researchers have concluded that Oswald's activities in New Orleans point to the former Marine being involved in some sort of legend being created. The lone nut believers say Oswald was just a confused malcontent trying to draw attention to himself. While Oswald certainly did draw attention to himself the questions is, and remains, why?

The mystery of Oswald continues to deepen when we look at his supposed trip to Mexico City. As the story, goes Oswald traveled to Mexico City to visit the Soviet and Mexican Consulates with the idea that he would obtain a visa to travel to Cuba and then on to the Soviet Union. Oswald applied for a visa to travel to Mexico on September 17, 1963. Standing in line in front of him was William Gaudet, who was an agent for the CIA. This fact came to light years later due to a bureaucratic blunder. Gaudet claims that the fact that his proximity was just a "coincidence." When Lee Oswald reached Mexico City, he allegedly visited the Cuban and Soviet Embassies where he attempted once again to defect to the Soviet Union. Many critics of the Warren Commission believe that it was not Oswald, but an impostor who visited the two embassies. This man (who may or may have not been Oswald) seemed to want to draw attention to himself. He visits the Cuban Embassy and requests an "in transit" visa to allow him to travel through Cuba and on to the Soviet Union. He puts on a display of leftism. He frantically talks about returning to the Soviet Union. He gets into a shouting match with the Cuban counsel there, and is asked to leave.

When the CIA forwarded photographs from surveillance cameras in the Cuban Consulate, it was of a man that clearly was not Lee Harvey Oswald. The man was much heavier, did not look like Oswald and apparently had thin blond hair. When it was found that the images of the man in the photographs were not of Lee Harvey Oswald the CIA claimed it had made a mistake, and they had no pictures of Oswald at all. David Phillips testified that the cameras at the consulate were not in operation at the time Oswald visited. Tape recordings of conversations were made between the man who called himself Oswald and Soviet Embassy personnel. If the tapes could be heard and analyzed, we the public could then be certain, whether or not, it was indeed Lee Harvey Oswald who was in Mexico City. But the tapes have vanished. David Phillips, who was in charge of photo surveillance at the Mexico City CIA station said the tapes were "routinely destroyed" before the assassination. Critics site this as evidence that Oswald was being set up to paint him as a dangerous, communist fanatic.

There is the strange tale of what has become known as the Odio incident. Sylvia Odio was the daughter of a prominent anti-Castro activist who was jailed in Castro's Cuba. In September Odio was living in Dallas when three men visited her at her apartment. Her sister Annie opened the door. "They were in a small hallway with bright lights overhead," said Annie.

Sylvia Odio said, "There were three men, the taller man introduced the other two men. Leopoldo he said was his name. He introduced the American who was in the middle as Leon Oswald, and introduced the one that seemed Mexican and spoke with a Mexican accent as Angelo." Sylvia Odio went on to say that "The American was introduced as Leon Oswald. That will always be in my mind very clearly. I think it was two days after that, Leopoldo, who had clearly a Cuban accent, called me on the phone and he tried to be very friendly and was trying to sell me on the idea of the American. The first thing he asked was 'What did you think of the American?' and actually, I had not formed any opinion of the American at the time. He said 'Well, you know we don't know what to make of him, he is kind of loco, he has been telling us that the Cubans should have murdered or should have assassinated President Kennedy right after the Bay of Pigs and they didn't have any guts to do it. They should do it.' It was a very easy thing to do at the time. The reason that I remember so clearly was because that same night, or I think later that night, or that night afterwards, I wrote my father and I also told a friend of mine who was my father confessor, about the visit. They were trying to sell me on the American because they spoke that he was a marksman, that he had been an ex-Marine, and that he was someone who could be used and who could be an asset to any organization."[2]

Sylvia Odio told this story to the Warren Commission but they dismissed what she had to say, because of course, Lee Harvey Oswald was in Mexico City at the time of the incident. By October 3, 1963, Lee Harvey Oswald is back in the U.S. – if he was ever out of it, checking into the YMCA, and later in the day he files a claim at the employment office. The next day, October 4th, he hitch-hikes to Ruth Paine's house in Irving, Texas where his wife and baby are living. On October 7th, Ruth Paine drives Oswald to the bus station and he returns to Dallas to look for work. He rents a room at 621 Marcella Street. Apparently, Oswald's landlady didn't like him and when he leaves to go to Ruth Paine's for the weekend, he is asked not to return. On October 14th Paine drives Oswald to Dallas where he rents a new room on North Beckley, and he registers under the name of O.H. Lee. Ruth Paine, as she tells it, mentions to a group of neighbors that Oswald is having trouble finding work. Linnie May Randle tells Paine there is a possible job opening at the Dallas Schoolbook Depository. When Lee calls the Paine home that evening, Ruth informs him of the job opening. The next day, October 15th, Lee applies for the job and is hired.

November 1st, James Hosty of the FBI who is in charge of keeping an eye on Oswald, locates where Marina is living at the Paine residence, and interviews her. Hosty interviews her again on November 5th and when Lee finds this out, it angers him so much he delivers a note to Hosty. We don't know what Lee said in the note, nor does the Warren Commission because Hosty, under orders from his superior Gordon Shanklin destroys the note after Oswald is shot dead. This fact does not come to light until 1975, when Hosty testifies at the House Select Committee on Assassinations. I had many conversations over the years with Jim Hosty and although he was more than a little gruff when I first talked to him many years ago, he loosened up and was quite amiable in later discussions. Hosty in talking about the note from a mock trial of Lee Harvey Oswald on 1966 ... " I was ordered to destroy [the note]. I was told by the agent in charge, Gordon Shanklin, he handed it to me, he said 'Here, I don't ever want to say this again.' ... I got rid of it, I destroyed it." Hosty did as he was instructed, but what the note contained, we shall never know – leading to more questions.

On Thursday November 21, 1963 Oswald breaks routine and asks Buell Wesley Frazier to give him a ride to the Paine residence on Thursday the 21st.

2. PBS Special Frontline: *Who was Lee Harvey Oswald?* Air date: November 19th 2013.

He spends the night, and has a fight with his wife Marina, whom to some of the "Oswald did it alone" crowd means that because Marina refuses to have sex with him, he decides to kill JFK – indeed, William Manchester describes Oswald in his book, *The Death of a President*, as "going quite mad." Buell Wesley Frazier drives Oswald to work on Friday, November 22 – Oswald is carrying a package made of brown paper under his right arm, cupping the bottom of the package in his hand. Oswald tells Frazier it is curtain rods for his apartment on Beckley Street. Oswald put the package in the back seat of Frazier's car. Frazier later says that the package was "under his arm, but the other [end] was cupped in his hand. I know it has been said that Lee brought the rifle to work with him that morning. There is no way he could have had that rifle in that package, because if you had one of those Italian rifles and you took the barrel off the wooden stock, neither one would fit in that package. As I have said, the package was around two feet long, it would take an inch or two. There is no way it would fit in there." None the less, the Warren Commission ruled that is how the rifle came to be in the Depository. The "Italian rifle" disassembled is about 35 inches. That is a discrepancy of 7 – 10 inches in length.

The official story of the assassination is as follows: After Lee Harvey Oswald enters the Depository building he is seen by a co-worker to be looking out toward the motorcade route. While the rest of his co-workers go to lunch, Oswald remains on the 6th floor, so he can assemble the weapon and creates the so-called "sniper's nest." At 12:30, Lee shoots JFK, getting off three rounds in less than six seconds. Oswald hides the rifle between some boxes, runs down four flights of stairs, goes into the lunch room where he buys a Coke from a machine. When he is confronted by patrolman Marion Baker, Baker draws his gun and he points it at Oswald. Roy Truly, manager of the Texas Schoolbook Depository, is with Baker and vouches for Oswald, telling him, "He is all right, he works here." Oswald walks out of the front of the building and boards a bus to make his escape, but the bus is slowed by traffic. Oswald gets off the bus, hails a cab, and tells the cab driver to take him to 500 North Beckley Street, but gets out of the cab at the 700 block. He walks the rest of the way to his rooming house, where he changes his shirt and retrieves his pistol. He leaves the rooming house, and while fleeing on foot, is noticed by patrolman J.D. Tippit. Oswald shoots Tippit and continues to flee on foot. Lee makes his way to the Texas Theatre where he goes into the theatre unnoticed by Julia Postal the ticket taker and finds a seat in the darkened movie house. Oswald is however, noticed going into the theatre without buying a ticket by shoe salesman Johnny Calvin Brewer.

Brewer calls the police, given Oswald's disheveled appearance and suspicious manner and when authorities arrive, Brewer goes up on the theatre stage and points out Oswald. Oswald is then surrounded by police and tries to shoot one of the officers, saying "Well, it is all over now." He is taken out of the theater in handcuffs and taken to Dallas Police Headquarters. He is questioned by the police and then taken to the basement for what is commonly referred to as a line up. Oswald is then taken back upstairs for questioning in Captain Will Fritz's office. Two hours later Oswald is taken for another police line-up and then returns upstairs for more questioning. By 7:10 PM Oswald has been arraigned for the murder of Officer J.D. Tippit. He is then taken for a third line-up. By 11:26 PM he is charged in the murder of the 35th President of the United States. There is a midnight press conference held in the basement of the jail where Oswald is surrounded by reporters as they shout out questions to him. Oswald later calls this press conference "short and sweet." The next day, Saturday, November 23rd, the questioning of Oswald starts again. In the afternoon, Marina and baby June visit Lee. Oswald tries to contact Attorney John Abt sometime after the visit from his wife and child, but is not successful. Lee has a fourth police line-up, and then with his permission, fingernail scraping and hair samples are taken. He is visited by his brother Robert and at some point Lee catches his brother looking at him and Oswald says, "Don't believe the so-called evidence."

Oswald later phones Ruth Paine and asks her to retain John Abt for his attorney. Paine tries but to no avail. The next day, Sunday the 24th of November, Lee Oswald is shot by Jack Ruby, a Dallas nightclub owner, while being transferred from the Dallas County Jail, and later dies at Parkland Hospital. Many who have studied this case over the last 50 years, believe that Lee Harvey Oswald was framed for the murder of John Kennedy. There are those who believe Oswald was working for the government and was set up by the powers that be (e.g., Military Industrial Complex, FBI, CIA, i.e. rogue elements in the government.) It is said that history often turns on a dime. Political leaders can be killed by one lone person. Oswald was not what we were told he was in 1963. There were, we now know, those who were on the Commission that didn't believe the single bullet scenario that the Commission tried to foist off on the American public.

> In the 1970's John Sherman Cooper, a member of the Commission said … "there were disagreements. The most serious one that comes to me most vividly of course, is the question of whether or not the first shot went through President Kennedy and then through Governor Connal-

ly who was sitting in the jump seat in front of him. I heard Governor Connally testify very strongly that he was not struck by the same bullet. And I could not convince myself that the same bullet struck them both, although we had experts that said it could ... I was not convinced by it." Senator Russell another commission member echoed Senator Cooper saying "I think someone else worked with Lee Harvey Oswald."

Let's take a look at the linchpin of the Warren Commission, the single bullet theory. According to the Warren Report, Oswald was able to fire the Manlicher Carcano three times in less than six seconds. The trouble for the Warren Commission was the Zapruder film. The Zapruder film is 26 seconds long, it purports to be a second by second, frame by frame look at the assassination itself.[3] The film runs through the Bell and Howell movie camera at 18.3 frames per second. Tests with the Manlicher Carcano rifle show that the fastest the bolt of the rifle can be cycled is 2.3 seconds. This does not allow time enough for Oswald to get off the required shots to kill Kennedy.

Arlen Specter, a junior Warren Commission lawyer, is credited with what is now known as the single bullet theory – one bullet goes through two men causing seven wounds and comes out if not exactly "pristine," then at least close. Joseph Dolce, a general surgeon and chief consultant for wound ballistics for the Army, worked for the Commission in 1964. Dolce performed tests with the Oswald rifle, firing at skeletons. Dolce's test produced "badly flattened bullets." Dolce is quoted in the *Palm Beach Post,* September 18, 1978: "No bullet could go through the President's neck, the Governor's chest, badly fracture the Governor's wrist and exit with only side slightly flattened." The Doctor's findings were published in the Army's final report – not declassified until 1971 – but the Warren report ... "stuck with the pristine bullet ... they didn't put it in the Warren report because they didn't want my test." The Warren Commission was a bit selective in what they wanted in the report.

There is the matter of the Dallas authorities not being able to place Lee Oswald in the Book Depository with the rifle, and we have that confession from Dallas Police Chief Jesse Currie. In a 1969 interview for the *Dallas Morning News,* Currie stated, "We don't have any proof that Oswald fired the rifle and never did. Nobody has yet been able to put him in that building with a gun in his hand."[4]

Then there are the paraffin tests that were performed on Oswald's hands and cheek. Jesse Currie announced on November 23: "that the paraffin test

3. For a good discussion of how this film could have been altered read Noel Twyman's *Bloody Treason* and Douglas Horne's magnum opus *Inside The ARRB.*
4. See *Reclaiming History* or *Reframing by Oswald* Gary Aguilar, December 21, 2007.

proved Oswald is the assassin." (In paraffin tests hot wax is applied to a person's skin; this creates a cast, and the cast is removed then tested for the presence of nitrate.) There were traces of nitrates found on Oswald's hands – but his cheek was found to have no traces of nitrates, leading to a conclusion that Oswald had not fired a rifle that day.

The questions that surround Lee Harvey Oswald's actions after the assassination of President Kennedy are many. Were there two shells or three shells found on the sixth floor? Was Oswald seen in the first floor lunchroom eating his lunch as some witnesses have said? Or was he indeed perched at the sixth floor window at the so-called "sniper's nest" waiting for his chance to change history? If he did assassinate President Kennedy how did he make it to the second floor lunch room with the speed that it would have taken? And why when he was discovered by Officer Marion Baker and Superintendent Roy Truly did he appear calm and collected and drinking a soda? How did he manage to get from his rooming house on North Beckley Street to the Texas Theatre as fast as he did? Was he waiting in the darkened theatre to greet a handler as some research suggests? Was his wallet found at the Tippit murder scene? Or was it on his person when he was arrested? Why, when questioned by the police for some twelve hours, were the brief notes made by Chief of Detectives Will Fritz lost for years? And why were there no tape recordings made of the sessions? Why was Domingo Benavides, the closest person to see Oswald shoot Officer J.D. Tippit, never asked to identify him in a line up? Why did Aquila Clemens, who also saw the Tippit shooting, give a description of two men – neither one matching the description of Oswald in physicality or dress? And questions abound as well about Jack Ruby. Did Oswald and Ruby know each other? There have been rumors for decades that they did. Ruby plainly had ties to the mob going back to the days of Al Capone in Chicago. These ties were never investigated. If the Warren Commission was correct in its findings, why was it afraid to delve deeper into these connections? Was Ruby truly there by chance as claimed by the Warren Commission? Or did Ruby intend to kill Oswald so the world would never know the "true facts" as Ruby later claimed? If the Warren Report is correct, why is nothing in the Kennedy case from start to finish cut and dried?

Indelible in my mind is the film taken of Lee Harvey Oswald at that "short and sweet" midnight press conference. Oswald stands surrounded by Dallas's finest. The din in the small room eases a bit as Oswald begins to talk. "I really don't know what the situation is about, except that I have been accused of murdering a policeman, I know nothing more than that. I do request someone to come forward to give me legal assistance." A reporter in the crowd throws Oswald a question, "Did you kill the President?" "No," Oswald replies, "I have not been charged with that, in fact nobody has said that to me yet. The first thing I heard about it is when newspaper reporters in the hall asked me that question." A voice from the crowd can be heard to say, "You have been charged." Oswald leans his head forward to try and hear against the noisy background of the crowd in the room. "Sir?" he questions. The voice in the crowd is heard again … "you have been charged." Oswald looks stunned like a man who has received an unexpected blow to the stomach. He is pulled out of the office by police.

That for me tells the story in a nutshell.

There are many reasons why a rational person might believe that Kennedy was killed by forces other than Oswald. The writer of the *New York Times* review of *Reclaiming History*, Brian Burrough, goes on to say, "what Bugliosi has done is a public service; these people should be ridiculed, even shamed. It's time we marginalized Kennedy conspiracy theorists the way we have marginalized smokers; next time one of your co-workers starts in about Oswald, and the CIA, make him stand in the rain with the rest of the outcasts."

I am willing to bet the writer of those words never spoke to a witness to the events in Dealey Plaza or one privy to the events at Bethesda, Maryland. I have.

Whatever Oswald's involvement in the events of November 22, 1963, he was not expecting to be accused of killing John Fitzgerald Kennedy.

Try talking face to face to a person like Malcolm Summers, who was confronted by a man dressed in a suit and tie, with a hat on his head and a raincoat over his arm, as he ran up the grassy knoll, after the sound of the shots rang out. "The man in the suit said, 'Don't come up here you might get shot.'" Malcolm Summers told me this at an accidental meeting, in Dea-

Malcom Summers and author.

ley Plaza in the early 2000's. There were no genuine Secret Service agents, FBI agents or Dallas police officers assigned or stationed in the grassy knoll area.[5] Does that raise any problems for the "lone nutters?" It appears that it does not.

Many eyewitnesses in Dealey Plaza saw the presidential limousine come to a complete stop during the gunfire – though it is not seen in the Zapruder film. Should we not wonder about that? Did Mr. Bugliosi talk to one witness who saw JFK's limousine stop? I did. Those of us who have questions about that shouldn't worry. After all, Vincent Bugliosi has proven conclusively, Lee Harvey Oswald assassinated John F. Kennedy. Don't question why Jack Ruby decided to shoot Oswald, in the basement of the police and courts building, the Dallas jail. Ruby, after all, was just a nut who wanted to avenge his president's death. He wanted to be famous. Ruby figured he would be a hero for killing Oswald, the toast of the town. He would finally gain the respect and "class" that had eluded him all of his pitiful life. No one should question that.

So what, that Jack Ruby had ties to the mob going back to the days of Al Capone? Ruby made no less than seven phone calls to at least seven organized crime figures during the years 1962 and 1963. Simply coincidence? Read the testimony of one Dallas police officer, Don Archer, who was with Jack Ruby immediately after he shot Oswald. "His behavior to begin with, he was very hyper. He was sweating profusely, I could see his heart – of course we had stripped him down for security purposes –he asked me for one of my cigarettes. I gave him a cigarette. Finally, after about two hours had elapsed, which put it around one PM, the head of the Secret Service came up, I conferred with him and he told me, Oswald had in effect died and it should have shocked him, because it would mean the death penalty. I returned and said, 'Jack, it looks like it is going to be the electric chair for you.' Instead of being shocked, he became calm, he stopped sweating, his heart slowed down, I asked him if he wanted a cigarette, he advised me he didn't smoke. And I was just astonished that this was completely difference in behavior of what I expected. I would say his life had depended on his

5. Read the article "The Secret Service Agent on the Knoll," by Debra Conway, with contributions from Michael Parks and Mark Colgan.

getting Oswald." That's not just gibberish from a so-called conspiracy theorist, it is testimony from one of Dallas's finest. Who was in the jail cell – with Jack Ruby. He saw this behavior for himself. Not to worry, not to question. No conspiracy here. Jack Ruby acted alone. The Warren Commission and lawyer, Vincent Bugliosi, have proven it. Trust them. Never mind that after President Kennedy was taken into Trauma room one at Parkland Hospital, after his little ride through Dealey Plaza, he had a wound to the back of the head that was avulsed, meaning blown outward, torn off, and a small round wound in the front of his throat, that all the Dallas doctors thought was a wound of entrance, in Dr. Malcom Perry's words, the bullet "seemed to be coming at him." A statement that he made at a press conference just an hour after the President had expired. Don't think about the fact that all tape recordings of that event were taken, and never seen again, and that it was the diligent work of a researcher years later, that found an existing transcript of that press conference tucked away at the Johnson Library. We must not question this. It was just coincidence.

The mere fact that the wounds to President Kennedy's body appear as markedly different when the body reached Bethesda Hospital, well, the Dallas doctors had it wrong, that's all. It must have been an optical illusion.

I am, of course, being ironic. But no less sarcastic and condescending than Vincent Bugliosi in his screed, *Reclaiming History*. In his end notes, Bugliosi takes a swipe at me, calling me a "died in the wool conspiracy theorist." I'll take the title. I have met many fine conspiracy theorists in the 20 years I have been working on the JFK mystery. Many have devoted their time, money, compassion and skills in an effort to get to a closer truth, where the murder of a U.S. President can be understood.

Until we have all the truth about John F. Kennedy's assassination, I'll just have to wait in the rain with the rest of the outcasts.

William Matson Law
June 28, 2015
Central Oregon

Chapter One

HOTEL CALIFORNIA

" *On a dark desert highway, cool wind in my hair, warm smell of colitas rising up in the air.*" I reached over and cranked the volume on my car radio up and at the same time I pushed the accelerator pedal almost to the floor so I could take the steep grade leading out of my little central Oregon town.

I smiled listening to the Eagles singing "Hotel California."I had spent the last couple of years working with filmmaker Mark Sobel on a documentary on the assassination of Senator Robert F. Kennedy and trying to write about the experience. Kennedy had run for the democratic nomination for the presidency of the United States and had been shot in the kitchen pantry of the Ambassador hotel in the early morning hours of June 5, 1968, and I had read somewhere that the song had been inspired by the event.

"Last thing I remember, I was running for the door I had to find the passage back to the place I was before. Relax said the night man, we are programmed to receive, you can check-out anytime you like, but you can never leave."

Robert Francis Kennedy never got to leave Hotel California in a very real sense. Just as Robert Kennedy's brother John Fitzgerald Kennedy has never really left Dealey Plaza in Dallas, Texas.

Both Kennedy brothers are locked in the collective consciousness of the world: JFK riding into ambush in Dealey Plaza, November 22, 1963, and Robert Kennedy, lying in a pool of his own blood on a dirty pantry floor on June 5, 1968. My book on John Kennedy's autopsy had been published a couple of years before, and I was pleased that the book had garnered mostly positive reviews from the public, but I was more gratified that the autopsy personnel Paul O'Connor and Jim Jenkins had thought that I had done a good job of letting them tell their story, and Dennis David, who had been on the periphery of the Kennedy autopsy, had said the same.

It was Dennis David who had alerted me to the fact that Vincent Bugliosi had just published his opus, *Reclaiming History*, his twenty year study of the JFK assassination. From the tone of David's email I had the impression

1

that I had not come out on the favorite end of the assassination stick, as it were, with Bugliosi, and another not so promising note from the publisher at JFK Lancer persuaded me that I would have to see (rather read) for myself what all the noise was about, so I drove the forty miles to the "local" Barnes and Noble.

During the drive, I had time to reflect on what time had wrought since my book had been published. Dennis David had lost his beloved wife Dorothy to cancer. Dennis called me just after Dorothy's passing. He hadn't even arrived home from the hospital when he phoned me to tell me of the news. "We just lost mama," he'd said, his voice catching in his throat. I listened, stunned. I had known of "Dot's" illness of course, but one is never prepared for that kind of news. I'm happy to report as of this writing that Dennis David has remarried, is doing very well and has moved to Indiana.

James Jenkins has continued to live in the Deep South, spending his time between Alabama and Mississippi.[1] He continues to live with his wife Jackie, two dogs, and in his words "several cats."

Paul O'Connor called me one day in June of 2006, and started off the conversation with his normal salutation: "How you doing, buddy?"

"I'm good," I said. "What's new with you?"

"Buddy," O'Connor said, "You're never going to guess what happened?" I started to chuckle and waited for what I was sure was going to be one of Paul's latest stories of the trials of dealing with crazy researchers of the Kennedy assassination who had called Paul to give him their ideas of "what had really happened" to JFK. Paul had received several of these calls over the years and he would often call me and tell me of his telephone adventures and we would have a good laugh or have a serious conversation about the assassination. I heard Paul say:"I was walking in the door of my own house and I tripped and fell and I fractured my hip and I didn't know it, and I tried to get up and fell again and broke my wrist!" And then I heard an explosion of laughter from O'Connor.

I was taken aback, and said, "Oh God, Paul, are you all right?"

"Yeah, I'm okay," I heard him say. "My son was with me." He was still recovering from the fall, but was feeling well enough to call me and tell me of his plight. We talked about what was going on in our lives at the moment and we tried to firm up a date for going on vacation together with our families to the Smoky Mountains of West Virginia. "Where you live reminds me

---

1. Jim created quite a stir on the 50th anniversary of the Kennedy Assassination when out of his friendship for me, he turned up at a conference in Dallas, Texas, telling his story to an overflowing crowd at the Adolphus Hotel. Due to that experience, he has begun writing his memoirs of the events of November 22, 1963.

a lot of the Smokys," Paul told me. "We'll have a great time," he said. I agreed we would. I wish we had had time to take that trip. I had no idea it would be the last time I would talk to Paul O'Connor. About a month and a half later I came home to find James Jenkins had called me, but had not left a message. I had an uneasy feeling. I didn't take Jim's call as a good sign. Jim Jenkins and I had formed a bit of a bond over the years, but I still had to be the one to initiate contact between us, but when I did call, Jim always to took my call or called me back if I got his answering machine. And he always seemed genuinely glad to hear from me.

A day went by and Jenkins called me the next morning. "William," Jim said after I answered the phone, "I wish we were talking under different circumstances, but I called to tell you Paul has died." I shouldn't have been shocked or surprised given Paul O'Connor's many health problems over the years, but I was. After Jim and I ended our phone conversation, I sat on the side of my bed stunned. And before I realized what had happened, I felt hot tears sting my eyes and trickle down my face. I had talked to O'Connor years before about his feelings about death. Paul had told me of the time he had had an operation. "I died on the operating table and I felt myself drifting. It was dark and quiet and from a long, long way up I heard the doctor calling my name. I heard him say: "Hey, O'Connor, are you in there?" and it brought me back. If that's what death is like, it's real calm, real peaceful and I don't have any fear of it."

Paul O'Connor was a person who enjoyed his life, and had learned to live with pain on a daily basis, and tried hard to have a sense of humor about his troubles. He liked to share funny memories of his time in the service and was a natural at telling them.

In the late-1990s I had arranged to have Paul and Dennis David attend a conference on the Kennedy assassination with me. (I was still working on the book at the time.) Paul and Dennis were sharing a room together at the hotel where the conference was being held and as luck would have it their flights had delivered them to Dallas earlier than my flight. Somehow, I had overlooked booking myself a room. The hotel at that point was full with little option left to me. I asked for the room number where Paul and Dennis were ensconced. I took the elevator up to their floor, trudged down the hallway and to the door of their room. I pounded on the door and Dennis opened it. He looked at me standing there with my suitcase in one had, my briefcase clutched in the other and said "Hey, we wondered when you were going to get here." I walked into the hotel room. Paul was sitting at a table having a drink, and if I remembered right, smoking a cigarette. "Hey Buddy, how are ya?" Paul rose from where he was sitting to give me a hug. "Jesus, you've gotten fat!" he said laughing. I'd admitted I put on a few pounds since we had last seen each other. I explained my plight.

"That's no problem," Dennis David said taking the comforter off his bed and throwing it to me, and Paul gave me one of the pillows from his bed.

We stayed up till the early morning hours, O'Connor and David sitting around in their skivvies telling stories of their time in the military. At one point Paul got down on his hands and knees and began crawling toward me, making sounds like an animal to illustrate a funny prank he and some of the other enlisted men had played on a buddy while Paul was stationed at Guantanamo Bay, Cuba, leaving Dennis and I howling with laughter.

Paul Kelly O'Connor was that rare individual who was comfortable in his own skin. He liked country and western music and "some" of the old rock and roll.. He liked a good beer now and then and anchovies on his pizza. He could be a total gentlemen while in the presence of women and use "colorful" language like the old swabbie he used to be and in his heart, still was, when he was in the company of men he considered his "buddies." Paul loved to study history. I still remember, when being driven at night from Portland to the town I live, my brother-in-law Bob drove on a stretch of freeway that ran along the side of the Columbia River where Lewis and Clark had once made an encampment while on their search of the Northwest Territories. When Bob pointed out the general area to Paul, Paul said, "Really." Like a little kid, craning his neck, his eyes wide behind the brown frames of his glasses, peering into the night.

Paul O'Connor knew his own place in history due to his involvement in President Kennedy's autopsy. Sometimes relishing the attention it brought him, sometimes hating it for the same reason. He paid a price for being part of the Kennedy legacy, having to put up with endless questions from people like me. Some he considered reasonable researchers, and some he considered to be – in his words "cuckoos and nuts." He had to live with naysayers questioning his motives and his memory. Paul O'Connor always had an answer to those questions. "We were there, they weren't," he would say. And sometimes he would add: "They don't know shit."

Paul's wife told me later that she'd come home to find him dead in his bed. Paul had died in his sleep. The cause of death was listed as natural causes.

I had fought with myself whether to attend the funeral or not. I did not attend. I'd lost too many people I had loved in years past, and unlike Paul, I had not learned, nor have I, to accept the deaths of those close to me. Paul O'Connor left us too soon, before we could say good-bye and before we were willing to let him go. But wherever Paul is now, I hope it's calm. I hope it's peaceful.

Arriving at the bookstore, I paid the $50.00, minus the 20% discount (I recently had a friend of mine living in California who told me he'd found a copy of Bugliosi's book in a discount bin for $2.00. I guess I should have waited) and lugged the monstrous tome to my car. Once home, I started to leaf through the 1600-plus pages, paying close attention to the section with Bugliosi's writing on the autopsy.

I remembered a call I received some months earlier from Andy Winiarczyk, owner of The Last Hurrah bookshop in Williamsport, Pennsylvania. "There's good news and bad news," Andy opined. Feeling like I was in an old Bud Abbott/Lou Costello routine, I said: "Okay, give me the good news first." "Vincent Bugliosi just bought a copy of your book," he replied. Feeling a bit shocked that the great attorney-prosecutor of Charles Mason and author of *Helter Skelter* had bothered with my little oral history offering, I asked, "O.K., what's the bad news?" Dead-pan Andy answered, "Vincent Bugliosi bought a copy of your book." I started to laugh as Andy continued "and he's been pouring through it looking for information. He wants to know if you have dates and times for the interviews you did." Some I did and some I didn't and I told Andy so. "Well, he wants to talk to you. Is it O.K. if I give him your phone number?" I said, "Yes," and I'd waited for Bugliosi to call me, but he never did. I'd wondered how he was going to deal with what the Navy corpsmen had told me. Andy had told me that Bugliosi had already made up his mind that Lee Harvey Oswald had acted alone and I remembered thinking, "Well he's going to have a hell of a time dealing with the medical testimony of 'the boys' as I came to think of them as a group."

As I was to learn, it wasn't difficult for Vincent Bugliosi to deal with any of the things I had written or any of Jenkins's, O'Connor's, Custer's or David's testimony, or anyone else's testimony I had gathered for the book. He simply dealt with any problems that he faced with his preconceived "lone nut" scenario by largely ignoring anything he didn't like. For example, on page 385 of *Reclaiming History* Bugliosi writes about who was in the autopsy room during the Kennedy autopsy.

FBI Special Agents Francis X. O'Neill, Jr. and James W. Sibert recorded the names of all those present, including the admirals and generals of whom there were only four. In addition to their report, which identifies them, listen to what O'Neill said in an October 2001 interview:

"There was the commanding officer of the hospital, [Admiral Calvin B. Galloway]; there was a rear-admiral [Admiral George C. Burkley, the president's personal physician]. There was a general [Godfrey McHugh] who was on the (continued on page 386) airplane with Kennedy and was his military attaché; he was a general and there was a Major-General Philip Wehle [commanding officer of the U.S. Military District, Washington, D.C.] who tried to enter and I kicked him out and he came back and told me he was there to get another casket because the other one was broken. There was no-one else." If someone could find a likely conspirator in this group, who was covering up the assassination, please let me know, Bugliosi writes. Bugliosi has quoted directly from my book. I was the interviewer. It fits with his "Oswald did it alone" approach, and so he uses the passages from my interview with Frank O'Neill because it suits his purposes. In the following paragraph, he quotes from *In the Eye of History* again. This time, it's Paul O'Connor he cites. "Bethesda medical corpsman Paul Kelly O'Connor told an interviewer (me) that he remembers the "I am" (meaning "who is charge"), coming from the area of Admiral Burkley."

Question: "So you think Admiral Burkley is the one who said 'I'm in charge'?" "Yes." Bugliosi then goes on to explain to the reader that it was James Humes that was in charge of the autopsy.

First of all, just because the list of names made by Special Agent Sibert and O'Neill contain the names of certain individuals doesn't mean that the agents captured the names of everyone present in the morgue that night. James Sibert told Debra Conway and I on June 5, 2001 at his home in Florida that: "We went around. But if someone was busy or got away, we asked. Most of it was eye-to-eye contact." Hardly a fool-proof method of getting every name in the morgue the night of Friday, November 22, 1963. There could have been, and probably were, people in the Bethesda morgue we will never know. From what I've been told by Jenkins, O'Connor and Jerrol Custer, the morgue was over-crowded, described by some as "chaos." I doubt very much whether Sibert or O'Neill had time to get every name by asking each individual personally, and if the FBI agents did, for example, pass around a piece of paper for people to sign, anyone could put down whatever name they wished, or not put down anything. The agents wouldn't have known the difference. And if the FBI agents did have time to check everyone in the morgue, persons or person unknown still could have lied about who they were. Has anyone ever found out who George Bakeman was? Not to my knowledge. (For discussion of this see the Jerrol Custer Chapter.)

The mere fact that Frank O'Neill told me or anyone else that "that's all there was" concerning admirals and generals in the morgue does not make it so. Francis X. O'Neill, as I learned in my research for this book, had his own reasons and bias for going along with the lone-nut scenario, and therefore his statements cannot always be taken at face value. The point here is not to savage Frank O'Neill, but to simply point out that Vincent Bugliosi chooses to believe what he chooses to believe. Bugliosi knows from reading my book that O'Neill professes to me that Oswald assassinated JFK, and did it alone. He also said things or wrote things himself that lead a person to believe otherwise. Bugliosi uses none of the testimony from anyone I have interviewed that did not help him prove that he is "reclaiming history." That kind of research is called "cherry picking." In other words, he's being a lawyer. Bugliosi had a telephone conversation lasting a few minutes with James Sibert in 2000, but no face-to-face interview, and instead, uses Sibert's interviews with the House Select Committee as testimony he gave before the Records Review Board to make the point he wants to make.

Bugliosi did not write in his book of the fact that Jim Sibert's recollection of the casket entry (at least the one they were involved in) on that night differs markedly from Frank O'Neill's memory of the event. As I point out, O'Neill's version of the casket entry jibed with Jim Sibert's in interviews conducted with both agents by Andrew Purdy of the House Select Committee, but after O'Neill became aware of discrepancies pointed out by David S. Lifton in his seminal work on the assassination, *Best Evidence,* published in 1981, Frank O'Neill changed his version of the casket entry to match with the "official" version in the history of the event, i.e., the display casket taken in by a military honor guard, etc. I have spent many hours with former FBI Agent Jim Sibert, on three separate visits to his home in Florida. Does Vincent Bugliosi relay to the reader any of what James Sibert and I discussed? That Sibert literally despised Arlen Specter, the so-called father of the single-bullet theory? That Sibert came right out and called Specter a "liar"? That Sibert is "adamant" that the single-bullet scenario "did not happen?"

Jim Sibert told me in an on camera interview in 2001: "I stood a mere two feet from that bullet wound that was in the back, the one that they eventually moved up to the base of the neck. There is no way that that bullet could have gone that low then rise up and come out of the front of the neck." Or did Mr. Bugliosi report that James Sibert, in the same on camera interview, told me "I've often wondered, whoever that marksman was if he had used an exploding bullet?" It hardly sounds as if former agent Sibert believes Lee Harvey Oswald killed Kennedy, does it?

Does Bugliosi tell the reader of James Jenkins and what he told me about what he saw and heard that night in the Bethesda morgue? On page 149 of his book, Bugliosi writes: "Paul O'Connor and James Curtis Jenkins, student lab technicians in charge of the admission and discharge of morgue bodies, lift the body out of the casket and placed it on the autopsy table where the bloody wrappings are removed." Then on page 409, the reader will find this passage: "For instance James Curtis Jenkins, a lab technician during the autopsy told HSCA investigators that the large head wound was to the 'middle temporal region back to the occipital'" That's all. The reader will not find anything on Jenkins's testimony to me – all reported in the first edition of *In the Eye of History* – where Jenkins claims that: "The brain stem had already been severed. Some [areas of the skull] that were fragmented along the sagittal sutures looked like – then there was some comment that it looked like [the head wound] had been surgically extended." Jenkins also said to me that: "My impression that the damage done to the area of the brain, the extensiveness of it, did not quite match the extensiveness of the wound ... the damage done to the brain seemed to be a little less than you would expect from the damage to skull." Nor does Bugliosi tell his readers that Jenkins felt the autopsy doctors were trying to do their jobs but were "being directed from the gallery" or any of the other myriad of things that Jenkins had to say. When I asked Jim Jenkins if, as it was claimed by Doctor Humes that he, Humes, was in charge of the autopsy and no one else, Jenkins told me "Humes was not in charge of the autopsy." Jenkins agreed with his partner in the morgue duties that night, Paul O'Connor. And who did Paul O'Connor claim was "in charge" of the autopsy? Admiral George Burkley, President Kennedy's personal physician.

Jerrol Custer, the x-ray technician who took x-rays of Kennedy's body, and whom James Jenkins assisted that night, believes the same thing. Why is it important to know why these men believe that Burkley was in charge of the Kennedy autopsy and not Doctor James Humes? Because a number of researchers, "conspiracy nuts" as lawyer Bugliosi is fond of calling anyone who does not believe in the "lone-nut" scenario, it stands to reason that if Humes or Boswell were not in charge of the autopsy, then the military personnel were in charge of the autopsy, and that would point to government control of the event, and give weight to Pierre Finck's testimony[2] at the Clay Shaw trial held in 1969. Read how Finck was questioned by Al Oser, lawyer and staff member of the Garrison team.

Oser: "How many other military personnel where present in the autopsy room?"

Finck: "That autopsy room was quite crowded. It's a small autopsy room, and when you are called in circumstances like that to look at the wound of the President of the United States who is dead, you don't look around too much to ask people for their names and take notes of who they are and how many they are. I

---

2. Finck was chief of the wound ballistics pathology branch of the armed forces institute in Washington, D.C.

did not do so. The room was crowded with military and civilian personnel and federal agents, secret service agents, FBI agents who were part of the autopsy but I could not give you a precise breakdown as regards to the attendance of the people in the autopsy room at Bethesda Naval Hospital."

Oser: "Colonel did you find that you had to take orders from this Army general that was there directing the autopsy?"

Finck: "No, because there were admirals."

Oser: "There were admirals?"

Finck: "Oh, yes! There were admirals and when you are a lieutenant Colonel in the Army, you just follow orders."

Bugliosi has to stay away from the information in my book, because he can't deal with the witnesses' testimony about the Kennedy autopsy. Vincent Bugliosi builds upon his peculiar logic stick by stick. Example: This footnote in the chapter entitled "Summary of Oswald's Guilt," page 953: *For instance, since we know that Oswald shot and killed Kennedy we also know that questions such as what is the small object resembling a bullet fragment that Dr. David Mantik has become obsessed with, believing it was planted in an autopsy x-ray to frame Oswald by indicating a shot from the rear? What ever happened to the missing autopsy photos? Was Oswald a good shot, or not? Why wasn't Commission Exhibit No. 399 damaged more than it was? Whom did Roger Craig see running out of the Book Depository Building fifteen minutes after the assassination and getting into a Nash Rambler? Did Oswald have time to get to Tenth and Patton from his rooming house in time to kill Officer Tippit? Why Drs. Gary Aguilar, Cyril Wecht and Rex Bradford want to know, did a test-bullet fired through a test-skull cause more damage to the right side of the skull than Commission Exhibit No. 399 caused to the right side of Kennedy's skull? What is the reason Josiah Thompson believes would have prevented it from being loaded into Oswald's rifle? And hundreds upon hundreds of other questions and problems the critics have with the case against Oswald – are all irrelevant. Why, because we know that Oswald killed Kennedy. So by definition there has to be a satisfactory answer for all of these questions and preconceived discrepancies and problems with the case. This is not my opinion I am giving. This is an incontrovertible fact of life and logic. They would have relevance only if the guilt of Oswald hadn't already been established beyond all reasonable doubt. But it has.*

Bugliosi has summed up for me in this footnote of *Reclaiming History* the problem(s) with his work. Like the Warren Commission, he started out with a preconceived conclusion to John F. Kennedy's assassination and presented a lopsided view of what he, Bugliosi, holds to be the truth, and pounds the table railing against anyone or anything (Read: conflicts in the evidence) that points out "problems" with the Kennedy case. Above all, his blatant unabashed unapologetic arrogance the words "conspiracy theorist" is used over, over and over throughout the text, and grates upon the nerves of the reader. I do not and have never considered myself a "conspiracy theorist." My job, as I see it, is to report. I have no fear of being wrong in making any assumptions about what happened at the autopsy of John F. Kennedy. *I don't know what happened at Kennedy's autopsy.* I can conjecture as anyone can – and that may be good for a guessing game, but that's all it would be: a kind of mental masturbation, worthless to lay persons or historians or anyone else who cares about truth in history. It is intellectual arrogance from the Warren Commission (read: lawyers) and those in government that keep documents locked in dark, airless vaults, who believe that they are qualified to tell the rest of us, we the people of the United States, exactly what happened in John F. Kennedy's assassination and why it happened. They have kept real answers from ever seeing the light of day more than anything else.

Paul O'Connor, during our first interview, said, "You know, most interviews don't want to hear my voice; they want to hear their voice." In every interview I have done since, I have always tried to remember to be humble and stay out of the way of the person speaking. And to *listen* to what the person is telling me. To hear their voice.

It is the voices of the witness to the events of the Kennedy assassination, from Parkland Hospital in Dallas, Texas and the Bethesda Morgue in Maryland (and those unknown witnesses in between) that have the best chance of giving us the clues through their memories of that long ago tragedy in this country's history that can lead to real answer: the truth.

In Bugliosi's massive tome, he included a CD with hundreds of end notes. In the section titled "Kennedy's autopsy and the gunshot wounds to Kennedy and Connally," I found this: James E. Metzler, a third class corpsman, who was at the autopsy for around five to ten minutes before the autopsy commenced, claimed the [head] wound was located toward the back of the head. (Lifton *Best Evidence* PP 631 – 633) I had, of course, read Lifton's account, but I had never personally talked to Jim Metzler before, but reading the end note made me curious. I contacted Mr. Metzler on October 26th, 2009. I explained who I was and that I had written a book on the Kennedy autopsy and I'd never talked to him and would he mind sharing some of his memories from that night in 1963.

"What do you want to know?" Metzler asked.

"What do you remember?"

"We were in lab school at the time," Metzler told me. "It is a 14 month school, and half of it, the first seven months are all theory, all classroom. The last seven months are all practical, actually working in each one of the departments." Metzler told me in essence what Paul O'Connor told me in 1998. Metzler had been in class when he and the other students were told President Kennedy had been killed. Classes were canceled. "Metzler went back to the barracks and watched television." He "heard talk" that Kennedy's body was going to be taken to Walter Reed. But Meltzer felt they would take the body to Bethesda because "Kennedy was a navy man."

He told me that he, Jim Jenkins and Paul O'Connor "volunteered" for the morgue, saying "you could stand fire watch at the barracks or 'assist' the pathologist at autopsies." Thinking on it, Metzler decided Kennedy was definitely going to be brought to Bethesda. "I knew Paul had the morgue watch that night, and I thought he's going to need some help." He walked over to the morgue, helped O'Connor set up for autopsies. "A little while later, the phone rang and the voice on the other end of the phone said. 'You're going to have a visitor tonight' and I knew what he meant." There was another call "a fair amount of time later," as best as Jim Meltzer could now remember. The second caller said. "He's coming in around the back." So Metzler went out on the platform at the loading dock and waited. After "waiting quite a while" he saw a pick up truck with a bunch of uniformed guys in it.

They passed the rear entrance of the hospital. "A little later, the men in the pickup truck, came around again, and pulled into the driveway there," with a navy ambulance or a hearse. Metzler wasn't sure. The men in the pickup truck unloaded the casket. Metzler told me he opened the door for them and showed them which door to go in. "The rear door of the hospital immediately to the left is a double door that goes into the refrigerated room where they keep the bodies, and you would make a right and go through the other set of double doors into the morgue itself. Anyway, they came in past the refrigerated room, into the morgue and they set the coffin down on the floor, near the corner. In other words, as you just come through the door to your immediate right was where they set the coffin down."

I interrupted Jim Metzler with: "They went into the autopsy room with it?"

"Yes, this was the autopsy room." Metzler's story was kind of a weird hybrid of both the display casket entry and the cheap metal shipping casket scenario to some extent. In the display casket scenario, the casket had been brought in to the "atrium" and put on a gurney and rolled into the morgue.

In the shipping casket scenario, the casket had been carried directly into the morgue and set down on the floor. Not to mention this would be a fourth version of how the coffin/casket came into the morgue. We have Paul O'Connor who said the body came into the morgue in a cheap metal shipping casket. There is Jim Sibert's version where Sibert, O'Neill, Kellerman and Greer carried in the expensive display casket. Remember Frank O'Neill went along with Sibert's version, but changed it later to match with the official casket entry, the one with the honor guard carrying the display casket in, and now one with Metzler directing the display casket being unloaded and carried directly into the morgue and set directly on the morgue floor.

"They sent everyone out," said Metzler, "that had brought the coffin in. There was an admiral that was with them. I don't remember if the admiral stayed. I kind of think the admiral stayed, though I'm not sure." I asked Metzler if he was talking about the display casket, just to be sure. "Yeah, David Lifton asked me that," he said. "He said what did the coffin look like? I said it was a large casket and [Lifton] asked what color was it?" I said, "I think it was brown, but I'm not sure. I pretty much remember it being brown." "Right," I said. "I could hear the silence (from Lifton) you know." And [Lifton] said: "Are you sure about that?" And I said, "No, I think it was brown, but I don't know for sure, right?" But he sent me a copy of his book (*Best Evidence*) and I read it in the book and he put in that [I said] it was "definitely brown." Well, gee, because that was my preference. I thought if anything, it would be brown. But he put in there it "was definitely brown."

I could hear the amusement in Jim Metzler's voice and it made me smile. "My memory, as best as I can remember, is that it looked like an expensive casket and it was brown.[3] Jim Metzler then told me of helping open up the casket and seeing the president's body. It was wrapped in a sheet. They unwrapped that sheet and the president was nude. Kennedy's head was wrapped with another sheet. "A second sheet was wrapped around his head." They unwrapped the head and picked up his body and carried it over to the autopsy table "face up." Metzler could then see some of the head wounds. "I was carrying him on his right side, so I was on the right side of him. I could see the wound on the side of his head. It looked like it started somewhere

---

3. Paul O'Connor's memory of course is that the casket was a cheap metal shipping casket. Jim Jenkins's memory was just seeing the tip of the casket coming through the door and when I asked Jenkins if it was a metal shipping casket, he said "Well, it was government, so … " There is the story of there being a casket brought in a hour or so before Kennedy's casket arrived, containing the body of an air force colonel. That casket was reported to be brown in color. Could Jim Metzler have had a memory merge of the cheap shipping casket being put on the floor of the morgue and the brown casket of the air force colonel, that caused his "memory" of Kennedy's body being removed from a brown display casket?

around the top of the [right] ear and it went down. (Jim's speech slowed, I could almost see him thinking about the scene in his head as he was telling me what he remembered of the head wound) and to the back of his head. It looked like somebody had opened his head with a can opener. It wasn't a precise cut. It was jagged; you could see white material under the hairline."

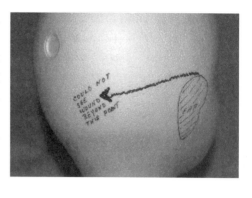

I asked Jim if he could see the president's brain.

"No, I didn't see the back of the president's head because he was face up. So I couldn't see what kind of damage was done to the back of his head."

"Did you see any damage to the top portion of his head?" I asked.

"No. What I saw was on the side." Metzler told me the top portion of Kennedy's head was intact. "The only thing I could see as far as a wound was starting somewhere near the top of the ear, and going a bit downward – not much – but downward to the rear. It looked like a jagged cut." Metzler reiterated "A tear and I could see white material. I don't know if it was brain or it was the bottom of his skin, I don't know, but it was white. There were pieces of it below the hairline." Jim then clarified he was talking about the part of the wound that he saw at the side of Kennedy's head. Metzler then told me Dr. Boswell came over and said "Thank you for coming, but we have plenty of help for right now."

Jim let out a short whoop of laughter. "He said 'You can leave, we've got plenty of help here.'" Metzler's laughter started again. "I could see that," he said. "There were quite a few people in the [morgue] room by then. And when I went to leave, I left through the refrigerated room. There's also another door that goes out to the passageway at the other end of the morgue, but I left by the door where they brought the coffin in and when I opened the door to walk into the refrigerated room there were quite a few men there in suits and ties. They weren't military, they weren't in uniform. This one guy had a clip board and he said, 'What's your name?' I told him. He wanted to see my I.D. card. So I showed him my I.D. and, he goes down this list he had and said 'this guy's not on the list,' steps in front of the door that goes out to the passageway – everybody looked like they were starting to get nervous – and I thought "Uh-oh." I said: "I'm in trouble now. It was spooky, you know? And then he said: 'Why are you here?' and I explained that I was in lab school and that I did stand the board watch and I came over to help

Paul. I said, 'But little did I know that you had plenty of help here', and then they let me go. I was only there maybe five, ten minutes. You know what's funny?" Jim Metzler asked me. "When I think back, some things are very clear, and other things, you're not sure about."

"Well, yes." I answered. "That's the human memory, isn't it?"

"Yes, but it just makes you feel stupid. When you remember something crystal clear and something that should be obvious, you don't."

"Now, I'm going to ask you this," I said to Jim. "I don't look for conspiracy, I let people talk for themselves."

"Right," I heard Jim Metzler say. "What's your opinion on [conspiracy]? I'm sure you've read [David] Lifton's book."

"I've read Lifton, I've read Harry Livingstone's book."

"One thing." Jim Metzler said, "I've found to be very interesting. In the video store they had a VHS tape about the assassination. I forget the name of it, but they interviewed Aubrey Rike from the funeral parlor in Dallas. And he described how they wrapped up the body and put it in the coffin. And that's exactly how I remember seeing it, when we took it out. The head was wrapped with a sheet and the body was wrapped with a second sheet."

"See," I said "that's where it gets weird. I had a little conference. I brought all the guys together," I told Metzler, that were willing to come, including Jim Sibert, one of the FBI agents, and we met in Florida (because Jim Siebert lived in the state and was in his 80's at that time and he didn't want to travel.) So Jim Jenkins, Paul O'Connor, Dennis David came and Dr. David Mantik who's done a lot of research and writing on this case, we all went in and sat around the table and talked about the autopsy pictures and things like that. We tried to get a timeline, I told Metzler, for different things that happened [that night]. You know the controversy, about the so-called metal shipping casket that Paul [O'Connor] talked about, and that Jim [Jenkins] thinks he might have seen, versus people like you that saw the ornate display casket, plus the different wrappings [on the body] and we've never been able to get a handle on – were people's memories were just fuzzy on that, and Jim thought it was a metal shipping casket they saw, but it really was the display casket? I don't know, it's hard to pin down."

I then said to Jim Metzler with some trepidation: "What do you think? Do you think shenanigans were going on that night [with Kennedy's body]? Do you think it was just confusion because of different people doing different jobs?"

"Harry Livingstone asked me to come to Westchester to talk about it, and I had mentioned to him that I didn't think it was quite dark. In other words, it was more dark but not totally pitch black, not totally dark when I was watching on the platform for the coffin and the guys to arrive. I don't know." I could hear the frustration in Jim Metzler's voice as he was telling me this. "I thought it just seemed – because the official autopsy they said didn't start until eight o'clock and I thought it doesn't seem…." There was a long pause from Metzler…. "Like it would be that late you know, it was just a feeling."

"I understand" I said.

"And when I watched one of the videos of the assassination, when the president's plane landed at Andrews Air Force Base, and when the people and the coffin were being removed from the plane, I noticed that it was dark. The first time I watched that movie, something bothered me about the movie and I didn't know what it was. I must have watched it a dozen times. But something didn't seem right – and then it dawned on me – It's dark at Andrews when the plane touched down. And I was thinking it wasn't quite dark when they brought the body in. I could be wrong about it. I don't know. It just bothers me that it didn't seem that it wasn't quite dark when the casket arrived. I said to Donna, my wife, "Something's not right; something's bothering me about this video. And then it dawned on me. It was dark." It was pitch black at Andrews, I think it was right around six p.m. when the plane touched down."

I asked Metzler to give me his perspective of the president's head wound, his opinion, if he thought that the scenario of Lee Harvey Oswald shooting, from the sixth floor of the School Book Depository Building was possible? Metzler said: "My opinion of the head wound is that it couldn't have happened! He [Kennedy] could not have been shot from the rear. He had to have been shot from the front side, from the knoll thing. That would be the most likely spot that would have produced a wound like that. If he was shot from behind, you'd see more damage to either the front of the face or at the side in front of the ear."

I asked, "Have you seen some of the autopsy photographs?"

"Harry showed them to me," he answered.

"You've seen that one where they've got [Kennedy] on the table?" I said. "And his head's all laid open on the top?" (See photo section, photo #3.)

"Yes."

"It didn't look that way to you, did it?"

"No," Metzler answered. I could hear amusement in his voice. "No, it didn't."

"That's the sixty-four thousand dollar question, isn't it?" I said. "What went on, to make the head look like that?" Some have speculated that [the hair] was so matted with blood that the hair stuck together, obscuring the size of the head wound. Would you think that's possible?" I asked.

There was a long pause. Then Jim Metzler said, "I" ... another pause. "I didn't *see any thing* like that ... top of the head wound that they show in those [pictures]."

I interrupted with: "Blasted open?"

"It was basically over the right ear and down into the back?" I asked.

Metzler answered, "Yes, starting near the top of the ear. Somewhere around that area, and then dipping down a little bit, not a lot, and running toward the back of the head. But, like I said, I couldn't see the damage in the back of his head because he was on his back and his face was facing up toward the ceiling." I told Jim Metzler that I was glad to have had the chance to talk to him. I then asked him if I could use his name when quoting him.

"If not," I said, "I'll just use you as a source that was there but would not let me use their name."

"You can use my name," he said. "It's just that ... sometimes you talk to people like Harry Livingstone or you talk to David Lifton, and it's not really quite what you told them." We both started to laugh, and then Jim told me, "You know what impression I get from some of the people that I talk to? It seems like – no disrespect to you, this probably doesn't even apply to you. But I got the impression that they pretty much know what happened. Their theories pretty much carved in stone and if what you tell them runs along with what they thought, Oh! Okay! But if you tell them something that doesn't, well, then, you can't be right about that." "I remember a woman called me one time, I forget her name – she asked me – I don't even know what the question was – and I told her the answers the best I could, and she says 'Well, you couldn't be right about that!' I said, 'Well I was there!'" I heard Jim Metzler's laughter. Metzler's experience with the "woman" illustrates perfectly the 'why and how' of the research and writing I do. To me, witness testimony is the closest thing to the actual "truth" of an event.

The people who witnessed President Kennedy's assassination in Dealey Plaza and the doctors and nurses who saw the wounds to the President's body at Parkland Hospital in Dallas, Texas and the witnesses at the Bethesda Naval Hospital autopsy are the best evidence of what happened to John F. Kennedy. This volume deals mainly with witnesses' memories of the wounds to President Kennedy's body, Dallas vs. Bethesda. Let's go back to the description of President Kennedy's body as seen in Dallas, Texas after the shooting in Dealey Plaza, after his arrival at Parkland Hospital. Dr. Malcolm O. Perry said this at a press conference held at Parkland Hospital on 11/22/63, an hour after President Kennedy died: "Concerning the wound in his throat ... there was an entrance wound in the neck.... It appeared to be coming at him ... the wound happened to be an entrance wound in the neck." Dr. Perry, of course, is the one who made a small slit across the wound in the throat to insert the trach tube to allow the president to breathe. And what did Dr. Perry say about the wound to Kennedy's head? "I then examined the wound in the back of the president's head. This was a large gaping wound in the right posterior part, with cerebrum and cerebellum tissue being damaged and exposed.... " And this from Dr. Marion "Pepper" Jenkins: "There was ... obvious tracheal damage.... There was a great laceration in the right side of the head (temporal and occipital) causing a great defect in the skull plate. So that there was herniation and laceration of great areas of the brain, even to the extent that the part of the right cerebellum had protruded from the wound."

The following information is taken directly from the Dallas doctors' handwritten notes and/or Warren Commission testimony:

Dr. Charles Carrico, in a handwritten report dated 11/22/63, stated: "The skull wound had avulsed the calvarium and shredded brain tissue present with profuse oozing." Dr. Ronald Jones' handwritten report dated 11/22/63: "Severe skull and brain injury was noted as well as small hole in anterior middle of neck thought to be a bullet wound..."

Dr. Gene Coleman Akin, resident anesthesiologist testimony: "The back right occipital parietal portion of his head was smattered with brain substance extruding.... This [neck wound] must have been an entrance wound.."

Dr. Paul Peters, urologist: "We saw the wound of entry in the throat and noted the large occipital wound..."

Dr. Charles Crenshaw, resident surgeon: From his book *Conspiracy of Silence*: "I walked to the president's head to get a clear look. His entire cerebrum hemisphere appeared to be gone. It looked like a crater ... an empty cavity ... from the damage that I saw there was no doubt in my mind that a bullet had entered his head through the front, as it surgically passed through his cranium. The missile obliterated part of the temporal and all of the parietal and occipital lobes before it lacerated his cerebellum." [Page 79] "I also identified a small opening about the diameter of a pencil at the midline of his throat to be an entry bullet hole. There was no doubt in my mind about that wound."

Dr. Charles Baxter, attending surgeon: In a letter to researcher and author Harrison Livingstone, Baxter wrote: "There were two wounds to the president that we observed at Parkland. The first was a small and neat entrance wound to the throat which Dr. Malcolm Perry made an incision to put in a trach tube. The [head wound] ... resulted in a gaping hole the size of a baseball in the back of the head, and the cerebellum was hanging on a thread of tissue outside the wound."

Dr. Richard Brooks Delaney, resident surgeon: The wound in the neck was "no more than a pin point. It was made by a small caliber weapon and it was an entry wound. Testimony 3/25/64 ... he had a large head wound – this was the first thing I noticed."

Dr. Kenneth Salyer, resident surgeon: "He did have some sucking wound of some type on his neck.... Nothing, other than he did have a gaping scalp wound."

Nurse Patricia Hutton: Report of activity on 11/22/63. "Mr. Kennedy was bleeding profusely from a wound in the back of his head." Interview by David Lifton *Best Evidence*, page 706. "The large throat wound shown in the [autopsy] photographs was not the tracheotomy incision that she saw on November 22, 1963. (It doesn't look like any that I've taken part in, let me put it that way.) And the head wound was in the back, not as shown in the pictures. I was standing behind him when I was putting pressure on the head," she said, "and it was right in front of me. It wasn't around the side and on top."

Nurse Audrey Bell, interview with David Lifton *Best Evidence*, page 704. "The wound she saw was so lacerated at the rear that, from her position on the righthand side, with Kennedy laying face up, she couldn't see any damage." Shown a photograph of the trach: "Looks like somebody has enlarged it.... You don't make trachs that big. Not if you've got as much experience as Perry has."

Dr. Philip Williams, *High Treason II*, 4/16/91 unreleased video: "Certainly the president's cerebellum was severely damaged and swinging in the breeze."

Nurse Margaret Hinchliffe, on the throat wound: "It was just a little hole in the middle of his neck ... about as big around as the end of my little finger ... that looked like an entrance wound."

Now, this testimony from the Dallas doctors and nurses from attendance at Parkland Hospital who saw Kennedy's body, i.e., throat wound and head wound, described the throat wound as a small round wound of entrance. The head wound at Dallas and Bethesda was described as being in the back of the head. However, the back of the head wound seen in Dallas was a "low" wound, and the head wound as seen at Bethesda can be characterized as a "high" wound. The throat wound seen at Bethesda Naval Hospital was a large gaping gash with irregular edges.

The autopsy doctors did not know if the small round wound in the throat as seen in Dallas, was a bullet wound and assumed it was a tracheotomy. The difficulties in the throat wound and the head wound as seen in Dallas, Texas and Bethesda Naval Hospital in Maryland, give rise, of course, to the speculation that the president's body had been surgically altered or tampered with during the time span it took Kennedy's body to travel from

Dallas to Washington. And why would anyone need to "tamper" or alter the wounds on Kennedy's body? The small round wound of "entrance" as seen in Dallas would imply that Kennedy was hit from the front. The "low" wound in the back of Kennedy's head, as seen in Dallas was reported to be about the size of an egg, would also imply a shot from the front (and in order for the so-called single bullet theory to work, one bullet hitting both Kennedy and Connally, causing seven wounds on two men, the throat wound has to be an exit wound.) right side of the "grassy knoll" area. And a "high" back of the head wound including the right side and top, some four times larger than seen in Dallas, would imply a shot from the back, that the president was shot from the area of the Texas School Book Depository, and hence, Lee Harvey Oswald.

The throat wound had to be seen as an exit wound and in my opinion that is why Dr. Perry received a visit from the Secret Service to try and get Perry to change his mind about Kennedy's bullet wound being one of entrance. Richard Dudman of the *St. Louis Dispatch* released an article on December 1st, 1963 titled "Secret Service gets Revision of Kennedy's Wound." The article in the *Dispatch* said in part: "Two secret service agents called last week on Dallas surgeons who attended President John F. Kennedy and obtained a reversal of their original view that the bullet in his neck entered from the front. The investigators did so by showing the surgeons a document described as an autopsy report from the U.S. Naval Hospital at Bethesda. The surgeons changed their original view to conform with the report they were shown."

The "visit" got the desired effect, at least from Malcolm Perry. David S. Lifton described Dr. Perry's change of heart in his book *Best Evidence*: "by the time Dr. Perry testified before the Warren Commission his attitude had changed markedly.... Although he was still describing the throat wound anatomically as a small pencil size hole, just a quarter of inch in diameter, Perry no longer maintained it was a wound of entry. 'It could have been either,' he said. And he apparently subscribed to the theory that he had been misquoted at the press conference. Dr. Malcolm Perry could speak to that and other things such as the tracheotomy incision he made across the bullet wound on President Kennedy's throat, but he chooses not to."

The few researchers I know who have managed to talk to him over the years have found that Perry claims that he was misquoted about the throat wound and it could have been an entrance or an exit wound. But one certainly does not get that impression from reading Dr. Perry's earlier statement about the throat wound.

It has been said that Dr. Robert McClelland was in the best position to see the president's wounds. Here are some of Dr. McClelland's early statements about the wounds to Kennedy's body in a report written 11/22/63: "A massive gun shot wound of the head with a fragment wound of the trachea ... the cause of death was due to a massive head and brain injury from a gun shot wound to the left temple" – of course Dr. McClelland had a slip of memory or tongue here – there was no wound to the president's left temple.

"I could very clearly examine the head wound, and I noted that the right posterior portion of the skull had been extremely blasted ... Probably a third or so at least of the brain tissue posterior cerebral tissue and some of the cerebellum had been blasted out.... There was definitely a piece of cerebellum extruded from the wound.... The lost cerebral and cerebellum tissue where so great.... Massive head injuries with loss of large amounts of cerebral and cerebellum.... The mental impression that we had was that perhaps the wound in the neck, the anterior part of the neck, was an entrance wound and that it had perhaps taken a trajectory off the interior vertebral body and again into the skull itself, exiting out the back to produce the massive injury in the head."

I met Dr. McClelland in 2008 at a conference. I had the opportunity of spending several hours with him and had the chance to ask several questions about what he remembered about the President's wounds.

I had not seen or talked to Dr. McClelland since that night almost a year earlier. I decided to see if I couldn't get him to talk to me briefly, as there were a few things about his participation in trying to save President Kennedy's life I wanted to ask him. I emailed the doctor a brief note and received a reply the next day telling me he did indeed remember me and would be glad to answer any questions I might have.

When I called him, he was ready and willing to tell me of that day, and of his experiences in trauma room one. "How did the day start for you?" I asked.

"Well, I was in the operating room at Parkland – actually, a conference room in the operating room at Parkland showing a movie of how to repair a hernia to some of the surgery residents when I heard a little tap on the conference room door and went to the door and it was Dr. Chuck Crenshaw, who was a senior surgery resident at that time, and he asked me to come out, he wanted to tell me something. So, I stepped outside the door, and he told me that they had just received a message in the emergency room that President Kennedy had been shot and that they were bringing him in now, any moment – to the emergency room, and they wanted all the faculty, which at that time was a very small faculty, in surgery including myself, Dr.

Charles Baxter, Dr. Malcolm Perry" – the doctor's voice stopped as luck would have it, the phone went dead and I had to call Dr. McClelland back and we picked up the conversation.

"You were telling me about the doctors in attendance," I said.

"They asked us to come down to the emergency room and Dr. Crenshaw and I did just that. We got in the elevator there in the operating room and went down two floors just below us where the emergency room was and that was were I got into the whole process that I was involved in." "So tell me about that." I said. "Well, when we got off the elevator, I walked into the area we called 'the pit', the emergency room at that time was about one quarter of the size it is now. It's been remodeled two or three times since that time. But at that time, there was a central area that was all of about 50 by 50 feet that we called the pit, where every kind of emergency case was brought in. And that was encircled by little cubicles where patients were seen, then, just off that, a kind of little straight hall off of the pit, where four other rooms called trauma rooms, one, two, three and four. This is where serious gunshot wounds and automobile accidents and whatnot were first evaluated in the emergency area. And, so I saw in that big pit area, oddly, something that I had never seen before. It was jammed with men in suits and hats, standing almost shoulder to shoulder, and I thought to myself, and said to Chuck: 'Well, I've never seen anything like this down here' and about that time, that crowd of people parted and I could look down through that little corridor that that part made off of trauma room one off a little hall that I mentioned and Jackie Kennedy was sitting on a folding chair outside of trauma room one. And so I went in there and passed by her"

I broke into Dr. McClelland's narrative to ask. "What was your feeling when you saw Jacqueline Kennedy sitting there?"

Dr. McClelland replied, "People always ask me what my feelings are, that kind of in my mind involves where I stand back and stroke my chin and say, 'now what are my feelings here?' You don't do that, you don't have any feelings. You're just reacting. You're almost on automation. I recognized, 'yeah, that's who she is' and it was a real shock to me, I guess you could say that was what my feeling was. Shock." I asked him to continue his narrative. "I went on into the room and I saw immediately when I opened the door, the first sight that confronted me was the president's face, which was intact, but swollen. He was lying on the gurney on his back, and was a little bit propped up so that I could see his face. Dr. Perry and Dr. Baxter had entered the room a few minutes before me and had already started doing a tracheotomy. So I passed by the left side of the gurney where the president was lying

21

and Dr. Perry reached across and he handed me a little retractor and he said, 'Bob, would you go to the head of the gurney here and put this retractor in the upper edge of the tracheotomy wound we are making and hold it there?' So I did that, and that placed me in a position where I was only about eighteen inches immediately above the president's head wound, so, I had the best view of it of anybody in that room. Since I stood there for ten or twelve minutes while the tracheotomy was being completed, with nothing to do but hold that retractor. And that didn't take that much attention. And so my attention was mostly devoted to looking at that wound, and that is still emblazoned in my memory, exactly how it appeared all these years later."

"So tell me?" I said. "Tell me in your own words – I read your testimony and I've seen the picture of the drawing you drew [of the head wound]. But tell me in your own words."

"Well, basically," Dr. McClelland answered. "All of us, including myself, said that the wound involved the occipital parietal area of the skull. What that means is that the back part of the skull, which the back most extreme bone in the back part of the skull is the occipital bone. That right side of that because the wound came out of the right side had been extremely blasted away. In the back part, that is the posterior half of the parietal bone, which is right next to the occipital bone, which comprises part of the back of the head, but is mostly the side of the head, so in essence, what we're saying is that the wound involved the back, the posterior part of the side of the head. It was probably about, I would estimate, something like two to three inches in diameter. A very large wound."

I then asked Dr. McClelland, "You didn't see an opening in the top part of his head, did you?"

To which he answered, "Well, actually that was part of the top of his head, the back part of the top of his head, and the back of his head was blasted out. It was a very large hole. That's what makes me think it was an exit wound and not an entrance wound. You've seen the autopsy photographs, I'm sure?"

I said. "Yes. Did the wound look like that?"

Dr. McClelland's answer surprised me. "It looked pretty much like that, except in one of the pictures they showed.[4] There seems to be no hole there (*See photo number 6A in the photo section.) [in the back of the head] and the reason there wasn't, I assumed, is because it looked like the pathologist was pulling a flap of scalp up over that large hole. And I suggested that to someone, and then one person said, 'No, that's not a flap, there just wasn't any hole there, and I said, 'Yes there was, too, you know.'

4. I'm assuming that was the presentation shown on PBS *Nova*, in 1988.

That's what I thought it was. In fact, I could see the prosector, the autopsy prosector, the pathologist's thumb and forefinger, pulling the flap forward over the hole, so I think that what it was."

"So the pictures were pretty much like you remembered the body, [looking like it did at Parkland]?"

"Yes, except for that flap business."

I then asked Dr. McClelland about President Kennedy's throat wound.

"Well, there's been a lot – too much made of that throat wound, I think. [5]And my ideas about this have developed over the years as I've learned more things and seen the Zapruder film several years later. And if you want, in a nutshell, what I think happened that made that throat wound, initially we didn't know what it was, because we knew none of the circumstances when we were first seeing the president in trauma room one, and so Dr. Perry, that day, said it appeared to him like an entrance wound. Well, it was small like an entrance wound. But what I think happened after a long period of time, and putting all of the different things together, from the Zapruder film, the way the wound looked and so on, I think the bullet – there were two bullets at least that hit the president."

What follows is Dr. McClelland's speculation on what happened to JFK in Dealey Plaza:

"The first bullet made the hole in his throat, but it came from a fragment from behind. If you'll recall the Zapruder film when you see the president's motorcade motoring down Elm Street, he's moving along and nothing's happened yet, and the motorcade is just about to pass behind a big sign that temporarily briefly obscures the [president's car] but just before the president's car disappears behind that sign, he is hit by the first bullet. And you can see his reaction. His hands, both of them, his arms go up to his throat – do you recall that?" Dr. McClelland asked me.

"Oh yes, I've seen [the Zapruder film] many times."

"As if something hit his throat," McClelland continued. "Well, I think what happened is that Oswald, who was in on this – he was just a patsy, but he was in on it, (my thought on Dr. McClelland's statement that Oswald was just a patsy, but was in on it, gave me pause, but I remained silent as he continued)

5. The doctor is apparently not aware that the case for conspiracy depends on the wound to Kennedy's throat. The back wound was not seen at Parkland as the Dallas doctors did not turn Kennedy's body over. The bullet either went in Kennedy's back, went up and out his throat or it did not. The Bethesda prosectors did not dissect the neck, an absolute must if the pathway of the bullet was to be found. James Jenkins, who helped Boswell dissect the body and remove the internal organs told me "There was very little blood in the chest cavity," which led Jenkins to believe there were no real penetrating wounds in the chest cavity and they found none. Read more of the discussion on page 230.

he was in the sixth floor window alright, and that first bullet was probably fired by him from that window. And it went into the president's back and a little fragment from that bullet exited out the president's throat. And that's what that first bullet wound was, and the thing that made that hole in his throat. In other words, it was an exit, not an entrance wound. The little throat wound. Then the motorcade disappears behind the sign for about one or two seconds, and as he comes out from behind the sign, one or two seconds after that, if you will recall, all of a sudden, the President's head explodes violently, and he's thrown violently back and to the left. As you would expect him to do if he were hit from a bullet from the picket fence [area] which is where I think the bullet that made that head wound, and it killed him, came from. And then I met the man Mr. Hoffman, Ed Hoffman, a deaf-mute who accidentally saw this happen. His car was parked on Stemmons behind the picket fence."[6]

A little stunned by all the revelations, mostly hearing Dr. McClelland say that he thought the wound to Kennedy's throat was caused by a bullet fragment – and was an exit wound, and not an entrance wound, I stuttered: "Ah, so – but –you – are – You do think the wound in the back of the head was an exit wound?"

Dr. McClelland answered, "Yes, very definitely."

"What about the rest of your colleagues?" I asked him. "I know there's been mixed reaction from them."

"Well," Dr. McClelland said. "I really can't speak for them at all, and I'd rather not say one thing or the other about what the others thought. Dr. Perry, in fact, categorically refuses to say anything about it to any of us."

I decided to go on a bit of a fishing expedition and see if Dr. McClelland was one of the doctors that "received a visit" by the secret service and got a reversal of the direction of the shots from the doctors, Dr. Perry being one we actually know about.[7] I said to Dr. McClelland, "Now as I recall, there was an article that came out shortly after the assassination that said you'd had a visit from some secret service agents?"

"No, I didn't," Dr. McClelland interrupted. "Dr. Perry may have. Dr. Perry was the one that was most prominently identified as the surgeon of record."

"You weren't involved in that then [secret service] didn't interview you?"

"No," he said. "No secret service agents did."

"How about FBI agents?" I asked, still fishing.

---

6. Casey J. Quinlan and Brian K. Edwards, *Beyond the Fence Line: The Eyewitness Account of Ed Hoffman and the Murder of President John F. Kennedy*, JFK Lancer Production (2008).
7. Dr. Perry died December 5, 2009 in Tyler, TX.

"No, the only interview I had was with Arlen Specter who was sort of a low-level member of the Warren Commission, who came to Dallas and took my testimony and the testimony of several other people."

"How did he treat you?" I asked.

"He treated me just fine. It was a very straight-forward thirty minute interview."

Dr. McClelland told me that he had no pressure from anyone at any-time to change his testimony. I thanked Dr. McClelland for his time and said that I hoped we would meet again. "I hope so too," he said.

Later, I realized that I had neglected to ask Dr. McClelland for his impression of President Kennedy's brain, with special focus on the cerebellum. "That's an important point," he said, when I called him and talked to the doctor the next day. "And as you know, cerebellum is very distinguishable from the rest of the brain. The portion that fell out on the gurney which was probably a good bit of the right half of the cerebellum, did appear intact, and clearly looked like cerebellum. I have no doubt about that, even though Dr. Jenkins changed his story on that."

"You've seen the Ida Dox drawing – there's a drawing of a brain [supposedly of President Kennedy's] and the cerebellum looks undamaged and intact."

"That's not the case," the doctor shot back. "From what I saw, the cerebellum, a piece of it, fell out of the president's skull – and of course, the reason to me that that's a significant point, as to whether it was cerebellum or cerebrum, is that that means to me, that's further indication that the hole in the back of his head was far back in the head and low down and toward the base of his skull, whereas if it had been further forward, you wouldn't have expected cerebellum, but perhaps would have expected cerebrum to have fallen out."

Dr. McClelland is of course correct. If cerebellum fell out of the wound in President Kennedy's skull, again, that would point to a shot to the front of Kennedy because the hole in his skull would have to have been low enough for the cerebellum to have been seen. "And as Dr. McClelland has pointed out, the texture of the cerebellum is quite different from the rest of the brain. Virtually all of the Dallas doctors reported seeing cerebellum oozing from the back head wound. Although, some doctors in later years did say they were mistaken about seeing the cerebellum oozing or "protruding" from the head wound, most notably "Pepper" Jenkins and he only changed his mind after being shown the autopsy pictures from the "Nova" program in 1988. Clearly the drawing of the brain by Ida Dox, reported to be a representation of President Kennedy's brain shows the cerebellum is intact and undamaged. James Jenkins, who told me that he was given a brain to infuse that night, said the cerebellum was undamaged. An undamaged cerebellum is in conflict with what was seen in Dallas, Texas. There seems to be no convergence with the medical evidence (as you would expect with the passage of time) anywhere along the line in this case, and so despite Vincent Bugliosi's claim that we know that Oswald shot and killed Kennedy we *also know* that … hundreds upon hundreds of these questions and problems with the critics have with the case against Oswald are irrelevant … There has to be a satisfactory answer for all of their questions and preconceived discrepancies and problems with the case. On that point I would agree. There should be clear cut answers as to what happened to President Kennedy, but the only thing that seems to be clear about the president's assassination is that he was shot. And that is not because there are so called "conspiracy nuts" studying the minutiae of the case and making up problems with the "evidence" – it's because the problems do indeed exist.

After I talked with Dr. McClelland, I decided to see if I couldn't get Dr. Ronald Jones to talk to me about his memories of President Kennedy's wounds. I called his office at Baylor University and talked with his receptionist, Annie, who took my name and number and with a very cheery "great" from Annie, I waited for Dr. Jones to call me back. A week went by and I had decided that the doctor had for whatever reason decided not to return my call, when I received a message on my answering machine to please call Dr. Jones. I did the next day and once again found myself talking to Dr. Jones's bubbly receptionist Annie.

"Hello, William this is Annie from Dr. Jones's office. Can you speak with Dr. Jones?"

"You bet," I said.

Annie asked me to hold for a moment and Jones came on the line. I introduced myself and explained what I wanted.

"Okay," the doctor said. "I know you've told the story countless times," I told him.

"Basically, I'd like your opinion on President Kennedy's head wound and your feeling about the matter all these years later."

"Okay," I heard him say. "The head wounds, I couldn't get a good look at. I was standing to his left side; his left arm was out on an arm board, so I was standing below his left arm. He is flat on a cart, and about all that I know is that there was blood and brain, a little bit on the stretcher, but I couldn't – I never did go around to the top of the table and you know pull all the hair apart and look at the wound. So, from the description of the head wound, I can't help you much in terms of details because I just know that he had something back there, but I didn't know the extent of it, or the size of it, or anything at the time. We just knew that he had a wound there that initially we thought was an exit wound. And I think everybody that afternoon thought the entrance wound was in the front of the neck and the exit wound was in the back of the head. That, subsequently, was not thought to be the case, as you know. But, I can't give you much description of the head wound itself."

"Would you still say all this time later that the cerebellum was disrupted, or damaged?" I asked.

"I can't, I don't know what part of the brain, I just know that the back of the head would be all that I could say and I don't know which part of the brain this could have come from."

"Do you believe all this time later that the head wound, the large head wound in the back was an exit wound? Do you have an opinion on that?"

"Well, all I can say is that *initially,* that was what I thought. That's what everyone thought. I think Dr. Perry made that comment early on that first afternoon. That's what I thought and, I think Dr. McClelland testified that had he seen what was described, that's what he would have thought, too. But as you know, there was a lot of ballistics done, and we didn't know that he was shot in the back and they didn't at autopsy, didn't know he was shot in the neck, so – or that there was a wound in the neck. So we were [all] short one piece of information on both ends. Both at the autopsy initially, because they called the next day to find out, you know, where the exit – where they thought they knew there was a wound in the back, but they didn't know where it exited. Initially cause they didn't know there was a injury to the front of the neck, cause that's where the tracheotomy incision had been made through that wound and they didn't pick that up."

"So," I asked again, "do you have an opinion all these years later, do you?"

"Well," the doctor answered, "I, you know, I can't change what I initially thought, because that's what I initially thought that the neck wound was an entrance wound and the head wound was an exit wound. But, we didn't know at the time that there was a back wound – as you probably know, there were ballistic studies done. One arsenal group did that, and they show that the wound – exit wound – or the neck wound could never be as small for an exit wound as had been described. The smallest that they could produce was in centimeters, and we described it as a quarter of an inch, which was smaller than what they were able to show. But then, you know, somebody else came in, a ballistic expert, and said, 'Well, the government test was not the right way to do it', or that his shirt was so tight that it prevented the wound from being larger than it was. Whether or not, with a high-power rifle a shirt can make that much difference I don't know. The pristine-bullet theory was a mystery to me as to how you could hit that many things and have no damage to the bullet and then it be found on the cart. So I've never understood that. I can't explain that. You sort of have to accept it, but you've seen pictures of other bullets that have struck bone and there was significant damage to the nose of the bullet."

"Have you ever had a case," I asked, "all these years later, where [you saw] a bullet could do that and cause those kinds of wounds?"

"Probably not," Dr. Jones replied. "Number one, after I left Parkland in 1987 as Chief of Surgery at Baylor in Dallas, I didn't do any more trauma, but I don't recall between '63 and '87 of seeing any – we didn't see a lot of high-power rifle injuries, number one. We saw a lot of gunshot wounds, occasionally one from a deer rifle. But you don't have so many questions about an entrance and an exit wound in most of those that struck bone and caused a lot of damage, so, no, I haven't had another case similar to that and as I'd said on Paula Zahn's show one time, you know, if there ever is evidential evidence that should come forth that would state that he was shot from the front, I could accept that based on what I saw, but, I guess we'd have to go with what the Warren Commission Report said at this time."

"Were you there for any of the coffin controversy? Did you see the president placed in the casket?"

"No, I left the room before they placed him in the coffin."

"You've seen the so-called 'stare or death' photograph haven't you?" I asked. "On the autopsy table?"

"Yes."

"Do you remember – I know you said you didn't see the extent of the [head wound]."

"Uh-huh," I heard Dr. Jones say.

"But," I said, "it appears to go down into his forehead a bit."

"Yeah, I did not – I did get a good look at his face, and I do not remember any damage to the forehead."

"At all?" I ask.

"At all."

"I've questioned a lot of the people that were there at Bethesda and they don't recall any damage to the [president's] forehead, including the FBI agents that were sent there by J. Edgar Hoover, so it's a little interesting."

"Uh-huh."

"Given all the controversy of this whole thing, you would think that something from point 'A' to point 'B', to point 'C', to point 'D', would add up over all the years, and it just doesn't seem to do that."

"No," Jones replied, "but that stare, as I recall, his eyes were open when we saw him. I don't remember his eyes being closed. But, you know, over forty-six years, now, things begin to not be as crisp as they once were, and you begin to see other photos that interfere with your memory to some extent. And you see it so much that it sorts of fades away. But I think the autopsy photo of him on the (autopsy table) looks from the front, looks (Dr. Jones drew out the word looks) loooksss real except for that triangle nick in the right forehead. I don't remember that, and you know, hair could be over that or something at the time, where we wouldn't have seen it, maybe that's a possibility. But I don't recall that being there."

"That's part of the mystery, isn't it?" I said. "And I deal extensively with trying to figure out about the medical evidence and why it doesn't converge [with Dallas]. The wounds look so different or have been described so differently from Parkland to Bethesda."

"And another guy that never got interviewed," said Dr. Jones, breaking into my reverie, "was the neurosurgeon resident, Lito Porto."

I felt my excitement rise. "I've heard that name," I told Dr. Jones.

"And," the doctor said, "he initially said, I think he's still alive, and around Arlington, Texas here. He thought he put his finger in a wound in the temple, but that all sort of faded away, but he mentioned that that afternoon."

"Did he say which side?" I asked.

"There's been some controversy to me," said Dr. Jones, "it would have been on the left. And I don't know, do you have his phone number?"

"I don't," I said. With that, the doctor told me to wait a minute, when he came back to the phone he had an address where he worked, but no phone number. Dr. Jones did not know if Dr. Porto was still practicing medicine.

"Have you had discussions with your colleagues over the years? Do they basically feel the same way that they did that day? Disregarding any information that you have may picked up from books or ballistic experts?"

"Well, I think," answered Dr. Jones, "that most of them did accept the Warren Commission Report. So many of them are dead now. Dr. Jenkins, who was chief of anesthesia, and was at the head of the table, is dead. Paul Peters, who was with me, he was on the opposite side of the table, he was the chief of urology and he's dead. And Kemp Clark was a neurosurgeon and he's dead and Charlie Baxter helped Dr. Perry do the tracheotomy, and he's dead."

"Oh," I said disappointed. "I didn't know he had passed."

"Uh-huh."

"As I understand it," I told the doctor, "Dr. Perry is extremely reluctant to talk."

"Probably," he said. "I haven't seen him in a few years. He seemed to have changed his mind about the wound to the throat."

"That's a good point," I said to myself. "You saw the neck wound, correct?'

"Uh-huh."

"You saw it after Dr. Perry did the -?"

"I saw it before," Dr. Jones told me. "We went down together."

"So you've seen the stare of death photograph. Does it look basically the same?"

"Yeah," he answered. "I don't think there's too much difference. Are you talking about that incision?"

"Yes," I said. "You know, you just make an incision for a tracheotomy, and I don't remember – somebody asked me one time how many centimeters it was. I didn't do the procedure, I was right below it putting in chest tubes, doing a cut down, getting a catheter into the arm to get fluids in, while Perry was doing that. But that seems about right. The wound, you can see that little divot?"

"Yes," I said. "In the bottom, that's how big that wound was, it's pretty small. So when I first saw it, I would not have thought that it was from a high powered rifle. But all indications are it was, at least from the Warren Report. And you've got all the testimony from various people that said they saw him shot from the front and off the railroad trestle or something like that. I think Arlen Specter told me that he tended to disregard that as not worthwhile. He told me after I gave my testimony here in Dallas; he called me out in the hall and said. 'We have people, I don't want you to say anything about it, but we have people who will testify that he was shot from the bridge or the trestle of the railroad area, somewhere in that area, but we have discounted that testimony as unreliable.'"

"What was your opinion of Arlen Specter?" I asked.

"Well, I don't know, I was a young guy, I was thirty-one, he was an attorney and I don't know, in retrospect, that he was much older than I was, any older than I was, but he certainly, you know, with the Warren Commission and things as serious as they were at the time, commanded and demanded a lot of respect. He came to Dallas and I testified in Mr. Price's, the administrator's office or conference room – I guess we were in a conference room, and I testified individually with Arlen Specter questioning me, and I'm sure you've seen that in the Warren Commission Report."

"Yes," I said. "Did he treat you decently? Did he try to bully you into anything?"

"No, no," the doctor answered. "Well, you can read his report and get the gist of what the questions were like." 'You gave him steroids; what happened if he wouldn't have needed them? What damage would that have caused him?' There were a couple of innuendos there that were somewhat aggressive."

I broke in with, "a little uncomfortable?"

"Yes."

"There was a story by Richard Dudman that he has claimed that a couple of secret service agents came and talked to Dr. Perry, and maybe some of the other doctors, and bullied them into changing their testimony about the throat wound. Did you hear anything about that?" I asked.

"No, I don't know anything about that. The Secret Service came by from San Francisco, oh, about January as I recall, after the assassination in November, and wanted to know where my handwritten note was about what I did and I said, 'Well, I turned it in to Kemp Clark.' And they said it never reached Washington. And for a long time I don't think it did and then they found it in Jack Price's administrative office safe, somebody said, and it eventually got – I know, I know I got a copy of it back from Charlie Crenshaw one time and it was stamped top secret. That he had gotten access to, but, where the original report went in by Kemp Clark, they mentioned there three or four people's names that had participated and they said all of the other reports were not legible; they could not read them. Mine being one of them, but mine was put on display down at the JFK museum here three or four years ago, along with my coat and shoes and some other things and some pictures that I had. And it's pretty easy to read, so I can't buy that, because it's not tremendous handwriting, but anybody could take a little time and easily read what it says."

"Did you read Dr. Crenshaw's book?"

"I've scanned it quite a bit. I don't know that I've read it cover-to-cover," Dr. Jones said. "He's dead too, as you probably know."

"Did you agree with what his conclusion [was]?"

"Well, I couldn't remember that Crenshaw was in the room. But I did read a *Dallas Morning News* newspaper, kept an article two or three days later and it gave the people that were listed – I can't remember whether he was listed or not, but I did not remember him being in the room, but he could have been. There were a lot of people in the room and I could have missed him."

"So all these years later," I asked, "do you live with it? You don't think about it a lot, do you?"

"No, I don't." I heard a little laugh escape from the doctor. "I was watching TV Sunday night and they had a little special on it – many of the same photos. It was narrated by Jane Pauley and it was pretty good. It didn't change anything, there was nothing new in it, maybe a few pictures that I hadn't seen before. But [Robert] Schieffer, the news guy was on, and I had been on *Larry King Live* show with him once before, 3 or 4 years ago."

"I don't do conspiracy theories," I said. "I'm not a conspiracy theorist. I try to stick with what people say. But do you believe that there was a conspiracy, just based on what you know?"

"I – I don't know," Jones answered. "I don't know what to believe."

In his forward to his 2004 edition of this work, Dr. David Mantik wrote: "the higher in the hierarchy someone stands, the more susceptible he or she is to social pressure. The more the individual has to lose both in prestige, money, and future success, the less likely he or she is to risk." Such a loss, I believe, is a large part of the reason that there is such confusion along the line in Dallas to Bethesda. The minute it was realized that John F. Kennedy had been killed, individuals went into C.Y.A. (cover your ass) mode. Once the Dallas police had Lee Harvey Oswald in their grip, they were not about to let him go. The police had their man; the Dallas doctors with a little "arm twisting" to paraphrase James W. Sibert, changed their opinion and became unsure of how Kennedy's wounds appeared at Parkland. (Though not all.)

And the secret service, if you read chapter 8 of the ARRB's final report in 1998, the reader will find this: Congress passed the JFK Act of 1992. One month later, the secret service began its compliance efforts. However, in January 1995, the secret service destroyed Presidential Protection Service Reports for some of President Kennedy's trips in the fall of 1963. The review board learned of the destruction approximately one week after the secret service destroyed them. When the board was drafting its request for additional information, the board believed that the secret service files on the president's travel in the weeks preceding his murder would be relevant. Records review analyst, Doug Horne wrote in a memo dated April 16th, 1996: "The final decision to approve the Texas trip made later Tuesday night indicates the decision came on September 24, 1963." The Secret Service Protection Service Reports ... which were destroyed in 1995, changed with trip files starting on this same date; September 24, 1963.

As noted by Vince Palamara, in his fine work, *Survivors Guilt*: In addition the ARRB's John Chinerman noted in a May 1st, 1977 memorandum to file: "Therefore the U.S. Secret Service collection is in six gray archive boxes of documents, seven large flat gray boxes with newspapers and clippings, and one small box with the tape cassette … In box five there are three folders marked 'trip files'. All are empty." The chairman of the ARRB, Judge Jack Tunheim stated: "The secret service destroyed records after we were on the job and working. They claimed it was a mistake that it was just by the normal procedures of records destruction."

Vince Palamara writes: "Only the Secret Service – no other agency, not even the CIA is on record as having intentionally destroyed key filed 1963 records during the ARRB tenure." Why did the Secret Service destroy files they were asked to keep sacrosanct? Does that mean that everyone that was a Secret Service agent in 1963 is complicit in the murder of the President of the United States? No. But it's damn suspicious behavior on the part of the powers that be.

I once interviewed a Secret Service agent that was in the motorcade in Dallas for the film director Brian McKenna. After several phone calls over a long period of time, the ex-agent said to me. "You know, I thought the Kennedys were a bunch of users, and I didn't want anything to do with them." I was stunned by what the ex-agent said. I've talked to half a dozen agents over the years that were connected to Kennedy's detail in one way or another, and I definitely got the feeling that Kennedy's womanizing lowered the agents respect to almost nothing for JFK.

It's well known there were agents that left the president guarded by local fireman in Fort Worth while they went out drinking at a local night spot, The Cellar, the night before the assassination. I spoke to former FBI agent James Hosty via phone in 2004 and he gave me his opinion: "There was no protection. Kennedy made it impossible for the Secret Service to protect him. So they just gave up and were holding their breath hoping they could get from point A to point B without him getting killed. He made it impossible," Hosty repeated. "I watched him go by that day, I was standing on the curb as a spectator and I almost missed them because I was looking at the wrong car. I looked at the car Kennedy was in and everyone else had protection except for him. I maintained he would not have gotten through the 1964 campaign the way he was going. Somebody would have shot him."

"You think so?" I asked.

"Oh yes," Mr. Hosty answered. "It was wide open with all the hatred toward Kennedy. Sure!"

"I guess they didn't have enough people to guard him?" I said.

"They hired off duty firemen," James Hosty told me. "See, one of the off duty firemen, he continued one of the Secret Service agents from Dallas, Mike Howard, his brother was a Fort Worth fireman, Pat Howard. And through Pat Howard they were able to get these off-duty firemen. TheSecret Service could do that, they could deputize people. And rather than go to the FBI or to the ATF or to somebody else, who would have done it for free, they deputized these people and that's how they covered themselves."

"That seems so strange," I said.

"I guess it was just the times." Hosty answered me by saying: "The secret service didn't have enough man power. They were so worried about being absorbed by the FBI, they didn't want the FBI coming anywhere near them. They didn't tell us that he was coming to town. We read it in the newspaper."

"Really," I said. "They didn't make an effort?"

"No, and they didn't tell us the parade route. I read that in the paper the night before. You can see the Secret Service was fearful. They didn't have the manpower and they couldn't do the job. And they were afraid to tell anybody that they couldn't do it."

Well perhaps. The revelation from James Hosty that he had seen the president's motorcade, "while everyone else had protection but him," startled me more than a little. I don't guess it crossed Mr. Hosty's mind that there may have been a reason that everyone but the president had protection that day.

Perhaps the most famous secret service agent since the time the secret service was created in 1865, is Clint Hill, immortalized in Abraham Zapruder's 26-second home movie of President Kennedy's assassination. Hill can be seen running from the follow-up car to the presidential limousine after the fatal head shot – where he grips the handle on the back of the car and almost falls to his own death, as Bill Greer accelerates the limousine and then, once he is aboard, watches as Jacqueline Kennedy crawls back into the back seat of the limousine. First Lady Jacqueline Kennedy had climbed out onto the trunk to recover what was reportedly a piece of the president's skull or brain. If Clint Hill had not acted when he did it is quite possible the first lady could have been seriously injured or killed. Clint Hill did, however, admit he was one of the agents who participated in the "drinking incident" the night before President Kennedy was murdered. In any event, by almost anyone's standard, Clint Hill acted with true heroism that dark day in Dallas.

While working for Gala Films in Canada, my job was to try and contact as many people as I could that were involved with Kennedy or his administration. One day after speaking with a former secret service agent from the

Kennedy era, I laughingly and not expected to be taken seriously asked the ex-agent if he had Clint Hill's phone number. "No, I don't," he said. Then I heard the man say "ah – oh well, just a minute." He left the phone for a couple of minutes and when the agent returned, he said: "Listen – I'm going to give you Clint's number, and Clint's going to ask you where you got this from and if you tell him, you're a dead man." He made the statement without a trace of humor. But he did give me Clint Hill's number.

When I called, he answered the phone saying "Hills." I was a bit taken aback at the speed with which Clint Hill answered the phone, but I managed to introduce myself and tell Clint Hill where I was calling from and I whom I was working for.

"They would very much like to have you be a participant in the project," I heard myself say.

There was a pause. Hill then said, "Well, what's the film about?"

"The 1960s, the whole era," I said. "They're going to cover the civil rights movement, the Kennedy era."

Another pause, "I'm not interested," I heard Hill say. I heard another voice in the background, I took to be Mr. Hill's wife say, "Ask him what company it is." Mr. Hill then repeated his wife's question. "What company is it?"

I told him. "Gala," said Hill spelling it. "Yes," I explained. "The company was based out of Canada and they asked me to get ahold of you and some others."

"I'm not interested in participating," Hill told me again. I then told Clint Hill that I was working on a book about the assassination and asked him if he would be interested in meeting with me. "No," he said, "I'm sorry, but I just don't discuss the assassination."

To keep him on the line I said, "Could you discuss other things?" I asked.

"No, not really."

"I haven't seen but a couple of things you've done," trying to keep him on the phone. "One was on the Secret Service."

"What, you mean on TV?" Hill asked.

"Yes."

"Only when it was requested by the Secret Service did I do anything."

"So, you just don't do anything at all?"

"I don't do interviews," Clint Hill told me.

"You've never done any interviews other than that?" I said stalling for time.

"No, I did *60 Minutes* once. I did two or three *60 Minutes* [episodes]."

"I think," I said, "I've only seen the one." I had seen the first *60 Minutes* interview when it was broadcast in 1975 on CBS. It's heart-wrenching to watch.

The interviewer, Mike Wallace, sits across from Clint Hill and his wife. They are sitting on a couch; the camera is on Wallace as he asks Hill, "Just let me take you back to November 22, 1963." The camera now settles on Hill's face in a medium-tight shot. Clint Hill is sitting slouched on the couch; he looks extremely uncomfortable. His eyes are cast downward. "You were on the fender of the secret service car right behind President Kennedy's car? The first shot, you ran forward and jumped on the back of the President's car *in less than two* seconds, pushing Mrs. Kennedy down into her seat, protecting her." Clint takes a long nervous drag off of his cigarette. Wallace continues, "first of all, she was out on the trunk of that car." "She was in the back seat of that car, not on the trunk of that car."

Clint breaks in, "Well, she had climbed out of the back and she was on the way back, right? And because of that fact that her husband's – part of her husband's head had been shot off and gone off into the street." The camera has now focused in close on Hill's face. One can see the pain, the raw emotion Clint Hill can no longer hold in.

"She wasn't trying to climb out of the car?" Wallace asks.

"No," Hill answers. "She was simply trying to reach that head – part of the head."

"To bring it back," Wallace rhetorically says.

"It's the only thing," Hill answers.

"In the twelve years since that assassination, undoubtedly you have thought and thought and thought again about it, and studied it. Do you have any reason to believe that there was more than one gun, more than one assassin? Was Lee Harvey Oswald alone or were there others with him?"

"There were only three shots," Hill answers.

"And it was one gun three shots? You're satisfied Lee Harvey Oswald acted alone," says Mike Wallace. "Completely." "Is there any way, is there anything that the Secret Service, or that Clint Hill could have done to keep that from happening?"

A long pause then: "Clint Hill, yes."

"Clint Hill yes, what do you mean?" Wallace asks.

"If he had reacted about 5/10ths of a second faster or maybe a second faster, I wouldn't be here today." Hill looks at Mike Wallace.

"You mean you would have gotten there and you would have taken the shot?"

"The third shot, yes sir."

"And that would have been alright with you." It's more of a statement from Wallace than a question.

Clint Hill, his face full of pain, his emotions so raw it seems to come at the viewer in waves, looks at Wallace and says: "That would have been (a pause) fine with me."

"But you couldn't, you got there in less than two seconds, Clint. You couldn't have gotten there … You surely don't have any sense of guilt about that?"

"Yes, I certainly do," Clint Hill answers. "I have a great deal about that. If I turned in a different direction, I'd have made it. It was my fault." Clint Hill's voice is choked with emotion. It hurts to watch Hill, his emotions laid so bare it feels as if one is looking at the man's soul.

"Oh," Mike Wallace says in disbelief. "No-one has ever suggested that for an instant. What you did was show great bravery and great presence of mind. What was on the citation that was given to you, for your work on November 22, 1963, extraordinary courage and heroic effort in the face of maximum danger!"

"Mike, I don't care about that! If I had reacted a little bit quicker, and I could have, I guess." Clint Hill's voice cracks, "and I'll live with that to my grave." The interview ends.

My own "interview" with Clint Hill was coming to an end. I had not convinced him to sit before the camera for Gala Films or to talk to me about what he knew of those times and of the Kennedy tragedy. I did ask for an autographed picture. He agreed to send me one, taking down my name and address very carefully, asking me to repeat it twice. I never received the picture.

Not receiving the autographed picture from Clint Hill didn't bother me half as much as when at the very end of our conversation, I said with more than a little resignation in my voice: "Is there any time at all that I could meet you? – ever?"

"I doubt that very much, Mr. Law," he said. I would use the fact that I had asked Mr. Hill for an autographed picture and did not receive it as a reason to call him back and press for answers to questions if it had been anyone else. But with Clint Hill, I couldn't do it. I once wrote that while trying to get James Sibert to talk to me about what he knew, that I was torn between pushing him just as hard as I could to get as much information as I could – no matter what, damn the cost, no matter to whom – and realizing there comes a point where you have to draw a line.

The trouble for me was, and is, that ever since having been drawn into the JFK mystery, I had never been able to draw lines. In any case, aren't lines meant to be crossed? But with Clint Hill, I had reached the limit. I could not cross the line. I had seen the Hill interview originally in 1975 when it had first been broadcast. I had never forgotten the emotion I had seen pour from Clint Hill, and it had stayed with me ever since. I was extremely affected by Hill and try as I might, I could not press Clint Hill any further. However I would talk to Clint Hill again two years later, for a bizarre reason. A researcher sent me an email put out by Vince Palamara, claiming that he had received a phone call from Clint Hill, and Hill had called him a "bastard" because of a book he had written about the secret service, and Clint Hill was angry with him for "hurting the agency." I know the writer fairly well, and I was curious as to why the book had elicited such a response from Hill. The e-mail was my excuse for calling Clint Hill one more time. I agonized over contacting Hill; I had made up my mind to let the former secret service agent live his life in peace. I felt he had been through enough pain and guilt over the years for what had happened in Dallas, and through no fault of his own, and I did not want to be responsible for opening those old wounds again. But I did. I crossed the line.

"Hills."

I introduced myself telling him; "I called you a couple years of ago when I was working for a film company about a project we were doing, and you were very kind to me and then turned me down. I have a question I'd like to ask – or something I'd like to read to you." I waited for Clint Hill's response, but none came. "Somebody sent me this over my email and it's by Vince Palamara." "He wrote a book [about the secret service] and [he said] you were unhappy with it, he put out this email. Can I read it to you?" I asked.

"Go ahead."

I read Mr. Hill the email.

"Who wrote this?" Clint Hill asked. "What's his name?"

I said it again and spelled it for him.

"Where's he from?"

I told him.

"Well, I don't know who he is because I've never had any contact with him. I don't know anything about this fellow."

"Really," I said surprised. "I had no idea what he said until you told me." "Really," I said again, at a loss for words. "In this email he says you called him."

"No, that's not true."

Greatly surprised by Clint Hill's revelation, I decided not to press the matter further. And then I did what I vowed I would not do, I pushed Clint. "I know you don't give interviews, and I didn't want to bother you again, but I thought if this guy's putting this stuff out, maybe you'd like the opportunity because–

Clint Hill interrupted me with, "Maybe he's right, because I apparently turned him down or something, I don't know."

"The thing about this is," I said. "I know you don't like questions–"

Hill interrupted me, unable to let the claim about the Palamara e-mail go. "Let me just say this, if he even wrote to me, I usually don't even respond to a written request, so … "

"So he's putting out something that is absolutely not true?" I asked.

"Absolutely," Hill replied.

"Well, I was reading this email and I thought it was kind of strange, so I thought I would give you a call and get your opinion on it."

"You've got it," Clint Hill told me.

"Let me make a pitch, one more time," I said. "You turned me down for my first project I was doing with Gala Films, but at some point, I would like to talk to you. I know you've done interviews with *60 Minutes*."

"That was years ago," Hill replied. "And I just don't do that anymore."

"Is there a reason why?" I asked.

"Because," Hill said, "I've said everything there is that I'm ever going to say, there is nothing more for me to say about it."

"I understand – that you were just doing your job – every person I've ever talked to dealing with this subject – [feels that way], but unfortunately you got caught up in this historical event, and that makes you a historical figure. Caught in this thing that is a very big part of our country, and you are a hero to most people in this country, and they don't know your story all that much, because you don't talk."

"That's exactly the way it should be," Hill said to me.

I took an exasperated breath, "I've talked to other Secret Service agents and you're all pretty tight-lipped, but from a point of view from a person who loves history – talking to you is the only way I can touch the event, do you understand?" I asked. "And I don't understand why you don't understand that you are important to history and if you don't tell the story *your way*, some nut's going to tell it."

"A lot of people have told the stories," Clint Hill said. "I mean many different ones."

"Well, you're the only one who can really set the record straight … "

"All they have to do," Hill told me, "is read what I said to the Warren Commission, and it's all right there."

"But, you know people, they read things into that and so the only way that it's really going to get cleared up is for you to come out and talk about it."

"I don't know what's so unclear," Hill shot back. "What's so unclear?"

"Well, God there's so many things." I was struggling to tell him something that would make him want to continue talking to me. Jim Sibert popped into my mind. "Okay," I said. "I interviewed an FBI agent who had never talked to a private researcher before. His name is Jim Sibert."

"Sibert?" I heard Clint Hill say.

"Jim Sibert, I met him at his home in Florida. He had never come forward before, outside of a governmental inquiry."

"Who was he?" Hill asked.

"He was an FBI agent, sent there by J. Edgar Hoover to stay with the president's body."

"Sent where?" Hill interrupted.

"The morgue," I answered, "after the assassination."

Clint Hill then asked, "What morgue?"

"The morgue in Bethesda."

"Alright," he said.

"So," I continued, "he was in the morgue, and he agreed to see me, so I flew down to Florida. So I sat with him in his office and he told me the story and he was really angry, about the single-bullet theory." I quoted Sibert. "The single-bullet theory did not happen; this was something that was concocted by Arlen Specter," he said. "I was two feet from the body. I looked at that back wound, and it was way down in the shoulder.[8] So, he's at odds with the single-bullet theory. All these things keep getting stirred up and stirred around, and I'm the first person to come along and say, 'just tell me the story.' I won't embellish it, I won't put things in it that aren't true, just tell me the story. And so, – he's just as much of a historical figure as you are," I said, groping for the right words to convince Hill to talk to me. "Because he (Sibert) became involved in the events, so when he put his story out there, there's no way that people could say, 'Well, I know what really happened.' He's the only person who could tell what happened [from his point of view]. He's the only person who could really tell me what his thoughts were."

"It doesn't matter how many times," Hill replied, "he says that, or how many times you put that story out, people are still going to say what they want to say, believe what they want to believe. It doesn't change anything."

---

8. I was paraphrasing Sibert, as I did not have his interview to read from.

"But at least," I started to say, but Clint Hill was having none of it.

"The only person it changes anything to, is you," he said.

"Well, I guess that's why I do it." I couldn't help but give a little laugh, "because it's a big deal to me, to talk to people like you and I treat it with respect."

"I understand that," Hill said, "and I respect that, but as I said before I just am not going to be interviewed."

"Not ever?"

"Never," he sounded adamant.

Still, I kept trying, "and that just because you feel it's all been said?" I asked. "Everything has been that … "

"There is nothing else to say. I mean, how many times can you say the thing over and over?"

"Well," I said, "the only thing that I know from you is your testimony before the Warren Commission."

"That's exactly the point! And that's where anybody that wants to know anything gotta look!"

I felt terrible pressing Clint Hill for more, but I found myself doing just that. "Just answer this one for me," I said. "Do you think the FBI agent Sibert was right, that the back wound was too low for the single-bullet theory to have happened?"

"I don't have any idea *what he* saw," Clint Hill answered. "I mean, I was in the morgue."

"All he said was 'that I was two feet from that wound.'" I said.

"So was I," Clint Hill interrupted.

I kept talking. "He said that back wound was too low to have come out the throat."

Hill replied, "It's very difficult to have someone look at the body, lying on a slab in a morgue and tell you exactly what had happened. You'd have to see so many different things to disprove or prove anything. You can't just visually see something, you know, and from a distance without a lot of other things being done to give you any proof of anything."

"And I agree with you," I said. "But the closest thing we can get is [to talk] to the people that were there. So that's what we are left with."

"Then go right back to the Warren Commission Report," Clint Hill told me. "Read what it says, it will answer all your questions."

In the end, I could not convince Hill, and I was defeated. We said good-bye to each other; I thanked him for his time. He thanked me, and I let him go. But I did take Clint Hill's advice; I went back to the Warren Commission Report, to Clint Hill's testimony:

Mr. Hill: "Well, as we came out of the turn and began to straighten up, I was viewing the area which looked to be a park. There were people scattered throughout the entire park and I heard a noise from my right rear, which to me seemed to be a firecracker. I immediately looked to my right and in so doing, my eyes had to cross the presidential limousine and I saw President Kennedy grab at himself and lunge forward to his left.

Mr. Specter: "Why don't you just proceed in narrative form to tell us?"

Representative Boggs: "This was the first shot?"

Mr. Hill: "This is the first sound that I heard, yes sir. I jumped from the car realizing something was wrong, ran to the presidential limousine. Just about as I reached it, there was another sound which was different from the first sound. I think I described it in my statement as though someone was shooting a revolver into a hard object. It seemed to have some type of an echo. I put my right foot, I believe it was, on the left rear step of the automobile and I had to hold the hand grip between with my hand when the car lurched forward."

Toward the end of Clint Hill's testimony, Specter again asks him about the shot.

Mr. Specter: "I believe you testified as to the impression you had as to the source of the first shot. To be sure that the record is complete, what was your reaction as to where the first shot came from, Mr. Hill?"

Mr. Hill: "Right rear."

Mr. Specter: "And did you have a reaction or impression as to the source or point of origin of the second shot you described?"

Mr. Hill: "It was right, but I cannot say for sure that it was rear, because when I mounted the car it was – It had a different sound, first of all, than this first sound that I heard. The second one had almost a double sound – as though you were standing against something metal and firing into it. And you hear both the sound of the gun going off and the sound of the cartridge hitting the metal place which could have been caused probably by the hard surface of the head but, I am not sure if that is what caused it."

Mr. Specter: "Are you describing the double sound with respect with what you heard on the occasion of the second shot?"

Mr. Hill: "The second shot that I heard, yes sir."

Mr. Specter: "Now, do you now, or have you ever had the impression or reaction that there was a shot which originated from the front of the presidential car?"

Mr. Hill: "No."

Mr. Specter: "That is all I have."

Note that Specter did not ask Hill if he thought a shot had originated from the right side of the presidential car, from the "grassy knoll" area. That not withstanding, there were a number of people who heard the "double bang."

In an article written and sourced by John S. Craig entitled "The Guns of Dealey Plaza," Craig explains in a section called "Double Bang" Secret Service Agent Roy Kellerman described the shots as a "flurry." Two of the shots were often described by witnesses as "so closely spaced" they sound simultaneous and have practically no time element between them. Additionally, there is a substantial amount of testimony … that describes the later shots as sounding different from the first shots. Governor Connally's initial reaction to the gunfire was that there was either two or three people or more involved in this, or someone was shooting with an automatic rifle.

Craig points out that: "A double sound or bang is described by three secret service agents." (Hill being one of the three, of course). Two of these agents sat within feet of Kennedy as occupants of the limousine. A double shot was reported by one of the witnesses standing on the overpass. Special Agent William Greer, the limousine driver, testified that the last two shots seemed to be just simultaneously one behind the other. The other secret service man in the limousine was Roy Kellerman. Agent Kellerman sat next to Greer and was intimately familiar with the sound of weapons. He described the first shot like many others had as sounding like a firecracker. But the other two shots which he officially reported as a "flurry," sounded different than the first shot. Asked by Mr. Specter if Kellerman could describe the sound of the flurry by way of description of the first shot, Kellerman replied, "If I remember correctly, there were two sharp reports, sir." "Did they sound different from the first shot?" asked Specter. "Yes, definitely," Kellerman added, "Let me give you one illustration, you have heard the sound of a plane breaking the sound barrier? Bang, bang? That is it, it was like, a double bang." Craig lists at least twenty-one more ear witnesses to the "double bang."

So much for answering all of my questions, reading Hill's testimony before the Warren Commission, only made me have more questions for Clint Hill.[9]

---

9. On April 3rd, 2012, Clint Hill did in fact give an interview to writer Lisa McCubbin, who was writing a book with former secret service agent Jerry Blaine. Hill wrote the forward to *The Kennedy Detail*, and then would go on to write: *Mrs. Kennedy and Me, An Intimate Memoir* published in 2012. Then a year later in 2013 he went on to write *Five Days in November*.

Years ago, while working on this book, I received a very late night phone call from a well-known researcher and author of a best selling work on the assassination. I was asleep, and the ringing of the telephone startled me into consciousness. I groped in the dark for the phone on my night stand next to the bed and held the receiver to my ear. "Hello," I managed to say through the fog of sleep. "What's better," I heard a voice say, "The history I've created or the history you are creating now?" (I recognized the voice, we had had many "discussions" about the Kennedy assassination and even considered working on the Kennedy case together, but I found trying to work with the author an impossible task, so the "relationship" hsd been terminated.)

Taken aback by the person not saying "hello" or even can I talk to you, just the direct question, I managed to give him an answer. "History isn't created," I said, "History just is."

I am grateful for the question from the writer, if somewhat rudely asked because it made me think about the phrase creating history. "Creating history" would be what those involved in the assassination and subsequent cover-up did. Create history. Take away the peoples' right to choose a leader of their government, because "they" knew what was best, what was "good" and "necessary" for the people. Bullets were used to make history instead of ballots. It has been my attempt through research and writing to come as close to the best possible "truth" to be found about the Kennedy assassination by listening to those witnesses involved in the aftermath of the assassination itself. Let them tell of their memories, with the hope one can get a sense of direction and for a sense of balance to make a judgment as to whether or not there was a conspiracy in John F. Kennedy's death. I have chosen the road less traveled: let the witnesses to this history speak their truths, their way, and hope to find solid ground in whatever direction the memories, the voices of the men and women who were there in that extraordinary time, take us.

History, after all, just is.

Chapter Two

THE WHITE HOUSE WITNESS

It had started like this: I handed the woman a drawing I was proud of. I had just finished the book I had been working on the last six years. The text was now complete, and I was putting the final touches to the photographic section. "This is an original drawing done especially for this book by Warren Commission medical artist Harold Rydberg," I told her. The drawing showed the inside of the Bethesda morgue where the JFK autopsy had been performed. Rydberg had sketched out the autopsy tables, complete with the body, a weigh scale for internal organs, shelves on the walls, the clock, telephone, the railing in front of the gallery, and the gallery benches, with "Kennedy" spelled out in precise neat letters. For the first time, people were going to get to see the inside of the autopsy room, and I was excited about it.

The woman looked up at me, her brown eyes sparkling. "Wow! This is really interesting!" she said. "You know my father-in-law would really like to see this." "Yes, him and a lot of other people," I thought to myself. "Well, because," she continued, "he was involved in all that, you know." It took a second for the import of what she is said to sink in.

"What?" I asked. "Yes," she said, "My father-in-law. He was there. He was in front of the motorcade in a van or something?" She made it sound like a question, "At the head of the motorcade in Dallas?" "He worked in the White House. He tells us stories about President Kennedy all the time. He has pictures of himself with President Kennedy and everything." "OK," I managed to stammer, "do you think you could get your father-in-law to talk to me sometime?" The woman told me she would ask him the next time they talked.

I then thought it was a shame my friend's relative was in a van away from the motorcade. He had missed witnessing one of the greatest historical events of our time. Still, he would be able to give me unknown bits of history about that day, and tell me some great stories about working in the White House. No matter how peripheral his job or contact with the President, it would be interesting. However, it would be weeks before I heard from my friend again and when she called, I casually asked her if she had talked to her father-in-law about me and my research on John Kennedy. "No, I haven't," she replied honestly. "Why don't I give you his phone number and you can call him and tell him you're a friend of mine. I'm sure he'll talk to you. He's a great guy and one of the nicest people I know."

In the end, I called him almost as a lark to see if there really was anything new the man could add to the record of what happened to Kennedy in Dallas. I didn't know how the van story my friend had related fit into what was already known. In all my research on the Kennedy years, I hadn't studied much material on how communications in the White House worked, not that I had really looked for any. It was an untapped area for me "Probably some little low-level person, the closest he's ever been to the White House is when he drove his communications van to the underground parking garage to have it serviced," I thought to myself as I dialed the number.

"Hello," I heard a male voice say pleasantly. I explained who I was, that I was a friend of his daughter in-law, and that I had written a book on the Kennedy assassination. I explained I had been told by his daughter-in-law that he had been involved in the aftermath of what happened in Dallas. "Yes," the man's voice came back, "I was involved in that somewhat. We set up communications for the President wherever he traveled." The man's voice had the caramel over ice cream smoothness of a radio announcer, a light baritone, every word perfectly enunciated. I asked about what his daughter-in-law had said to me about his being ahead of the Dallas motorcade in a communications van.

"No," he said, "I wasn't in a van. I was at the foot of Air Force One when he was shot, and I was taken by police car to Parkland Hospital." I felt my left hand tighten around the phone receiver. "Just give me a little background on it," I quickly requested. "To talk to someone like you who the public doesn't know about is a rare thing." I heard the man chuckle and then begin again, "I was at the nose of Air Force One when the call came in that Kennedy was shot and so I was told to have a police escort take me to Parkland Hospital." The man went on to describe the scene at Parkland as "complete chaos." "I had never seen anything like it," he told me.

At Parkland, he was given over to another agent who told him to go to the end of a hallway in the hospital and hold a pay phone open and not to let anyone use it, "As it had not been announced that President Kennedy had died," he explained. After the announcement had been made, he was told to go with an agent and follow in another vehicle while the agent drove the Presidential limousine back to the airport to be loaded onboard the cargo plane to Washington, D.C. "So that's what I did," he told me. The man explained how he saw the condition of the car, "Pieces of scalp on the floor, pieces of scalp in the seat, blood, hair, bits of bone on the trunk." After the limousine was loaded aboard the cargo plane he remembering being, " taken back to the nose of Air Force One. Sometime elapsed and the ambulance arrived with Kennedy's body in a casket. Then Jacqueline Kennedy got out of the ambulance," the man said. He was "beckoned to come over," and helped load the casket aboard the airplane. "There was a body in the casket," he said with finality. I questioned him with, "Then you're familiar with David Lifton's theory (of body theft and alteration)?" The man replied, "Yes, I've heard that. There was a body in the casket, believe me."

He then described helping Jacqueline Kennedy aboard Air Force One, taking her by the arm and gently sitting her down next to the casket. He was present for the swearing-in of the new President Lyndon Johnson. "I was probably ten feet away," he said. He could see the casket, "the whole time the swearing-in was taking place. I'm ninety-nine and nine-tenths sure the cargo doors were never opened inside or out." (Another theory told of possibly hiding the President's body in the cargo bay of the plane.)

The man went on to describe the atmosphere inside of Air Force One as "rushed chaos, with a lot of people who were scared." I was startled and my breath caught in my throat as I heard him say, "I'll be honest with you, there are things that I will take to the grave that I can't … " the man paused, "That I will never say. I guess that's fortunate or unfortunate. I won't put my family and that kind of jeopardy." It was at that point I realized that I wasn't breathing. I had been holding my breath, so caught up in what the man was saying, that when I did let my breath out, it was in a long explosive sigh. I hoped he hadn't heard it. "For a fellow like me, that just grabs me by the throat. Can you understand that?" I explained. " Oh, I know that," he shot back.

There was a few seconds of silence on the phone line, then, "Lee Harvey Oswald had nothing to do with that assassination." "What makes you say that?" I asked, shocked. I felt my chest start to tighten, my heart start to pound. The man answered back, "The talk I heard when I got back to Washington." "Yes," I interrupted. "There was talk all over Washington," With in a dead, quite voice the man continued, "I mean among the people that were there. People I trusted with my life. That I still trust with my life. The Secret Service agents," he went on, "tell one story for public consumption, but what they told me later, back in Washington, was a whole different story." "I have to be careful with my past," he explained. "I had to cope with the assassination for a long time. I spent a lot of restless, sleepless nights. There are a lot of things I've put on the shelf."

We talked a little more, and at the end of our conversation I asked to meet with him sometime. " Stay close to my daughter-in-law," the man said.

" She will know the next time were going to be visiting. Maybe we can talk then." Thanking him, our conversation over, I put the phone receiver down gently in its cradle.

I never sleep well before an interview. It was to be no different this time, tossing and turning throughout the night, my head full of questions I wanted to ask, excited at the prospect of turning up new information in the Kennedy case. My appointment with the man was set for midmorning. I carefully followed the directions I had been given. I turned off onto a short gravel road and there off to my left sat the house I had been told to look for. I pulled up across from the house, opened the door of my minivan, got out, gathered my hand-held tape recorder, the black leather folder containing drawings of Kennedy's head by Harold Rydberg, and pictures taken of President Kennedy's casket being loaded onto Air Force One at Love Field in Dallas, and of Jacqueline Kennedy following up the same steps up into the plane. I wanted to see if the man could point himself out to me in those now historic pictures. Normally, for an interview, I would be lugging a video camera as well, but part of the man's agreement to talk to me was not to tell where in the country he lived, give his name or to film our conversation. So, the small handheld tape recorder was all I was allowed to bring to preserve the meeting.

I walk up the sidewalk that leads to the door of the house and ring the doorbell. The door opens, the man stands before me. Everything about him bespeaks order. Neatness. He is a large man in his mid-60s, salt and pepper hair is neatly combed, every hair in place. He wears a neatly trimmed mustache. Piercing deep green eyes look at me from behind steel frame glasses. His bearing is that of a military man. I, on the other hand am dressed in a pair of not too faded jeans and an ancient pullover short-sleeved polo shirt. The town that I live in, is not Washington D.C., or Dallas Texas, for that matter, because if I had to travel to another state for the interview with the witness, I would've taken more care in my dress. But because I'm a friend of this man's relative, and I'm on home ground, my guard is down.

Now, standing in the doorway with man dressed in crisply pressed clothing, creases on his pants so sharp one could cut one's finger, I now feel like a pizza delivery boy about to enter the hollowed halls of West Point. Even so, the man invites me in, and steps aside as I enter the living room. "Where would you like to do the interview?" he asks, "The couch, or we could sit at the table." The man looks towards a large dining room table dominating a small dining area off of the kitchen. I choose the table. The man walks ahead of me moving with easy grace. I move without grace, but aptly enough across the beige carpet of the living room, the tiredness I felt earlier has now vanished.

My body is flooded with adrenaline now that the interview is at hand; my senses are on hyper alert. Sights and sounds are magnified.

I take my black leather bound folder and sit it down the on the left side of the table along with my cassette tape recorder. I pulled out one of the heavy wooden chairs and settled uncomfortably in the seat. The man sits to my right. "You'll have to ask me questions," he says. " I don't know how to … " I flash a big smile at him, trying to be reassuring. " I will ask you questions if I need to know more about something," I said, "but for the most part, I just want you to talk about your experiences."

I picked up the tape recorder and held in my hand." Your more important than I am," I said. "So let's put this closer to you." I placed tape recorder closer to the man. He smiles shyly at me, biting his lower lip, hands folded in front of him. I reached out with my left hand and pushed the play record buttons on the recorder.

"Tell me," I said. "Tell me what you remember."

LAW: First of all, tell me how you came to be in the White House?

WHW: Well, a lot of that I really don't know. Basically I just was called in a really big room and there were people sitting at the end of this long table, and they told me that President Kennedy wanted me to be on his Communication Staff. Now, I don't know exactly what they did as far as a background check – they did one after I accepted, of course, but how they originally chose me I don't know. There was about fifty-some men that were interviewed for that, and three of us made it. So, some of those questions I can't answer because I really don't know, but it really was an experience. It really was.

Law: You're in the White House now. Tell me your first experience meeting President Kennedy.

WHW: We arrived in Washington, D.C., my wife and I, and we finally found a place to live in Silver Springs, Maryland. So we had what we call, the "White House Communications" building down on the Potomac, right next to that was a Watergate Inn (which now all of that is gone) and it's now the Watergate Inn Hotel, which is famous for other things. But my first recollection was that I was taken to the West Wing of the White House where all the press people go and I was told that I was to meet President Kennedy that morning.

We waited outside in a little alcove until a lady came and told us that the President was ready to see us. There were two of us, and we were taken in the Oval Office where he got up from behind his desk and came out and shook our hands. He welcomed us to the White House, saying, "It's good to have you here." He asked us a little about each one of us, our families, where we came from, and a little bit of our backgrounds.

The thing I remember most is he said, "I want you to always remember my door is open to you. You can come and see me anytime, and I want you to always remember that. I'm glad to have you here, and we look forward to working together."

I noticed his rocking chair. I noticed a book shelf close to his desk off to one side, of course, because there's windows right behind his desk, but I just noticed how clean the desk area was and I remember his good willingness to meet us and his attitude was very, very positive.

Another thing I remember about Kennedy as I look back on this now, I remember going to places after he had been there, because in communication we always have to pick up and clean up after he had been there. I remember little doodle papers and stuff that were lying there and we just kind of tossed them not knowing that they would be valuable later. You don't think of that when you're doing that sort of thing, but lots of stuff we could have just picked up and kept as souvenirs, but we didn't. We really respected him, and one thing I do remember was, he knew everybody by name and when he saw me it was "Mr. WHW," and when I saw him it was "Mr. President." No matter how low or high on the totem pole of importance you were there – he always knew your name and he respected you, and it was something we always remembered, and something we really remembered often.

The President also remembered little things that we had done for him and little things that occurred. He always came back, maybe a day or two later, and thanked us. I remember one trip where we went to Alabama. The name I think, White Sands Proving Ground [in New Mexico], or something down in that area [probably Redstone Arsenal], it was a military installation. Anyway, one of the things that all of us remember about President Kennedy was he was always willing to dodge under the rope and go into the crowd, and of course, that drives the Secret Service people crazy. Once he does that the crowd starts generating to the center where he is and that can become very troublesome and cause a lot of panic or injury. So, as we were leaving that area and going to his motorcade, he dodged underneath the rope and went into the crowd and the Secret Service Agents just tore their hair out. One grabbed me and said, "You go on one side, hold his arm, and take his arm, lift him up, and I'll do it on the other side, and we'll take him right through here while the two agents in front of us will just clear the path." So, I took his arm and picked him up gently and the other Service Agent picked him up on the other side and we just quickly pushed him through and got him back to where we thought he was safe again.

Law: When you were on duty you actually wound up sort of being like a Secret Service man or bodyguard. What was going through your head?

WHW: Well, we work together very closely because all the communications that the Secret Service had we took care of, and so we worked very closely together. They knew who we were, and we knew who they were, and we respected that. We knew how far we could go, and they knew how much they could call upon us, so there was a real commendatory there that helped us to work together well. I think it was two or three days later, I was walking through the main Mansion, through the Rose Garden over where the Oval Office is located, and President Kennedy was outside. I don't know what he was doing out there, maybe just taking a little break or something, but he said, "Mr. WHW." Which is kind of unusual because I didn't expect that right at that time and so I said, "Yes, Mr. President?" He said, "Come on over. Let me talk to you a minute." So I went over there. He said, "Did you ever play football when you were in high school?" I replied, "Well, yes sir, I did, but it was a very small school in Montana and it wasn't significant, but I did play a little bit." He said, "Well I figured you did." He said, "When you took a hold of my shoulder and arm the other day I felt there was a little football image behind that," he continued, "I just want you to know that I appreciate that." I think you got me out of a little trouble there." And I responded, "Well, Mr. President, I'm glad to help anyway that I can." He kind of laughed, and I kind of laughed, and I just walked on to other things. That's just kind of like how he was, very personable and he treated his staff with much respect. I think that's why, when he was assassinated, there was a great exodus of people leaving – not only that but politically wise too, but because Mr. Johnson was a much different, different person, but that is a whole different story in itself.

But that was one instance. There was another instance where I was repairing and putting in a phone recording service in the Oval Office underneath his desk and there was a gentleman helping me from the department, from the same department I was in. This might come to a shock to you, but President Kennedy recorded everything that went on in the Oval Office. Three stories down below, underneath the White House in a very secret situation, every time the President lifted the phone or talked on the phone or the First Lady talked on the phone it was always recorded unbeknown to those who were talking to him. So, that's just a little bit of sideline that may be interesting to you.

Law: How did they tell you? Was it, "I want you to come in here and put this recording system in?" Were you shocked?

WHW: No, because it was an ongoing thing at that time. We inherited the recording when I got there. To tell you how at ease I was, when I got the assignment, my supervisor just said, "You need to go up there. There's something wrong with the recording system in the Oval Office. Could you fix that?" That was just sort of the way it was treated. It wasn't like, "Don't tell anybody," and "Don't do this." Or, "You know to be very careful," because it wasn't that way at all. It was just an open situation. Anyway, I was underneath this desk (in a very precarious situation) and trying to get this thing, and my companion in work evidently left the room, and me not knowing that, I called out, "Would you hand me the damn screwdriver, please. I need it!" And this hand came down with the screwdriver in it. As I turned I could barely see the hand, and I thought, "That's not my companion's hand!" So when I got through doing what I had to do underneath the desk, I came out and President Kennedy was standing there with a big grin on his face. Of course I immediately apologized for what I said, and the President answered, "Don't worry about it Mr. WHW, I say that occasionally too." And we laughed and kind of joked with each other a little bit and that was the end of that. It was just those little things where he seemed like he was just a part of the boys, and he was just a human being. Those are a couple of experiences that I can relate, to tell you about.

Law: Do you remember any various trips where anything happened? I talked to a Secret Service Agent once that told me he went with President Kennedy to Germany where he gave the famous "Ich bin ein Berliner" speech and he was there for all of it.

WHW: I was in Berlin for that.

Law: Where you there for that?

WHW: I wasn't there in the stadium where he talked, but I was there about two-and-a-half weeks before he arrived because we had to set up a communication systems. You have to remember though, at that time, there were no computers, no satellites, there was nothing of those sorts. So, we had to set up sideband radio, and we used the underground transatlantic telephone communications when we could, so there was a lot of expensive equipment being set up for that visit. We had to be there about two-and-a-half weeks early before Kennedy arrived.

Law: Really? So you would go in a couple of weeks before?

WHW: We would either go in before or right then if it was a short stop, and we could set up with a very portable unit, and sometimes we flew with him on Air Force One because we knew we could take care of it at things time because of the short stop situation. But if he was going to stay overnight some of us had to go prior to that stay and set it up. For instance if we felt that when he went to Hotel Carlisle in New York City, there wasn't the communication access necessary because there were so many tall buildings. What we had to do was go up to the very top of the Hotel Carlisle, outside, way up top. I can't remember how many stories it was, but I know it's 70 or 80 stories, somewhere in that area – we had to go outside on the very narrow ramp and put up an antenna that would cover that whole area for when he was in a motorcade, in his limousine, or coming in from the airport. All of those things had to be set up. We later changed the setup to the Pan Am Building that, at that time, next to the Empire State Building, was probably one of the tallest buildings in New York City, but now it isn't. At that time the Pan Am Building was a pretty tall building. We had to look out for those things all time. Then we took care of all the radios and all the White House cars to make sure if they got any new cars we put radios in them too, and that the new cars were being put away, or put in retirement, so of speak, before we would take all the radios and equipment out. We had a vast area to take care of, but we did travel with the President or go ahead of him.

We did a lot of hop scotching, especially during campaigning. For instance, if he was going to Atlanta, Palm Beach, and Texas, some of us would go to Atlanta, then when we'd get down to Texas, and somebody else would pick up Florida. That way we would hopscotch into different areas every other stop, and the President would be all set communication-wise. Sometimes we had time to pick up our gear and put it in the Cargo plane and then we would sometimes fly back on Air Force One or sometimes go with him.

Law: I'm not sure how this works or how communication works. Was there an area in Air Force One?

WHW: There was an area in Air Force One, but we could go anywhere in the plane because of what our assignment was, but normally we respected that, and there was more of a living quarters (at that time, this is the old Air Force One remember) so I have not been in the new one, but in the old Air Force One there was kind of a respected living area where the President and his First Family were always there. We didn't really go in there unless we were asked to go in there, so we were more in the front of the plane while the rest of them were in the back of the plane.

When Kennedy was shot, when we loaded the casket in the back of Air Force One, it was in the back there, and so that was mainly understood that we really didn't go back there unless we were asked.

Law: So, in your travels with President Kennedy you told me a little story about being in West Palm Beach, Florida and bringing a plate of cookies?

WHW: We were in a communications trailer on the property on West Palm Beach, Florida, so after "the Boss" (which we called him) retired for the night we just undid our ties' and took off our suit coats and kind of relaxed a little bit. This time, just as we did that a knock came at the door and we wondered what was going on because it was a kind of late. Then we opened the door and there was Mrs. Kennedy and the President who had come out with some soft drinks and a plate of cookies for us. I don't know whether she cooked them or not, it wasn't important to me, but again it was a respect issue for us, to come out and visit with us for about 10 minutes or so. Then they told us good night and went back to the main Mansion. Those are just little things that they did.

Law: How does that feel to be in the presence of the President of the United States?

WHW: At first it's a very overwhelming situation because you've never been there before, but we who worked with him and became very close to him, you just kind of accepted him, and you respected him. Don't get me wrong, he was always the President and we always respected that, but he became one of the crew who helped us accomplish what we were assigned to do, and even though he wasn't there all the time (you know with a plate of cookies or whatever) we always respected him and gave him the respect he deserved. We knew that he was on the same frequency as we were.

Law: That's a good point because over the years there have been lots of books written that said President Kennedy would basically do what he wanted to do if he wanted to do it. The story of when he was in Dallas it is claimed he said, "Keep those Ivy League Charlatans off my car!" I haven't met a Secret Service Agent or talked to a Secret Service Agent yet that says he said that. Would that be out of character for the President?

WHW: It would be out of character for the President to speak ill of any race or any situation that he knew would be heard. Now whether he thought that or not personally, I couldn't tell you, but I know when I worked for him there was never any of that going on.

Now, his own mind! Yes, he did have his own mind. And I think that bore out during the Bay of Pigs situation and the Missile Crisis situation when Russia was sending missiles to Cuba. I think that people don't realize how close we were to a very terrible World War III. And if he hadn't of stuck-by-his-guns, and if he hadn't had the personality that he did, I don't know whether Russia would have backed down or not, I really don't.

Law: How involved in that were we?

WHW: Very close. We had evacuation plans ready for him to go.

Law: Really?

WHW: Yes. We had things standing by to take him and his family away. That's how close we were. I'm not sure the normal public, and maybe that's okay, too, but I don't think the normal public knew how close we were at that time. If he hadn't of stuck by his guns and said, "You either turn those boats around or that's it!"

Law: The staff had things going on at the White House. Was that loosely run? I mean it wasn't a tense atmosphere, I guess is what I'm asking? Because it was a new time and a new President coming in give me a little flavor of the air of that. Your comfort level at being there and others' comfort level.

WHW: Well, everybody was happy working there. I can't think of anybody that was griping about something or had un-pleasantries about something. As far as I'm aware everybody was in good spirits and happy to be there because of the work environment. Now, the other past Presidents … I must say when Johnson took over it was much different. It was terrible. It was absolutely terrible. I think that's one of the things that occurred to me because I could have stayed there for as long as I wanted because it was a non-political assignment-so I could have been there today, but one of the things that made me really think seriously was President Johnson.

Law: I'm going to ask you about President Johnson in a little bit. Let's talk about the Secret Service. Did you have close contact with them?

WHW: Close ties.

Law: Tell me a little about the Secret Service. A lot of blame has been heaped upon them over the years for not doing their job correctly, and I don't know that that's true.

WHW: You know there's no organization that's perfect because we're all humans, but I've never met more committed men. I've never met men with more respect for the person they were working for (at that time) President Kennedy, than I did with the Secret Service people. They were very into their job. They knew what had to be done, and they did it, and sometimes feelings were hurt, but they did it!

Law: How did feelings get hurt?

WHW: Well you're working in a political environment so there's maybe a member of Congress or maybe there's a House Speaker or maybe there's somebody in a high esteem position, but watch this situation. I remember one time when we were lining up the motorcade in Berlin, and we were doing a run through motorcade.

Law: What does that mean?

WHW: Well we would set up the motorcade and this is where the President's car is and this is where the executive car would be and this is where this leader would be.

Law: Did they have a standard set of things that they dealt with in each trip?

WHW: Most of the time there was a standard. Now that changed, because of the environment and because of the country-that changed because of lots of things, but the Secret Service Agents, and us, were in charge of setting up those motorcades when I was there helping with that.

Law: Did you help a lot with the setting up?

WHW: In some situations we did. Not all the time, but the main decision was made by the Secret Service. I must tell you I do not know who made the final decision to take the Bubble Top off the car in Dallas. I don't know who did that.

Law: There are a couple of agents who have taken the responsibility.

WHW: Yea, I think that is basically where it comes from, but I think that they were guided by the sense of direction that President Kennedy wanted. You know ... I think that what happened was President Kennedy said, "Hey, if it's going to be sunshine and you feel like the bubble top should come off, take it off." It was kind of up to them to make that decision, but it was under his guidelines of what he wanted.

Law: You probably know this more than most. If it came down to the Secret Service wanting something and the President wanting something, who would win out? I mean if they went and said, "Sir, this is for your protection and this is what we need to do ... " Would he contradict that or would he go with it?

WHW: Most the time he would go with it because he respected that. Now, as the thing like 'under the rope' and we held it, now he would do that against his Secret Service Agent wishes, but we would work through those things ... you know, but once in a while that would happen. I still say that the Bubble Top came off because of how they thought the President wanted it at that time, but you've got to remember that that morning, that was a strange morning because as he left Fort Worth the clouds in Dallas where–

I was at the airport as the plane was approaching the clouds started disappointing away. It was unbelievable.

Law: OK. Let's pick up there then. The plans had been set to go to Texas. Take me to the morning that everybody left Washington to go to do this trip.

WHW: OK. I think that there was myself and one other communication person who went to Dallas and we were there, if I remember correctly, two or three days before Kennedy arrived. I know it was at least two … maybe three. In fact I still have my room key. I forgot to turn that back in.

Law: You've had it all these years.

WHW: I've had it all these years. I think it was the Hilton. I think that's what it was. Jeez, it's amazing how you just sort of lose sense to that. Anyway, we were there at least two or three days before he arrived so we had to set up communications. We put an antenna on top of the tallest building, which was our hotel if I'm not mistaken. We worked closely with the telephone company and so our first contact when we get there was with the telephone company because we use telephone lines. So we're in close contact with the telephone company, and so we set up what we call our "Base Station" which is a little portable thing about the size of a 25 or 27 inch television, and we would pack that and put it in a high place and put an antenna on it and then we would set up our base station, and make sure it covers the area, especially the motorcade. Now we knew where that the motorcade was going to be. We know that because we have to make sure that it is covered by the radio system that we have.

Law: Do you remember the line up? Give me a standard if you can remember. I know that I'm asking you to go back decades, but can you give me a basic of while he's in America?

WHW: Usually there are police cars or motorcycles, policemen ahead of the first Secret Service car. There's always a Secret Service car in front of the President's limousine and there's always one behind.

Law: OK, but is there a standard procedure for the lead car that may have a local politician?

WHW: The lead car never has a local politician. The limousine where the President is riding may have a local politician, but the Secret Service car in front of him, never has a politician, that's Secret Service and the Secret Service car behind-remember when the Secret Service Agents ride in the back of the limousine, that's only for Secret Service too. Now behind that Secret Service car, then I think it was Johnson's car, and then it goes from there on a scale from how important you are to the further back you are, the least important you are. Well that's just the way it is.

Law: I've been told by other researchers, I don't know if this is true or not, it has been written that the press usually rode, the camera people, on a flat bed truck in front of the motorcade so they could get photographs. I'm not talking about the 22nd, because we know that one changed.

WHW: No. No. Sometimes that does happen. Sometimes the press people ride behind the Vice President's car, and sometimes depending upon the stop and depending upon the circumstances they could be in front, but very seldom they're in front because if something happens there has to be a way clear to get them out of the situation. So, the press people usually are behind the President's limousine. Now whether that's been changed over the years or not I have no idea.

Law: Do you remember the motorcycle formation? Do you remember how they usually did that?

WHW: There's usually two or four. Yes, usually there were that many.

Law: Just around his car?

WHW: They tried to stay away from the side of the car because they didn't want to get in the way of people seeing him. I don't know if that was the President's request or whether that was the Secret Service request or whatever, but you have motorcycles or police cars in front, and then you have Secret Service car and then you have the President's limousine, then you have another Secret Service car and then normally you may have press people there or you may have the Vice President's limousine there if he's on that trip. Sometimes the Vice President doesn't accompany him. So behind that last Secret Service car could be the press people.

Law: Do you remember whether President Kennedy traveled most of the time with an aide in the car with him?

WHW: No, because when he left the airport–

Law: I'm talking in standard motorcades not–

WHW: There's usually not an aide. There wasn't then Again, whether that's been changed or not, I don't know. In the Dallas motorcade there was only him and Mrs. Kennedy and the Connallys' and the Secret Service Agents, and that was normally the way it was. And sometimes he would travel by himself, with his wife, or he would travel with somebody in the jump seats, like Connally did.

Law: Greer and Kellerman, did you know them well? Did you ever get to meet them? They were the drivers of the limousine.

WHW: I knew them. I wouldn't say I knew them personally, but I could recognize them immediately and Hill who jumped on the back of the limousine, I knew him. He went on a lot of trips with the President also.

Law: What kind of person was Clinton [Hill]?

WHW: Very down to earth, and "this is the way it has to be done." As they all were. Namely all of them had that same attitude which you know you have to have.

Law: OK. So let's continue. Take me back to the 22nd. You arrived a couple of days early to set up the communications, so you have all that done, what happens next?

WHW: We'd wait in the morning for him to arrive, and we'd be at the airport early. Secret Service would have set up a barrier and worked very closely with the local law enforcement. There was law enforcement on top of the airport. There was local law enforcement on top of any kind of tall building that existed in that area. There was law enforcement on the ground. There were Secret Service agents right where the plane was to land, and like I said, as the plane was getting ready to land the decision was made to take the bubble top off of the limousine, and it was taken off. As the airplane landed, the President and First Lady embarked. This was the first time that Mrs. Kennedy had accompanied him for quite awhile because she had been ill, so this was not only a big political trip for him, but it was a trip that was good because they were together again.

As the President and Mrs. Kennedy walked from the airplane it never ceased to amaze me how the people clamored and screamed and yelled. As he stepped off from the airplane he shook hands with the dignitaries that were waiting there and he came over closer to the limousine but then he began to walk away and instead went to the fence area where people were lined up. Even Mrs. Kennedy shook hands for a few minutes and then they went over to the limousine, if I remember correctly, – this is the limousine (showing photo) – and then he was inside the limousine. There were some things that I had to do, which I can't tell you at this time what those things were because of the secrets …

Law: It was just putting it together?

WHW: Yes, that's right. It was just putting it together, that's all it was. As Kennedy got in the limousine he sat down and he looked up at me and his last words to me were like, "It's going to be a nice day today Mr. WHW." And I said, "Yes, it does Mr. President." And that was it. As he sat there for just a few seconds and then his wife got in the other side, and then the Connally's got in. The President continued to wave at the people and the hustle and the bustle that normally accompanied a trip of that situation, wherever he goes actually. And then within a few minutes they started to pull away. As they pulled away he continued to wave and he left in the motorcade.

I went to the nose of Air Force One, where we just kind of made a little meeting and were talking, because we were getting ready to go to the Trade Center where the President was going to speak. So, we were just kind of killing a little time there until we were going in a little motorcade of our own to the Trade Center. I would imagine 15 or 20 minutes or something went by and we heard something over the radio that was – we couldn't quite understand what it was, it had something to do with the President, but we couldn't quite understand – and then we did get the complete situation. "The President has been shot. We're taking him to Parkland Hospital!"

Well, at that time, you've got to understand, that this is what you fear more than anything that something would have happened to him. You go through this knowing that it will probably never happen, but if it does happen.... But if it does happen, how are you going to respond to it? So, here we are. The President has been shot. We didn't know if he was alive or dead, and so immediately there were decisions made. They came to me and said, "You go to Parkland Hospital. This policeman is taking you to Parkland, and you do what they tell you there. OK?" So, I was taken by escort to Parkland Hospital, and when I arrived – this is so vivid in my mind – there were people sitting on the curbs and holding their head and their hands crying out loud, literally crying out loud. Pandemonium like I've never seen before. Older men crying, women hugging each other, men hugging each other, tears flowing all over the place. It was just unbelievable and I stood there for a moment.

My head couldn't comprehend what was going on because of the significance of what was happening. I have great faith that I was raised with and I depended upon that faith a lot at that point and time. It gave me great comfort. It really did.

I was taken into Parkland Hospital and the Secret Service agent said to me, "Go down the hallway and hold that phone open. Don't let anyone use the phone because the press is going crazy." So I immediately went down the hallway, and as I went down this little hallway, I can't remember if it was a hallway or what it was exactly, but I remember going towards that pay telephone and as I went by I looked into this room and there President Kennedy was laying on this table and Mrs. Kennedy was on the other side of the casket. I remember seeing part of his skull, even though it was on the other side. I remember seeing part of his head, and debris from his head lying on this table. I couldn't stop, and I couldn't look at it because I didn't feel comfortable with that, but I remember seeing the pandemonium in that room, but I remember seeing the blood on his shirt and everything that I could see within a few seconds, and as I went by there I remember that vividly. I continued to the phone and held that phone open.

Law: How many minutes, after this all happened, did they come to you and get you?

WHW: Probably 10 minutes or 15 minutes had elapsed. Then he told me, another Secret Service agent (not the same one that sent me there) told me that the President was dead. He was very emotional when he told me that, and of course, we were all very emotional during this whole period. I mean it was just unbelievable.

Law: So, they were saying he was dead even before–

WHW: They told me he was dead, and I don't know whether they announced that to the Press at that time, but I know it was announced either before that or right after that ... OK, I think it was announced right after that, because as I was walking out the Secret Service agent had seemed to be acting like that was what was going on. Then the Secret Service agent told me, "We have to take this car that he was shot in back and load it in the Cargo Plane. OK! You take this car and drive it so you can bring me cross back over to the Air Force One."

Law: He drove the limousine, and you drove the backup car?

WHW: Right. Now I didn't get a chance to see the limousine until we got to Love Field, and as he pulled the limousine up to the ramp to load it in the Cargo Plane I stopped the car I was in and I walked over to the limousine. Now, I didn't know what to expect. I hadn't thought about it, I guess, but as I saw this limousine it come to my mind that there was more than one shooter. Why that came to my mind, I don't know, because at this point and time no one knew anything, as far as I knew. As I saw the limousine I walked over to this side of the limousine where he had been shot and I saw scalp on the floor. The thing that I really noticed was on the back of the trunk lid was a large area that you could tell that a bullet had taken half his scalp and actually just pulled it across the trunk lid.

Law: Can you do me a favor? Do you remember it enough to–?

WHW: I remember pretty much–

Law: Could you maybe, from memory, just give me a little sketch? OK, you're drawing it for me.

WHW: OK, this is where Mr. Kennedy was sitting. This was the trunk lid (which is kind of exaggerated in the drawing). This is the Secret Service agents (front seats) and this is the Connally's (middle jump seats) and this is Mrs. Kennedy, and here is where President Kennedy was (rear seats). There was a pattern like this, on the back–

Law: That's how it looked?

WHW: That's how it looked. And there were pieces of scalp and matter and everything on the back.

Law: So, it was more or less a half-moon that looked to you like it had been blown back?

WHW: Right. Oh, definitely.

Law: So you could tell?

WHW: Yes. It was so obvious that it made an impression upon me immediately that there must have been somebody from the top that had shot him. I mean it was just obvious. It was just there. There was no conversation about it whatsoever.

Law: Did you see the car afterward? I mean, after they took it back to the White House garage?

WHW: My understanding was – and I have no way of verifying this – that when this car was taken back to Washington, D.C. it was taken and washed.

Law: There's a picture that was taken that showed a dent in the chrome, and I was wondering if maybe you saw the limousine after that to see the dent. Did you ever inspect it?

WHW: I never did see it. No, but that is the way it was at that point and time. And there was, of course, on the floor here, there were pieces of scalp and pieces of matter here and, of course, there was blood over here because Mrs. Kennedy just pulled him over on top of her.

Law: You mean over on the left side?

WHW: Right, on this side to the left seat.

Law: I brought this picture along because that's the picture where they loaded the … I wondered, because you told me that you had assisted Mrs. Kennedy, so this is you right here?

WHW: Right. As we loaded the plane – this is after we'd gone in the plane – as we loaded the casket into the plane, I started to come out and I ran right into her. I mean, I just literally just face-to-face. I merely took her arm and set her down next to the casket.

I wrote a little bit in your book last night glancing, just glancing through it, about how there are some people who think that the body was removed from the casket at this point in time. That never did happen. Never! Never did happen!

Law: How can you be certain?

WHW: Well, because that cargo bay was never open.

Law: And your certain of that because?

WHW: You bet. You bet. Because there was somebody at that casket at all time.

Law: Were you pretty much inside of there the whole time?

WHW: Yes. Yes.

Law: So you were basically on the plane?

WHW: Until it left. Until it left, and Mrs. Kennedy was by that casket the whole time and the only time she wasn't was when she went up … She didn't want to go up to the swearing-in. She fought that, didn't want to.

Law: You were there and it took off and you were still on the plane?

WHW: No, no, no. I was there until the plane took off. And then we were taken off the plane.

Law: So you weren't on the plane on the way back?

WHW: No. No.

Law: OK, so tell me some of the things aboard the plane as you put this casket in. You were there for the swearing-in? Tell me about that?

WHW: Well, Mrs. Kennedy didn't want to go up there, but she did, under pressure, and as she went up there–

Law: When you say "under pressure"?

WHW: She wanted to stay with her husband.

Law: Did you see her being pressured?

WHW: I saw her saying, "I don't want to go there!" You've got to understand that she was under very heavy medication. Now, how much medication I have no idea, but she was. Because of the situation I understand that, believe me. If your husband's body is blown across your … I can understand that you would need to be medicated.

Law: I can't remember if read anything about medication. I think it was Dave Powers or someone fixed her a drink.

WHW: Yes, but she was given medication. Because that may not be well known, but they had given her medication to help her calm down a little bit. When she was taken from the casket up to the swearing-in, one of my companions stayed with the casket.

Law: One of your companions?

WHW: Right.

Law: Was he in communications or was he a Secret Service guy?

WHW: Right. He was in communications.

Law: Right.

WHW: And in order to get into the bay of that airplane you have to open it from the outside. You can't go in from the inside so that body in that casket was never taken out of that casket.

Law: In Lifton's book, where this picture came out, David Lifton has a drawing, oh, could be some other, I've read so many books over the years, that you could lift from the inside of the plane into the cargo hold. That's not possible?

WHW: Ah, that is, but I don't think it's big enough for a casket. I think it's big enough for a person, but not a casket. I could assure you that his body was not removed from the casket in Air Force One in Dallas.

Law: How did you know there was a body in the casket as you were loading it?

WHW: Um, well we could feel it, and then Mrs. Kennedy certainly knew that the body was there, and she was with the body all the time.

Law: So, tell me after you set the casket down, what happened after that?

WHW: We set the casket down. We seated Mrs. Kennedy down next to the casket where she wanted to be. We stood there until the decision was made, evidently, to swear President Johnson in, and then within a matter, of oh – it wasn't more than thirty seconds or a minute in discussion to whether she wanted to go up front or not. That was the end of it, and so she got up. They helped her up to the front of the swearing-in and I was standing towards the back of that group of people that you see. I'm not in the photograph, thank heavens, and so when that swearing-in …

Law: Were you just out of range?

WHW: Right.

Law: The cabin portion is kind of disoriented for somebody that doesn't know the area. I've never been there. I've only seen it in pictures.

WHW: I was just standing more behind everybody. And so when the swearing in was done, she immediately wanted to go back to the casket. The gentleman that I worked with stayed there with the casket. In fact, I think of our conversation I said, "Do you want to stay here or do you want me to go up with her?" He said, "No, I'll stay here. You go on up." So, that was kind of the end of the conversation.

Law: So what happened after the swearing in?

WHW: After the swearing in, the decision was made for them to fly back to Washington, D.C., and the plane started up and disembarked at the back of the plane, and they took off.

Law: I know that you said that you weren't paying attention to things that you may have to remember twenty years ago, but I'm interested in the sense of how everybody was acting. Did you see Johnson?

WHW: Johnson was very scared. In fact, when they took him from his car … he came before, if I remember correctly. He came before the casket arrived with Kennedy's body in it. As they took him out of the car and put him in Air Force One they actually huddled over him with arms and body, so that, I guess they felt he was terribly afraid that he would be next. I don't know what the conversation was at that high level, but I know that the look on his face was scared.

Law: How were the actions of the Secret Service agents you viewed? How were they doing?

WHW: Demanding and it was done. In this situation that's just the way it's going to be and there's not going to be any arguing about it. Which is the only way to take care of it under those circumstances, and it was just the way it was going to be. You know, I would not have wanted to get into an argument with one of them at that point and time because they were beyond their ability to cope to what had really happened. I think it just pushed them up several notches.

Law: So very tense, very–

WHW: Oh boy, yes. They seemed to keep their professionalism, but it was very close. Normally you could kid and joke, but at this point there was none of that, none of it whatsoever.

Law: What was your own personal feeling when you're there, and you just set this casket down, and you told me that you took Jacqueline Kennedy by the arm and sat her down next to the casket-what's going through, you were in your twenty's at the point?

WHW: I was twenty-four, I think.

Law: What's going through a young twenty-four year olds' mind?

WHW: You know, I don't even know if I can relate that or not. I kept thinking, "What am I doing here? Is this a dream? How is this going to affect my life? Is anybody every going to come back to visit Dallas again? This is going to be a ghost town! What's going to happen to our government? How's my wife? Hope she's OK!"

You know so many things go through your mind at that time because of the terrible significance of what's occurred, and so you try to cope with all these things that come into your mind. I wondered how my mom and dad are doing in Montana. I wondered, you know!

And after a few days of this I was thinking why would I think of all this, but I think it's the way your mind has of coping. You try and put things in perspective and try to think about things and people that are close to you that give you comfort. I don't know what I really thought. I knew that I was scared. I knew I wanted to get home. I depended a lot upon my faith and that gave me great comfort. That was probably the thing that gave me the biggest comfort of all was knowing that I had somebody of a higher power that could comfort me and give me peace and that did come over me. It really did, and that was a very enlightening situation in my life. So, I thought about a lot of things.

I thought, I've got to remember this to tell my kids and my grandkids, but, you know, I don't know whether I … I guess that you just go through those emotions and those feelings. I don't think really comprehended the whole thing as it was going on, in depth. I kind of picked up little scrimmages here and little thoughts there. If affected me for a long time afterwards.

Lots of nights I couldn't sleep. I kept thinking about seeing him and hearing his last words to me and remembering all the things that transpired with him that were fun, exciting, and uplifting, and I did wonder why. Were all of us partly to blame or was it just something that happened, and who was to blame for this and they should be punished terribly. How is our government going to react to all of this–?

Law: Let's go back to Parkland now for a moment. You said, as you were passing the doorway, you looked in and saw the President on the table and you saw the wound on his head. This was a little bit after. The doctors were not trying to do life-saving procedures at this moment?

WHW: Like I said, that was just a brief second. So, as far as I could remember, I could not see tubes or anything on his face. It just seemed to be kind of a hustle and bustle, and I guess the thing that stood out was to see his wound and to see the blood and especially Mrs. Kennedy. I guess I felt sorry for her. It was just a terrible situation. I felt sorry for her when we helped her in the back of the plane. I … you know … I just wondered what this lady was going though. I wondered what her emotions were and how she'd held together though all of this.

Law: Since you mentioned this, loading the ... was Clint Hill down here or any of the–

WHW: If I remember ... I think Clint Hill was there, and the two Secret Service agents that were in the front of the limousine were there, but I don't know that for sure. It seems to me that Clint Hill was there.

Law: They just said, "Come on over here and help lift this up!"

WHW: Right ... right ... right!

Law: You know things like this are frozen in time for people like me, and so have I poured over these pictures, and so they're kind of frozen in my head, but for a young fellow it was just a few seconds.

WHW: Right ... right!

Law: What I've noticed about people like yourself, and others that I've interviewed, while I'm somewhat obsessed about this particular area in our government, you've moved on.

WHW: Right!

Law: It was a part of your life and you didn't really study it, you just moved on. I've always been taken back a little bit by that because I'm so focused on that, so I expect everybody to want to know ...

WHW: Well, I appreciate that and I think the reason for that, because I didn't want to continue on and do what you're doing. And believe me, what you're doing I admire, and I think it's great, but I think a lot of us just didn't want to ... we tried to put it to bed. We tried to get it out of our minds to somewhat degree, because to me, anyway, and all I can talk about is how I feel. It made such a drastic impression upon my mind that I didn't want to dwell in it anymore. It took me ... it took me ... when the movie *JFK* came out, it took me a year before I could even look at any of that, because what that does is it opens up the whole wound again.

Law: Does it take you right back there?

WHW: It takes you right back into the center of that. Right back in the center of it. So all of the emotions you fought with over the years, and all of these things you tried to cope with, and all of the feelings that you tried to deal with are all there again. That's the reason most of us don't do that. I saw a movie afterwards, and I don't know if you can even get the movie anymore, it's called, *Executive Action*.

Law: I've seen it.

WHW: I saw that and I think ... according to what I believe and what I've observed, and everything that I sort of read up to a certain point, that's probably the closest that I think happened to some degree, but I'm not sure of that. I just ... I just ... I know that there was a bullet that came from the front. That was very obvious to me; there was no miscalculation of that. Now, whether Oswald comes from the back, whether he shot from twice from the back, I have no way of knowing that, but I know there was one from the front, and I'll go to my death saying that.

Law: Well, now we're going to come to this place, and I'll turn off the recorder if you want me to, but you made a statement to me a long time ago that said, "I saw things and I know things that I'll take to my grave."

WHW: And I will!

Law: And for a person like me that tries to delve into this just as hard as I can, that just makes me crazy.

WHW: I know. I know it does, and I'm not the only one probably who will do that, but I think there's just certain things that you kind of throw out of your mind because it has such a significance or has such a weight upon your mind that you just don't cope with it, and the reason you don't cope with it – it's because you just don't want to be bothered with it anymore. Maybe it has to do with intelligence or whatever, and there's not a great amount of things that I'll take to my grave, but there are a few things that I've never told my wife. I've never told my family. There are lots of times that I've sat down in the evening with my family, with my grandkids, and they'll ask, "Grandpa, why don't you talk with us about Kennedy." And I will. I'll just sit there and talk about things, but there are certain things that I will not discuss, and I won't. I just … there are certain things that happened in Dallas that, unfortunately … I won't talk about.

Law: Things that you saw yourself?

WHW: Right.

Law: Things that others may have told you later connected to Secret Service agents? I know that you knew some of them fairly well.

WHW: Not necessarily that, but just certain things that I observed and certain things that I heard after the assassination.

Law: After the assassination?

WHW: Right … right!

Law: You made a statement to me once that, if I get this right, you said …

WHW: What's the statement?

Law: I don't have it written down, but it stuck with me for some time. It goes something along the lines of, "Secret Service agents, what they say publicly was totally different than what they told me privately."

WHW: That's true. That's true, but that can happen even in a non-assassination situation. A Secret Service agent came up to me, during Johnson, and said, "I don't feel like I have enough respect to protect this 'blankety-blank' anymore!" He spoke to me in private. Not that he would say that in public. He never would say it in public.

Law: But this pertained to what this agent saw?

WHW: Right!

Law: And he believed one way in private or saw things in private that would lead him in a direction of perhaps conspiracy, but publicly he has a whole different story or they have a whole different story.

WHW: That's true. You have to understand that there is a certain aspect. Well, let me tell you what was told to me. Then maybe you'll understand what I'm telling you. I was told when I got back to Washington, D.C. "You are not to speak of this or discuss this; we know where your family is."

Law: And this came from?

WHW: This came from government officials.

Law: Government officials? They actually physically took you and said …

WHW: One-by-one.

Law: One-by-one?

WHW: That's right.

Law: And they said, say it again for me.

WHW: "You will not discuss what happened down there. You will not talk about it. We know where your family is!"

Law: Tell me a little bit about Lyndon Johnson now. We're past Dallas.

WHW: Well, Johnson, of course, was a different President.

Law: Tell me your first impression of Johnson.

WHW: We never had much affiliation of Johnson as a Vice President, but boy did we have an affiliation with him when he became President. Johnson came from a different cloth. He wasn't educated like Kennedy. He came up basically on his wife's skirts, basically. He never had a great amount of money of his own.

Law: She had a lot of money from what I understand.

WHW: But she had a lot of money through broadcasting and investments. I think she owned, at that time, every television station in Texas, but I'm not sure. Anyway, Johnson came from a completely different mold, and he wasn't the "knowing everybody's name" type of person. He used vulgar language and he wasn't afraid to use it in public or in private, and he didn't care about you. He didn't respect you. As far as he was concerned, you're just somebody to help him achieve something greater. I stayed in Johnson City for two and a half months, and that's probably the worst two and a half months I ever spent in my life.

Law: Tell me what happened?

WHW: Because Johnson City is nothing but a hole in the ground and the only thing there is a house that's cut in half, a drive-in theatre, and they barbeque's goat. Their big thing during the weekend was they have beer and barbecue goat, and the only thing there was Johnson Ranch. Now the Johnson Ranch was very pretty. We were at the hotel; I think it was the last time Johnson stayed in The Hotel Carlisle before he moved to the Waldorf Astoria. He came out of the Presidential Suite here, there's a corridor and there's an elevator right here, and as he came out of the Presidential Suite–

Now, you've got to understand that this is the President of the United States. Okay? The largest free country of the world is what he represents in private or in public, and as he came out of this Presidential Suite, this elevator door was not opened waiting for him. Now, again, I've got to tell you, this is the President of the United States, he walks over to this door and he kicks this door with his foot, and his words were, "Get the God-damn elevator up here. I'm the President and when I want the elevator make sure that God-damn elevator is here." The Secret Service agent and I looked at each other and we just … I know he was thinking the same thing as me. That this is the President of the United States acting like a ten-year-old kid! And that's just some of the things that transpired. You know, he had no respect. He got up and he talked about Civil Rights, about to treat the black people equally. Do you know how they lived on his ranch?

Law: How?

WHW: They lived on dirt floors. They had little houses, and he treated them like they were some kind of little pieces of cattle that he had to deal with. That's how he treated them.

Law: Do you know personally that it was true? Well, it's well known that he used government funding, governmental materials to fix up his ranch.

WHW: Oh, it was obvious.

Law: And used Secret Service as babysitters.

WHW: It was obvious. He could care less what people thought of him.

Law: So, he just basically felt he was the President and he could do anything that he wanted?

WHW: That's exactly right.

Law: Now you're aware of some of the stories about Johnson, I'm sure, "Landslide Lyndon," they called him. There's been a great amount of rumor about Johnson having a hand in President Kennedy's assassination.

WHW: Yes, I thought about that. That was one of the first things I thought about.

Law: When this all happened, that thought was in your head?

WHW: I thought … "I wonder if Johnson had something to do with this?" Because there was not a great amicable feeling between Johnson and Kennedy, there really wasn't. I'm not saying its hatred, but there wasn't any great love between those two men. There really wasn't. And so immediately, maybe I wasn't the only one, but you think, "I wonder if Johnson had anything to do with this?" And then you think, "I wonder if Johnson is the next one killed?" I mean you think about those two things immediately.

Law: In discussions with your friends at the Secret Service or FBI agents or anybody you knew there, was that a common thread of thought among the fellows?

WHW: Oh yes. It was just like, "Good morning!" That was just the way it was.

Law: It was accepted?

WHW: It as accepted as much as it was accepted that Kennedy respected you.

Law: Did a lot of the guys think that maybe Johnson had something to do with it? Did you all discuss?

WHW: Well, that was discussed, but I don't think there was a great serious belief that maybe that, and the other thing that I thought maybe he didn't because when he got out of the car to go to Air Force One that man was scared to death. You could tell that man was scared.

Law: He was scared?

WHW: Now, was he scared that he might get caught or was he scared because he might be next? I don't know.

Law: That's a good point too.

WHW: I really don't know that, but I don't think that Johnson had anything to do with it. I really don't. There were maybe moments that I thought maybe he did, over the years but–

Law: Anything in particular that would.... How did he act right after the assassination? I don't know if you had any immediate contact with him.

WHW: Not a lot of contact, but in talking to people afterward he was concerned; he was scared and he wanted to get out of Dallas.

Law: Did you ever meet Director Hoover?

WHW: No. No.

Law: Now let me ask a question. We were just talking about President Kennedy and the cancellation of the motorcade. There was one in Florida, I believe, and one in Chicago. What can you tell me about that?

WHW: Ah, the one in Florida, I was on that trip, and I think the motorcade was canceled, and I think, you know that was so many years ago. I know it was canceled but I don't remember whether it was rerouted. [It was rerouted.] I just don't remember that. The one in Chicago I was not on, but I remember the gentleman that went on that, and that was canceled completely.

Law: Did you hear any rumors about that?

WHW: Only because of security reasons.

Law: They canceled it for security reasons?

WHW: Right.

Law: And that's basically all you ever heard about that one?

WHW: Right.

Law: I'm doing a book on Bobby Kennedy right now. Did you ever get to meet Bobby Kennedy?

WHW: I was in the room with him two or three times, but I didn't get to know him very much.

Law: Well that doesn't help me much with my next book. (Laughs)

WHW: Sorry about that. (Laughs)

Law: One thread that I hear while talking to you and in talking to some Secret Service Agents is when I'll ask, "What kind of man was President Johnson like?" I've had two agents give me almost verbatim statements. One agent said, "Awe … he was the most deplorable man I ever knew." Two agents, separate, said almost the exact same thing. And that's why they moved on.

WHW: I guess the thing that blows my mind is we elect people like that to be political leaders and unfortunately we have that today. I just don't understand why people … there's a certain power mode you have to have to get into politics, and if you don't have that power mode you cannot succeed. And what I mean by power mode you have to make [your goal] everything. Everything that you breathe, what you sleep, what you eat. Everything! If you don't live up to that situation you'll never make it in national politics. So here you have these power-hungry people that go to the Congress, to the Presidency and the Executive Office, and all these people have this power thing in their system, and that's all they want. One of the examples was Nixon. He wanted so much power that he made mistakes; unfortunately that brought him down.

Law: He could have been a really good President.

WHW: And he still was in as far as Foreign Relations was concerned, and he could have done an excellent job, but the power struggle got in his way.

Law: My family comes from a whole line of Democrats, so Nixon, to me, was like the National Boogie Man. Having grown up the way I have, watching politics, and being interested in them, Nixon almost seems like an angel today.

WHW: Right.

Law: Now, did you … you left after Johnson came in?

WHW: I left after Johnson got elected in the second term. I left just as he was approaching his term.

Law: Any regrets about that?

WHW: No! (Laughs) Didn't have to think about that, did I?

Law: So, how has this affected you over the years? How has this changed your life?

WHW: Like I said earlier, I had a hard time coping with this for several months. I must tell you that there's never a week that doesn't go by since then that I don't think of that day. Never a week! Never a week! One time during the week, I think about that.

Law: Does it make you look at your government differently? I know it affected some people that I interviewed like that.

WHW: Well, you know, there are conflicts with that question. The government I respect and I think it was formed under Godly principles, and the people that run the government whom I don't have a lot of respect for. There are certain people that I do, but for the majority I lost a lot of respect for the government.

Law: Going back to the Kennedy's time, there's been a lot of talk about Joint Chiefs of Staff were always trying to push him in a way, they were trying to push him into a corner. Did you ever get to see any of that?

WHW: No, but I must say, knowing Kennedy as I did, and having the contact that I did, which was not like, believe me, was not like other people like the higher echelon had contact with him, but it would be hard for me to believe that anybody could push Kennedy into doing anything that he didn't believe in. I mean if he believed the Bay of Pigs was right, no matter what the military said, he would go through with it. He was his own person. Not that he didn't listen, not that he wouldn't change his mind, but when he really believed in something, that's the way it was, and maybe that's what it takes. When you look at today, President Bush, you can agree or disagree, but you know where he's coming from.

Law: You do, and I respect that. I don't like it though.

WHW: You can argue about the war, and you can argue about weapons of Mass Destruction, but in my mind I know where he's going, I know what he has in mind and I know what he's thinking.

Law: Yes, you do.

WHW: And you may disagree or agree with that, but you know that's the way he is, and he's never changed. Now, the President before him, that's a different story, but I just feel sometimes that Kennedy was – how should I say this? Kennedy was blamed for some things or some ideals or whatever that maybe didn't really exists. Maybe they just took that has something he was because he was a Kennedy. You know I don't think it was as easy growing up in the Kennedy household as most people think it was. Joseph Kennedy wasn't really an honorable man. He had a lot of things going on in his life that were not all that honorable.

Law: Did you ever meet Joseph Kennedy?

WHW: No. So those boys grew up around stuff like that all the time and so you have to take that into consideration.

Law: Does it lessen your opinion of President Kennedy at all? The different things that came out about, things that transpired, mostly with women?

WHW: It doesn't affect mine, because you have to separate, and again … I'm going to make a comparison here, maybe it's not fair, but if Kennedy did those things it was done out of the premise of the White House, away from the public image. Where the last President that got into that situation; it was done in my house, basically. It was done in a very sacred situation to where it should have never been done. If he wants to do that kind of thing, then go away and do it, and that's his own choice. But, to do that within the realms of the White House, which is America's House, then I guess I have a problem with that. I guess that's where I have a real struggle with that kind of stuff. People in power like that just take advantage and really don't care. That's the way Johnson was, not that he did [women] kind of stuff, and I'm not saying that, the power struggle is what I'm talking about. The disrespect for people, the disrespect for those who work with you, that, I have a real problem with.

Law: Is there anything for historical record that you would like people to know about President Kennedy that you don't think they don't know, or anything that comes to mind now that you would like to tell them?

WHW: I think, and maybe a lot of people already know this, but I feel President Kennedy had a heart and he cared, and he wanted America to succeed in so many areas. I didn't agree with him politically and everything, but there's not a President that I can think of that I do. I think for the time he was "the man," and I think he gave the ultimate sacrifice to prove that.

Chapter Three

JIM SIBERT AND DOUG HORNE

I hadn't contacted James "Si" Sibert in five years and the last time I had talked to Sibert I had been in California doing research for a documentary and hopefully a book on Robert F. Kennedy. My partner Mark Sobel and I were trying to find the location of William Bailey, a former FBI agent, whom had been in the pantry where Robert F. Kennedy had been shot at the Ambassador hotel and had examined a door jamb where he had claimed to have seen bullet holes. Having no information as to have where Bailey might be located, I decided to call Si and see if he could help us.

"Well, William, still alive are ya?" Si said when I contacted him. I explained my plight to Jim and he responded with, "Just a moment while I check my directory." Si gave me every name containing the last name of Bailey in his FBI directory. I thanked him, and said I would stay in touch. Now five years had gone by. I was now working on this update for *In the Eye of History,* and there was the new work by Doug Horne that I felt needed to be mentioned. He'd written a five volume set on his time with the Assassination Records Review Board and had come to some startling conclusions, or maybe not so startling in regards to the Kennedy autopsy. Jim Sibert had, of course, been part of that piece of history.

The key to Horne's analysis of the autopsy was what FBI agent Sibert, along with his partner Frank O'Neill, had written in their FD302 report.

> A tight security was immediately placed around the autopsy room by the Naval facility and U.S. Secret Service. The Bureau agents made contact with Roy Kellerman, the assistant secret service agent in charge of the White House detail, and advised him of the Bureau's interest in that in this matter. He advised that he had been, he had already received instructions from the director Rowley as to the presence of Bureau agents.

To Horne, those lines in the agent's report were code for FBI agents being kept out of the morgue room so the agents would not see the pre-autopsy on the President's body. I had asked Sibert about he and O'Neill being kept out of the morgue when I interviewed him at his home in Florida in 2002, which Sibert had denied. I needed to tell him of Horne's work and ask him again to hear what he would say.

"I am still putting one foot in front of the other," he told me, when I called. I told Jim I was putting out a new edition of the book. Jim replied with "that's good." He told me that he had recently had a call from a researcher.

"And I said, well, you know. That's it." This has been going on for 47 years now. I cut it off back when I was 90. I'm 91 now. I'll be 92 in August. I get letters. Some guy wrote me from somewhere up in New England. And he sent me 5 postcards and all of them had pictures of Kennedy on them. I don't know where he got them. He wanted me to initial each one. And I told him I didn't know where they came from and I don't initial anything that I don't know the origin on, you know."

"I had this one guy that called me down here at Fort Myer's Beach. He read about me in the paper. There was an article in the paper here about my presence at the Kennedy autopsy. He said, "I just want to meet you. Shake hands with you.""

"The thing is," I said to Jim, "You are an historical figure. You really are. You are part of that history of the Kennedy situation. And people just like I did, want to reach out and connect with some part of that. So I'm afraid you're stuck."

"Yeah," I heard Si say. "I'll get out of it one of these days, when I start looking up at the roots of green grass."[1] Laughing I said, "Let's hope that's a long, long time for both of us, huh?" Si joined me in laughter. "Yeah, I am laboring to have it come quick," he replied. I asked Si if he was still working out at the community weight room at the continuing care facility where he lived. "Yeah, I worked out today. I try to use the gym three times a week."

I told Si I had taken on Vincent Bugliosi in a new chapter of the re-issue of the book. "He came after me a little bit," I said.

"He's the guy who wrote *Helter Skelter*," Si said.

"Yeah," I replied. Bugliosi came after me a little bit in his endnotes, so I had to take him on a little. He called me a "dyed in the wool conspiracy theorist."

"No kidding." Si said.

"That's the reason I let everyone in the book speak for themselves, so I wouldn't get caught up in all that stuff," I answered.

"You know what I tell everybody?" Jim Sibert asked. "There was a guy that came out and interviewed me for the press, our local paper, the Gannet

---

1. James Sibert passed away on April 6, 2012 at the age of 93.

paper here, and he asked me, 'Now, what do you think about a conspiracy to kill Kennedy?' I said, 'Well, I won't go so far to say there was a conspiracy, but there is no way I will buy any part of the single bullet theory that Specter was responsible for.' "(I noted when Jim said the name Specter it sounded like he was spitting out the name – his contempt for the Pennsylvania Senator still evident.)

"Right." I said.

"And I don't," he continued. "Boy, that Specter, he lied. He wrote that 'Sibert didn't make any notes at all.' And that 'O'Neill said he made quite a few and destroyed them'. He must of thought I was a genius to remember all those notes, measurements and everything that was in that report."

I smiled listening to Jim. What he was telling me was almost verbatim what he had said about Arlen Specter when Debra Conway and I had interviewed him in June of 2001. Specter's dubious behavior in 1964 when he interviewed the two agents was still sticking in his craw in 2010, 45 years later. I told Jim that I hoped to meet Specter one day.

"Well I don't want to meet him," Jim told me. "Because I don't think I could be courteous and give him the respect he is due, if he is due any."

"I don't think he is due any," I told Jim, laughing. "But that's just my opinion." I heard Jim Sibert return my laughter.

"Now one thing I've got to ask you," I said. "Do you know the name of Douglas Horne?"

"That one I've never run across before," Si answered[1].

I explained to Jim who Doug Horne was and the fact that Horne had written about Si's experiences while part of the Records Review Board. I told Sibert that it was Horne's analysis that he and O'Neill had been kept out of the autopsy room and that the line in their 302 report, "We expressed an interest in this matter," was code that the agents had indeed been kept out of the morgue room. (Thus giving the conspirators time to do whatever they did with JFK's remains and the cheap metal shipping casket.) Jim Sibert, as I knew he would, denied being kept out of the morgue room.

"No we were never kept out of the room. We were there when they put the casket in the anteroom and they opened the casket and put the body up on the autopsy table – the medical person did that. And then after they finished that they cleared the room because they were going to take X-rays and photographs, you know?"

I decided not to push him further, and asked about Jim's wife, Ester. Jim, much to my surprise, told me his beloved wife had passed away five years earlier in 2005. "I have been getting along for a while," Jim said. "I have

Jim Siebert, September 2002.

a goldfish. I wrote to people at Christmas time and told them I wasn't living alone anymore. I left a blank space and I wrote 'I have a goldfish!'" I heard Jim laughing and I joined in. Our conversation turned to Frank O'Neill at this point.

"You know, Frank died."

"I had heard that he had."

Jim said, "I've written to his wife Liz. She had written to me and I sent her a copy of the interview of me I did here locally, and they mentioned O'Neill. I got his book."

I broke in with, "Oh, it came out?"

"Yeah it's out." Sibert told me. "I got "a copy of it. Bought it over here at the bookstore."

"What did you think?" I asked.

"Well some of the stuff … I wonder if he was getting a little start of Alzheimer's, because, he wrote it and it was *all O'Neill*. He didn't mention me much."

"Really?" I exclaimed.

"Yeah," Jim answered. "And he said later on he called Hoover and told him that Oswald was the right man and he was responsible for the assassination. Well, he never called Hoover that night. I know."

I heard Si give a small chuckle. I could sense his puzzlement and disappointment as he told me about his old FBI partner and what O'Neill had written – and/or perhaps what O'Neill did not write. But to my mind, going over the conversations I had with Frank X. O'Neill, it fit the man to a T. O'Neill was going to have his way, tell it his way, and he did. All the way to the grave.

"Jim," I said toward the end of the conversation. "You know if there is anything I can do for you, I am here." Si replied, "Oh, I know that, Bill."

I was reluctant for our telephone visit to end and I was sorry that I had let so much time lapse since I had talked to the ex-FBI agent.

I remember the first visit I had with Jim Sibert at his home in Florida, when he allowed Debra Conway and I to invade he and his wife's privacy and bring us into their home. The first thing Sibert did was show us their small kitchen off the living room.

"Look at this," Jim said, taking out a small fold out table and chair, placing them in the middle of the kitchen floor. Si sat down and with a great big smile said: "See, I can reach the sink and the refrigerator and never have to get up from the table." Jim gave Debra and I a demonstration by reaching for the facet with one hand while reaching for the refrigerator with the other. Later during a break during their interview, Si and Ester took us on a tour of their community where they lived, complete with its own post office, beauty salon and barbershop, restaurant, weight room, and hospital. While touring the gym at the complex, Sibert sat down at one of the nautilus machines and demonstrated how to do a shoulder press.

"I've always been a health nut," he said. "I had a degree in physical education before I joined the FBI," he explained as we all walked back to their apartment.

Later, after the major portion of the interview, the Sibert's took us to dinner at the restaurant in the complex. As we sat at a dining room table, friends of the Sibert's trickled in, stopping by to say hello, and see who the new visitors were. In turn, Si and Ester pointed out some of the residents of the community complex including a famous World War II pilot, former agents of the OSS, FBI, and CIA, as well. One of the people introduced to us, one of his and Ester's friends, was a big bear of a man. Si told Debra and I, "He is 90 years old and was with the OSS from the beginning." "Yeah, I'm hiding out," the man said with a laugh and a wave of his hand as he lumbered by.

Later that evening back at the Sibert's apartment, the interview over, Ester joined us, and Debra and I listened as Jim told us of some of his exploits in the FBI, raising a family, and married life. As Debra and I were about to say goodnight and make the short drive to our hotel for an early morning flight, Jim called me over to his desk, where he had a large, hardbound book laid open.

"Look at this, Bill," he said.

Sibert explained that the book had been put together and privately published by one of his friends that had been in his same squadron during the war. Jim pointed to a black and white photograph. "That's me," he said. Pictures showed a proud, handsome young man in his early 20s, in uniform, smiling into the camera, hair tousled by the wind.

Jim Sibert knows of his importance to the case of the assassination. How do I know? I asked him during my third visit to his home, when I accompanied film director Brian McKenna and a film crew, working on a documentary of the Kennedy case.

While Brian and the film crew were packing up, I had a few minutes alone with Si in his home office. Sitting across from him, I thanked him for letting me and my companions invade his closely-held privacy. And then I asked, "Jim, are you aware of how important you are to history, to this case?"

"Oh, yeah, I understand that," he said.

But I also know from talking with James William Sibert, his greatest pride, what he considers to be his greatest contribution to the history of this country, is his military service in World War II, not his role in the aftermath of the murder of the 35th president of the United States. We, as a people, who care about this country can be grateful and thankful that he was involved in both.

There are some students of the case that feel the FBI agents were part of a cover up where their part in that autopsy was concerned either wittingly or unwittingly. Most notably, Doug Horne, the military records analyst from the Records Review Board. His five-volume opus titled, "Inside the Assassination Records Review Board," in Horne's words to me in an e-mail, "So damn long it had to be split into five volumes."

I first met Horne in 1998 behind the picket fence in Dealey Plaza, when we were both attending the JFK Lancer conference on the assassination. I happened to walk behind the picket fence as Horne was talking with David S. Lifton, author of *Best Evidence*. When Lifton noticed me standing there not so subtly listening to the conversation, he paused, looking at me for a few seconds, and then he recognized me. "Oh, yeah yeah, William, you can listen to this." And then he introduced me to Doug.

Horne was at that point getting some recognition and attention for his 32-page memo on his analysis that there had been two different medical exams on two different brains on two different days. Both reportedly were JFK's brain, an impossibility, and therefore, a cover-up had taken place.

Now twelve years had gone by, and Horne had published his book(s) on his work with the ARRB. Horne gives his analysis of the autopsy doctors, Humes, Boswell and Finck, through their ARRB depositions. He was present during most of the depositions. But I find Horne's work fascinating for the back-story, getting these illusive doctors before the Board, and his impressions of these men, describing their body language, temperament, etc., while being interviewed. In my opinion, this makes the work invaluable to researchers and historians alike.

Horne describes the doctors in Volume One:

"Dr. Humes was an extremely large man, about 6' 4 inches tall with very large hands and a huge head. He was ultimately arrogant, diffident, evasive, testy, and cryptic and seemed just barely able to control his anger and frustration at several points during the deposition. After his deposition, Jeremy Gunn and I agreed, that he had obliviously been prevaricating on several occasions – the only question was which occasions. He seemed like a man who was hiding something during the deposition, and who was more then willing to give nonsensical answers to probing questions rather that reveal what he was hiding. There was an "I've got a secret" aspect to Humes' personality that was frustratingly hard to get at. And yet at times he did exhibit genuine bafflement and confusion when viewing the autopsy photos and x-rays. Dr. Humes made it known to us that he stayed at the home of "J." Thorton Boswell, his former colleague, when he traveled from Florida to Washington, for his deposition and it was Dr. Boswell who drove him to the deposition in College Park and picked him up when it was over.

Doug Horne's description of Boswell was short and succinct.

Boswell was a very different man from his former colleague, Jim Humes. He was a medium size man, soft spoken, unemotional, and rather laconic and seemed to carefully consider all of his answers before speaking. He spoke with precision and without the bluster characteristic of Humes on occasion. Dr. Boswell seemed the most credible and forth coming of the three pathologists, where as the level of tension during the Humes deposition had often been quite high, the Boswell deposition preceded for the most part in a very congenial manner, almost completely devoid of conflict or emotion.

I found Horne's description of Pierre Finck, informative, and delightfully amusing.

Dr. Finck was a most unusual and memorable personality. We had considerable difficulty contacting him where he lived in Switzerland, primarily because he had been in the United States for some time on an extended visit to his daughter in Dallas, but once he returned to Switzerland, and our mail caught up with him, we finally persuaded him to come to Washington without issuing a subpoena. David Marwell deserves great credit for this, for Dr. Finck really did not want to discuss the Kennedy assassination again before any government bodies; He had unpleasant memories of his testimony in 1969 at the Clay Shaw trial in New Orleans, and of his testimony before the government's HSCA forensic pathology panel in 1978.

Nevertheless, the ARRB prevailed, thanks to David Marwell's persuasive talents, and the day finally arrived. He was a small, rather wiry man and seemed to have some gigantic spring inside of him wound nearly the breaking point – he was a very "uptight and nervous individual. He reminded me of a little bantam rooster, but one without a barnyard to rule over. Several times during his deposition, when handed documents to re-view by Jeremy Gunn, Dr. Finck exhibited what I call 'startle reactions,' an indication of how nervous he was about the whole affair- several times he grabbed documents out of Jeremy's hand as they were being handed to him, scrutinized them most intensely very close to his face with his piercing, bird like gaze, then slam them down nosily upon the table with the palm of his hand before beginning to slowly read them.

Even when Jeremy would ask Dr. Finck to briefly peruse a docu-ment and simply tell us whether he had seen it before, or to please just read one particular paragraph or sentence, Dr. Finck would laboriously read the entire document from start to finish. (We went" off the record" several times while he slowly read through documents in their entirety even though we had told him it was not necessary to our question to do so.) His manner was most peculiar. He would not answer questions un-less he was 100% sure that he could give a precise answer. Many of our questions were answered with the response, "I can't remember" or "I can't answer that." Finck expressed off the record that he was not forbid-den or prohibited from answering such questions, but that he did not always have a firm enough recollection of events to give a precise an-swer, therefore, he could give no answer at all to many of our questions.

Dr. Finck seemed to have suffered a massive memory lapse com-pared to the time he testified at the Clay Shaw trial in New Orleans in 1969. Whether this was intentional, or a function of old age, I could not tell for sure, but I suspected on more than one occasion, that his "forgetfulness" about so many areas of the autopsy about which he had once been quite certain was simply a defense mechanism. Furthermore, Finck seemed so "anally retentive," to use the new vernacular, that he re-sisted giving generalized characterizations of anything; If he could not quote specific numbers or measurements, he would provide no answer, saying once again "I can't answer that."

As Jeremy would read through prepared questions in his outline, Dr. Finck would angle his head from side to side at a 30-degree angle and what as I can only describe as resembling the way a dog looks at his master when being asked to run and to go get his chew toy. He was so nervous that he exhibited what animal behaviorist call 'displacement activity' during his deposition, repeatedly pulling out a large European design lip balm applicator the size of a fountain pen and repeatedly cov-ering his lips with a white, waxy substance while being questioned by Jeremy. By the end of the deposition he appeared to have a thin line of foam around his mouth, and slightly resembled a mad dog.

Dr. Finck suffered from a stiff knee, and consequently he suddenly jumped up out of his chair at one point during the deposition, in the middle of the question, and began hopping around the room on one leg! We did not know why he was doing this at the time, so I am afraid that on this one occasion Jeremy and I exhibited' startle reactions' of our own. (On several occasions, despite the gravity of the proceeding and its purpose, I almost burst out laughing, and I believe Jeremy, usually the very model of emotionless self-control, almost did so once or twice himself.)

Dr. Finck seemed the least forthcoming and least "useful" of our three pathologists deponents, but he still provided valuable answers to some key questions. I would characterize Dr. Finck as intentionally evasive, but would not characterize him as being intentionally dishonest, as Jeremy and I felt Dr. Humes had been on numerous occasions. With one exception, which I will discuss later in this chapter, Finck seemed to prefer not answering a question to lying about it.

I felt Horne's work was so important that I had to try and get him to talk to me. I had been warned that Horne was a very private person and although he had given a very much-publicized interview to Dick Russell for his book *The Man Who Knew Too Much*, he was not going to give any more interviews. He was not talking to researchers. I decided I would send Doug Horne an email and at least ask for an interview. And if not, ask him why he wouldn't. A day or so later, I received Horne's reply. He wrote he considered my work to be "worthy" and that he would give me an interview with certain provisions.

I was pleased and surprised with Horne's reply and we exchanged a few more emails setting up the date and time that I was to call and he would answer my questions over the phone. Horne's book consists of nearly 2000 pages. The work is, to say the least, massive, mostly dealing with the medical evidence regarding President Kennedy's wounds. (Indeed there are parallels to the work I have done, but Horn had the enviable experience of being in the catbird's seat of history as far as the work of the ARRB.) Horne includes great chunks of the medical depositions and uses them to connect the dots of some of the greater mysteries of the Kennedy autopsy, and to my mind with great success. Horne's material is wide ranging and would be impossible to cover it all in one interview, even several. So naturally I decided to dive into the heart of the casket controversy and the so-called alteration of Kennedy's body. I wrote to Doug in a follow up email on what areas I wanted to question him on. He wrote me back, "Nothing complicated there, eh?"

Chapter Four

Interview with Douglas Horne

When It Happened

Law: Doug, would you tell me when your interest in the JFK assassination began?

Doug: Okay. I have vivid memories not only of the assassination, which occurred when I was eleven and a half years old, but I also have vivid memories of election eve in November 1960 – I can remember the election returns coming in. My household was split. My dad was still in the Marine Corps at the time, was a Republican, and my mom was a Democrat, and a Kennedy supporter. I can still remember their interest in that election, since they each voted for a different candidate. And I can remember it being fascinating because the election was so close. I clearly recall them watching co-anchors Chet Huntley and David Brinkley on NBC, and I remember staying up very late in an attempt to learn who won. I can also still remember what I was doing that night – drawing dinosaur pictures. It's really interesting, these vivid memories from the age of eight and one half years old. Then after President Kennedy was inaugurated, sometime in 1961, I wrote a letter, just a fan letter from a kid, you know, to President Kennedy in the White House, and I got an answer. It was signed by some secretary on White House letterhead stationery, it thanked me for my interest in the President and First Lady, and thanked me for my good wishes. The secretary signed it – no, not the President, of course. I wish I still had it today, but I don't have it anymore.

So, I had an early interest in the election returns and I had an early interest in the President and his wife, I think, because of their youthful appearance, glamour and style. As I wrote in my book later on, my appreciation and interest in the Kennedy Presidency later broadened, and became more mature, based on things other than glamour and style and appearance. But I had an early interest at the age of eight and nine years old.

The assassination occurred when I was living in Phoenix, Arizona. My father had just gotten out of the military in 1962 after spending 13 years in the Marine Corps, and I remember the Cuban Missile Crisis, and the uproar that caused in the nation – and in my own household – in 1962. (I remember my mom filling the bathtub with water – for drinking purposes – because she was sure there was going to be a nuclear war.) I also vividly remember the assassination in 1963. I remember it because of the cruel way I learned about it. I was living in Gold-water country. I didn't know it was called "Goldwater country" at the time. I'm not sure that at that time I had any firm sense of who Barry Goldwater was, but I was definitely living in Goldwater country, a hotbed of radical conservatism. I remember seeing the flag at half-staff at recess and we all wondered why. Kids were running up and saying "Kennedy's been shot" or "Kennedy's been killed" or something like that and they were laughing, and thought it was funny. I could not understand why they thought it was funny. The school administration re-called us to our classrooms, and the announcement was made that Kennedy was dead. Everyone was upset, the teacher cried and said a prayer, and we were sent home. I remember the long walk home and I remember my mother – she was a Kennedy supporter – waiting at the back door for me when I walked in the gate, through the back door fence.

I have strong memories of that entire weekend after the assassination. My father certainly showed no glee or happiness, even though he was a Nixon sup-porter. I remember how sober and really intensely serious he was and how we were all glued to the TV for three days. I remember Oswald getting shot by Ruby on Sunday, and I also remember watching the arrival of the Dallas casket at An-drews Air Force Base the previous Friday night, the evening of the assassination. I remember seeing Lyndon Johnson make some brief remarks at a microphone at Andrews AFB on TV, and being disappointed. I vividly remember that.

As I said, I remember accused assassin Lee Harvey Oswald getting shot in the Dallas Police Department basement on national television. How did that af-fect a little kid? Well, my mouth was hanging open. I was not afraid – I was just stunned. It was like – oh my God! – and I remember my mother saying, "That proves there was a conspiracy," a reaction that most people had. I remember a lot about the televised funeral on Monday, as well. And so my interest continued. A couple of years later in grade school, I ordered a paperback abridged edition of the Warren Report simply because I wanted to know all that I could possibly know about it. I remember reading the parts about the medical evidence and that's the truth – I actually did – so at that time I would have been about 13 years old, and I remember wondering, "Geez, is that all there is to it? Why are there no pictures?" I wanted to know why I couldn't relate what I was reading to any pictures and it bothered me that I could not do that. Then in 1966 and 1967, I became aware that books were being written, books critical of the "official find-ings," and then I was hooked. I remember buying a paperback copy of *Rush to Judgment*. At that time I was not aware of [Harold] Weisberg's books, but I defi-nitely remember *Rush to Judgment*. Then the next year *Six Seconds in Dallas* came out, and I remember learning about it from a copy of *The Saturday Evening Post*

– the cover story stated "Three Assassins Killed Kennedy," and a lengthy book excerpt was published in that issue. Those books made a big impression on me, so from 1966-1967, I was truly hooked in terms of interest. I was "hooked for life" well before I saw the Zapruder film, but when I saw the Zapruder film on national TV in 1975, I believe it was '75, my interest was renewed, and increased by a factor of ten or so.

Law: it was '75.

Doug: Yes, on "Good Night America." I remember Geraldo Rivera, the moderator or host, with his long hair, and Bob Groden and Dick Gregory, who presented the film to the audience. Seeing the Zapruder film as a motion picture was really captivating because what I was observing didn't seem to match the official story at all. Afterwards, while the House Select Commission on Assassinations was in session, from late 1976 through the end of 1978, I had no idea how that investigation was proceeding. I was then a junior officer on active duty in the Navy, was very busy, and I was at sea most of the time on a surface ship (USS *Ouellet*, a frigate), so I missed all of that. I never got to see any of the public hearings that were televised on PBS.

The final event that captivated me "for life" was purchasing a copy of Lifton's book, *Best Evidence*, in January of 1981, right before I got transferred to the new Royal Saudi Naval Base at Jubail, Saudi Arabia. I was assigned to Saudi Arabia for my first tour of shore duty, and I bought the book the week before I got on the airplane to leave Hawaii and the United States. In fact, I was reading the book on the plane when a man across the aisle spoke to me and said, "I notice what you are reading and I work for the publisher, I work for Macmillan. I am real pleased to see that you bought our book. I would like to give you a coupon good for any three books you like." So I was able to order three free books by mail! *Best Evidence* was a big event for Macmillan. I remember not only being blown away by this detailed piece of research, but I also remember thinking at the time how courageous the publisher was to publish a book of that nature, accusing the U.S. government of a major medical cover-up in the JFK assassination, and implying that his assassination was a covert operation. I will always feel indebted to Macmillan for having the courage to do that. So I guess that is a real long answer to your question.

Law: So after you read Lifton's book – what happened then? The same thing happened to me when I stumbled across Lifton's book in the late 1980's. It literally changed my life.

Doug: I believe you.

Law: It did. It actually changed my life in the sense that the book made me continue my research and read everything I could get my hands on. Like you, I was sitting in front of the TV as a teenager watching "Good Night America" and I was stunned, but didn't do anything with it. I read some books and articles, but it took David Lifton's work to light the fire and I have never been the same since.

Doug: Me too. I have never viewed politics the same since, and I no longer automatically believe what I hear on the news. I read the book twice in 1981, because after I read it for the first time I thought, "This is so fantastic! Could this really be true? Could wounds really be altered by surgery before an autopsy, because that would be a crime of the worst possible magnitude." I was more or less convinced that the basics of Lifton's hypothesis were likely true, but I had some problems with his timeline: some things about the timeline – such as the speculative diversionary trip to Walter Reed Hospital prior to the body's arrival at Bethesda – looked a little too tight to me. So I read it a second time, and then when Stone's movie "JFK" came out in a decade later I read it two more times: a third time in 1991, and a fourth time in 1992. And so here we are. The more I studied his hypothesis the more skeptical I was about "reconstructive surgery" – it seemed to me that there was no room in his timeline for anything of that complex nature to have taken place prior to the commencement of the autopsy – but I was convinced, based on the evidence he presented, that there had been post-mortem surgery somewhere to simply expand JFK's head wounds and gain access to the evidence (the brain and bullet fragments). In other words, my final assessment after reading his book so many times was that there had been obstruction of justice (in the form of clandestine post-mortem surgery, prior to the autopsy), and that the autopsy results were therefore legally invalid.

Becoming Involved

Law: So now it's years later, tell me about the Assassinations Records Review Board being formed and how you had an opportunity to be part of that.

Doug: Sure. I guess I became an activist when I went to my first research symposium. It was in 1993. I went to something called "ASK" in Dallas but I didn't know anything about it at the time. I viewed it as an opportunity to learn more about the evidence. It was organized by a company that held the meeting for profit (but which was advised by Kennedy researchers) and it was called "Assassination Symposium on John F. Kennedy." They shortened it to "ASK," which was clever because it was common for people to ask questions about the assassination. That was a major event for me because it was the 30th anniversary of the assassination – our culture makes round number anniversaries into a big deal – and many of the authors of the books I had read were there and I thought that was really fascinating. I got to meet Gaeton Fonzi, John Newman, Peter Dale Scott and got to hear many other speakers on stage. Even though many of them had not published a book yet many of them were medical doctors, historians, or teachers. I was impressed by the education and the sobriety of the presenters, even though there were some presenters that starkly disagreed with each other. I was really impressed overall with the serious tone of the symposium, by how much I learned, and by the intelligence of the leading lights of the research community. I could tell they didn't all like each other, but they were all intelligent people, and so that made me want to do something – I didn't know what I wanted to do, but something. I was driven to make a contribution of some kind to this ongoing independent American research effort, which to me seemed emblematic of democracy in its truest form, and of freedom of the press and of association, in its truest form.

In 1994, the following year, I went to the first symposium held by COPA, the "Coalition on Political Assassinations" in Washington D.C. (ASK was in Dallas) – organized by political activist John Judge – and one of the speakers was Jack Tunheim, the Chairman of the newly empaneled Assassination Records Review Board (ARRB). Jack Tunheim was the person selected by his peers – his fellow board members (there were five Board Members) – to be the Chairman of the newly formed ARRB, and therefore its public face. All five board members had just recently been confirmed by the Senate. John ("Jack") Tunheim had been the nominee of the American Bar Association. (Two other board members were nominated by professional historical societies; one by a national society of archivists; and one by the White House.) The Assassination Records Review Board had just received some startup money from President Clinton, from a contingency fund, so Tunheim's immediate goal was to find an office and hire a staff. This was in October '94. So at the symposium he gave what I call his stump speech, a standard address that he gave to public gatherings who wanted to know what the ARRB was all about. He addressed the big questions: "What is the JFK Records Act? What is the Review Board? What is the Review Board empowered to do and what is it not authorized to do?" He gave that talk, and there was a question and answer period that was rather lengthy. One of the people in the audience asked if he was still hiring staff and he answered, "Yes, we are still hiring staff. They will have to get a high level clearance, they cannot have worked for any previous investigation into the JFK assassination, and they can't be present government employees." He implied there were ways around the prohibition against hiring current government employees, but I know he said they could not be present employees of the government or have worked for any previous investigations.

I immediately knew that I wanted to be involved in this effort. The day after Tunheim spoke to COPA, I knew that the Review Board was going to have its first public hearing at the Old National Archives building. I went back to my hotel room, borrowed a typewriter from the hotel desk clerk, took it up to my room, and typed up a letter expressing my interest in employment with the ARRB. Then I went to the public hearing the following day in the National Archives building. As I arrived, I gave my letter of interest to David Marwell, who had just recently been hired as staff Executive Director, and who had also been present the day before at the COPA conference. Marwell had spoken at COPA as well as Tunheim, so I gave my letter of interest to the newly hired staff Executive Director, saying "I would like to apply for a job on your staff." We shook hands and both went into the fifth floor auditorium in the old Archives building on the Mall. I sat and listened to the first public hearing of the ARRB. The subject was: "How do we define an assassination record?" That hearing was really interesting. There were many notable speakers present from the JFK research community, including John Newman, Peter Dale Scott, Jim Lesar, Dan Alcorn, and John Judge.

Back in my Navy civil service job in Hawaii, I was forced to wait for a decision about possible employment with the ARRB over the course of about half a year. I was asked to submit two different resumes, which I did – one in civilian format and the other in the standard government format. I recall that I participated in six telephone interviews. It took half a year to get hired, quite some time, but, of course, I was ecstatic. I knew I would be taking a big pay cut, and I was right – it turned out to be a 42% pay cut. (That was enough to give anyone serious pause, no matter how brightly the fires of zeal burned in his belly.) The conditions of the job offer given to me by this underfunded agency were extreme: I would have to leave my family in Hawaii, go east, pay for my own transportation, my own move, and take a 42% pay cut. I still wanted to do this because I knew in my bones and in my gut that this would be the last time the government would do did anything about this matter. That is the way it was being advertised – that is the way the JFK Records Act was sold to Congress – "This is the last time the government will do anything with the Kennedy assassination. The Board is not going to reinvestigate the assassination, it's just going to look for and collect documents and get them declassified to the maximum extent possible, and place them in the National Archives for people to study on their own, so they can draw their own conclusions about what happened in 1963." I thought, OK, this is it then, and I want to be part of the final effort, just to learn all I can as an individual about the case and yes, specifically, the medical evidence, which was the main focus of my interest. I didn't know what I would learn or how I would learn it, but I wanted to learn all I could about the assassination because for me, most of the evidence did not come together in a way that supported the Warren Commission's official conclusions that JFK was felled by a lone assassin, and that there was "no credible evidence" of conspiracy.

Law: From the descriptions in your book, it wasn't quite what you thought it was going to be as far as the attitude of the other staff members, was it?

Doug: No, it wasn't. I went into this with open eyes, knowing that we were not going to officially reinvestigate, and knowing there would be no findings of facts or conclusions in our final report – I knew that. I understood that our primary role was to find records and get them declassified, but I nevertheless began my new job with the expectation that probably at least 75 or 80% of the staff would believe there had been a conspiracy, and would be burning with curiosity, as I was, to know just what had really happened.

Law: Was that the case?

Doug: It was not the case. I was shocked and dismayed to find out that well over half the staff – and when I say staff I am talking about a maximum of 25 to 30 people employed full-time, serving a Review Board of five part-time VIPs – well over half the staff had no burning interest or curiosity about the case or the evidence whatsoever. Later I came to terms with it by understanding how most of the staff was hired. Most of those people that didn't have the curiosity that I had were much younger than me; they had no memory of JFK or of the assassination, and had grown up being fed the pabulum about Lee Harvey Oswald being the lone assassin in America's watered down, sanitized history books in high school. I was 43 when I joined the staff, the same age as JFK when he was elected president. But two-thirds of the staff were much younger than me, and many had just obtained their master's degree in one specialty or another, or had just completed law school, and needed a job, and so to them this was simply a great "resume builder." And it was the fact that they were so young and not established yet professionally, most of them with no families to support yet, that allowed the staff Executive Director David Marwell to "low-ball" these people from the standpoint of salary. His overall agenda was apparently to hire people that didn't know much about the case – he didn't want zealots on the staff, people who would be determined to quote solve the case unquote, or who would bring with them predetermined agendas or strong points of view. That goal of his was also a goal of the Board Members themselves. But I think an unspoken agenda was also to hire people that didn't have a job (or who didn't have a well-paying job), so the ARRB could get away with not having to pay them as much as someone who was 35-40 years old, and had a family to support.

Well over half the staff didn't care that much about the assassination, and viewed their role as rather a passive one, like librarians looking for records. I would say about twenty-five percent of the staff was as intensely interested in the assassination as I was. I would say maybe two thirds of the staff, maybe more then two thirds, thought the Warren Commission got it right. That was a big shock – the biggest shock of all. Somewhere between a fourth and a third of the staff wondered why a lot of the evidence didn't come together to support the official conclusions (like it does in a normal homicide case) and suspected that there was some kind of conspiracy, or cover-up, or both. So I was in a minority in terms of my intense interest, and I was in a minority in terms of my distrust of the Warren Commission's conclusions. That came as a great surprise to me. This built-in "bias" on the staff reflected the bias of the Board Members and of David Marwell – they all publicly pronounced themselves as agnostics about the assassination, but I soon learned that they all were firmly convinced the Warren Commission had gotten it right. The ARRB was to be officially and publicly neutral about what happened in 1963 – all of us understood that – but the management team running the show thought Lee Harvey Oswald had been the lone assassin, and that most assassination researchers were "off their rockers," and couldn't handle the truth. As Marwell once attempted to joke with me, he thought many assassination researchers had a "pathological" problem! (No, I didn't laugh.)

When I arrived on the staff in August of 1995, there were no pictures of President Kennedy anywhere on anyone's wall – none in the lobby, none in the hallway, and none in anyone's office. I thought that was extremely peculiar. This was an overt and telling indicator of the sterility of the work environment at the ARRB (no emotion permitted!), and of the extreme lengths to which the Board Members and David Marwell were going to present an appearance of neutrality. I just didn't think that hanging one or two pictures of the dead 35th President in the public spaces in the office (such as the lobby where we received visitors, and the conference room where we interviewed witnesses and met with other government officials) would present an impression of bias, or of hagiography. After all, we were concerned with this man's death, weren't we? Thank God that Jeremy Gunn was allowed by David Marwell to hire me. At the time Jeremy extended a job offer to me in March of 1995 (on St. Patrick's day, as it turned out), he was David Marwell's number one assistant: he was the Head of Research and Analysis (all of the analysts, who comprised about half of the staff), and had just assumed the additional role of General Counsel as well, after winning a power struggle with Cheryl Walters. (She was the previous General Counsel, and had lost a power struggle with Jeremy prior to my hiring. She had also opposed my hiring, for reasons unknown. Her resignation cleared the way for Jeremy to bring me onboard.) Why did Jeremy hire me? Ostensibly it was to be a member of the military records team, since I had 20 years of varied Navy experience under my belt. But he also knew I shared with him an intense interest in the medical evidence. He had read the same books I had, such as Lifton's *Best Evidence*, Josiah Thompson's *Six Seconds in Dallas*, Weisberg's *Post Mortem*, and others. He was as interested as I was in the evidentiary conflicts that prevented the case from coming together like a normal murder case. Like me, he was unwilling to accept that state of affairs, and thought it meant something was terribly wrong with some of the evidence, as I did. So, looking back on it, I knew from my interview with him that he had great hopes of conducting some depositions, in an attempt to gather new evidence and resolve evidentiary conflicts, but I had not been promised any involvement in that during the interview process. I was just hoping that the ARRB would interview and depose some of the key medical witnesses. I think Jeremy probably had his own preferred scenario for what the ARRB might do in this area – namely, at least depositions of the three pathologists. So to summarize here, I am really glad that he decided to hire me. He knew I was so enthusiastic and so intensely interested in the assassination that he pulled me aside a couple of times, during my first weeks on the staff, and told me, "You really should not talk about conspiracy or conspiracy issues, and not talk about a cover-up as if you believed it to be a fact, while you are anywhere near the Board Members." He first told me this in the fall of 1995. (I certainly had not consciously done so, but "walls have ears.") He explained that none of the Board Members believed there was a conspiracy – that was a bit of a stunner – and that it would not be in my best interests to talk that way within earshot of any of the Board Members. He advised that the less I talked that way around my peers, the better it would be, since the staff was split on these issues – and reassured me that it truly doesn't matter what your private beliefs are, that you are certainly permitted to have any private beliefs you wish about the assassination – but that there was a certain professional decorum that you want to maintain with the public, and with any witnesses we engage with, as well as the Board Members. With the Board Members it was because of their built-in bias, and of course, with the public we did very much want to present ourselves as a neutral, unbiased agency that just wanted to find records and get them released, no matter what they contained. I believed in that cause and so did Jeremy, and thank God, so did the Board Members. It was the cement that bound people of disparate beliefs and judgments and life experiences on the ARRB together: the desire to get as many documents and as much evidence as possible about the assassination released, and placed in the Archives, no matter what the content was and no matter what its impact was likely to be upon one theory, or official finding, or another. Jeremy's friendly and sage advice to a green staff member hinted at the probability that he had a very open mind himself about possible conspiracy and cover-up, but that he kept most of those thoughts to himself as a matter of self-preservation. It simply wasn't politically correct to say such things too loudly or too often within the hallways of the ARRB's offices.

Anyway, if I may revisit some earlier remarks I made, the lack of any photographs whatsoever of President John F. Kennedy in the office, when I arrived in August of 1995, was part of a studied attempt by David Marwell and Jeremy Gunn, the two leaders of the staff, and the Board Members, to ensure that we did not appear to visitors to be an agency full of zealots, and to avoid the possible impression that we considered President Kennedy to have been a saint. I think they went way too far in this direction, in an attempt to avoid looking like the Kennedy Library in Boston. (Now, I still have not yet been there. This may surprise some of my critics and opponents, who seem to think I have engaged in hagiography myself.) The desire by David and Jeremy was to present the impression of a detached, unbiased, academic environment, but the unintended consequence, in my view, was to create the impression of uncaring sterility.

Law: Yes

Doug: As I wrote in the book, I finally did put up some pictures in my office (an office that I shared with three other people on the military records team), but beforehand, I was politely reminded by Jeremy: "Don't go overboard." But management had already gone overboard, in the opposite direction. Consequently, I put up twice as many JFK photos in my office as I had originally intended (5 or 6 as

I recall). It was very ironic, therefore, about two years later, on an occasion when Jack Tunheim was doing one of his television interviews, when one of our ARRB communications staff came running to me out of breath and wanted a framed picture of president Kennedy so they could hang it in the background during the Tunheim interview, because the TV people wanted the dead president in the background. I almost denied the request – the spiteful part of me wanted to say "no way in hell" – but I relented and said "OK, sure, here," loaned them the Knudsen portrait taken just before the inauguration in January of 1961, the one published in the Warren Report. Later, I managed to get permission to put up that portrait in the conference room where we did witness interviews, and where the Board Meetings were held – I figured that if the photo was dignified enough for Jack Tunheim to appear with it displayed behind him on national TV, it was good enough to put in our conference room. Everyone agreed.

Obstruction of Justice at Bethesda Naval Hospital

Law: Do you want to talk next about Dallas and what you think happened in trauma room 1, or do you want to skip ahead to the pathologists at Bethesda where the autopsy was conducted?

Doug: Let's skip on ahead to the pathologists at Bethesda Naval Hospital.

Law: After the shooting in Dealey Plaza, President Kennedy was driven to Parkland Hospital and then of course they tried to save the President's life, and couldn't succeed. After death he was placed in a 400 pound Britannia casket after being wrapped in sheets, and there was a bit of a fight – between the local coroner, who wanted to do a Texas autopsy, and the Secret Service, who wanted the body taken back to Washington immediately – to get him out to the ambulance and get him on board the plane and this of course is where it gets complicated. Air Force One flies the Dallas Casket to Andrews Air Force Base, it's unloaded in public view, and there is a 40 – 45 minute drive to Bethesda Naval Hospital. Why don't we pick it up there?

Doug: Let me began with the arrival of the body on Air Force One at Love Field in Dallas, can I do that?

Law: Sure.

Doug: I've given this matter additional thought since my book was published. I have wondered what happened to the President's body after the Britannia casket was loaded into Air Force One at Love Field, what specifically happened to it before the aircraft took off? We know now, with great assurance, that when the bronze viewing coffin was publicly offloaded at Andrews Air Force Base it had to be empty, which we will go into in a few minutes. If it was empty at that time, then what happened to the body before the airplane took off from Dallas?

Since the publication of my book, I have spoken with a researcher named Jamie Sawa, who has become a self-educated expert on Air Force One, on its design and interior layout, and who is really an impressive individual in terms of what he knows. He has visited the plane at the Air Force Museum at Wright-Patterson Air Force Base in Dayton, Ohio. He photographed the interior of the plane and he was also allowed brief access to the forward and aft luggage compartments: he was allowed to stand on a ladder and stick a camera inside the aft luggage compartment, and also allowed to stand on a ladder and stick a camera inside the forward luggage compartment, in order to photograph them both. It seems that in 2003 he gave a presentation on the layout of AF1 at the Wecht Conference in Pittsburgh, which I knew nothing about when my book was published in 2009. He contacted me right after my book came out, so we discussed this problem of what probably happened to the body after it was loaded on SAM 26000 at Love Field. Much outside research has confirmed that the Dallas casket was placed in the aft passenger compartment after some seats had been removed; he says it was placed on the left-hand side of the aft passenger compartment in the fuselage, with the hinge of the casket alongside the left-hand or portside wall of the airplane, which would have allowed the lid of the casket to be opened. He and I came to the joint conclusion that the body of JFK was probably removed from the bronze Britannia casket prior to, or during, the swearing in of Lyndon Johnson. I would imagine this probably occurred prior to the swearing in, and that the body was probably then taken out of the starboard aft galley door by Secret Service agents and then placed in either the forward or aft luggage compartment prior to takeoff. You see, in this aft passenger compartment there is a passenger door on the left side, the portside to use a Navy term; there is also a passenger door up forward on the portside, that's the left side, just behind the crew compartment where the pilot, co-pilot, and flight engineer sit. The aft portside passenger door, near the tail of the aircraft, is where the national TV audience saw Jackie and Bobby Kennedy standing when the door was opened and the scissors lift was raised up to the door to offload the Dallas casket at Andrews AFB. But on the starboard side there are two galley doors: there is a forward galley door on the starboard side and there is an aft galley door. The aft galley door, according to Jamie Sawa, is in the same area of the plane where the casket was placed prior to the flight from Dallas to Washington.

Right after the president's casket was taken on board, we know that Jackie Kennedy went into the stateroom and closed the door to compose herself, right after she went on board the airplane at Love Field. Then, the swearing in didn't happen for several minutes, because Lyndon Johnson was waiting for Judge [Sara] Hughes and his big photo-op; and when the swearing-in ceremony began, people went to the center of the aircraft. So the body almost certainly was removed from that casket either before or during the swearing in, and was taken out of the aft passenger compartment via the starboard aft galley door. Then it's a little uncertain whether it was placed in the aft luggage compartment or the forward luggage compartment. I had always assumed, since first reading Best

Evidence, that it was placed in the forward luggage compartment because that was the assumption that David Lifton made; he made it very clear to me in many phone calls during the 1990's that he was convinced that the body was transported from Dallas to Washington D.C. inside the forward luggage compartment. I don't really know which compartment it was placed in, but I am sure it was one of those two.

The photos that Jamie Sawa took of the aft luggage compartment show a shelf – a long shelf that runs fore and aft along the length of the plane, which would have been ideal to place a body on. His photos of the forward luggage compartment were surprising to me, because it looked unbelievably cramped and crowded. He explained to me that the Air Force had installed an APU (an auxiliary power unit) in there, making the interior extremely hot. It would get so hot, Sawa told me, that sometimes the heat from the APU would melt the plastic carrying bags that people would use for their suits while traveling. There were also sections in the forward luggage compartment that held a lot of special communication equipment used on SAM 26000, and that allowed much less available space than was present in a commercial variant of the 707, or in the aft luggage compartment of SAM 26000. The body could have been put in the forward baggage compartment, but what I learned from Sawa is that another candidate was the aft luggage compartment, which means that the transfer would then have been much quicker. If you had taken the body out of the aft starboard galley door, the aft luggage compartment is very close by; you're just moving the body down a few feet, and a little bit forward, I believe. And, of course, if you're going to put it in the forward luggage compartment you would have had to move it the length of the plane, in broad daylight. To reiterate, I am convinced that the body was removed from the casket at Love Field, simply because we know today that when the bronze casket from Dallas arrived at Bethesda Naval Hospital it had to be empty, the proof of which I will go into in a few minutes. This certainty that the bronze Dallas was empty when it was driven up to the front of Bethesda Naval Hospital about 6:55 PM, is what drives the discussion above, about when JFK's body was removed from the Britannia casket and where it was placed on the aircraft. But I honestly don't know to this day whether it was flown from Dallas to Washington, D.C. in the *forward* or *aft* luggage compartment. Perhaps some new evidence will surface some day from some researcher that will definitively resolve this issue.

Law: You wrote there are limits as to what we can know.

Doug: Yes, exactly. There are limits to we can know. The one thing that Jamie and I agreed on is that the president's body was not taken down the center of the plane; too many people would have seen that. I reject that as a possibility. So I have made this statement three times now: we know that the bronze Dallas casket was empty when it arrived at Bethesda Naval Hospital from Andrews Air Force Base. We do know that today, and we know that because of a new piece of evidence, a new document received by the Review Board staff from a Marine Corps Sergeant who was the NCOIC, the noncommissioned officer-in-charge of a work detail from the Marine Barracks in Washington D.C., named Roger Boyajian. I want to give the proper credit here – the tip was given to us by Kathy Cunningham, an LPN, who I know in the past has worked with Dr. Gary Aguilar on a couple of JFK assassination research projects. She provided us with the lead on this gentleman and told us he had written an "after action report" about receiving a casket that the president's body was in at the Bethesda morgue loading dock. Using her tip we located Roger Boyajian, using our staff investigator, Dave Montague. First I spoke with him on the phone, and then I wrote a letter which forwarded to him information about the ARRB. I interviewed him on the phone, and he confirmed he did have a report that he had written about the activities of his detail on November 22-23, 1963, and he agreed to send us a photocopy, an authenticated photocopy. He had an onionskin copy, from the old typewriters; they used carbon paper for reproduction and he had an original carbon, typed on that very thin onionskin paper. He was not willing to part with that, but he did send us a very good photocopy of it. He authenticated the photocopy by means of a cover letter with his signature on it. As I recall, it was a two-page document. The key entry in the report is that the president's casket arrived at 1835 hours at the Bethesda morgue loading dock, and of course that is 6:35 PM, civilian time. This means we were finally able to pin a precise time on the Dennis David event. The crucial thing to understand here is that if the casket that President Kennedy's body arrived in at the morgue loading dock (a cheap aluminum shipping casket, per Dennis David) arrived at 6:35 PM per the Boyajian report, then the bronze Dallas casket that arrived at 6:55 PM and sat out in front of the Hospital (without moving) for 12 minutes, had to be empty.

Law: It is very close to what Dennis stated.

Doug: It was remarkably close, since Dennis David had estimated in 1975 that the black hearse he offloaded at the Bethesda loading dock had arrived at about 6:40 or 6:45 PM. It seems to me that it emphasizes how important, how reliable, Dennis David is as a witness. His account, first given to a newspaper in 1975, and then again to David Lifton in 1979 on audiotape, and in 1980 on film, has been corroborated by a contemporaneous written document prepared by Roger Boyajian on November 26, 1963. Since Dennis David was correct about the early arrival of President Kennedy's body at the Bethesda morgue loading dock, he seems likely to credible on a number of other matters as well.

Law: Yes.

Doug: Dennis David has consistently recalled meeting a hearse, which is a black Cadillac used for funerals, at the morgue loading dock at the back of Bethesda Naval Hospital with a working party of sailors. He was an E6 then, but he was filling the duty slot called "Chief of the Day," even though he was not yet a Chief

Petty Officer and was "only" an E6 Navy corpsman. His work party of sailors off-loaded a cheap metal shipping casket from a black hearse, sat it on the floor in the morgue anteroom outside the morgue, and walked away. That was their part of the story. But as you know and I know, he had always equated that as 15 or 20 minutes before he saw the motorcade from Andrews arrive out front, so that always placed that at about 6:40 PM, roughly speaking. It was always a little uncertain whether his event occurred at 6:40 or 6:45 PM, or five minutes either way, but his estimate turned out to be remarkably accurate. It's clear to me that Dennis David's event is the same the event that Sgt. Boyajian wrote about in his report. By the way, his report was written the day after the funeral on November 26, 1963 – that's the same day the two FBI agents wrote their famous report about what they witnessed and heard at JFK's autopsy. So to me it's "gold" – a contemporaneous record that is better than anyone's memory, because it's clearly made from notes that Boyajian took that night. Every military man had a "wheel book," a little green book designed for memoranda, kept in his back pocket or shirt pocket. Clearly, Boyajian took notes that night, and wrote his report the day after the funeral, based on the notes he took – that is why he was able to come up with a precise time of 1835 for when the casket arrived. His report puts a precise time on the Dennis David event, which was the offloading of a cheap aluminum shipping casket from a black hearse.

The problem with the historical record is that the casket offloaded from Air Force One at Andrews Air Force base on national TV was not a cheap aluminum shipping casket, and it was not transported in a hearse, in a black ambulance. It was an expensive bronze ornate viewing coffin, and it was transported in a light-gray, almost white, Navy ambulance. To me this is one of the most important aspects of the whole assassination case right here, because it destroys the chain of custody for the Presidents body. We know that the Andrews AFB motorcade arrived at the front of Bethesda naval hospital at about 5 minutes to 7. One source wrote 6:55 and one source wrote 6:53 PM – at any rate the two reports were within 2 minutes of each other. So let's call it 5 minutes to 7 that the motorcade arrives out front, and this is 15 minutes after the black hearse offloaded the President's body at the rear of the hospital, so therefore the casket that was driven up out front must have been empty, by definition.

Law: So this is where it starts to get a little more complicated.

Doug: This is where it gets very complicated, and as my good friend Dr. David Mantik has said, "If it was not such an important subject this would read like a French farce-comedy movie." Because you have a casket being driven up out front, the public is observing it, the newspaper reporters are observing it, high level dignitaries are out there observing it and riding with it and unbeknown to all of them (or certainly most of them) – the casket supposedly containing the body of the slain President is empty. And the bronze Dallas casket sits in the light gray Navy ambulance for 12 minutes, and goes nowhere until about seven minutes after seven; we know this because of the times recorded by the newspaper reporters and published the next day. So after sitting there for 12 minutes (of course, I am reconstructing this from knowledge obtained later during the ARRB's FBI agent depositions), one of the FBI agents in the motorcade from Andrews AFB (either Sibert or O'Neill, I forget which one) approached Navy ambulance driver William Greer. (Secret Service agent Greer was not only the driver of the limo in Dallas, but he was the driver of the gray Navy ambulance from Andrews to Bethesda, as well.) The FBI agent approached him and said "Why are you still sitting here with the casket in the vehicle? Everyone else has gone inside." Greer responded, "I don't know where the morgue is." The FBI agent said, "Well, we know where it is, we get our physical done over here every year." So the FBI agents went back and got in the car they had ridden in from Andrews AFB. I believe it was O'Neill that told us this during his deposition.

Greer, driving the light-gray Navy ambulance containing the bronze Britannia casket, followed the car the FBI agents were in around to the back of the complex. It is a very large building, and the Bethesda National Naval Medical Center (NNMC) is a very large compound, and at night it would be a little confusing. Greer followed them around the back to the morgue loading dock, and shortly after the arrival of the light-gray Navy ambulance, Secret Service agent Roy Kellerman (who had entered the hospital with Jackie Kennedy immediately after the motorcade's arrival at 6:55 PM) walks out on the morgue loading dock and the four of them, William Greer and Roy Kellerman, who had also been in the front seat of the limo during the shooting, and these two FBI agents from the Hyattsville, Maryland FBI office (they were really not major players in FBI history except for this one evening). These two men from the FBI and these two men from the Secret Service offloaded this extremely heavy bronze casket from Dallas using some kind of wheeled conveyance, and moved it to the general vicinity of the morgue proper. When O'Neill was interviewed by the HSCA staff in the late 1970s, I believe he referred to the wheeled conveyance as "a dolly."

While I was writing my book, I spoke with someone who had been in the Army and had met the remains of the deceased coming into Dover Air Force Base from the battlefields in Iraq and Afghanistan. He told me that these conveyances are called "church trucks." He said it's a standard terminology used in the funeral trade. They are used to transport heavy objects like caskets and that is probably what the FBI agents used, a church truck. It made sense to me; this is speculation, but it is intelligent speculation. I don't think it was a normal dolly like you would find in a warehouse because you can raise and lower the heights of these church trucks to accommodate repositioning the body in the casket. It would make sense to find a church truck, therefore, at a morgue entrance. The bodies being received have to be raised and lowered either into chill boxes, or onto examination tables in the autopsy room. These four men probably only lifted this heavy casket – which according to William Manchester was probably slightly over 400 lbs. – out of the gray ambulance just a couple of inches and then slid it onto the church truck. My father was buried in a solid bronze casket and I was astounded at how heavy it was. I was one of the eight pallbearers and I could barely handle my part of the heavy load of the casket. I was amazed, and during my own father's funeral I was thinking of this very subject – I could not help but think of it. I was astounded at how heavy it was even with eight of us carrying it. Because of that experience, I knew the truth of what O'Neill had told the HSCA: there was "no way" that just the four of those men, all by themselves, could have handled that casket, unless they had a wheeled conveyance to assist them. Furthermore, the two FBI agents would not have known that there was no body in that casket. Most of its journey into the morgue was on the wheeled conveyance – they only lifted it a few inches, or perhaps a foot, to get if from the ambulance to the church truck. And it is the use of the church truck, and the identity of the four men who unloaded the casket at about a quarter past 7 PM (none of them was in the military or wearing a military uniform), that distinguishes this second "casket event" or "casket entry" from the first one earlier that evening, in which Dennis David's working party of *Navy sailors* (all in working uniform) offloaded an *aluminum shipping casket* from a *black hearse*.

Law: Now Sibert said in his interview with Andrew Purdy from the HSCA, that O'Neill, him, Greer, Kellerman and maybe some people from the unit there, or hospital, came out to help unload the casket because four men could not unload it alone.

Doug: That's interesting – I don't recall that at this time, but I do specifically recall that O'Neill named only Sibert, himself, Kellerman, and Greer in his HSCA interview. This was wonderful for me, and would be for any oral historian, because O'Neill not only provided conformation that the casket was offloaded by just four people (using a "dolly"), and that two of them were Secret Service, but O'Neill actually gave the names of the Secret Service agents. So, I am going to differ with you slightly on that. I think to the HSCA Sibert and O'Neill only talked about four people unloading the casket in the Navy ambulance. It was later, I believe, after the passage of additional years and after reading books, when they have had a chance to think about it too much, that they have muddied up their own earlier account. After they think about what they reported to the HSCA in the late 1970s, and are troubled by the implications of that when they learn about two other casket entries that night, this is when I believe these two guys began to muddy the record, and their own memories. The earliest memories are generally the most reliable.

Law: I think Sibert stayed with it, and also O'Neill did too, until he learned what came out in *Best Evidence* – then they changed their story.

Doug: O'Neill was just adamantly against Lifton's hypothesis, which posited that the FBI agents had unknowingly lost control and custody over the President's body, and had been fooled by an empty casket. O'Neill told me this off the record, and may also have said so on the record during his ARRB deposition. I think the two FBI agents had no real opportunity to notice that the bronze casket from Dallas was empty because it was so heavy, and also because they didn't lift it very high or very far, as they put it on the church truck. In most cases you do that by just sliding it out of the vehicle right on top of the church truck dolly (which is covered with little rollers), and you can then raise and lower the dolly as needed, after you position the casket. It is unclear whether the two FBI agents and the two Secret Service agents deposited the coffin in the anteroom outside the morgue, or in the morgue examination room. I believe it was in the anteroom for a couple of reasons; the primary reason I believe it was the anteroom is because Sibert recalled during his Review Board deposition, "I think we put it in the anteroom," or words very similar to that. Because that fit with my own reconstruction of events, I found that statement on his part particularly illuminating. And we have a definitive time that is assigned to this event. That time is 7:17 PM. David Lifton was the trailblazer here. He discovered that O'Neill and Sibert, in an internal FBI recapitulation of their interview by Arlen Specter of the Warren Commission, described 7:17 PM as the time of "preparation for the autopsy." Since the Navy ambulance left the front of Bethesda hospital at 7:07 PM, this time of 7:17 PM would seem to mark the time when they probably finished unloading the bronze Dallas casket and set it down in the anteroom.

Law: So basically, you think at that point (7:17 PM) that the cheap metal shipping casket is inside the morgue examination room, and during this period, from 6:35 PM until sometime after 7:30 PM, that's when the clandestine surgery was performed on JFK's body? Then, the body was transferred from the examination table in the morgue proper back into the bronze Dallas casket again, correct? Have I got that right?

Doug: Yes, that's right. I guess this is a perfect time to go into that.

Law: Yes, as you said in your book there has to be an audience one and an audience two.

Doug: Right, audience one was waiting for the initial arrival of the President's body: they saw it offloaded in a cheap aluminum shipping casket that was taken out of a black hearse at 6:35 pm, and taken into the morgue anteroom by Dennis David's working party of uniformed sailors. Audience one (outside the morgue) was reportedly Humes, Boswell, General Wehle, Captain [John] Stover, Captain [Robert] Canada, Commander Ebersole, Paul O'Connor, and possibly James Jenkins – in his case it is unclear simply because he has no recollection of the shipping casket – but that does not mean that he was not there, it just means that the type of casket was not important to him and that he therefore does not remember it, if he was indeed present on the loading dock. He may not have gone out on the loading dock – Jenkins may have remained in the morgue proper when the casket arrived at 6:35 PM.

Law: His words were that he caught just a glimpse of it coming through the door.

Doug: OK, then this pretty much nails it down – he may have been inside the morgue instead of out on the loading dock at 6:35 PM.

Law: Yes, he said he was inside the morgue, not in the atrium.

Doug: I understand, then, why he has no memory of the black hearse – he was not out back on the loading dock. There is something very important to me that I didn't mention earlier, which is that Dennis David has consistently told the same story over and over. And part of the story that he has consistently told is that he asked Dr. Boswell, way after midnight, after the autopsy was over, something to the effect, "When did the President arrive?" or "What casket was the body in?" or something to that effect and Boswell replied, "You should know, you were there." Boswell thereby confirmed that the casket offloaded by Dennis David's working party of sailors contained the President's body, and that is critical information. This is also additional corroboration that the bronze casket ferried from Andrews AFB in the light-gray Navy ambulance, which arrived at Bethesda 20 minutes later, had to be empty.

Law: These doctors had to know.

Doug: Yes, that's right, Humes and Boswell, the two navy pathologists (and surely their superiors, Admirals [Edward] Kenney and Galloway, and Captains Stover and Canada) knew what they were involved in from the beginning. They were all involved in a subterfuge which involved an impossibly early, secret arrival of President Kennedy's body so that wounds could be privately inspected, clandestinely altered, and evidence removed from the body, prior to the start of the "public" autopsy. Since we are discussing casket entries right now, it is time to point out that there was a second entry for the bronze Dallas casket, at 20:00 hours military time (or 8:00 PM civilian time). That time of 20:00 hours (8 PM) is written in an "After Action" Report published by the Military District of Washington after the funeral was over. The After Action Report covered everything imaginable on Friday night, Saturday, Sunday, and Monday that involved military honor guards, or anyone else belonging to the military district, from the time Air Force One landed on Friday night until the time the funeral was over Monday afternoon. On the pertinent page of that report (provided to me by David Lifton, who got it from the Archives in the 1970's) it reads: "The joint casket team carried the president's casket into the morgue at 20:00 hours." It is confusing when you first read about it, if you have already learned about the Boyajian report unearthed by the ARRB. But the only written evidence of a casket entry the world at large knew about prior to 1981 was the joint service casket team's report which recorded that they took the casket into the morgue at 8 o'clock at night. When Lifton's book came out, he documented the earlier casket entry (of the aluminum shipping casket) through numerous eyewitnesses, Dennis David and Donald Rebentisch and others, and this fact then became "problematic" for the establishment. Following the illicit, clandestine surgery on President Kennedy's body at Bethesda to remove bullet fragments and all evidence of frontal shots – severely altering the size and location of his skull wound in the process – his body was placed back into the bronze Dallas casket so that it could formally be delivered to the morgue (at 8 PM) by the joint service casket team, whose job it was to transport and then safeguard the body of the slain commander-in-chief. This allowed them to perform their function, and also allowed Drs. Humes and Boswell to carry out a charade of monumental proportions, in which the wounds they had previously altered (after 18:35 and prior to 20:00) were presented to a second audience, audience # 2 if you will, as if they were the pristine, unaltered bullet wounds inflicted by the Dallas assassin. After the second Dallas casket entry at 20:00 hours, Humes and Boswell carried out a three-hour charade called an "autopsy," during which the grossly expanded cranial defect and other wounds were examined before a huge, noisy, and somewhat skeptical, morgue audience sitting in the gallery.

The famous FBI FD-302 report written by FBI agents James Sibert and Francis O'Neill on the day after the funeral (November 26, 1963) – which David Lifton appropriately made very famous: the "Sibert-O'Neill Report" – only records what audience # 2 witnessed and heard after the "public autopsy" began after 8 PM following the second entry of the Dallas casket. It's their report of what they observed during the official or "public" autopsy on the body. (It parenthetically also describes their being barred from entering the morgue by the Secret Service after the two of them and Kellerman and Greer delivered the empty Dallas casket to the morgue anteroom at about 7:17 PM.) After Lifton's book came out, O'Neill and Sibert spent decades vociferously denying that they were ever separated from JFK's body or that they were ever barred from the morgue – but even the stilted bureaucratic language in their report makes it pretty clear that there was a significant period of time when the Secret Service would not let them enter the morgue, and that they argued about it with the Secret Service before it was resolved. It was resolved simply by letting the two FBI agents enter the morgue immediately after the 8:00 PM entry of the Dallas casket, which had just been brought in by the joint service casket team. They saw the bronze casket on the floor, saw it opened, and saw JFK inside, and never knew anything was amiss or that there had been any clandestine surgery prior to the "autopsy" they were witnessing. Another victim of this ruse was Army pathologist Pierre Finck, who arrived at the morgue at 8:30 PM and who knew nothing that night about the clandestine surgery which had been performed to remove bullet fragments, and evidence of frontal entry, from JFK's skull.

I covered this extensively in my book but I'm going to make it much shorter here. We know now that the autopsy procedures that Sibert and O'Neill were writing about begin at 8 o'clock, following the second entry of the bronze Dallas casket, and ended at 11 o'clock when they left the morgue. In other words, they left rather early that evening, before Humes, Boswell, and Finck had finished their examinations, and before any of the embalming work had begun. As far as they were concerned the autopsy was completed when they departed, and in their minds their FD-302 report was about "the autopsy," period. What they did not know was that Humes talked to Dr. Perry in Dallas on the phone immediately after they left at 11:00 PM, and then revised the earlier 2-hit scenario given before the FBI, to a three-hit scenario. [The three-hit scenario was heard by General Wehle's aide, Richard Lipsey, who recounted it to the HSCA in great detail.] This three hit scenario became the basis of the first (unsigned) draft of the autopsy report, which was found unacceptable on Saturday, and was then burned on Sunday morning by Humes. But the two FBI agents knew nothing of this at the time, or subsequently. They stuck by their report of what they saw and heard the rest of their lives, simply because that is what they saw and heard. I agree totally with Lifton about the veracity of the key statements in their report. There were two key statements (one about being barred from the morgue, and the second about "surgery of the head area" discovered by Humes on JFK's cranium) first, they were barred from entering the morgue as soon as they offloaded the casket from the Navy ambulance, writing these approximate words: "A tight security was placed around the morgue by the U.S Navy and the Secret Service." I think the words they then used were something like: "We advised the Secret Service of the Bureau's interest in this matter." The clear implication is that they were barred from entering the morgue by the U.S. Navy and the Secret Service.

Law: That's correct.

Doug: That means there was one hell of an argument, Lifton is absolutely correct about that. That is bureaucratic language for "They would not let us in and we had one hell of a discussion about it; we eventually won; and were finally permitted to go inside." In order to avoid embarrassment to themselves and to the Bureau, which was always the number one requirement by Hoover, they did not overtly report that the mighty FBI was temporarily barred from entering the morgue by the smaller and less important Secret Service, and that they lost control of the President's body, which was their chief assignment – to stay with the body and get the bullets from the body (for examination by the FBI lab).

Law: I have asked Sibert about this recently and he still says they were not barred from the room.

Doug: I don't believe it. He may believe it now, this many years later, but if so that is just denial, or cognitive dissonance. Stonewalling, if you will. But I don't believe that is the case, because they would not have written it in the report if it didn't happen. I will tell you why I don't believe him. There are reasons I say this: Sibert and O'Neill were covering their asses and have never been willing to admit that they failed in their primary mission: their primary job was to maintain the chain-of-custody on the body and get the evidence (bullets and bullet fragments) removed from the body. I think those are Sibert's own words to the House Committee staff, and probably ever since then. I just don't see these guys admitting that they failed in their primary mission. I wrote about this in my book: Dr. Humes told one of his neighbors that the FBI agents were never in the morgue at all during the autopsy in the first place, that they were kept in a separate room. Now clearly, this is not totally true either – it is a half-truth. I have demonstrated in my book that Humes was surely referring to the period during the illicit post-mortem surgery (after 18:35 and prior to 20:00) when the FBI agents were not present; yet clearly they were present later, between 8 and 11 PM, for they observed the "public autopsy," took notes about what they saw and heard, and then wrote a report from their notes on November 26, 1963.

I think in this case that the FD-302 document (the "Sibert-O'Neill report") speaks much louder than any later denials by the two FBI agents. No matter how kindly I feel toward Sibert – and I feel very kindly toward him, because he is a real gentleman – I do not believe his assertion that they were never barred from the morgue. I believe the reason they were temporarily barred from entering the morgue was because when they delivered the empty casket on the church truck at about 7:15 or 7:17, the surgery on the body had just been completed and x-rays were being taken of the skull. These two guys – who knew nothing about the covert operation underway (the clandestine surgery to expand wounds and obliterate or remove evidence) – could not be allowed inside the morgue while that illicit activity was underway. They would have seen the president's body lying there on a table with his skull being X-rayed. These guys would have "lost it," they would have gone berserk, and the whole cover-up would have been blown. (After all, they thought that JFK's body was in the Dallas casket they had just brought in on a church truck.) So I am convinced this is why they were barred from the morgue. By the way, when Navy x-ray tech Jerrol Custer was deposed by the ARRB, he testified that only when he left the morgue after taking the 5 skull x-rays he exposed, only then did he see another casket (certainly the empty bronze Dallas casket) sitting out in the anteroom. This is highly significant. This is the bronze Dallas casket (empty, of course) delivered to the morgue anteroom by the two FBI men and two Secret Service agents while Custer was inside the morgue, taking x-rays of the expanded cranial defect in JFK's skull.

Law: Let's move on to the "why" and the "how" and "when" of the X-rays and autopsy photographs.

Doug: I will describe for you what I believe happened – this, I am convinced, is one of my two major contributions to the research in the medical evidence arena. It's one I am proud of because it came out of a lot of work done by the Review Board in terms of interviews and depositions. I believe that shortly after the President's body arrived after 6:35 PM, there was a cursory inspection of his wounds with high level people attending (Admiral Galloway, Admiral Kenney, Captains Stover and Canada) and, of course, Humes and Boswell were there on the loading dock, by their own admission, when the body arrived. They were present on the morgue loading dock when the body arrived at 6:35 PM, so you know they were certainly there when the body was first examined, to receive instructions from their military superiors. I think that the first cursory examination of JFK's body must have quickly confirmed what they had likely already been told: "The President has been killed by a crossfire in Dallas, and it was an ambush. We can't tell that to the American people, can't admit JFK was killed by an international communist conspiracy, because if we do, the people will demand that his death be avenged and we will have World War III on our hands, and millions will be killed in a nuclear exchange." I think they were given a very nice, simple national security cover story, very similar to the one above. I think it was the "WWIII cover story," because it's the same one Lyndon Johnson used on Chief Justice Earl Warren, to get him to chair the Warren Commission. So, I think that from the moment the body arrived, and perhaps prior to that, Drs. Humes and Boswell already had their marching orders, and those marching orders were, "You are going to inspect the damage and remove any evidence of shots from the front, and you are only going to put in the record the evidence you find of shots from behind."

The autopsy report is most peculiar in the way it is written because it starts out like a newspaper article. It says something to the effect, "Three shots were heard and they were fired from behind the president." I remember Jeremy Gunn, our General Counsel, being very concerned about this and asking Dr. Humes, during his deposition, how this got into the autopsy report. Jeremy's point was that the autopsy report was supposed to be about wounds on the body. Entrance wounds, exit wounds and trauma. What's this stuff? Dr. Humes didn't give a very good answer to that. But clearly someone instructed them to put those words in the report – and if someone instructed them to put that in the report it's clear to me exactly what was driving all of their actions that night – the official cover story: "A man in a tall building shot the president while riding in his car, from above and behind." So, language about three shots from behind ended up in the autopsy report, which is really unusual, since Dr. Humes was not in Dealey Plaza and knew nothing about what people heard or didn't hear. The many shots heard from the vicinity of the grassy knoll were not recorded in the autopsy report, but the point is that shots were heard coming both from the front and behind, as many eyewitnesses told the police that day. I think this mention of only three shots, and only shots from behind, is a clue to what was driving the actions at Bethesda – the necessity for the autopsy report, one way or another, to conform with the official cover story.

David Lifton was correct, I'm convinced, absolutely correct, about the fact that wounds on the president's skull were altered by surgery. A comparison of the Parkland wound descriptions with the autopsy report led him to that conclusion – the differences between the two descriptions are quite stark. I think he was incorrect about when and where that cranial surgery occurred. He believed the skull wounds were altered by post mortem surgery before the body arrived at Bethesda, and he also believed in 1981 that the brain had already been removed before the body arrived at Bethesda. He still believes these things by the way – I have not been able to convince him of his error yet – but I am absolutely convinced I have got this part of the sequence of events corrected and clarified now. As I reconstruct this cover up, when people first saw the president's head wound at Bethesda they saw the same head wound that had been seen in Dallas by the treating physicians. They saw an avulsed exit wound in the right rear quadrant of the head, about three inches wide, about the size of a baseball (a hardball), or a small orange, or a closed fist. The reason I am convinced they initially saw the same wounds that were seen in Dallas at Parkland Hospital is because Dr. Canada (Commanding Officer of the treatment hospital at Bethesda) said so, and Dr. Burkley (JFK's military physician) said so – to researchers many years later – but they didn't tell the Warren Commission, they only told researchers Michael Kurtz and Henry Hurt, respectively. Of course, Burkley saw the wounds at both locations. He rode in the same ambulance, I believe, that the casket was in, with Jackie and Robert Kennedy, on the way from Andrews. As soon as they arrived at five minutes to seven, he went into the building, presumably straight to the morgue. Canada not only told Kurtz about the avulsed, localized exit wound in the right rear of the head in the late 1960's, but he also blithely told him that not mentioning it in the autopsy report was 'part of the cover-up,' or words to that effect. Kurtz, obeying Canada's wishes, did not publish the information until 2006! Burkley told Henry Hurt about the exit wound in the right rear of the skull in the early or mid 1980's. Presumably, Burkley was describing what he had seen in trauma room one in Dallas, since by the time he arrived at the morgue about 7 PM Friday night, the clandestine surgery was surely underway. One other physician, Dr. [John] Ebersole (the radiologist that night), also described the wound as 'occipital' and said the back of the head was missing, during his deposition before the HSCA (which the HSCA refused to publish in 1979 and sealed for 50 years). His deposition was liberated by the JFK Records Act. Furthermore, mortician Tom Robinson, in drawings made for both the HSCA and the ARRB, drew a blowout in the rear of JFK's head very consistent with the wound descriptions from Dallas. He was present along with the body as soon as it first arrived, so he is another crucial witness to the way the head wound looked prior to the illicit surgery at Bethesda.

In his 1981 book, *Best Evidence*, Lifton also came (reluctantly) to believe that after the initial post mortem surgery was performed on JFK's skull to gain access to the brain and to remove evidence, that reconstructive surgery was performed afterwards so that the back of the head would appear intact in the autopsy photos and in the cranial x-rays. He was led down this incorrect path by the HSCA's firm assertions in Volume 7 of its report that ALL of the Bethesda autopsy witnesses agreed with the wounds as portrayed in the autopsy photos, and that NO EVIDENCE of alteration of those images had been detected by the HSCA's expert photographic and x-ray panels. Lifton believed the wound accounts from Parkland Hospital of a blowout in the right rear of the head – whereas the HSCA did not, and amazingly, concluded that all of the Dallas medical personnel were in error. Since Lifton believed the Parkland wound descriptions, he concluded that it was reconstructive surgery that had allowed the camera and the x-ray machine to record an intact back of the head at Bethesda. As he put it in his Best Evidence video, "the body lied to the doctors." We now know that he was wrong: the ARRB uncovered two Bethesda witnesses to the illicit post mortem cranial surgery at Bethesda: Gawler's mortician Tom Robinson and Navy x-ray tech Ed Reed. And they were not describing reconstructive surgery – they were simply describing a radical expansion of the original exit wound to the enormous one seen in the "autopsy" photos today – a modified craniotomy, if you will. Furthermore, the pioneering work of Dr. David Mantik, M.D., PhD., during his nine visits to the National Archives to examine the three extant skull x-rays, has proven that the three surviving skull x-rays (two are missing) are not originals, but are copy films: altered copy films, which obscure the original blowout in the right rear of the head. (I have written about his work extensively in my book, and have provided the key empirical measurements made at the Archives to prove the point.) In 1993 the JFK Records Act liberated all of the HSCA's own staff interviews of autopsy witnesses (which like Dr. Ebersole's deposition transcript, had been sealed for 50 years), and its big lie became exposed: twelve of the autopsy witnesses interviewed by the HSCA staff gave wound descriptions (or drew diagrams) that disagreed vehemently with the autopsy photos, and agreed with the exit wound in the rear of the head seen in Dallas. So to conclude this digression, David Lifton was wrong about reconstructive surgery, and in fact he has admitted this to me in a telephone conversation. But he was led down the primrose path in 1981 by the big lie in the HSCA report. We are smarter today than we were in 1981, when Best Evidence was published, because we have more evidence available to us today.

As I reconstruct the cover up, I imagine an early inspection of the wounds on the body and quick decisions being made as to how to perform the damage control. Admiral Kenney or Galloway might have phrased it thusly: "What are we going to do? We have what is clearly an exit wound in the back of the skull and that is not compatible with a shooter from behind. We also have an entrance wound high in the right forehead, above the right eye, just below the hairline." Their decision: the entrance wound above the right eye had to be surgically obliterated, removed. (It was, but the evidence of its removal – a bright red, bloody "V" shaped incision, remained as evidence of post mortem surgery.) The exit wound in the rear of the skull had to be grossly expanded, for two reasons: (1) to gain access to the brain and remove all noteworthy bullet fragments from the cranium, so as to remove all gross evidence of crossfire; and (2) this modified craniotomy, or radical expansion of the Dallas exit wound to five times its original size, to include the top and right side of the head, created a truly massive cranial defect that could then be represented as an "exit wound" in the top and right side of the skull, as if it had resulted from a shot from behind. [This is what Lifton referred to as 'changing the geometry of the shooting.'] Any brain tissue that showed a clear bullet track consistent with a shot from the front would have been removed also. I am convinced that when we look at the autopsy photographs today, the surviving autopsy photographs, that is, about two thirds of those photos that are in the record today, were taken immediately after this postmortem cranial surgery. So, instead of the entry wound high above the right eye (which was obscured by the President's bangs in Dallas), an entry that was recalled by Dennis David (in the Pitzer photos), seen by Tom Robinson in the morgue, and recalled by USIA photographer Joe O'Donnell from a post mortem photo shown to him by Robert Knudsen, what we see now (instead of an entry wound high above the right eye) is a rather dramatic, bright red V-shaped incision, that to me is evidence of postmortem surgery and removal of an entrance wound high above the right eye. Behind the "V" shaped incision are two pieces of white bone that appear to have been split apart and pushed aside by the force of the frontal bullet as it entered. The "V" shaped incision is startlingly clear in the color positive transparencies in the National Archives.

When Dr. Peters, the Parkland trauma room one treatment physician, saw the autopsy photos (color positive transparencies) in person in 1988 for the NOVA documentary "Who Shot President Kennedy?," he referred to this lesion as "an incision." It was that simple – it looks like an incision, and it was certainly not present in Dallas when he saw the body – and so that was a significant statement by Dr. Peters, since we know there was no surgery of the head area in Dallas. [On the color positive transparencies it is clearly a bright red incision, whereas on the multi-generational, B&W bootleg autopsy photos printed in many books, it looks more like a black triangle. The "black triangle" effect is contrast buildup on multigenerational bootleg photos, where red has also turned to black in the black and white image.]

At one point during his deposition with the ARRB, Dr. Boswell slipped up, and told the truth about this incision. During his deposition, Dr. Boswell talked at length about a very long laceration which went from the cowlick area all the way forward into the right forehead, but on one occasion during his deposition Boswell referred to the trauma above the right eye as an "incised wound," instead of as a laceration – in other words, as an incision. So, to me that was a significant slip wherein he actually used the correct terminology for once during his deposition (instead of calling it the end of a laceration). And, of course, if it was an incision like Dr. Boswell and Dr. Peters both said it was, then there is only one place where that post mortem surgery could have occurred, and that is Bethesda

Naval Hospital, because Dennis David and Joe O'Donnell both saw photos after the president's funeral depicting a small entry hole in that area, and no incision. They saw the "before" photos of that pristine entrance wound above the right eye, and today in the official autopsy collection we are only left with the "after" image, reflecting the results of post mortem surgery at Bethesda to remove that entrance wound. Since the before and after images were both taken at Bethesda, therefore the surgery must also have been performed at Bethesda.

When we look at the autopsy photos in the collection today, two-thirds of that collection, I would say, just about all of the images except the back of the head and the open cranium view that is out of focus, that is, in all the images where we see the Bethesda towel with the blue stripe, and the metal head rest or stirrup, holding the head of the president while his body is lying supine on the examination table – in those images we are looking at the results of the radical, illicit, clandestine, post mortem cranial surgery. That is why the head wound is so large – you are actually looking at the results of a modified craniotomy done to gain access to the brain so that forensic evidence (bullet fragments and brain tissue) could be removed. In all of these photos JFK's head is resting in a metal stirrup so that you can't see the back of his head in the photos. This was an intentional subterfuge, and it did not require any visual special effects. All these "head in the stirrup" photos, it is clear to me, were taken immediately after the conclusion of the clandestine post mortem cranial surgery, and before the beginning of the "public autopsy." This is why no one present at the "public autopsy" remembers seeing such a metal head brace. For example, neither of the two Navy enlisted autopsy technicians who assisted Humes and Boswell with the autopsy from 8:00 PM until 11:00 PM – Paul O'Connor and James Jenkins – neither of them ever recalled it being used that night at the autopsy (or at any other time, for that matter). It was apparently used only for a quick ten minute photo shoot when very few people were present in the morgue, and then quickly disassembled. The photos taken with JFK's head in the U-shaped head brace, with the pristine towel underneath the head brace, are a con job, meant to persuade the viewer that the enormous damage he is seeing in the images was caused "by the assassin's bullet." The pristine towels are meant to convey the impression that the President's body has just arrived and has not yet been touched by the pathologists. Similarly, the autopsy sketch of the top of the skull made by Boswell on the reverse side of the body diagram (Autopsy Descriptive Sheet) is also a con job, made during the "public autopsy" as he sketched the head trauma supposedly caused by the "assassin's bullet" for posterity. You will note that although Humes said he destroyed – burned – autopsy notes to prevent any documents with blood on them from becoming objects of morbid curiosity, he most certainly did NOT destroy Boswell's sketch of the "head wound," which had blood stains all over it. Of course not! Boswell's drawing had to survive to provide support for the official cover story.

I have stated numerous times already in this interview that I am positive the post mortem cranial surgery on JFK – obstruction of justice – took place at Bethesda, and the reason is because the ARRB discovered two witnesses who said so, in rather matter-of-fact terms, simply describing what they had seen with their own eyes. In his deposition before us in 1997, Navy x-ray tech Ed Reed described how Dr. Humes had taken a scalpel and cut open JFK's scalp from left to right, high in the frontal bone above what the layman would call the forehead, just inside the hairline. After making this incision, Reed testified that Humes then took a circular bone saw to the same area and began cutting the bone. At this point, Reed says, he and Custer were summarily dismissed. [They were recalled to the morgue a short time later, to take the skull x-rays – which like the surviving autopsy photos, were taken AFTER the cranial surgery was completed.] This is extremely significant since Humes testified before the Warren Commission in 1964 that he never had to perform a craniotomy, since the skull wound was so large. (He repeated this incredible fish story before both the HSCA and the ARRB.) What Ed Reed witnessed, of course, was the commencement of a craniotomy, or rather a modified craniotomy. Gawler's mortician Tom Robinson is the other witness to post mortem cranial surgery, and he told both the HSCA staff in 1977, and the ARRB staff in 1996, that he witnessed the doctors saw open the skull to get to the brain, and that he then saw the brain removed. (He had what he described as a "50-yardline seat" in the morgue gallery. When the black hearse arrived at 18:35 with the aluminum shipping casket, there were two persons in the front seat wearing white operating room smocks, according to Dennis David. One of them was surely Joe Hagan, the Gawler's supervisor that night, and the other was undoubtedly young Tom Robinson, one of the four working members of his team. Having arrived with the body at 18:35, Robinson was present in the morgue to actually witness the clandestine surgery, the obstruction of justice. Someone was obviously stupid enough and careless enough to view him as "a nobody," as someone who was not a threat to the cover-up.)

Now Robinson, as it turns out, made a diagram of the head wound he recalled for both the HSCA and for the ARRB. His HSCA drawing was a crude sketch made on a blank sheet of paper without any anatomical reference points available, but seemed to depict a circular wound about the size of an orange in what he described was the back of the head. The ARRB staff gave him an anatomical template of the back of the human skull copied from an anatomy textbook, and on this he drew a circular wound about the size of an orange squarely in the back of the head. Above it and below it he drew horizontal dotted lines. Jeremy Gunn (who was conducting the questioning that day) asked Tom Robinson what the dotted lines represented, and he immediately answered, "That's where the doctors sawed the skull open to get to the brain." This was an electrifying moment, I can tell you, for it confirmed that the post mortem cranial surgery took place at Bethesda Naval Hospital. [One year later, in 1997 (as recounted above), Ed Reed provided independent corroboration of this.]

Law: Did shivers go up your spine when you heard Robinson say this?

Doug: Yes, actually I did get chicken-skin. Jeremy Gunn and I exchanged significant glances when Robinson made that statement about the doctors having to saw open the skull to get to the brain; we knew we had achieved a significant breakthrough in the case. Post mortem surgery had been confirmed, and its location had been confirmed: Bethesda Naval Hospital. Next, we showed Tom Robinson the two separate autopsy photos (from the bootleg Fox set – we were at the ARRB office, not at the National Archives, so we had to use the standard bootleg photos used by all researchers) that show almost the entire top of JFK's head removed, with the rear of the skull resting in the U-shaped metal head brace, and a good two-thirds of the cranial skull cap removed, with nothing but lacerated scalp and brain tissue visible. He immediately frowned with disapproval and said, "This makes it look like the bullet did that. But all this [damage] was what the doctors did." Now, THAT was an electrifying moment. The hair stood up on the back of my neck – it was one of only three or four times when that happened while I was on the staff of the ARRB. This was the moment I knew that there had been a cover-up of the medical evidence by the U.S. government, for Humes denied until his death that he had ever performed a craniotomy to gain access to the brain. Those denials were the lies of a guilty man who was carrying out the orders of his superiors to sanitize a crime scene.

One final aspect of the clandestine surgery needs to be addressed here. The other significant statement in the "Sibert-O'Neill report" that I alluded to earlier is their quotation of Dr. Humes saying at one point early in the autopsy that there had been "surgery of the head area, namely, in the top of the skull." Sibert and O'Neill confirmed internally to the FBI in 1966 that they had indeed written down the exact words of the head prosector [a person who performs autopsies] to establish the cause of death, Dr. Humes, and that this was not their opinion. It was a direct quotation of the chief pathologist, they assured their FBI superiors. David Lifton made a big deal about this in 1966 when he discovered it, as well he should have. Lifton has always interpreted it as a statement of shock and amazement from Humes when he discovered evidence that JFK's skull had been tampered with by others – an attempt by Humes to leave clues in the official record that something was amiss. (If it was, why did Humes not write about it in the autopsy report?) I strongly disagree with Lifton's interpretation of Humes' excited oral utterance. First of all, Humes made the statement AFTER 8:00 PM, or else it would not have been in the notes taken by O'Neill and Sibert. By then, Humes had been with the body since 6:35 PM (when it had first arrived) and knew damn well what was going on. In fact, he had performed the surgery, as stated by Ed Reed under oath to the ARRB. In front of the large morgue audience following the second Dallas casket entry at 8:00 PM – remember, this is audience # 2, who knew nothing about the clandestine surgery that Humes had performed earlier that evening – it is clear to me that Humes panicked, and to combat the astonishment and no-doubt skeptical comments from the gallery about the enormous head wound supposedly caused by one bullet, he blurted out a cover for himself, declaring that "someone" (clearly not him!) had performed surgery on the top of the skull. At least one other witness in the morgue recalls him asking if surgery had been performed in Dallas (Humes clearly knew that was not the case, since he had performed it himself at Bethesda). I recently spoke with an experienced clinical psychologist who concurred in my assessment of Humes' major gaffe; he told me, "When people who are not accustomed to lying are caught in extremely stressful situations, they exhibit regression, and do and say things that cannot be defended later – this is exactly consistent with Humes' untimely outburst." My professional source has informed me that the clinical term for Humes' excited oral utterance is dissociation, and that his publicly expressed statement about his 'discovery' of "surgery of the head area, namely in the top of the skull" on JFK's body was a psychological self-preservation response to extreme stress. As I see it, Humes was attempting to explain away the enormous "head wound" to a skeptical morgue audience of his peers by saying, in effect: "Sure, this is a huge cranial defect and it is extremely shocking; it does look too big to have been caused by one bullet; I can see that somebody has performed surgery at the top of JFK's skull, but [since I just discovered that and reported it] it cannot have been me!" James C. Jenkins has confirmed to both Harry Livingstone and to you, William, that JFK's brain fell out of the cranium into Humes' hands without Humes having to perform a craniotomy or sever the brain stem. No wonder Humes felt like he needed to cover his ass with such a ludicrous remark about "surgery." No brain in the history of pathology ever just "fell out of the cranium" at an autopsy without a craniotomy being performed prior to its removal.

Law: How do you explain the intact back-of-the-head photos in the autopsy collection?

Doug: I believe they were taken after Sibert and O'Neill left the morgue at 11:00 PM. This is because Sibert and O'Neill both told us in emphatic terms that they never saw anything at the autopsy that looked like the intact back-of-the-head photos. They literally disowned those photographs, under oath. Instead, when viewing the head at that angle they saw a large defect in the right rear of the head (the part of the cranial defect that represented the original exit wound seen in Dallas). I personally believe that these photos were taken by moving more or less intact scalp from elsewhere on the head, and simply holding it in place for a few moments to cover up the enormous amount of missing skull in the right rear of the cranium. In the photos of these images you can see several hands holding the scalp in place, and even pushing it out from behind, toward the camera lens, as if to suggest that the brain was still present. I examined these images on high-definition monitors at the Kodak lab in Rochester in November of 1997, and saw no blatant evidence of photographic forgery: no matte lines, no out of focus areas, and no discontinuities between the hairs around the circumference of the image. Neither did the Kodak technicians. I also seem to be almost alone in my conclusion that these images are not photographic forgeries. (I believe they are dishonest, but that they are not forgeries, not produced by visual special effects.) Dr. David Mantik has concluded that they are indeed photographic forgeries, because he created his own home-made stereoscopic viewer at the National Archives and has stated that the intact area on the back of the head in these photos appears *two-dimensional* in a stereoscopic viewer, not three-dimensional as it should. In contrast to his own personal subjective experience, however, the HSCA photographic panel stated that they saw no evidence of photographic alteration in any of the autopsy images, after viewing them stereoscopically. Should we believe what the HSCA published about its photographic panel, given its other lies and distortions? I really don't know.

So, we are left with a puzzle here. Both Mantik and I, and most JFK assassination researchers, believe that the back-of-the-head images are dishonest and do not reflect reality; Mantik and I just disagree on whether they represent manipulated and relocated scalp (moved only long enough to snap a few photos), or whether they represent the employment of photographic fakery. I believe that they are authentic photos of relocated scalp, taken after the FBI agents left at 11:00 PM and before the Gawler's funeral home team began its work at 11:45 PM. I believe that all of these post-11:00 PM photos were taken by Robert Knudsen, a Navy Chief who normally took only social photographs of the President and his family, but who was employed on this occasion to take additional post-mortem photographs after the formal conclusion of the "public autopsy." He repeatedly told his family, and he also told a photo magazine during an interview in the late 1970's, that he had photographed the autopsy of President Kennedy and that it was "the hardest thing he had ever had to do in his life." He seemed unaware that the official photographer of record was Navy civilian John Stringer, assisted by HM2 Floyd Riebe, a corpsman who was being trained as a medical photographer by Stringer at the time. And if he was there that night, they were certainly unaware of him. But that is what one would expect if a compartmentalized operation was being run by the Secret Service and the CIA.

Knudsen served four Presidents, and according to his widow, was a man of sterling integrity "who would take secrets to the grave with him if ordered to do so by higher authority." He had no reason to lie about photographing what he thought was the autopsy, and therefore I have concluded he did not lie. This could explain why none of the autopsy photos display the normal identification cards (showing the autopsy number) that Stinger normally employed; why so many of them are partially or grossly out of focus (Knudsen as a social photographer was not accustomed to macro-photography); why wide establishing shots and medium shots (normal progressions in autopsy photography) are missing; and could explain why Stringer was not allowed to develop his own autopsy photographs, as he normally did. Knudsen may well have been the photographer at the early session (immediately after the clandestine surgery), and at the late session, as well. If that is the case, then none of Stringer's or Riebe's photos ever made it into the official record. Riebe has been adamant over the years about the fact that none of the photos he took are in the official collection. My own analysis of which photographic views are missing, based on testimony and interviews of key autopsy witnesses, shows that possibly as many as 18 different views are not in the official collection. (Three or four photos were usually taken of each view.) I suspect that those missing views are the ones that show the true wounds to the cranium, including the blowout at the right rear of the skull, as well as probes in the body. Let me wrap up this discussion of autopsy photography by saying that at my request, Jeremy Gunn asked Dr. Boswell to examine his sketch of the damage to JFK's skull that he made at the autopsy, and make a three-dimensional rendering of it on a human skull model during his ARRB deposition. (Our reason for doing so was related to whether or not we should have any confidence in the intact back-of-the-head photos.) Boswell did so, and for the first time clarified that not only was two-thirds of the entire top of JFK's skull missing, and part of the right side above the ear, but also that the entire right rear side of the skull was missing as well. [The skull model he drew on can be seen at the National Archives, and I have reproduced hand-renderings of his three-dimensional skull markings in my book.]

Boswell's position, of course, has always been that all of this bone was missing when JFK's body first arrived at Bethesda. But as I have previously stated, that is part of the big con job he and Humes were perpetrating upon history and the American people: passing off the results of clandestine surgery they performed themselves as "damage from the assassin's bullet." We know from the multiple Parkland hospital observations that this was not the case in Dallas, therefore Boswell is engaging in falsehood whenever he declares that most of the top of the skull bone, much of the right side, and the right rear side of JFK's skull was missing when Kennedy's body arrived at Bethesda. No such massive damage was reported at Parkland hospital on the day JFK died. Boswell lied for decades to cover-up his and Humes' involvement in obstruction of justice. In conclusion, this confirmation by Boswell that the right rear of the cranium was missing, as well as the top of the skull, and part of the right side, was another truly electrifying moment for Jeremy and I, for it provided unintended corroboration of all the Parkland Hospital medical reports of a baseball-sized exit wound in the right rear of the skull. Quite simply, this damage to the right rear of the skull was not shown on Boswell's autopsy sketch because his sketch only depicted the TOP of the skull as the President was lying supine on the examination table. (Intentionally, no doubt.)

Two Brain Exams

Law: Can you please explain how you came to the conclusion that there had been two brain exams following the President's autopsy, and the significance of that? It seems to me that this is a major aspect of the medical cover-up.

Doug: It is. And quite frankly, it is my discovery. It was significant enough to be reported on the AP wire and in the *Washington Post* in November of 1998. The discovery came about in about May of 1996, as Jeremy and I were preparing for the deposition of Dr. Pierre Finck. (We had already deposed Humes and Boswell.) We were both working in the office on a quiet Sunday morning, undisturbed. Jeremy asked me to do a timeline of all events surrounding "the brain exam." Meanwhile, he was studying what Humes had written about the damage to the brain in the supplementary autopsy report, and attempting, unsuccessfully, to reconcile that verbiage with the photos in the Archives. (In cases of death due to head trauma like gunshots to the brain, the brain is examined separately well after the autopsy on the body is finished, and a separate report is written about the condition of the brain afterwards.) My timeline analysis of all known testimony revealed that there had been two separate events. Brain exam number one (JFK's real brain) took place on Monday morning, November 25th, the day of the funeral, just three days after the President's assassination. (Photographer Stringer and Dr. Boswell were quite sure about that. So was a pathology technician named Benson who processed JFK's brain tissue that morning.) Brain exam number two took place between Nov 29th and Dec 2nd, and this timing was confirmed by Dr. Finck (who was called by Humes on Nov 29th and told to attend the brain exam) and by Navy Chief [Chester] Boyers, who processed the brain tissue (on Dec 2nd). The second brain exam, I have concluded, was of a substitute brain, a fraudulent specimen. (After all, Bethesda was a teaching hospital, and brain "cuttings" were performed there every week for students to observe. It would not have been difficult to come up with a brain at a teaching hospital.) It is the pictures taken of this fraudulent specimen which reside in the Archives today. JFK's real brain is missing, and so are the photographs taken of it on November 25th by John Stringer.

How do I know this? Because the ARRB deposed Stringer and asked him to describe the type of views he had shot of JFK's brain and the type of film he had used. Under oath. Then we showed him the extant brain photos in the official collection, and everything about them was wrong – different from what he had testified to earlier in the day. He had shot only views of the top (superior) surface of JFK's brain, yet half of the extant photos were of the underside of the brain (basilar views). He had shot many views of coronal or serial sections of JFK's brain, yet there were no photographs of sections in the extant collection in the Archives. He had shot the photos using Ektachrome color positive transparencies and Pan-X Kodak B&W film, yet the extant photos were shot on Ansco B&W film and the color positive transparencies in the Archives were *not* Ektachrome film (Stringer could tell this from the fact that the notches in the corner were not consistent with Ektachrome notches). Finally, Stinger had used duplex film in holders, not a press pack. Yet the black and white negatives in the Archives were shot on a press pack, for each frame was numbered (in the factory, unlike film in duplex holders which is never numbered). *Case closed.* This was starling courtroom evidence, gathered under oath, which would impugn the authenticity of the "JFK" brain photos in any trial. There is no better expert witness than the man who took the images.

When FBI agent Frank O'Neill viewed the brain images at the Archives during his deposition, he disowned them, saying that there was too much brain tissue present for them to be JFK's brain. He said he recalled that over half of JFK's brain was missing when it was removed at the autopsy, and that the biggest loss of mass had occurred at the right rear of the brain (entirely consistent with the Parkland hospital observations of a blown out right occipital cortex and macerated, partially blown out cerebellum). Tom Robinson had also told the ARRB staff that most of the missing mass in JFK's brain was in the right rear. The brain photos in the Archives depict a completely intact right cerebellum, and damage seemingly consistent with a shot from above and behind.

So the game being played here by the cover-up artists is pretty obvious. The damage so clearly caused by a frontal shot (or shots) in Dallas could not be displayed because it contradicted the official cover story, and had to be suppressed forever; pictures of damage to a different brain that was consistent with a shot from *behind* had to be inserted into the official record. The means of doing this was the substitute brain so obviously used at the second brain exam. And that substitute brain, of course, as well as the authentic JFK brain, is now missing.

The particularly damning fact for both Humes and Boswell is that they were present at *both brain exams*. They engineered the whole charade, and this also proves their complicity in a medical cover-up. Poor Dr. Finck was present at only the second one – he was the dupe who could testify, if need be, that the photos in the Archives were indeed photos of what he had examined about a week after JFK's death. He never needed to. (It's just as well, for in his notes he wrote that the appearance of the brain at the brain exam he attended was different from the way it appeared at the autopsy!) The conspirators got away with the "big switch" – until 1996 when Jeremy and I discovered their legerdemain. When I told Jeremy Gunn that I was convinced there had been two brain examinations – one fraudulent – he agreed with me. He had come to the conclusion that the brain photos in the Archives were not authentic by comparing Humes' description of damage to the brain, with the photos in the Archives. I had reached the conclusion that there were two exams by studying the timeline of brain events. Jeremy's masterful performance at Stinger's deposition forever destroyed the presumed authenticity of the brain photos in the National Archives. (Even the HSCA wrote that it could not authenticate the brain images as being those of JFK.) Another Big Lie has been exposed.

Wrap-Up

Law: What concluding thoughts do you have about the state of the medical evidence in the JFK assassination?

Doug: The evidence in the JFK assassination (not only the medical evidence, but also the ballistics evidence and photographic evidence) can be likened to a 500-piece jigsaw puzzle for which 250 of the pieces have been thrown out, and substitute pieces from the wrong puzzle have been introduced into the box to keep us forever confused, and unable to assemble an accurate picture. In short, the reason the JFK assassination does not "come together" like a normal homicide case is because there is *fraud in the evidence*. Much evidence is just plain missing, and much of that which remains is seriously tainted, and suspect. That is the major theme we should be focused on as we approach the 50th anniversary of President Kennedy's death.

At a time when the mainstream media is solely intent upon continuing its character assassination of President Kennedy, in an obvious attempt to get people to care less about who murdered him in 1963 and why, the JFK research community should be reminding all Americans that a major cover-up was implemented by the U.S. government immediately after his death (particularly in the medical evidence arena), to hide the fact that America experienced a coup d'état in 1963, an illegal transfer of power. This illegal transfer of power was engineered by those who were afraid of, and despised, JFK's foreign policy at the height of the Cold War with the USSR. He wanted to end the Cold War and engage in serious détente with the USSR, while his domestic opponents in the intelligence community and the military wanted to win the Cold War, preferably by engineering victories in proxy wars on the battlefield (in places such as Cuba and Vietnam). The heroes of World War II had learned the wrong lessons, and sought purely military solutions to all problems in a nuclear age. As JFK knew, this was folly, and madness. They disagreed, and despised him as a weak, communist-influenced, naïve one-worlder. History has shown that they were wrong, and he was right: he was a generation ahead of his time, in wanting to end the Cold War and place human rights at home and abroad ahead of national prestige and jingoism. I cover all of this quite thoroughly in volume 5 of my book, Inside the Assassination Records Review Board. (For those who wish to purchase my five-volume work, please go to Amazon.com and enter the search keywords "Horne JFK.")

The medical cover-up's goal was to suppress all medico-legal evidence of shots from the front, and to only record evidence of shots from behind. It has failed miserably, and as David Mantik has said, the cover-up was so abysmal, and so poorly coordinated, that if it were not such a serious subject, the cover-up could be likened to a French farce – high comedy. Many autopsy photos were destroyed, and two skull x-rays were destroyed. The three remaining skull x-rays are altered copy films (forged composites). Many of the surviving "autopsy photos" do not resemble anything that witnesses to the autopsy recall seeing. The President's brain is missing. So are skull fragments (including the Harper fragment and the Burros fragment, sent to Washington from Dallas). The brain photos in the Archives are a fraud and are demonstrably photos of a substitute brain, not JFK's brain. The substitute brain which was photographed is missing also – and it has to remain missing – otherwise DNA tests would prove that it bears no relation to the Kennedy family. Three separate casket entries at Bethesda Naval Hospital (when there should only have been one) should serve as the final proof that this was a poorly coordinated, inept cover-up, being arranged on the fly.

I quoted Shakespeare in my book, expressing confidence that "The Truth Will Out" eventually. And it has. But it should be of the deepest concern to us all that the establishment in this country remains out of step with the 80% or so of the American people who KNOW John F. Kennedy was killed by a conspiracy and who *know* that the U.S. government covered it up. Two venal men, Lyndon Baines Johnson, and J. Edgar Hoover, were the willing and essential keys to the success of the coup, men I have called "essential enablers." They were not the masterminds of the conspiracy, but they went along willingly and with foreknowledge, and without their cooperation beforehand and afterwards, the CIA officials and their military allies in the assassination cabal could not have gotten away with the crime. The U.S. government today remains in the same cowardly mindset it has been in since the mid-1970's: unwilling to admit the truth about the Kennedy assassination. (The cover-up in the 1960's was imposed by guilty men; since the mid-1970's it has been perpetuated by cowards.) Now, instead of lying to us outright or blatantly and arrogantly withholding information from the American people like the HSCA did in so many instances (i.e., the Ebersole and Knudsen depositions, and its own staff interviews of autopsy and other medical witnesses), the government hides behind walls of silence (since the government has no credibility anymore) and prefers to let third party surrogates (in the media and in Internet chatrooms) do its dirty work – these insidious specialists in the ad hominem attack, in ridicule, and in the use of distorted argument, and bald-faced misrepresentations. Shame, shame. If only the U.S. government could come to understand that the only way for America to cleanse its soul is to confront what really happened in 1963 in an adult manner. We are not children anymore in this country – we have survived three dastardly political assassinations in the 1960's, and Vietnam, and Watergate, and the Iran-Contra scandal – we do not need to be "protected from the truth." What we cannot handle are continued lies and evasions, for they are extremely corrosive to the true spirit of democracy. The longer the stonewalling and evasion continues, the less faith we will have in our own government. The lies perpetuated by the media and the government about the JFK assassination constitute a cancer on the soul of America, and that cancer must be excised.

Above: Paul O'Connor and author standing at the end of the old Oregon Trail. Paul O'Connor opened up a Pandora's box with his revelation in 1981 that Kennedy's body was actually brought into the Bethesda morgue in a cheap metal shipping casket. Below – left to right: Dennis David, Jim Jenkins, Mark Young (film director & writer), Jim Metzler, Robert Groden, and author at the Westmont conference, where new clues were found within the mystery of the JFK autopsy.

AFTERWORD

If you're in darkness, step into the light!
– Hip Hop artist Ryelo, aka Ryan Law
Come Correct
2.0 Project

D arkness and light. Truth and lies. That is what one is faced with when approaching the abyss that is the Kennedy assassination. I have been trying for almost twenty-five years now to cast light into the dark mystery. Rather than do nothing but curse the darkness. To quote the Grateful Dead, "What a long strange trip it's been."

I had been reading everything I could on the assassination, and calling witnesses to the event for a couple of years, when I got the notion in my head that I had to put a stop to my obsession. After all, grown men with a family and approaching 40 years old don't act this way. I don't remember how I came to find out about the conferences held in Dallas, but I found myself at one in 1997. My plan was to go to this one event, learn what I could, visit the hallowed ground that was Dealey Plaza, the site of the crime, then go home. Forget it. Be a rational human being and not think about the Kennedy assassination anymore. But that is not what happened. Instead of leaving the Kennedy assassination behind me, some months after the conference I attended, I found myself in Pittsburgh, Pennsylvania at the home of Jerrol Francis Custer, the x-ray technician who had taken the x-rays of the late President, as he lay on the morgue table at the Bethesda Naval Hospital. How can I relay to the reader how I felt, as Jerrol Custer held up one of the frontal head x-rays of Kennedy and said, "They wanted this man dead. They did a good job of it." How do I relay to you, the reader, that I now believe that the x-ray that Custer held up for the camera (I filmed the interview with Custer's permission) is a composite x-ray and not an original? I do believe Dr. David Mantik's work on the Kennedy x-rays held at the National Archives prove that they are composites. I believe that most, if not all of the

119

evidence in the Kennedy assassination, has been tainted. One can virtually trust nothing in "the so-called evidence" – to quote Lee Harvey Oswald.

For skeptics: remember that no one I have interviewed who was at the Bethesda Naval Hospital, in the morgue, remembered seeing the frontal x-ray with the apparent metal fragment, circular in shape, with a notch out of it, that just happens to be the same size of a 6.5-mm. bullet. Humes, Boswell and Finck, the three autopsy doctors themselves, testified under oath to the Assassination Records Review Board, that they did not recall this bright fragment on the skull x-rays at the autopsy. Kennedy's hair was combed through thoroughly to find bullet fragments, but none were found. And there is the fact that no metal headrest is seen in the x-rays of the head that survive. The headrest should show up on the head x-rays as it is made of metal, but Kennedy's skull – if it is indeed Kennedy's skull – seems to be floating in air. And as you have read earlier, at the gathering in Westmont, Illinois, Hugh Clark, who was guarding one of the morgue doors, said while the door was open for several seconds, he looked in and saw the President's remains on one of the autopsy tables.

The President's neck was on what is referred to in the funeral trade as a "block" – no resemblance to the metal headrest as seen in the supposed autopsy photographs – something Paul O'Connor and Jim Jenkins have been saying for years. Jerrol Custer claimed to me in 1998, that there was a headrest on the autopsy table and it was removable. But Jerrol also told Sylvia Chase in the 1988 documentary "An Unsolved Murder" on KRON TV in San Francisco when shown the head x-rays by Chase, that they were not the x-rays he had taken. Custer's credibility at least on whether or not there was a metal headrest is questionable. There is further corroboration that the President's neck, at the time of autopsy, was resting on a "block." James Felder, one of the Honor Guard, claimed to Phil Singer and myself, at the Westmont gathering, that he was in the morgue from time to time and also saw the President's neck on a block.

In a conference in Florida, held in 2002, consisting of Paul O'Connor, James Jenkins, Dennis David, James Sibert, with guest Dr. David Mantik, and myself, retired FBI agent James Sibert did not remember Kennedy's head in a metal headrest. Both Jenkins and O'Connor said in an interview on film, that they did not think that the existing photographs of Kennedy's body, real or not, were taken in the Bethesda morgue the night of November 22, 1963. If the Kennedy autopsy pictures are open to question, then all of the evidence in the case is open to question. Let's not forget Dennis David's account of supervising the carry of, by a crew of six or seven enlisted men, a cheap metal shipping casket into the morgue. I tried to contact Donald Rebentisch, who had claimed to be one of the enlisted men who helped bring in the metal shipping casket, to see if I could get him to come to the gathering at Westmont, Illinois. But when I did find a phone number for him, I found that Donald had passed away two years before. I talked to Mrs. Rebeintisch, Donald's wife, and asked her if Don had ever told her the story about helping to take a metal shipping casket into the morgue on the evening of November 22, 1963. She replied, "Oh yes, many times." So, there is indeed corroboration for Dennis David's experience of giving orders to unload a metal shipping casket at the Bethesda morgue. How could this have happened? The best scenario we now have is through the work of David S. Lifton, and Assassination Records Review Board analyst Douglas P. Horne.[1]

I do believe David S. Lifton, who first brought the description of Kennedy's body being altered or probed before the official autopsy started, to the attention of the public in 1981, in the publication of his ground breaking work, *Best Evidence*. And Horne, with his work with the ARRB, for the most part got it right. (There are things we will never know.) It's the best explanation of how President Kennedy's remains were brought into the morgue at Bethesda, at 6:35 p.m. in an aluminum shipping casket. And then the two FBI agents helped carry the Dallas casket into the morgue at 7:17 p.m. (the casket was empty), and the Honor Guard carried the Dallas casket in at 8:00 p.m.

There was indeed a "shell game" with Kennedy's remains. The shell game continued with Humes and Boswell doing alterations, or another word can be used here – tampering – with JFK's remains. The only way the wounds on the President's body could have happened is if the autopsy doctors were in on the ruse, and I believe they were. Dennis David has said that the Doctors Humes and Boswell were out on the loading dock when the cheap metal shipping casket was brought into the morgue. The doctors had to know about the different casket entries into the morgue and therefore had to be part of the cover-up. I want to be clear here: I am not accusing the doctors of President Kennedy's murder. The doctors were probably given a story along the lines of what Lyndon Johnson told Earl Warren, that Johnson was concerned about the wild conspiracy theories circulating around the world that would lead to World War III. He insisted it was Earl Warren's patriotic duty "in this hour of trouble." As in most things having to do with this case, there is another version of how Johnson coerced Warren into heading up the Commission. In a telephone call with Richard Russell, Johnson claimed: "Warren told me he would not do it

1. For more on this, see the Douglas Horne chapter.

under any circumstances. I called him and ordered him down here, and he told me 'no' twice, and I just pulled out what Hoover told me about a little incident in Mexico City and he started crying and said, 'Well, I won't turn you down. I will do whatever you say.'" In any event, the autopsy doctors went along with whatever they needed to, to keep their rank, their jobs and their pensions. Douglas Horne, military analyst for the Records Review Board, in Volume IV of his 5-volume set of books, *Inside the ARRB,* and who was present for the board's depositions of Humes, Boswell and Finck, said, "He [Humes] seemed like a man who was hiding something." And indeed I believe he was hiding something. He was hiding the truth that he knew there were different caskets and different times for the entries of those caskets, and that he along with Boswell, altered and tampered with the wounds on the President's body. Don't think the doctors would have participated in such a heinous deed? We already know that Humes, who was in charge of writing the autopsy report on President Kennedy's death, burned his original notes he took in the morgue the night of the autopsy. To quote Humes: "I, James J. Humes, certify that I have destroyed by burning certain preliminary draft notes relating to Naval medical school autopsy report A63-272 and have officially transmitted all other papers related to this report to a higher authority." Before the HSCA, Humes said that he destroyed his working notes because the notes had the President's blood on it, and he didn't want the notes to become an object of future morbid curiosity, such as the Lincoln assassination had.

What follows are excerpts from James Humes's testimony before the Assassination Records Review Board, taken from Volume I of Doug Horne's *Inside the AARB,* where Jeremy Gunn questions Humes about his handwritten notes:

Gunn: Now, I presume the notes that you took during the autopsy did not resemble in any way the document you have in your hand now, Exhibit 2 (a photocopy of the handwritten draft of the typed autopsy report)

Humes: Well, they did, yes. I mean, I didn't dream this up out of whole cloth.

Gunn: Certainly, I understand the content ... what I am interested in is what the two or three pages of notes look like.

<Break>

Gunn: ... I assume that the notes you made while at Bethesda during the autopsy were not written in sentence and paragraph form.

Humes: No. They were shorthand.

<Break>

Gunn: So when you drafted – well, first, was there any other draft of the autopsy protocol other than the one that you're holding in your hand right now-

Humes: No. No. There was not.

<Break>

Gunn: Was there any information that was contained on the handwritten notes that was not included on [sic] in the document [the handwritten draft] –

Humes: I don't believe so.

Gunn: Have you ever observed the document now marked Exhibit 1 (the Autopsy Descriptive Sheet) in the original appears to have blood stains on it as well?

Humes: Yes, I do notice it now. These [the two-sided Autopsy Descriptive Sheet, or body chart, reproduced in Exhibit form as a 2-page document] were "J"s [meaning "J" Thornton Boswell]. I am sure I gave these back to "J." I presume that I did. I don't know where they came from.

Gunn: Did you ever have any concern about the President's blood being on the document that's now marked Exhibit 1?

Humes: I can't recall to tell you the truth. [To me, Humes's attitude here was flippant and dismissive.]

Gunn: Do you see any inconsistency at all between destroying some handwritten notes that contained blood on them but preserving other handwritten notes that also had blood on them?

Humes: Well only that the others were of my own making. I didn't – wouldn't have the habit of destroying something someone else prepared. That is the only difference I can conceive of. I don't know where these went. I have no idea. I certainly didn't keep them. I kept nothing, as a matter of fact.

Gunn: I'd like to show you the testimony that you offered before the Warren Commission ... I'll read that into the record while you are reading it yourself. Mr. Specter asked the question: "And what do these consist of?" The question is referring to some notes. Answer: "In the privacy of my own home, early in the morning of Sunday, November 24, I made a draft of this report, which I later revised and of which this represents the revision. *That draft I personally burned in the fireplace of my recreation room.*" Do you see Mr. Specter's question and your answer? (emphasis added) [Note: Remember, the "certificate" Humes had typed and signed stated that he destroyed "preliminary draft notes," and Gunn here was trying to establish whether Humes had destroyed working notes with blood on them, or a first draft of the autopsy report that may have contained different conclusions than are in the final autopsy report we have in evidence today, or both.]

Humes: Yes.

Gunn: Does that help refresh your recollection of what was burned in your home?

Humes: Whatever I had, as far as I know, that was burned was everything exclusive of the finished draft that you have as Exhibit – whatever it is [Exhibit 2].

Gunn: My question will go to the issue of whether it was a draft of the report that was burned or whether it was –

Humes: I think it was –

Gunn: – handwritten notes-

Humes: It was handwritten notes and the first draft that was burned.

<Break>

Gunn: Dr. Humes, let me show you part of your testimony to the HSCA. Question by Mr. [Gary] Cornwell – I will read this into the record ... Mr. Cornwell: "And you finally began to write the autopsy report at what time?" Dr. Humes: "It was decided that three people couldn't write the report simultaneously, so I assumed the responsibility for writing the report, which I began about 11 o'clock in the evening of Saturday November 23, having wrestled with it for four or five, six hours in the afternoon, and worked on it until three or four o'clock in the morning of Sunday, the 24th." Mr. Cornwell: "Did you have any notes or records at that point as to the exact location of the –"Dr. Humes: "I had the draft notes which we had prepared in the autopsy room which I copied." Now, again the question would be: Did you copy the notes so that you would have a version of the notes without blood on them but still notes rather than a draft report?

Humes: Yes, precisely. Yes. And from that I made a first draft, and then I destroyed the first draft and the notes.

Gunn: So there were, then, two sorts of documents that were burned: one, the draft notes, and two, a draft report?

Humes: Right.

Gunn: Is that correct?

Humes: That's right. So the only thing remaining was the one that you have [meaning Exhibit 2, the handwritten draft of the typed autopsy report in evidence today].

Gunn: Why did you burn the draft report as opposed to the draft notes?

Humes: I don't recall. I don't know. There was no reason – see, we're splitting hairs here, and I'll tell you, it's getting to me a little bit, as you may be able to detect. [At this point I felt Humes was almost ready to explode – to walk out of the deposition and terminate the proceeding.] The only thing I wanted to finish to hand over to whomever, in this case Admiral Burkley, was my completed version. So I burned everything else. Now, why I didn't burn the thing that "J" wrote, I have no way of knowing. But whether it was a draft, or whether it was the notes, I don't know. There was nothing left when I got finished with it, in any event, but the thing [the handwritten draft, Exhibit 2] that you have.

Gunn: Well, the concern of course, is if there is a record related to the autopsy that is destroyed, were interested in finding out the exact circumstances–

Humes: [Angry and defensive] I've told you what the circumstances were. I used it only as an aide-memoir to do what I was doing and then destroy it. Is that hard to understand?

Gunn: When I first asked you the question, you explained that the reason that you had destroyed it was that it had the blood of the President on it.

Humes: Right.

Gunn: The draft report of course, would not have had the blood of –

Humes: Well, it may have had errors of spelling or I don't know what was the matter with it, or whether I even did that. [Humes by this point was arrogant, and blustering.] I don't know. I can't recall. I absolutely can't recall, and I apologize for that. But that's the way the cookie crumbles. I didn't want anything to remain that some squirrel would grab on and make whatever use they might. Now, whether you felt that was reasonable or not, I don't know. But it doesn't make any difference, because that was my decision, and nobody else's.

Gunn: Did you talk to anyone about your decision –

Humes: No, absolutely not. No. It was my own materials. Why – I don't feel a need to talk to anybody about it.

Humes, Boswell and Finck – were in so deep at this point that they had no choice but to go along and obfuscate any attempt by any governmental body that was formed to investigate the Kennedy assassination and the above exchange between Humes and Jeremy Gunn is a good example.

Don't take my word for it – read and compare Humes, Boswell and Finck's testimony before the Warren Commission, the House Select Committee and the Assassination Records Review Board. Read for yourself the contradictions in their testimonies, obfuscation and so-called "confusion" while they try to orientate the wounds as seen in the autopsy photographs. The photographs in question do not depict the wounds as they really were on Kennedy's body – and I believe I have laid to rest any ques-

The Gathering – left to right: William Law, James Sibert, Dennis David, Paul O'Connor, Debra Conway, James Jenkins, Dr. David Mantik, Kelly Kreech – September 28, 2002, Fort Meyers, Florida.

tions having to do with the autopsy pictures being altered – see my film *The Gathering*. Humes and Boswell should have had no trouble in finding where the so-called bullet entry was on Kennedy's skull that night; they were after all trained physicians and had the basic skills of anatomy and had their hands on the body and their eyes to see with. Humes has stated in an interview on CBS with Dan Rather circa 1964, that the markings on the autopsy face sheet were not meant to be exact but approximations of where the wounds were. Is that a reasonable statement? No. That's why coroners have autopsy face sheets, so markings can be placed on them correlating with wounds on a body with accuracy. But Humes is always acting like a man on a hot plate, never really answering any kind of question put to him by any kind of governmental body doing an investigation, because he might get caught in a lie. And while I am on the subject of the autopsy face sheet, on the 50th anniversary of Kennedy's murder, James Jenkins said in a public forum what he has been telling me for years: that the autopsy face sheet that is now housed in the National Archives in Washington, D.C., is not the original one from that night. The face sheet that is in evidence today depicts two body charts on the front side of the document and the back side of the form which was originally blank and was used by Dr. Boswell to make a historically important sketch depicting the damage to the top of President Kennedy's skull. The autopsy face sheet that James Jenkins helped to fill out was a two sided form with a single body chart of the front of a human body on the first page and another body chart of the back of a human form on the reverse side. There are erasures and amendments of original weights on the extant form in the archives which James Jenkins did not make and which were contrary to the conventions for such entries in 1963.

Boswell claimed that he made most of the notes on the autopsy face sheet. James Jenkins told me that he helped fill out the autopsy face sheet. He does not see his handwriting on the existing face sheet in evidence today. And there is the little problem of Finck's missing notes. It was reported by David D. Saslaw, PhD, who was employed by the Armed Forces Institute of Pathology in Washington D.C., that Saslaw, immediately after the assassination, while he was in the lunch room of the AFTB at an adjoining table between Pierre Finck and two other individuals, when he overheard a conversation between the three gentlemen. Saslaw claimed that he heard Finck complain that after washing up following the autopsy that Finck looked everywhere for his handwritten autopsy notes but couldn't find them anywhere and had to reconstitute them from memory. Did Humes or Boswell take Finck's notes? It seems likely. Remember Doug Horne, military analyst for the Assassination Records Review Board, has concluded that there was a brain exam held three days after the conclusion of the autopsy on the body. The brain was photographed by civilian navy photographer John Stringer, on November 25, 1963. Horne's conclusion is that Stringer's photographs of JFK's brain would have provided proof that JFK was shot from the front and that a bullet exited from the back of his skull. These photographs were suppressed by the federal government and are not the brain photographs found in the archives today. The second brain exam took place as late as December 2, 1963. Humes and Boswell testified before the Warren Commission that Humes, Boswell and Finck were present when the brain was examined. But when Humes testified before the Assassination Records Review Board in 1996, Humes did not list Finck among those present at the brain exam. Boswell said Finck was not there. Finck, on the other hand, said the brain exam occurred much later. Fourteen months after Kennedy's assassination, Finck wrote a memo to his superior, Bloomberg, that Humes called him on November 29, 1963, seven days after Kennedy's death to say it was time to examine Kennedy's brain. Finck reported that all three pathologists examined the brain together, and that color and black and white photographs were taken. The following are the conclusions of Douglas P. Horne:

Pertinent facts regarding the two brain examinations are as follows:

First brain exam Monday November 25, 1963.

Attendees: Dr. Humes, Dr. Boswell and John Stringer.

Events: John Stringer testified to the Assassination Records Review Board that he used both Ektachrome E3 color positive transparency film, and black and white portrait PAN Negative film; both were 4" x 5" format films exposed using duplex film holders; he only shot superior views of the intact specimen – no inferior views; the pathologists sectioned the brain, as is normal for death-by-gunshot wounds, with traverse or "coronal" incisions – sometimes called "bread loaf" incisions – in order to trace the track of the bullet or bullets; and after each section of tissue was cut from the brain, Stringer photographed that section on a light box to show the damage.

Second brain exam between November 29 and December 2, 1963.

Attendees: Dr. Humes, Dr. Boswell, Dr. Finck and an unknown Navy photographer

Events: Per the testimony of all three pathologists, the brain was not sectioned, as should have been normal procedure for any gunshot wound to the head – that is traverse or coronal sections were not made. The brain looked different than it did at the autopsy on November 22, 1963 and Dr. Finck wrote about this in a report to his military superior on February 1, 1965. The color slides of the brain specimen in the National Archives were exposed on "Ansco" film not Ektachrome E3 film; and the black and white negatives are also on "Ansco" film and originated in a film pack (or magazine), not duplex holders. The brain photographs in the Archives show both superior and inferior views, contrary to what John Stringer remembers shooting, and there are no photographs of sections among the archives' brain photographs, which is inconsistent with Stringer's sworn testimony about what he photographed. Furthermore, Horne goes on to write: "That finally the weight of the brain recorded in the supplemental autopsy report was 1500 grams, which exceeds the average weight of a normal, undamaged male brain. This is extremely inconsistent with a brain that was missing over half of its mass when observed at autopsy."

That one fact alone, that the brain weight was recorded at 1500 grams, should be enough "proof" that there was something horribly wrong with the JFK autopsy evidence. But as you have already read, there is more – much more evidence that there was disguise and subterfuge in Kennedy's autopsy. And if there was subterfuge at the autopsy, then there had to be subterfuge in Dallas, Texas, starting with the planning of the Texas trip and continuing with Lee Harvey Oswald as the "lone assassin."

I ask this of writers and researchers and the public at large that believe Oswald was alone in the killing of John F. Kennedy: how is it to be explained that the Dallas doctors all believe that Kennedy had been shot from the front when they saw him in trauma room one? Several Dallas doctors said that Kennedy's cerebellum could be seen and was damaged. How is it that the Ida Dox drawing supposedly of JFK's brain shows no such damage to the cerebellum? Why do the wounds to Kennedy's body have a different appearance than when his remains were seen at the Bethesda Naval morgue?

What is the explanation of Kennedy's body being brought in to the Bethesda morgue in a cheap metal shipping casket inside a body bag delivered by Dennis David and six or seven enlisted men at 6:35 p.m.? Why do we have differing stories of when and who brought in the Dallas casket? There is the 7:17 p.m. entrance of the Dallas casket recorded by Sibert and O'Neill and the 8:00 p.m. entrance by the Honor Guard.

What happened inside the Bethesda morgue is the subject of this book, and I won't go into all of the discrepancies, but surely even to the most hardened skeptic there must be doubt that we know all of the truth about the why and how of John Fitzgerald Kennedy's death – and autopsy.

William Matson Law
July 10, 2015
Central Oregon

Appendix One

THE HISTORIC BETHESDA SEVEN

WESTMONT, IL • FEBRUARY 2015

Deedee Cheek was hoping for some snow. She said that she had never seen it. At 63, she wasn't sure if she'd ever actually get to see it, to touch it, to play in it. To make a snowball. Living in Florida, it just didn't seem too likely to happen. It was January of 2015. Our event was scheduled for early February, just a few weeks away. She said to me on the phone, "Do you think it'll be snowing when we come out?" Our event was to take place in Westmont, Illinois – a suburb of Chicago. I said, "Well, I hope that there'll be some snow on the ground. But I don't want it to be snowing that particular day. We'll see." I was worried about the possibility of flights being cancelled or postponed. And getting people to the hotel from the airports. I didn't want anything to go wrong or mess up our plans. The weather could screw everything up. More on Deedee, the snow and our event a bit later.

In 2005, ten years ago, William Law published a tremendous book about the JFK case. In particular, about the autopsy of the President. The book, *In the Eye of History,* had several interviews with people that were present at the autopsy of President Kennedy at the Bethesda Naval Hospital. I read it. Enjoyed it. And learned a lot about the strange events that night. The book was, and is, a big contribution to the case. David Lifton, Doug Horne and some others have done tremendous research and writing on this very complicated aspect on the case as well. They too deserve a ton of credit for helping us to understand the confusing and often seemingly contradictory events of that terrible day and night. But many questions still remain to this day.

I have been studying the Kennedy case since it happened. I was nine at the time. I started collecting newspapers and magazines about the assassination of our President in November of 1963. Then the books started to come out: *Whitewash* by Harold Weisberg, *Rush to Judgment* by Mark Lane, *In-*

quest by Edward Jay Epstein, *Six Seconds In Dallas* by Josiah Thompson, *Accessories After the Fact* by Sylvia Meagher and many others. I was reading and learning what I could to educate myself on this tragic historical event. Basically, I discovered that there were some pretty big discrepancies between what people saw and heard and what the government told us had happened on Elm Street in Dealey Plaza in Dallas on November 22nd of 1963. As with many people, I'm sure, this bothered me greatly.

In 1975, I was twenty and attending Knox College in Galesburg, Illinois. I was participating in three sports, running a group called The Ghetto, writing some articles for the school newspaper and studying the Kennedy case on the side. I found out that Mark Lane was gonna be coming to visit our school to give a lecture about the case. I inquired about exactly when he was to arrive and found out that he was gonna be flying in to a local airport, just outside of town. I arranged to go with a friend, Mitch Baker, who had a car, to pick-up Lane. So we drove out to the small airport. Lane, sure enough, arrived in a little plane. He was by himself. I introduced myself and Mitch. And I said, "Well, what d'ya wanna do? Go get something to eat? See the town? Meet some students? See the campus?" Lane said, "Let's shoot some baskets." That was pretty cool. So we headed to the school gym – the basketball courts – and I got him some stuff to wear and we shot around for awhile. Later that evening, Lane gave a lecture and showed his documentary film "Rush to Judgment" to many of the students and faculty. The black & white film was – and still is – very powerful. He had numerous eyewitnesses to the assassination describing their recollections of the events. There was a big disconnect with what they saw and heard and with what we were told by the government. Lane answered questions from the audience. I joined his organization, The Citizens Commission of Inquiry, or for short: The CCI. We worked on trying to get the JFK case reopened in Congress. I gave some local talks on the case, showed the Zapruder film of the shooting and was writing and sending letters to Congressmen and Senators, urging them to reopen the case. Our efforts, along with that of many others, resulted in the formation of the House Select Committee on Assassination – or the HSCA., as it is often called – in the late-1970s. After several years, they concluded that Kennedy was killed most likely by a conspiracy. Based primarily upon the acoustical evidence, the HSCA. said that a shot was fired from the grassy knoll to Kennedy's right-front. But that that shot missed. They, like The Warren Commission in 1964, also locked up a whole lot of information for many, many years. Some of this material is still unavailable to be seen by the public today.

The years went by and I continued to study the case. I helped some other researchers with their work. I met and interviewed many witnesses to the various events of that weekend in Dallas in 1963. My goal was to get closer to the truth of what really happened to our President. It became obvious to me that there was a conspiracy to kill Kennedy, to frame Lee Harvey Oswald and to cover it up. To me, that's where the facts led. But I didn't – and still don't – consider myself a Conspiracy Nut. I do view myself as a Truth Seeker though. I go where the evidence leads me. But the problem with the Kennedy case is: what evidence? 'Cause everywhere one turns, there is contradictory and conflicting evidence. There are many, many unresolved areas in this case. It's all very confusing. Ultimately, one has to pick and choose what seems to be the most credible evidence. For example, just to pick out a few of these areas: What happened in Mexico City in the fall of '63 with Oswald? Was Oswald even there? Or was it a "double"? The Tippit killing? Who was on the 6th floor of the Texas School Book Depository Building at 12:30 p.m. on November 22nd, 1963? Wasn't a German Mauser rifle initially found on the sixth floor of the Book Depository? What was going on behind the picket fence at the top of the grassy knoll when the shooting occurred? Didn't several people claim to see a puff of smoke at the corner of the picket fence lingering in the air for several seconds? What was Oswald doing in New Orleans in the summer of 1963 passing out pro-Castro leaflets on Canal Street? Was he really a loner? Or was he working for some agency? Et cetera. Et cetera. Et cetera.

William Law's book was about what happened at Bethesda that night. This is, of course, another of these mysterious, confusing areas of the case: the wounds on the body of JFK But also, different caskets and different casket entries into the morgue. Different vehicles: one – an unmarked black hearse and another – a gray Navy ambulance with naval markings on the side. Weird stuff seemed to be going on. I contacted William Law with some questions about some of his interviews. We would talk on the phone from time to time. And then I heard that there was going to be an updated version of his book. I probably heard about this around 2010 or so. Maybe even earlier. I was anxious to get it. And learn more. Well, the updated version wasn't yet completed and available. And so we continued to talk periodically about the case. William and I became friends to a degree, even though we had never met one another face-to-face.

In the fall of 2013, during the 50th anniversary of JFK's assassination, I got an e-mail from an old college friend who remembered my interest in the case. She had been seeing a bunch of articles in the newspapers in her town about

Kennedy, Oswald and others. I e-mailed her back and requested that she mail me whatever she could about the case. Well, one of the newspaper articles that I received was about a man that had been present at the autopsy of JFK And my old college friend knew him personally. They had a business relationship. I asked her if she might be able to hook me up with this guy that had attended the autopsy of the President that night at Bethesda. She said that she'd try to do it. And she asked me, "Well, what should I tell him?" And I said, "Just tell him the truth. That I'm an old college friend. And that I've been studying the JFK case for many years. And would like to talk with him about it." After many e-mails between this lady and me, and then between me and this witness to history, I arranged to call him on the phone at exactly eight p.m. one weeknight. We spoke for two hours and five minutes.

This was in May of 2014. He told me that he didn't want his name used. So I'm not using it. Let's just call him "the Bethesda witness." He told me how he knew Kennedy and found him to be very friendly and bright. He told me about how he and his superior, a General, would brief the President on ceremonial functions. The Bethesda witness told me about how he had to sign a secrecy agreement after the autopsy, but was told that he might want to read it first. We discussed many different things on the phone. He and the President were on a first-name basis. He told me about the security in Washington, D.C. for the Civil Rights March in the summer of 1963. He said that there were 80,000 troops within ten minutes of Washington. He was given a loaded pistol by his superior prior to arriving at Bethesda that night and was told to use it if necessary. He was thinking, "When's the last time I used a pistol?" He said that his instructions were, "Do not leave the body."

The Bethesda witness described seeing the President's left arm cocked at an angle at the elbow before the autopsy started. He told me that he had never seen a dead man before. And that he helped put JFK into the casket when the embalmers from the funeral home were done. He made a point of letting me know that he thought that Oswald had done it alone. The Bethesda witness said, "The guy was a freaky guy. A misfit. Oswald was out to prove he was capable of killing the President. This guy acted alone." Just before our phone conversation ended, I asked him if he'd want to get together with some of the other guys that were also at Bethesda that night. I figured that he'd most likely be too busy or not interested in something like that. But he said that yes, he would like to do that. It sort of surprised me a bit. I told him that I would get back to him about it. And he reminded me that "I don't want to read about your notes [concerning this conversation] being on the internet tomorrow." It was now 10:05 p.m.

I told William Law about this Bethesda witness prior to my interview of the man. He said, "Call me as soon as you get off the phone with him. Tell me how it went. Fill me in." He was pretty excited about it. This led to a conversation about having a small get-together with the Bethesda witness and two others – Jim Jenkins and Jim Metzler – who had been at Bethesda that night too. William had the contact information on them. William and I continued to talk about this idea over a number of months. We spoke about getting his updated book finished off and out there, as well. I got back to the Bethesda witness in the fall of 2014. I asked him if he would still be interested in hooking up with some others that were there "that night." He said that he was still interested. William and I talked some more about pulling off some kind of get-together. We both felt it was important to get the Bethesda witness there. So I contacted him. And found out what dates would work for him. Eventually, we picked a time-frame: February 3rd, 4th and 5th, 2015 – a Tuesday, Wednesday and Thursday. I felt that if we were actually gonna do it, we needed to pick a date and make it happen. No more talking about it. No-one was getting any younger. The clock was ticking. I felt that if we were gonna have this event, maybe we could get more than just the three guys.

I started tracking down some others. I reached one guy here. And then another guy over there. And then one more. Before you knew it, we had seven Bethesda guys committed to attending our event in Westmont, Illinois. I actually tried to get some more people, but there were some conflicts and some issues that prevented them from coming. All seven of these men were at Bethesda that night in various capacities: Jim Jenkins. Jim Metzler. The Bethesda witness. Dennis David. James Felder. Tim Cheek. And Hubert Clark. Basically, they hadn't seen each other in 51-plus years. Over half a century.

Adam Smrokowski, a friend of mine at the local health club, helped me immensely with coordinating and booking the flights. Then I had to find a hotel and book rooms and secure a conference room. And get videographers. And make photocopies of material. And track down Styrofoam heads to draw on. And get ahold of a chock block. And some still photographers too. A couple of people cancelled on us. In fact, the Bethesda witness changed his mind. He wasn't gonna be coming. I stayed in touch with him and eventually, at almost the last minute, he decided that he would join us. Whew! All in all, it was pretty exciting. I was hoping that we wouldn't have any serious weather-related issues for the event. William and I were talking on the phone at least once or twice every day as we got closer and closer to the event. It was gonna happen.

I flew the guys in to Chicago and got them from Midway and O'Hare airports to The Clubhouse Inn in Westmont, Illinois with the help of some friends, Dennis Kroll and Bob Smith. William Law had arrived a day early with his friend, Mark Young. Glenn Bybee, a teacher and JFK researcher, was there. Robert Groden, a famous author in this case, made it too. We had three people there to film it: Matt Kliegman, J.B. Schiess and Michael Gleeson. John Boda and Darold Drew took still photos during parts of the three days together. One-by-one, our Bethesda Seven started to arrive at the hotel. These guys were all in their seventies now. They were young military men at the time and got "thrown into history" – as I like to call it. They woke up that Friday morning of November 22nd, 1963 and thought they knew what their day was gonna be like. The weekend was coming up. A chance to relax. Rest up. Have some fun maybe. Do some personal things.

The Bethesda Seven – left to right: James Jenkins, Hugh Clark, Tim Cheek, a Bethesda witness, James Felder, Dennis David, Jim Metzler in February 2015 at Westmont, Illinois

Well, that all changed at 1:30 p.m. Eastern time for these guys when Kennedy got shot. Within sixty to ninety minutes, they found out that Kennedy was dead. And they were receiving orders from superiors in the military. Report here. Do this. Do that. Some of these guys already worked at the Bethesda Naval Hospital. The others ended up reporting there for the autopsy. It was an event that changed their lives forever. Some of these men were in the morgue for the autopsy, others helped with arrangements and carried the caskets – plural – or guarded the door to the autopsy room. Three of these men buried the President at Arlington National Cemetery – they carried the casket and folded the flag – on Monday, November 25th, 1963. And this was, by far, the heaviest casket these Honor Guard men ever had to deal with. Normally, six men could handle a casket. In this case, they needed nine guys. And it was still tough. All seven of these men who attended our event performed under immense pressure and scrutiny. A future book and documentary film will be detailing this historic gathering of the Bethesda Seven that got "thrown into history" – but to follow are some of the highlights from the February 2015 Westmont, Illinois event:

One. At least some of the purported "official" autopsy photographs of President Kennedy cannot be of him that night at that morgue in Bethesda.

Two. The President's neck was on a "chock block" during the autopsy and his head was not being supported by a curved metal stirrup, as seen in some of the purported "official" autopsy photos while he is lying on his back.

Three. The Honor Guard guys were in the back of a pick-up truck chasing a Navy ambulance that supposedly had the bronze Dallas casket in it containing the body of JFK It was dark and cold and for a period of time they lost the Navy ambulance – or more accurately, the Navy ambulance seems to have lost the pick-up truck on the grounds of Bethesda.

Four. One of the Bethesda Seven men saw the pick-up truck driving by outside the back of the morgue and someone in the pick-up truck yelled out something like, "Have ya seen the ambulance go by?" Our guy hadn't seen it and he told them, "No." The pick-up truck kept on going.

Five. A plain gray shipping casket was received from a black unmarked hearse around 6:35 p.m. or so at the morgue loading dock. This clearly wasn't the bronze Dallas casket or the gray Navy ambulance seen at Andrews Air Force base just a half-hour earlier with Jackie and Bobby Kennedy and the Honor Guard. Another one of the Bethesda Seven confirmed seeing the black unmarked hearse that night on the grounds of the Naval Hospital.

Six. The autopsy "face sheet" of JFK – which is really a full-body sheet – that has been released by the government as being authentic is not the original one made that night by one of our Bethesda Seven autopsy participants. He said that it's not his writing.

Seven. Several men in suits in the anteroom just outside – and adjacent to – the morgue were checking people from a sheet on a clipboard and writing down names apparently of who came and went into and out of the morgue that night. One of our participants was detained by these mysterious men in suits. Later, he had to sign a secrecy agreement with the Navy.

Eight. The body of JFK was alone with two young autopsy technicians after it entered the morgue. The body was fully wrapped in sheets, essentially from head to toe like a mummy. Everyone else left the room. The two guys were ordered not to touch the body until the doctors returned. A full 20 to 30 minutes went by.

Nine. One of the Bethesda Seven guys was ordered by a military superior to cut out a page and then alter his official log book entry for that night. This took place on Saturday, November 23rd – the day after the autopsy. He falsified the record as he was ordered to do.

Ten. There seems to have been some cover story concerning an Air Force officer in a casket that night in the Bethesda morgue. One of the attendees described how he was told not to log in this casket and not to open it.

Eleven. At one point that evening while two Secret Service agents were standing in the hallway at Bethesda, one of them said to the other something like, "Well, from now on we won't have to feel like pimps." This was heard by one of the Bethesda Seven during his rounds throughout the building.

Twelve. The morgue log book disappeared that evening.

Thirteen. The back wound to the President was probed. It never penetrated the pleural lining around the lungs. And never exited out the front of JFK. The wound was in the back, about six inches down from the collar area and to the right of the spine. If it had exited the President's body, it would have come out just below his right nipple, based upon the location of the entrance wound in the back and the steep downward angle. The wound in the back was around two to three inches in depth. It was not in the back of the neck, but clearly several inches below that. There was only one back wound on the President's body.

Fourteen. At our event, drawings were made on white Styrofoam heads with black permanent ink markers to illustrate the wounds seen on the President that night, by several of the participants that actually saw JFK's body in the morgue.

Fifteen. One of the Bethesda Seven guys discussed how he and another autopsy participant had to sign a secrecy agreement the next morning. And then minutes later he was ordered to return the papers that they had just signed. He was told that the Captain needed the documents back.

Sixteen. An autopsy participant at our event saw what appeared to be a small entrance wound just to the right of the top of Kennedy's right ear. He saw what appeared to be an exit wound in the right rear of the President's head. He felt that these two wounds were connected. Upon leaving the autopsy room the following morning, this young man was certain that JFK had been hit from two different directions – from the right-front and from the back.

Tim Cheek is one of the Honor Guard men who attended our event. His wife, Deedee, mentioned at the beginning of this narrative, had asked me just weeks before our February 2015 event if it'd be snowing when they arrived in the Chicago area. Well, on Sunday, February 1st – which was Super Bowl Sunday – we literally got hit with about two feet of snow. I didn't even bother going out that day. What a mess! A massive blizzard. I was worried that our whole event might be cancelled due to flight delays, cancellation issues and more weather problems. So, sure enough when the Cheeks – and everyone else started arriving two days later – there was a whole lotta snow still on the ground. The streets had been ploughed by then and traffic was moving along pretty well. So I guess we got lucky. And then it did snow a little during our event: kinda sideways to Deedee's amazement. She got to touch the snow and make some snowballs for the first time in her life. And she even played in the snow, making a "snow angel" on the ground just outside the hotel. That alone, made the event for her. And me too.

Thank you, "Ms. Culpepper," for your help behind the scenes. It is greatly appreciated. Thanks, K-Lo, for your help too. Both William and I thank the Bethesda Seven – Jim Jenkins, Jim Metzler, Dennis David [and his wife Marian], Hubert Clark, Tim Cheek [and his wife Deedee], James Felder [and his friend Lillie Johnson] and the Bethesda witness [who left his ill daughter at the hospital] – for joining us in Westmont, Illinois and participating in this historic gathering of eyewitnesses to history. They got thrown into history and did their jobs. And did it well. Under a lot of pressure. Thank you, guys, for sharing your experiences from November of 1963 with us. We learned a whole lot from you guys. And we hope that you-all got something out of the event as well. William and I feel that our collective efforts will help us all to get closer to the truth of what happened to our President that day in Dallas. And that night at Bethesda.

–Phil Singer
July 2015
Illinois.

The 2005 Edition

ACKNOWLEDGMENTS-2005

My love of oral history comes from my mother and father. Indeed, the first stories I learned were those my parents told of growing up in the south. I would sit at their feet, legs crossed, wide-eyed as my mother told of her life on one of the last plantations, of picking cotton until her back ached and her fingers bled. My father would regale my big sister Kay and me with stories of the Great Depression, adventures in the CCC camps as a young man and later as a solder in World War II. My mother usually told her tales from her easy chair, working her crochet, a smile or frown playing upon on her face, depending on the narrative. My father was at times greatly animated, sitting on the couch or at the dinner table, leaning forward looking you right in the eye for emphasis, using his hands as much as his voice. I see them now in my mind's eye and hear the southern drawl as I write these lines, and it makes me smile.

The style of this volume owes much to those stories. Both my mother and father had the ability to take me back in time and give me the feeling of actually being in the tale. There is nothing like that feeling, and I have attempted to pass it along to you, the reader. My father, Jesse Dean Law passed on nearly a decade ago and my mother Dorothy Elizabeth Law has been gone half that long, leaving legacies of love and stories that I now tell my children about their grandparents' lives in a faraway place called Arkansas.

The love of my life and mother of three of my children, Lori Ann, has shown the utmost understanding and patience as I have crisscrossed the United States in search of answers to the Great Mystery. Without her, this book would not have been possible. Childhood is fleeting, both for parent and for child, and in this personal search for balance to history I have stolen precious time away from my youngest children and grandchildren. Ryan Matson Law, Shawn Garrison Law, and Haylee Elizabeth Law (Sissy), and my grandchildren Christian Dean Law and Trey Eliot Law deserve my gratitude. I hope that when they are adults they will feel my efforts were worth it. My love and thanks to my sister Jessie Kay Wilson. Her passing has left a hole in my being that cannot be filled. I miss the sound of her laughter.

This was truly a family project. My eldest son Trevit Clay Law helped to prepare me for interviews, as did my nephew Wesley Dean White. My brother-in-law Robert Dale White did double duty helping with video equipment, and along with my sister Elizabeth Ann White, helped to entertain Paul O'Connor and Dennis David during their all-too-short stays with us for their interviews. Elizabeth Ann also typed a large portion of the manuscript. I have been grateful for their love and support during this project, and throughout my life.

Words cannot express the debt I owe my editor, Allan Eaglesham. Allan took this project on at a time when he was already overburdened with work. He has given of his time to make this book a reality. His has been a firm, guiding hand. Raymond Wiiki was there when Allan and I needed him to make the final push to ready the manuscript's layout for printing. Debra Conway has been a generous sounding-board, offering her support and gathering background materials, and has been a welcome traveling companion on some of my adventures. Her contribution is incalculable. My thanks to David Mantik for his wonderful foreword. A man of great courage and intellect, if the Kennedy assassination is ever solved, it will be due in no small measure to Dr. Mantik's groundbreaking work with the autopsy X-rays and photographs. David Lifton is due thanks for his masterwork *Best Evidence* (Carrol & Graf, 1988). Mr. Lifton and I have had our disagreements over one point or another about this case; in the process I learned much and I am in his debt. Noel Twyman has been very helpful in my research; I consider his book, *Bloody Treason* (Laurel, 1997), to be the new cornerstone in the continuing inquiry into Kennedy's murder. I thank Walt Brown, editor and publisher of *JFK/Deep Politics Quarterly*, for kindly and promptly providing copies of the autopsy photographs that appear in this volume. My friend from across the "big pond," Matthew Smith, author of *The Second Plot* (Mainstream, 1992), has also been extremely supportive – reading a late draft of the manuscript and offering advice; I treasure his friendship. Robert Gagermeier has been of great assistance in putting his typing skills at my disposal, copying documents and offering his expertise to induce my aged computer to do my bidding.

I also thank Steve Conway, Beverly Oliver Massagee, the late Madeleine Brown, Bill Newman, Gayle Newman, Mark Oakes, Vince Palamara, Douglas R Horne, Robert Groden, Laura Chaput, Ian Griggs, Jerry Robertson, Donna Edwards, Mark Rowe and Johnny Young.

Lastly, but most importantly, I owe very special thanks to Dennis and Dorothy David, Paul and Sandy O'Connor, Jim and Jackie Jenkins, the late-Jerrol Custer and his widow Marilyn, James and Ester Sibert, Francis X. O'Neill, Harold Rydberg and Saundra Spencer.

William Matson Law
Central Oregon

Author's Note – 2005

*I was always under the impression that Oswald had killed the president.
That was just taken as read, you know. There it was. It's in tablets of stone.*
— Gary Oldman, who played Lee Harvey Oswald
in Oliver Stone's movie *JFK*.

The gentlemen interviewed for this book are among the most important figures involved in the aftermath of one of the darkest turning points in this nation's history: the assassination of President John F. Kennedy. Thousands of articles and books have been written about the murder of the thirty-fifth president of the United States. Even some of the best are long on theory and short on fact.

My idea was simple: contact those who had been involved in the events at Bethesda Naval Hospital on the evening and night of November 22 – 23,1963, and ask them to take me, step by step, through their recollections of what they had seen, done and heard and put their words on record. I wanted to meet these individuals face to face, to look into their eyes and get an impression of how they had felt during those momentous events.

I tried to start with a clean slate as far as my own opinions on the Kennedy assassination were concerned. However, try as I might, I have not been able to remain neutral. "You have to make a choice," former FBI agent Francis X. O'Neill told me when I explained that I was not taking any side in the controversy, just reporting what I was told. "You have to make choices when putting together pieces from first-, second- or sixth-hand information," he told me. Mr. O'Neill may or may not be surprised to learn that he pushed me to the side of conspiracy (despite his forcefully expressed opinions to the contrary).

I learned what most people have learned who have studied the case in depth: things just don't add up. From Lee Harvey Oswald's murky life as a marine, Russian defector, pro/anti-Castroite, until the day he wound up in the Texas School Book Depository on Elm street, and his death in the basement of the Dallas County jail, it doesn't add up. Similarly, the differing descriptions of the wounds on the president's body as seen in Parkland Memorial Hospital, the differing types of caskets that the body was seen in, the differing descriptions of the wrappings on the body, the amateurish autopsy photographs supposedly taken by civilian photographer John Stringer (who has been described as one of the best medical photographers in the world), the X-rays of the skull showing a large fragment of bullet that the autopsy doctors looked for but never found – the list goes on and on – just don't add up.

The men I interviewed have had parts of their accounts published elsewhere, and to a certain extent their words have been used to bolster authors' pet theories. I had, and still have, no theory to present to the reader as to who was behind the deed. Herein you will find, simply, the words of those who happened to find themselves involved in the aftermath of the assassination of a president. For the first time, they provide analyses of autopsy photos.

In 2000, documents were released that reveal that the ceremonial casket – in which Kennedy's body was supposedly transferred from Dallas to Bethesda – was drilled with holes, weighted with bags of sand and dumped into the Atlantic Ocean. Other documents, reviewed by Douglas P. Horne, late of the Assassination Records Review Board, apparently show that two different brains were examined on two different days, both supposedly belonging to the late president. Clearly, some kind of weird shell game was going on with the president's remains.

While I am not prepared to declare that white is black and black is white in the assassination of John Fitzgerald Kennedy – as was stated by Kevin Costner in his role as Jim Garrison in Oliver Stone's movie *JFK* – I do believe that historical "fact" is not necessarily set in tablets of stone.

FOREWORD-2005

I am exceptionally pleased that William Law, with the able assistance
of Allan Eaglesham, has submitted this work for future historians. My
primary concern, too, has been that the tragic events of November 22,
1963, should be accurately recounted for future generations. To date, textbooks and media have fallen far short of the mark, due mostly to closed
minds and insincere efforts. They have instead chosen the broad and easy
road – endlessly echoing the now-terminal Warren Report rather than listening to those who were there.

In this volume Law brings us the actual words of autopsy participants
as well as others, such as Harold Rydberg, who played his role later. The
mysterious role played by William Pitzer is revisited by Allan Eaglesham.
The efforts of Law and Eaglesham extend over six years and plainly required
immense persistence and dedication. That the two FBI agents, James Sibert
and Frank O'Neill, finally agreed to go on the record is a remarkable testimony to the tenacity of Law, in particular. I am delighted to introduce this
historic set of interviews to the public, and especially to future historians.
For anyone who wants a first-hand look at that long-ago night, this is as
close as we can now get.

During my decade-long curiosity about these events, I have had the
pleasure of meeting many of these interviewees, often speaking to them at
length. As a result, when I first read their interviews here, I felt that I already
knew them – I could visualize their facial expressions, feel their passion,
and recognize their nuances of expression. I met Jerrol Custer, the radiology technician, in New York City in 1993, and then later often spoke to him
on the phone. I immediately recognized Paul O'Connor's demeanor from
Law's description; I had met Paul both in Dallas and in Florida, the latter
during a lengthy panel discussion. I also met James Jenkins and Jim Sibert at the same time in Florida, discussing details with them both formally
(during the videotaped panel discussion) as well as informally. I had the
pleasure of a detailed and intimate discussion with Dennis David while in

Dallas several years ago. On the other hand, I have never met Frank O'Neill or Harold Rydberg. I have, however, read all of the transcripts of these men (some several times over) and listened to all of their audiotaped interviews with the Assassination Records Review Board (ARRB).

My personal encounters with these men leave no doubt that they are both sincere and passionate in their recollections. There is no attempt to bend the facts to fit some preordained conclusion or some specific theme. They were there – they are merely telling it as they remember it.

After I reviewed the transcripts that appear in this book, I suggested no substantive revisions.[1] The words that I read were consistent with what these individuals had told me and also consistent with their narratives to the ARRB. Although they disagree with one another at times on details (as they recognize), sometimes surprisingly so, the common theme is unmistakable and consistent – the Warren Report does not describe what happened that day or that night.

Dennis David tells a remarkably compelling story of two caskets: one arriving at the loading dock in a black non-military ambulance and a second arriving later at the front of the National Naval Medical Center, Bethesda. He personally assisted and arranged for some of his men to unload the first casket. He is certain that it was a plain gray shipping casket, not the ornate casket that left Dallas. He personally observed the official (gray) ambulance drive up to the front entrance some time later; he watched as the Kennedy entourage left that vehicle. Because he was Chief of the Day, he included his observations in a log. As Officer of the Day, J. Thornton Boswell, one of Kennedy's pathologists, also signed that document. That log has never since been seen.

David, because of his security clearance, was selected that night to type an official memorandum that described four pieces of lead, between one and two bullets in total mass, supposedly removed from Kennedy's head. He actually held these in his hand. Neither these fragments nor the memo have been seen since. Curiously, Jenkins recalls that a small plastic bag containing bullet fragments was placed on the autopsy table near Kennedy's head. (Officially, only two tiny lead fragments from the skull were entered into evidence, far less than one bullet in total mass.)

Several days later, David encountered his good friend, William Pitzer (head of the Audio-Visual Department at Bethesda), reviewing a 16-mm film of the autopsy as well as both b&w and color stills and 35-mm slides (all presumably made from the 16-mm film). Pitzer and David both observed and discussed a small hole in the hairline, directly above the pupil of the right eye. Based also on a large hole at the right rear of the skull, they

---

1. The chapter on Saundra Spencer was under preparation when Dr. Mantik wrote this foreword.

both concluded that a shot had struck from the front and exited at the rear. This was particularly arresting for me, as I had concluded early in my own work, based solely on the X-rays, that a shot must have entered from the front almost precisely at the hairline, above the right eye.

David offered yet one more astonishing observation: the name of Pierre Finck (the third pathologist at Kennedy's autopsy) appears on the cover page of William Pitzer's autopsy.

Paul O'Connor notes that he had assisted in fifty to sixty autopsies before Kennedy's. His experience with death by then was extraordinary – he had begun working at a funeral home at age 13. Like David, he also recalls a plain shipping casket. Like several other members of the autopsy team, he has no recollection of the wooden frame in the background of one autopsy photograph, thereby casting some doubt on the authenticity of that photograph. O'Connor saw hardly any brain inside the skull, thereby echoing the comments of Jerrol Custer, but disagreeing with Jenkins. He agrees with Jenkins that the probe placed into the back wound did not penetrate the pleura, going in at most IV4 inches. (Under oath, Kennedy's chief pathologist, James J. Humes, confirmed this to the ARRB.) O'Connor repeatedly states that the exit from this wound would surely have been through the sternum, near the level of the heart. By explicitly stating that the back wound was three inches below the seventh cervical vertebra, he violently disagrees with the Warren Report's single-bullet scenario.

James Jenkins also saw a plain shipping casket. He places the back wound at the fourth thoracic vertebra (precisely where the autopsy radiologist, John Ebersole, placed it when I spoke to him). Like O'Connor, Jenkins saw the probe going into the back wound and reaching the pleura, but not penetrating it.

Jenkins still has the impression that the brain had been surreptitiously removed before the autopsy and then replaced: he did not need to perform the usual skullcap incision (that was his job) and he had the impression that the scalp wound had been extended by a scalpel. Also (this was eye-catching for me since I had not heard it before), Jenkins saw that the cut through the brain stem was at different levels on the two sides (as opposed to a single level from a single cut, as would be standard). One final observation by Jenkins also implied to him a prior (illegal) brain removal: the carotid arteries were severely retracted, which suggested to him that they had been transected quite a while before the autopsy.

Like other autopsy personnel, he also does not recognize the wooden frame in the background of an official autopsy photograph. And, like so many who commented on it, the headrest was totally unfamiliar to him; he recalled that the Bethesda morgue routinely used an aluminum block that was scalloped for different sizes, but never such a headrest. Such a consistent recollection by so many calls into question the authenticity of at least the photographs that display the headrest.

His comments about James J. Humes, the chief pathologist, are memorable: Humes was "totally navy." He implies that Humes was totally beholden to the navy for his expertise and professional standing. Jenkins also notes that, in his eighteen months at Bethesda, this was the only autopsy that he saw Humes (or Boswell, for that matter) do.

Jenkins, only about age 20 at the time, later earned a master's degree in combined sciences, including pathology and anatomy. In light of this subsequent training, his foregoing comments must be taken seriously.

Jerrol Custer, the X-ray technician, also recalls a cheap shipping casket. As he has told me and others, several skull X-rays are missing from the current set, most especially an oblique view. (Astonishingly, the autopsy radiologist, John Ebersole MD, in a conversation with me, also recalled more skull films than the three in the current official set. His recollections were quite independent of Custer's – they never compared accounts.)

Custer recalls an entry wound above the mid-right eyebrow. During this conversation with Law, he pointed only about half an inch above the eyebrow, in apparent disagreement with David, who placed it at the hairline. But this may not be a true disagreement; I would challenge anyone, without use of a mirror or some means of measuring distance, accurately to identify a precise site on his own forehead. In further disagreement with the official conclusions, and in view of what he saw that night, Custer also cannot accept the single-bullet theory.

Custer's impression of Humes matched that of Jenkins: "Humes was a politician; knew how to manipulate things. Humes was a career person. He knew how to protect Humes's back."

As in his ARRB appearance, when Frank O'Neill described the official photographs as showing too much brain, he also recalled for Law that the brain was mostly missing – there was only a portion of a brain left. Based on the (low) position of the back wound, he insists that the single-bullet theory is impossible. (In his ARRB conversation, he even ridicules Boswell for raising the level of this wound from where Boswell had placed it in his official drawing.)

Jim Sibert notes that Kennedy's head looks too clean in some autopsy photographs – especially where the large rear hole was located. He felt vindicated when he learned that Gerald Ford, one of seven members of the Warren

Commission, had moved the back wound up (so as to salvage the single-bullet theory) to the base of the neck. For Sibert that explained a deep mystery, since the back wound that he saw could not possibly fit with an exit at the tracheotomy site. Sibert adds that the level of the back wound was entirely consistent with the holes in the shirt and coat. When questioned about the single-bullet theory and Arlen Specter, Sibert responded: "What a liar. I feel he got his orders from above – how far above I don't know." He adds that Specter even misspelled both his name (as Siebert) and O'Neill's (as Oneal).

He does not recall seeing a brain that night that looked anything like photographs in textbooks (i.e., he saw nothing like a nearly intact brain). Neither he nor O'Neill recalled seeing the 6.5-mm metal-like object within the right orbit that is so obvious on the extant frontal X-ray. Furthermore, neither of them recalls any discussion of this object at the autopsy. (In my view, that is devastating, since the entire purpose of the X-rays was to register precisely such objects. Prior readers will recall my firm conviction that this object was later added to the X- rays; precisely matching the caliber of Oswald's rifle and lying on the back of the skull, this fake object by itself made a strong case against Oswald.)

Eaglesham updates us on the strange case of William Pitzer, who was shot to death at the Bethesda Naval Hospital (officially a suicide) on Saturday, October 29, 1966, just a few months before his scheduled retirement and literally days before an official review of the autopsy materials by the autopsy personnel. According to Eaglesham, the FBI concluded, from the absence of powder burns, that the gun may have been held at least three feet away when fired. Eaglesham, again quoting the FBI documents, reports that the absence of muzzle marks – as described by the autopsy doctors – rules out direct contact of the gun with the skin. The myth that Bill Pitzer was left-handed is corrected. It is possible, given his expertise, that he recorded the Kennedy autopsy via closed circuit television. Finally, and somewhat curiously, the Pitzer residence was searched by the navy after his strange death.

Adding to the striking possibility that Pitzer did indeed record the autopsy on closed circuit television is a statement made, under oath, by Humes:

> Routinely, at the end of a week, we would retain the organs from the autopsies of the week. In fact, not only did we review them there, but there was a closed-circuit television. They went to Andrews Air Force Base, NIH, and it was a closed-circuit instruction program. (ARRB deposition of Dr. James Joseph Humes, College Park, Maryland, February 13, 1996, p. 58.)

However, when specifically asked by the ARRB, Humes denied that the Kennedy autopsy had been recorded by closed circuit television.

Harold Rydberg, director of the medical illustration school at Bethesda, describes how he was detained on a Friday in early 1964 to draw the now-official Warren Commission diagrams of Kennedy's wounds. This was so impromptu that Rydberg even had to cancel a date for that night. As Humes verbally described these wounds, Rydberg tried to display them. This was done without any photographs or other images, the only time in his entire career that Rydberg was asked to prepare images from words alone. He specifically recalls that Humes told him to blacken Kennedy's right eye, an odd request since it is not especially dark in the autopsy photographs.

Rydberg witnessed the official gray navy ambulance arrive at the front of the hospital, where he saw Jackie Kennedy holding the side of the flag-draped coffin.

He recalls that John Stringer, the autopsy photographer, played navy politics well. Although he was not intimate with Stringer, in his (Rydberg's) role as head of medical illustration, he often worked with Stringer. (He recalls that Captain John "Smoky" Stover, Pitzer, Humes and Boswell – but not Stringer or Finck – all attended his (Rydberg's) wedding.) He is quite certain that the extant autopsy photographs do not accurately reflect the photographs that Stringer took that night; he has the greatest respect for Stringer's professionalism and does not believe that the photographs reflect the usual quality of his work.

Most striking, though, are Rydberg's comments about the pathologists. Both Humes and Boswell were facing navy retirement and did not want to lose their benefits. According to Rydberg, they both were soon awarded promotions in rank. Though he did not know Finck well personally, he occasionally worked with him. Rydberg notes that Finck was involved in the case of Lt. William L. Calley, Jr., of MyLai massacre fame (March 16, 1968). [2]Jim DiEugenio has previously noted Finck's cover-up in the case of Captain

2. The MyLai cover-up has strong psychological parallels to the JFK cover-up. One obvious parallel is that leading roles in both cases were played by military personnel. Believers in Oswald as a lone gunman often object to conspiracy on the grounds that too many individuals would have known the truth if there had been a conspiracy. Yet in the MyLai case, M. Scott Peck (*People of the Lie*, 1983) informs us that at least 500 personnel knew that war crimes had been committed, yet no one said anything. This event became known only because Ron Ridenhour, a nonparticipant, sent a letter (March 1969) to several congressmen. I have previously pointed out that no one went public during the Manhattan Project either, and Gary Aguilar has noted a similar situation for the Pentagon Papers. In spring 1972, Peck chaired a committee of three psychologists. Their research proposals, intended to avoid future MyLais, were rejected by the military because they (1) could not be kept secret and (2) might prove embarrassing to the administration. Peck also notes that, to a considerable degree, those guilty at MyLai did not confess because they were not aware of their crime. Although they

John McCarthy, which I have recounted in *Murder in Dealey Plaza* (edited by James Fetzer, 2000, p. 286). Some readers will also recall that Boswell informed the ARRB that he was sent to New Orleans during the Garrison investigation, prepared to refute Finck in case Finck strayed too far off the official path. That never occurred, however. Even more curiously, Boswell was invited, but declined, to supervise the autopsy of Martin Luther King, Jr., a request that he himself disclosed to the ARRB.

Of all the interviewees, Rydberg provides the most insight into the pathologists. He describes Boswell as a very good, albeit reserved, doctor. Rydberg apparently had a comfortable relationship with Humes, as evidenced by the respect Humes paid to Rydberg's wedding, but also by Humes's unexpected appearance at Rydberg's office sometime later in Chapel Hill, after which they had a fine dinner together, joking, drinking, and eating roast beef, with Humes paying the bill. To encapsulate Humes's dilemma, Rydberg employs the metaphor of a chess game: on November 22, 1963, Humes was checkmated. However, he was never happy "that he had to knuckle under." Even though Rydberg is no believer in the lone-assassin theory, he agrees that Humes had no choice and that perhaps it was the better part of valor for Humes to do what he did.

Law cites a book (unnamed) in which Humes is described as trying to communicate via subtle language; phrases had to be read carefully to discern the true meaning. Rydberg agrees that this characterizes Humes; he believes that in this case Humes was trying to go along, but at the same

---

recalled the details of their acts, they did not appreciate the meaning and effect of their deeds. (Also see *Individual and Collective Responsibility: The Massacre at MyLai*, 1972, edited by Peter A. French.) For me, the chief example of this psychological state in the JFK case is Robert Knudsen, the White House photographer. He told his family that he had photographed the autopsy (though no one saw him there) and he became quite distraught after viewing autopsy photographs, claiming that they had been altered and that he knew who had done it. He was not at home that night, so he himself may well have immediately altered autopsy photographs, possibly accepting the cover story that they needed to be cleaned up a bit – either for the public or for the Kennedys. His friend and fellow government photographer, Joe O'Donnell, recalled for the ARRB that Knudsen had shown him two successive photographs of the back of the head shortly after the event – one with the large posterior hole (that all the witnesses recalled) and the second with the head intact, covered by clean hair (as seen in the extant collection). As in the MyLai case, many of those involved in the JFK cover-up, too, did not understand the full implications of their acts; they simply followed orders. Not knowing they were guilty, they had nothing to confess. Peck makes one final point that bears directly on the JFK case. Warren Commission supporters often argue that the seven honorable Americans on the Commission could not possibly have misled their fellow countrymen. But we know that in the case of the Vietnam war, many respectable Americans tragically misled their country. One has only to read *In Retrospect: The Tragedy and Lessons of Vietnam*, 1995, by Robert S. McNamara, to understand the degree to which this self-deception was practiced at the highest levels of the government. Lyndon Johnson even had ongoing recourse to a group of "Wise Men," an appellation rarely applied to the seven Warren Commissioners. High office, even for honorable men, is no warranty against error.

time trying desperately to save his own reputation. He believes Humes did not want to go down quietly, but left encoded messages to transmit what he could not say explicitly. Rydberg is persuaded that Humes was an honorable man – and so likewise was Boswell, though Boswell, in his view, was the weak link, the one who would have buckled under pressure.

This snapshot of the pathologists is entirely consistent with my own picture of them, as I have sketched it in *Murder in Dealey Plaza* (pp. 283-290). These were competent, honorable men, who earned respect throughout their lives, but on this one occasion they were thoroughly boxed into a corner – checkmated, as Rydberg says. The only other option was to throw away all they had earned during a lifetime in the military. Few individuals would so rashly risk all they had achieved. The pathologists told the truth when they could, but when trapped they went along. Boswell raised the back wound from where he had placed it on his autopsy diagram. Humes radically lowered the trail of metallic debris on the lateral skull X-ray; after all, a correct placement at the top of the skull, coexisting with an entry wound low on the skull (which the pathologists saw and felt) would unambiguously have meant two shots to the head – and unmistakable conspiracy. That was an intolerable conclusion – radically inconsistent with the developing official view. The bullet trail therefore had to be displaced downward by over ten cm. When asked under oath by the ARRB about this incredible discrepancy in his autopsy report (with the disagreeable X-rays staring him in the face), Humes had no explanation whatsoever. In fact, Doug Horne, who was present, advised me that Humes nearly walked out of the interview, so frustrated had he become by that point.

I am not without sympathy for these unfortunate doctors. But they hardly stand alone in infamy. The Parkland doctors, too, changed their statements about the throat wound – even without seeing any new evidence. After merely being told that the official autopsy reported an exit (not an entrance) in the throat they, too, went along.

Doctors (of whom I am one) have no special birthrights of courage – nor even of moral uprightness. For example, by January 1933, before Hitler rose to power, 3000 doctors (6% of the total) had joined the Nazi party By 1942, more than 38,000 were members, about half of the total. It is not, however, only doctors who were subverted by National Socialism. F.A. Hayek (*The Road to Serfdom*, 1944) reports: "The way in which ... with few exceptions, [Germany's] scholars and scientists put themselves readily at the service of the new rulers is one of the most depressing and shameful spectacles ... " Perhaps the lesson is merely one that applies to all of us: we humans are at amazing risk for social pressure.

This is no longer speculation. In 1963, the results of a startling psychological experiment offered proof of this conjecture. A headline in the *New York Times* (October 26, 1963) read: "Sixty-five Percent in Test Blindly Obey Order to Inflict Pain." Stanley Milgram's research at Yale University had shown that the majority of participants willingly inflicted electric shocks up to 450 volts on presumably real (but actually sham) participants who made mistakes on word-matching tests. These participants obeyed only because they were told to do so, not because they were under any specific threats. Later, at the University of San Diego, twenty-three of twenty-four law students told a client (who was only an actress, but the law students did not know this) to perjure herself, merely because law professor Steven Hartwell suggested this presumably authentic legal advice as the only hope for the client. Milgram's experiments demonstrated with frightening lucidity that ordinary humans can be led to act immorally – even without physical threats – and, furthermore, that these humans need not be innately evil to act reprehensibly. While most of us prefer to believe that we would not mislead or distort, as Kennedy's pathologists certainly did, the fact is that Milgram was right: when powerful social constraints enter the scene, our common moral senses become overwhelmed. Milgram specifically warned that when someone joins " ... an organizational structure, a new creature replaces autonomous man, unhindered by the limitations of individual morality, freed of human inhibition, mindful only of the sanctions of authority. " Moreover, Milgram claimed that obedience to authority flowed naturally from the logic of social structures: "If we are to have [a] ... society – then we must have members of society amenable to organizational imperatives."

Milgram's work has had both recreational and serious consequences. In 1973, British playwright Dannie Abse produced a play, "The Dogs of Pavlov," based on Milgram's work. In 1976, CBS aired "The Tenth Level," starring William Shatner as a Milgram facsimile. In 1985, the U.S. Military Academy introduced two new mandatory psychology courses based on Milgram's work. In 1986, musician Peter Gabriel recorded a song, "We Do What We're Told (Milgram's 37)."[3]

M. Scott Peck echoes the same theme heard in Milgram's work:

> Whenever the roles of individuals within a group become specialized, it becomes both possible and easy for the individual to pass the moral buck to some other part of the group. In this way, not only does the individual forsake his conscience but the conscience of the group

3. Interested readers may consult *Psychology Today*, March/April 2002, or www.stanleymilgram.com or the book, *Obedience to Authority: An Experimental View*, 1974, by Stanley Milgram.

as a whole can become so fragmented and diluted as to be nonexistent … any group will remain inevitably potentially conscienceless and evil until such time each and every individual holds himself or herself directly responsible for the behavior of the whole group – the organism – of which he or she is apart.

We have not yet begun to arrive at that point. [4]

I would add one final, personal observation: the higher in the hierarchy someone stands, the more susceptible he or she is to social pressure. The more this individual has to lose – both in prestige, money, and future success – the less likely he or she is to risk such a loss. That the paramedical personnel interviewed for this volume have stood so resolutely by the truth as they saw it on November 22, 1963, while their superiors have offered only half-truths, is clear confirmation of this general principle. We should be particularly grateful for their presence at the autopsy and for their willingness to speak forthrightly about this unnecessarily confusing event. And hats off, too, to Law and Eaglesham for caring so intensely. History is now deeply indebted to them. The case now lies before the bar of history. If we can seek truth in advertising, why can we not have truth in history? Surely our children deserve no less.

David W Mantik MD, PhD
Idyllwild, CA, August 1, 2003

---

4. M. Scott Peck, *People of the Lie: Hope for Healing Human Evil,* 1983, p. 218.

Prologue-2005

This volume of oral history on the aftermath of the Kennedy assassination – as experienced by enlisted men and FBI agents on duty at Bethesda Naval Hospital, where the president's body was taken for autopsy after the events in Dallas Texas, on 11/22/63 – came about as a direct result of my reading David Lifton's book *Best Evidence: Disguise And Deception In The Assassination of John F. Kennedy* (Carrol & Graf, 1988). I had stumbled across it while browsing at a local bookstore at the end of the 1980s. Like most Americans, my interest in the assassination, up until that time, was confined to reading a few books and watching the occasional documentary on TV and wondering whether Lee Harvey Oswald acted alone in shooting the president from the sixth floor of the Texas School Book Depository. Or, in conflict with official history, did he act with others as part of a conspiracy, or was he merely an innocent bystander cornered by circumstances in the wrong place and time?

The one person with the answer – Lee Oswald – was himself murdered at the hand of Jacob Rubenstein, a/k/a Jack Ruby, operator of the Carousel Club, a sleazy strip-joint in Dallas. Oswald was shot while being transferred from the City Hall lock-up to the county jail, walking through the basement handcuffed to a member of the Dallas Police Department, while other policemen and a room full of reporters from around the world looked on in stunned incredulity.

Vice-President Lyndon Baines Johnson became the thirty-sixth President of the United States, and almost immediately formed a panel, later known as the Warren Commission after its chairman Earl Warren, Chief Justice of the Supreme Court, to study the facts behind the assassination and to reach conclusions as to what had happened and why.

The report, issued on September 24, 1964, soon came under attack by citizens across the nation who took the time to study it and its accompanying twenty-six volumes of testimony and exhibits.

Not quite a year after the assassination, David Lifton, a 25-year-old graduate student at UCLA, while on a visit to New York to see his parents, attended a lecture on the Kennedy assassination presented by Mark Lane, one of the first critics of the Warren Report. What Lifton learned from the Lane presentation sent him on his own search for the truth about what had happened to President Kennedy. In studying the report and the twenty-six volumes in detail, he found that testimony by doctors at Parkland Memorial Hospital in Dallas, who first saw the wounds on Kennedy's body, differed greatly from that of the Bethesda doctors who performed the autopsy.

DALLAS VS. BETHESDA

Item: When President Kennedy's body arrived at Parkland, the wound to his head was described as being in the right rear of the skull and roughly two inches by 2¾ inches. "The bones were sprung outward," according to one of the doctors who worked vainly to save the president's life.

Item: When the body was examined at Bethesda Naval Hospital during the autopsy, the wound to the head was described as some four times larger than was observed at Parkland. The hole was huge – approximately six inches across the top of the head, extending from the rear of the skull towards the front – and completely uncovered by scalp.

Item: In Dallas, Kennedy had a bullet wound low in his throat, approximately at the level of the knot in the tie, which was described by nurse Margaret Hinchcliff as, "about as round as the end of my little finger and looked to be an entrance bullet hole." Doctor Malcolm Perry made an incision across the wound in the throat of about three-quarters of an inch to insert a tracheostomy tube to aid the president's breathing.

Item: At Bethesda, the wound to the Kennedy's throat was described by Dr. James Humes, who was nominally in charge of the autopsy, as "6.5 centimeters (i.e., 2½ inches) and had widely gaping irregular edges."

The president's body was placed in a 400-lb bronze Brittania casket from O'Neal's Funeral Home. After a struggle between secret-service agents and local authorities about removal of the president's remains from Dallas, the casket was driven in an O'Neal hearse to Love Field airport and placed aboard Air Force One. When the presidential jet touched down at Andrews Air Force Base near Washington, D.C., the casket was unloaded onto a cargo lift, then placed in an gray navy ambulance and driven to Bethesda Naval Hospital.

Over the years, many theories have been posited as to the circumstances underpinning the assassination, centering mostly on Dallas and on the movements of Lee Harvey Oswald. With the publication of *Best Evidence,* focus shifted. Lifton's discovery of the differing descriptions of the wounds on the body (i.e., Parkland vs. Bethesda) and interviews he conducted by telephone and in person with witnesses in Dallas and Bethesda, caused him to formulate a theory that, briefly, is as follows:

> The casket that was unloaded in public view from Air Force One was empty. At some point, probably during the time when Air Force One was at Love Field and everyone was at the front of the plane witnessing the swearing in of Lyndon Johnson, the body was taken from the casket and hidden in a compartment in the floor of the airplane. Upon arrival at Andrews Air Force Base, while the off-loading of the Brittania casket was the focus of attention, the body was removed from the other side of the plane, out of view of the television cameras, and was taken to an unknown location where a "pre-autopsy" by conspirators altered the body to hide the true direction of the shots that had taken the president's life.

At face value, it is a preposterous theory, and, certainly, I did not wish to believe it. But, Lifton had found a statement in a report filed by two FBI agents, James W. Sibert and Francis X. O'Neill, who were in attendance at the autopsy, and who recorded oral utterances of the attending pathologists. One such utterance included in that report was (paraphrased): "It is apparent that a tracheotomy has been performed, as well as surgery of the head area, namely in the top of the skull."

The only "surgery" done at Parkland Hospital, was the three-quarter-inch incision across the bullet hole in Kennedy's throat, cuts made on either side of the chest for drainage tubes, and cut-downs on the right ankle and left arm for administration of fluids. David Lifton's discovery of the FBI agents' words was potentially explosive – and strong indication that the American people had not been told the whole truth about the events of November 22, 1963.

Just as Mark Lane's lecture had been a turning point in David Lifton's life in 1964, so Lifton's research became a turning point in mine. The core of his conclusions, and his theory of body alteration, originated with verbal accounts of the men who saw, and had their hands on, the body of President Kennedy. Because of the enormity of the theory, I found it hard to accept it at face value and could not help but wonder if Lifton

Author and Mark Lane, 2003.

had slanted what witnesses had to say. In any case, *Best Evidence* ignited a fire in my belly. After reading and rereading it over for the next several years, and reading everything else I could find on Kennedy's assassination, I discovered that other researchers had followed up on Lifton's work. Some agreed with the body alteration theory, some did not. One writer proclaimed that it wasn't Kennedy's body that had been altered, but the autopsy photographs that had been airbrushed or retouched. The Kennedy autopsy photos have a strange history in and of themselves, and I am not sure anyone knows – or will admit to – how they began to float around research circles.

DEALEY PLAZA

There are also claims by some assassination researchers that the 26-second home movie taken of the assassination by Abraham Zapruder, then a 56-year-old clothing manufacturer, has been altered. That was one supposition I was unwilling to accept until I went to Dallas for a symposium on the assassination and was granted an interview by Bill Newman, one of the closest witnesses to the president at the moment of the fatal head shot.

With an easy, down-home manner and an open friendly face, Newman sat behind his desk in his office in Mesquite, Texas, and freely shared his memories of the events of November 22, 1963. He took me through his narrative up to the point where he and his wife and children were standing on the north side of Elm street and heard gun-fire. "And then I can remember that when we were on the ground – I'd like to bring this up if I may – looking back over my shoulder I can remember, I believe it was the passenger in the front seat – there were two men in the front seat – had a telephone or something to his ear and the car momentarily stopped. Now, everywhere that you read about it, you don't read anything about the car stopping. And when I say stopped I mean very momentarily, like they hit the brakes and just a few seconds passed and then they floor-boarded and accelerated on." I said, "But you don't really see that in the Zapruder film." He replied, "No you don't. But that's the impression I'm left with."

At no point in the Zapruder film – known popularly as the "Z-film" – does the presidential limousine come to a stop. Nevertheless, I tended to believe Bill Newman. He was a close witness at the moment of the shot that tore into Kennedy's head. Surely he would be able to tell if the limo stopped or not. If he was right, it forced me to consider the authenticity of the Z-film. If it could be called into question, then so could just about everything else to do with the assassination.

A few days after my interview with Newman, the conference over, I found myself in Dealey Plaza. Also there was author Robert Groden, who had been the first to peak my interest in the Kennedy assassination by showing the Z-film to a nationwide audience on Geraldo Rivera's *Goodnight America* television program in 1975. Groden's enhanced version of Zapruder's home movie was ultimately responsible for the forming of the House Select Committee on Assassinations in 1977, and he served as a consultant to that committee. Next to him was Beverly Oliver Massagee, known as the "Babushka Lady" for the head-scarf she wore as she watched President Kennedy being assassinated through the view finder of her movie camera. At least, Beverly Oliver claims to be the woman who was captured on the Z-film, in long coat and head-scarf; none of the pictures that are in the record of the event clearly shows the woman's face. No one knew who the woman in the photographs was – hence the moniker "Babushka Lady" – until Beverly made the claim in the 1970s. As for the movie she took of the assassination, she claims that two men came to her workplace, identified themselves as FBI agents, and took her film, telling her it would be returned in a few days. Oliver, then a singer at the Colony Club next door to Jack Ruby's Carousel Club, is still waiting for the return of her film. If her story is true, that film could have cleared up myriad questions, but, like so many aspects of the Kennedy case, firm answers seem to be out of reach.

As I stood in Dealey Plaza watching the cars pass along infamous Elm Street and under the triple underpass, feeling the warm Texas breeze in my face, I thought of the events that had brought me to this place, now and forever linked with the legacy of John F. Kennedy. I thought about my interview with Bill Newman, how I had listened as he talked of Kennedy's head being torn apart by a sniper's bullet as the limousine passed directly in front of him, his wife Gayle and their two small children Billy and Clayton: " ... the shots were coming from behind us, directly over the top of our heads ... and then the car stopped."

My thoughts drifted back to the year before, and my first trip to Dealey Plaza. Walking on the grassy knoll, looking at the triple underpass, I heard shots. Boom- boom ... boom. I whipped around, thinking I had been caught in some weird time warp. There was John Kennedy in the blue presidential limo! It took me a second or two to realize that it was a reenactment of sorts of the assassination. For $25 you can ride in an exact replica of the limousine taking the same route President Kennedy did then, complete with a recording of gun-fire after the car passes the Texas School Depository. Startled, I quickly looked around, hoping that others had not noticed how shaken those seconds of unreality had left me. It provided an impression of what some of the Dealey Plaza witnesses must have felt and a real sense of how fast it all took place. A mere six seconds. I could see how witnesses could be confused or mistaken about their particular perception of events. But Bill Newman's words again rang in my ears: " … the shots were coming from behind us, directly over the top of our heads."

It was evening now. Daylight was fading. The globed streetlights blinked on, casting the plaza in a soft eerie glow. Transfixed, I stared at the spot where the thirty-fifth president had taken the final, fatal blow that shattered his dreams – and ours. Despite the warm breeze, I felt chilled. The Texas School Book Depository now loomed in front of me; an archaic specter in the gathering shadows. Had Lee Harvey Oswald shot at President Kennedy from its sixth floor window 34 years before, in an insane desire for infamy? Had he acted with others as part of a conspiracy to take the president's life? Or was he, as he later claimed, "just a patsy?" That building had seen all. Knew all. But held its secrets. I turned my head and looked over my left shoulder at the corner of the picket fence. Bill Newman and his family had been standing at the bottom of the grassy knoll on the sidewalk at the curb, with the picket fence behind them: " … from behind us directly over the top of our heads … "

Zapruder's film is silent, but I've seen and read so many interviews of the survivors in the limousine that I can hear their voices as they slowly roll towards destiny. Nellie Connally points to the triple overpass and says, "We're almost through. It's just beyond that. " Jackie, warm in her winter suit, thinks, "How pleasant the cool tunnel will be." The president is looking to his left, smiling and waving. "Thank you. Thank you very much," he says over and over, surprised at the large turn out, bathed in the smiles, the clapping and cheering of the crowd. Nellie Connally turns to say: "You can't say Dallas doesn't love you, Mr. President." He smiles: "No, you certainly can't."

Kennedy suddenly stops waving. He turns his head towards Zapruder's position and the grassy knoll, a look of puzzlement crossing his features. Speculatively, he has just heard the first rifle shot. Governor Connally also hears the shot, and starts to turn to his right. Kennedy begins to wave again. Connally is unable to see into the back seat, and starts turning to his left. Another rifle shot rings out in the early Texas afternoon. The president's right arm begins to drop. The view of the governor and the president is obstructed as they disappear behind the Stemmons Freeway road-sign. Connally reappears, apparently unaffected, whereas, as President Kennedy reappears, it is clear that he has been hit – his arms are raised, his elbows splayed up and out, his hands at his throat in a protective manner, a so-called football stance. A man standing near the Stemmons sign opens a black umbrella and pumps it up and down as the limo rolls past. Another, standing next to "umbrella man," raises his right arm in a close-fisted salute. At some point another shot is fired, chipping a piece of cement from the curb near the overpass that strikes onlooker James Tague on the cheek. President Kennedy's back is against the seat. Apparently hit from behind by another shot, he is pushed downward and forward. Governor Connally now shows signs of being hit. His right shoulder drops, his cheeks puff out, and his hair becomes disheveled. He screams, "My God they're going to kill us all," falling into the lap of his wife who leans over, hugging him to her. "Be still," she says. "It will be alright."

Kennedy had confronted death several times in his forty-six years upon the earth: childhood illnesses, the sinking of his PT boat during World War II, Addison's disease since 1946, and serious back surgery in 1956. This day, as he sags to his left against his wife, death finally claims him. In an explosion of flesh, bone, and blood, the thirty-fifth president of the United States is transformed from a mortal man to immortal legend.

I closed my eyes tight, willing the image from my mind. There are times when I wish I had not watched Zapruder's film so closely over the years, sometimes frame by frame by frame. That night was one of those times, but it was too late. Its images are now part of me like my own heartbeat.

I knew I could not determine whether Beverly Oliver's story was true, or if Robert Groden's enhanced version of the Z-film showed the true direction of the shots. (Who can forget the courtroom scene in Oliver Stone's film JFK where Kevin Costner in the guise of Jim Garrison has the projectionist – Groden himself – play that terrible moment when John Kennedy's head is struck, knocking him "back and to the left, back and to the left." Nor could I determine if Bill Newman's memories were accurate, or if the autopsy photos are forgeries. I had neither the means nor the expertise. But before I left Dealey Plaza that evening, I decided to delve as deeply as I possibly could into John Kennedy's murder, beginning with the men who had been present at his autopsy.

What I would learn would take me down dark, cobwebbed hallways of an alternative history, not the one that was taught to my generation and is told to our children, but one that is glimpsed only by those who dare to look beyond the official version of the events of that terrible November weekend in 1963.

Dennis David and James Jenkins talking together in February 2015 at Westmont, Illinois

Chapter Five

DENNIS D. DAVID

T he hour was late, the night was black, and, because of night-blindness, I was having trouble seeing the road. By leaning closer to the steering wheel and squinting, I was able to stay on my side of the white line. I hoped my passenger wouldn't notice my difficulty. Dennis Duane David was relating his experiences as an executive for Van DeCamp's foods, and I was trying to pay attention. But my main concern was to get him to central Oregon safely so that I could interview him about his experiences on the evening of November 22, 1963. Dennis's account of what he'd seen that night, 35 years before, was important. He was on the second floor of the "saltshaker" – the aptly named tower above the main entrance of the Bethesda Naval Hospital complex – when through a window he saw a gray navy ambulance pull up. This vehicle carried a bronze ceremonial casket, which by the official, historical account, contained the body of the slain President of the United States, John F. Kennedy.

The critical part of Dennis's story is that, some 20 minutes before, he had supervised a formal detail of seven or eight men as they unloaded a slate-gray metal shipping casket at the entrance to the morgue at the rear of the building. The shipping casket had arrived in a black hearse. Not the standard vehicle that the navy would use for transport, it bore no distinguishing markings. Nevertheless, Dennis had been led to believe that this casket contained the president's body. If his recollections are accurate, there is something dreadfully wrong with the official version of the arrival of Kennedy's body at Bethesda Naval Hospital.

Another reason Dennis David's account is important is that later that evening he typed a memorandum for a government agent to the effect that four bullet fragments had been removed from John Kennedy's head. After the memorandum was typed, the agent took all copies of it along with the carbon paper, removed the typewriter ribbon, and said, "Forget I was here." Dennis had held the pieces of metal in his hand – enough for one bullet, but probably not enough for two – which fits with nothing in the official autopsy report. No fragments large enough to be recognized as bullets were found, at least not according to other members of the Bethesda team I had spoken to, with the notable exception of X-ray technician Jerrol F. Custer. According to Mr. Custer, a whole bullet was found. Again, this points to the official version of the events of the night of November 22, 1963 being less than accurate. The Warren Report makes mention of the removal of just two fragments from the skull.

I had almost missed Dennis at the airport. The plane was early, and, as luck would have it, the arrival gate was at the far end of Portland airport. As I hurried through the terminal, I ran past him, belatedly recognizing him from a photograph. I called his name and he turned around. Standing about 5'9," he is of slight build, what is usually termed "wiry." His strawberry blonde hair, graying at the temples, was parted on the left and worn long enough to cover the tips of his ears. His face was angular, his eyes blue, and he had a mustache that gave him a prominent lower lip. He was in a blue short-sleeved shirt, blue dress slacks, and a pair of shining black dress shoes. "Hello William." The voice was familiar from our many telephone conversations. With a firm handshake and warm greetings, we headed out. And, after a quick bite to eat, we were on the road.

If Dennis was aware of my driving troubles, he didn't show it as I dropped him off at the hotel. The next morning after breakfast, I took him to the local "viewpoint" overlooking the town. I thought it would make a good background for filming with natural light. Since it was early, I hoped we would miss the tourists, which we did, but I hadn't taken into account that the road traffic below us would make so much noise. There were train whistles as an added bonus, and a helicopter passed overhead, making filming disjointed and interfering with the flow of our conversation. We gave up and I took him to my home to go through documents on William Pitzer that he had brought with him, and to continue filming indoors.

William Bruce Pitzer (photo 9) was head of the Audio/Visual Department at Bethesda Naval Medical School, which, with the Naval Hospital, is part of the National Naval Medical Center (NNMC). Dennis maintains that two or three days after the assassination, he dropped by Pitzer's office, and found him bent over a hand-cranked film-editing machine. The movie was of the Kennedy autopsy. Dennis claims he helped Pitzer edit the film. There were black and white photographs also – he assumed Bill pulled them off the film – similar to autopsy pictures that have been published in several books. One of the black and whites was similar to the "stare of death photograph" (see photo 1), but with the difference that a small bullet hole could plainly be seen in the president's right forehead. Such a wound would be in conflict with the Warren Commission finding that Lee Oswald, shooting from the Texas School Book Depository Building behind the president, was the lone assassin. No movie film of the autopsy has seen the light of day.

Lieutenant Commander Pitzer died at the NNMC as a result of a gunshot wound to the head, on October 29, 1966, just months before he was to retire. Two naval investigations and one by the FBI ruled it a suicide, yet there are indications of murder (See appendix two).

One day while pondering how to present the Pitzer section in Dennis David's interview, I received a telephone call from researcher Jones Harris, seeking information on an ancillary subject. During our conversation, he told me that he had interviewed William Pitzer's wife some years earlier. He stated that she had collected insurance money upon the death of her husband. "As you know," he said, "insurance companies don't pay off if you commit suicide!"

I looked up from the Pitzer documents to see Dennis David with my youngest son's red cowboy hat perched upon his head. Here was the "Lake County Informant" – as he was named in a newspaper article in the 1970s – playing with my children, and it was hard to tell who was having the most fun. Although he is the oldest of the Bethesda witnesses I interviewed, he seemed in some ways the youngest. He walked at a pace that I had trouble keeping up with, and he belied his age when I chose to drive him around town in my two-seater soft-top convertible. Obviously having fun, he chided me: "Have you ever had the top down?" For me, this was what it was all about. Getting to know these witnesses to history as people. Living, breathing human beings. Much more than lifeless words from a dusty tome on a shelf.

Dennis Duane David was the fourth of those I interviewed. For reasons of chronology, that interview is presented first.

Law: Mr. David (photo 13), give us a little of your educational background and how you came to be at Bethesda Naval Hospital.

David: I graduated from high school in 1955, and right after that I attended one semester at the University of Illinois. To back up a little, I had joined the Naval Reserve in '54 as a junior in high school when I was 18, or 17, partially because I wanted to go to Korea. My dad said not only "No," but "Hell no!" But he let me join the reserves and, you know, it was a little income, but I didn't have enough money to continue after that first semester.

So I went on active duty in the navy in '56, and after they ran me through the battery of tests they told me I could have any job I wanted as an enlisted man. I asked to go to Hospital Corps School, and they tried to talk me out of it. They said, "You can go into electronics, you can go into nuclear physics, anything." Nope, I wanted to be a corpsman. Primarily because I'd been in pre-med at the University of Illinois. So, I went to Bainbridge, Maryland, to Hospital Corps School, and graduated out of there in December of '56. I went for duty, then, to a naval hospital in Memphis. I was one of the lucky few – right out of Corps School I made HM 3, Hospital Corpsmen Third Class Petty Officer. Which, as an E4, you became almost career-oriented at that time, and I had made up my mind to do so, to make a career out of the navy. They sent me overseas to Morocco, North Africa, and I was stationed over there for thirty months. Then, I came back in July of '61 and they sent me to MAT, or Medical Administrative Tech School, at Portsmouth, Virginia.

There, again, they asked me – I and two other corpsmen who were in the class at MAT school – we had qualified so high on the nuclear test programs they tried to get us to go into submarine medicine and nuclear submarines, which were popular at the time. But none of the three of us wanted to spend six or seven months out at sea, under water, so we turned them down. Then I got orders to go to the Naval Medical School at Bethesda. And, again, because of the schooling, I was selected and made promotion to HM 1 Hospital Corpsman First Class Petty Officer, and was an Administrative Tech.

When I reported there – in my initial work at Bethesda – I worked for the Commanding Administrative Officer George W. Weise. And I was in his office for about a year, until the summer of '62 when they needed a Senior Petty Officer in the correspondence training division. In Commander Weise's office I handled correspondence for the command, typed, maintained the files, that type of general clerical administrative function.

Then, when they moved me over to the correspondence training division, I would take current text books in the field of medicine and read through them, and, usually using a highlighter pen, would highlight the important parts of each paragraph. Then, I would go back and write questions on the areas that were highlighted, which then would be taken and a question booklet would be made up. If a reserve doctor, or a physician in the reserves or civilian practice, or medical corpsmen in the reserves, or active duty doctors – if they wanted – they could write and ask and they could get this correspondence course, could fill it out, either for self-education or for promotional points. The reserve people particularly were required to do so many of these a year to earn retirement points.

The head of the correspondence division was Captain Giaconda R. Saranerio, one of the few female physician captains in the navy at the time. Her immediate assistant would have been an ensign and then I was the next senior, if you will, in that particular division. As a leading Petty Officer, my job would be to make sure that all enlisted people reported in on time and make work assignments for them, what job they were to do, make sure that they did them. On the particular day in question, on the 22nd of November (1963), I was sitting at my desk reading and highlighting a book on hematology, and listening to a local FM station – there was classical music on it – and it was interrupted about 1:15[1] PM to announce that the President had been shot in Dallas. And so, of course, I immediately listened, and then it said he was dead.

Law: What were your feelings at that point?

David: I was crying like a baby. I looked over at the ensign sitting across from me, he'd been doing a crossword puzzle. Tears were running down his face. So I suddenly realized I was too, I was just crying. Both of us just sat there sobbing, crying.

A few minutes after the news, I went up to the next floor and there was a Lieutenant Barb Munroe, who I played bridge with occasionally and who was in charge of the physical therapy classes up there. So I walked in and said, "Kennedy's been assassinated." She turned around and looked at me. She said, "Denny, that's not funny." And I said, "Ma'am, I'm not kidding. Turn on your radio and listen." She did, and then started crying. Then I went back down and just tried – we listened to the radio – and tried to concentrate on work, but I never did do any more work that day, in that respect.

About two o'clock, we got word to set the watch – as a First Class Petty Officer I was on the Chief-of-the-Day list – and to stand my duties. At any military facility the workday, of course, was usually eight to four, eight to four thirty, whatever, but after hours you always had a duty section. These were individuals who maintained the command, primarily for security purposes. In the case of the hospital, if you were on duty in the emergency room you took care of patients who came in after hours. We were not a treatment facility; the hospital took care of that. So, as a duty, our primary purpose was just maintaining security. We were a training institution. At the Naval Medical School, the laboratories, the X-ray facilities, the medical photography facilities were all under our command, and we supported the Naval Hospital with these services. For instance, if a person came in from the emergency room at the hospital after hours and needed X-rays, then one of our people would go down, or they would bring them up to the X-ray department, and we would do the X-rays. In a regular hospital, these services would fall under the command of the hospital. In this particular case, they fell under the Naval Medical School because we trained people who had just come out of medical school in various internships, in the lab or in pathology procedures, et cetera. We also trained enlisted men in laboratory procedures assisting in pathology procedures, making tissue slides, whatever. We also had training in how to take X-rays, various technical methods of doing that – and medical photography.

Law: So, in essence, Bethesda functioned as a training center?

David: Exactly. The title, of course, is the National Naval Medical Center and it is the center point – at least it was at that time – of all navy medicine. The Bureau of Medicine and Surgery, our senior institution, was downtown. But, if you were

1. President Kennedy was shot at 12:30 PM local time, i.e., 1:30 PM EST.

a career person, to be assigned to the medical center was one of the things you needed to move up in the ranks – that was a primary assignment. It was a choice billet, if you will.

Law: Basically, if you were at Bethesda Hospital, you were at the creme de la crime so to speak.

David: Exactly. How I managed to get there … (laughing) but I got there. Even when I was in med school, whenever I was state-side I also went to night school. Because I'd made up my mind I was going to get a college degree one way or the other. It took me 11 years, but I finally did get a Bachelors degree in Health Care Administration. It was a lot of hard work, but in retrospect it was a lot of fun too. I met a lot of people.

Law: Now as I understand it, you were what's termed – on the night of November 22 – Chief of the Day. Can you explain to me what that entails?

David: Every command has a duty section for after hours, and the Chief of the Day would be your senior enlisted man on duty that night. You would have a doctor or an officer who would be the Officer of the Day. Then you would have the Chief of the Day, and then there would be several enlisted people who would be in the duty section. The enlisted men probably would stand one night out of four or one night out of five – Chief of the Day, we stood probably one day out of every fifteen to seventeen days. So, in other words, I might stand the duty twice in one month. It depended on how many First Class Chiefs we had.

On the day of the assassination, the Officer of the Day was Doctor Boswell. And, as luck would have it, I was the Chief of the Day. So, about two to two-thirty, when the word came down from the Commanding Officer's office to set the watch – what then happened – all the people who did not have duty, civilians, everybody attached to the Naval Medical School, all throughout the command – there were seven commands at Bethesda at that time – everybody went home except the duty sections. So then I went over to the Finance Liaison Office in the basement of the main building, where we stood our watches. Doctor Boswell had come down and he and I were sitting there, listening to the radio, on the local news to what was transpiring in Dallas, when the reporter on the news stated that the body of President Kennedy was going to be flown back to Bethesda for autopsy.

Law: Did this surprise you at all?

David: Yes. We didn't expect it. I had no inkling that that might transpire. I looked at Boswell and said, "It's going to be one hell of a night," because the morgue facilities fell under our bailiwick, if you will, under our command. Commander Humes was the head of the laboratories and Lieutenant Commander Boswell was the number-two man. So, when that happened – I went up about twenty or thirty minutes after that, roughly five-thirty – I got a call from my counterpart at the Naval Hospital, Chief Ledbetter, and he said, "Come on up, there's some men that need to talk to us." So when I went up – the Chief of the Day for the Naval Dental School, Chief of the Day Ledbetter for the Naval Hospital, myself, and the Chief of the Day for the Naval Medical Research Unit were there, and the Chief of the Day from the Naval School for Healthcare Administration – when I walked in, there were several men in suits who identified themselves as government agents. I don't remember if they were Secret Service or FBI, but Secret Service is what sticks out in my mind. And they told us that the body of the president was being flown back and then would be brought over to the Naval Hospital or Medical School, if you will, for autopsy. I then went back down to Finance Liaison and informed Dr. Boswell of what the agents had said. At his directions I called Captain Stover (see photo 9), the Commanding Officer, whose response was, "I heard. I'm on my way in. "

Law: Now was Captain Stover a doctor as well?

David: Yes, he was. He was the Commanding Officer of the Naval Medical School, but he was a physician. He said, "David, I'm on my way in. I'll be there in less than twenty minutes." Then I went, and called my duty section over from the barracks, and assigned the various men to whatever – our facilities, outside doors, windows – wherever anybody might come in, I put a guard, if you will, and gave instructions, "No one is to come in unless they're on duty. If you have any problems you get on the horn and call me and I'll come up." And then – and this probably took forty-five minutes – less than an hour – about six-twenty I got a call that said, "Your visitor's on his way."

Law: What did that mean to you?

David: It meant that the president's body was being brought in, that it was going to be arriving. That it would be arriving very shortly – fifteen minutes – and that they needed people to offload the casket. So, I had three men left who were not assigned. They were in the barracks and I called them over, and then I called the Chief of the Day of the Navy Dental School and asked him if he had some men I could borrow. He told me, "Sure. How many?" I told him three would be enough, and he said, "Fine, where do you want them?" And, as I had told my men, I said, "Tell them to report to the loading dock in the back of the morgue, and I'll meet them down there. " As soon as I made those phone calls, I immediately went down to the morgue, then the six enlisted men arrived. We just stood there for five, ten minutes, and about six-thirty, six-thirty-five, a black hearse pulled up and backed up to the jetty. A driver and another man riding shotgun, if you will – riding in the other seat, an attendant – got out and opened the back door, and five or six men in blue suits got out of the back of the hearse. They never identified themselves, I presumed they were government agents of some kind, perhaps Secret Service or whoever. I and the attendant and the driver and my men moved out on the jetty and they kind of pulled the shipping casket out of the hearse, my men picked it up, walked in through the entrance into the passageway there, off the jetty, came in probably ten, fifteen feet, turned to the right and went into the anteroom of the morgue. I stood near the doorway watching. They set the casket down in the middle of the floor and then they came back out, I didn't need them anymore so I told them to go back to the barracks. And the dental students, I told them to report back to the dental Chief and tell him they were back, and I told my men to go on back to the barracks and if I needed them I would call them.

Law: What happened next?

David: While we were standing there, I talked to the driver and I'm sure he was a civilian. He had on a smock, much similar to what we used in the OR [operating room], but their shoes – I don't know why, I guess because it wasn't a military vehicle and because of the way the men were dressed – I assumed they were civilians, the driver and the attendant. The driver told me they had just come up Sixteenth Avenue, across Jones Bridge Road and in the back entrance off of Jones Bridge by the Officers' Club. They came in the back and pulled up to the morgue entrance. It didn't sound strange to me. I didn't question it.

Law: Now you're talking about the morgue entrance at the back?

David: The morgue entrance at the back of the hospital. I went on up to the front of the main building, to the front of the Naval Medical Center, and I stopped on the way to check on my men who were guarding doors to see if they needed to be relieved for obvious reasons, you know – standing in one place or one spot for a long period of time. It was probably five minutes to seven, five after seven, somewhere in that time frame, and I was up on the second floor of the main building, in the rotunda area.

I'd walked over and was looking out at the front of the hospital at the mass of people standing out in front. There is kind of a semicircle drive that comes in off of Wisconsin Avenue then back to Wisconsin Avenue again. Both sides of that driveway were lined with Prince County, Bethesda, Rockville, and Maryland State Police. Motorcycles and cars. Lined up like a huge guard or maybe keeping the people back from coming into the Naval Medical Center building. They were all civilians. That was one of the things that was remarkable. Between the semicircle drive and Wisconsin Avenue there's about, oh, four or five acres of land – and there is a well called the Well of Bethesda that gets its name from when Franklin Roosevelt called it that when they built the Naval Center in the '40s or late '30s – but that was one solid mass of humanity. You could not see a bit of ground. There were people standing shoulder to shoulder, back to back. It was unbelievable. Something you can never forget.

Anyway, when I was looking at this, I saw the flashing red lights of a D.C. police car pull in from Wisconsin Avenue with a gray navy ambulance immediately behind it, and then an entourage of official cars. I didn't count them, but I watched them pull in, they pulled in up to the front of the Naval Medical Center. Mrs. Kennedy got out of the back of the ambulance. Admiral Galloway got out of the driver's side. I presume he'd been driving the ambulance. Some other people got out of some of the official cars – McNamara for one, Bobby Kennedy for another, and some others who I think were Senators.

Law: But you recognized all these people.

David: The ones I've mentioned I recognized.

Law: From your position?

David: Yes. And then I turned around and went back, and was standing immediately across the rotunda, up on the second floor looking down, looking right straight down at the front door when Mrs. Kennedy and McNamara and others came in – Admiral Galloway – and I can still see that dress and the pillbox hat – blood on her dress, on her skirt – and McNamara looking like he could bite railroad spikes in two, the expression on his face. These are some of the things that stick out in my mind the most.

They came across the lobby, went right under where I was standing and into the elevator. Then I turned around and watched the elevator until it hit the seventeenth floor, which was the presidential suite.

Law: So you actually watched the elevator all the way up?

David: All the way up. I didn't see them enter the elevator because where I was standing I couldn't see that far underneath. But they went in and the next thing I know – I see the elevator going up – and I learned later from other sources that yes, they did go to the seventeenth floor. So I'm fairly confident that's who it was. And yes, I watched the elevator until I saw the light click on seventeen. So I knew that's where they were.

Law: Now, the controversy comes in because, as the story goes, you already had unloaded a coffin, or a casket, at the back entrance before the official ambulance pulled up in front. Is this correct?

David: That's correct – exactly what happened. We offloaded a gray casket. A gray shipping casket. The kind that we later used to ship bodies back from Vietnam in. Even civilians in civilian life, they use a similar type of casket to ship bodies, say from state to state. Especially if it's going on the airlines or anything like that. It's just a plain, simple, gray metal box.

Law: Now, officially, weren't all ambulances having to do with official business at Bethesda – weren't they gray?

David: I never saw a navy ambulance that wasn't gray or a military ambulance that wasn't gray.

Law: And so, what color was the vehicle that came to the morgue.

David: It was black. I might also add that all military vehicles had black letters, numbers, if you will. It's really an inventory number you know, depending upon the area, which indicates for inventory purposes the type of vehicle. The black hearse or black ambulance that I saw, had no such markings, and I'm almost certain that I remember seeing a license plate on the hearse. I can't remember whether it was a D.C. plate or a Maryland plate, but a military vehicle would not have had such a plate on it.

Law: So this basically had to be some type of civilian –

David: Yes. I'm positive it was a civilian vehicle. It was not a military vehicle.

Law: What happened at that point – did you see them carry any kind of casket in from the official vehicle at the front?

David: No. As soon as Mrs. Kennedy got out of the vehicle, and, from the front of the driveway, if you will, to the dock of the main entrance of Bethesda, about thirty, thirty-five feet up this set of steps, maybe four or five steps up – you get out on a curb, walk across the side walk – six, eight feet wide – to a set of steps, five or six steps. Then, you walk across a platform, another twenty feet, and then you come to the doors. The gray navy ambulance I saw that she got out of pulled away and went off. See, as I was facing, it would have gone off to my right. Where it went I did not watch, because I turned around and started back. I went and I stood and watched Mrs. Kennedy come in.

After I'd watched Mrs. Kennedy go up to the seventeenth floor, I went on about my duties for the rest of the evening, just checking to make sure that my job as Chief of Security – that people were watching what they were supposed to be. And then also, I would keep a rough log; every command with a duty section would keep a log of events: phone calls, unusual occurrences, whatever, rounds made – all quiet, something to that effect. Some people get a little more fancy than others, go into details, whatever. So, I'd keep a rough log, and then, under normal procedures, after the watch was over, say in the morning, I would write up the log, in the official log, I would write it up, take it to the Officer of the Day, whoever that might be, in this case it was Doctor Boswell, he would have reviewed it. If there were no questions he would have signed off on the log. I would have signed it on one side, he would have signed off on the other. This would then – the next day or in the future if anyone had any questions about any events that transpired that night – they would come and ask, you know, is this what happened? Did you make these entries? See, every command had to do that.

Law: And so did you do that?

David: Yes, I did.

Law: You made your usual log of the events that had happened. Did you mention what you had seen?

David: Yes.

Law: So you put that you had seen a black ambulance/hearse, drive up at the back?

David: Right.

Law: And to your knowledge was this handed over to Doctor Boswell?

David: Yes, the following morning.

Law: Do you know if he signed off on it?

David: Yes he did.

Law: And do you know if it's still in existence?

David: No, I don't. I'm sorry I don't know where it's at. I have no idea whether it's still in existence or not.

Law: You don't know if it was called for by the Warren Commission?

David: I do not. I have no knowledge of it, other than that night.

Law: But you know that you did make one?

David: I know, oh yes, I know that I made one.

Law: This was regular routine for you.

David: It was part of my duties, part of my responsibilities.

Law: All right. So, what happened from the point that you were up on the second floor, what happened after you saw the ambulance drive up and then drive away? What did you do after that?

David: Then I went about, as I said, making sure my log was up to date, and making rounds, periodically checking my people. Seeing if they needed to be relieved to go the bathroom or whatever. About twenty-three hundred, eleven o'clock at night, I was on rounds, down in the passageway outside the morgue. And there was a lieutenant who, I believe, was the Administrative Watch Officer for the Naval Hospital. He was an MSC Officer, he was a Lieutenant Medical Service Corpsman, as opposed to being a physician.

Law: Do you remember his name?

David: No, I do not. He was standing there with a man in civilian clothes and said, "David, do you know anyone who has a security clearance and can type?" And I said, "Yes, I'm an MAT Tech and I'm cleared up through and including secret. " Now an MAT Tech is Medical Administrative Tech, and by definition you'd better be able to type. Anyway, then he introduced me or identified the gentleman with him, and I think it was Sibert, it might have been O'Neill, but I don't remember to this day clearly who it was. But I do remember that he was an official agent of the government. And he said: "Mr. so-and-so needs to have a memorandum typed." The lieutenant asks, "Where can we do it?" I said, "Well, we can utilize the Administrator Officer's office at the Medical School up on the second floor." He said, "Fine." So then all three of us went up there, and the agent put a pill vial down beside the desk and I started to type a memorandum as he dictated it – verbally dictated it to me. It was a memorandum you know, the date and time, to the effect: "To whom it may concern, this date during the postmortem conducted upon the body of President John Fitzgerald Kennedy, the following described pieces of metallic or lead removed from … " – and proceeded to describe four pieces of lead. He then had a signature, and I don't remember what the signature was, and when I completed it, he took it out of the typewriter and he reviewed it and signed it. Then he made sure he had all the copies, and I think two or three copies were made. Then he took the typewriter I was using – it was an IBM typewriter with a use-only-once tape, which he took out of the typewriter. I guess somebody could have taken and unwound the tape and then could have made out what was on the tape because of the way it was typed. And while he was doing that, I picked up the pill vial and was looking at it. He said, "Go ahead, you can look at it." So I poured the pieces of lead out in the palm of my hand.

Law: How many were there?

David: There were four pieces. The exact dimensions – they were about a millimeter thick – one of them was probably two by three millimeters, one was maybe three by four millimeters, one was two to five millimeters – those figures … exactly, I can't remember. There were more particles than would have constituted one bullet, but maybe not enough for two. I know enough about ammunition to know there was more lead there than would constitute one bullet. So, after that I put them back in the vial, capped it, and handed it to the agent. And then, you know, he said, "Thank you for your assistance." He looked at me and said, "Remember this is considered to be classified information. You know what that means?" I said, "Of course I do."

Law: So he didn't say it – the words went unspoken that you were not to talk about this.

David: Exactly. Anybody who is classified for – I had handled classified documents when I was in Commander Weise's office, and when I went back to Captain Stover's office in '64 and '65 when they moved me up again and I worked with the Commanding Officer – I knew that if you were handling classified documents or if you were in possession of classified information, you did not tell anybody, unless it was authorized to be released. And then only if the person was qualified to get that information – and you had to be damned sure that he was qualified. In other words, you just didn't walk out and say, "Hey, I just read this document. " You didn't say anything unless you had it in writing that this could be released or you had authority to. Now, of course, if my commanding officer would come in and say, "Dennis did we get a classified document such and such? Well, what did it say?" Well, obviously you know, I could tell him because he was the Commanding Officer.

Law: What would have happened to you had you, just as scuttlebutt, said: "Guess what I did tonight?" And that would have gotten out? What would have happened?

David: If someone had overheard it? I could have been brought up on charges – could have been court-martialed and, depending, could have gotten anything from a slap on the wrist to spending a little time in Kansas, in prison (chuckles).

Law: How did it feel to dump this pill vial? Did you have any kind of feeling as you were holding these fragments? What was that like?

David: I remember it seemed a little weird. I don't remember exactly what I thought, but just looking at them – you know, I really don't remember. I was probably depressed, and thinking, "You know, so this is what did the deed," or something like that. Exactly how I felt, I don't remember.

Law: What happened after the agent took the pill vial with these pieces of metal and the typewriter ribbon and the memorandum?

David: We walked out, then he and the lieutenant went downstairs. We all three did. We walked back down to the basement and then they headed to the back, I presume. I could be wrong, but I presume they went back to the morgue area. I don't know. I went to the Finance Liaison Office and made a notation in the log as to what had transpired. I did not log typing the memorandum.

Law: You didn't? You left that out of there?

David: It was classified information. And that log is not classified.

Law: Anything that would be classified you could not put in an ordinary log?

David: I could not do that, no. So, I just made an entry. I don't remember exactly, but I made an entry, probably something like: "Rounds complete. All secure." Something of that nature.

Law: And then what happened from that point?

David: Again, I just continued the rest of the night making rounds. About two in the morning, I went into the geedunk, which is navy lingo for snack-bar.

Law: Okay.

David: (laughter) Don't ask me where the term geedunk comes from, but it's old navy. I got a cup of coffee and went over and sat down with some other enlisted men, and obviously we were discussing the events of the night.

Law: And what do you recall from that? Do you remember anything specific?

David: (animated) Yes, one man said something. "Hey, did you know there were two caskets?" … "Yes, wonder why?" … "Well I heard for security purposes. They were afraid someone might try to kidnap the body." The other guy says, "Well, yes. See all those people out front? I heard it was to avoid all the crowds; all those morbid assholes out there." And that's the term that was used (chuckles), and perhaps you don't want this to be recorded but, you know, that's exactly the way we talked about it. And another guy says, "They brought a brain in through the emergency room of the Naval Hospital – it was in a pan and they put it on a gurney covered it with a towel and took it down towards the morgue."

Law: Now, do you remember who this was?

David: No, I don't. Just one of the comments.

Law: But he said he knew that this had happened, or he said that he heard it?

David: Yes. He said, "Have you heard?"

Law: So there were all kinds of rumors floating around that night?

David: All kinds of rumors.

Law: And with the men there, you – the enlisted personnel – you were tossing back and forth these stories or rumors about what had happened – you were overhearing and sharing with each other.

David: Right. Exactly. It was just a gossip session if you will, about the things going around. Yeah.

Law: And so, as things transpired through the night, did you continue with your duties or did anything special happen after that?

David: After that I made rounds yet again and finally, ah, I think about four-thirty I finally went to the room that we had where we could go to bed. I remember all I did was take off my jumper, kick off my shoes, and laid down on the rack, and literally passed out. 'Cause I was beat. I guess about six-thirty, one of the men woke me up and I went in and checked the log over, made any corrections that were necessary and got the log ready. About seven-thirty or so, Dr. Boswell came down and took the log and went up to Captain Stover's office at eight o'clock, because at the end of every shift once the log was done, you took it to the Commanding Officer. He may read it or not, but you make your report of things that were going on.

Law: There's a story about a man named Bill Pitzer, and I'd like you to go into that a little. I want you to tell me who Bill Pitzer was, what your relationship was with him, and what you saw one to two days after the assassination of the president.

David: When I came out of the Corps School in '56, my father had asked if I was going to make a career in the navy and I said, "Yes, sir, but I'm not going to retire as a white hat. " Meaning I was going to become a commissioned officer, and I told him what steps I was going to take to achieve that.

When I got to Bethesda, I had achieved being First Class, and in the Naval Medical Service, as a First Class or a Chief, you could apply for a commission as a Medical Case Service Officer in the Service Procurement Program. They had a program where you take a series of tests, physical, personal, and interviews. If you were lucky – and God knows, I was – you would have some of the MSC officers who would take a liking to you and would help you. I had four who were basically my mentors. Lieutenant Commander Bill Pitzer (photo 9) was one of those, and at that time, in '63, '64, '65 and '66, he was head of the Audio-Visual Department of the Naval Medical School and, as such, made training films that were utilized to train fleet marine force corpsmen – navy corpsmen, chaplains, and dental techs from the navy, supporting the Marine Corps – if they don't have that type of individual in their own command. Bill, as I said, was head of the Audio-Visual Department and was one of my mentors – and I would stop in two, three, four times a week, and ask him questions, and he would tell me, "Okay now, study this, or study that." And sometimes he would question me and say, "Well, maybe you should bone up on this area." In other words, helping me to become an MSC officer.

Law: What's an MSC officer?

David: Medical Service Corps – the administrative people in the Naval Medical Service. The physicians treat the patients, and the Medical Service Corps people make sure they've got supplies and the assistance – usually the head of the personnel departments, the patients' affairs departments – we make sure that the records are maintained and that the doctors have the supplies to accomplish what they needed to do.

Also, Lieutenant Commander Munroe – who was a physical therapist and also an MSC officer – Bill Pitzer and myself and the physical therapist used to play bridge together at noon damn near every day. Bill was not only my mentor, but he was also a good friend. A very good friend. A couple, three days after the assassination – I don't remember if it was Monday, Tuesday, Wednesday – it was two or three days after – I stopped in to see Bill about something about the MSC exams that would be coming up – and, again, I just walked in. He was working on a sixteen-millimeter film, and on his desk he had some black and whites, some color photos and some thirty-five-millimeter slides. All of these were from the autopsy. There was, you know – one of them I recall was – I saw years later – was the so-called death-stare photo of President Kennedy on the table at the morgue.

Law· Now, these are pictures.

David: These were pictures. They were black and whites, and colored.

Law: So he actually had these with him?

David: Yes he did. And he was editing a film, a sixteen-millimeter film. I watched him do several reels. I got the impression that he was pulling some of the frames off of the film to make slides with. I could be wrong. You know, I helped him. And, you know, watched some of these. We were looking at various aspects, and we made some comments. Number one, it was our distinct impression – impression, hell, it was our opinion, actual opinion – that the shot that killed the president had to have come from the front.

Law: And why do you say that?

David: Because we both noted a small entry wound here (points to the right side of his forehead) from another photo, and a large exit wound back in this area (indicates right rear of head). I had seen gunshot wounds before, and so had Bill. I've seen a lot of them since, and I can assure you that it definitely was an entry wound in the forehead.

Law: Now I'm going to hand you a picture, the "stare-of-death" photograph (photo 1). Is this the picture that you remember seeing with Bill Pitzer?

David: Very similar, except that it seems to me that there was more to it – the camera seemed to be at an angle like this (indicating a right-profile perspective). What I saw, there seemed to be more of a ninety-degree shot to it. But there was a small hole that looked like an entry wound. It was about the size of the tip of my finger. Maybe a little over a quarter of an inch, five-sixteenths of an inch in diameter. It was located right in this area right here (indicates a point at the hairline above the pupil of the right eye).

Law: Now, is there anything else about that picture that looks different? Does it look about the same?

David: I don't recall seeing this (neck wound) at the time. I may have. But I do know one comment that has been made about this is that if that was supposed to be a tracheotomy incision, it was a Goddamned sloppy job! Because, I had done tracheotomies – I am not a physician – but I did a tracheotomy on a young lad in Memphis in 1957, it was the first time I ever did one, in the back of an ambulance – and I sure as hell didn't need a two-and-a-half-inch diameter incision! Besides, the incision should have been vertical to get into the cartilage so that the trach tube could be inserted.

Law: Would you say that that's a big tracheotomy?

David: That's a very large tracheotomy.

Law: You wouldn't normally see that?

David: No.

Law: If you were doing that, you wouldn't do it like that?

David: No I would not have done it like that.

Law: You were at Bethesda. Were you ever in the morgue itself?

David: I was only in the morgue perhaps two or three times. This bothers me a little, because I don't ever remember seeing anything like that there.

Law: You're pointing to what Paul O'Connor would refer to as "a wooden structure" (photo 1b).

David: It's some kind of a structure, but I don't know what it is. I don't remember seeing that.

Law: That wasn't in the morgue that you can recall?

David: No.

Law: Looking at the floor, does that look like the morgue tile?

David: William, I can't remember. I –

Law: I know I'm asking you to remember from a very long period. What about the forehead itself? Did it look like that from what you recall from the film and the pictures that you saw?

David: It didn't seem to be as clean.

Law: Was there damage to the forehead that you can recall?

David: Well, again, the picture that I remember seeing really was kind of more of an angle … the right eye seemed to be a little more prominent than it is here in this picture.

Law: More prominent as to what?

David: Protruded.

Law: So it was popped.

David: You could say that.

Law: Okay.

Dennis David, September 2002.

David: But this one seems to be almost in a natural position.

Law: All right. So maybe there were some differences then?

David: Yes. Some differences between this photo and the one that I saw on Bill's desk, and on the film…. And also, I might add that this area back here, that is so shadowy? (motioning with a ballpoint pen in the right rear area of Kennedy's head) I don't recall that. You could clearly see the outline of the skull, of the head.

Law: So then it was a clear – ?

David: Much clearer picture.

Law: It wasn't as dark?

David: No, it wasn't nearly this dark.

Law: I'm going to show you a series of autopsy photographs now.

David: Okay.

Law: Just for clarification, to see if they are anything like what you remember. I believe that's a shot of the cranium (photo 5).

David: I don't ever recall seeing this.

Law: How about this next one (photo 4)?

David: Let's get this thing in perspective. Again, I presume that this is a flap of scalp or something (above the right ear). The picture that I saw, it would have been back more in this area, the exit wound (points to the rear of the skull behind the right ear).

Law: Did this particular picture look anything like what you remember?

David: No.

Law: What is different about this picture?

David: Number one, this – whatever it is – looks like a flap of scalp or something (circles the flap of scalp above the right ear) is protruding. There was more of a gaping hole back in this – about … oh, about that wide, two to two and a half inches wide by maybe an inch or an inch and three quarters – not a rectangular hole, I mean it was kind of blown out (points to the lower portion of the back of the head).

Law: Right. How about that little speck down there at the bottom (photo 4a)? Some have said it was an entrance wound, some have said it was a piece of brain matter. Did you see that on the photograph?

David: I don't recall. I don't recall, William.

Law: Can you tell me anything else about this photograph you might find interesting?

David: The hand that's holding it up. Be nice to know whose hand that is.

Law: But basically, you're telling me there was a defect back there?

David: The picture that I saw – I don't know whether I remember the hand being there – but, the picture I saw – that Bill had – showed a hole. This almost looks to be slightly forward of the right ear. My recollection of what I saw – the exit wound – was more to the rear of the right ear. Behind it, not forward of it.

Law: This next one (photo 3) – what can you tell me about it, and was it one of the ones –

David: Now this is closer to what I remember seeing.

Law: Now I notice you said closer. Is there something different about –

David: I don't remember seeing all this matter down there (pointing to the shredded tissue hanging down). It may have been cleaned out or something. But, there was more – the head was held up more. The shot – this looks like it's almost a direct head-on view. But this is the area – in this area – is where I remember seeing the gaping exit wound.

Law: Okay, so –

David: This looks like bone. Apparently brain tissue or something in there.

Law: Was that small metal table there? Do you remember that?

David: I don't remember this, no. I don't remember this (head) support here.

Law: Again, how about the small metal table over the body do you remember that? I know I'm asking you to remember an awful lot.

David: I can't remember that or whether they ever used such an apparatus at the morgue, I don't know. But I don't believe the morgue table at Bethesda was equipped with this type of headrest.

Law: How about the background of the photograph? It seems to be awfully dark. Do you remember if it looked like that? Was it dark in the background?

David: I can't remember, William.

Law: That's fine. How about this photograph (photo 6)?

David: I remember seeing something similar to this. One of the pictures that I saw, that Bill had, was very similar to this. It showed – they have it encircled here (pointing to the back wound) – the head was more – the head seems to be craned back, the one I saw was almost on a flat level as though he were laying flat looking down. That's why –

Law: Show me on your own head again.

David: You could see the entrance wound here. That's what I am talking about – you could see the wound that was back here (takes his pen and encircles the lower rear portion of his own head).

Law: Okay. Back in this area.

David: Again, I don't remember seeing the hands or anything like that. And I may well have, but this looked like an entry wound also (pointing to the back wound, photo 6a, arrow A).

Law: But you do remember that being there?

David: Yes I do.

Law: Okay, and this last one (photo 2). Is that anything like what you recall?

David: I did not see this picture, no.

Law: You didn't see that picture.

David: Seen it many times since.

Law: But at that particular time in '63, no?

David: This was a view of the left side of the head. There, again, this headrest is, you know – but, I was never in the morgue – I was not a pathology tech and was never in the morgue that often – maybe two, three times in my life have I ever been in there. This may well be a part of it, but I don't recall ever seeing it.

Law: Okay. Now you've had a chance to look over the pictures. As the story goes, you went in and saw Bill Pitzer.

David: Right.

Law: And he had film that he was editing and he also had some pictures on his desk. Would you say that these photographs show basically what you saw?

David: They were similar.

Law: They were similar, but there were not exactly the same.

David: Not exact. They were similar pictures. They were clearer, more definitive, which is the reason Bill and I came to the conclusion that he'd been shot from the front.

Law: So, they actually showed – did they show, like, a hole?

David: Yes.

Law: Did they show an entrance? Point to your own head and tell me where you think –

David: Right about there. Just slightly to the back of the eye. If you drew a line straight from the corner of the eye and came back about maybe a half-inch, right in this area. Almost in the hairline. As I said it was about as big as the end of my finger like that. Just like that. Right in that area there (pointing to the extreme right side of his own forehead at the hairline).

Law: What did he say as he was editing this film. Do you remember any of the conversation?

David: Oh, not exact words, no. Comments, you know: "That looks like an entrance wound." "Yeah, like the one I saw in Morocco where the kid was shot with an M-l. Like he was shot right here, just below the breast plate (pointing to his chest). I couldn't put my finger into it, but where it came back out here, I could put both fists in it."

Law: Okay.

David: That type of thing. And then again when I was in 'Nam, I saw a lot of gunshot wounds, and so on. There's absolutely no question in my mind that that was an entry wound up here (again pointing to the right side of his own forehead).

Law: So what did Bill Pitzer say? Did he tell you that he took this film?

David: No.

Law: He didn't tell you that?

David: I never asked him. He was head of the Audio-Visual Department. I just assumed he had done it, he had taken it.

Law: So that would have been part of his duties.

David: It could have been, yes.

Law: Did he tell you how this transpired?

David: He just said that he was editing and kind of, in a round about way, that it was to be used partly for the investigation into the death, for autopsy studies you know, as back up to the autopsy – whatever. Exactly what he said, I don't recall. It was just light conversation about it. Remarking upon the extent of the injuries – what size of a weapon would have made that kind of a hole – you know, whether it would have been a hollow point, or whether it would have been a solid jacketed bullet, or what. And neither he nor I were ammunitions experts, so a lot of it was just guesswork and supposition on our part.

Law: Do you remember a Y-incision?

David: I don't recall seeing a picture that Bill had that showed a Y-incision, no.

Law: How about on the film itself?

David: No.

Law: How was he editing this?

David: With a little monitor and a hand-crank. You could crank it and you could advance it. The faster you cranked it the faster it went, but you could crank it slow enough that you could do one frame at a time.

Law: Did you notice anybody – movement of people. Did you see anybody in the background that he filmed?

David: Yes, in some of the pictures, faintly in the background. Bear in mind you're looking at sixteen-millimeter film and the viewing screen has perhaps three by five or two and a half by three inches, something like that – about that size – and till you put it on a projector where you could blow it up on a large screen, you could see what looked like figures in the background – ah, not that I could identify any of them, no.

Law: Did he mention that anybody had tried to stop him from taking film?

David: No, he did not say anything to me.

Law: He didn't say anything about "no camera." See, there's a story that, at some point, some film had been taken away from someone. Just out of the peripheral vision of these fellows.

David: I heard about that later, yes.

Law: But you didn't know that he was the one that –

David: No, I do not. And again – because of Bill's position – I logically assumed that he had taken the pictures. He may not have, but, at that time, I just assumed that he did. I never did say, "Yes he did," or "No he did not take them."[2]

Law: What happened to Bill Pitzer?

---

2. Sometime after my interview with Dennis David, David Lifton confided that the story was true and the person who had had his film confiscated was medical photographer Floyd Riebe.

David: As I said, Bill was one of my mentors – and I took the program for MSC in '64 then – starting early '61 – and missed it. They selected forty – I was forty-third on the list. In 1965 I applied for and took the program again. And there were sixty selected that year, and I was number two on the selection list. So then, in late August of '65, Congress passed the bill and the president signed the bill, and I became an officer and a gentleman (laughter). I used to laugh about that because I used to say, "Well, they made me an officer, but my mother made me a gentlemen." At least I tried to be, before that. I left Bethesda in the first week in December of '65 to go to Officer's School and Naval Justice School in Newport, Rhode Island. And shortly before I left, Bill indicated to me that he was getting ready to retire – probably in '66 – and he would have had, I think, thirty years at that time. He had been through the second world war for one thing. So I left, and reported in at Newport, Rhode Island, in the early part of January.

I went through the three weeks at Officer's Training School and Naval Justice School, and was assigned to a naval hospital in Great Lakes – one of the jobs I had there was as an assistant to one of the department heads. I was in the lobby of the hospital at Great Lakes when Lieutenant Commander Barb Munroe came in and saw me and came over, and of course we renewed old friendships. And she said, "By the way, did you know Bill's dead?" And I said, "No, what happened?" Then she said, "Well, he shot himself." I said, "I don't believe that." And she said, "Well they found him with a gun in his right hand, and he blew his brains out." And I said, "But Bill's left-handed … " That's what I recall, because sometimes – back at Bethesda, Barb, Bill, and I would play bridge together – he sometimes would deal the cards in reverse, you know instead of dealing them clockwise he would deal them counter clockwise (with his left hand) and we'd kid him about it.

That was the first time I had heard he was dead. I asked, "Well, why did he commit suicide?" And she said "It's highly questionable that he did." I said, "Well, it stands to reason." And then she said something to me about, "Did you know that he'd had some pretty good job offers?" And I said I had, and that just before the last time I'd seen him, just before I'd left Bethesda, he'd told me that he had some very lucrative offers from a couple of the national networks like ABC, CBS, to go to work for them. I said, "I suspect it was probably because of some of the films and the material he had from the assassination." She said, "You know he had those?" And I said, "Yes, because I was over there a couple, three days after the autopsy and saw them." She kind of nodded her head as though she agreed with me, or something like that.

Law: Did she apparently know that he had the film?

David: I don't know whether she did. She seemed surprised when I told her that I knew about it though. Now whatever that was – the reaction – that was the first time she heard … we really didn't discuss it too much after that, because even in '67 – excuse me, in '66 May or June[3] – you still didn't talk about what you

3. Lieutenant Commander Pitzer died October 29, 1966.

knew, your experiences on the night of the assassination. It was still classified information.

Law: It's not so unusual that somebody would commit suicide. It happens every day. Why do you feel that Bill Pitzer would not have done this?

David: Because I knew the man. You can say well, he wasn't the type to commit suicide. Well, what type will commit suicide? I don't know, it was just a gut feeling.

I didn't think that he would do it. He had been through too many stressful situations in his life. Second World War – he had been in and out of Vietnam for various and sundry reasons – dealing with classified information and I didn't think – you know, he was not a weak personality type, or type of person who would ever run into anything he couldn't handle, whether it be stressful or whatever, mental. I knew he had some problems with his kids, but he generally had a "well you know it will work itself out" attitude towards that. So I don't know. I just didn't feel like he was the kind of man who would commit suicide.

Law: Did you ever talk to his wife about it?

David: No. Enlisted and officer don't really socialize – at least back in those days – don't socialize that much. I had met his wife at a Med School picnic one time, but only enough to say, "How are you Mrs. Pitzer? Nice to know you." That type of thing. I did talk to her later, around '94, but that was only the second time in my life I'd ever talked to her.

Law: Did you ever discuss it?

David: In '94? Yes.

Law: And what were her feelings? Did she tell you anything about the way she felt?

David: She was being pressured or being pushed by some investigators and researchers at that time, but she did not want to push the government to release the information on Bill's death.

Law: As I understand it she had trouble just even getting the death certificate.

David: To my knowledge the first time she ever received a copy of the death certificate – or autopsy report – was in '92, '93, largely due to the efforts of (author) Harrison Livingstone after I had talked with him in '89, '90, '91. I had told the reporter from the *Waukegan Sun* back in the '70s and David Lifton. And other researchers have always brought up Bill Pitzer's name, but Livingstone was the first one who really attempted to find out more details, if you will, about it. He contacted Mrs. Pitzer. In fact, it was through him and Rick Russo that I got Mrs. Pitzer's number. I called her and told her who I was. I think she remembered me at least she seemed to indicate so. And we talked about it, because in '90 – well, I had given the story to a number of researchers and Rick Russo called me – we were in Pittsburgh in '92 and for a hypnotic regression a year or so after that.

One night I'm sitting there, having a cup of coffee about nine or nine-thirty at home in the kitchen, and the phone rings and my wife answered and she said, "It's Rick Russo." I picked up the phone and he asked, "Are you sitting down?" And I said, "Yes." He said, "I just completed going through a little seminar here in Chicago on the assassination." And he said, "I walked out and a man walked up to me and he asked, 'Have you ever heard of a man named William Pitzer?'" And Rick said, "I looked at him because that name had not been mentioned or even brought up in the seminar." And Rick said, "Yeah, I've heard it. In fact I know a good friend of his." And the man said, "Well, I know who killed him." And Rick kind of says to me, "Are you all right?" Well I wasn't … but then he proceeded to tell me: "The guy didn't give me any names, but he told me the name of somebody who could."

So then, a few weeks later, Rick called me back and he said, "There's a Lieutenant Colonel Dan Marvin who says that in the early part of the summer of '66 he was asked by a man who identified himself as a CIA agent to assassinate William Pitzer."[4] I said, "I want the man's name and phone number," which he gave to me. And then he told me – Rick told me – that he had talked to Lieutenant Colonel Marvin who had insisted that he had turned it down. But there was another man who had been called out of class (at Fort Bragg, NC) at the same time, and after he (Marvin) had turned the job down, the CIA man then went over and talked to the other man. He (Rick Russo) told me that Marvin had said, "Now I don't know whether he took the job or whether he did it, or whether he (the CIA agent) even talked to him about it. All I know is that he talked to me and he went over." And so I contacted Colonel Marvin.

Law: Now for the record is this Dan Marvin?

David: Yes, this is Colonel Marvin, Dan Marvin (holding up a newspaper with Marvin's picture). He was a Green Beret.

Law: So let me ask you a question: If "Bill Pitzer committed suicide" is the official version, why would somebody offer this man a contract to kill this man?

David: Because he didn't commit suicide. Exactly right. It just doesn't make sense.

Law: What happened to Bill Pitzer's film? What's the official line on Bill Pitzer?

David: The official line is that Bill Pitzer was never in the autopsy room and that the film never existed. No government agency has told me that, but researchers who I have told my story to later on got back with me and said that, when they asked officials about it, Pitzer was never even in the morgue, he never took the pictures, the films don't exist, they were never taken.

Law: So, in essence, what we're hearing from the government is this never happened to begin with.

4. According to Lieutenant Colonel Marvin, he met with a CIA agent in early August, 1965.

David: Exactly right. Total denial.

Law: Would it surprise you to know that I did an interview some months ago back with Jerrol Custer, and he told me that he knew what Bill Pitzer looked like and Bill Pitzer was in the morgue and that he was taking film. (However, see footnote 6, page 259).

David: I think you can recall my reaction when you first called me and told me about that. I damn near cried. In fact I did cry. Because it was – really everything that I have ever told anyone about my experiences with the assassination committee and Bill Pitzer – everything had been corroborated except for that one little thing. And that completely corroborated everything that I had ever told anybody. I was not making things up out of my head. This is what happened. This is the way it went.

Law: This is the real reason you keep doing this isn't it?

David: Exactly right. I would like to see the man responsible – and I don't think Dan Marvin did it – I would like to see the man who killed Bill Pitzer brought to trial.

Law: So this is the real reason you keep going through this isn't it?

David: Yes, it is.

Law: It's really the reason you are talking about this, isn't it?

David: Yes, it is, very much so. Very much so. And, if he's ever identified and brought to trial, rest assured I'll be in the front row of that courtroom every God-damned day!

Law: Is there anything for the historical record that you would like to tell me?

David: Well, I had an opportunity to go out and talk with Dan Marvin in February (1998). I might also add that after I initially contacted Dan, he sent me a copy of official letters, orders – official orders which showed his name and further on down the list, a name of the individual he says was also called out by the CIA and asked to do this. We went back and asked for the current address of this gentleman and the army said no such man exists or ever existed, even though we've got a set of official orders here, name, rank, serial number, no such man ever existed. Eighteen months after we contacted the army on that, and this was about a year ago, we found out that this lieutenant docs exist. He is now a practicing physician living in Salt Lake City, Utah, and denies everything.[5] Refuses to talk to Dan Marvin or anybody else about it. At least that's what I'm told.

I don't know what else to tell you. That brings me to today, really – talking to you and the opportunity to help write a book that tells exactly from my words

5. Then-Captain David V. Vanek, the individual under discussion, resides in Idaho. Although he went through Special Forces training at Fort Bragg, NC, he has denied knowing Marvin or that he was solicited by a CIA agent to terminate William Pitzer.

and Paul O'Connor's words and Jim Jenkins – and you can hear it straight from the horse's mouth. I know Paul and Jim and some of the others have testified before the committees. I've never been contacted by an official government agency except for the Assassination Review Board and all I wanted was to provide them with any documentation I had, and, unfortunately, I don't have anything in writing, or pictures or anything. All I have is my memory and you know I'm not senile yet. (laughter)

Law: Tell me about – somebody sent you a death certificate of Bill Pitzer?

David: I have a copy of the death certificate and a copy of the postmortem proceedings, which was sent to me by Harrison Livingstone.

Law: You told me a strange little thing about that. Can you relate that?

David: There's another gentleman, Allan Eaglesham, who lives in Ithaca – and he had worked with Dan Marvin and Robin Palmer in putting an article in the *Fourth Decade* publication, and when I was in Ithaca, New York, in February this year, I spent some time with him. In October of 1997, Allan obtained, from his own sources, a copy of William Pitzer's autopsy report bearing the name of Pierre Finck on the cover page:

Law: Finck?

David: Lieutenant Colonel Finck – one of the pathologists for the JFK autopsy. It's rather strange.

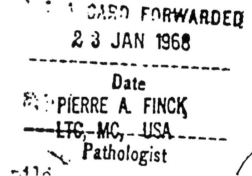

Law: There exists a copy of the autopsy report on William Pitzer that is stamped with Colonel Pierre Finck's name?

David: Exactly. Yes, that's exactly right. Something strange. It's intriguing to say the least. Interesting.

Law: Well, Mr. David, I appreciate your time.

David: It's been my pleasure.

Law: Thank you very much.

David: You're welcome, sir.

Chapter Six

PAUL K. O'CONNOR

P aul Kelly O'Connor was a 22-year-old medical corpsman stationed at
Bethesda Naval Hospital on November 22, 1963. On that particular
night, he had duty in the morgue; as fate would have it, he was in a
position to serve history well.

O'Connor first worked in a mortuary at the age of 13, for Mr. V.L. Poindexter. In correspondence, he explained: "I did anything and everything a
young kid could do. I washed hearses and ambulances, and anything else that
needed cleaning. I went on ambulance runs to car wrecks, and saw people who
had been injured or killed. Mr. Poindexter taught me about death. He was a
stern man, and expected you to do what you were told. " O'Connor worked
in another funeral home before graduating from high school in 1959. He enlisted in the U.S. Navy, saw duty at Guantanamo Bay, Cuba, and came close to
being involved in the Bay of Pigs fiasco. With his platoon, he was awaiting the
order to invade when President Kennedy canceled the action.

After his overseas stint, he re-enlisted and applied for duty at the Clinical Laboratory and Blood Bank School at the National Naval Medical Center
at Bethesda, Maryland, of which the Naval Hospital and Medical School are
part. "I was one of only fourteen selected from the whole hospital corps," he
wrote me in 1998. "It was one of the most prestigious schools in the navy.
Eighteen months of long, hard study – our class was broken up into 24-hour
duty units. Every day we attended school from 7:30 AM to 5:00 PM, except
weekends, then work duty from 5:00 PM to 6:00 AM the next day. It was rough
trying to study and do the duty watch. My partner and I were assigned to the
pathology department, and we assisted in fifty to sixty autopsies before November 22, 1963. And then our lives were changed forever."

O'Connor's experience in funeral homes from a young age and his
duty in the navy working as a physician's assistant in the field, enabled him
to keep his head and pay close attention to events as they unfolded in the
Bethesda autopsy room on the evening of the assassination of President
Kennedy. He opened up a literal Pandora's box for assassination research-

191

ers when he went public with his testimony in 1980, revealing that not only did the president's body arrive at the morgue in a shipping casket, but that removal of the lid of the casket revealed a body bag. O'Connor told researcher David Lifton: "You know, a crash bag, like they brought bodies home in from Vietnam. " This was in stark contrast with the description of how the body had been prepared for removal from Parkland Memorial Hospital in Dallas.

Mr. O'Connor was one of the people I most wanted to interview. I contacted him at his home in Florida. The rich baritone voice I recalled from David Lifton's *Best Evidence* video (Rhino Home Video, 1990) and *The Men Who Killed Kennedy* (A&E Home Video) came on the line. After introducing myself and explaining the project that I had in mind, O'Connor told me with a chuckle, "I don't have much to do with the Kennedy assassination anymore. I've retired. I've got all my papers and documents in a box up in my attic. " It took more phone calls over several weeks to convince him to come out of his self-imposed "retirement. "

* * *

I stood back from the debarking throng, and waited until I was sure it was he. "Paul," I said. With a smile, he offered his hand. "Well, Bill Law! I was wondering where you were." Standing about six feet in height, his grip was firm and his face was adorned with brown-framed glasses and a short-cropped graying beard. His hair was cut not unlike in the military picture I had seen of him taken circa 1963. He was dressed casually in a blazer, polo shirt and jeans. I had read that he had been wounded in Vietnam, his back painfully injured. As he stood before me, I could see he was in some discomfort, and as we waited outside the terminal building for our car, he placed his hand on his lower back to stretch and find some relief. During the drive from the Portland airport to Central Oregon, Paul kept my brother- in-law, Robert White, and I entertained with tales of his time as a deputy sheriff in Florida after being medically retired from the navy.

The next morning over breakfast, I invited his opinions on some of the books he'd been interviewed for over the years. "David Lifton was a ground breaker, although I don't agree with all he wrote." I asked if Lifton had quoted him correctly in *Best Evidence* (Carroll & Graf, 1988). "Yes, he did. One thing he did – I didn't know of at the time – when he first called me, he tape-recorded our conversation without telling me, and put it in his book. I felt he made me sound silly, how I described the casket and all. I like Robert

Groden[1] a great deal. As for Harrison Livingstone,[2] he sent me a copy of his latest book and I threw it in the trash. In one of his books, he tore all of us up (i.e., the autopsy team). I told him never to call me again." O'Connor is unflinching in expressing his views on, in his words, "the so-called experts" on the Kennedy assassination: "We were there, they weren't. "

At that stage, I avoided direct discussion of the assassination, saving my questions for the on-camera interview. By the time I had set up for the shoot, got the lighting right, done sound and video tests, it was late evening. Paul was tired. The trip had taken a lot out of him. I knew his back was hurting, but he bore the pain with grace.

I had expected Paul O'Connor to be a serious, conservative man, based on previous interviews I had seen of him. Instead, I found a man of warm personality with a salty no-holds-barred sense of humor. This dichotomy was explained as I turned on the camera: he took a deep breath and said, "Okay, time for my interview face. "

Law: Mr. O'Connor, where were you on November 22, 1963?

O'Connor: I was a naval hospital corpsman, stationed in the National Naval Medical Center in Bethesda, Maryland, attending Medical Technology School. During a break from one of our classes, before noon actually, we all left and went down the hallway to the coffee shop when I noticed a bunch of people – we had a security office in the Naval Hospital – talking in loud voices. I stuck my head in the office to see what was going on and they said that President Kennedy had been wounded in Dallas, Texas. I was one of the first out of the classroom, so I ran back and told the rest of the class. We got our coffee and came back sometime later, and people were very excited and agitated. I looked back into the office and they said that President Kennedy had been assassinated. He was dead.

Law: What was the feeling at that point?

O'Connor: I was in total shock, and so was the rest of the class and the rest of the personnel around us. We aimlessly wandered back to our classroom, wondering what had happened. Actually we were in a state of shock. Several minutes later, it was announced over the PA system that all personnel not on duty that night were to be dismissed and go home, and all duty personnel were to report to their stations. Of course this was a Friday, and I and another hospital corpsman, James Curtis Jenkins, had duty that night. My duty station at that time, in school, was in the pathology department of the Naval Hospital in the morgue, where I helped

---

1. Author of *The Killing of a President* (Viking Studio Books, 1993) and *The Search for Lee Harvey Oswald* (Penguin Studio Books, 1995) and co-author with Harrison Livingstone of *High Treason* (Berkley Books, 1990).
2. Author of *High Treason 2* (Carroll & Graf, 1992), *Killing the Truth* (Carroll & Graf, 1993), and *Killing Kennedy* (Carroll & Graf, 1995), and co-author with Robert Groden of *High Treason* (Berkley Books, 1990).

perform autopsies in my off hours. Everybody else left and went home and my partner and I went down and assumed duty at the morgue.

Law: What did "duty in the morgue" encompass?

O'Connor: We made sure we had all the supplies and chemicals for autopsies.

Law: Now did you do this with a doctor present?

O'Connor: No.

Law: You did this on your own?

O'Connor: We knew our duties and we did them on our own. The morgue was in the lower part of the Naval Hospital in the rear. We went in and checked our supplies and made sure we were ready for anything that came up, then sat around and did nothing for about ten minutes until Admiral Galloway, the chief of the hospital command, walked in himself. I had never seen Admiral Galloway except from a distance, and never conversed with him because I was a junior enlisted man and he was an admiral. He asked – and I remember distinctly – "Is your name O'Connor?" I said, "Yes, sir." He turned to Mr. Jenkins and asked, "Is your name Mr. James Jenkins?" And he said, "Yes, sir." This floored us to death. He said, "Gentlemen, you are now confined to the morgue from this time out because you have a very important visitor coming in tonight."

Law: What did that mean to you?

O'Connor: We knew in a flash that we were going to receive the body of the slain President John F. Kennedy.

Law: After he told you that, what did you do?

O'Connor: Well it was a kind of numbing experience. It was surreal. We knew we had everything prepared for any autopsy that came in, so there was nothing for us to do but sit around. The afternoon wore on very slowly. Finally, in the evening, we heard that the president's body was being brought back to Bethesda. Of course, we knew that. It was confirmed. Then the morgue doctors came in. There were doctors and high-ranking officials. We had Commander Boswell. Commander Humes came in. They were instructed that they were going to perform something on the president. They didn't mention autopsy. They mentioned something on the president's body. So we set up the morgue with all the equipment we needed to perform an autopsy. About eight o'clock, a bunch of us in the morgue heard helicopters coming over the top of the hospital. Now at that time the morgue had filled up with the highest-ranking officers and the highest-ranking political figures in the nation.

Law: Can you tell me a few of the people who were there? Do you remember anybody specifically?

O'Connor: Yes. I remember there was Admiral Burkley, the president's personal physician. He came in and was very agitated – giving orders to everybody, including higher-ranking officers.

Law: What kind of orders?

O'Connor: Be prepared to do what I tell you to do, when I tell you to do it.

Law: So he, in effect, assumed command?

O'Connor: He was entirely in command over admirals, over generals. I remember one general who was sitting in the gallery. It was a teaching morgue and we had a big gallery. I remember Curtis LeMay sitting there with a big cigar in his hand.

Law: How did you know it was Curtis LeMay?

O'Connor: I knew Curtis LeMay by seeing him before and by the big cigar he smoked all the time.

Law: What was his manner when you saw him?

O'Connor: Nonchalant. Kind of, "well let's get this show on the road."

Law: You didn't see him nervous, upset?

O'Connor: No. He was just –

Law: Just there in the gallery smoking a cigar.

O'Connor: Right. After we heard the helicopters come over, I distinctly heard one land in the back of the hospital, which was the Officers' Club parking lot. There was a big parking lot. I heard one helicopter land there. I heard another helicopter land at the north side of the hospital where there was a normal helicopter-landing pad. Several minutes later, I can't give you a definite, time – maybe five minutes – the back of the morgue opened up and a crew of hospital corpsmen and a higher ranking corpsman brought in a plain pinkish-gray, what I call a shipping casket. It was not ornate. It was not damaged. It was just a pinkish-gray casket. They brought it up into the morgue and set it – we had two tables in the morgue – autopsy tables – and they were back to front. They weren't side by side. They were back to front. They brought it up front where we were. At that time we opened up the coffin. Inside was the body bag.

Law: Now you're sure there was a body bag.

O'Connor: Absolutely sure there was a body bag. We unzipped it quickly. Inside was a nude body with a bloody sheet wrapped around the head of the body. We lifted the body onto the table.

Law: Who helped you? Do you remember?

O'Connor: There were probably six or seven people who grabbed a hold and helped lift him. I don't remember who they were. After we put him on the table, I started unwrapping this bloody sheet around the head. Now, you have to remember we knew that President Kennedy had been assassinated. Shot. Dead. But we didn't know where he was shot, or how he was shot or anything. When I saw the bloody sheet I had a feeling he was hit in the head someplace, or in the face or upper torso. I helped unwrap the bloody sheet and Commander Humes grabbed it and threw it in the corner. I remember I was astounded to look down and see that President Kennedy's head was half blown off. And when I say "half blown off" – I put my fingers at the rough proximity of the damage done where it was completely struck.

"I put my fingers at the rough proximity of the damage done where it was completely struck ... "

Law: So that much – parts of the top, back and side – were gone?

O'Connor: Were gone. The skin was all macerated and torn. It was a terrible sight, because I could look straight down and into his cranium. What I could see at that time was completely empty. No brains.

Law: Now are you absolutely certain there were no brains in his head?

O'Connor: When I say "absolutely certain he had no brains in his head," I was looking at an angle from which no brain was visible. The whole right side was gone. After that, Admiral Burkley got extremely agitated because we had found out that Jackie Kennedy and the Kennedy family did not want an autopsy done. He persuaded them to have an autopsy done, so they agreed at the last minute.

Law: Okay. He's on the table. What happened then?

O'Connor: There was uproar in the room. You have to realize we were in a large morgue, a teaching morgue, with high-ranking officials – both military and civilian.

Law: When you say a teaching morgue –

O'Connor: At the Bethesda Naval Hospital we were teaching young doctors who had come out of medical school how to be pathologists. The morgue had a big gallery along one wall where students and young doctors could sit and watch autopsies being performed. It was a large place. At that time of night, when the body was brought in, the morgue was jam-packed full of people. Not only the gallery was jam-packed, but all around our tables and everywhere. Anybody with any business there, was there.

Law: So you have the body and are trying to set up for an autopsy, and you've got all these people running around – high-ranking officials, lots of people in the morgue. That's not usually the way things were done was it?

O'Connor: No.

Law: Didn't you usually do something like that in a quiet controlled manner? Nobody allowed except the pathologist?

O'Connor: Normal autopsies were done by three people. Myself, Mr. Jenkins, and a pathologist. It's a quiet affair. You go in and you do what you have to do. You start your autopsy off by examining the body on the outside for scars, bruises, contusions, any abnormalities. We measure the body, weigh the body, and then start the actual physical autopsy, which included making an incision from below both nipples to the sternum, which is the center part of the chest, and down to the pubic area. Then the body is opened up. Rib cutters are taken and we cut all the ribs down the sides and lift off the sternum completely, revealing the heart and the lungs. Of course, when the lower position, the bowel cavity, is opened, the abdominal organs, the intestines, are shown. At that point, we start dissecting the body parts. Usually what I did – not usually, always – my job was to make an incision from ear to ear, across the top of the head, and peel back the scalp toward the front and towards the back. And take a bone saw and cut around the cranium, and take the lid off the cranium and open up the dura, which is a thick membrane around the brain. Then slowly lift up the front part of the skull where the optical nerves come into the brain, snip those and then go to the rear of the skull and pull the back of the brain up and reach in with a pair of long scissors and cut the spinal column. Then I could lift the whole brain out, intact. We had what they called brain buckets – it sounds kind of crude – but it wasn't, because it was a stainless steel bucket, about a four-gallon bucket. Before the autopsy, we had it lined with gauze, like a bridge and we would put the brain onto the bridge upside down and attach formaldehyde intravenous solution to the carotid arteries and the major veins so we could fix the brain. Fixing means the formaldehyde would actually preserve the brain permanently. The same as being embalmed. Formaldehyde is used for embalming fluid.

Law: How many autopsies have you done or assisted?

O'Connor: Probably at that time fifty to sixty.

Law: You knew what you were doing when you were in there?

O'Connor: Absolutely.

Law: Do you feel that you got an opportunity to follow a normal autopsy?

O'Connor: On the brain?

Law: On any of it.

O'Connor: No.

Law: What was different about it?

O'Connor: Number one, as I said before, the wound was so massive inside of his head there was hardly any brain matter left. There was no brain really. There was no brain really for us, for myself, to take out. There was no need for me to open up the cranium because the cranium was completely shattered. When I say "shattered," not only was the brain blown open, where nothing was left, but the rest of the cranium – the skull cap – was totally fractured. By "totally fractured," I mean it was comminuted. Comminution means if you took a hard-boiled egg and dropped it on the floor, there are hundreds of fractures in the shell and that's the way the president's skull was. It was just malleable – moved back and forth – and what was left of the cranium was completely shattered. His right eye, as I remember, was poked completely out of the orbit, the eye casing. I remember that Dr. Boswell and I looked into the back of the cranium, looking towards the front, and the orbit – the bony casing around where the eye sits was completely fractured.

Law: When you saw there was no brain, what took place then?

O'Connor: It got very tense. Admiral Galloway started getting very agitated again, because there was a wound in his neck. Now the wound – and of course I had seen tracheotomies, where you make an incision and you make it up to down to put in a tube to help a person breathe – the wound was a big gash and more horizontal – and I remember the doctors were going to check that out when Admiral Galloway told them, "Leave it alone. Don't touch it. It's just a tracheotomy" (photo 1).

Law: So he basically stopped anyone from going further?

O'Connor: He stopped anybody from going further. Drs. Humes and Boswell, Dr. Finck, were told to leave it alone, let's go to other things.

Law: Now you've seen tracheotomies before. You've dealt with them. What was your thought when you saw that? The hole in the president's throat that was said to be a tracheotomy?

O'Connor: It looked very sloppy, very nasty, very ugly. Usually a tracheotomy is made with a very sharp, pointed knife and it's very clean. This tracheotomy, or so-called tracheotomy was all macerated and torn apart, and it went this way, both sides, which is very dangerous. If you do a tracheotomy across the throat, you stand a chance of killing a person, because you have on each side of the trachea two large arteries, the carotid arteries, and right beside them are the jugular veins. Arteries run the blood up into the brain and the jugular veins run the blood down back into the heart and lungs. If you make a horizontal incision, you stand a good chance of severing those arteries, which would make a person bleed to death immediately.

Law: Having been told to leave the tracheotomy alone, what happened next?

O'Connor: When we started an autopsy, the first thing we always did – and we never deviated from our procedures – was to weigh and measure the body. We'd check for any scars, contusions, any abnormalities, and so on. But, in this case, we didn't turn the body over to look at the back while we were doing that. Finally we turned the body over, and there was a bullet wound – an entrance wound – in his back, on the right side of his spinal column (photo 6a). To emphasize where it was in proximity to the rest of his body: if you bend your neck down and feel back, you feel a lump and that's the seventh cervical vertebra. This bullet wound was about three inches down and an inch or two to the right of the seventh cervical vertebra. I remember that there was a big gush of surprise that nobody had actually thought about turning him over right away, you know after we had done our initial investigation of the president's body. Dr. Humes took his finger and poked it in the hole – the bullet-wound hole, the entrance-wound hole – and said it didn't go anywhere. There was a very big argument, a lot of consternation, that he shouldn't have stuck his finger in the hole.

Law: What difference would it make?

O'Connor: Well, when you take your finger and stick it into a bullet wound, you avulse the wound, which means that you make the wound abnormal.

Law: You think that happened when he stuck his finger in the back?

O'Connor: Yes.

Law: Could it have created a false track?

O'Connor: Well, not necessarily a false track as much as a false impression of the entrance of the missile that went into his back.

Law: Who was arguing?

O'Connor: Dr. Finck had come over from the Armed Forces Institute of Pathology at Walter Reed Army Hospital. He was a forensic pathologist and he strongly objected to Commander Humes doing what he did. He took a sound. Now a sound is a probe, a metal malleable, non-rigid probe. Malleable means you can move it back and forth and bend it a little bit and trace a bullet path through the body. Now, there are high-powered weapons that will drive a bullet straight through a body and a rigid probe will trace its path all the way through. We started out with a rigid probe and found that it only went in so far. I'd say maybe an inch and a quarter. It didn't go any further than that. So we used a malleable probe and bent it a little bit and found out that the bullet entered the body, went through the intercostal muscles – the muscles in between the ribs. The bullet went in through the muscles, didn't touch any of the ribs, arched downwards, hit the back of the pleural cavity, which encases the lungs, both front and back. It bounced off that cavity and stopped. It actually went down and stopped. Went through the ribs and stopped (photo 10). So we didn't know the track of the bullet until we eviscerated the body later. That's what happened at that time. We traced the bullet path down and found out it didn't traverse the body. It did not go in one side and come out the other side of the body.

Law: You can be reasonably sure of that?

O'Connor: Absolutely.

Law: It was just from the probe then?

O'Connor: Oh yes.

Law: And these doctors knew that?

O'Connor: Absolutely.

Law: While it happened?

Paul O'Connor, September 2002.

O'Connor: Absolutely. And another thing, we found out, while the autopsy was proceeding, that he was shot from a high building, which meant the bullet had to be traveling in a downward trajectory and we also realized that this bullet – that hit him in the back – is what we called in the military a "short shot," which means that the powder in the bullet was defective so it didn't have the power to push the projectile – the bullet – clear through the body. If it had been a full shot at the angle he was shot, it would have come out through his heart and through his sternum.

Law: After you traced the wound, what happened then?

O'Connor: After that, we looked at the head wound and found that there were no bullets in the cranium. Minute fragments were scattered through the bone area of the cranium front and back. I remember distinctly because, having worked in funeral homes since I was thirteen years old, I had seen bullet wounds before, and also I served in Vietnam and saw bullet wounds there. It looked to me like a bomb had exploded inside his brain and blew out the whole side of his head (photo 22). I've never seen a more horrendous destruction of the cranium, unless it was done by a very high caliber weapon. I found out later that it was done by a Manlicher Carcano – a cheap Italian rifle – just about what I would call a thirty caliber or a thirty-thirty caliber rifle.

Law: In your opinion is it capable of doing that kind of damage?

O'Connor: Absolutely not.

Law: N ow you were there in the morgue. I know some people came in and took some X-rays. Can you give me a little information on who they were and what happened at that point?

O'Connor: The first person to come in was Mr. Floyd Riebe, a medical photographer.

Law: What can you tell me about him?

O'Connor: Floyd Riebe was a student in Medical Photography School and in the same command I was at Bethesda Naval Hospital. He was called down to take pictures of the body of President Kennedy. He and a civilian photographer – I can't remember his name – came down and Floyd used a big Pentax camera with a big flash and took pictures of his whole body. The exterior part of his body, and also took pictures of the wounds in his head, in his back, his throat, and probably many more pictures that I didn't see. After Floyd was done, X-ray technicians came down. Jerry Custer was a member of the staff of the Naval Medical Center, the Radiology Department. Jerry came down along with his assistant and took X- rays of the whole body. In the process of taking the X-rays, I left the morgue and went into what they called an anteroom or cooler room. It was inside the morgue, but it was outside the main morgue where we could look through the small windows and watch them take X-rays. I didn't want to get X-rayed too much.

Law: You could see through this window what was going on?

O'Connor: Yes. Mostly I could. You have to remember the morgue was still full of people who didn't want to leave. My partner Jim Jenkins, and Jerry Custer and this other young fellow started taking X-rays. They had to use a portable machine because we didn't have a main X-ray machine in the morgue. It had to be rolled in like they do in the hospitals.

Law: So Jerry Custer rolled in a portable X-ray machine.

O'Connor: Rolled in a portable machine and started taking X-rays. I remember watching some of it and some of it I didn't watch. Then, after he left, we started the main autopsy. The main autopsy is started by making two incisions from below the nipples down to the middle of the chest, the sternum, and from the sternum down to the pubic area. Then the body is opened up, which we did and then we had to take chest cutters and cut the ribs on the far sides of each part of the sternum. Then we could lift the whole chest, sternum, ribs and all, off to expose the internal organs of the top part of the body. Of course, we had already made incisions on the bottom part of the body and there were no bones to go through. After that, usually, and I've done many, many autopsies, we used to start taking one organ out at a time – weighing it, studying it, taking little samples of tissue for microscopic examination later on, through chemical analysis. Admiral Burkley intervened again and was very adamant in the fact that we were to "Christmas tree" the body.

Law: What did that mean?

O'Connor: "Christmas tree" is slang – after the body is opened up – for severing the trachea and all the arteries and the veins in the neck, going down into the shoulders and severing all the arteries in the shoulders and main arteries and connective tissues down into the abdominal cavity and reaching down and severing the lower part of the intestines and bringing all the organs out en masse. Then you lay all the organs on the table – and they did a perfunctory examination, because Admiral Burkley kept yelling that the Kennedy family wanted just so much done and that's all and nothing else.

Law: Normally when you're doing an autopsy does the family have the right to be interjecting what they want?

O'Connor: Absolutely not.

Law: Was this unusual?

O'Connor: Very unusual. I had never actually worked on an autopsy where we did this procedure before and never have done it since. So, all the organs were taken out – and, when you do that, you've got an absolutely empty cavity where all the organs were and you could stare down and see the spinal column inside. Now they were very interested in one thing. They were very interested in his back surgery. He was hurt in World War II during the crash of PT 109,[3] resulting in extensive back surgery in the early fifties or late forties. I think it was the early fifties. At that time, back surgery was very, very risky, which almost ended his life. So they wanted to see how much damage was done to his spinal column, which they did. There was extensive scarring. At the same time that Dr. Finck and Dr. Humes and Mr. Jenkins were examining that area there, I didn't have too much to do. My duties were to remove the brain and take care of the top part of the body. We were ordered by Admiral Burkley to leave the throat wound alone: it was nothing but a tracheotomy. Well I had seen tracheotomies before I'd gone to Bethesda. The tracheotomy just didn't look right and it worried me. We didn't touch it. We couldn't touch it. Same thing with the back wound: leave it alone, don't mess with it. I did notice something that struck me. After all the organs were taken out of the body you could look back through and see the interior rib muscles and ribs. The intercostal muscles are those I was talking about that connect the ribs together, and there was a lot of hemorrhaging in the inner spaces of the intercostal muscles, which I thought was very strange because we didn't know that the back wound had not penetrated. We were told (i.e., in the report of the Warren Commission) that he was shot in the back and it came out of his throat. That didn't jibe with what we saw, and when I say we, I'm talking about Dr. Boswell and myself.

Then the other doctors decided to check on top of each kidney – the adrenal glands – for some reason. I didn't know at the time he had an adrenal deficiency, which I learned is called Addison's disease. The glands were essentially not there. They had atrophied to nothing.

Law: So, they did check the adrenals?

O'Connor: They did a small check of the adrenals. The organs were then put back into the body en masse. The body was sutured completely up. As far as the skull went, we had problems.

Law: Like what?

O'Connor: We found out through the X-rays Mr. Custer took that the skull was completely fractured. Not only was part of it blown, gone, but the whole rest of the skull was fractured completely.

Law: Everywhere?

3. In August 1943, a Japanese destroyer rammed U.S. Navy patrol torpedo boat 109 skippered by John F. Kennedy..

O'Connor: Everywhere. It was malleable. So they sent me up to the central supply room, which is two floors or one floor above the morgue area, to get plaster of Paris. I brought it back down and they filled his cranium with plaster of Paris to get conformity so that the skull wouldn't be misshapen. Because Admiral Burkley told us that the president's family wanted to view the body. I thought, "My gosh how are you going to do this?" Well, we filled the cranium with plaster of Paris – they put too much plaster in and we had to chip half of it out. We finally got it out and they colored the plaster of Paris with some sort of brown substance that closely resembled his hair. You have to realize, President Kennedy had a large amount of hair, and it was all combed to the right. So it was combed over an area that was devoid of tissue, just plaster of Paris. The rest of the tissue was gone. That area was combed over and cleaned up, and the throat wound was sutured up.

Law: Now this was after the autopsy and after you put the plaster of Paris in?

O'Connor: Right. Everything was just kind of follow up and clean up. Then we found out that he was not going to be taken to a funeral home for embalming and fixing up for burial. They brought in people from Gawler's Funeral Home, one of the most respected in Washington, D.C., to do the embalming and to prepare the body for burial, right in the morgue. Now we had two tables and they were head to foot. The first one was the one we did the autopsy on. We moved him to the second clean one. The gentlemen from Gawler's were very prim and proper. I thought it was very odd because they were wearing bowler hats that you see people wearing in Britain – and they brought all their equipment in, and I stayed and assisted those guys. They did the most extraordinary things I've ever seen with preparing a body for embalming. Number one, when I started working in funeral homes when I was thirteen years old, when the deceased was brought in they would bring in the clothing they wanted to be buried in, and we'd take the dress or the coat, the suit and the shirt, and cut it down the back completely in half so we could stuff one part this way and one part this way – because rigor mortis, stiffening of the body, has already set in. Well, we didn't do that. We dressed his whole body in his inaugural suit. They brought his inaugural suit in.[4]

Law: You personally helped put this on him?

O'Connor: Yes. It was very, very difficult, because when a body is in rigor mortis the arms are very stiff and you can't pry them apart hardly at all to do anything. And we're talking about long-sleeve shirts with French cuffs, and we dressed him in his shirt. Same thing with the pants. They weren't cut down the back – he was dressed completely, just like you and I would dress in the morning.

Law: Now had everybody left the gallery by this time?

O'Connor: Just about everybody had left, except for a few of us.

4. A blue suit brought from the White House

Law: Had it calmed down?

O'Connor: Oh yes. Everybody was gone.

Law: Now how did it make all of you react when you had all these people in there and this is not the normal procedure. You're looking at the President of the United States. There's chaos all around you. Could you do your jobs that night?

O'Connor: No. We weren't able to do our jobs the way we were supposed to. That's another thing that upset me terribly – the fact that we weren't able to do certain critical things like probe the throat wound that we thought was a bullet wound. We found out it was a bullet wound years later. We weren't able to do certain procedures like take each organ out, examine them and do microscopic examinations by taking slides. Every organ is usually taken out and weighed. They were weighed en masse. We had a chart that had a sketch of a body on one side and on the other side were entries for each organ and what it weighed. And every organ and what they weighed were put in there but they weren't weighed separately. They were weighed en masse.

Law: Oh really?

O'Connor: Except the brain. The brain was left blank.

Law: It was?

O'Connor: As far as weighing the brain.

Law: It was left blank?

O'Connor: Yes.

Law: I believe it was recorded at fifteen hundred grams.[5]

O'Connor: Fourteen hundred grams I think it was – more than a normal brain.

Law: What do you think about that?

O'Connor: I knew something was terribly wrong, but I was not in a position to comment – being a junior enlisted person – about what senior officers were doing. So, I kept my mouth shut. Then, after he was embalmed completely and dressed, another thing was odd. When I worked in funeral homes we never put shoes on people, and they put his shoes on too. Socks and shoes, sock garters, everything was put on just like he was getting ready to walk out of the room to be inaugurated again.

Law: The whole thing?

O'Connor: Yeah, the whole thing. Then they brought in – actually it was already in the cooler room – a huge mahogany casket that he was to be buried in, called a Marsellus casket. Handmade mahogany.

Law: Were you there when the casket was brought in – the ornate casket?

---

5. Officially, the weight of the brain was 1,500 g, determined at the brain autopsy, not on 11/22/63. On average, the adult brain weighs 1,300 to 1,400 g.

O'Connor: No. It was brought in some time after we had just about finished the autopsy and embalming. They had it in the cooler room, the anteroom. We picked up the body of the president, and put him in the casket, with, of course, his hands in the funeral position, and I remember that somebody in a civilian suit asked, "Your name is O'Connor?" And I said, "Yes." And he said, "You must be Catholic. Put this rosary in his hands properly. " I wasn't really sure how a rosary went, but I did it. Wrapped it around his hands. Black onyx. The casket was closed and the casket left.

Law: So what happened after that? What did you do?

O'Connor: Cleaned up the morgue. It was a terrible mess.

Law: What was running through your head?

O'Connor: It was early in the morning, and I'd been up all day in school and all night in the morgue, and I was exhausted. And all Mr. Jenkins and I wanted to do was to get the morgue cleaned up as quickly as possible, and get away and go home. Which we did. I think it was eight-thirty or nine o'clock in the morning.

Law: So that was the end of it for you basically?

O'Connor: For me, basically it was.

Law: Now, in talking to some of the other fellows who were with you, some of your colleagues, I'm struck with the fact that all of you know bits and pieces. It's like you're all on different frequencies. You all noticed different things. Did you all get together at one point and share any kind of information? I mean early on, not years later. I'm talking about within that week, within a few days?

O'Connor: No. What happened was – that took place on a Friday, of course, he was buried on the Monday and on Tuesday of that next week we were called into Captain Stover's office – who was one of the commanders of the Naval Medical School – where we were instructed and told that we were going to sign orders of silence under the penalty of general court martial, and other dreadful things like going to prison, if we talked to anybody about anything that happened that night. Period.

Law: So you were threatened basically with being thrown in jail?

O'Connor: In prison.

Law: In prison if you talked about this to anybody?

O'Connor: To anybody. Now that was the worst experience of my life. The Kennedy assassination autopsy was bad. But that scared me to death because I was a good loyal navy hospital corpsman, had done nothing wrong and was thrown into a situation that I couldn't control. And all of a sudden I was told that if I was to say something to anybody, anybody – and they left that wide open – anybody – that, if found out, we'd go to prison and be dishonorably discharged from the navy.

Law: So what happened to you in the years after? Did you think about this often? Did it affect your life? Did you have nightmares from this experience?

O'Connor: No.

Law: Did you just forget about it?

O'Connor: I forgot about it. Matter of fact I put it completely out of my mind. I knew what I had to do. I didn't want to go to prison. I wanted to continue my navy career. So I kept my mouth shut and continued my navy career.

Law: So what happened – when did you first – who did you first reveal this to – that you had been involved in this, and how did these circumstances come about?

O'Connor: Actually I was married soon after school and transferred to a naval base in Florida, and I mentioned it briefly to my wife. I was scared to death to do that, but I did. I figure a husband and wife have the most intimate secrets in the world they can share with each other without anybody knowing anything about them, so that's what we did. She was a little bit doubtful about what I was talking about, but she didn't say anything and I didn't say anything else anymore.

Law: So what happened – did you get calls over the years? Did anyone know who you were? How did it come about that people knew who you were?

O'Connor: Well, after I was stationed in southern Florida, I got orders to go to Vietnam in 1965. And I served with the United States Marine Corps in combat over in Vietnam, was wounded in Vietnam and eventually was discharged medically from service. After I was out of the service, I knew I could talk to anybody I wanted to about it, because the military had no sway over me. But, I never said anything, because I didn't think anyone would believe anything I had to say about seeing this. So I didn't say anything for years, until the mid-seventies I think. Correct me if I'm wrong – the Freedom of Information Act was passed and my name was released with the files and all the autopsy crew. I started getting calls from people all over the United States and Canada and Europe. They wanted to talk about what I saw during the Kennedy autopsy. A lot of them were very strange people, what we call cuckoos and nuts. A lot of them were very honest people, with a lot of integrity. I finally started talking to an author who was going to write a book on the assassination named David Lifton. We corresponded for, I guess, over a year or so, before he came out with a book on the Kennedy assassination, which opened up new chapters for me because I found out through talking to other people, who were ordered to keep silent, that a lot of things weren't right.

Law: As far as?

O'Connor: The autopsy, the bullet wounds, the massive destruction of the cranium. I was able to talk to the doctors in Parkland Hospital in Dallas several years later. We collaborated and talked about our experiences: Parkland vs. Bethesda.

Law: Did you do this on your own?

O'Connor: No. Actually we were brought together by different groups. Mr. Lifton and other people who were getting more interested in the idiosyncrasies of what had happened at that time. There was a group that started a big conference in Dallas back in the seventies, late seventies I guess it was, or early eighties, I can't remember really. That's when we found out – when the Dallas doctors and I got together – that something was terribly, terribly wrong between Parkland and Bethesda. What they saw in Parkland – what they did in Parkland – did not jibe with what we saw in Bethesda. What astounded me was the doctor who first got to JFK in the emergency room in Parkland said he had a bullet wound – an entrance wound – in his throat.

Law: Was he adamant that it was an entrance wound?

O'Connor: Adamant. Very. He had been an emergency room physician at Parkland for a number of years, treated a multitude of gunshot wounds. He knew what an entrance wound looked like, knew what an exit wound looked like. Entrance goes in small and neat and comes out big and nasty. If it comes out; a lot of them don't. He explained to me that he saw a bullet wound in the president's throat and made an incision through the bullet wound into his trachea to insert the endotracheal tube to inflate his lungs. They worked on that. They did several life-saving procedures for quite a long time. I guess several, maybe five or ten, minutes, until a neurosurgeon declared the president dead. According to the Dallas doctors, the wound they saw was approximately this big and the wound we saw in Bethesda was this big, and so we were both in a kind of state of complete puzzlement at what had been going on. You know – what happened? Did something happen between Parkland hospital and Bethesda? Then I found out that the casket I saw come into our morgue in Bethesda wasn't the same coffin that he was put in at Parkland to ship to Bethesda. He was put into a bronze, ornate casket at

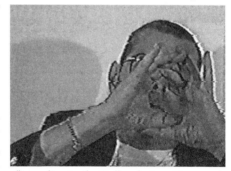

"According to the Dallas doctors, the wound they saw was approximately this big … "

Parkland that came from the O'Neal's Funeral Home. I found out also – which was amazing – that the Secret Service and the Dallas police department almost had a gun battle on who the body belonged to. Did it belong to the State of Texas or the United States Government? Well, actually it belonged to the State of Texas because the president was killed, murdered in the State of Texas. They had a big fight. There were no guns drawn, but a friend of mine – can't remember his name now, he was the ambulance driver –

Law: Aubrey Rike?

O'Connor: Aubrey Rike. He was an ambulance driver for the O'Neal Funeral Home. They were at Parkland at the time the body was brought in and they were told to call Mr. O'Neal at the Funeral Home and have him bring his best, most expensive, casket to Parkland Hospital, post haste. When they got it there, Aubrey Rike told me they put him in a bed liner. Now a bed liner is something that goes over a bed – it's a plastic covering that keeps bodily fluids from bleeding into the mattress. It's not a body bag. A body bag is a bag that a body is put into and zipped from the head to the toe. He was wrapped in sheets around his chest and his torso, and when we received him he was not in a bed liner. He was in a body bag, but nothing wrapped around his torso. It was an unclothed body. The only thing on his body was a bloody sheet around his head. So that was another thing that was extremely disturbing to hear about.

Law: How did that make you feel?

O'Connor: That somebody, somewhere high up in government – it had to be the government – was concealing evidence, vital evidence, from the American public about what actually transpired between Parkland and Bethesda.

Law: I want to go back to the morgue for a minute. I want to go back to what the atmosphere was like. I've been told by one of your colleagues, James Jenkins, in a telephone conversation, that he felt that there was supposed to be a little scenario of what was to happen during the autopsy, but when the doctors started finding out other things and doing other things – other than what they were told to do – that that's what started Burkley or some of the generals, or some of the people that were in there, getting angry and having hostile feelings and "You're not supposed to do that." What do you think about that and do you agree?

O'Connor: Well, I know that's for a fact and I do agree one hundred percent because Admiral Burkley was the president's personal physician. The president's family, Bobby, Jackie – and, I don't know, some other higher-ranking members of the family – were taken to Bethesda Naval Hospital – it has a seventeen-story tower in front – were taken up to the executive suites where Admiral Burkley was directly on the phone with, I found out later, Bobby Kennedy and Jackie Kennedy – about what to do and what not to do about the autopsy. So he, Admiral Burkley, controlled what happened in that room that night, through Bobby Kennedy and the rest of the Kennedy family.

Law: So you believe that Admiral Burkley was getting his orders from some of the Kennedy family?

O'Connor: Yes. Absolutely.

Law: What other things took place there that night?

O'Connor: One other thing – after I was out of the military for several years, I met Dennis David, who is now a good friend of mine. Now, at the time of the assassination he was a member of the hospital med-school staff – we had about three different staffs in that hospital, med-school staff, regular hospital staff and several other staffs that were all under the command of Admiral Galloway. And he was ordered that night, early, before the president even landed at Andrews to get a crew of six men and himself together and be ready on a back loading dock of the hospital, which was right outside our morgue, to pick up the body of the president and bring him into the morgue. That's when I, and not only myself but Mr. Jenkins[6] and several other people, heard helicopters flying over. Now the president was brought into Andrews Air Force Base, located southeast of Washington, D.C., and Bethesda Naval Hospital is northwest of Washington, D.C. Supposedly the casket was off-loaded from Air Force One and placed in a marked navy-gray ambulance. And supposedly driven with Jackie in the ambulance and Admiral Burkley was supposed to be in the ambulance too. Andrews Air Force Base is twenty-five miles or more from Bethesda Naval Hospital. At that time there were no interstates or beltways in Washington, D.C. When the whole country, the whole world, knew that the president was dead and Washington was going crazy – the whole city was in a frenzy – why would they drive his body in a marked navy ambulance from Andrews Air Force Base all the way up Pennsylvania Avenue through the middle of the city into Wisconsin Avenue which runs due north to Bethesda Naval Hospital? Well, we will digress a little bit and say that after the helicopters landed, a black hearse drove up from one of the helicopters in the dark where it was met by Mr. Dennis David and his crew of six men. A black hearse, not a navy ambulance, where a plain casket was taken out and rushed right into the morgue, which is no more than ten feet from the loading dock, where we opened it immediately and took out the president's body in a body bag.

Law: Years later you became a sheriff?

O'Connor: A deputy sheriff.

Law: Did things happen to you on your job over the course of the years that made you look back and think, "Wow! This makes me understand that the president's wounds couldn't have been the way they were when I saw his body?" Did it make you think at all?

O'Connor: Oh absolutely. As a matter of fact, I had seen head wounds. I was stationed at the naval hospital in Guantanamo Bay, Cuba, in 1960, and saw a military person who had been shot point blank in the head with a forty-five caliber pistol. Now a forty-five caliber pistol bullet is twice as big as a 30-30 which was just about the caliber of the projectile that was supposed to have caused all this extensive damage to President Kennedy's head. This guy was shot in the head at point-blank range, and it made a medium-sized hole and we saved him in the operating room. I remember saying to myself when I first saw the sheet unwrapped from his head, I thought to myself that it looked like a bomb went off inside of his head (photo 22). It stayed with me. It still stays with me to this day. It looked like a bomb went

---

6. James Jenkins has no memory of a helicopter (page 223)..

off inside of his head instead of a bullet. I just could not envision – after they told me what kind of caliber rifle that they used – how it could do that much damage. One bullet. Another thing: I talked to several learned forensic pathologists, doctors who said that the trajectory of the bullet coming down from the sixth floor (of the Texas School Book Depository, Dallas) that entered his back would have come out through his sternum, through his heart, and probably would have gone into the floor of the car. But, according to the official Warren Report, this one bullet – pristine bullet they called it, and I put emphasis on the word pristine – entered below his collar bone, did an upward turn, came out his throat, did a ninety-degree turn to the right and a ninety-degree turn to the left and passed completely through John Connally's body, through his chest, breaking bones, shattering his wrist and finally lodging in his thigh – and still being pristine – when I've seen bullets that hit a watermelon and were deformed. Anytime a bullet of that high a caliber hits something it starts deforming no matter what surface it's hitting. It just cannot stay pristine. So, I guess you have to sit back and think about the evidence that's been brought forth over the years and say to yourself:

"Who's hiding what from who and why?" Will we ever know? I doubt it. We know that a terrible wrong has been done to the American people considering what happened on that day in Dallas and Bethesda. And, after thirty-five years, I don't think that any of us know what really happened. Too many people are now dead, some people have left the country, and the government does not really care, or seem to care, about any of the new evidence brought out. It's like, "Just don't worry about it. It's a non-event."

Law: Does it make you angry at your government?

O'Connor: Absolutely. I'm still angry at my government. Every time I see my government in action I get angry. Not to the point where I would want to assassinate somebody or see anybody else assassinated, but I get angry that so many things are covered up.

Law: Now going back to the morgue that night. I know you've seen the movie *JFK*. Were the scenes in the morgue a fair representation?

O'Connor: No.

Law: Tell me about it.

O'Connor: If you remember, all the doctors were dressed in white gowns and masks and gloves, and none of us ever did autopsies in any kind of white uniforms. We all wore green – scrub clothes they called them – and no masks. Although it was before the AIDS epidemic, we did wear gloves. So that wasn't a fair representation of the autopsy scene.

Law: Was that the only thing? Or were there other things Oliver Stone got wrong, that weren't quite right? I'm just interested on a personal level now.

O'Connor: On a personal level that's the only thing I can think of, because that was the only thing I was tuned to, the medical aspect of what we did and what they showed. There was one funny thing that they did show: this big finger getting stuck in the hole, the bullet hole in the back of the president's body, and wiggled around a little bit. Somebody said, "Well, this doesn't go anywhere at all." Name's unknown. Of course, I knew who did it.

Law: All right. What about the person that said, "Who's in charge here?" Did you hear that said?

O'Connor: I don't distinctly remember that. I do remember somebody saying "I am," and it came from the area of Admiral Burkley.

Law: So you think Admiral Burkley is the one who said, "I'm in charge"?

O'Connor: Yes. You have to realize the morgue was jam-packed full of people. Everybody talking at one time. It was a mad house. I had two FBI agents behind me, watching every move that was being made, and they were talking and carrying on. Frances X. O'Neill was one of them. Sibert was the other one. I remember Burkley, I remember Boswell, Dr. Humes, Dr. Finck who is now not a member of our American community anymore.

Law: What happened to Dr. Finck?

O'Connor: He decided to suddenly resign his commission and move to Switzerland or another European country.

Law: Was this some time after the assassination.

O'Connor: Yes, it was.

Law: Going back to Boswell and Humes, what was their demeanor? What do you remember about them when they had to perform this autopsy? From my understanding, they were more paper pushers than anything else.

O'Connor: Dr. Humes was the commander of our Medical Technology School. And yes, at that time, the higher you got up in rank, the less you did except push papers around. You're more of a commanding person than an acting person. And Dr Boswell was a lieutenant commander who was more of a scientific person, a scientist who worked with students and the staff. Neither of these gentlemen had performed autopsies for a long time. And neither had ever performed a murder autopsy. Neither one was a forensic pathologist.

Law: Were you a little surprised that they would use these two doctors.

O'Connor: No. At that time I didn't know that forensic pathologists do murder investigations. The procedures are so much different. Things are filmed, everything is taped. Every time there is a murder there are several different witnesses in there and, like I said, they are taped and filmed and so everything is ready for court.

Law: That night – getting back to that – we all know they film and have microphones. Did they have microphones in the morgue that night?

O'Connor: No.

Law: Did they normally though?

O'Connor: No.

Law: They never had microphones in the morgue?

O'Connor: They had no microphones, no cameras, no nothing.[7]

Law: So they didn't tape things?

O'Connor: No.

Law: Not at all?

O'Connor: Not at all.

Law: Is there anything else that you word – suspicious, now that you look morgue? Anyone in particular?

O'Connor: Not in the morgue so much as what I gleaned over the years from hearsay evidence only. When I say "hearsay" – I mean that I can't prove anything and nobody else can either that the president's body was intercepted and the wound in his cranium was beaten open by a hammer to enlarge it, to mask the original wounds.

Law: By a hammer?

O'Connor: By a hammer, or some blunt object.

Law: You were told this some years later?

O'Connor: By several different sources. Yes.

Law: That there was a hammer taken to the skull of the president?

O'Connor: Yes. And not in Bethesda Naval Hospital.

Law: Where was it supposed to have been done?

O'Connor: I have talked to several people about that, and Bethesda Naval Hospital was a big hospital complex and behind the complex we had an animal research complex that had a morgue just about the same size as our morgue, where they did surgeries and autopsies on experimental animals.

Law: Right in the same building?

O'Connor: No. It was down the road a little bit behind the hospital.

Law: But it was in the same general area?

O'Connor: In the same general area, yes.

Law: The complex was in this area and you had another separate morgue area?

---

7. Asked later, Mr. O'Connor stated that he does not believe that the autopsy room was equipped with a closed-circuit television system. However, see pages 151 and 448.

O'Connor: Another separate morgue area that was for animals. Also, that he was flown by helicopter. Another was that the ceremonial casket from O'Neal's Funeral Home in Dallas was put aboard a marked navy ambulance, the ambulance sped off and disappeared in the compound at the Andrews Air Force Base for I don't know how many minutes, ten minutes or so or more.

Law: Is this just rumor from other people?

O'Connor: This is all hearsay. I wouldn't call them rumors as much as hearsay. So what I mean by hearsay is that when I get three or four unrelated people talking about the same thing, something is odd. Something is not right. Maybe somebody has really got something going and he knows what he's talking about. You have to put all these things together because there are too many discrepancies between what happened between Parkland and Bethesda. They were ignored. They were all ignored. Everybody still ignores it. It's like it never even took place. The Warren Commission ignored it. The Warren Commission – out of all the autopsy personnel – interviewed one person and that was Commander James Humes[8] who stated that, the day after the autopsy, he felt bad about the autopsy and burned all his autopsy papers and writings, voluntarily. Why? Why did this person do that?

Law: What kind of person was Humes, do you know?

O'Connor: Yes. I considered him a very moody, uncaring person. The kind of officer that considered enlisted personnel less than dirt, and considered himself superior to everything else on earth.

Law: Do you find any inconsistencies in the available autopsy photographs?

O'Connor: Absolutely. I think just about every photograph that was released has been altered by air brushing. And there are some I don't even know if they were taken in the morgue that we were in.

Law: Do you have any experience with pictures?

O'Connor: I'm not a photographer, a professional photographer, but I've consulted with professional photographers and photographic studios, and have shown the pictures to them and they pointed out what they call air-brushing and shading of the pictures to make them a little different.

Law: Could you show us what you mean? Give us some details about the pictures. Please go through whatever ones you want and tell us about them.

O'Connor: Okay. Let's start off with the famous "death stare" (photo 1). The picture of JFK laying on the morgue table which shows a wound in his throat – what they said is the tracheotomy wound – which actually turned out to be a bullet wound with a tracheotomy incision made through it. Now, if you'll look at this picture, it shows the table, it shows the floor and it shows a wooden object

8. Humes, Boswell and Finck all gave testimony to the Warren Commission.

213

that I can't actually tell what it really is (photo 1b). We didn't have anything like this at all.[9] The morgue was all stainless steel and tile. This actually would be sitting in front of the main door into the morgue. The raised area on the right is part of the three-tiered gallery along the side of the morgue where junior pathologists sat for instruction, where you stepped up to the benches.

The second picture (photo 2) shows JFK on the table from the left side. I don't remember this metal headrest. It's fastened onto the table here. All the autopsies we did – and I remember later that night – we used a rubber chock block that had different levels on it, to raise or lower the head to any level you want. The rest of the picture looks normal.

Law: Do you remember this phone on the wall?

O'Connor: Yeah, this phone was on the wall there.[10]

Law: It was? Does it look normal? There are books that I've read that say it's a composite because you can tell by the grouting that it's not quite matched, or there was no phone in the autopsy room.

O'Connor: Oh yes, there was a phone in the autopsy room. Matter of fact, right in this corner there was a desk.

Law: So this does look like your morgue area?

O'Connor: Yes, it does. It looks like our morgue area. You know it's been thirty-five years and I couldn't tell you if the phone was green, black, purple or pink, but we did have a phone there.

Law: Okay.

O'Connor: The third picture (photo 3) is looking down at his head toward his feet, showing the destructiveness of the wound. All this white tissue inside of the scalp, was torn out and all macerated, torn in pieces, shredded. Another thing strange about this picture is this instrument table that comes up and over him. If you look closely – you'll see there's a bar going down here and a second bar that comes out and goes down here, and the table we used that night had just one bar in the center, and we usually kept it sideways. We never put it over the top of the body at all because when you're working on a body you don't need it in your way. You'd have to push it out of your way all the time. We kept it sideways. Again I don't know where this picture was taken.

Law: You just don't recognize it?

O'Connor: I don't recognize that.

Law: How about the head wound itself? Does it look like what you remember?

O'Connor: Yes, it does.

9. Mr. O'Connor later stated his belief that Jerrol Custer was mistaken in his contention that the wooden object (photo 1b) was the base of a portable X-ray machine.

10. In later conversation, Mr. O'Connor was less certain that the phone was on the wall; he recalled a telephone on a desk in a back room (photo 11).

Law: Now there appears to be something in the middle of JFK's head. Do you know what that is? It looks like some kind of instrument (photo 3a).

O'Connor. Right, here. I've been asked about that a hundred times, and I just don't know what it is. I don't have an answer for it. But we didn't have any instruments or anything like that inside of his cranium.

Law: Do you recognize the towels? Did you use that kind of towel.

O'Connor: Yes we did. They have a blue stripe down the middle and USN on both sides. That was the towel we put underneath his head.

Law: Anything else you'd like to tell us about this photograph?

O'Connor: No. That's about it as far as this photograph is concerned. This next one (photo 4) is another of his head, and here again if you compare this photograph with this one (photo 6) you can see that the back of his head is completely intact. It's not all torn and macerated. A lot of people have talked about this little white object down here (photo 4a, arrow) being an entrance wound.

Law: What was that?

O'Connor: It was actually a piece of brain matter.

Law: Did you see that yourself?

O'Connor: Yes.

Law: You know that was brain matter?

O'Connor: Yeah, but this – if you look at his hair – it's all nice and shiny and dark and it's all together. You don't see any rips or tears like you do in this picture (photo 3) here of the back of his head. So this picture (photo 4) has been touched up. It shouldn't be like that, completely intact.

Law: Were you there when they were taking some pictures?

O'Connor: All the pictures.

Law: Do you remember them posing him like this?

O'Connor: Yes. Not necessarily this way. Now this large flap right here is part of the temporal bone and parietal bone and actually attached by tissue, and as they were positioning the body for these pictures, the flap fell off.

Now this next picture is very bad (photo 5). It's difficult for me to explain. This is actually looking at the back of the president's skull. It shows the wound looking into the cranium. This is the right side of the president's head looking from the head down towards the feet. This was all blown away, all gone. If this picture were a little clearer you could see that the cranium was empty.

Law: Do you know who reflected the scalp back on that?

O'Connor: The scalp wasn't reflected back, it was just laid back. Now the other photograph (photo 6) is another that has clearly been doctored.

Law: Tell me where.

O'Connor: This, if you notice the back of the president's head, he's got a cowlick here; it's not a bullet wound, it's a cowlick (photo 6a, arrow D). The hair is all nice and shiny like it's been freshly washed, wet.

Law: Was there anything back there that could be washed?

O'Connor: No, because you have to remember – and every photograph I showed you – this was all torn and macerated and fallen down. And, in this picture here, it looks like the whole back of his head is intact, the right side of his head is intact, just about. You can see what is in an earlier photograph – part of his skull hanging out the side. Now, right here next to this ruler is a back entrance wound (photo 6a, arrow A), a bullet wound.

Law: That is the only wound on the back?

O'Connor: The only wound on the back.

Law: What's that little area down below there (photo 6a, arrow B)?

O'Connor: Blood. Just like the areas further below: blood and wrinkles. That's a very accurate portrayal of the entrance wound to his back, which, as you know, is quite a ways down from his neck. The Warren Report of course said he was shot in the back and it came out his throat. At the angle he was shot – if he was shot from the sixth floor of the depository – the laws of physics will not let a bullet strike there and go up and go out his throat.

Law: I know this isn't your department, but I was told by one of your colleagues who took the X-rays that, at this point, they weren't allowed to do what they wanted to do and so they just started playing with him, playing with the body in terms of "We're just going to do our jobs," and that's why you see some of these strange angles. This wasn't like normal procedure to just raise a person. When you try to look for a wound – do you normally have a set procedure? They didn't just roll him around to different areas did they?

O'Connor: Yeah, they did.

Law: They did?

O'Connor: An autopsy starts not by opening the body. The autopsy starts with an examination of the outside of the body before you examine the inside of the body, so that you get all the marks, scars, bruises, contusions, and everything recorded. So, after you look at the front part of the body, we always rolled him over and looked at the back part of the body.

Law: So that would have been normal for them to do?

O'Connor: Yes.

Law: So this isn't something that you think someone is trying to hide or make the markings different (photo 6)? It's just a standard thing?

O'Connor: It's standard. Yeah. There's nothing strange or odd about what they did. I remember they did roll him over.

Law: They did?

O'Connor: I helped roll him over, matter of fact.

Law: Did you help when they lifted him up like this? Were you watching?

O'Connor: One of these arms might have been mine. Because I was at the head of the body and I helped roll him over.

Law: How soon into the autopsy did they do this, if this (photo 6) is an original?

O'Connor: Actually the funny thing about this autopsy was that when we examined the front part of his body for a long time. He wasn't rolled over on his back until quite a ways into the autopsy, and that's when they discovered the bullet wound which caused a big stir in the autopsy suite because they weren't expecting a wound in his back, especially that low.

Law: So they said it was a low wound?

O'Connor: It was low, yeah. It's a low wound. It's actually – about three inches lower than the seventh cervical vertebra to the right of his spine. It missed his spinal cord and didn't penetrate his body, all the way through.

Law: Authors have suggested that this ruler isn't showing you anything and it's probably there to cover up a bullet wound they're trying to hide. Do you agree with that?

O'Connor: I disagree.

Law: You just think they're trying to –

O'Connor: There was only one wound in his back and that was it right here.

Law: So basically they're just trying to show at what vertebra the bullet went in?

O'Connor: Exactly. Like I said they use the seventh cervical vertebra as a starting point, a reference point to reference how far down and over this wound was.

Law: I see.

O'Connor: Now, I had this picture made at the University of Florida showing his back wound and this is exactly what happened (photo 10). The bullet struck him in the back as shown in the previous photograph. It passed through the outer layer of muscle and through the inner layer of muscle between the vertebrae. These are the intercostal muscles and they connect the spinal column together. This bullet came in, arched downward, and bulged against what they called the pleural cavity, which is a protective cavity around both lungs. It did not penetrate that lung area. It just bruised it real badly. I had it highlighted showing there was bruising on the right lung. The back of the right lung was bruised, but wasn't torn. It was bruised badly enough to hemorrhage in the tissues, but not enough to tear the lung or the cavity. As I said before, during the X-ray procedure after the photographs were taken, X-ray technician Jerrol Custer was turning the body over and this bullet or bullet fragment fell out on the table and was retrieved. I didn't see that because I was out of the room when they were taking X-rays.

Law: You were in the anteroom.

O'Connor: I was in the anteroom. As I said before, this shows a short shot, which didn't get a clean burn or have enough punch to send the bullet completely into the body. If it had, at that angle, it would have passed through the lung and probably through his heart and killed him. It would have been a fatal shot if it had gone through the body. But, then again, it wouldn't have passed through his neck.

Law: Why, when you were taking organs out and they were being weighed, didn't you see any fragments?

O'Connor: Matter of fact, I understand that Jerrol Custer found on his X-rays several minute fragments. Metal fragments. He couldn't identify what kind of fragments they were, except they were metal. They were very, very small. As for any intact bullets, there were none recovered from the president's body. The largest fragment in his body, this fragment here, that I never got to see, which was possibly retrieved by somebody standing around the table at the time the X-rays were taken, and was taken away before I got back into the room.

Law: Do you know a David Osborne? Wasn't there someone named Osborne in the autopsy room who said a bullet fell out of the wrappings? Do you remember that at all?

O'Connor: Yes I do. This Osborne, I don't know what he's talking about. I think he was fantasizing or something, because we didn't have any wrappings on the body at all. The body was unclothed and nude. So there was no chance of anything falling out of any wrapping that was on his body, because there was no wrapping on his body. Period.

Law: Is there anything else you'd like to state about these pictures for the historical record?

O'Connor: Just that I talked to the photographer, Mr. Floyd Riebe, and showed these photographs to him several years ago and he adamantly said he didn't take these pictures.

Law: Well, thank you for your time.

O'Connor: You're quite welcome.

Chapter Seven

JAMES C. JENKINS

What I knew of James Curtis Jenkins had come from David Lifton's book *Best Evidence* and from the work of Harrison Livingstone. As far as I was aware, he'd had little contact with other assassination researchers. Reading *Best Evidence*, I got the impression that Jenkins was, to say the least, uncomfortable talking about what he saw and did on the night of November 22, 1963, so when I first called him, I was not hopeful that his response would be positive.

Far from what I was expecting, Jenkins was friendly, albeit somewhat reserved. When I told him I was a Kennedy assassination researcher, he told me candidly, "I've decided not to talk to researchers anymore." The voice was smooth and mellow with a trace of a southern accent. Apparently he had been taken advantage of by a team that had made arrangements to interview him where he worked, with promises that they would give him a copy of the film. "They came in and they spent hours and hours here. And then I found out – not from them but another source – that all they did was edit it and sell it for educational TV So at that point and time I decided well, I don't want to get involved in this anymore. " Who could blame him? But then Jenkins surprised me by staying on the phone and telling me of his experiences on that fateful night in November.

The notes I made after our conversation include the following:

> Believes Livingstone is correct. Thinks Ford and Specter concocted something to fit the situation. The assassination committee was nothing but show. Basically agrees with O'Connor. Does not remember body bag. Body taken from gurney to table. Wrapped in sheets, pillowcases and towels. Lots of civilians and brass in morgue.

But the striking thing that made me feel connected with Jim Jenkins was the emotion I felt from him when he said, "I was 19 or 20 years old, and all at once I understood that my country was not much better than a third world

219

country. From that point on in time, I have had no trust, no respect for the government. And this was the start of it."

I kept in touch with him, and eventually worked up the courage to ask if he would meet with me for an interview. To my complete surprise he told me he would drive from his home in Alabama and meet with me in New Orleans. It was with great anticipation that I made arrangements for the flight.

I first planned to visit New Orleans to interview Perry Raymond Russo. "Come to New Orleans," he said to me in 1993. "Bring a camera and sound equipment and we'll talk." Russo, of course, was famous (or infamous) for his role in the Jim Garrison affair in which Clay La Verne Shaw was brought to trial for complicity in the death of President Kennedy. However, a few years passed and before I could take Perry up on his offer, he passed away. I thought then that I would never have the chance to visit New Orleans, a city with several nicknames, but known widely – and for good reason – as the "Big Easy."

I got off the plane lugging a heavy briefcase of JFK documents, X-ray prints, autopsy photos, and several depositions just released by the Assassination Records Review Board, as well as camcorder equipment and other essentials for the interview. I had anticipated, but found I wasn't really prepared for, the overwhelming heat and constant oppressive humidity of New Orleans.

By the time I reached the hotel shuttle bus, I was soaked with sweat, tired, wishing for a nice room, a cool drink and a good night's sleep to ready myself for the interview. This was not to happen easily. I nearly got on the wrong shuttle, which would have taken me the wrong way into downtown. At the Best Western, the desk clerk had a hard time finding my reservation, but with a little time and luck, things were straightened out. Finding room #336 was also stressful. I got to #335 and the hall reached a dead end. What now? So far, the Big Easy was anything but!

I eventually stumbled onto room #336, and after a good five minutes of trying, dripping with sweat and frustration, the key card finally opened the door. Ah, my home away from home.... I turned on the air conditioner, stripped down, fell on the bed, and tuned into CNN to catch the latest gripping installment of the Monica Lewinsky show. After making the usual calls to my family, it was time to get down to business, to collect my thoughts and go through my notes for the interview with James Curtis Jenkins.

I fiddled with my new Sony camcorder, and found I had lost a piece from the top of my tripod. It was now 1:30 in the morning New Orleans time, and Jim and I were scheduled to meet at 11:00 AM. Sleep finally came, but I got up bright and early to ready myself for our meeting.

I was trying to figure out how to fix the tripod when the phone rang. "Hello William, it's Jim." It was 10:30, and for a split second I was afraid that he was calling to cancel. "I'm in the lobby," he said. "Great, I'll be right down." Knowing he was there I felt the trepidation melt away that something was going to go wrong at the last minute. With breath held, I walked through the double doors of the lobby to find him staring at a picture on the wall, hands deep in his pockets.

He was bigger than I had expected at well over 6'. With a shock of white hair and a full neatly trimmed beard and mustache of the same color, he was dressed casually in black slacks, socks and shoes, which contrasted with a crisp white buttoned-down shirt. Dark eyes behind steel-framed glasses looked directly at me. He could have been a college history professor. "Jim?" I said. He stepped forward and in the soft voice that I had come to know from our telephone conversations, he said, "Well, hello William. " We shook hands and agreed to go for a late breakfast nearby. "I'm not really hungry," he said. "I'll just have a coke." Although I was eager to get to the topic of experiences on the evening of November 22, 1963 , I was starving, having eaten little the day before.

From our telephone conversations I was aware that he was distrustful of the government and he broached this again in a matter-of-fact tone, without anger or apparent malice. "The government is there to protect itself. … It's certainly not for the people anymore. " I had assumed that we would spend part if not all of the afternoon together, and was shocked when Jenkins informed me that his wife would be back from shopping at around 11:30. "Okay, let's go put this on the record," I said, trying to sound cheerful, but sensing what was coming next. "William, I'd just as soon sit here, drink a soda and talk – without filming it."

I was stunned. For months I had put enormous effort into persuading and arranging for enlisted Bethesda personnel to go fully on the record. Paul O'Connor, Jerrol Custer, and Dennis David had learned to trust me and agreed to relate their experiences on film. (Medical photographer Floyd Riebe had declined at the outset.)

Now that Jim Jenkins had finally agreed to see me and to talk about what he had seen and done on that night of November in the Bethesda morgue, I simply could not let it end like that. Desperation gripped me. I felt my shoulders slump. I felt like I had been clobbered with a two by four, and managed only: "Jim, I've come all the way here. … " I was at a loss. He looked at me for what seemed a long, long time, but was probably only about ten seconds. "Alright, William, I'll do it for you. " The world jumped back into focus. "Great! Let's go do it," I said as I jumped up from the table.

In the room, I scrambled to get things ready. I'd had little experience with the Sony camera. Knowing my time was now limited, as Jim's wife would soon arrive, I inserted the tape, mounted the camera on the tripod and set the focus and the light on automatic. Praying that the settings would be right, and with a notepad and a set of roughly drafted questions, I took a deep breath, sat down behind the camera and started the interview.

Law: Mr. Jenkins, give me your educational background. How did you come to be at Bethesda?

Jenkins: I was in the navy at the time I was in Bethesda. I was in their clinical laboratory blood bank.

Law: What happened to you on the night of November 22, 1963? How did you become involved in that?

Jenkins: I had the duty. And when we had duty we assisted with autopsies. Either I had changed the duty that night with someone, or Paul had changed. I'm not sure which. But normally Paul and I didn't work together as a team.

Law: By Paul you mean?

Jenkins: Paul O'Connor. Usually my teammate was a guy out of Meridian, Mississippi, Stanley Miller. But we were always changing duties. So I assume that's what happened. I don't specifically remember that.

Law: What were you doing when you first heard that President Kennedy had been shot?

Jenkins: We were in class and we had a friend – or I had a friend that was kind of a jokester – and he came in and told us the president had been shot and everybody said, "Naw, naw, you're just joking again." The Chief who was teaching us serology came in and told us classes were dismissed and the people on duty should report to the morgue. At that time he told us the president had been shot. We did not know for sure that he was coming to Bethesda. We were just told to go to the morgue and get it ready. We did not know until the body actually arrived.

Law: How did this make you feel when you heard that John Kennedy had been assassinated?

Jenkins: I don't remember having any strong or specific feelings about this, other than the fact that someone had been killed, but I didn't really have any strong feelings one way or the other about John Kennedy.

Law: So this didn't throw you into any kind of shock or anything like that?

Jenkins: No, no.

Law: Not other than a normal American would feel with their president being killed?

Jenkins: No, it didn't affect me in any dramatic ways. I didn't have any really sorrowing remorse in the sense that it was debilitating or anything of that nature. Like I said, it was no more so than someone dying.

Law: Okay. At the point you were told that the president was coming to Bethesda, what did you do after that?

Jenkins: We really were never told that he was coming to Bethesda. We were told there was a possibility that he would be there, and we should ready the morgue, which is what we did. Paul and I went to the morgue. The duty NCO went with us. I think he was a first-class. We did the normal stuff: labeling the specimen bottles, you know, basically setting up the morgue for an autopsy.

Law: Were you asked not to leave the morgue?

Jenkins: I did not leave the morgue.

Law: I'm talking before, now.

Jenkins: We were not allowed to leave.

Law: Was that by Admiral Galloway?

Jenkins: Admiral Galloway really didn't come down to the morgue until the autopsy started.

Law: Did you hear any helicopters?

James Jenkins, September 2002.

Jenkins: I don't remember hearing any helicopters.

Law: Okay. I'm interested in the atmosphere in the morgue itself. Tell me what happened from the point that you knew the president was going to arrive and things started.

Jenkins: Well, actually I guess, in reality, we first knew the president was coming when he came through the door. That was the first reality. Now, I don't have a very clear memory of him coming through the door. Just a glimpse of the coffin. I wasn't in the atrium. I was in the morgue proper at the table when they came in, so the transfer of the body and so forth is something I don't have a clear memory of.

Law: Do you remember what kind of coffin it was?

Jenkins: I remember that the casket was kind of a – if possible, silver bronze. It was a plain coffin. It was kind of like the ones they used to transport bodies in.

Law: A so-called shipping casket?

Jenkins: Yes, I guess you could call it a shipping casket.

Law: A cheap casket?

Jenkins: Well, I'm not sure. It's the government so – (look of amusement passes over his face). That's really all I remember about it. I guess probably the clearer memory I have is after he was received and was placed on the table.

Law: Okay. Let's go to that. He's placed on the table. People gather around. Is this correct?

Jenkins: Well, not really, because he was placed on the table and he was still wrapped in the sheets and so forth.

Law: How was he wrapped?

Jenkins: Well, he was wrapped in sheets, and I remember that when they unwrapped his head – "they" being Boswell and Humes and so forth – Humes actually took some towels and threw them on the floor, against the wall. I guess being a corpsman and young, and the person who had to clean that up, it stayed with me for a while. Over the years I talked to people at Parkland about that, and of course the lady who had prepared the body had died. They couldn't tell me whether they had those types of towels at Parkland or not. I remember the towel. The towel was basically a terry cloth towel, similar to what we called a shaving cloth in the military.

Law: Do you remember if the body was wrapped in a body bag? There is some controversy about that.

Jenkins: I don't know. I don't. Paul and I have talked about this several times. Paul said it was in a body bag. I don't remember a body bag. But again, like I said, I wasn't specifically involved in taking the body out of the casket. My earliest memory of the body is a clear memory of it being on the table and wrapped in sheets. We were removing the sheets from the body and leaving the head wrapped. And then we began to do the face sheet, [recording] the body marks and so forth.

Law: So while you were doing the face sheet, the head remained wrapped?

Jenkins: Yes. And then Dr. Humes came in. Dr. Humes, Finck, and Dr. Boswell. I think Dr. Boswell may have come first. If I remember correctly, they actually unwrapped the head themselves. I also have a very vague memory of someone telling us not to unwrap the head until they came in. I don't have a clear memory of that.

Law: After that was done, and you saw the wound, what was the reaction of yourself and the people in the morgue in general?

Jenkins: I think that most of us were kind of – I hesitate to say, shocked by a wound – but I think the size of the wound was the most impressive thing.

Law: How big do you estimate the wound was?

Jenkins: It would be difficult to estimate because a lot of the hair was still attached to the skull fragments – the skull was fragmented. But I would say that if you take your hand and you put the heel of your thumb behind your ear, that would cover the basic part of the wound with the open hole approximately in that area.

Law: Do you remember if any of the president's forehead or face was damaged?

"...that would cover the basic part of the wound..."

"...with the open hole approximately in that area."

Jenkins: There were none.

Law: There was no damage?

Jenkins: No. And the only thing is that when they were preparing the body for burial, they had to put a suture in the right eyelid in order to keep it closed because apparently there may have been some bone fracture in that area, but there was no externally visible wound or fracturing there.

Law: Did the front of his head look normal?

Jenkins: Yes.

Law: There were no cracks or missing skin from any of his forehead?

Jenkins: No. It was basically – it probably ran from the temporal right above the ear to the sagittal suture and then back, maybe to the occipital – in the occipital area.

Law: So after they unwrapped the head, they started doing the face sheet.

Jenkins: Well, we did the face sheet – when I'm saying the face sheet, it's just the face sheet of the autopsy. It has drawings of the bodies on them and you put scars, measurements, that type of thing. Unusual scars like the back, you know the injury that he had. The fact is that I believe his left leg was shorter than the right, and that type of thing. I started that. Dr. Boswell continued it, with me writing what Dr. Boswell said. Then we did X-rays. We sat the body up and turned the body over.

Law: You did turn the body over?

Jenkins: Yes, I don't know how many times.

Law: So you moved the body back and forth?

Jenkins: Yes, we moved the body around and, like I said, we sat the body up, we rolled the body over on its side to do the AP, laterals. Most of the X-rays were located kind of in the head area, and then the upper body area. Then, after that, the head was examined. I can remember the positions of the pathologists. [Humes and Boswell] were both standing at the head of the table looking down on the head and Dr. Finck was closest to me. I was at his right shoulder. They were speculating about a lot of things.

Jenkins: Well, about a hole actually above the right ear. The speculation was that it had some gray substance on it and of course the speculation at that point in time that it was from a bullet.

Law: Did they ever discuss whether it was the metal from the bullet? Could they tell if it had come from the front? Did they discuss a frontal entry? Did they make a decision?

Jenkins: No, I think – from my assumption – that it was an entry wound.

Law: In the side of the head?

Jenkins: Yes. You know, I've told people this before. I had seen a similar type wound that I think helped to give me a better perception of the wound. And also, the summer before that I was stationed at Cecil Field, Florida. I was working one night in the dispensary. We were called to the gate because we were told a sailor had been shot. It turned out to be a civilian. He was in white clothes. He was a butcher. He and a friend were rustling his brother-in-law's cattle. And his brother-in-law had shot him through the side of a pick-up truck window. When I went to take this individual out of the back seat of the car, I put my hand under his head and it went inside his brain. It went inside of his head. And so, that was kind of traumatic. This wound seemed to be similar to that. Later on I was told there was a wound below the nuchal line in the back of Kennedy's head (see photo 19).

Law: Tell me what that is.

Jenkins: The nuchal line runs through here (pointing to the rear of the skull, just above the hairline). And it's possible that I could have missed that when we were moving the body around because of the hair and the blood and so forth. But I would have thought that it would be fairly evident. I have to say I never saw that wound.

Law: The depositions of Dr. Humes and Boswell have been released by the Records Review Board. I believe it was Dr. Boswell who said they made decisions that night of where the bullet entered and exited. Would you say that's true?

Jenkins: To my knowledge, no. Again, like I said, I came out of the autopsy that night and I was sure that the bullet entered the right side of the head and exited in this area (touching the back of his head above his right ear), and that there was a bullet wound around the scapula in the back.

"… and exited in this area…"

Law: How far down do you say that was. Give me an estimate: Tl, T2 – ?

Jenkins: Probably … (he thinks, reaching around touching his back) … I would say about T4 [i.e., the fourth thoracic vertebra].

Law: Giving your opinion based on your experiences, would you say that a bullet could enter the back like that and go out the president's throat?

Jenkins: I wouldn't think so because it was below that wound. Later in the autopsy I helped Dr. Boswell remove the organs from the body and we were sectioning the organs and weighing them. And Dr. Humes and Dr. Finck were trying to probe that wound.

Law: And what did they probe it with?

Jenkins: Humes probed it, to begin with, with his little finger. Humes has huge hands. Humes is a big man. And then they used a probe. I could see his finger and I could see the probes behind the pleural area in the back and it never did break into the pleural cavity. And the wound actually went down and stopped.

Law: In essence, from what you saw, the wound did not go upwards toward the throat? You feel that it went down?

Jenkins: It seemed to have gone down and then stopped. It didn't break into the pleural cavity.

Law: Did they have a discussion about this?

Jenkins: They were a little upset about it. There was something else about it [the lung] on the right middle lobe. There was a purple spot, which might have been a bruise. I know the comment was made when we removed the lungs that they were awful pink and someone had asked had he been a smoker. And the comment was that he smoked cigars. That was about the only discussion they had. I do know they did not find any bullet – we didn't find any bullet fragments. The bullet fragments were the ones that were brought in after the autopsy started.

Law: Were you there during any of the X-rays that Jerrol Custer took?

Jenkins: Yes, I was there during everything.

Law: Tell me the basic story from the time that the body was taken from the casket.

Jenkins: Basically, they unwrapped the head and they started taking X-rays and photographs.

Law: Immediately after they –

Jenkins: After they looked at it. The X-ray people got there and, from the conversation, they were looking for bullet fragments, or metal fragments really, I guess is more appropriate. And they kept doing X-rays and going back and finally one of the radiologists came in. There was a lot of discussion and so forth about them not being able to find fragments and there was some direction and so forth being given from the gallery, which is where Admiral Galloway was.

Law: When you say direction from the gallery, tell me how the morgue was set up.

Jenkins: The morgue was set up basically – you had an atrium that had morgue boxes in it. The morgue proper had two tables. The body was placed on the first table (see photo 11).

Law: Were these tables side by side?

Jenkins: No, they were end to end. Number one table was at the front of the morgue. There was a table behind it and an autoclave behind that. Standing at the head of the table, on your right you would have a passageway that went into the back where the dressing lockers were. There was also a little room to the left where they stored the brains and tissue and so forth. And there was a little supply room, and a room to the right of that. Coming back into the morgue, you had a deep sink and a counter space all the way to the back of the morgue with overhead storage. And as I said previously, at the back of the morgue there was a large autoclave. Now, standing at the head of the first table, to the left, there was a gallery where people would come in and watch the autopsies, for training purposes or whatever.

Law: And how many people would you estimate in the gallery besides the doctors and technicians?

Jenkins: It was full.

Law: It was full?

Jenkins: The gallery ran almost the length of the morgue, and I would say that the morgue was probably 18 to 20 feet.

Law: An estimate of people – fifteen, twenty, thirty?

Jenkins: I would say probably more than thirty people.

Law: Do you remember any of the Joint Chiefs of Staff being there?

Jenkins: No, I wouldn't have known them.

Law: You wouldn't have known Curtis LeMay by chance?

Jenkins: No.

Law: Did you think there were high-ranking officials there?

Jenkins: Everything was flagged above.[1] Actually, I felt sorry for the people on the floor because Humes was a commander and Boswell was a lieutenant commander and Finck, I think, was a major.

Law: Do you feel that these doctors felt extraordinary pressure? It was the President of the United States –

Jenkins: Sure, I think that they were pressured toward a conclusion that had already been established and they were not finding evidence to support that, and were under a tremendous amount of pressure.

Law: What do you mean by "the conclusion had already been established"? That Oswald had shot Kennedy? One man shooting another man?

Jenkins: One man shooting another man.

Law: And they weren't exactly finding that in evidence?

---

1. Meaning: all present were of high rank.

Jenkins: They weren't. Like I said, we were finding no bullet fragments, no metal fragments.

Law: Anywhere? No large pieces?

Jenkins: No. The only bullet fragments or any type of metal fragments I saw were brought to us by a man in a suit and tie and he had some small pieces of bone. Not so much like the ziplocks we know today, but in specimen bags that used to have the ties on them. And it was placed down the side of the president's head on the right side, next to his ear on the table. And later on they tried to fit some of the bone fragments into the skull. I don't remember them being very successful at that.

Law: My understanding is that you helped Jerrol Custer move the president's body around for X-rays. Is this correct?

Jenkins: Yes.

Law: Give me the procedure for that. What happened that you were the person to take X-rays. Now, did they take X-rays first and then pictures?

Jenkins: I think they were doing everything – kind of –

Law: However, they could get it done?

Jenkins: Jerrol was the X-ray tech who came in. He needed help and I happened to be the corpsman who was detailed there at the table, and as an enlisted man it was my job to help him do whatever he needed to do, and we moved the body around for the various angles that he needed to take.

Law: Now, at this point everyone had left the room?

Jenkins: No.

Law: I mean technician-wise because they didn't want to be zapped with X-rays.

Jenkins: I don't know about the gallery, but …

Law: The gallery basically stayed in while this was being performed?

Jenkins: I don't really remember that everybody left. I know that probably some of us couldn't leave. But, I think Jerrol gave me a lead apron. I'm not sure. And I'm sure that probably what happened is that everybody backed off. I don't think that they left the room. I'm not sure.

Law: What did you think when you were moving the body around and you saw the wounds. What were your general impressions?

Jenkins: Well, I think really that my feeling was, it was basically something we'd been directed to do and we were doing. The wounds – I had seen the wounds before the X-rays ever started, when the head was unwrapped and so forth. I had seen the wounds.

Law: Did anybody tell you not to probe the throat wound? Was there any talk – no one said, "Don't probe the throat wound," or "Leave it alone"?

Jenkins: No, because – we went through the whole autopsy on the premise that the throat wound was a trach [tracheotomy]. The only examination of the throat area that I remember was that Dr. Boswell kind of pulled the flap back as far as he could, the chest flap, and kind of looked in that area. There was no probing for that, that I could ever remember. The neck wound was –

Law: Was it totally left alone?

Jenkins: As far as I remember, it was. I don't remember any intensive probing or examination of it.

Law: Did anybody dissect the neck?

Jenkins: No.

Law: That was left totally alone?

Jenkins: Right.

Law: How many X-rays would you estimate were taken by Jerrol Custer?

Jenkins: I have no idea.

Law: Do you know if he X-rayed the total body?

Jenkins: I don't remember him X-raying the total body. I remember him basically, like I said, from his thorax up.

Law: Do you remember – at any point – a bullet fragment falling out of the back of the president?

Jenkins: No.

Law: Absolutely not?

Jenkins: Absolutely not.

Law: What happened after you completed the job with the X-rays?

Jenkins: After the X-rays, photographs and so forth, we started the autopsy

Law: Tell me about that.

Jenkins: Well, Dr. Boswell and I started the incisions. I worked with him to remove, weigh, and dissect the organs. And we were doing that, basically, over the chest cavity. One of the things that was a little unusual for me was that there was very little blood in the chest cavity.

Law: What does that signify?

Jenkins: I would probably think that there was no real penetrating wounds in the chest cavity. And we found none.

Law: No penetrating wounds in the chest cavity?

Jenkins: The organs in the chest cavity, other than a slight, like I said, blue spot or purple spot, which would have been a hematoma on the right lung – it could have been insignificant – there was no major amount of blood in the cavity.

Law: Let me ask you this. From the wound in the back, it's been speculated that the bullet went into the back, and the reason the lung was bruised on the top, was that the bullet may have hit the lung and went out the throat. In your estimation is this possible?

Jenkins: There would have had to have been an entry into the pleural cavity in order for it to hit the lung. Actually, there would have had to have been a lot of damage done. Because it wouldn't just come into there, it would have – it couldn't hit the lung, per se, in exit because it would have had to have gone down and then bounced up at a 90 degree angle, come up, and then come out. I assume the probability may be such, but I would have thought that it would have had to have been deflected by a rib or something solid.

Law: You just don't feel that the scenario is possible?

Jenkins: No, I don't think so. Not from what I saw.

Law: Okay. Continue with the autopsy work you did.

Jenkins: Well, Dr. Boswell and I took the organs out. He dissected them and weighed them. I wrote in the information and once we finished that, and once they finished probing the head, they began to remove the brain.

Law: Now, during this time the brain had not been removed? The brain was in the cranium at this point?

Jenkins: Right.

Law: Did you see who took out the brain? Who cut the brain and stem and brought it out?

Jenkins: That's something that's a little strange. We normally did a skullcap. We didn't really have to do a skullcap on this because, as they expanded the wound, it was large enough for the brain to come out. And Dr. Humes removed the brain and made a kind of an exclamatory statement. I think what he said was, "The damn thing fell out in my hand."

Law: What would this mean to you?

Jenkins: It would mean that the brain stem had already been severed. And that, with some other statements and our conversations about some areas that were fragmented, along the sagittal suture looked like – there was some comment that it looked like it had been surgically extended.

Law: Surgically extended? What does that mean?

Jenkins: I think what they were talking about was some of the fragmented area up in here (top, right side of the head), that it looked like it had been cut with a scalpel to expand it a little bit.

Law: The wound itself?

Jenkins: Yes. To me that indicated that the brain had been removed and re-placed. To further support that, when Dr. Humes gave the brain to Dr. Boswell, I'd been asked what my impression of the brain was. My impression of the brain was that the damage to the area of the brain, the extensiveness of it, did not quite match the extensiveness of the wound. In other words, the damage to the brain seemed to be a little less then you would expect from [the damage to the skull].

Law: So we're talking massive damage to the head, but not so much damage to the brain?

Jenkins: Right. And I think that is possible because we were talking about a tra-jectory that rapidly transverses something. And the brain tissue – whenever you traumatize brain tissue it gets kind of soft and jelly-like – and again this could just be my perception because I thought, like probably most other people, when I saw the president's body I thought it was small, probably due to my expectations of it. And I thought the brain was small.

Law: You thought the brain was small?

Jenkins: Right. But the brain was taken – Dr. Humes took it and went to the bucket. And the vessels in the base of the brain – there were two things that were a little strange to me. Where the brain stem had been severed, it looked almost like it had been severed on the one side to a certain point, then maybe severed on the other side, but not quite at the same level. To me it was a little bit unusual. But you have to understand, I am a third-class hospital corpsman. I'm twenty years old and everything in there could have had me shot tomorrow. So we took it to the bucket and there was a pathology resident who came in and helped us with it because the vessels at the base of the brain – which we infused, which was internal carotids – they were retracted. It was like they had been severed and a short period of time after – when you sever a blood vessel, especially an artery, it retracts. And the longer it is severed, the more it retracts and it was kind of mangled a little bit so we had problems with that.

Law: So it was hard to infuse this brain because it had been severed for a long period of time?

Jenkins: That was my feeling, okay? I think over the years I've increased my ed-ucation and so forth and I feel like that's probable.

Law: But you did see the brain?

Jenkins: I did see the brain.

Law: There was damage on the right hemisphere of the brain?

Jenkins: Right anterior.

Law: Okay. It was not whole and undamaged?

Jenkins: No, it was not whole.

Law: There was damage to the brain. What happened after you put the brain into the bucket?

Jenkins: Well, our normal procedure was we start the infusion through the needles and we made a gauze sling across the top of the bucket. The bucket had formaldehyde in it also, or formalin. Then once they're infused for a while we just drop them in the bucket and normally we would have labeled the bucket and then it would have gone to the brain conference, which was basically a dissection of the brains by the attending pathologist, who would have probably been Boswell in his residence, as a teaching exercise, and, other than that, as far as I remember, the brain was still in the bucket when I left at nine the next morning.

Law: The brain now has been put in the bucket. What was the procedure at that point?

Jenkins: To leave it there.

Law: Regarding the rest of the body, what did you do?

Jenkins: The rest of the body at that point in time, they – I think it was probably one or two o'clock in the morning – they concluded their autopsy, notes and everything, examination of the head, the body, the organs, everything was concluded, and then the mortician came and took over.

Law: Are you saying that the morticians came in after everything had been done?

Jenkins: There was only one mortician.[2]

Law: There was only one mortician? But, there wasn't any make-up person there?

Jenkins: He did everything.

Law: Did he come in after everything had been completed.

Jenkins: He was there, I think, before the autopsy was completed.

Law: I've been told that even as pictures were being taken, and after the X-rays and things were going on, that he was basically there doing work just as soon as he could do it.

Jenkins: No.

Law: That's not true?

Jenkins: He did not have access to the body until after the autopsy was completed. My duty was to stand by and help him if he needed it.

Law: And you were there with the body for most of the time?

Jenkins: I was there from the time it started. I was in the morgue from three to nine the next morning. From three that afternoon. The only time I left the table was sometime after Dr. Boswell and I had finished with the organs. Dr. Stover, who was sitting behind me, told me to get a sandwich. And the sandwiches were right behind him in the morgue.

---

2. Four moricians are listed in photo 18

Law: You ate the sandwich in the morgue?

Jenkins: Well, I washed my hands first (smiles). I took the gloves off. I remember not really having an appetite for it. So I just took a couple of bites and went back to the table.

Law: Let's go back to the atmosphere of the morgue. I'm very interested in that part of it.

Jenkins: The atmosphere of the morgue was extremely tense. At least I felt like it was.

Law: It's been called by one of the doctors, "a circus." Would you say that was true?

Jenkins: Yes, I think that would be. The autopsy at the table was being directed by the end of the gallery, which consists of the person I recognized as Galloway. The couple of other officers – one, I'm told, was Burkley.

Law: But you wouldn't know them necessarily otherwise?

Jenkins: I didn't know them. The only officers I knew were the ones I was working with at the table, and I really didn't know Dr. Finck. When I asked, I was told he was an expert on managing wounds from downtown. Captain Stover was my commanding officer in the Medical School – and Admiral Galloway, who was actually the commanding officer [of the National Naval Medical Center]. All the other people were – I don't know.

Law: It's been said that there was a comment made of "Who's in charge?" and someone said, "I am." Do you know who that was?

Jenkins: I don't remember who that was.

Law: Do you remember hearing that statement?

Jenkins: No.

Law: Do you feel that Dr. Humes was basically fully in charge of the autopsy? Was he giving most of the orders?

Jenkins: No.

Law: He was not in charge of the autopsy.

Jenkins: I think he was being directed.

Law: By someone in the gallery?

Jenkins: If the individual they told me it was, was Burkley, then I think he was probably being directed by Burkley through Galloway.

Law: You don't think that Humes was basically in charge and giving the orders. He was basically taking them?

Jenkins: Yes. I think so. I mean, technically he was in charge of the autopsy. But –

Law: Technically?

Jenkins: Yes. He was a senior ranking doctor there, plus he was also the director of a laboratory. But he certainly was being directed by someone else.

Law: And do you think he was taking these orders –

Jenkins: I think they were frustrating him. All of the doctors at the table were being frustrated by this.

Law: Do you think they were actually trying to do their jobs to the best of their ability?

Jenkins: I think so. I think they were trying to do their jobs. And I think they were trying to honestly come up with as much as their ability allowed them, as to what happened – where the bullet wounds were, and to categorize them in terms of direction and so forth.

Law: So you don't feel they were trying to hide anything?

Jenkins: The autopsy? No. No I don't think so.

Law: They were just doing their job. They were trying to get through this the best way they could. Did they do the best job they could in your opinion?

Jenkins: They did. I agree. I think that's probably the scenario.

Law: Do you feel that anybody was trying to stop them from doing their job to the best of their ability?

Jenkins: I think that there were people who were directing them and trying to direct them toward a conclusion. And I think that's probably what happened.

Law: So you think that there was a preconceived conclusion, and that conclusion was not being reached.

Jenkins: I think so. I think that's putting it very well.

Law: Is this part of what you feel was causing the tension in the morgue?

Jenkins: Yes. I think so. There were a lot of things going on in the morgue, in the sense that you had – on the floor with us – two FBI agents. They were standing off behind Dr. Humes and Dr. Finck and Dr. Boswell. They were kind of some distance back, you know. Basically within hearing range, but without getting in the way.

Law: Do you remember who they were?

Jenkins: I have been told that their names were Sibert and O'Neill. Again I would not –

Law: You didn't know at that time?

Jenkins: No. I remember kind of a scuffle. I'm not sure that it was a scuffle per se, but I was later told that someone had a camera taken away.

Law: A camera? A picture camera or a movie camera?

Jenkins: I don't know. Because I had been told the disturbance was someone who had taken a camera away from somebody.

Law: Do you remember there being a person taking any kind of movie film? There has been a story about a William Pitzer taking –

Jenkins: I don't remember him doing that. I mean he may have been doing it.

Law: Would you know who William Pitzer was?

Jenkins: I think he was public relations or something.

Law: Would you know him by sight?

Jenkins: No.

Law: So you wouldn't have known him anyway?

Jenkins: No, but I probably would have recognized him because he would have been in uniform.

Law: He would have been in uniform?

Jenkins: From my understanding he was a Lieutenant Commander so he would have stood out fairly well.

Law: But you don't remember him being there?

Jenkins: No, I don't remember. It's possible, but I don't remember. The only other officers that I remember that were not – at least, maybe – captain or above, were the escorts, the honor guards. Most of them were in the army or dress army.

Law: Can you remember anything specific? Little bits of conversation amongst the doctors or amongst the people in the gallery?

Jenkins: I was across the table from the gallery. And the [people in] the gallery – they were not – they were basically not speaking in very loud, audible terms. They were pretty well directing Dr. Humes and Boswell from over that side of the table.

Law: Were these doctors – Boswell and Humes – were they acting nervous in any way? Would you say they were frightened by what was going on? Or was it just normal, average pressure?

Jenkins: No, I don't think they were frightened. I think that, as I said, they were beginning to get frustrated.

Law: Basically they were just angry that they weren't allowed to do their jobs, or frustrated?

Jenkins: I think they were frustrated because the directions that they were being given – I think the frustration in the gallery was the fact that they were not finding any metal fragments.

Law: Was there any comment that they were not finding any metal fragments?

Jenkins: I think that was the reason for the continuation of the X-rays.

Law: Did they seem surprised that they didn't find metal fragments?

Jenkins: I'm not sure that I really paid that much attention to that. Most of my concentration was – I was there at the table to help the doctors and my attention was directed to what they were doing – not so much to the other things. The rest were just peripheral-type things. I remember the frustration and tension and so forth, but I felt it also.

Law: You felt the tension?

Jenkins: Yes, because it was the way that during the X-rays – it was almost like they brought the radiologist in out of frustration.

Law: From not finding fragments?

Jenkins: Yes, like well, you know this guy is missing something. Then the radiologist came in and I think he directed some more X-rays. But they didn't show anything either.

Law: So, after that, you weighed the organs. Is this correct?

Jenkins: Yes.

Law: Were they weighed en masse or were they weighed separately?

Jenkins: Individually.

Law: They were weighed individually?

Jenkins: Yes, the weights are on the face sheet.

Law: Would you say they were average for a man?

Jenkins: I would think so.

Law: Nothing was smaller or abnormal?

Jenkins: I don't remember There was a question, I think, about the adrenals, but I –

Law: Was there a big thing about the adrenals?

Jenkins: No.

Law: Did they find any adrenals?

Jenkins: There was no major discussion or anything on that.

Law: Did you know if they did an examination on the adrenals?

Jenkins: Well, we removed the kidneys.

Law: You would have known about adrenal glands. You would have known what they look like, right?

Jenkins: Yes.

Law: I know that I'm asking you to remember from 35 years ago. But, do you remember there being any adrenal glands?

Jenkins: No, I don't remember one way or the other. Remember we were focusing on the area where the wounds would have been. Now, I'm sure that Dr. Boswell would have – and the kidneys may not have gone back in the body.

Law: Do you think most of the organs were put back? Did you see anybody put organs back? Did they save the organs?

Jenkins: Actually, no I didn't. I remember forming the body cavity, filling it with plaster. And I remember the mortician actually cutting up the bowel.

Law: The mortician did this?

Jenkins: Yes, and adding it [the bowel] to it [the plaster], apparently for the moisture. I'm not sure why. I remember him cutting the bowel up. We basically stripped the bowel and checked for lesions and that kind of stuff.

Law: Would you say the body was bloody at this point? I've had it described to me by colleagues of yours that if you even went near him or touched him you were bloody. Would you say that is accurate?

Jenkins: No.

Law: No, there wasn't that much blood then?

Jenkins: Most of the blood was in the head and upper chest area around the neck.

Law: So you wouldn't say that the body was literally drenched?

Jenkins: No, not at all.

Law: Do you remember the hair itself? Did it look like it had been previously cleaned? Do you think –

Jenkins: No, I don't think so.

Law: You don't think that the hair could have been cleaned at this point?

Jenkins: You mean cleaned before, as the body was being prepared?

Law: Well, Saundra Spencer, who had at some point developed negatives of President Kennedy, has said these are – how she described it was – a set of "more tasteful" pictures. Not the pictures that were taken at the autopsy. She said these aren't like the autopsy pictures at all, that the hair had been cleaned and there is no blood. The interesting part is she said that the throat wound was about thumbnail size. And, from my understanding, when you received the body on the night of November 22nd, the wound was a big, open, gaping –

Jenkins: The wound was a gash. It was about this wide (indicates approximately 3 inches with fingers).

Law: Would you say that was the normal size of a tracheotomy?

Jenkins: Considering the statement that was made, that it was done in an emergency and so forth, I would think that would probably be a little large.

Law: Do you think it would have endangered the patient?

Jenkins: No. You have to understand this was an emergency procedure. All they were trying to do was get to the trachea. It was a little wide, and according to what I learned later at Parkland – in Parkland normal trachs were done basically vertically, as opposed to horizontally. But, like I said, I think the doctors who did this, did it over a bullet wound.

Law: Did you see any evidence of a bullet wound?

Jenkins: No.

Law: In the so-called "stare-of-death" photograph, and I believe I have a copy of it –

Jenkins: I've seen it.

Law: Would you mind looking at it (photo 1)?

Jenkins: It looks basically about the same size.

Law: Now there is a small point at the bottom. There has been some talk about that being part of a bullet wound (photo la, arrow C).

Jenkins: I'm not sure. It would just be speculation on my part. But just to me, as I said before, I went through the whole autopsy, and I think so did the pathology people, assuming that was the trach. That it was an emergency trach.

Law: Would you say that is valid?

Jenkins: This looks a little wider (indicating the vertical distance, top to the bottom of the wound). It seems, a little larger than I remember, but the width across the neck seems to be about the same.

Law: You don't think that that's been painted in or enlarged by painting? Would you say that's possible?

Jenkins: Well, I don't see much definition in the area within the wound and there should be more definition of the tissue, I would think. But again we're talking about black and white, we're talking about lighting – this photograph always bothers me.

Law: What bothers you about it the most?

Jenkins: This area right here (pointing to what Paul O'Connor termed a "wooden object" in the background of photo 1). That item (photo lb) was not in our morgue.

Law: I have been told by one of your colleagues, the X-ray technician, Mr. Jerrol Custer, that this was a portable X-ray machine and he put it there.

Jenkins: There was a portable X-ray machine in there, but –

Jenkins: This doesn't look like a portable X-ray machine.

Law: What do you think it looks like?

Jenkins: It looks like either a box or a cage … or maybe – my first impression when I looked at it, when I looked at these photographs, was that it was maybe a shower stall, but I don't – it doesn't look like … (silence)

Law: You would know what a portable X-ray machine would look like?

Jenkins: Yes, there was one in the morgue most of the time.

Law: But you would say, based on your memory, that that is not a portable X-ray machine?

Jenkins: I wouldn't say that is a portable X-ray machine. First of all I would say it's a little small. I don't see … I would have to say that I couldn't identify this as a portable X-ray machine.

Law: Now this next picture (photo 2): does that look like what you remember from the left side?

Jenkins: Yes. Yes, it seems like it. You can see the hair hanging down here and so forth. This one really bothers me too, because in our morgue we did not use this type of headrest.

Law: What did you use?

Jenkins: We used an aluminum block that was scalloped for different sizes, for the neck and so forth. And the headrest really, unless they used it for the photograph, would have gone underneath the neck.

Law: Underneath the neck itself?

Jenkins: Right.

Law: So basically you used a block, you did not use a metal head holder?

Jenkins: In the eighteen months that I did autopsies in that morgue, I don't even remember seeing anything like this.

Law: How about the phone? Was the phone there on the wall (photo 2)

Jenkins: There was a phone, but I remember that it was next to the deep sink, right in the passageway (top left of photo 2).

Law: Does this look like your morgue to you?

Jenkins: It's hard to say. The passageway is in the right place.… The other things too.… This also is something I don't remember – I don't remember this towel underneath the body or anything.

Law: To your recollection, was that ever put underneath the body while you were there?

Jenkins: It's possible, but I don't remember.

240

Law: Were you there for all the pictures?

Jenkins: I was there from the start of the autopsy to the end of the autopsy.

Law: Do you remember these pictures? Do they show the body that you remember?

Jenkins: I am fairly sure that this is the body (picking up photo 1). The reason why I am sure is – see there is a small incision here and one on the other side (pointing to marks on either side of the chest, reportedly made by the Dallas doctors; photo 1a, arrows A and B).

Law: Does the face look the same as it did?

Jenkins: I would say probably. Again, like I said, these are black and white photographs and it's been a long time.

Law: Right. The reason I ask these questions is that I'm trying to clear up misperceptions voiced by other people. And there have been speculations – writers have stated that that particular picture, the "stare of death" photograph, may be of a wax face because there are no pores in the skin. I've been told by other persons who were there that the camera flash was so bright that it took the pores out of the skin.

Jenkins: I wouldn't know. That's not within my realm of knowledge and expertise. I really don't know and I can't even speculate on that.

Law: How about this one (photo 3)? I've always wondered about the clip or whatever it is inside the head (photo 3a, arrow). Do you remember anything like that?

Jenkins: This is unusual if you look at the brain tissue. The brain tissue is intact.

Law: It is intact?

Jenkins: This is the brain tissue. With an injury like this, the brain would have had to have been affected, traumatized in some manner.

Law: Right.

Jenkins: This looks like the normal softness in the wrinkles of the brain.

Law: Really? So you can basically see brain in there?

Jenkins: Yes. Right here. Right in here (pointing to the top center on both sides of the so-called clip inside the head).

Law: There seems to be some kind of foreign object in the middle of the head. Have you ever been able to ascertain what that might be?

Jenkins: I had looked at one once before – that looked like a suture needle.

Law: A suture needle?

Jenkins: I haven't seen one in a long time. It could have been to hold the scalp back for this. So it looks like that right here. Maybe a hook. It could have been something to hold the scalp back.

Law: I always thought it was something they put in because the skull was so crushed that they needed something –

Jenkins: Well, you can see what I was describing before. This is all tissue, skin and so forth with hair attached to it (pointing to the extruded material). There was really only a portion that was gone in the brain, about this size in the skull (indicating an area of about two and a half inches in diameter with his fingers).

Law: Missing from the brain?

Jenkins: That was the hole in the skull. It was in this area (touching the rear right side of his head). I think several other people have corroborated that. I think this (photo 3) was actually taken with the skin, the tissue, and the fragmented skull opened up.

Law: Would it make up part of the so-called flap, this part hanging down?

Jenkins: No, the flap itself was an area over the ear, I remember, and it was kind of – well, actually it was kind of just flapped out because it was totally broken from the scalp and the skull.

Law: Would you say you can take that, whatever, flap, and basically hide some of the wound with it?

Jenkins: I would think you could do it, but it would cover the area over the ear.

Law: So there would be a lot – that much – missing? Just over the ear, it wouldn't have covered the back part?

Jenkins: No, you could cover everything on the wound with the exception of the small area that I described.

Law: There seems to be a small table, a metal table, over the president.

Jenkins: That's probably the dissecting table but I – I'm sure that's what it is.

Law: Did you use that in your morgue?

Jenkins: We did use it. As a matter of fact it had a scale on it and when we dissected organs that's where we did it. The only thing I would probably think about this is that if this was the original photograph it must have been one that was taken later, later on, during the autopsy than I remember.

Law: I'll just show you one more (photo 4). A lot has been made of this particular photograph because the hair looks clean and shiny, and everything I've ever read or talked about with people said it was bloody.

Jenkins: It was bloody. This is the flap (pointing to the avulsed skull bone over the right ear).

Law: Okay.

Jenkins: That seems about right because it actually would've been pulled back on to the skull.

Law: So we're not seeing all of that, are we?

Jenkins: No.

Law: That's just a piece we're seeing in the picture there. It would cover more of an area than it seems to in that picture. Is that what you're saying?

Jenkins: The flap would have filled in this area right in here (pointing to the area in the back of the skull behind the flap).

Law: Right.

Jenkins: I think we're just seeing the flap as it's protruding out. The thing that I don't understand is that this area would've been where the wound was (pointing to the back of the head).

Law: That was, at that point, a large gaping wound?

Jenkins: That was a large gaping wound.

Law: From this picture (photo 4) you don't see that.

Jenkins: No, I don't.

Law: Was there enough scalp back there? It looks like someone is pulling that forward.

Jenkins: They probably could have picked up some of the scalp and filled it in, but there was enough missing. I guess they could have stretched the scalp that was there without the bone and covered it, but this was an area without bone; [it] was gone. This was actually the hole.

Law: That was actually the hole?

Jenkins: Right. That was actually the hole (pointing to the rear right side of the head in photo 4),

Law: I know this is opinion, but this is part of what I'd like to straighten out – I've been told there wasn't enough scalp there in the back to cover that up and I've been told by two different people that there was enough to cover that.

Jenkins: I think that, to clarify it, I think there was probably enough scalp and tissue and hair that they could've covered everything with it, but they would not have had a bone basis.

Law: So even though the bone was missing –

Jenkins: They would have had to stretch the scalp that was there because there was a hole that was – there was nothing left. It was like, well, getting into the controversy, it was like it had been blown out.

Law: A blowout in the back of the head?

Jenkins: Right. And I think that that's probably part of the bone fragment that had been brought into the autopsy.

Law: So, there was a blowout in the back of the head.

Jenkins: I think so.

Law: A curious statement was made by Dr. Humes when the House Select Committee in 1977 asked him about the wound in the head, and he said it had to come in from behind and exited from behind. I've never understood that statement.

Jenkins: I've looked at probably most of the theories on trajectory that have been published. To me they defy mathematical projections and probabilities, and physics, actually. And there are things that I have looked at over the years, these photographs for one. I have been asked basically the same thing: "Do you think those things were doctored?" I don't know. It would only be conjecture on my part, but I know there are some differences from what I remember and what these photographs show.

Law: This is for clarification (photo 6). The back wound?

Jenkins: I think the back wound (photo 6a, arrow A) appears higher up on the torso than it was, probably because of the positioning of the neck, and the head is straight and back.

Law: Now, it's my understanding that they took him and pulled him from his shoulders from the table. Is this correct? He was lying on the table and they kind of pulled him up to show the wound?

Jenkins: Right. And the area is close to where I remembered it. But I think this gives the impression it is a little higher than it really was.

Law: With the large wound, was there only one?

Jenkins: It was the only one I saw.

Law: And the small? It seems like a smaller entrance there (photo 6a, arrow B). Is that just a speck of blood?

Jenkins: I really don't know what that is.

Law: It's just an artifact. You really don't know what that is?

Jenkins: It could very well have been blood, because as you see there is dried blood down through here. It could have been an artifact of him being laid on his back. His rigor mortis set in.

Law: Now going back to the back of the head – his hair seems to be washed and shiny.

Jenkins: Yes, and this also seemed to have some type of metal retaining – whether it's a hook or needle, or whatever.

Law: Where is that?

Jenkins: Here (photo 6a, arrow C).

Law: I've never really noticed that. That might explain some things, truly.

Jenkins: You can see again in this – here's the flap (pointing to the area above the right ear).

Law: Right, but that was the smaller flap, right?

Jenkins: That was the one above the ear, and you can see this is above the ear, because here's the external ear, the auricle, and above it is the beginning of the flap.

Law: So we have a flap at the side and a big hole in the back. I know you're not a ballistics expert, but let me ask you this. Would a Manlicher-Carcano – I don't even know how big the shells are – could it cause that kind of damage?

Jenkins: I personally don't think he could've hit the president with it.

Law: You don't think so. Conceding that it could, would it crack the skull in this –

Jenkins: A bullet, unless it is designed as a dumdum or something like that, makes a small entrance and a large exit. Especially in a skull where you basically have a hollow cavity filled with brain tissue. So as it goes in, the skull going in would deform it a little. As it was coming out it would push more. As it goes in, its basically solid. And as it goes in, the brain tissue is not really that dense. Coming out it would go from a less dense to a more dense type thing. In relating back to the night that I described to you, before I went to Bethesda, that kid had been shot with a 30/30.

Law: We're talking about the man who got shot through a car window?

Jenkins: Right. The wounds were similar.

Law: The wounds were similar? And again, he shot him through the side of the head?

Jenkins: He shot him through a pick-up truck window. He was apparently in front of or to the side of the truck.

Law: From that experience and from what you saw at Bethesda that night, those wounds were similar?

Jenkins: Yes.

Law: I'm going to show you one more, and this is just for my own understanding. The beveling of the wounds – see I don't know much about this kind of thing. I have to go to people that know.

Jenkins: This has always been controversial (photo 5). ... I assume that this is the internal auditory capsule.

Law: What does that mean?

Jenkins: The internal part of the ear. The nuchal line would be somewhere in this area (photo 5a, line A). Like I said, it is extremely difficult to orientate this picture and I may be totally off.

Law: What about – I think they said the notch is in the bone. Do you see this? That notch and the notch down below here. There seem to be two round beveled wounds (photo 5a, arrows B and C).

Jenkins: I think this is purposely done where you can't hardly see any neckline, shoulders or reference points that would help you.

Law: Well, couldn't this just be through inept picture-taking?

Jenkins: It could be, but I'm sure this has been copied a number of times, so I don't really know. Of course this (ruler) is also placed in a very opportune place.

Law: Why would you say that?

Jenkins: Well, it gives you no reference over here – and see this is all blacked out so you have no reference there. The reference that I would try to use would be this, which may be the mid-line but I can't follow it into the occipital area. And the nuchal line (approximately at line A, photo 5a) – this looks like it may be an area where they had said there was a wound (c.g. photo 19, "entrance of bullet #2"). If that's the case, it would be at the nuchal line

Law: Now, did you see the skull like that? Did they reflect the scalp back in your presence? Do you remember that?

Jenkins: This one I didn't pay any particular attention to. Understand that I'm standing here and the head is there. And Dr. Finck is standing next to me there (i.e., Finck was between Jenkins and the head), examining the [president's] head and I'm listening to these comments. Basically because I'm anticipating their needs.

Law: Now this last thing was something that Paul O'Connor had drawn up (photo 10). Would you agree with that?

Jenkins: I would say that's probably what happened. I think this is certainly plausible in the fact that there is an entrance wound here, and it goes between the ribs and stops here. The probing that I saw indicated that there was a dead end behind the pleural cavity.

Law: So it did indicate that there was a dead end?

Jenkins: Yes, that there was no entrance into the pleural cavity, which would have been here. And before they were pressing on the pleura with the probes and their fingers.

Law: So when the body was laid open, if those bullets had stopped there, wouldn't there have been fragments to be seen?

Jenkins: Theoretically there should have been bullet fragments in the head. There should have been a thoroughly intact bullet in this (i.e., the back wound). At the termination of this one.

Law: But there were no fragments?

Jenkins: There were no fragments. And that was part of the frustration that the pathologists were having, and the reason for the continuing X-rays.

Law: So they kept this up because they could not understand why there were no bullet fragments in the body. Usually you would have bullet fragments in the body?

Jenkins: Sure. You would have at least fragments where it hit a rib or bones. Like I said, there was some discussion as to whether some grayish type of matter that was on the skull, here on the right side (pointing to his head above the right ear), were actually particles of a bullet or not.

Law: Do you remember talking to Jerrol Custer? You worked with him. Did he give you any indication as to what he thought, or did you basically keep to yourselves?

Jenkins: No, there was no conversation between –

Law: It was like, let's get this job done?

Jenkins: Well, we were just technicians doing the job we were supposed to do. And it was best at that time to keep your thoughts and your opinions to yourself.

Law: So you didn't offer any opinions?

Jenkins: No.

Law: You didn't offer any opinions to anyone about what you thought?

Jenkins: I didn't. After I received the orders, I did not even discuss this with my wife.

Law: How long was it before you discussed it with your wife?

Jenkins: Probably not before Lifton got it.

Law: Really, that long?

Jenkins: I didn't discuss it with anyone. First of all, let's face it, if I told people that I helped do the Kennedy autopsy they would have thought I was crazy. The other thing was that I really didn't want anybody knowing, because at the time that all this finally came out and was going, too many coincidences were happening. At that time it was when Garrison was doing his investigation and the papers were full of all of that.

Law: Were you ever called for the Garrison investigation?

Jenkins: No, I really believe that neither myself, Paul, Jerrol or Floyd – I didn't think our names had ever been –

Law: Released before the '70s?

Jenkins: Released before the assassination committee hearing. I think it only came out then because it had to be in the transcripts.

Law: Let me ask you this: do you have any fear today?

Jenkins: No.

Law: I know in 1977 – we discussed this earlier – we all know that 1977 was not a good year for people who had anything to do with the JFK assassination. It doesn't bother you today?

Jenkins: No. I've watched a pattern since I was actually brought into this, as far as information is concerned. For example, Paul, and I believe Jerrol too, indicated there was no brain. I say there was a brain, and I helped infuse it. Then Dr. Crenshaw's book, I felt, gave more credibility to what I remember.[3] And immediately after Crenshaw's book came out, the AMA (American Medical Association) came out with their big deal. They basically tried to crucify Crenshaw's credibility, which I felt was political.

Law: Have you talked to Dr. Crenshaw?

Jenkins: No.

Law: Do you feel, from reading his book, that he was accurate?

Jenkins: I think his observations were fairly accurate. I think it certainly had more credibility with me than anything else I have seen. Any other reports and so forth. And after reading some of the transcripts from the various government investigations, things began to stay with me like from Ramsey Clark's panel where they stopped the tapes and the neuropathologist got frustrated and left because they wouldn't let him tell what he felt like the fragments were for. It's still an editing of information to the public. It's information and disinformation.

Law: Do you think that's still going on?

Jenkins: Yes.

Law: Do you feel it has been going on ever since this thing started?

Jenkins: Yes I do, because it's almost like when someone who has credibility like Dr. Crenshaw comes out and it doesn't fit the scenario that the government put out, then almost immediately, or shortly thereafter, some other authority comes out to discredit it. It's not only the Dr. Crenshaw and AMA-type thing. You know, it's happened before.

Law: Do you think that any of your colleagues, such as Paul O'Connor, Jerrol Custer, Dennis David, or yourself have ever felt you've been discredited in any way?

Jenkins: I think the probable differences between what I saw, and what Paul and they saw, plus the fact is that we have all been portrayed as very insignificant, menial players in this – so I don't think that at any one time the people, whoever is doing the disinformation, thought we were that much of a –

Law: That much of a threat to them?

Jenkins: Right, because first of all we don't really have credibility. I don't know what the educational background of the others is, but I have a masters in combined sciences and that includes pathology and anatomy.

Law: Now you had some of this training before –

Jenkins: I had most of that training afterwards.

Law: Has it given you – looking back on it now with all the training you've had, now being an older man –

---

3. Charles A. Crenshaw MD, *JFK: Conspiracy of Silence*, Signet 1992.

Jenkins: I think it's given me, probably it's given me a better perspective on what I saw that night – the things that I remember – certainly gives me a better anatomical perspective of it.

Law: Would you say that things just weren't right when it comes right down to it?

Jenkins: They weren't. I felt what we saw that night was nothing related to the pathology report. There was no relation to it. I came out of the autopsy totally expecting them to say there were two shooters. One from the right front and one from behind. And over the years I, by the description of the throat, I think there probably was another [implied third] shooter. I don't know if that was a bullet wound or a trach, that was never clarified.

(break)

Jenkins: Even though we differ, Paul, Jerrol and I, if you look overall, it's the same. I think the things that we remember are the things that we focused on. I don't remember much about the coffin, the body bag or whatever. I didn't participate in that directly. Paul did, so I would say his memory of that is much better than mine. The brain – it's hard to say at what time they actually looked at the skull – I would think that the brain was in the skull for more than a short period of time after the autopsy began.

Law: So this brain was in the skull for a lot of the time while it was being X-rayed and so on?

Jenkins: Yes, because X-rays were being taken, I think, after the brain was removed. The time-frame just doesn't – as I said before, things I remember were the things I was focusing on and the X-rays were just basically an assist-type thing, and some of the conversations were things that I didn't really focus on, but kind of heard.

Law: Right. Have you seen the AP[4] X-ray (photo 7)?

Jenkins: I've seen that.

Law: Did Jerrol, at any time, tell you that was the one he took?

Jenkins: No.

Law: Did you say it was one that he didn't take?

Jenkins: No, I haven't –

Law: You haven't discussed it. The thing that really amazes me is that people think that you all know each other and that you knew each other on that night, and maybe some of you did –

Jenkins: I didn't know Jerrol.

Law: You were all drawn into this event and I think part of the controversy is the belief that you all knew each other and you discussed this and that. Yet, I find one of you saying something and others don't know anything about it.

---

4. Front to rear.

Jenkins: See, one of the things they have to realize is that I didn't know Jerrol Custer. I didn't know Floyd Riebe.

Law: You weren't friends for whatever reason, you didn't pal around together. You just all were drawn into this event. Is this correct?

Jenkins: Paul and I were in school together. This was in November, so we had known each other for a little more than two months. I was married, living off base. Paul was single and living on base. So knowing each other as friends – that's not what happened. I actually got to know Paul after he married my wife's cousin.

Law: There's an interesting little twist.

Jenkins: And you know, that's been over the years – I guess we know each other better now than we did back then, but at that point in time Paul was just another individual in my class.

Law: Did any of you discuss these events? I'm not talking months or years. I'm talking within weeks or days. Did any of you get together and discuss the strangeness of this whole thing?

Jenkins: I didn't.

Law: I've asked this of others. Given the circumstances of the morgue being called a circus that night – do you feel that this was the way a normal autopsy is handled?

Jenkins: No.

Law: Do you feel you were able to do your job fully in that atmosphere?

Jenkins: I probably would have done more.

Law: More as far as – ?

Jenkins: Participating in the autopsy, more than I did.

Law: As I understand you and Paul had done several autopsies at that point yourselves.

Jenkins: Yes. That was not what we were supposed to do. But, there were certain residents who would tell you go ahead and remove the organs and brains and so forth, write down the scars and so forth.

Law: Now this is not your normal procedure that you are supposed to do, but you were allowed to do these things?

Jenkins: Yes.

Law: You had to do that anyway at some point, didn't you?

Jenkins: Well we did, but we had to do it under supervision.

Law: I see, and basically you did some of it without supervision?

Jenkins: Yes, well at two in the morning it's hard to get a resident to come down to the morgue. Basically, most of us, every time we had duty we had autopsies to do all night. For a while there we got a little paranoid. We felt that the people during the day were leaving them – particularly one individual. But, by that time we had a fair amount of experience in what we were doing and what was going on (smiles).

Law: So basically you knew how an autopsy was run?

Jenkins: Yes, well, at least there.

Law: In your opinion, what kind of men were Boswell and Humes?

Jenkins: I think Humes was totally navy.

Law: Meaning?

Jenkins: Meaning the fact is the navy had actually probably made Humes. I'm not sure if he was educated in the navy, but I had often gotten that feeling that what Humes was, the navy had made him. Boswell? I feel that he was probably a little bit more of an individual than Humes was, and more interested in his teaching and so forth. And that's probably the reason Humes was the medical director of the laboratory there, was probably due to the politics in the military. I don't want to put Dr. Humes' abilities down because I've really never observed him in his job well enough to make an opinion of how well it was done. I do know that from the time that I was there, this was the only autopsy that I ever saw him participate in. In reality this was the only autopsy I ever saw Dr. Boswell participate in, physically participate in.

Law: Do you find it a little strange that they would take two people that probably were quote-unquote "paper pushers" and put them in this kind of situation?

Jenkins: I find it rather strange in a lot of areas. In the fact that they had a huge forensic center at Parkland – yet they took him and brought him back to Bethesda. In retrospect, I think it was a controlling factor. They could control Humes, Boswell, and Finck because they were military.

Law: And you think this was deliberately done?

Jenkins: Yes.

Law: That they were controlled by outside forces, purposely?

Jenkins: I think so. I think they were controlled. So were we. We were all military, we could be controlled. And if we weren't controlled, we could be punished and that kept us away from the public.

Law: Is there anything, for the historical record, that you would like to state about your involvement, that you feel needs to be said?

Jenkins: I would like history to really understand what was going on, as much inside that morgue as in the nation, in the political arena. I am convinced that John Kennedy was shot at least two times by two separate people, and possibly a third time. Relating to the wound in the back – the entrance wound that I feel was at the right side of the head just above the ear, a little bit forward, and exited in the large expanse at the back. The other wound from the back of the head, which has been reported (e.g., photo 19) as I said, right around the base of the skull or the nuchal line, I never saw that. I'm not saying it wasn't there, but I never saw it. I had an opportunity to see it. So I think what history needs to understand – I feel really frustrated that nobody would come and do a thorough investigation of this – people need to understand that this was a cover-up. For what reason, I can only speculate, but certainly the evidence – presented by Humes to the public, from the Warren Commission to the public – was not the evidence that we found at the autopsy.

Law: I know you don't like to participate in this because of the experiences you have been through before. Why are you doing it now? Is that part of the reason?

Jenkins: To be quite honest, I'm not really sure why I'm doing it. I guess that somewhere there's some hope that ultimately the truth in all this will be found – that it will be presented to us as a people to let us make our own decisions and evaluations. At this point in time I haven't seen that. Plus, there are the people who have said, "Okay, well, there was a wound on the side of the head," and so forth, and they can prove it scientifically, with demonstrations and so forth. The government has never been able to do anything but speculate on it basically. I'm really not sure how the general populace looks at this. I kind of feel they look at it as a dead issue, it's the past, it's over with and they really don't want to get involved with it anymore.

Law: Take heart in the fact that not all of us feel that way.

Jenkins: Well, we are a very small minority. History is written by historians. So I think this is going to be written into history by historians who take the easiest route, which is the perspective of the Warren Commission and so forth. And my feeling is that it's a real shame because that is not valid. I've been asked why would the government want to do this. I think, at this point in time, the credibility factor is important for the government, especially today. So, I think the government covered it up, for whatever reason. If you go with Lyndon Johnson, it was for the good of the people because they couldn't handle it, which I don't believe. I believe that the people, if you get angry about something that's well and good, there's something to get angry about. If you force the government to do something about it and you do it as a people, then that's what the government should do. Those types of decisions should not be made for the people, the general populace. They should be presented to the people and the people should make their own judgments and I don't think it has ever happened – and, being pessimistic, I don't think it ever will.

Law: I thank you for your time.

Jenkins: Thank you.

Chapter Eight

JERROL F. CUSTER[1]

J errol Francis Custer was a radiology technician stationed at the National Naval Medical Center, Bethesda, and happened to be on call on
the evening of November 22, 1963, when President Kennedy's body
was brought in for autopsy. I first contacted him early in 1998, hoping he
would consent to an interview. He was friendly over the phone and took
time to answer some questions. I asked flat out what his feelings were regarding John Kennedy's assassination: "I think he was set up by a CIA hit
squad … " I was taken aback by his candor. It is one thing to read pro-conspiracy books about the assassination, but to have someone who participated in the autopsy, who had seen the wounds for himself at close quarters
and who had placed his own hands on the cadaver, say without equivoca-
tion that there had been a plot was quite a different matter.

Custer went on to tell me that he had recently returned from Washington, D.C., where he had been deposed by the Assassination Records Review
Board (ARRB). "My deposition is going to point fingers and bring out some
issues that I saw." He intrigued me further, saying, "There's a lot of conspiracy stuff here. You don't know about a radiologist going to the White House
and being briefed on what to do and what not to do … I do." He went on:
"On my little trip to the ARRB, they kept me busy for six and a half hours
nonstop. I was in this room in the archives and there was four men there
plus a transcriber. Maybe you would know one of these men? Douglas P.
Horne?" I told him I didn't. "He's Chief Analyst for Medical Records. He
and Jeremy Gunn, who's with the Attorney General's Office. They were
questioning me on different things that I brought with me plus on other
things they have at the archives."

Custer then told me he was writing a book on his experiences in the Bethesda morgue. When I said I would like to go to Pittsburgh and interview him, he
was receptive. I had met Debra Conway of JFK Lancer Productions and Publications at a conference in Dallas, held yearly, for students of the assassination,

---

1. Mr. Custer died July 28, 2000.

and it was to her I turned for advice. I explained that I had arranged to interview Mr. Custer and needed help, as I knew no one in Pittsburgh. She arranged for me to stay at the home of Vincent Palamara and his wife Jessica. Palamara, also a researcher of the Kennedy assassination, is author of a well received book on the role of the Secret Service before and after the events in Dallas.

A few months later, I found myself in Pittsburgh in the back seat of the Palamara's car with Vince at the wheel and Jessica beside him, bumping down the road looking for the Custer residence. "I interviewed Custer once," Palamara told me. "I did the camera work for Harrison Livingstone when he interviewed him. I was so star-struck I didn't say anything to him."

The Custers lived in a suburb of Pittsburgh. While Vince retrieved the camcorder from the car, I stretched my legs. It was a crisp Pennsylvania evening. I surveyed the house, aware that David Lifton had filmed Custer there for *Best Evidence: The Research Video* (Rhino Video, 1990). Lifton had used only snippets of Custer's testimony, focusing on the theory of alteration of President Kennedy's corpse. I wanted to hear all of what Custer had to say for myself, and this was my chance.

We were met at the door by Marilyn Custer – attractive with a pleasant smile. With her "Hello, we've been waiting for you while having coffee and desert," I felt immediately at ease. Jerrol rose from the kitchen table to greet us. He was older than I had expected. The only interview I had seen of him had taken place almost 20 years before, and I had expected him to be frozen in time, forgetting that historical figures age just like the rest of us. He was of medium height and heavy set, wore steel-frame glasses and was clean-shaven. Hair, once coal black, was now graying, cut short on the sides and long on top, combed straight back. He was dressed casually in a yellow polo shirt, black dress pants, and black loafers. Introductions were made all round, then we went into the living room for coffee and to discuss where we should set up the equipment. It was decided that the first part of the interview would be in a sparsely furnished room off the living room. Chairs were brought in for Vince and me. Although Palamara and I had put together a list of questions, I wanted the exchange with Jerrol to be as free-form as possible. I retrieved the so-called Fox set of Kennedy autopsy photographs from my briefcase while Vince readied the camera. I also had a diagram of the Bethesda morgue – as set up on November 22, 1963 – that had been sketched by Paul O'Connor, and made sure that copies of the Kennedy-skull X-rays from the National Archives were within easy reach. Custer settled into a recliner and I sat beside him. From behind the video camera, Vince said, "Okay, this is it. One, Two, Three, GO!!" And we began.

Custer: We'd had a busy day in the X-ray department, and one of my colleagues came and asked me, "Is there any possible way you can take my duty for me?" I was a twenty-two-year-old fellow, single, living on base and at least four and a half hours from home, and said, "Sure, why not?" It was his anniversary – a special night for him – he wanted to take his wife out. Little did I know that this night would change everything throughout the years for me.

During the day we had seen the news broadcasts and knew that Kennedy had been shot in Dallas. I thought, "No, they would never bring him here. Wouldn't happen." Around six thirty to eight thirty, in that time period, I was notified by the Officer of the Day that I was to take a portable X-ray machine and a bunch of films to the morgue, that a special person was coming in and they needed X-rays. They never told me exactly who, but the Officer of the Day said to me he was coming in from Walter Reed. I took the films and the cassettes to the morgue and I set everything up. We sat there and waited and waited; they said, "He should be arriving at any moment." They brought him in, in the casket, put the casket down, and opened it. So we proceeded to remove the body from the casket and place it on the autopsy table.

Law: What kind of casket did you see?

Custer: There were two different caskets there. One was a regular shipping casket, one was a ceremonial casket, and we were told the ceremonial casket was for later on for Kennedy's body to be placed in and taken to wherever he was to be taken.

Law: But you did see a cheap shipping casket?

Custer: Yes.

Law: All right. And so you were there when the body was taken out?

Custer: Correct.

Law: And you helped place him on the table?

Custer: Correct. One thing that I noticed in particular: the head was completely covered by a plastic bag and there was a sheet around it. The sheet, of course, was bloodied, and nothing was ever mentioned about that. When we placed him on the autopsy table we were told we would not be needed at that time – we could leave and go back up to the department. So we left. In a matter of an hour or two we came back and the Y-incision had already been made. Dr. Ebersole was there and I asked him, "What kind of X-rays do you want?" "I'll leave that to your discretion." Well, come on! I'm only an HM 3 technician. He's a radiologist. He should tell me what to take!

And I just proceeded to take X-ray films of the head. During this time we covered every cassette because there was a lot of body fluid. And this was brought out later by Dr. Ebersole during his deposition; he stated that there were a lot of artifacts due to dirty cassettes, which, in my estimation, was baloney because I knew we took precautions to avoid that.

We took an AP[2] film. We took a lateral film. Actually we took two lateral films. But here's one thing that was brought up later on: both laterals had the same marking on them. That was my fault. I was a young man, excited; trying to do the best possible job I could, and I totally mis-marked one film. But I was able to distinguish the films by the defect on the right side, which you can see here (photo 8). I knew this had to be the right lateral because I had the complete distance that I needed, which is 44 inches, a normal study distance for any film. The lateral that I had difficulty getting a decent distance with was the left lateral.[3] Because of the gallery, the way the table was situated, it was close to the gallery and I couldn't get the tube far enough away, so a portion of the back skull was cut off (pointing to the left of photo 8).

Law: Now you had to take this right in the amphitheater?

Custer: Right in the amphitheater.

Law: So, with pandemonium going on all around you –

Custer: Correct.

Law: – you had to take these X-rays?

Custer: Correct.

Law: What was the morgue like? To give people a better understanding, give us a little background. How were people acting, and what was the general atmosphere in the morgue that night?

Custer: (addressing the sketch of the morgue by Paul O'Connor, photo 11) You can see the outside loading dock, which is where they brought the coffin in. This was with an honor guard – brought the coffin in through the cooling room and then into the main morgue itself. All right, this was a table that was about five feet off the ground and that's where they did most of the dissecting, and then they had a regular weighing machine there to weigh the different organs.

They brought the coffin in and sat it right in front of the gallery. The gallery went along the back of the wall here; this is where all the joint chiefs, the Secret Service, and I'm sure that there was CIA there, and a lot of people dressed in suits and ties that night. They brought the coffin in, sat it here (photo 11). They opened the coffin, we took the body, brought him over here to autopsy table number 1. Now if you've ever seen an autopsy table they have like a head holder; it's a metal head holder that sits under the back portion of the skull. They set them on that and they dissect the body, but when I was taking my X-rays that head-holder (photo 2) was gone. They had taken it off. That has caused a lot of confusion with a lot of researchers who wanted to know, "How did you ever get X-rays

2. Front to rear
3. The left lateral X-ray is not public and was not available during this interview.

through that thing?" It was removable. Here's the problem I was trying to tell you about before: I was able to put my X-ray machine near the body to take the right lateral here with no trouble (pointing to the side of table #1 away from the gallery, photo 11). But once I got back here (between table #1 and the gallery, photo 11), I was too close to the gallery, I couldn't get the distance that I needed, plus rigor mortis played a big part.

Let me take you to the AP position (photo 7); look at the size of the orbits. Kind of enlarged, aren't they? You know why?

Law: Why?

Custer: Distortion. The head at the time, due to rigor mortis had been brought back and off to the side and it was kind of hard to get things situated. So a lot of researchers brought up later: "Maybe this was taken in a PA position.[4] But you have to remember this is a person that already has been autopsied. He has a Y- incision. How are you going to flip him over on his stomach? There's nothing to flip him on. Plus, you can see the skull fragments. What's going to hold the head together? Basically, you shoot them as they lie to get as much evidence as possible. Another thing that was brought out later was, "How come the orbits are so enlarged? " When you shoot an X-ray, you have diverging rays. And the way the body was tilted the rays were hitting on an angle and elongating the orbit – even though it was taken in an AP position – which deformed a lot of the bone fragments. It's not a typical good AP projection, but for that night, in that time, it told exactly what they wanted to see. Same thing on the lateral. There's a slight rotation, but it's kind of hard to tell. You got to look at the sella turcica, the keystone of the skull cap which holds the brain in. You see the thickening, there's minimal rotation there. So you are getting a kind of foggy picture. Let's put it that way. I want to keep it in as basic terms as possible. A foggy picture.

Law: Now I've noticed this area here. It looks like the skull is gone. Can you explain to me why we have this defect here (pointing to the blackened area on the AP X-ray, photo 7)?

Custer: You mean this complete defect?

Law: Yes.

Custer: What you're looking at, you've got to remember, is an AP projection. You're looking at an area that is right here or you could possibly be seeing a defect back here or defects here, (placing his right hand on the right of his own forehead then on the back of his head and then on the right side of his head). The only possible way to tell exactly where the defect is, is by taking a lateral film. Here's that area you were looking at (indicating the darkened area in photo 8). The fragments are traveling front to back and outward. It lifted everything up (motioning right to left to indicate the direction in which he feels the bullet

4. Rear to front.

fragments were traveling) – overlapped everything. Take a hard-boiled egg, run it in your hands. That's exactly what the skull fragments were like.

Law: By the way, is this an actual X-ray you took?

Custer: This is the actual X-ray I took.

Law: And you remember it being this way that night?

Custer: Absolutely!

Law: Okay. Is there anything else of interest about this X-ray that you can tell us?

Custer: Massive destruction. They wanted to make sure this man was dead. And they did a good job of it.

Law: How did you feel, when you first saw his body – you were 22 years old.

Custer: Right.

Law: How did you feel as the radiology technician – what you saw, taking the X-rays, putting your hands on the body of President of the United States, and the evidence telling you one thing, but yet the report (of the Warren Commission) says something different.

Custer: This is my country. I served in the United States Navy because I knew that they wanted me to serve and they needed me. But it was quite disillusioning in that I knew the truth of the matter. I knew why. I won't lie to you – during that time I did what I was told. And I kind of looked at it and thought, "Well, wait a minute. This isn't right. This can't be. " But as I've gotten older, I've looked at it more with experienced eyes, looked at the evidence a lot closer with experienced eyes. I've gotten a lot smarter and I've realized that the government can do what they want, when they want, and as often as they want. I kept my quiet for 35 years. One day my wife and I went to a movie and they brought the JFK assassination up and said it was a coincidence that so many witnesses had died for unknown reasons, or heart attacks, cerebral vascular accidents – and I just sat there and thought to myself, "My God! This could happen to me." Truthfully, the only thing I think that actually saved my tush, was they felt that I was too low on the totem pole to worry about. But it literally made me mad. Later on down the line, I thought, "Well, it's about time the truth should come out."

Law: Let's go step by step now through the photographs. What can you tell me about this particular one, the "stare of death" picture (photo 1). What sticks in your mind most about this photograph.

Custer: Basically, the wound on the neck, a tracheotomy wound. When we took pictures of the neck, we took two views of the neck. A straight-on view and a side view. Now, in the straight-on view, in that area, you actually saw bullet fragment, also bone fractures where the bullet had gone through. Same thing on the lateral, but it showed you the different perspective. Like I stated before, a good way to tell the depth of a specific fragment is by taking two planes of interest, and then measuring the distance.

When I first saw the body, the neck was exactly like this (photo 1); there were no suture marks. It was a big gaping hole.

Law: And in your opinion was that man-made?

Custer: Absolutely. You could see where this was man-made. Where they had taken a scalpel and went across and down you can see the down marking cut right here (pointing to the bottom portion of the wound; photo 1a, arrow C).

Law: So, in effect you think that's a scalpel mark?

Custer: Right.

Law: You don't think that's a part of a bullet entry wound?

Custer: No.

Law: Many researchers have said that – what you see down here – this little part right here (photo 1a, arrow C) is part of a bullet-entrance wound.

Custer: You could see the skin where the skin was separated. If a bullet fragment came through there – a bullet went through there – it would be separated, irregular. This was nice and neat like the skin was separated, like somebody took a ruler and just separated the skin. There were no serrations on it at all. It was perfect. This is one thing for the books.

Two films are missing: the AP and cervical spine. They are not in the archives. Basically, because that's a part of the evidence. One reason why Pitzer was killed is because he was taking movies of the body and the gallery. At that time, people had a fit: "What is your status? What is your clearance? Why are you here? Stop that now! Evict that man."[5]

Law: Who was William Pitzer? (photo 9)

Custer: At that time he was the chief in charge of the photographic department of the National Naval Medical Center. He and Dennis David were buddies, longterm friends. Dennis wasn't on duty that night, but Chief Pitzer[6] was. I remember seeing him that evening and he was all around. I mean everywhere you went, you saw Chief Pitzer.[7] He was there. And it's funny to the fact that the man

---

5. For more on William Pitzer, see the Appendix Two.

6. In November 1963, William Pitzer held the rank of lieutenant. Prior to that, he had been chief warrant officer.

7. Mr. Custer's apparent familiarity with "Chief Pitzer" contrasts with his testimony to the Assassination Records Review Board in October, 1997:

Q: In addition to Floyd Riebe's taking photographs, did you see anyone else take photographs?

A: There was a chief there that night that was taking movies ... he was the gentleman that had committed suicide, supposedly ...

Q: ... Do you remember the chief's name?

A: No I don't.

Q: Does the name Pitzer mean anything to you?

– he never noticed what was around him. He kind of turned the commotion off and he was doing his job. That's what he was paid to do.

Law: What was he doing exactly?

Custer: Taking movies.

Law: He was taking movie film of the autopsy?

Custer: Absolutely.

Law: And you saw this?

Custer: I saw this. Later on it was brought out that Commander Pitzer – well of course he made Commander farther down the line – had committed suicide by blowing his brains out by putting a gun in his right hand and shooting himself.

Law: What's so unusual about that if you're going to commit suicide?

Custer: Well, it's kind of funny. How can you commit suicide when you have a deformed right hand? That couldn't hold a gun? This was due to a birth defect. And Dennis David knew it.[8] Everybody that knew the chief knew it and it was evident that night. When he was taking the movies, you could see the hand was deformed. But suicide was the reason for the death on his death certificate, which, I felt, was part of the cover-up. See, you have to be there. You have to see what's going on. Everything is plain and simple. It's there! It's right in front of you! The government feels the experts, so-called experts, are going to look at everything but the nose on their faces. And if you just stop and look at what's right in front of you and not try and surmise, "Well this is why, this is why that happened." My God – Kennedy's skull was pushed backward! Basic physics! You had to have a force from the front! If you had a force from the back, everything would have been pushed forward. Common sense! Doesn't take a genius to figure that one out.

Law: Returning to photo 1. What does it show? What's its importance?

Custer: Well, like I had said before, it shows the tracheotomy wound, the opening, which was a bullet hole. The defect you can see around the eye – I have to bring this out right now. I cannot authenticate these pictures because I had really nothing to do with them. All I can say is what I happened to see. The eye was more protruded at the time, but there's nothing to say that the eye wasn't pushed back in. Because at that time also there was a mortician there doing his work, his job was fixing, making the body more presentable.

A: Yes. Now, it rings a bell, but I'm not quite sure. But that name "Pitzer" does ring a bell.

Q: Are you able to elaborate at all why you –

A: Not really. I'm not sure if it was – It could have been brought to my recollection that night that we had the get-together in Pittsburgh. I think it was Pittsburgh. Yes, it was.

Q: But did you know that name at all on the night of the –

A: No I didn't know that name at that time. No I didn't. Some of this stuff is starting to come back.

8. Dennis David has since said that William Pitzer had no deformation of either hand.

Let me go to the other pictures here to show the massive destruction of the skull. These are going to be kind of off-center here. If you'll notice a king-size opening (photo 5). What's that? You ever wonder?

Law: I wonder about all of them.

Custer: Look at that opening right here.

Law: What does that tell you?

Custer: That's a hole. This will be brought out in due course. See, I can only go so far with this. There's a lot more information that has to be brought out legally first. Then I will delve in a lot more. But that's a hole. And that can be proven by computer enhancement. Definitely: no ifs, ands, or buts about that. They can complain and say, "No, that's not what this is."

Law: And the next one? (photo 4)

Custer: You see Kennedy on his back. The condition of the scalp – how serrated it is, shredded. Due to fragmentation of the bullet, due to fragmentation of the bone. During the autopsy, the complete skull was held together by the skin alone. But you could take the scalp and pull it forward, backward, any way, shape or form you wanted to do. It wasn't totally attached.

Law: His face was mushy and movable at that point?

Custer: Mushy and move-able.

Law: Yes, but you couldn't perhaps pull it back enough to cover the defect in the back of the head?

Custer: You could drape it across the defect.

Law: You could?

Custer: Yes. There was enough of it there. But it was bloody. There were brain cells, brain fragments, all kinds of stuff. Nasty stuff. Now here's one thing that kind of gives a lot of the researchers nightmares. This little flap (above the right ear): a lot of people feel that was man-made. Truthfully, at that time, I did not see that flap.

Law: This flap was not there.

Custer: Not there. I cannot testify to what was done after I left. The mortician was there, things were being done, more parts of the skull were being received that night. Bullet fragments were received after I had left.

Law: Did you see a defect here, where there's scalp? (photo 4, pointing to the back of the head)

Custer: I saw the defect in this area. But not this (pointing to the flap). The only thing I can possibly think of was that the bone fragment (flap) was up and in place and later on the skin was cut and it released a fragment to fall. I'm surmising – but you've got to remember there was a lot of probing going on.

Law: Probing in what fashion – what parts?

Custer: All over. Specifically in the skull, and the neck, and the body itself. The pathologists were in there with their hands. Now if you know Dr. Humes – Dr. Humes had awfully big hands and he had his hands in the skull.

Law: He put, actually put, his hands in the skull?

Custer: Absolutely.

Law: Both of his hands would fit in the skull?

Custer: Well, I don't know about both, but he had at least one.

Law: That's how massive the wound was?

Custer: That's right. He had to be dead when they took him to Parkland hospital. There was no way, shape, or form he could have been breathing, with that much damage. Just the brain loss alone would be enough to drop him. Any man. It would stop him right in his tracks.

Law: Since you mentioned the brain. Did you happen to see it? I've heard that there was a brain that night. I've heard there wasn't a brain that night. I've heard the brains were blown out. I've heard they did have a brain and it was in a bucket. Did you see a bucket with a brain in formaldehyde?

Custer: No. I didn't. All I saw within the skull were fragments of the brain. The brain was already out.

Law: How much brain would you say was in the skull?

Custer: Oh, very little. Five, ten, fifteen (cubic centimeters).

Law: Which would be – we're talking a handful? Half a handful?

Custer: A half a handful. And that was only just attached to different parts of the scalp where it was blown out. So, it was a mess, literally.

> **Author's note:** At this point, we took a break, then continued the interview in the dining room around the kitchen table. Vince Palamara joined the conversation.

Palamara: What was your interaction, if any, with the Secret Service agents there – Greer and Kellerman.

Custer: Well, [FBI agents] Sibert and O'Neill were literally up my nose. We were attached at the hip, every place I went, they went. The morgue was in the basement of the National Naval Medical Center, and our X-ray department was on the fourth floor of the tower. I had to get on an elevator and go up to the main level then go down to the main rotunda (to get another elevator to the fourth floor). This is why I ran into Jacqueline Kennedy and the entourage. I had a handful of films and O'Neill was right in front of me.[9] He saw them coming and said, "Stop, I don't want you to run into the news people." And you could

9. When contacted 4/23/01, Francis X. O'Neill failed to corroborate this.

see them, the flashes going on from guys taking pictures of the Kennedys. In fact, I still remember the bloody suit that she had on. She hadn't had a chance to change. The main rotunda was like a circular hallway. There was a bank of elevators. A hallway went down the center (of the building) with the executive offices of the Commander in Chief of the National Naval Medical Center. And further down the hall was the emergency room, and then further down were more offices, and then one floor down was the cafeteria.

Palamara: How many skull fragments came in that night? Do you remember? There's a little bit of controversy about the exact number.

Custer: It's kind of hard to remember. There were at least four that I can remember right off the top of my head. At least four. And there were at least – one, two, three – three small bullet fragments. One fragment about the size of my little baby finger the top half of it – and this is when I had to tape them to the bone fragments.

Palamara: Let's talk a little bit about the Ebersole bust of Kennedy, and go into a little detail about that.

Custer: I don't know who Dr. Ebersole was blowing smoke up, but he came in that Monday and he said, "I need you to do a special duty. I have skull fragments here and I've got bullet fragments. I want you to tape the bullet fragments to the skull fragments – and take X-rays of the different densities. This is for a bust of Kennedy." I just looked at him again. When you're in the service, you don't question what an officer tells you to do. You do it!

Law: What were the thoughts in your head when this fellow came to you and said, "We're making a bust of Kennedy and we want you to tape those fragments to pieces of skull?

Custer: Well, let me put it this way, I won't say it on camera (laughter)!

Law: That speaks volumes. Tell me where the wound in the head was located, to the best of your recollection.

Custer: To the best of my recollection it was in the frontal sinus on the right hand side. Just above the orbit, right about here (points to a spot about half an inch above middle of the right eyebrow).

Palamara: Now you claim that was the entry wound?

Custer: That's the entry wound.

Palamara: How about the exit wound?

Custer: The exit wound. It's hard to tell because I was – I did not visualize it because the body was constantly kept on its back. You did not want to move the body any more than necessary because I felt every time I moved the body I changed the contour of the head. Therefore, I took the lateral films first, then I took the AP film. Then I took a tangential film. With a tangential film you bring the [X-ray source] to the [left] side [with the film on the right-rear] and you come in at an angle [i.e., semi-profile], just to show the gaping hole. By the way, those are missing too.

Law: Those are missing from the archives?

Custer: Yes, they are.

Palamara: But I've heard that you did say that the back of the head appeared to be gone, there was no scalp there –

Custer: Here's where a lot of researchers screw up. Not the back of the head. Here's the back of the head (indicating the area of the head in contact with the head-holder, photo 2). The occipital region. The defect was in the frontal-temporal region. Now, when you have the body lying like that, everybody points to it and says, "That's the back of the head." No! That's not the back of the head (pointing to the top of Kennedy's head in photo 2)! That's the top of the head!

Law: Now, explain to me: there's been a lot of controversy, and this is why some researchers point to forgery, that the back of the head was blown out. If the back of his head was blown out, how can the head rest on that [head-holder]?

Custer: Because the back of the head wasn't blown out. This was still intact (pointing to the lower portion of the back of the head in photo 2). It may not have been perfectly intact, there were fractures in there of course with all the destruction. If the back of the head was gone, there would be nothing there to hold the head up.

Law: But there was a –

Custer: This [head-holder] would have been all inside.

Law: Now, when you saw the body were there any chest marks, puncture wounds?

Custer: There was bruising on the thoracic-pleural area. Now I'm talking about a bruising, a slight discoloration, but at that time I did not notice any particular openings. All I saw was – yes, I did! I'll take that back! When we lifted him up to take the skull films, that's when a fragment fell out of the back.

Law: Out of the back wound? They're saying this is a back wound (photo 6a, arrow A), and this is a wound (arrow B).

Custer: That (arrow A) was a wound. This (arrow B) was not a wound.

Law: Okay. What was it?

Custer: A piece of blood.

Law: Let's talk about the X-ray films for a minute – I read somewhere, that you took extra sets of X-rays.

Custer: Well, not extra sets. I double-loaded.

Law: What does "double-loaded" mean?

Custer: You put two films in – you've got to remember an X-ray cassette has two screens and they are activated screens. When the X-ray goes through them, they lighten up and you get an image on the film. So if one film is a little bit too dark, one film is just right.

Law: Okay. So what did you do with them?

Custer: I ran [i.e., processed] one film and put the other film in the light-proof box. The processor was an old Pako unit. It was like a table where you ran your film in and underneath there was a light-proof box. You take one, put it in, and put the other in the box. I went through each film that I took and after everything was over and done that evening. I came back and ran the films in the light-proof box, those were all good too. I put them in one of the mailing folders. Tied them up and kept them there for the longest time.

Law: How long do you think they were there undiscovered?

Custer: Couple of months.

Law: And what happened to these films?

Custer: I destroyed them.

Law: Why did you do that?

Custer: Because of the gag order that I had signed. I didn't destroy them right away. After I'd thought on it and pondered on it a little bit, and thought, "Well, if these films happened to surface along the line somewhere, they're going to trace them back to me. And guess whose body is going to wind up in jail." I never thought that later on down the road that they could have been worth millions. Or they could have solved the whole problem.

Palamara: Because of the missing X-rays, missing materials, you could have resolved it.

Custer: But I also could be dead.

Law: Given that there have been several deaths over the years – some unexplainable things have happened to people who had a lot to do with this case – thirty-four years later, going on thirty-five, do you have any fear?

Custer: If I were to say no, I'd be lying. I still have a little bit. There still are people around that don't want to be implicated. Who came up with the one-bullet theory? Need I say more? One bullet? Come on. That bullet had to do a fantastic dance.

Law: Yes. Was there a George Bakeman present? Do you remember that name? His name has been tossed around.

Custer: No – there was so much confusion. The two FBI agents [James Sibert and Francis O'Neill] were going around taking names, and twisted [the spelling] one way and twisted another and, I think, it was just a mistake on their part.

265

Law: One of the witnesses that I've talked to, one of your colleagues, has told me that he felt that the body had been gotten to before it ever came into the morgue. What's your opinion on that?

Custer: Well, there again, all I can do is surmise that it's a possibility because when I was notified that the body was coming in, I was told that it was coming from Walter Reed.

Law: You were told by?

Custer: The Officer of the Day.

Law: Who was?

Custer: I can't remember his name right off the top of my head.

Law: Was it Smoky Stover (photo 9)?

Custer: No. This was just either a JG or an ensign.

Law: And this person told you personally that the body was coming from Walter Reed?

Custer: I feel that he told me something he shouldn't have, because he was later reprimanded for it. Now, stop and think. Where's Walter Reed Hospital? Alexandria, right?[10] What also is in Alexandria? Three initials. Need I say more?

Law: So, let's go back to the morgue for a second. I want a little more of the atmosphere of the morgue. I've been told by other people who were there – again, your colleagues – that it was absolute pandemonium. Would you say that's true?

Custer: Oh, absolutely! There was hollering and screaming, and orders being given and different people saying this and saying that.

Law: Who was in charge? Did anybody assume charge?

Custer: Absolutely. It was quite evident throughout the evening – JFK's personal physician.

Law: So, you're saying Dr. George Burkley.

Palamara: Admiral Burkley.

Custer: Full Admiral. He came right out and absolutely, positively said: "The Kennedy family wouldn't want that done, and I don't think you should follow that line." Baloney! It's a forensic pathology autopsy! You're looking for evidence! If you have to do that to the body, you have to do it; to find out what happened. I'll bring this up as a little anecdote. Many times when we were taking the different X-rays, I brought certain things to Dr. Ebersole's attention and I was told to shut up, do my own job, mind my own business: "That's his job. You do your job." I said, "Fine." And I walked away.

10. Walter Reed Army Medical Center is in NW Washington, D.C. The Central Intelligence Agency is located in Langley, VA, south of Washington, D.C.

Law: Is there anybody that you can recall specifically being in the morgue that night?

Custer: Kennedy's physician, that's the only one. Because he stuck out. I mean, he wasn't quiet at all. He made comments about everything.

Law: He didn't seem to be in any kind of shock or loss or mourning or – ?

Custer: No. He seemed like he was controlling everything.

Law: Every little step along the way?

Custer: Every step along the way. And this is one thing that I couldn't get over: what Ebersole brought out in his [HSCA] deposition. When he was asked, "Was anybody in control that night dictating to you what you could and couldn't do?" He said, "Oh, absolutely not, there was nobody in control." That was baloney. It was so evident. Everybody knew who was in control.

Law: Boswell and Humes, what was their demeanor while this was going on?

Custer: They did what they were told to do.

Law: And that was it? Was any kind of scenario going on where they went too far, or they were just following along trying not to make waves, for Burkley?

Custer: Absolutely! When they stepped over the line, they were smacked.

Law: So you don't feel that they hid anything. They just followed along and did what they were told to do?

Custer: They did what they were told to do. But it's funny, later on Humes destroyed his notes. Why did he keep such detailed notes? He did it for a reason. Humes was a politician. Humes knew how to manipulate things. Humes was a career person. He knew how to protect Humes's back. But, evidently somebody got to him, higher and more powerful, and he destroyed his notes. He had to be hiding something. Common sense tells you that.

Palamara: What's your take on the notion of a fifteen-hundred-gram brain? The weight being above average? What's your take on that?

Custer: Well you see, you're delving into something that's not my expertise. I really can't say. I never saw the brain. I didn't know the weight, shape, or form. I knew they were weighing particular different organs and stuff, but that's all.

Law: Going back to when they first brought the coffin in, and they took the lid off the coffin – and again we're talking about not an ornate coffin but a cheaply made coffin. When they took the lid off, what do you recall the body was wrapped in? Was the body in anything? I'm asking this because of the controversy about whether the body was in a body bag or not. Do you remember the body being in a body bag?

Custer: What struck me funny was the body was totally naked. No clothes on it at all. The only thing I can possibly remember and honestly say that really stuck out, was the head was completely covered down to the neck and there was a sheet wrapped around it and I could see the sheet through the clear – whatever it was. I won't say it was plastic, I don't really remember honestly. But I thought, "My God, the head must really be in disarray if they have something like that on it."

Law: Do you remember if it was a zipable cover?

Custer: Can't remember that.

Palamara: Did you recognize President Kennedy right away, was there any question about it?

Custer: Well, as soon as they took the cover off, I recognized him right away.

Palamara: Just from a human-interest standpoint, what did you feel like, just knowing this was –

Custer: See, the bad part about it is that I'd met the man prior. Well, you know he had a bad back?

Law: Yes.

Custer: I had taken some X-rays on his back and I'd talked to him.

Law: You had!

Custer: Yeah.

Law: You met him when he was alive?

Custer: Alive. Right. And he was just an average Joe. An average person. It wasn't, "I'm the President of the United States." Johnson: a typical politician (gestures as if pushing something away), "Get away from me, son." Kennedy wasn't that way. Walked up, shook my hand, "And what's your name?" And I told him, he said, "Where you from?" And I told him. He said, "How long you been there?" And I told him. He says, "Do you have any girlfriends?" (laughter) And I told him, and we had a heck of a conversation. But he did have an extremely bad back – a war injury.

Law: You took X-rays of his back?

Custer: Right.

Palamara: So this was even more poignant to see –

Custer: It kind of shocked me. I had to look at him twice because there was a deformation. He didn't actually look the way he normally looked. And you have to remember it's due to postmortem rigor mortis, bloating – look here, due to all that trauma (pointing to the lower neck region in photo 1).

Law: The "stare of death" photo (photo 1) – is this pretty much what he looked like? Would you say that is Kennedy? There's been speculation –

Custer: Look at his forehead here. Note how this all seems to indent (indicates the right-temple area)? Here again you've got to remember now, the mortician was there. He had putty and wax. You can't see any holes here. Look how thick that looks (points to the right side of the forehead in photo 1).

Law: And you think that's because of the mortician at this point –

Custer: Had started his job.

Law: I've never heard that before. I didn't know that the mortician had already been there and had started his work.

Custer: Oh, yes, as soon as I walked away from the body.

Palamara: Did the Gawler's funeral home people –

Custer: Yes, he was right there, in fact, like I'd said, there were two coffins there. One that they'd brought him in, and one they put him in and transported him to the funeral home. It wasn't the same coffin.

Law: You saw the ornate coffin and the so-called cheap shipping casket?

Custer: Right. Here's one thing a lot of researchers keep bringing up: "Well, was there another body in there that was supposed to be autopsied?" Baloney! No! Why would they put another body in there? This is the President of the United Sates. Security was so tight – guards all over the place. Nobody was allowed in. Literally every time I left the morgue, I had either Sibert or O'Neill with me.

Law: They stuck pretty close to you?

Custer: Like one was here (indicating his hips) and one was there.

Law: And they didn't leave you, they followed you?

Custer: They followed me. I think if I went to the john they would have followed me.

Law: I'm going to ask this simply so we can clear it up. For a lot of people – I know I keep harping on this, but is this (photo 1) basically how Kennedy looked?

Custer: Right.

Law: A lot has been made of the fact that you can't see pores in the skin in this photograph.

Custer: Right.

Law: And they say that – there have been writers that have written that this is a composite.

Custer: You know, why you can't see any pores?

Law: Why?

Custer: I can tell you right now. Just look at it. Look at all this! They used heavy flashes on it. They burnt the pores out. There's no detail.

Law: And that's basically because of the flash?

Custer: Right. Let me show you something else. What do you think this is? (pointing to the object in the background of photo 1; photo 1b)

Law: I've heard from Paul O'Connor that that is a wooden object that was not in the morgue that night.

Custer: That is like a lock. There is a screw there, there is a wheel there, and there's a wheel over here. It's an X-ray machine. There's the box to hold the films. Do you know why I know it's an X-ray machine? Because I put it there!

Law: You're the one that put it there?

Custer: Right!

Law: My God. That's amazing.

Custer: This whole washout [of the face] – ask any photographer – if you get too close with too strong of a flash, you get no skin detail at all. None.

Law: All right.

Custer: Do you want detail when you see wax up here (pointing to Kennedy's forehead in the "stare of death" photograph)?

> **Author's note:** At this point we broke taping until the next day. We resumed around the kitchen table.

Law: Just to clarify – when you had X-rays in your arms and were going down the hallway and you saw Jacqueline Kennedy – I'll let you tell it in your own words.

Custer: I'm not sure whether it was Sibert or O'Neill, but one of the two FBI agents was with us at the time they happened to stop us just before we came into the rotunda and we saw the entourage of Jacqueline Kennedy. Bobby Kennedy was there, and pictures were being taken.

Law: What were your feelings when you came out of there with an armload of X-rays and saw Jacqueline Kennedy coming in the front door?

Custer: It sort of surprised me. My white smock was bloody, and I had to literally destroy it. So, I was covered with blood, and I had to clean the X-rays off when I got back up to the department – but, I don't think she knew that the body was there.

Law: You don't.

Custer: No. I think she thought the body was with her at that time. So, the body had to be separated from her at one time or another, beyond her knowing what was going on.

Palamara: Do you think the body was tampered with in any fashion?

Law: I know this is opinion, but you are a medical person.

Custer: Let's put it this way. With as much stuff, as much cover up, as much influence, pressure was on that night, and I wouldn't put it past them. They had an inexperienced radiologist. They told him to look for bullets that went in and didn't come out. And a forensic pathologist would look at the person and say,

"You're crazy. We're looking for tracking, entrance, exits, degree of inclination." They had two administrative pathologists that hadn't done autopsies in umpteen years – all they did was process paper work, and had never done a forensic autopsy. They had an influencing force in the gallery that literally guided the autopsy throughout the evening. They had two FBI agents that created their own little pandemonium by questioning people that night.

Law: Let's back up a little. When you say there was an influence in the gallery are you talking about Burkley? Or are you talking about someone else? Let's clarify that.

Custer: Well, let's put it this way. I'm talking about JFK's personal physician. And he let it be known that night, "I am JFK's personal physician. You will listen to what I say. You will do what I say."

Law: Continue with what you were going to say about the Secret Service agents – did you say – FBI?

Custer: Now there were Secret Service agents there also.

Palamara: Kellerman and Greer – were you familiar with them? Did you really –

Custer: No. They didn't quite get involved with us. They stayed pretty much with the Joint Chiefs and that.

Law: Were they there in the gallery?

Custer: I seem to remember seeing the other two gentlemen there, also. But I know for a fact that Sibert and O'Neill were there because they were attached to my hip.[11] They were literally – how can I say it? Delegated to stay with me.

Law: What was their demeanor? They filed a report where they wrote: "Surgery of the head area." And there's been speculation that they wrote that because they heard it from a doctor there at the autopsy.

Custer: Right. Now here's the thing you have to remember: these two gentlemen were laymen. When an autopsy is performed, surgery of the wounds is performed so it is possible they could have heard it from Boswell or Humes, or Finck at that time, because he arrived later on and he was more aggressive.

Law: We're talking about Finck, now?

Custer: Right. He was more aggressive in his mannerisms and procedure than Boswell and Humes. Boswell and Humes were like puppets.

Law: Did he seem to be frustrated by being told, "No, you can't do this" or "You shouldn't do that" or "Only take this so far"?

Custer: That's kind of difficult to remember. Because he did what he was told, and if he was frustrated he kind of hid it.

11. See pages 286 and 322 for denials by Special Agents Sibert and O'Neill, respectively.

Law: So he just basically went along –

Custer: He went along.

Law: He didn't put up a fuss? I want to get to how all of you must have been under extreme pressure.

Custer: Oh, we were being watched constantly. Everybody watched us. Ah, there were times when I literally had to scream at people to move. In that close area, you're taking X-rays with a machine producing ionizing radiation, and you had to be at a distance of six feet to be safe.

Palamara: Were you aware of the allegations of – I don't know if it was Admiral or Captain David Osborne – about the bullet falling out of the body? During the autopsy? Did you see a whole bullet or a fragment fall out of President Kennedy?

Custer: Well, I wouldn't call it a fragment, I'd say it was a pretty good sized bullet. Because it created such a fuss. They ran over with a set of forceps – and they grabbed it, picked it up and put it in a little basin of water.

Law: Now is this the bullet – when you were doing the X-rays, and you had him on the table and moving him around, didn't you tell me at some point in an earlier conversation that a bullet fragment fell out of the president?

Custer: This was the time that they found that.

Law: Okay. And what happened? What was their demeanor? What happened when that bullet fragment fell out?

Custer: I called one of the pathologists over and said, "Hey, we have a bullet here." Soon as they heard that, they came down off the raised platform and they ran over and they picked it up. Then Sibert and O'Neill also came over and said, "Well, we want that, that's – "[12]

Palamara: Yes, they wrote out a receipt for a missile so people think it's semantics – was it a fragment? So you're saying it wasn't a whole bullet? It was a sizable fragment of a bullet?

Custer: It was about – see, you're getting in semantics here about the size. It was distinguishable enough to know it was a bullet. It wasn't complete because there was some fragmentation. Some area of destruction on the bullet.

Law: Just for clarification, what area of the body did it fall out of?

Custer: That was the upper thorax. The upper back.

Law: It literally fell out of the back wound.

Custer: Right.

Law: Well now, the single-bullet theory would have you believe that the bullet went in Kennedy's back, came out his throat, hit Connolly below the right arm-

12. See pages 286 and 323 for denials of Custer's assertion.

pit, came out the right side of his chest, broke his right wrist, and went into his left leg. So, if you're telling us that the bullet fragment fell out of the back, that blows the single bullet theory to hell right there.

Custer: Right.

Palamara: And also it was too low on the back to exit the neck.

Law: And you're absolutely certain that a bullet fragment fell out of the back?

Custer: Absolutely.

Law: The back wound itself. No doubt about it.

Custer: Absolutely. Right. We lifted him up and boom. That's when it came out.

Palamara: That's corroboration for David Osborne too.

Law: That would explain, "missile received" from Sibert and O'Neill.

Custer: Right.

Law: That's something that I've wanted to clear up.

Custer: They documented everything that happened that evening. If somebody got up and left, they documented it.

Law: Now to my understanding, the logbook, there was a logbook that is normally kept of people that go in and out of the area.

Custer: Right.

Law: Is this correct?

Custer: Right.

Law: Now, as I understand it, that's missing.

Custer: It's gone.

Law: And has been missing since that night.

Custer: Correct.

Palamara: Paul O'Connor memorized the number, remember that?

Law: Yes, that's correct, he could do it from memory.

Palamara: Right.

Custer: Yeah. It was gone. Totally disappeared.

Law: What do you feel about that?

Custer: Part of the cover-up. They don't want people to know. This is why the chief was taken care of, literally. He actually had photographic evidence they didn't want out.

Law: And by "chief," who are you talking about?

Custer: Chief Pitzer.

Law: I know we discussed William Pitzer (photo 9) a little bit last night. Pitzer was a mentor to Dennis David and they were basically best friends.

Custer: Right.

Law: I've been told by him that he helped edit film –

Custer: Correct.

Law: And there's been no corroboration for that except that you've said that you saw him and you do remember him.

Custer: Absolutely.

Law: Filming. And he – Dennis David – also told me that he saw pictures of a wound in the side of the president's head. A small bullet wound. In the right temple.

Custer: Now you've got to remember something, Dennis David is a layman. His [knowledge of] anatomy may sometimes leave a lot to be desired. What he considered the side of the head could be here or here (pointing to his own head in the right temple area). But I would say the side of the head would be in the temporal region. There was no bullet wound here (indicating the right temple).

Law: Really.

Palamara: He did mention on a documentary – he did point to here (Palamara points to the right side of his forehead), whether it was an entrance wound and it appeared that President Kennedy was shot from the front. Viewing this film.

Custer: Right.

Law: So would you say that's correct?

Custer: I would say that's pretty close to where it was. Actually, it was right in here (points to approximately half an inch above the middle of the right eyebrow). You can see where the fragment went in from the destruction. You have the picture, the AP skull X-ray (photo 7); look where the lines emanate from. There's a focal point. That's the shell entrance. Back to the same simple theory. Look at what you have. It's as plain as the nose on your face. Don't surmise the bullet looks like it's at the back of the head. No. Look at your fractures. Where do they come from? Where do they start at? Where's all the damage at? You see damage in the frontal sinuses. You see damage to the orbit. The floor of the orbit. The orbital ridge. If a bullet goes in the front you'd have fracturing in that area. If you've ever seen anybody that's been shot in the back of the head and the bullet exited from the face, there's not much of the face left.

Law: And you've seen such things?

Custer: I've seen such things.

Law: So you would know basically what a bullet would do if it hit you in the back of the head?

Custer: Correct.

Law: So you would know what to look for and you could tell that a man had been hit in the back of the head. There wouldn't be any question in your mind.

Custer: Right. You would see all the facial damage. When a bullet goes in, it expands, destroys tissue. You have fragments, bullets, tissue, bone coming forward. All that is one big mass and it just brings everything –

Palamara: And this (photo 1) is not indicative of someone who was shot in the back of the head.

Custer: No. This would all be gone (pointing to the right side of Kennedy's face).

Law: People are going to say, "But, it was a copper-jacketed bullet, it was made to stay in place" – talking about the Carcano now –

Custer: Okay That's fine. Let them say that – explain away all the (bullet) fragments.

Palamara: Yeah. There are dust-like fragments all over here, all over the place.

Law: If you had a jacketed bullet that remained intact or partially intact, you would not see this?

Custer: It was 99 percent intact. A jacketed bullet is meant to go in, kill, and come back out.

Law: So you're not going to see fragments, you're not going to see dust particles.

Custer: Right.

Law: You might see a little bit, but –

Custer: Right, but not that much. And you wouldn't see sizable fragments in there like that. That bullet went in and exploded. That's what it's used for.

Palamara: What about the notion – I think you said something yesterday, briefly – about his eye was hanging out.

Custer: Right. Right. That's basically from the destruction. Of all the tendons and fragments within the eye and the muscles that were destroyed by being severed when the bullet went in.

Palamara: That's what Sam Kinney – the driver of the follow-up car – said when he first saw him (Kennedy) at Parkland. His right eye was on his chin.

Custer: Right. Literally. It came straight out. There was nothing to hold it. The only thing that held it was maybe a few small muscles and the skin itself. Here, you can see the eye was placed back (photo 1). Like I said before, the mortician was already here. He started his work after I completed mine.

Law: All right.

Custer: I had nothing to do with these photos. I can't authenticate them. I can't say when they were taken. This could have been taken afterwards to help the mortician.

Law: Okay. That would explain stuff. Did you have anybody assisting you that night?

Custer: Yes I did. Ed Reed assisted me. He was my student. He was on call that evening and assisted me, to lift, place the films, clean the cassettes, cover them. Simple stuff.

Palamara: James Curtis Jenkins was another technician, helping out.

Custer: Right. So was Paul O'Connor. Floyd Riebe was also there. We all kind of helped each other.

Law: So basically you all pitched in and did some of the jobs others would ordinarily do? Because of the special circumstances –

Custer: Right.

Law: What is the strongest evidence just based on what you went through that stands out now, almost thirty-five years later that points to conspiracy?

Custer: Actually, there are two different things. Outside control, from the gallery. And Dr. Ebersole's actions.

Law: Let's talk about Dr. Ebersole a little bit. What in his actions points to that?

Custer: He wouldn't actually specify –

Law: Who was Dr. Ebersole and what was his demeanor?

Custer: Dr. Ebersole just at the time, during that period, was left in charge by Captain Brown. He (Brown) was off at a conference somewhere and Dr. Ebersole was, like myself – I'm the technician that was on call – he was the radiology resident on call. He had finished his residency. He was in the process of waiting to take his board certification. So he actually was not board certified at all. His expertise was radiation therapy. So he really had nothing to do with any forensic-type information: bullets, fragments, bullet wounds, gunshots, or anything like that. He just took care of any basic fractures, any basic carcinomas. At that time, we had radiologists that took turns, taking care of different situations, different facets of the radiology field. And that was their expertise, and they stayed within that region. So … ah … hum … the gentleman is dead and I do not want to cast any aspersions on him per se, but, I do not believe he was the best person for that position at that time. When he was told his duty was to find any bullets that went into the body and stayed there, he should've questioned that right away. He was a Lieutenant Commander. He was supposed to be there doing a particular job, gathering evidence. A couple of times I went to him and showed him: "Don't you think this is a fragment – what do you think about that?" [He said,] "Mind your own business, do your own job."

Law: So, basically, he fell in line with Boswell and Humes and Finck – "Do what you're told to do. Don't go any farther?"

Custer: Right. He was a career officer that did what he was told to do. He did no thinking on his own.

Law: Let me ask you this: you've all known each other – you all knew each other because you worked with each other – did any of you – all of you young men at this point in time – did any of you get together after the autopsy was over and say, "Jesus! What's going on here?" Did any of you get together and talk about your experience?

Custer: Well, you've got to remember the night was kind of draining. I know I went back up to the call room and I literally crashed. And I didn't wake up until, I think it was 6 o' clock the next morning when Captain Brown and Dr. Ebersole came into the call room, sat there on the bed and were talking to me and congratulating me on a job well done. But truthfully, the next day, we were summoned, each one of us to the Commander in Chief of the National Naval Medical Center – and told that we had to sign a gag order.

Law: Now, this was done separately? Each one of you separately went in and were told this?

Custer: Right.

Law: And what were your feelings when they said, "You're going to sign this gag order"?

Custer: Well, I knew that it was an important event that had happened. And they didn't want this to get out. But when I walked in the room I didn't realize the atmosphere – until actually I was there – the intimidation. We were meant to be intimidated.

Law: You got a feeling that you were – not so much in words but through their actions and the feeling you had – that basically you were being threatened.

Custer: Absolutely. You open your mouth, you're gone. We will forget you.

Custer: Court-martialed. And Fort Smith, the navy's jail.

Law: How long was it before you told anyone that you were the person that took the X-rays of the president?

Palamara: Like your wife, for example.

Custer: Well, the first time I actually said anything to anybody was when David Lifton came and proved to me that the gag order was rescinded.

Law: But you made sure that gag order was rescinded before you –

Custer: Absolutely. I saw the paper, in front of me.

Law: When Mr. Lifton came to you, did it frighten you? Was your wife frightened for you?

Custer: Well, see, all along, I was receiving phone calls, from different people and they were saying, "Well, the gag order's rescinded. Can you talk to me?" And I said, "No, I can't talk to you. I don't know it's rescinded. You're talking to me over the phone. I don't know you from Adam."

Law: Now, they rescinded it because of the House Select Committee on Assassinations in '77, correct?

Custer: Correct. And I voiced my opinion about it, and my wife would listen to me. She'd say, "What was that all about?" "Well, it's nothing, don't worry about it." And there we left it. We were married for quite a few years before she actually found out about it. And that night after Lifton left, she said, "Well, you mean to tell me you kept that secret all that long?" I said, "Yeah, I did."

Palamara: What was that like? Was she in disbelief at first?

Custer: She didn't realize I was there. Well, she knew I was at Bethesda, and she didn't put two and two together that I was involved in this until later. Much later.

Law: Is there anything else that you'd like to state for the historical record?

Custer: The more you think about the situation, even now thirty-five years later, a lot of the officials really don't want to hear the truth. When I went to Washington, D.C., and gave my deposition to the ARRB, I was told I was brought there to set the record correctly. During that time, I was told by the chief investigator that my deposition was the most important of all. And that kind of struck me as funny at the time, because they had Humes, Boswell, Finck, and Ebersole there – and to tell me mine was more important than theirs? You kind of say, "Well, wait a minute. Are you telling me you're going to believe me more, over and above these gentlemen?" They weren't very kindly to these other gentlemen. They felt they were kind of aloof and standoffish. They didn't want to be honest and truthful with the evidence they had. But they didn't consider it as evidence, it's historical artifacts. That's how it's listed. It should be listed as historical evidence of an assassination.

It makes you wonder, why a great country like ours would do something like that. Destroy a person that, just maybe, could have put this country on its feet to where it could have been totally well and respected by everyone throughout the world. The age of Camelot. Why did they call it Camelot? Because they wanted to go back to honest and decent ways, as at that chivalrous time. When a woman was worth something, when a man's word was his bond. Today, you cannot take people by their word. You have to have everything written out. Detailed. Everything plain and simple. Certified. Documented. Then again, you have to go through the same thing. No longer just a handshake – today you bring it back and you count your fingers.

Law: Well, here's my handshake, sir. It's been an honor. You said a lot.

Custer: Well thank you. I appreciate it.

Law: Thank you.

Palamara: Thank you.

* * *

Jerrol Custer was an enigma. Some months after our interview, Vince Palamara sent me a copy of a television documentary, *JFK: An Unsolved Murder*, broadcast in 1988 by KRON TV in San Fransisco, in which Custer was interviewed by Silvia Chase. Having been given a copy of the lateral X-ray (photo 8), Custer was asked, "Is this the X-ray picture that you took, and is this (pointing to the top of the skull) the wound that you saw on the president?" He replied, "This area was gone, not this [blackened on the right] area." He seemed perplexed as to what the X-ray showed, giving the impression that it was not an X-ray he had taken. Yet to Vince and me, Custer was quite sure that it was one of his exposures.

Another aspect of Mr. Custer's account that is troubling is the statement to us that William Pitzer had a congenital deformity of the right hand. It is doubtful whether Pitzer, who reached the rank of lieutenant commander, would have been inducted into military service with such a birth defect. Dennis David, who played cards with Pitzer on many occasions, has no recollection of a deformed right hand. I believe that Jerrol either heard or read that Mr. Pitzer's widow had been told by the U.S. Navy that Lieutenant Commander Pitzer's left hand was mangled and his wedding ring could not be removed. In his mind, Custer may have transformed this information to the "fact" that William Pitzer had a deformed hand, a birth defect.

Before the interview began, Jerrol told us that he was working on a book, and showed us a notebook of questions and answers that he and a researcher had assembled. When I asked him why the back of President Kennedy's skull appeared to be intact in the lateral X-ray, he stated, "In the next video, this comes out, then I'll discuss it more. See, legally I can't go much further with this." Before I had arranged to travel to Pittsburgh from the west coast, my understanding had been that he would go fully on the record, therefore I was disappointed that there were aspects that he would not discuss because of his book-in-progress. I tried to hide my irritation, and stuck with the task of obtaining as much information from him as possible.

I found this man to be more than a bit of a curmudgeon. I was aware from several telephone conversations with him before our meeting in Pittsburgh that, over the years, he felt he had been taken advantage of by re-searchers and authors. The first time we spoke, he said, "See, all these people take advantage of me. They write books, making millions, while I'm bust-ing my ass for pennies." Jerrol was working as an armed security guard at the time, having lost his position as a supervisory X-ray technician due to down-sizing. His bitterness at authors such as David Lifton and Harrison Livingstone was palpable. It was clear he felt he was entitled to some of the monies from their book sales. Certainly, it must have been hard to cope with past troubles with the IRS and a lost job, believing that his experiences had been used by others to make millions while he struggled to make ends meet.

The kindest possible light that I can shed on the dubious parts of Jerrol Custer's account is that he hoped to use the interview to promote the book he was working on. And he wanted to make his story more interesting by claiming that William Pitzer was in the morgue during the autopsy. He may have allowed his account to be influenced by the researcher he was working with on the book.

I contacted Jerrol after the discovery of apparent discrepancies in his story, in the hope of setting up an appointment for a more "hard-boiled" exchange. He agreed to the proposal of a follow-up interview but then can-celed, stating that he had started a new job and could not spare the time until he had settled into his new assignment.

Sadly, Jerrol never recovered from his longstanding financial difficulties, nor did he see the publication of his book. After receiving a call from Debra Conway passing along a rumor that Jerrol had died, I called the Custer resi-dence. At the moment I heard Marilyn's voice, I knew it was true: "Well Bill, it's no rumor. We lost Jerrol in July." He died as the result of a massive heart attack, leaving a wife of 30 years and two sons, one of school age at home.

Troubles continued for the Custers. Marilyn and her son moved to a small duplex, no longer able to afford the home that she and Jerrol had shared for many years. "One thing I am grateful for," she imparted. "Jerrol always said that he wished that he would go before me, because he couldn't stand to be without me. Also, he wanted to go quickly." He got both of his wishes.

Whatever Jerrol Custer really believed about his experiences at the Na-tional Naval Medical Center, Bethesda, as a young corpsman charged with the onerous task of X-raying the body of a slain president – to paraphrase Edwin M. Stanton – now belongs to the ages.

Chapter Nine

James W. Sibert &
Francis X. O'Neill

Part One

By November 22, 1963, James Sibert had been with the FBI for fourteen years and Francis O'Neill had been an agent since 1957. Both were in their forties when fate or some unseen hand placed them at the heart of the mystery of John Kennedy's murder.

According to O'Neill he was assigned to the Baltimore office because of his military background. When he learned President Kennedy's body was being flown to Andrews Air Force Base, in Maryland, he went there "to assume jurisdiction over any violations that might fall within our purview. " Jim Sibert was brought in "so there would be two of us to be a witness to whatever might happen." While waiting for Air Force One to taxi to a stop, O'Neill contacted Ed Tully at FBI headquarters who had a directive from J. Edgar Hoover to have the agents stay with the president's body, in agent Tully's words, quoted by O'Neill, "… so that if there is any evidence of what occurred, in the body, take that evidence back to our FBI laboratory." After Kennedy's casket was off-loaded from the cargo lift and placed in the gray navy ambulance, Sibert and O'Neill entered the third car in the motorcade that accompanied the coffin to Bethesda Naval Hospital. (However, if David Lifton, author of *Best Evidence*, is correct, the casket in the ambulance was empty; Kennedy's body already had been removed from the presidential jet so that it could be altered to hide the direction of the shots, and, from other indications, remove what was left of Kennedy's brain and replace it with another.)

As I sit typing these lines, my mind still tells me that this cannot be true! It still seems preposterous, even after interviewing the Bethesda technicians. The very thought of such a thing is so utterly repulsive, yet follow-

281

ing the paper trail of documents and witness testimony, there really is no other conclusion I can come to. Sherlock Holmes's adage has never been more true: "When you have eliminated the impossible, whatever remains, however improbable, must be the truth."

Perhaps the strongest clue to this mystery is provided by agents Sibert and O'Neill in their FD 302[1] report on events in the Bethesda morgue, including the autopsy doctors' description of the body at the start of the autopsy: "the clothing had been removed and it was apparent that a tracheotomy had been performed, as well as surgery of the head area, namely, in the top of the skull" (photo 21). This critical piece of evidence indicates that alterations had indeed been made on president's body between the time it left Parkland Memorial Hospital, Dallas, Texas, and arrived in the morgue at the Naval Medical Center, Bethesda, Maryland. One can argue about metal shipping caskets and body bags, but there is no argument that the appearance of the head suggested to Drs. Humes and Boswell that it had been altered surgically. This history-altering statement is in an official government record, placed there by two seasoned agents of the FBI.

I had to try to talk to Sibert and O'Neill, as with the other witnesses present at the Kennedy autopsy – they held the keys to the answers I sought. But, how to find them? The gods of fate were with me. Going back through documents from the HSCA, I found the general area where Sibert lived in Florida, and with help from a willing telephone operator, I obtained a number for a James W. Sibert. He answered the phone and, as I explained who I was, he interrupted with, "Just a minute, will you? I've just come back from the store and I've got an armload of groceries. Are you calling long distance?" I told him yes. He said, "Let me set these down." How many people would interrupt bringing in groceries to answer questions on the telephone? Was this a "cover story" to allow him to find a notepad and pencil? Soon he was back: "Okay, I'm sorry, go ahead."

I imagined Mr. Sibert, phone in one hand, scribbling with the other. As I explained my project, he listened patiently then offered only, "Everything I have to say is in the 302s Frank O'Neill and I did. I've been asked to give interviews by researchers over the years, but I never have. I was contacted by the House Select Committee [on Assassinations] in the 70s and told them what I could remember, and that was how many years ago now?" Sensing that I was losing him, I decided to ask directly about the statement in the 302 about surgery of the head area (photo 21). To my surprise, he answered: "We found out later that that statement was wrong. One of the doctors said

---

1. Jargon for the official typed-up report stored in the FBI archives.

there had been surgery done on the head from the way the wound looked. I wish we would have worded it better. It would have saved some confusion in some books." I then asked him if he would be interested in attending a conference on the assassination held each year in Dallas as my guest, and although I already knew the answer I would get, it was a way to keep him on the line. As expected, he declined: "You know, after I came back from testifying before the last one [Assassinations Records Review Board] I told my wife, 'That's it! No more. I'm done. I've testified enough.' " Never one to give up easily, I again appealed to Sibert to give me an interview because he was important to history. "Listen," he retorted, "I turned down David Lifton when he asked me for an interview. I don't need to be quoted in books. I dropped some of the first bombs over Europe during the war. I don't need to be famous. I don't have any stars in my eyes." I asked him if I could ask just a few questions before I let him go. Not waiting for an answer, I launched into Arlen Specter and the single-bullet theory. He told me Specter had made a false statement in his report to the Warren Commission: "What a liar. I feel he got his orders from above and how far above I don't know." Sibert went on to tell me he does not believe in the single-bullet theory. I then asked him about the casket Kennedy's body was in when it was brought into the morgue. Sibert said: "The casket was ornate with a broken handle. " Without my asking, he told me the body was not in a body bag. I asked him if I had any more questions would he mind if I called him again. He may have sensed my disappointment over his refusal to give me an on-camera interview, as he then told me kindly: "I don't want to do an interview but I'll tell you what. The next time you call, if you have a list of questions you want to ask, I'll do my best to answer them."

I was elated! The possibility of Jim Sibert sitting for an on-camera interview was remote, yet I had still had my foot in the door. I was still in the game.

I then asked if he had kept in touch with Francis X. O'Neill. The last time they had talked had been when the ARRB contacted them. I told Sibert I would like to talk to Mr. O'Neill about participating in my oral history project. "Just a minute," he said. "I think I have his number in my directory." Jim Sibert came back on the line. "Here it is," and proceeded to give me O'Neill's phone number and address in Connecticut.

The voice that came over the line was brusque and to the point: "This is Frank O'Neill." After I introduced myself and told him of my project, he said, "Would you wish to do this telephonically or in person?"

"Whatever is convenient for you," I said. "If you're willing to meet with me, I will come to you. If the telephone would be more convenient for you we could do it that way." O'Neill responded with, "I'm going to call Jim Sibert first. I'm going to call him as soon as I hang up from you. As to an interview, I'll have to think about it. " Instructing me to call him back within the week, Francis X. O'Neill hung up.

During the week to follow, I armed myself with as many questions as I could think of, starting with the "surgery of the head" statement. For me, this was still the key phrase, despite Sibert's insisting that what was in the FBI report was wrong. I suspected that he was reluctant to share his true feelings on the matter, and was hopeful that, in time, he would be more forthcoming. I was determined to draw him out. It might take weeks – it might take months – and many conversations before he would be sufficiently comfortable.

I waited out the week. I had his testimony to the HSCA and his 302 report at hand. Unfortunately, I did not yet have his ARRB testimony. I felt confident as I dialed the number – that Sibert and I had "connected" during our brief exchange. He had been at ease and friendly over the phone, even offering a picture of himself for the book. Full of goodwill toward the affable ex-agent, I burbled, "Hi Mr. Sibert. It's William Law." Silence. And then: "Yeah?" The voice was tinged with more than a little hostility. "Well, Sir, I called you last week, remember? About the book of oral history I am trying to put together? You said in our last conversation if I called you back with questions, you would answer them. " Sibert shot back, his voice strangely defiant, "Look, it's all in the 302s. I don't know what else I could tell you." Gone was the kindly demeanor of just seven days prior. Dazed, all I could manage was, "Does that mean, sir, that you won't answer my list of questions?" "Yes, that's what that means." He was obviously impatient and wanted to get off the phone. But, I was unwilling to relent. "Could I just ask you one question before I let you go?" Silence. "When you were shown the autopsy pictures before the Records Review Board – did President Kennedy's body look like what you remember from that night?" Silence … then: "The body looked cleaner than what I remember seeing. Maybe they were taken further along in the autopsy after the mortician's started working on it." "No, sir, I blurted. As far as we know, all the pictures we have were taken at the start of the autopsy." "Look," said Sibert. "I've already said I don't know what else I can tell you. Hell, I'll probably still be getting calls about this when I'm 90. I know you're interested in this – you'll just have to wait till all of the records on this are released and then you'll understand all of these things." With a terse goodbye, Sibert broke the connection.

I found Frank O'Neill to be even more hostile than Sibert! When he came on the line, he barked: "I've decided not to discuss the Kennedy matter further." Knowing I was going to be talking to dead air in a very short time, I said, "Could I please just ask you one question while I have you on the phone?" Obviously annoyed, he said, "I've already told you I've decided not to discuss the matter further, but go ahead."

"When you went before the Records Review Board and were shown the Kennedy autopsy photographs did they look like what you remembered?"

"Some of them did. Some of them didn't."

I pressed on, "Did the President's body look like what you remember?" O'Neill's angry reply came back.

"No!"

My mind went blank. "Well, th-thank you Mr. O'Neill," I stammered.

And there the matter of Sibert and O'Neill rested for three years.

It was my good fortune to be put in contact with Allan Eaglesham through Dennis David. I called Allan to discuss his research on Pitzer, and learned that he is an editor by trade. During the time I was trying to put the manuscript into cohesive form, I turned to Allan for help. He agreed to assist with the editing, and, as the book was being readied to go to press, I found myself once again thinking of Sibert and O'Neill. Obviously, they were central to the case. I had to try again to interview them, if only so that I could say that I'd given it my best shot. During my first call to Sibert he had said that he and his wife were planning to move to a retirement community. Therefore, I no longer had his telephone number or knew in what area of Florida he now lived. On the other hand, as far as I knew, O'Neill's number was still good. I hit upon the idea of calling O'Neill to invite his comments on some of Jerrol Custer's statements, and thus engage him in further discussion of his recollections of events in the autopsy room. Hopefully, enough time had gone by that he wouldn't remember who I was or his anger towards me.

I braced myself as I dialed the number, half afraid that the number had been disconnected since so much time had passed, and half afraid that he would answer the phone in the same brusque manner as before. I had decided to take an informal approach, and asked for Frank O'Neill, even though I recognized his voice. "Well, which one of us do you want? There is two of us," he said. "Well, senior, I guess." O'Neill replied, "Well, I'm junior, but you must want me." I introduced myself by name and told him I was a writer working on a book about the Kennedy assassination. I said: "I understand you were in attendance at President Kennedy's autopsy." "Yes, yes, I was." O'Neill said. Far from the short, clipped tone I had expected, he seemed open, relaxed, maybe even a little glad to hear from me! He started to give me a brief rundown on being a paratrooper in World War II, shifted to his tenure as an FBI agent and then, "I was a State Congressman for a number of years." I was trying to scribble things down, and at the same time take in every word.

I asked if he would mind my reading from the manuscript I was working on to get his comments. "This is from an interview I did with Jerrol Custer, sir. Let me read you this statement – " O'Neill interrupted to ask, "Was he the photographer?" I told him who Custer was. O'Neill said, "Oh, yes. I see." I read Custer's statement about going down the hall with an armload of X-rays and seeing Jackie Kennedy. "No, that wasn't me," he said. Next I read Custer's statement about a bullet fragment falling out of Kennedy's back when Custer put an X-ray plate underneath the president's back. "There was no fragment. The only fragments found that night were a sliver of metal taken from behind the right frontal sinus and a small sliver of metal from the brain. The man's hallucinating. He's sick." I then asked about Custer's claims that he or Jim Sibert had accompanied Custer to develop the X-rays. "No, that's not true. We weren't present for any of the X-rays. They were taken while we were out of the room." He then repeated: "He's sick." O'Neill also told me: "We weren't present for any of the pictures. They were taken while we were out of the room. " I said: "I read your testimony before the ARRB – you seemed to be saying the body looked different from what you remembered." He chuckled. "There were just a couple of different pictures we had not seen before." I said, "Then you don't believe there was any kind of conspiracy to kill Kennedy?" "Absolutely not! Look, Jim Sibert and I made six pages of notes. It's all in the 302s. Don't you think the Kennedys would have spent every last dime to find out who killed their brother? They all agreed with the report."

After I hung up, I felt strange. He seemed sincere, and was quite friendly. In contrast with what had happened three years earlier, although still somewhat brusque, he'd answered my questions and we'd parted on good terms. I may have to get my answers through several phone conversations, but I was determined to try again to question him face to face.

I needed an excuse to call again. It came in the form of Jim Jenkins. Jim had agreed some months previous to make some drawings and provide an analysis of the Kennedy autopsy pictures for the book, but he was putting in many extra hours at the hospital where he worked as a chief administrator. Jim told me, "I have to have time to go through this and do it right." I would call him every couple of weeks to see how far he had progressed. During one of our phone conversations I told him I had spoken to Frank O'Neill, one of the two FBI men present at the morgue that night. "I'd really like to talk to him sometime," Jim said, which seems the perfect excuse to contact Mr. O'Neill again. Thus I would kill two birds with one stone: hook Jim Jenkins up with Frank O'Neill and get a chance to ask questions.

O'Neill answered the phone and I started to tell him that someone in the autopsy room on the evening of November 22, 1963, wanted to talk to him. He wasn't interested. "There's nothing that he could add to what I know." I said: "Well it's not that he wants to add anything to what you know, he wants to hear from you on what you know." O'Neill replied curtly, "He can read it in my book [*A Fox Among Wolves*]." Never to miss an opportunity I asked him when it would be published. "I don't know. It's at two publishers at the present time, and they're kind of dickering on it. Listen, I'm really tied up, but I'd like to take your telephone number. I know I got it the last time, but I lost the piece of paper." I gave him it and he asked for my full name. I couldn't help but wonder if he was planning on running my name by one of his contacts at the FBI, but then, what the hell was he going to find out? That I was a middle-aged would-be writer, divorced twice, one grown son with three young children still at home, two cars, one mortgage, and one very serious obsession with what had happened to the thirty-fifth president of the United States.

As these thoughts passed through my head, O'Neill caught me off-guard with: "Did you have any cousins or brothers or uncles or aunts in the FBI at one time?" I replied in the negative. "Because I worked with a guy by the name of Willy Law years ago. Its just the name stuck with me." He then said, "Give me the name of this person (Jim Jenkins) because I made a record of most of the people who where there and I'd just like to know … " I interrupted: "It's because of your record taking that we found out that Jim Jenkins was there." I gave him Jim's name, spelling it for him. "Do I have him listed down?" He answered himself: "I'll have to check my notes and find out. Give me his telephone number, just in case I have a change of heart." "I wish you would, because he would really like to talk to you. I'd like to talk as well," I said, getting in another bid for a chance to get O'Neill to go on-camera. "You are talking to me," he answered. "Well, I am," I said. "But I'd really like to sit face to face with you." Laughing, O'Neill responded, "I'll send you one of my videos." Then he said: "I did a debate with two other gentlemen at Franklin Pierce Law School in Vermont about the Kennedy assassination. " I asked: "Is it available to the public?" "I don't know. They sent me a copy. I'll check and see. If so, I'll send you a copy. Not this instant, you know, but – I told O'Neill I understood, and that I was grateful for anything he was willing to do for me.

I let a couple of weeks go by. Still working on the manuscript for the book, I knew it had to include Francis X. O'Neill. I also knew I was verging on being a serious pain in the ass to the former FBI agent. I didn't want to alienate him, partly because I was beginning to rather like the man, although his manner had been somewhat tart – he did not beat around the bush. You may not like the answers O'Neill gives, but they are straight and to the point. The one time I caught a glimpse of a sense of humor was during an early conversation, referring to Mr. Sibert, he said: "You know, Jim is fifteen or twenty years older than I am." I tried to sound like I already knew that. "Right," I said. O'Neill retorted, "I'm joking, of course." No change in tone, no inflection of voice. Flat monotone: "I'm joking, of course." That exchange told me a lot about Mr. O'Neill.

I had to keep pushing. I wanted a meeting in person, but, thus far, my overtures regarding a get-together had been rebuffed. I decided to try a different tack. The next time I called, he didn't seem to remember me. I reminded him that I had called a couple off weeks prior.

"From Califo – ?"

"Oregon," I prompted.

"Yes, okay. I beg your pardon. I'm so mixed up with so many different things at the present time. I'm sorry that I didn't recognize you. "

"Could I just ask you a couple of questions?"

"Yeah," O'Neill replied. "I'm right in the middle of something right now, but go ahead. "

"Well, let me get to the point. I would like to have an interview with you – "

"You said that before, but go ahead."

"I realize you don't want to do it face to face."

"Correct."

"Could we do it through e-mails or something?" I asked.

"My basic point is this," O'Neill went on, "everything I have to say, I've already said. There's nothing new, in any respect, that can come out, one way or the other. And I'm sure you've seen my reports." There was no animosity in his voice; he seemed genuinely perplexed that I wanted an interview. "There is nothing in there that is different from what I would tell you." There wasn't a whole lot I could say in reply to that. I certainly could not say what was really in my head: Well, Mr. O'Neill, you don't realize that some of your words to me contradict the "official" version of the events in Bethesda, and if I can keep you talking long enough, you just might – by some slip of the tongue – tell me something significant that you don't grasp as being important, at which point, sir, I'll have more of the truth of what happened to the thirty-fifth president of the United States.

I wanted to say just that, and more, but, of course, I could not. Instead I offered: "Well, I understand that. I guess it's just a matter of my own curiosity of having you say it to me in person. Do you know what I mean?"

"Yes, I do," O'Neill answered.

"It's different to have the person who was there say it to you rather than read it in cold script. " I took the opportunity to expand on that point with: "There might be a point that I want to ask about, or need your clarification."

"And this would be for your own personal knowledge and nobody else's? " O'Neill asked. I told him again of the manuscript I was working on. "Well, let me think about it ... suppose I sent you a tape of a lecture I gave at the University of – let's see, it's up in Vermont – Franklin Pierce Law School? Let me see if I can get a copy of that and shoot it to you. You can tell me then if there's anything additional that you'd like to ask me. I will say one thing about you. You are persistent."

Of course, I needed a reason to call yet again, just in case he didn't get around to sending me the tape. While going through an encyclopedia of the medical evidence assembled by Vince Palamara – a compendium of the medical information with references on where to find the original source documents – I came across this CBS memorandum:

> 1/10/67 CBS Memo Robert Richter to Les Midgley: "Jim Snyder of the CBS bureau in D.C. told me today he is personally acquainted with Dr. Humes. They go to the same church and are personally friendly. Snyder also knows Humes's boss in Bethesda; he is a neighbor across the street from Snyder. Because of personal relationships, Snyder said he would not want any of the following to be traced back to him; nor would he feel he could be a middle-man in any CBS efforts to deal with Humes. Snyder said he has spoken with Humes about the assassination. In one conversation Humes said one X- ray of the Kennedy autopsy would answer many questions that have been raised about the path of the bullet going from Kennedy's back though his throat. Humes said FBI agents were not in the autopsy room during the autopsy; they were kept in the anteroom, and their report is simply wrong. Although initially in the autopsy procedure the back wound could only be penetrated to a finger length, a probe later was made – when no FBI men were present – that traced the path of the bullet from the back going downward, then upward, then downward as it was apparently taken with a metal probe that was left in the body to show the wound's path. Humes said that a wound from a high power rifle, once it enters a body, causes muscle, etc., to separate and later

contract; thus the difficulty in initially tracing the wound's path in the case of Kennedy. Also, once a bullet from a high power rifle enters a body, its course can be completely erratic; a neck wound could result in a bullet emerging in a person's leg or anywhere else. Humes refused to discuss with Snyder the 'single bullet' theory in which the Warren Commission contends the same bullet described above went through both Kennedy and Connolly. Humes also said he had orders from someone he refused to disclose – other then stating it was not Robert Kennedy – to not do a complete autopsy. Thus the autopsy did not go into JFK's kidney disease, etc. Humes's explanation for burning his autopsy notes was that they were essentially irrelevant details dealing with routine body measurements, and that he never thought any controversy would develop from his having done this. "

I hoped that my reading "the FBI were not even in the room" might get Frank's juices flowing and it might lead to something. The next time I called, I apologized for bothering him again, but said, "I just came across something the other day. Something I was reading and it's a statement attributed to Dr. Humes – " O'Neill interrupted: "Dr. Humes. He was one of the doctors." I agreed. "I just came across this quote and I wanted to get your opinion on it. With a sigh of resignation, he agreed to my request. "It says: 'FBI were not in the autopsy room at the time of the autopsy – ' " O'Neill interrupted again: "Absolutely wrong one hundred percent!" I continued: " 'They were kept in the anteroom. Their report was simply wrong.' " "Absolutely wrong." O'Neill said again. "Why would Humes say that?" I asked. "I have no idea. You'd have to ask him that. In fact I'd like to send you – in fact I might do it – I have a two hundred and seventy-six page affidavit that I gave to the government, which I did two years ago. Maybe I might be able to take that and shoot it out to you. But that remark by Dr. Humes is totally and irrevocably wrong."

He asked me where I got the quote from. I told him. "Totally wrong. That's one reason not to read that encyclopedia or things like that." I decided to push things a little farther. I knew I'd kept him on the phone longer then he'd wanted, but I felt I had touched a nerve by reading him the CBS memo. I delved into uncharted waters. "You interviewed Roy Kellerman, correct?" "Twice – once in the autopsy room, and once at the White House. Sibert and I made a decision amongst ourselves, he would take one agent and I would take the other. In the autopsy room I stayed with Kellerman and Jim stayed with Greer. We carried on with the same thing after Hoover told us to go back to the White House, two or three days later, which we did. And as a result of that we did another interview."

I asked O'Neill if he believed Kellerman's statement about hearing the president say, "My God I'm hit! Get me to a hospital." He answered "Not a single doubt in my mind, not a single doubt, because he reiterated it the next day: 'My God, I've been hit. Get me to a hospital.' The first thing he said. He told me there were other quotes from the back. Somebody said, 'My God they are killing him.' I don't know who that came from. Supposedly from somebody in the convertible. But those were the exact quotes from the two men who were with him [Kennedy] in the car at the time." Just to nail it down, I said, "So you did believe him when he said that?" "One hundred thousand percent. I asked him specifically, 'How do you know it was the president that said that?' He said: 'Frank, he was the only one in that back seat that had a Boston accent.' "

I then decided to take a bit of a plunge. "There are some people who have researched the case that feel Kellerman and Greer were part of the plot and that's why you interviewed them twice. " I waited. O'Neill was terse in reply. "They were good honorable agents." We parted on that note. I waited a week or so and wrote Mr. O'Neill a letter thanking him for his offer to send me a copy of the Franklin Pierce Law School debate, and enclosed a money order in the amount of thirty dollars to cover the cost of materials and postage.

I confess, I hoped that the money would obligate him to some extent, but, more so, I wanted him to understand that I am not an "assassination buff," although by almost any standard I would be considered one. I wanted O'Neill to get used to me, to be comfortable with me. I wanted to get to know him as a person and I could do that only by sustained contact. As with the other men I had interviewed who had been connected with the autopsy, I needed to know what he knew. I had to get past the usual facade the former FBI agent showed others, and, in so doing, get closer to the truth of the Kennedy mystery.

A week later, the letter came back to me unopened. I had used the address I had gotten from Jim Sibert during our first – and next to last – conversation, three years before. I had hoped it was still good. Now, I had to call him and ask about the tape, and tell him I wanted to reimburse him. As with all my other calls of late, he was cordial. I reminded him of our previous telephone conversation some weeks before and the tape of the debate at the Franklin Pierce Law School that he had said he would send me. "Yes, I remember. I just haven't had time to run you off a copy yet." I told him of the letter and money order I had enclosed to cover his costs for materials. "What address did you send it to?" he asked. I gave him the address I had for him in Connecticut. "Oh, no. That address hasn't been good for two years." He then gave me an address in Massachusetts, and added, "I'm glad you called me. After the last conversation we had, I went down to the library we have here and I looked through every book and document I could find, and nowhere could I find any statement attributed to any of the doctors." I was confused. Then I realized he was talking about the statement attributed to Dr. Humes about the FBI agents not being present in the autopsy room at the time of the autopsy and the agents' report being wrong. I reminded him of where I had gotten the statement. "I'll send you a copy of the page from Vince Palamara's book that has the statement, if you like. You probably wouldn't find it in your library because it is self-published. " "I see," said O'Neill. "I'd appreciate that very much."

As usual, I wanted to ask questions, and he indulged me. I asked him if he felt the autopsy doctors had been under any pressure that night, and if so, from whom. "No, they were not under any pressure – well, nothing more than what you would expect, considering the circumstances. Jim Sibert and I wanted a full autopsy. The doctors wanted a full autopsy. The Kennedy family did not want a full autopsy. There was an admiral who told the doctors to do a full autopsy – I can't remember his name." I asked, "Was it Dr. Burkley?" "No, it wasn't Burkley. He was the president's physician." I asked if Burkley was in charge of the autopsy. "No. Burkley wasn't in charge. He gave no orders."

There was one more question I wanted to ask before the call ended. The week before, I'd been sitting at my desk going through some notes I had made on O'Neill some three years earlier. With reference to the second brief and angry exchange we'd had, one of the notes read: Did the president's body look like what you remembered? Answer: *No.* I was beginning to like Frank O'Neill a great deal. His brusque manner had softened somewhat. He seemed sincere, and he had indulged me even when he was busy. This for me would be an acid test – a test I hoped O'Neill would pass: "In the autopsy pictures, does the president's body look like what you remembered?" "Oh, yes. It looked the same. There was just a picture or two Sibert and I had questions about is all." I didn't ask O'Neill what his and Sibert's questions had been. Oh, yes, the body had looked the same – a direct contradiction of the answer he had given me in 1998.

I mailed a new letter.

September 6, 2001

Mr. Francis X. O'Neill

Dear Mr. O'Neill:

> As per our conversation last week, here is the page from Vince Palamara's book, *JFK: Medical Evidence Reference*, where I obtained the

information concerning Dr. Humes statement that you and Agent James Sibert were not in the autopsy room on November 22, 1963. As I read the material over it seemed to me that I had read it somewhere else before. So I decided to dig through my stack of JFK documents, and after about an hour of going through them I ran across the original documents source for Mr. Palamara's information in his book. I thought you might like to have a copy for your records.

I want to thank you, Sir, for all your effort in my behalf concerning my interest in the JFK case. Please let me know if there is anything I can assist you with in this matter.

Sincerely,

William M. Law

On September 11, 2001, the World Trade Center and the Pentagon were attacked by terrorists. I sat, like all Americans, numb with shock and grief watching the images of the attacks and their aftermath flicker across my television screen. The following Saturday, I was working in my backyard when my fiancee Lori brought me the phone. "I have no idea who this is," she said, handing me the phone. "Mr. Law. This is Frank O'Neill." I was taken aback and blurted, "Well, hello, Fra – Mr. O'Neill. How are you, sir?" "I wasn't in too good of shape a few days ago, but I'm doing better now." It took me a few seconds to realize he was referring to what had happened on September 11. We spent some moments talking about the tragedy, two Americans concerned about the fate of their country. "Well, enough about that," he said. "I wanted to let you know I received the papers you sent me. I've read them, and I was quite disturbed by what I read. I have no idea who the person was that wrote this – Vince Palamara, huh?" "Well," I said, "Vince Palamara didn't write it, it was just a document he included in his book. It was a memorandum from somebody who worked at CBS who knew Dr. Humes from church. I think it was more or less third-hand information and you know how reliable that is." O'Neill replied: "I'm going to send you two interviews I did on one tape, plus other information I think you'll find interesting. And I'm sending you back your money order. It wasn't necessary to send that." I asked him to please keep it: "It's the proper thing to do." And, off the top of my head, I said, "Mr. O'Neill, you were the first FBI anti-terrorist agent in the United States. Do you think we'll be attacked again?" He responded, "It's not a matter of will we be attacked again, but where and when. We need to stick them back hard. It's like operating on cancer. You need to cut all the cancer out, or else it will kill you." I agreed. I then told him I was thinking of writing an article for my local paper about the attacks on our nation. "Perhaps because of your background on this I could call you and we could work on it together." "Perhaps we can," O'Neill said. Despite my doubts brought on by his giving me two different answers to the same question three years apart, it was hard for me not to like him, to remain neutral and not make a judgment on his veracity. He had told me that he would send the package immediately. True to his word, it arrived a few days later. The package contained a VHS videotape, some pages of documents and a letter typed in upper case.

Honorable Francis O'Neill Jr. Esq. September 17, 2001 MR. WILLIAM LAW

DEAR MR. LAW

AS I PROMISED ENCLOSED IS A COPY OF A TAPE MADE AT FRANKLY [sic] PIERCE MADE IN AN EVIDENCE CLASS WHEREIN I AM DISCUSSING MY ACTIONS DURING THE EVENING OF THE ASSASSINATION OF JFK. YOU WILL NOTE I DELETED THE COMMENTS OF THE 2 OTHER GENTLEMEN WHO PARTICIPATED DUE TO THEIR OBVIOUS LACK OF SOLID EVIDENCE TO ESTABLISH THEIR RIDICULOUS CONCLUSIONS.

ALSO ENCLOSED ARE COPIES OF ARTICLES OF THE AMERICAN MEDICAL ASSOC. RELATIVE TO AN INTERVIEW WITH DR. BOSWELL. YOU WILL ESPECIALLY NOTE HIS COMMENTS ON PAGE 5. INTERVIEWS WITH DR. HUMES, CRENSHAW AND OTHERS FOLLOW I AGREE WITH A SUBSTANTIAL PORTION OF THESE COMMENTS.

I HAVE ALSO INCLUDED A PORTION OF A CHAPTER IN MY MANUSCRIPT PERTAINING TO MY ACTIONS ON THE ARAB TERRORISM DESK. SHOULD BE INTERESTING READING

SINCERELY, FRANK O'NEILL

With great excitement, I loaded the videotape into my VCR ... *The JFK Assassination: Issues And Evidence.* Gary Hamilton copyright 1992. Gary Hamilton tells us that because of his interest in the JFK assassination he has put together a panel in a legal context. "We have quite a good panel and we should have a lively discussion tonight." Frank O'Neill is sitting off to Hamilton's left, looking through papers. "We want this to be a thoughtful discussion from a legal perspective, how lawyers look at the evidence, how juries look at the evidence, how judges look at the evidence, and we hope to have a lively discussion." O'Neill continues shuffling papers. The camera moves in, while Hamilton describes events surrounding the assassination and the Warren Commission, and then switches to the HSCA and their report. Hamilton is now in full close up with all else lost from view. "Tonight, we will look at the evidence and tonight you can be the jury. Let me introduce our panel." The screen goes blank, an obvious edit, and Frank O'Neill appears in close up, looking lawyerly and relaxed at his papers. "To my left," says Hamilton, "is a retired special agent with the FBI. Mr. O'Neill was present at the autopsy of President John F. Kennedy and participated in the FBI's investigation of the assassination.

"Mr. O'Neill has a law degree from the University of Baltimore Law School. Among his many experiences includes being the FBI liaison to the Secretary of State, the Secretary of Defense, Vice Presidents, he was also an FBI liaison to intelligence agencies all around the world." During his introduction, O'Neill continues to sit looking like a man of intellect, exuding quiet power. I'm excited now. A chance to see him in action! The screen goes blank. When images appear again, it's a close-up of Professor George Michael Evica of the University of Hartford, Connecticut. He tells us where he was on November 22, 1963. The camera now moves to O'Neill who briefly describes where he was when he heard of the assassination – in a Bureau car en route to Glen Arden, MD, he received the information from the FBI office in Baltimore – and the screen again goes blank. Next, Frank O'Neill is standing holding a microphone: "Credible evidence shows – not *theory*, but facts, facts that can be admitted in a court of law, facts that any reasonable jury would find one person and one person only responsible for the assassination of John Fitzgerald Kennedy. But I'll get into the subject in time. I just have some comments about the things that were discussed in the slideshow, which you saw,[2] which I thought, by the way, was excellent, and many which I had not seen before. I think both you gentlemen have done an admirable job in gathering – ." The video cuts to underwater film footage of a submarine; it's a National Geographic special with a voice-over by Tom Brokaw. And that was it. The end. Four minutes and forty seconds of video, with Frank O'Neill talking for all of one minute and three seconds.

I stared at the TV screen – in disbelief that he had gone to the bother and expense of sending me something so inconsequential – then looked again at his letter. "You will notice I have deleted the other gentlemen due to their lack of credible information to support their ridiculous claims." I burst

---

2. Of course I didn't get to see it, as Mr. O'Neill had deemed it necessary to delete it.

out laughing. "Yes, Mr. O'Neill," I said out loud. "You certainly did!" I had hoped to use the give-and-take between the individuals in the discussion on the assassination as a segue to my own questions. But, that would be impossible now. I had also wanted to see how he handled himself in the cut and thrust debate with two knowledgeable researchers of the Kennedy case. Also now impossible. Frank O'Neill's monotone joke about his and Sibert's ages, and his editing out "the other gentlemen" on the tape of the "debate" told me a lot.

I turned to the documents he had enclosed with the VHS tape. There, copied from his local library, were the articles for the Journal of the American Medical Association, from 1992. The next pages were labeled down the side of the page in black letters in printed hand: "TERRORISM." The last document was titled "ASSASSINATION OF JOHN E KENNEDY." My heart rate increased. "Surely he didn't send me ... from his book ... .?" The document consisted of twelve pages of script. Some pages looked newer than others. New pages mixed with older ones – possibly an old draft of a chapter mixed with a new one. I tried to slowly read though the pages. They describe the drive to Andrews Air Force Base; the contact with Ed Tully and Hoover's directions to stay with the president's body; the coffin being unloaded from Air Force One and put aboard a gray navy ambulance; he and Sibert getting into the second car in the motorcade; the ride to Bethesda Naval Hospital; and the unloading of the casket:

> The driver of the ambulance. Special Agent Bill Greer, Kellerman, Sibert and myself went to the rear of the vehicle, opened the door and proceeded to take out the casket. An honor guard arrived at this time and assisted us in placing the casket on a conveyance and moving it up a short flight of two or three steps onto the small landing just outside the corridor that Kellerman had just exited. An honor guard member opened the door to the corridor and we four with some members of the honor guard rolled the casket into the corridor. Immediately upon entrance several feet away was a door on our left. Pushing open the door took us into a small room with several morgue slots for bodies. I recall being told by a naval attendant who met us at the door that one of the slots contained a small child who had died that day.

He goes on to describe going through another door to the right, rolling the conveyance into the autopsy room, "where there were persons who immediately introduced themselves as the autopsy surgeons." The casket was moved to an autopsy table where it was opened "by the medical technicians." The casket was bronze – in essence, the casket that left Dallas. He describes the body: " … wrapped in a sheet, with another bloody sheet wrapped around his head. " The body "was lying on a plastic-type sheet" as described in Dallas to protect the inside of the lining of the casket becoming soiled with blood. "His hands were clenched, eyes opened, and his mouth in a grimace." He and Sibert helped to take the body out of the casket. At that point, "one of the physicians, Commander Humes, requested that all non-medical personnel who were to assist with the autopsy leave the room so that X-rays and pictures could be taken." O'Neill, Sibert, Kellerman, and Greer went into the anteroom and observed what went on through the window in the door. Upon completion of the X-rays and photographs, they returned to the autopsy room. O'Neill states: "Never at any time were the investigative agents kept out of the room as some uninformed authors suggested. " There follows a direct dart aimed at David Lifton's book Best Evidence. "It would have been a physical impossibility for anyone to have tampered with the casket or the body from the time it left Air Force One until the time we took the president out of his coffin."

The next part was basically what he had told me during our telephone conversations. Jackie Kennedy wanted a partial autopsy. The agents wanted a full autopsy to ascertain the exact cause of President Kennedy's death. The matter was resolved, O'Neill wrote, by Admiral Holloway [sic, Galloway] commanding officer in charge of the hospital. "Holloway" was also how it appeared in his contemporaneous notes. He also wrote of the interviews of Kellerman and Greer, noting that they had not had a chance to clean up after the shooting – both men had "blood and parts of brain tissue on the backs of their coats, evidence of the force which the president's head had, for want of a better word, 'exploded.' " He claimed to have kept General Philip Wehle out of the autopsy room briefly until he "properly identified himself. " Wehle left and came back with a coffin for burial, as the bronze casket had a broken handle, and Wehle did not feel it was appropriate for President Kennedy to be buried in a broken coffin. At some point that night, O'Neill and Sibert "hastily passed around a sheet of paper and directed that all present write down their names." If that's true, then a man named George Bakeman was present. The agents did not make a mistake, as Jerrol Custer suggested to Vince Palamara and me. God only knows who George Bakeman was or why he was there.

I read through the chapter at least three times and didn't see any significant contradiction with the "official" version. It took a couple more readings to catch it. After O'Neill tells us about passing paper for signatures, the next paragraph reads, "Immediately upon viewing the body it was evident that a tracheotomy had been performed." So far, it's close to the 302 report. He goes on: "Humes viewing the body indicate [sic] that some type of surgical procedure had been (done?) in the head region, possibly cutting of hair or removal of some slight tissue to view the massive would [sic, wound] in the right rear of the president's head." He tells us it was Humes who made the statement "as well as surgery of the head area, namely, in the top of the skull" (photo 21), which he had admitted to me in a phone conversation – so I wasn't surprised by this. But the key here is in his statement, " … possibly cutting of hair and removal of some slight tissue to view the massive wound in the right rear of the President's head." Surely, even a "paper pusher" such as James J. Humes, who hadn't done an autopsy in years, could tell the cut from a scalpel and cutting of hair versus tearing from a bullet.

O'Neill went on to say there was no cutting of the body of the president until the X-rays were developed. "Humes pointed out to Sibert and I the many fragments of bullets and skull that was in the skull cavity." He does not mention seeing the sliver of what appears to be a bullet in the right part of the skull, which is quite obvious in the frontal X-ray (photo 7) and should have been mentioned in the 302 report that Sibert and O'Neill made from their notes – nor does O'Neill remember seeing this metal fragment when the ARRB showed him the Kennedy AP X-ray during his testimony in 1997, indicating, I believe, that the X-rays now in the archives are indeed composites, as suggested by Dr. David Mantik. Mantik has run tests on the X-rays and believes they are composites, i.e., forgeries. I believe O'Neill holds part of the key to this and gives confirmation to Mantik's suspicions, even though, because of his nature and background as a government agent and later State Congressman, he is incapable of believing that John F. Kennedy was killed as a result of a government conspiracy. Plainly he has not studied the case in all aspects, e.g., the Dallas witnesses to the assassination, the paper trail of documents, the actions and inaction of the Secret Service in the days leading up to and including the aftermath of the assassination, and, of course, what happened at the Bethesda morgue. He holds keys he does not know he possesses, keys locked in memory.

The most stunning portion of the manuscript on Kennedy that O'Neill sent me was yet to come: "Humes pointed the many fragments of bullets or skull that was in the skull cavity. Parts of the brain were still within the cavity, but not much." (emphasis mine) This fits directly with Paul O'Connor's recollection that when President Kennedy was taken from the casket and the sheets were unwrapped from around the head, there was no brain to be removed; only fragments were left inside the cranium.

I went back to Frank O'Neill's deposition before the ARRB on September 12, 1997.

Q: And let me say, in the way of preface, these photographs have been identified as having been taken of President Kennedy's brain at some time after the autopsy – after they have been set in formalin. Can you identify that in any reasonable way as appearing to be the – what the brain looked like of President Kennedy?

A: No.

Q: In what regard does it appear to be different?

A: It appears to be too much.

Mr. Gunn: Could we now look at – let me ask a question.

Q: If you could elaborate a little bit on what you mean "It appears to be too much."

A: Well, from this particular photograph here, it would seem that the only section of the brain which is missing is this small section over here. To me, that's not consistent with the way I recall seeing it. I do recall a large amount of what was identified to me as brain matter being on the back of Kellerman's shirt – I mean, Kellerman's jacket and Greer's jacket. And to me, that was a larger portion than that section there. This looks almost like a complete brain or am I wrong on that? I don't know.

The testimony continued:

Mr. Gunn: Could we take a look – if we could keep this one out for just a moment, and take a look at the ninety view, which is described as the superior (top) view of the brain, color photograph #50.

Q: Just so it is clear to you, the basilar view is going to be the brain from the bottom. The superior view is going to be the brain from the top. And what I am showing you now would be the left hemisphere of the brain, and the portion over here is the right hemisphere of the brain. The correlation is the portion down there. Does that look approximately the size of what you recall President Kennedy's brain being when it was removed from the cranium?

A: In all honesty, I can't say that it looks like the brain that I saw quite frankly. I – as I described before, I did not recall it being that large. If other people say that this is what happened, so be it. To me, I don't recall it being that large. It could have been, but I can't swear to it on a stack of Bibles that it was.

Clearly, O'Neill suspected that it was not Kennedy's brain, which is confirmed by his own words in the chapter on JFK he sent me. "Parts of the brain were still within the cavity but not much." He did his best to convey to the ARRB without coming right out and directly saying it. But, he came close – as close as Frank O'Neill was able – to saying that something is terribly wrong. One can argue Paul O'Connor was not in the autopsy room at the time of the brain's removal from the cranium. It is known he was out of the room getting things for the doctors from time to time, and he could have missed the brain being removed, but, if O'Neill is being truthful, the only time he was out of the room was when the X-rays and pictures were being taken. He and Sibert were in the cooler room looking through the glass window in the door at what was going on in the autopsy room.

O'Neill says in his unpublished work that no cutting was done on the body until the X-rays were developed. "The X-rays were returned to a small room within the autopsy room and viewed." O'Neill goes on to say the head wound was "massive": "Humes pointed out to Sibert and myself the gaping wound at the right rear of the president's head and the tremendous damage done to the brain therein." He goes on to explain that Humes had started the autopsy by doing the Y-incision on the chest – "of course, after he dictated the normal procedural information relative to his observations in relation to the body." O'Neill then says that "Pierre Finck from the crimes institute [sic, Armed Forces Institute of Pathology] arrived at that time to help with the procedure." Humes then "indicated the bullet had fragmented upon hitting the skull" and removed two fragments of metal. "He measured one and told Sibert and me it was 7 by 2 millimeters. The other one was measured 1 by 3 millimeters." They placed the fragments in a glass jar. The agents then signed a receipt "for both missiles." O'Neill then claims that he and Sibert helped turn Kennedy's body over. "The first thing that everyone noticed was the large scar on the president's back due to an operative procedure." Jim Sibert is credited by O'Neill for noticing a small hole in the upper right rear of Kennedy's back. Humes and Finck probed the wound with a metal surgical probe "and their fingers." The depth of the wound could be felt with a finger and there was apparently no exit for the wound. O'Neill apparently saw Humes measure the back wound at approximately 2 inches to the right of the center line of the spinal column "just below the shoulder." Humes said that the entry of the bullet that caused the back wound "entered from the rear at a 45 to 60 degree angle." All the calculations were done by Humes. The doctors were at a loss to explain why they could not find the bullet that entered the back and only went a short distance. It was decided that Jim Sibert would call the FBI laboratory firearms section to see if they could come up with an explanation. He spoke with agent Chuck Killion who said that a bullet had been received from Dallas that had been found at Parkland Hospital on a stretcher that had been used by "the presidential party." O'Neill reports that when they came back to the autopsy room and told the doctors about the stretcher bullet "Humes appeared greatly relieved." It appeared "quite likely" Humes said, "and entirely possible" that the bullet found on the stretcher in Dallas accounted for the fact that the bullet that entered the back could not be found. Frank O'Neill goes on to say that Humes "grew more confident as he thought about it and appeared convinced that the Dallas bullet had worked its way out of the back through the external cardiac massage performed on the president in an effort to save his life. " O'Neill then writes that "at no time did the autopsy doctors give any other kind of explanation for the back wound. This probably accounts, at least partly, for Humes destroying his original draft notes in his fireplace at his home."

I marveled at what Mr. O'Neill's unpublished chapter contains. He told me that he does not believe there was any conspiracy to take John F. Kennedy's life. In his manuscript he states, " ... there has been no hard evidence to date, nothing to support any conspiracy theories in a court of law, nor a scintilla of fact that would prove otherwise." Yet, he puts the lie to his own argument against conspiracy in Kennedy's death by his own belief that the single-bullet theory is not possible. If the single-bullet theory is not possible – i.e., one bullet caused seven wounds in two men, going through skin and bone and falling out on a stretcher at Parkland Hospital, almost unscathed – then there was indeed more then one assassin in Dealey Plaza that day.

The next time I talked to Frank O'Neill, I would have to be prepared. I would have a detailed list of questions ready, and see how many of them I could get him to answer. How far could I push the envelope?

I contacted him again on October 12, 2001. He was cordial; the brusque manner of our earlier conversations was gone. We started off by discussing events that had occurred since September 11, and after telling me that an FBI man had been killed in the World Trade Center – the head of building security who also happened to have the last name of O'Neill (no relation), he said, "Well that's neither here nor there. What can I do for you?" Once again, we delved into the Kennedy assassination.

Law: Were you surprised you were not called before the Warren Commission?

O'Neill: Yes. Because we had pertinent information and the information that was given to the Warren Commission as a result of our interview with Mr. Specter was not a hundred percent accurate.

Law: I've been told that there were officers of high rank in the autopsy room that night. Is that true?

O'Neill: There was the commanding officer of the hospital. There was a rear admiral. There was a General Godfrey McHugh, who was on the airplane with Kennedy and was his military attache; he was a one-star general. And there was a Major General Wehle who tried to enter and I kicked him out and he came back in and told me he was there to get another casket because the other one was broken. There was no one else.

Law: I have your testimony to the ARRB. They asked you about the bullet wound in the throat and you said, "Well, I question it. I'll tell you more later." Why did you question the bullet wound to the throat?

O'Neill: Because there was no such thing as a bullet wound in the throat at that particular time. We only learned about the bullet wound in the throat in particular – well, let me see – we learned about that after the doctors – not "we" – but it was learned by the doctors who performed the autopsy after they had called down to Dallas to speak to the hospital. Ah, I think it was Malcolm Perry?

Law: Malcolm Perry was the attending physician.

O'Neill: That's the only time that they became aware that there was a bullet wound in the throat.

Law: Do you believe there was a bullet wound in the throat?

O'Neill: I have no idea. It was not a question – I mean it was a question – there was not a question in my mind about a bullet wound in the throat, it just never came up. It was a tracheotomy, period, until we found out that it was performed over the bullet wound – over a wound – because they weren't sure it was a bullet wound at that time.

Law: Greer – the driver of the limousine, and of the ambulance – was he under any great stress at that period?

O'Neill: Bill? No! No more so then anybody else. I thought they were very composed and I thought they were very effective in managing the situation as they saw it, and obviously – I mean obviously saw it, and I think I mentioned to you they both had brain matter on the back of their coats.

Law: Quite a lot of brain matter?

O'Neill: Sufficient to be noticed, let's put it that way.

Law: Okay. Now the reason I'm going to ask you this has to do with the supposed wound in the back. You said something in your testimony before the ARRB that one of Kennedy's fists was clenched when you first saw him in the casket. Were they both clenched?

O'Neill: His eyes were open – this is Kennedy when he's lying on his back – when we opened the casket, he was lying on his back, his eyes were open, and his mouth was in a grimace, and his hands were sort of clenched. Put it that way. Yes. In other words, they weren't lying down flat.

Law: Well, there's argument for when he was hit in the back of course – something called the Thorbum position –

O'Neill: Uh huh.

Law: – where your hands clench up? And that could be evidence of that.

O'Neill: Well, it wasn't on up into the shoulders. This was just his whole – I guess that when he was placed in the casket – I don't know whether they tried to arrange his hands or not, but they were in a clenched position. Not fully clenched at all.

Law: Do you remember how many pictures were taken?

O'Neill: Absolutely not.

Law: You've seen tracheotomies before, perhaps?

O'Neill: Yes.

Law: Did you ever see one that was that big?

O'Neill: You know, really when I got right down to it, I never really noticed the size of the tracheotomy.

Law: A lot of people I've spoken to said, "Well, it was done under emergency conditions. "

O'Neill: I never really noticed the size. I knew it was the tracheotomy. I mean, it was quite evident, but as to the size, I couldn't give you a definition as to what is a big one, what is a small one.

Law: In your ARRB testimony you referred a few times to a wound in the back of the head.

O'Neill: Yes, the massive wound on the back right side.

Law: There's been talk of a wound over the president's right (photo 4) ear by several people that I've talked to –

O'Neill: Well, that was a part of the wound itself.

Law: Of the wound in the head itself?

O'Neill: Yes.

Law: So you think that was just part of the blowout itself over the ear?

O'Neill: Yes.[3]

Law: The next question I have is: no damage to the forehead at all?

O'Neill: Absolutely none. There was no damage to the front of the face or the forehead. Absolutely none. I've heard some people say the right forehead was damaged. No way.

---

3. Note: Mr. O'Neill did not contradict my term "blowout."

Law: Well, I've seen some of those autopsy pictures and it does look like there has been some damage done down into the forehead.

O'Neill: None that I saw.

Law: You didn't see any damage that night?

O'Neill: No. I saw pictures, yes. But I didn't see any that night.

Law: You didn't see it *on the body when you saw the body?*

O'Neill: No

Law: The flap of scalp (photo 4). Now, I've heard that that was torn and macerated. And I've asked this of all the witnesses at Bethesda whom I've interviewed. Could you possibly take that flap of scalp and pull it back over the wound to hide the defect in the skull?

O'Neill: Not a 100%. In no way. No.

Law: But somewhat?

O'Neill: I would – now your going back 45 years – I would say that there was a possibility that could be done somewhat, but not 100%.[4] No.

Law: That's basically what I've been told before –

O'Neill: That's an error whoever told you that.

Law: Well, No. Every one of them has told me "yes," you could pull it up, but it wouldn't cover the whole wound.

O'Neill: That's right.

Law: The skull section brought from Dallas. Was that part of the back of the head?

O'Neill: (chuckles) Where else would it be from?

Law: Why I'm asking is: somebody interviewed Sam Kinney, one of the Secret Service agents who said that the piece of skull he saw was like a flower pot. It was basically the back of the head. And I'm wondering if that was the large section of skull that was brought in that night.

O'Neill: There was a section that was brought in at that particular time. I did note that there was a section brought in at that time, but quite frankly, it came in during the later stages of the autopsy, and we were more concerned with the completion of the autopsy rather than looking at a piece of skull.

Law: The next question concerns the brain itself. I've been told there was a brain, I've been told there wasn't a brain –

O'Neill: There was a brain. When I say a brain, I mean there was a portion of a brain.

4. I was actually going back 38 years.

Law: Just a portion of a brain? Did you see them cut whatever was inside of the head? Did you see them physically cut it to bring it out?

O'Neill: No I didn't see them physically cut it – well, logic would tell you that they just couldn't reach in and pull it out. It was attached to something.

Law: The AP X-ray (photo 7) –

O'Neill: I saw every one of the X-rays.

Law: Okay. When they showed it to you –

O'Neill: They didn't just show it to me, they took them and put them up on a dryer in that room, and they were all there and we were all looking at them at the same time. Myself, Sibert, the other two agents from the Secret Service and the other doctors who were in attendance. They all were looking and they were pointing them out and that's when we saw them.

Law: (looking at notes) I've written down: this indicates that the eye is gone –

O'Neill: No way! Where did you find that out?

Law: This is out of your testimony before the ARRB when you were trying to orientate the X-ray itself, and you were having trouble and you were talking about, "Does this indicate this is gone? This part is gone in the face. "

O'Neill: When did I say this, supposedly?

Law: Well, that's what I took it – as when you were answering questions from the Records Review Board.

O'Neill: Where?

Law: That dark section on the right side – a lot of people think that that indicates that the face was blown out.

O'Neill: No, the face was not blown out. As I'd mentioned before.

Law: Right. I guess the main part of the question is: is that the X-ray that you remember looking at that night?

O'Neill: I remember looking at – what was it? – twenty-six X-rays or something like that?

Law: I've only seen two.

O'Neill: No – but I mean I remember looking at every single X-ray that day. And I think I put that on my report.

Law: Okay. You've looked at them all and so that maybe –

O'Neill: Every single one.

Law: The so-called midsection piece round object that was on the AP X-ray? The frontal part? There is a big object, an artifact that looks like a piece of bullet and –

O'Neill: Where would this be?

Law: That would be in the AP X-ray (photo 7a).

O'Neill: I don't recall any. If there was something such as that, it certainly wasn't pointed out to me. But they did point out all of the various pieces of skull matter, or bullets or fragments of bullets which were in the skull cavity. That's what they specifically pointed out. And I think I made mention of that in my 302.

Law: And that's not necessarily in the frontal X-ray. Are we talking about the side X-ray now (photo 8)?

O'Neill: We're talking about all the X-rays. They pointed all these particular situations out and I do recall specifically when they were talking about the number of – what do you call them – shooting stars or something such as that. And you've got to remember, too, there were two pieces of shrapnel which were taken out of the head. They did not take them all out, I guess because they could not get them out. But there were two pieces taken out and given to me. And given to Sibert.

Law: The back wound. Do you agree with Humes and Boswell's original autopsy face sheet for the placement of the wound?

O'Neill: Which one are you talking about now?

Law: Well, his original notes we know he burned in his fireplace for whatever reason. But the autopsy sheet that you saw, or have seen –

O'Neill: The one I saw which was the – yeah, I think they went along with that. They went right straight along. It was in the position – well, take a look at it yourself, and if you think you can take a bullet (amused tone in his voice) from that particular shot and put it in through the neck – no way. This was in the upper right shoulder strap muscle.

Law: (reading from the list of questions) Confusion about the wound in the back of the head.

O'Neill: No confusion.

Law: Well, I'm only telling you from what I've read. That's what I'm trying to clear up. I'm not saying you are confused or that anybody that was there is confused –

O'Neill: Where do they say the confusion is?

Law: This is my own question.

O'Neill: Shoot.

Law: From different things I've read about Boswell and Humes, they kept moving the placement of the head wound (i.e., bullet entrance). At some point, they said it was in the back hairline and that it blew out the top of the skull, in other testimony (HSCA) they said it was above the occipital protuberance. So, I'm just trying to pin that down a little bit.

O'Neill: Quite frankly, I'm not a medical man. I don't know the medical terms. I do know the bullet wound was exactly where I said it was because they gave me the information and I put it down on paper. This was in the upper back strap muscles, so many centimeters over from the center. Now, as far as the back wound was concerned, and what they were saying, I don't exactly know what they were saying.

Law: I'm talking about the wound in the back of the head itself.

O'Neill: You mean the one single wound in the back of the head?

Law: Yes. The doctors have said the wound was in the hairline at the back of the head –

O'Neill: If someone has it recorded exactly where it was, possibly it was, but I don't recall writing down exactly where they said it was. There was no need for me to take it because I'm not a medical person and I'm not recording the medical terms for the thing. It was a large gaping wound in the back of the head. They did say that it came from the upper – it came from above and back and they said part of the skull was beveled in and part was beveled out.

Law: Now at some point you said there was some washing of the body to begin with.

O'Neill: Yes, they did wash the body.

Law: I've been told by somebody else or have heard that a bucket of water and Tide was brought in at the beginning and they washed it down. Do you remember that? (I was trying to get O'Neill to react to "beginning of the autopsy and they washed it down," the significance being that Sibert had told me the body looked cleaner then what he had remembered when he had viewed the autopsy pictures for the ARRB, and O'Neill had said "no" to me three years earlier when I had asked him if the body looked the same in the autopsy pictures as he remembered.)

O'Neill: They had to get the water from somewhere (amused tone in his voice). On the autopsy table, by the way, they do have an automatic, ah – they have to have drain pipes which they did have on the autopsy table – did you ever see an autopsy?

Law: Only on film.

O'Neill: No, I don't mean on film. They do have – the body is placed on the autopsy table and when it's finished, or at the beginning, whenever it is, to clear up a spot they will go ahead and hose it down. If they don't hose it down then they'll sponge it down.

Law: Well, that makes sense doesn't it? I just pick out things that aren't clear to me, it may be clear to someone else. There has been a lot of controversy about the head-holder. The thing that the head was resting on. Do you remember there being a headrest, a head-holder there?

O'Neill: There might have been, but I don't recall it.

Law: People there have told me they used a metal block with different lengths on it.

O'Neill: There might have been, but for my part I don't recall it. But there well could have been.

Law: I know you have seen the autopsy pictures. Do you remember the white spot down near the hairline? (photo 4a)

O'Neill: No, I don't recall that.

Law: Some people have said it's a wound, some people have said that it is a piece of brain matter.

O'Neill: No, there were no wounds other than the ones we described.

Law: (pushing the point) Some people say it's a wound in the hairline –

O'Neill: There was no wound in the hairline. No wounds other than what we described.

Law: Okay. I've got it written down here: Can you describe in any reasonable way the brain appearing like what you would remember?

O'Neill: Give me that again. What about the brain?

Law: When the ARRB asked you about the brain, and showed you the pictures they have in the National Archives that are reportedly of President Kennedy's brain, you said it appeared to be "too much brain."

O'Neill: Was this a picture supposedly of brain being pulled out of the head? Or spilling out?

Law: I don't know, because the transcriber puts down what you're talking about, but we can't see exhibits. I guess they handed you a picture that was in the archives and said this is what we have of the brain, and you said this appears to be too much brain.

O'Neill: Okay. Then that is what I said.

Law: Doesn't that seem a little strange?

O'Neill: No. What for? Why?

Law: That you would see a brain –

O'Neill: Brain! Brain! You keep saying a brain. We're not talking about a brain! We're talking about a portion – a small portion of the brain and then brain matter.

Law: I understand, I'm sorry, I'm not making myself clear.[5]

---

5. I believe I had made myself perfectly clear; Mr. O'Neill may have been trying to dodge the question

O'Neill: Yeah.

Law: I guess I'm talking about the picture they have in the archives. From what I understand from what you have said, there appears to be too much of a brain.

O'Neill: This was a picture that was shown to me – good God – twenty years ago.

Law: Did they show it to you at the Records Review Board?

O'Neill: Which board now? I had three different interviews.

Law: I think this is the one you did in 1996.

O'Neill: No, I did nothing in 1996. I did something in 1998 I know.

Law: '98? Was it 1998?

O'Neill: '96 or '98. Something like that, yeah.

Law: Well, did they show you the pictures that were in the archives?

O'Neill: They showed me several pictures. I don't know if it was all the pictures that were in the archives or not, but they showed me what they thought – several pictures. They thought, and I thought and Sibert thought it was not as we recalled it whatsoever.

Law: This is what a lot of people jump on, you see. This is why they say there has to be a conspiracy because the brain wasn't as big as it should have been, or there was more damage to the brain or there was less damage to the brain than there should have been. This is what some of these researchers jump on –

O'Neill: Are you one of those?

Law: I don't consider myself to be, I mean if that were true then I wouldn't want to hear anything from anyone who wasn't pro-conspiracy.

O'Neill: Right.

Law: Then I would just want to hear, "Well, of course there was conspiracy." I'm not interested in that. I'm interested in just what people saw and what people heard. So, I don't consider myself to be a "buff."

O'Neill: Did you recognize the individual who was on that television show with me at Franklin Pierce Law School?

Law: George Michael Evica?

O'Neill: Yes.

Law: I've met him a couple of times.

O'Neill: Have you really?

Law: Seems to be a sweet guy.

O'Neill: Yes. He and I don't get along together at all.

by feigning confusion.

Law: Oh, is that right?

O'Neill: Yeah.

Law: Well, I have heard from one source that – now I don't know if this is true or just hearsay – he believes that it was Officer Tippit's body not John Kennedy that was at the Bethesda morgue that night.

O'Neill: Which body?

Law: The body that was seen in the autopsy.

O'Neill: Good God almighty!

Law: Now that's just what I've heard –

O'Neill: I've never heard that at all from anyone!

Law: I've never discussed that with him at all. I just heard that from somebody else.

O'Neill: Why would they think that when they had the individuals who were there in the car with him and stayed with him all the time, never leaving him and taking him right to the autopsy room?

Law: But there are people out there that believe that.

O'Neill: They're out there, but the poor people need a mental examination.

Law: And that's why I like to try to talk to people that were there so that some of that stuff can go by the wayside. I do not believe this –

O'Neill: Good. You're very wise not to.

Law: But people do believe this kind of thing. I just want to explain why people get into this stuff about conspiracy. Agent Greer said that the president said, "My God, I've been hit," and because of the Zapruder film –

O'Neill: That wasn't Greer that said that –

Law: Oh, was it Kellerman? It was Kellerman. Because of the Zapruder film, and the shots, that he couldn't have been able to say this, they bring in the fact that the agent had to be in on it and that kind of thing –

O'Neill: Well, all I can say to that (laughing) – those individuals, agents, were speaking just as we recorded it, not after the Zapruder film was developed and then whatever was done to the Zapruder film, but within four and a half hours after the incident occurred itself, and I would have to go to on-the-spot testimony.

Law: Well you know, because of the hit to the throat people ask would he be able to say anything –

O'Neill: That's a question, isn't it?

Law: It is a question.

O'Neill: I've wondered about that myself. (His tone suggests he doesn't for one moment believe that Kennedy could have said, "My God! I've been hit! Get

JAMES W. SIBERT & FRANCIS X. O'NEILL-PART ONE

me to a hospital.") And that is one of the reasons that I believe, ah, that's the only thing in the Warren Commission [Report] that I don't agree with, the single-bullet theory. That's Arlen Specter's theory. And Arlen Specter – I guess you didn't see the report that he sent to Rankin. Rankin was the lead attorney for the Warren Commission. The other individual was the chief of the Warren Commission. They did no work whatsoever. They just took the information furnished to them by all the attorneys which went through Rankin; and he did not get the information because Mr. Specter did not tell him that we had told Specter that the person had said, "My God I've been hit." But he had our reports. Now, that eventually went over to the Warren Commission, but not immediately.

Law: Right. Well that's why people jump on anything they don't understand.

O'Neill: Who killed Christ? Was it the Romans or was it the Jewish people, or was it some fanatic group? They'll be arguing all their life. All I can tell you that the information I gave you is exactly what it was.

Law: I believe you. I absolutely believe you.

O'Neill: (chuckling) I hope so.

Law: (trying to be good cop and bad cop here, walking a tightrope) I guess what I'm trying to get at is that people see bits and pieces and they try and put them together. And if somebody makes a claim that they don't agree with, or they don't understand, the first thing they do is jump to conspiracy.

O'Neill: That's correct. And what proof do they have?

Law: Well, I guess that the only thing that they have is your testimonies. As far as I'm concerned, I don't know anything about what went on in that room.

O'Neill: Well, they don't have any information or anything that any attorney would allow in the court of law.

Law: Is there anything unusual at all that has struck you to indicate that there could have been conspiracy?

O'Neill: None.

Law: Do you still believe that there was no conspiracy?

O'Neill: Listen. Let's go back though. Let's go back to the time the incident occurred. There is various information about well, the lights went out in Washington D.C., and so forth, which is a lot of bull. They never did. So many different things. So you do take it into consideration because there's a possibility of it. But nothing has turned up to indicate any aspect, as the days and the weeks went on, that there was conspiracy. We looked at that angle to begin with – we being the Bureau – looked at that angle in the beginning.

Law: Sure. If you wanted to cover something up, you could have just covered it up. Plain and simple.

O'Neill: I'm the biggest cover up right there.

Law: You could have done whatever with your notes and the only reason we have all the information we do is because you took it down.

O'Neill: That's correct.

Law: So, if you wanted to hide something, you could have done it.

O'Neill: Correct.

Law: I think people get confused because they have been told that it takes 2.3 seconds or something to fire the bolt-action rifle –

O'Neill: Oh, that's the most ridiculous thing, for God's sake. They forget that there was one shell in the chamber already, there's one in there and then you have the remainder of the time to go ahead and get the other two shots off.

Law: Yes, that's true, and I've been up in that building. If he had wanted to do it, he certainly could have done that, and I tell that to people. If it was Oswald, he could have certainly done it.

O'Neill: See, you and I differ right there. You said, "If it was." There's not the slightest scintilla of evidence, there's not the slightest doubt in my mind it was anyone other then Oswald.

Law: Well, that's comforting to know. I try to stay away from having any kind of opinion –

O'Neill: You can't stay away from it if your trying to piece together information – second, third, fourth, fifth, or sixth hand – you have to make a decision: "Well, which one has the greater amount of veracity as far as what they saw or did not see?"

Law: I guess I'm trying to stay away from opinion until I'm done with the project. Basically, it's just been an opportunity for me to meet people who were there.

O'Neill: Good.

Law: One thing before I let you go. I bring it up because of the chapter you sent me. I've had Mr. Sibert tell me this some time ago, that the reason you put "surgery of the head area" in your report was because of the way the head looked. And David Lifton has made a great deal of this, but you said it looked like there had been some sort of – I don't have it in front of me –

O'Neill: I think some sort of surgery to the head area, but you've got to remember: we're not giving our own specific thoughts on this. It looked that way to us, but the doctors are the ones who also said that to us. It did look like it. But that was immediately during a cursory examination or something like that.

Law: So that was just on the first examination that they had –

O'Neill: Yes, but … that … it was not an exam. First viewing, put it that way.

Law: When they immediately unwrapped the head, that was when they said it?

O'Neill: Yes. Yes. Yeah. But then, again, when they unwrapped the head, that piece of cloth around it, or that sheet around it, was saturated with blood and I think that was before the washing of the head, too.

Law: Was there a sheet and towels or just sheets? I've had some people say there were towels and sheets, I've had some people say it was just towels. Do you remember any towels?

O'Neill: I think it was a sheet, but a bloody sheet. It could have been a towel, but whatever the head covering was, it was loaded with blood. This was the first viewing of it. And then you can – you could understand: Oh jeez, it looks like there might have been some surgery. Maybe because of the amount of blood, maybe because of something in there. But it turned out there was no surgery, when the doctors did their final examination.

Law: Did you ever hear them talk about gray matter over the right ear possibly being from a bullet.

O'Neill: No, nothing.

Law: Have you read David Lifton's *Best Evidence*?

O'Neill: I did read his book.

Law: Most of it is theory.

O'Neill: This is the whole definition: conspiracy theory.

Law: I can look at it and say, look I've been in that building, I know Oswald could have fired the shots. Where people are getting conspiracy – and I'm not saying they're wrong and I'm not saying they're right – I'm just saying I think where people get conspiracy is they study these details and it comes out that two shots had to have caused seven wounds in two men – the single-bullet theory. And the FBI doesn't believe in the single-bullet theory.

O'Neill: I think the Bureau itself doesn't believe in it. I've never sat down and said: Mr. Bureau do you believe in the single-bullet theory (laughter) or don't you?

Law: Well, how can they?

O'Neill: Well, they know Jim and I do not.

Law: Well, the problem comes in: if you don't believe in the single-bullet theory, then they say you've got conspiracy –

O'Neill: How?

Law: Given the firing time of the rifle, and given the –

O'Neill: People are seeing this because of a piece of film.

Law: Yes.

O'Neill: There are so many things that can go wrong with the film, I mean, I think most people know that with any kind of photography there are so many different things – you can't pinpoint the exact situation because of the film.

Law: There are two camps of thought –

O'Neill: Yeah, well, wait – I don't have time to go into all of them because we've been on the (amused tone) –

Law: I know. I'm sorry But basically that's why they say there's conspiracy because of the Zapruder film, that you have "x" amount of seconds to fire "x" amount of shots and you have seven wounds in two men and you have this pristine bullet show up on a stretcher – and they don't even know what stretcher it was.

O'Neill: Well, it's very simple. The bullet that was on the stretcher was the one that came out of Kennedy's back.

Law: But the doctors themselves have said that's the bullet that hit Kennedy in the back, came out his throat, hit Governor Connally in the back, came out below his nipple –

O'Neill: This is after the body is gone.

Law: I understand that, sir, and you understand it, and I know you were there, I'm just trying to tell you why people get all stressed about this.

O'Neill: If people would read what has been said and what has not been said, I think they'll follow through what's correct when they find out what the doctors conjectured after the body had been gone, that it worked its way through the strap muscles and things such as that. They didn't see that (sarcastically) they only said that after they – oh, then they went back and checked the X-ray pictures again. No way! I saw them check the X-ray pictures. I saw them view it. And in my eye view there, they never went back – well, let me rephrase that, they went back to check it as they were doing the autopsy. If they went back later on, and if they went back, and I can't – you know, I'm just saying this off the top of my head – if they went back later on and then they changed their minds about the X-ray pictures then what else did they change their minds about?

Law: Well, that's the ticket. And the doctors don't talk to people that I know of.

O'Neill: Well, they can't. One of them is dead.

Law: Yes, Humes passed away. But I think that's where people get concerned and then they all start trying to – take Greer and Kellerman. Would a reasonable person – if they were part of a conspiracy – would put himself in a limousine that he knows is going to be fired on?

O'Neill: Of course not.

Law: What makes it suspicious is that Kellerman claims he heard the president say, "My God I've been hit. "

O'Neill: That's right.

Law: Then people say: "Now wait a minute. He was hit in the throat by a bullet – "

O'Neill: He wasn't hit in the throat. When you say hit in the throat, you're conjecturing something being fired from the front.

Law: Right. Well, I know that you've seen the Zapruder film.

O'Neill: Yes.

Law: You've had to have seen it. Well, you've seen the part where he appears – I won't say he grabs at it, but – he appears to grab at his throat –

O'Neill: Um, hum.

Law: And that's where people get – of course there's no sound to the film –

O'Neill: Well, you could have doctors from the other side of this thing. There is a physical thing which can occur where the body can move forward and move back and things such as that when they get hit. I've seen doctors talking about that back and forth. Nobody, has a clear idea exactly what happened. You have something on film, it doesn't show exactly what happened. All you have is the eyewitness testimony of individuals and then you go back to the veracity of the individuals who were eyewitnesses to it. To me the two Secret Service agents – people keep forgetting Mr. Connally, Governor Connally, denied the single-bullet theory one hundred percent. He's an eyewitness. He's right there! People overlook his testimony on that, then say, "Well, the movie shows something else." I don't give a damn about the movie! This is the man who was there. He was the one who was hit. He should know what happened.

Law: It brings us full circle again. The people that say "because of the timing problem, because of the film – " and we don't even know if all the film is there, do we?

O'Neill: No, you do not. All you know is that somebody said, "I took this film." And somebody has another picture I think of somebody standing out there. Is that him? I don't know. And then you have these pictures of people on the grassy knoll. I don't know how anybody can conjecture that there was somebody up on the grassy knoll from one age-old Polaroid film taken by somebody.[6]

Law: Have you ever talked to Bill Newman?

O'Neill: Who?

Law: Bill Newman. He was standing directly in front of the limousine with his wife and children.

O'Neill: Nope. Never spoke to anybody like that. Never spoke to anybody who said that they were there or who had pictures of themselves there.

Law: He told me, and he has told other people, that at the moment of the shot he said the president was hit in the head. And he won't say if he –

---

6. Mary Moorman took a black and white Polaroid photograph from the left rear of the limousine, showing the grassy knoll beyond, close to the instant at which the president was hit in the head.

O'Neill: When he said moment of the shot, that was the last shot.

Law: Right.

O'Neill: What did he say about the first two?

Law: I can't remember what he said about the first two shots. The one that he's emphatic about is the one that hit the president in the head –

O'Neill: Oh, sure. Everybody is.

Law: He said it knocked him across the seat as if he had been hit by a baseball bat, and people take that to mean that he was hit in the side of the head.

O'Neill: The right rear. The right rear side. Put it that way. When we – you see, were talking about terminology here. When we said it was the right rear, we were talking about the right rear side, not the whole back of the head. I don't think anybody ever said he was hit in the back of the head.

Law: Well, for Bill Newman, of course, it was a momentary thing and he can only go on what he saw.

O'Neill: Well, he saw it from the other side of it, didn't he?

Law: What's that?

O'Neill: He saw it from the other side. The president was hit in the right rear, and he was on the left side of the car.

Law: No, he was on the right.

O'Neill: Well, then in other words – was he in front of, ah, the Zapruder people?

Law: Yes. He was somewhat down the street from them, I think, and right at the moment of the head shot, according to him, and according to pictures taken that day, Newman was standing there and he said that he saw the president's head open up, and saw the white and saw the red, saw the president knocked across the seat, and he turned to his wife and said, "That's it, hit the ground." And at that point, they hit the ground. And he also told me an interesting thing. He told me that the car momentarily stopped.

O'Neill: I don't think anybody says the car momentarily stopped. It might have slowed down, but I don't think it momentarily stopped. It did not stop (O'Neill's emphasis) I can assure you it did not stop.

Law: I tried to pin him on this and he said, "Well, when I say stopped, I mean just for a very few seconds and then it shot on through the underpass. And, of course you've done this before, you've questioned witnesses and in a moment of panic there are different things seen by different people, so who knows?

O'Neill: Was he one of the people – was it three shots or four shots or the five shots or six shots?

Law: I think he said he heard three shots.

O'Neill: I think the majority of the people – in fact I know – the majority of the people said that three shots were fired, or they heard three shots. But Bill, I've got to go, I'm going to have to take off, really now.

Law: Yes. I'm sorry for taking so much of your time. I just want you to know how very much I enjoyed what you sent me, and I very much appreciate your time. You've been very cordial.

O'Neill: Don't overdo it, now. Take care.

And, with that, the connection was broken.

* * *

There were times while talking to Frank O'Neill when I felt like I had fallen through the looking glass and into Lewis Carroll's Wonderland.

O'Neill and Sibert are adamant that the single-bullet theory is wrong. "That's Arlen Specter's theory," O'Neill told me. It's quite evident from my conversations with them that they have no respect for the one-time assistant counsel to the Warren Commission, now Senator from Pennsylvania. When I questioned Jim Sibert about the single-bullet theory and Arlen Specter, he went as far as to say, "What a liar. I feel he got his orders from above – how far above I don't know." When I suggested to O'Neill that his description to the ARRB of President Kennedy's hands being "clenched" was possible confirmation of Thorburn's position,[7] he took pains to tell me, " … .his hands were sort of clenched, put it that way. Yes, in other words, they weren't laying down flat – I don't know whether they tried to arrange his hands or not, but they were in a clenched position. Not fully clenched at all." The single-bullet theory is key to the "lone-nut" scenario. If, in fact, a bullet did not hit Kennedy in the back, come out his throat, hit Governor Connally in the back, exit his right chest, slam into his right wrist, breaking the bone and cutting the radial nerve, and then pierce his left thigh and fall out in remarkably pristine condition onto a stretcher at Parkland Hospital, then there was more than one assassin and, hence, conspiracy. The single-bullet theory is the linchpin of the government's case against Lee Harvey Oswald. If the theory is false, the lone-assassin concept crumbles to dust.

Governor Connally said, "It is not conceivable to me that I could have been hit by the first bullet, and then I felt the blow from something which was obviously a bullet, which I assumed was a bullet, and I never heard the

---

7. As proposed by John K. Lattimer in *Kennedy and Lincoln: Medical and Ballistic Comparisons of their Assassinations* (Harcourt Brace Jovanovich, New York and London, 1980) page 244.

second shot – didn't hear it. I didn't hear but two shots. I think I heard the first shot and the third shot." To the end of his life Connally rejected the single-bullet theory. And Frank O'Neill said: "You go back to the veracity of the individuals who were eye witnesses – Governor Connally denied the single-bullet theory one hundred percent. He's an eyewitness. He's right there – this is the man who was there. He was the one who was hit. He should know what happened."

Darrell Tomlinson, who found the bullet at Parkland Hospital, refused to identify it as Warren Commission Exhibit 399 and insisted that the bullet he found came from neither Connally's nor Kennedy's stretcher.[8] There is evidence that the bullet was actually on a stretcher used that day by little Ronald Fuller.[9] The FBI report by Sibert and O'Neill stated, " … a bullet entered a short distance … the end of the opening could be felt with a finger." At the Clay Shaw trial in 1969, Pierre Finck said, "The back wound's depth was the first fraction of an inch."

More metal remained in Connally's body, in the wrist and thigh wounds, than is missing from CE 399.

Surely this is enough evidence to damn the single-bullet theory!

I was pushed further into Carroll's mad world when I said to Frank O'Neill, "I've seen some of those autopsy pictures, and there does seem to be damage to the forehead." He replied: "I've heard people say there was damage to the right forehead. No way!" Yet, there is clearly damage to Kennedy's forehead in the autopsy photographs. By his own admission, O'Neill has seen the autopsy photographs, therefore, he has to know there is a problem with how Kennedy's body appears in them. He cannot have it both ways. He cannot say, "There is not one scintilla of proof of a conspiracy" having told me there was no damage to Kennedy's forehead when he saw the body, and yet there is damage to the forehead in the autopsy photographs. And consider O'Neill's statement before the ARRB, when he was shown pictures of the brain from the National Archives – purportedly Kennedy's – and was asked by Jeremy Gunn, "Can you identify that in any reasonable way as appearing to be – what the brain looked like of President Kennedy?," he replied, "It appears to be too much brain." O'Neill's own recollections, which he committed to paper for a chapter on Kennedy in his unpublished memoir, casts significant doubt on his supposed belief that there was no conspiracy. Compounding all of this is Sibert and O'Neill's statement in their 302 report that, upon removal of the wrapping from the head, it was ascertained that a tracheotomy had been performed,

---

8. Robert J. Groden and Harrison Edward Livingstone, *High Treason* (Berkley Books, 1989) page 66.

9. Josiah Thompson, Six Seconds in Dallas (Bernard Geis Associates, 1967) pages 161–164.

as well as surgery of the head area, namely in the top of the skull (photo 21). When asked about this, Sibert told me, "We found out later we were wrong. I wish we would have worded it better. It would have saved some confusion in some books." And from Mr. O'Neill: "That was from the first cursory examination." If that is true, why was it not so stated in the 302 report? I believe they did not include information that they were in error about "surgery of the head area" because it is what they believed that night, and what they continued to believe when they dictated their 302 report from their notes on November 26.

But the piece of information that is every bit as explosive as the statement in the 302 report is the passage in O'Neill's memoir concerning the condition of President Kennedy's head:

> Immediately upon viewing the body it was evident that a tracheotomy had been performed. Humes, viewing the body, indicated that some type of surgical procedure had been performed in the head region, possibly cutting of hair or removal of some slight tissue to view the massive wound in the right rear of the president's head. The information relative to the surgical procedure was made by the physicians not by the FBI agents. We merely reported what we heard.

I had been handed direct confirmation from one of the FBI agents present in the autopsy room that David Lifton was at least partially right in his body-alteration theory. There had been no "slight removal of tissue or cutting of hair" at Parkland Hospital. I find it hard to believe that Humes or Boswell, never mind Finck – a forensic pathologist – could confuse haircutting on the president's head with surgery. Despite the agents' denials that there was no "surgery" to Kennedy's head, they do, at least to some extent, understand that something is not quite right with all of this.

David Mantik, who possesses an MD, with specialization in oncology, and a PhD in physics, has been called the most qualified person to ever study the case. After reviewing a draft of this chapter, Dr. Mantik observed: "They have to know something is wrong, but how much they are willing to admit, even to themselves, we will never know." The old saying comes to mind: when you're up to your ass in alligators, it's hard to remember that your initial objective was to drain the swamp. Sibert and O'Neill are picking their way across the swamp that is the Kennedy assassination, and if they don't know where the pitfalls lie, they will more than likely fall in, and it's slippery footing indeed. The trouble for the FBI agents is that they keep tripping over their own statements. O'Neill's anger when I kept questioning him about the brain: "Brain! Brain! You keep saying brain. We're not talking about a brain! We're talking about a small portion of the brain and then brain matter." And to the ARRB: "It appears to be too much brain." Also, in 1998 when I asked if the body looked like what he remembered from the autopsy pictures, his succinct response was: "No! " Did Frank O'Neill, in his anger at me – for whatever reason – let his guard down and tell me the truth? Did he misspeak?

And Jim Sibert – when asked for his memory of Kennedy's body versus what he saw in the autopsy photographs – responded cautiously, "The body was cleaner than what I remembered. Maybe [the photographs] were taken further along in the autopsy after the morticians started working on it. " Most of the people present at the Kennedy autopsy – at least those inter-viewed by the ARRB – said the photographs were taken at the beginning of the autopsy. When Sibert was confronted with the autopsy photographs, did the body look so different to him from what he remembered? Did he conclude that it must be a different set of pictures that were taken when he and O'Neill were no longer in the autopsy room? Questions. No answers. The closest thing to answers that I had at that point, at least, lay in Sibert and O'Neill's 302 report from 1963, and in Mr. O'Neill's memoir – written years later – which he shared with me in 2001. I'd had the unpublished chapter some six months, and was unsure of how to make use of it. As far as I knew, he had not given it to anyone else, and I was excited about what it contained. I went back to his ARRB testimony. Near the beginning is this statement:

> This is a document which I am writing at the present time. But this is a chapter of a document – let me put it that way – about various things which occurred in my life since starting with my birth. This particular section of it pertains to the assassination of the President. I started this in 1971 and have brought it up to date as of yesterday.

Jeremy Gunn had the document marked Exhibit 189. I had a good idea what it was.

I contacted Matt Fulghum at the Special Records Access at the Nation-al Archives and explained what I was looking for. Within the hour, Matt called me back. "It's a document of about ten pages." I asked him to read the beginning paragraph to me: "In November, 1963, Camelot in the form of John F. Kennedy … ." "That's it!" I said. "That's what I'm looking for." I made arrangements to have the document sent to me. I couldn't wait for conformation of what I suspected, so I called Debra Conway of JFK Lancer Publications and asked her to look through her collection of documents from the ARRB. I gave her the document number and the section of records it should be in. "Just a minute, let me go to my computer and see what I can find." After a few minutes she came upon document 189. "Read me the first paragraph, will you?" She began to read: "In January, 1961, Camelot came to Washington D.C. in the … " "That's it!" I asked Debra to scan the rest of the document. "There should be a description of Kennedy in the casket."

She found the passage and read it. "Oh, my – ," I heard her say. I said, "There should be a sentence further on that reads, 'Immediately upon viewing the body.' " I waited while she looked for the passage I hoped was in there somewhere. She said, "Okay. Here it is." Silence ensued as she read on. Then I heard a sharp intake of breath: "There it is! Confirmation of surgery of the head!" Confirmation of surgery? Or tampering? Either way, something was done to the body of John F. Kennedy before it reached Bethesda Naval Hospital. And Frank O'Neill, had, unwittingly I'm sure, made it part of the public record, albeit buried amongst thousands of other documents released by the ARRB.[10]

My excitement about what I had in my possession was high, and though I didn't know it, my research was about to take an unexpected turn. I would get answers to my questions, in the form of none other than James W. Sibert. On March 12, 2002, while discussing the information I had with Allan Eaglesham, he asked, "Have you thought about trying to talk to Sibert again?" I wanted to contact him again, but had been so disheartened by his comments in 1998, and given the fact he was getting on in years, I was torn between pushing it just as hard as I could to get as much information as I could – no matter what, damn the cost, no matter to whom – and realizing there comes a point where you have to draw a line. The trouble for me was, and is, ever since being drawn into the JFK mystery, I have never been able to do draw lines. In any case, aren't lines meant to be crossed?

Sibert had moved since my last contact with him and all I knew was that he was in a retirement community somewhere in Florida. "Do you have his old address?" Allan asked. I still had the old address in my personal directory, and I gave it to him. "Give me a little time," he said. "I'll see what I can find." With some sleuthing, he found a telephone number for a James Sibert. Still, I was reluctant to try it, remembering the anger in his aged voice

10. Mr. O'Neill had, in fact, made mention of it on page 70, line 3, in his testimony before the ARRB: "Humes said it was evident that there was some type of a surgical procedure which would have been done to the head area or something like that. Those were not words that we were making up ourselves. These were words that were said by the doctor at that time. Now, as I understand it, that could have been cutting of the hair, or something to do with this – this thing in the back. But certainly, there was no type of mutilation. I could not make a determination what he meant by that, quite frankly." He is still traversing the swamp, giving us information, putting it all back on Humes, so he can refute what he and Sibert wrote in their 302 file or said in testimony before the ARRB.

in that last short and not-so-sweet conversation: "Hell, I'll probably still be getting calls about this when I'm ninety." In the end, my desire to probe further won out over feelings of trepidation.

I spent the next day going over Sibert and O'Neill's FD 302 report, summaries of their HSCA interviews the ARRB testimony and notes on my conversations with O'Neill, to have the information fresh in my mind and to list the topics I wanted to ask Sibert, if I was lucky enough to get him to talk to me. I decided to use the same tactic I had with Frank O'Neill: read Jerrol Custer's statement about them as a way to get my foot in the door, and see if I could use that as a catalyst to further conversation and questions.

I nervously dialed the number that Allan had found. A voice came on the line. After introducing myself, and, as with Frank O'Neill, hoping he wouldn't remember me from our previous conversations, I said, "I'm working on a manuscript about the JFK assassination and your name has come up a couple of times and I thought before I sent this out I better get conformation. Could I do that?" I waited, hoping that it was ex-FBI Special Agent James Sibert I was talking to.

Sibert: Yeah.

Law: This is out of my manuscript. I've talked to the X-ray technician who was in the Bethesda autopsy room, and I asked him a question about – he said Secret Service agents – actually this question was from a partner of mine who asked it when we were doing the interview: "What was your interaction with the Secret Service agents if any, Greer, Kellermen? And Mr. Custer replied: 'Well Sibert and O'Neill were literally up my nose.'" I think he got you confused.

Sibert: Yeah. Because we were FBI. Kellermen was the Secret Service agent. And he was the one riding in the front seat of the limousine, you know.

I felt confident that Sibert did not remember me. His tone was relaxed and friendly. I continued to read from my manuscript:

Law: " ... literally up my nose. They were attached to the hip. Every place I went, they went. It got to the point that after the first set of films I had taken and headed up toward the – ." He's talking about going upstairs to develop the X-ray plates.

Sibert: Yeah.

Law: Then later on in the manuscript, he says: "I'm not sure whether it was Sibert or O'Neill, but one of the two FBI agents were with us at the time, they happened to stop us just before we came into the rotunda." He claims that he had an armload of X-rays and that he – I don't know how Bethesda is laid out, I have no idea – but he said that they came through a hallway and he saw Jacqueline Kennedy and Bobby Kennedy. Were you one of the people who was with him when that happened?

Sibert: No, In fact, when they took the photographs and X-rays, in fact, in the FD 302, you know, that five and a half page –

Law: Yes, I've read it.

Sibert: Well, we were excluded. We weren't in there when the photographs were taken or the X-rays, and the photographs were never developed. They were turned over to the Secret Service.

Law: Here's a piece I don't know what to think of. He said – Custer again – he's talking about finding a bullet fragment in the autopsy room. I've talked to quite a few people and no one else remembers this: " I called one of the pathologists over and said, Hey, we have a bullet here.' As soon as they heard that, they came down off the raised platform, they ran over and then picked it up. Then Sibert and O'Neill also came over and said, 'Well, we want that.' "

Sibert: (small chuckle) We never – the only thing we took position of, William, was a little jar with [bullet] fragments that had been removed from the brain. You know, metal particles?

Law: That's the only thing I've ever had reported to me, and Mr. Custer has since passed away.

Sibert: I don't remember anything about a bullet – you know they couldn't find that bullet – wound in the back – and they probed that and there was no exit. So, I said, "Well, let me go and call over at the lab, see if there is any kind of an ice bullet that might have fragmentized completely." That was when I called agent Killion over at the lab, and he said, "Have you learned about the bullet they found under the stretcher over at Parkland?" Now, I came back and reported that to Humes, the chief pathologist, and that's the only – I never saw that bullet. They were sending that bullet in, but it didn't come into the autopsy room. I think they flew it into the Washington area, and that went directly to the FBI laboratory, the firearms section.

Law: I've talked to Mr. O'Neill quite a bit about this and asked him about his belief in the single-bullet theory, and he said, "Absolutely not, it did not happen!"

Sibert: Well, you can put me in the same category! Have you read Arlen Specter's latest book, *Passion For Truth*?[11]

Law: No, I haven't. I do not believe in the single bullet theory from all I've read, and how can –

Sibert: I told them before they asked me to come up for the [ARRB] deposition, I said: "Well, before I come up, I want to tell you one thing: I don't buy the single-bullet theory." And they said, "We don't expect you to." (laughter)

---

11. Arlen Specter with Charles Robbins, *Passion for Truth* (Harper Collins, 2000).

Law: Yes, when I talked to Mr. O'Neill, he was adamant that it did not happen.

Sibert: In the first place, they moved the bullet wound, the one in the back. See, I don't know if you recall, but over at Parkland, they weren't even aware of the back wound, because they had a big fight over there as to who had jurisdiction. Texas had a law that any kind of a murder done in Texas, the autopsy had to be performed there. They didn't know about the back wound. But they get to Bethesda – here's the pathetic part – they found the wound in the back, of course, they took the wound in the neck as a straight tracheotomy and they didn't find out that it was a bullet wound until the next morning when they called Parkland.

Law: Do you think it was a straight tracheotomy?

Sibert: Oh! They said over there that the – I forget who the doctor was there – but he said he made that tracheotomy right over a bullet wound.

Law: That was Malcolm Perry.

Sibert: Perry, yeah. And you know, a lot of them over there said first that they thought it was an entrance wound. So, you had Parkland not knowing about the back wound, you had Bethesda not knowing about the bullet wound in the neck, taking it as a tracheotomy, which really gets you off on the right foot.

Law: Were you surprised you weren't called before the Warren Commission?

Sibert: I was at the time, but now I can understand why (laughing).

Law: Why do you think you weren't called?

Sibert: Why? In other words, with that single-bullet theory, if they went in there and asked us to pinpoint where the bullet entered the back and the measurements and all that stuff, how are you going to work it? See, the way they got the single-bullet theory, was by moving that back wound up to the base of the neck.

Law: I've been told by other people that there were officers of high rank in the autopsy room. Do you remember –

Sibert: Oh, sure! You had generals in there and admirals and I mean the highest in the Military District of Washington, and General McHugh, the air force general who was Kennedy's aide. They had more rank in there then you could shake a stick at.

Law: Was the autopsy room full? I've had most people tell me it was fifteen people, I've had some say thirty people –

Sibert: Well, I don't know just how many, because they were in and out, you know? I mean you had [Admiral George] Burkley who was the president's personal physician there part of the time, up talking to Jacqueline part of the time, and back and forth.

Law: Is that right?

Sibert: Yeah. And you had people from the hospital coming in there, running for other things, you know, like caskets and that type thing.

Law: Do you remember somebody saying, "Who's in charge here?" And somebody said, "I am?"

Sibert: No

Law: Can you give me some information on the head wound. How big was it?

Sibert: Oh, it was a good size, in the back part of the head there. Well, I think about three and a half inches, as I saw – about three and a half inches one way and then quite a bit the other.

Law: Do you remember damage to the top of his head?

Sibert: (pause) … No, I just remember this one massive wound –

Law: Right in the back part?

Sibert: Yeah.

Law: Do you remember a flap of scalp? Some people say there was a flap of scalp that you could pull this way and that way –

Sibert: I don't remember that either. I'll tell you, we weren't thinking too much about – and another thing – now you know, it's interesting – have you ever read the interviews of Humes and Boswell by a doctor from Bethesda – it was in JAMA, the *Journal of the American Medical Association*.[12]

Law: I have read that.

Sibert: Yeah. Now those two stayed there till about 5:30 in the morning as I recall. That was their admission – that they had stayed and helped the morticians. In other words, they must have taken some other pictures, too, because they showed me pictures at that deposition that were neat in appearance, and boy, I don't remember anything like that.

Law: Well, that was the next question I was going to ask. Did the body look like what you remember from the autopsy pictures you were shown before the ARRB?

Sibert: Well, the ones that they showed me up there, the later ones didn't, no.

Law: They didn't look like what you remembered?

Sibert: No, they were neater. I stated that in my deposition. That's all up there in the archives I said it was much neater in appearance. That was my recollection, and I imagine O'Neill said the same thing.

Law: Yes, he did, and he said something else that was interesting. He said that when they showed him pictures of the brain, that the brain didn't look the same that he remembered, and he said that you said it didn't look the same, either.

12. *Journal of the American Medical Association*, 27 May 1992, pp. 2791–2807; 7 October 1992, pp. 1736–1738 and 1748–1754; 24/31 March 1993, pp. 1540–1547..

Sibert: Yeah.

Law: Isn't that weird?

Sibert: Oh, yeah. Well … (chuckles)

Law: There's been some talk about skull pieces. Do you remember those? Mr. O'Neill told me they came in at the latter stages of the autopsy.

Sibert: Well, this one big piece came in, yeah.

Law: A friend of mine did an interview with Sam Kinney who was a Secret Service agent, I think, and he said he found a piece in the back seat of the limousine.

Sibert: It was supposed to be from the limousine, they flew that in to the autopsy at Bethesda. It got there before the autopsy was over.

Law: Kinney said it was like a flowerpot.

Sibert: I didn't get that close to it. Humes had it and everything –

Law: Did they know if it was from the top or the back of the head?

Sibert: I don't think he even commented on it at that time.

Law: How about those guys. Do you think they were just obtuse? Or do you think they were hurried so much they just couldn't do their job?

Sibert: Did you read Wecht's book? I forget who it was, but he said if this had been a king or queen, you wouldn't have had an incision made until you had the top pathologists, gunshot pathologists in attendance. I want to insert that "gunshot" too, backed up by the number-two man.

Law: As I understand it from people I've talked to, they hadn't done an autopsy in many years.

Sibert: Well, much of their responsibility, I think, was reviewing autopsies that had been done.

Law: I think that's what they did, yes.

Sibert: I don't know how many, I really don't. You hate to criticize the guys because I think in that [JAMA article] they said they really shouldn't have done the autopsy. I think Humes said that in that interview in JAMA.

Law: I'll have to go back and read that.

Sibert: He said it should have been done at Walter Reed.

Law: The interesting thing is the HSCA testimony they gave –

Sibert: I was interviewed by them, too, down here in Fort Myers.

Law: – in that they couldn't make up their minds where they said the entrance hole was in the back of the head. At times they said it was above the occipital protuberance – the small bump at the back of the head – and then they said it was down in the hairline. And when I talked to Frank O'Neill, he said there was no wound in the hairline at all.

Sibert: None pointed out to us. Of course, we wouldn't have been down there moving hair around looking for it, because we would have been out of place there, you know. But nobody made any remark about a wound in the hairline.

Law: Do you remember any washing of the body?

Sibert: No. I don't remember that. I don't remember that at all. See, here's the sequence: O'Neill and I helped the Secret Service go in with the body into the room adjacent to the autopsy room there.

Law: The little anteroom there?

Sibert: Yeah. We put the casket down on the floor. Opened the casket – here it was wrapped in sheets. Then the medical corpsmen took over and put the body up on the autopsy table. Then they were going to take X-rays and photographs and that's when they cleared everybody out into the next room and that's when they took all the pictures that we know about. Yeah. And X-rays.

Law: Is there anything else you can remember?

Sibert: Another thing – Specter misspelled O'Neill's name and he misspelled mine on one occasion in that book there.

Law: Is that right? I'm going to have to get a copy of that. If I have any questions from that, could I call you back and ask you?

Sibert: Yeah.

Law: I don't particularly like Arlen Specter –

Sibert: You know, when somebody misquotes you that way and lies before the Warren Commission when he said we didn't – he said that Sibert didn't make any notes and O'Neill said he made just a few and then destroyed them after we'd dictated and checked them against typing and everything that came back.

Law: It's so silly for him to do something like that.

Sibert: But as I say, see, that sounds good if I'm working on the single-bullet theory and I tell the members of the Commission, the other members there, all the notes have been destroyed, Sibert didn't make any notes. What credence can we give to this?

Law: Mr. O'Neill took pains to point out to me that – concerning the single-bullet theory – they had changed their minds after the body was gone.

Sibert: Yeah.

Law: And he could not understand why they had changed their minds and then they made up all this stuff about the bullet –

Sibert: I've laughingly said that – when talking to people on this, groups and stuff.

327

Law: Oh, do you give lectures?

Sibert: Oh, yeah. Church groups and stuff like that. But I've said that when you perform an autopsy without the body, you're getting out of medicine and into magic!

* * *

With that, I took my leave. It was a good place to say goodbye, and when I hung up the phone, my mind was reeling. "Mother of babbling God!" I thought. "I've hit the jackpot!" As I'd hoped, Jim Sibert had not remembered our two conversations from three years before – I still carried with me the anger in his voice from 1998 when he responded to my question, "Does that mean you won't answer my list of questions?" to which he replied, "Yes, that's what that means! Hell, I'll probably still be getting calls about this when I'm ninety!" But he had answered my questions, and quite willingly. I'd had to wait a few years, but it had been worth it. My next step was to get a copy of Specter's book, *Passion for Truth*, and read it thoroughly so I could call Mr. Sibert back and ask him questions about it. Hopefully, he would share more of his recollections of the autopsy. Reading *Passion For Truth* was like swimming in wet cement. It can be done, but it takes a strong constitution. When I was sure I had a good grasp of the chapter on the single-bullet theory, I called Mr. Sibert again. He was warm and friendly: "Hi, Bill. How are you?" I explained I had read Specter's book and had a few questions. "Let me get my copy. There was stuff in there that I disagreed with when I read it."

Law: Please tell me what you've written down. I'd like to hear your opinion.

Sibert: Well, I've got here on page 47, second paragraph, line five, that's where he's misspelled both our names as O-N-E-A-L, and S-I-E-B-E-R-T. (reading) "[They] concluded three shots." Now, we never concluded there were three shots. That was never even mentioned, that night at the autopsy. The doctors said there were two shots: one in the back that they couldn't account for, and the massive head wound in the back of the head. Of course, they didn't even know about the gunshot wound in the throat. They didn't find out about that until the next day.

Law: They thought that was a tracheotomy all the way through?

Sibert: The whole night there, that was just treated as a straight tracheotomy. Now then, I put down here (reading from his notes): "Compare with ARRB – that's the Assassination Record Review Board – the FD 302s that O'Neill and I did 11/22/63." And I've got here: "Dr. Humes stated that the pattern was clear that one bullet entered the president's back, and worked its way out of the body during cardiac massage, external cardiac massage, and that a second high velocity bullet had entered the rear of the skull, and had fragmented prior to exit from the top of the skull." No mention made of a third shot, or of Connally or of the neck or anything like that. But he [later] said that the first bullet hit Kennedy's neck, the second hit Connally, and the third hit the President's head. That theory would remain doctrine for months.

Law: And you don't agree with that?

Sibert: No.

Law: What's your own personal take?

Sibert: Well, we never mentioned – there's nothing in that 302 that mentions three shots.

Law: So he just put that in there.

Sibert: Yeah. You can read. You've got a copy of that FD 302, haven't you?

Law: Yeah, I do.

Sibert: I think when you check that –

Law: I'll have to go back over it.

Sibert: Yeah.

Law: I've noticed where he (Specter) says: "The head shot had blown out 70 percent of the right hemisphere of his brain."

Sibert: I see, yeah: "Blown out 70 percent of the right hemisphere of his brain." I don't know where he got that from.

Law: Of course, he seems to imply things all the way through about the Kennedys. I don't think he likes the Kennedys very much.

Sibert: (laughter) Could be. Now on page 67, that's the next thing, sixth paragraph, line 5: "I was interested to know whether President Kennedy wore an undershirt because his clothes could indicate the direction and the location of the bullet. Fibers in the back of the president's shirt had been pressed forward indicating that the bullet had come from the rear." I don't know where he got that.
   "The controversy over the hole in his body versus the hole in his clothing." Of course, when you get back and you see where they inspected that clothing, it measures exactly five and a half, five and a third inches down from the top of the collar, you know, down in the back.

Law: He's trying to say that it doesn't.

Sibert: Here. Wait a minute. Let's see (reading): "Some critics have seized on the location of the holes in the suit jacket and shirt to argue that the hole was lower on the president's back than the reports asserted." Well, when you compare what Humes gave us that night, and what the actual measurements were on the coat and shirt, they jibe.

Law: Yes.

Sibert: On page 92 of the Warren Report, second and third paragraphs (reading): " … a roughly circular hole … on the rear of the coat, 5 3/8; inches below the top of the collar. The shirt worn by the president contained a hole on the back side 5¾ inches below the top of the collar … " These were the actual measurements of the bullet holes when they got to the lab. The clothing went to the lab, the agents over there in the lab measured that, and that's what those measured. The measurements on that face-sheet that Boswell made that night there at Bethesda – those measurements were the same.

Law: They were accurate.

Sibert: Yeah. In other words, the holes in the clothing, the holes in both the coat and the shirt matched the distance down that Boswell and Humes found that night when they gave the measurements on [the back wound].

Law: Right.

Sibert: Now, let's see, page 70 (of Specter's book). I mentioned that face sheet of Boswell's. It's just a schematic drawing of the back of the body and he made notations and everything. But that also fits in. Those measurements are the same that Humes gave us. That's where they got the measurements from.

Law: Did you notice anything else in Specter's book?

Sibert: Well, let's see. On page 79 there's a statement that's sort of misleading: "As the autopsy progressed, the surgeons realized that the bullet had passed further through the president's neck. They saw the muscles." Now, I was there until midnight, for all practical purposes the autopsy had been completed, and there was nothing mentioned about this going on through the neck and all that, muscles and stuff. I don't know when that was.

Law: If they didn't dissect the neck that night, how could they know that?

Sibert: That's it. They didn't.

Law: Everybody I've talked to said they never touched it.

Sibert: No, they never touched that tracheotomy. As I said, the opinion was that the one in the back had been worked out by cardiac manipulation over at Parkland and fell out on the stretcher, you see?

Law: Right. That's where the single-bullet theory gets confusing, because you can't have a bullet falling out on Kennedy's stretcher and being able to cause the wound in the throat.

Sibert: Well, the way they got that was by moving that bullet hole in the back, keeping moving it until they got it to the base of the neck so it would come out in the anterior part of the neck, you know, as an exit wound.

Law: And that was Gerald Ford –

Sibert: And, boy, when I say once you get rid of the body, and it goes to the funeral directors, any autopsy conclusions after that – it's magic rather than medicine.

Law: Here's one I have on page 83. It says: "Continuing to question Humes about matters outside of his sphere, I also asked about the president's clothing. The FBI found that the bullet had entered the back of Kennedy's suit jacket and exited through the front of his shirt by his tie. The tie showed a mark where it had been nicked. The caliber of the bullet could not be gauged from holes in the jacket or shirt. But those holes were consistent with damage from a 6.5-mm slug."

Sibert: That was done over at the lab. I wouldn't have any knowledge. I heard at the time it was nicked, you know, which would indicate – there was even some conjecture by some writers that it may have been a part of a bone that had been forced out by a bullet in the back or something.

Law: Somebody wrote it may have been a scalpel mark.

Sibert: I had some other notations. I'll read them to you: "See ARRB exhibit 44 51/2 – Bethesda surgeons considered the opening in the anterior neck as a tracheotomy and were not aware of it being made through a bullet wound until calling Parkland Hospital in Dallas the following morning, Saturday – " Now, that's verified. " – at which time JFK's body was in the Gawler funeral home. " In other words, the Bethesda autopsy physicians had turned it over to the funeral home. "It is noted in a reprint of JAMA" – *Journal of the American Medical Association* that I told you about, dated 5/27/92 – you know, when the doctor interviewed Humes? – where Humes and Boswell were interviewed by JAMA editor George D. Lundburg MD, Humes stated that he and Boswell stayed at the medical center until 5:00 AM. Now, this is important, because we left there about midnight. And evidently they stayed to help. Helping to embalm and restore the president's head structure, I guess, (reading) "Humes said he called Parkland at 7:30 AM." Now, that would be Saturday morning, they left at 5:00 AM, and he called Parkland and spoke with Dr. Malcolm Perry, "learning of the tracheotomy made over a bullet wound." This is coming straight from Humes when he was interviewed for that JAMA article.

Law: Right. Well, that brings us back to the fact, though, that he burned his first report. And his draft notes. He gives the excuse –

Sibert: He didn't want them to become a collector's item.

Law: Yes, but the face-sheet had blood stains on it and so it doesn't make any sense from that standpoint. Why do you think he did it?

Sibert: Why he destroyed them? I could only put myself in that place. If I'd been the pathologist, and then I find out after I'd come to those conclusions and everything, and find out that I treated this as a straight tracheotomy, and find out this had actually been made over a bullet wound, either an entrance or an exit wound I would have to think, "Boy!"

Law: Pretty silly looking, huh?

Sibert: So then he destroyed those original notes – I don't know what – but he admitted that, even in testimony you know?

Law: Yeah. I read that. I did have something marked on page 88 second paragraph, where Specter claims: "Tom Kelly the Secret Service liaison officer to the Commission tried to ease my concern about the photos" – he's talking about the autopsy photos and he said they "traveled to Dallas to conduct an on-site test – "

Sibert: Tom Kelly …

Law: Yes, and he says that Tom Kelly showed him a picture, a small picture that showed –

Sibert: (reading) " … a man's body with a bullet hole in the base of the neck, just where the autopsy doctors said Kennedy had been shot."

Law: Yes, except we know there was no hole in the base of the neck!

Sibert: None that we saw that night. Or that was pointed out that night by the autopsy –

Law: So, I wonder where he's coming up with –

Sibert: I don't know.

Law: Just another one of his –

Sibert: And then I had on page 93: "We disagreed with the initial FBI report which said two bullets had hit Kennedy and a third had hit Connally – and we wound up supplanting it with the single-bullet conclusion." Now, I don't know where he got the FBI report that two bullets had hit Connally, because certainly there were no statements of that kind made that night.

Law: More of his exaggerations.

Sibert: " … wound up supplanting it with the single-bullet conclusion. But we simply did not have the time or the resources to recruit and train our own crew of investigators."

Law: When he says things like this, you doubt everything else he's written. Here's one question that I wanted to ask. It's on page 99, and he talks about: "The president had a full head of hair. It was bloody and matted making it difficult to find his wounds. "

Sibert: Yes, I see it.

Law: Did you find that to be true?

Sibert: Oh, yeah. He had a full head of hair and it was matted – blood, you know. You can imagine. But that's one thing that impressed me when I first saw him when they took him out of those sheets there. When they brought him in that casket, you know, from Air Force One, and we got him there to Bethesda. They opened up that casket and then took the sheets off and that heavy head of hair – in the pictures, some of the original pictures – I'm sure you've seen some of those – Lifton's book –

Law: Yes.

Sibert: How matted that was. But when the pieces from the skull were blown out, it took the hair with it, so, there was no question about a big wound there, you know? The photographs I saw, that they showed me there at the ARRB and said, "Do you ever remember seeing photographs like this?" I said no. I said nothing that neat. In other words – and I think O'Neill probably felt the same way – I haven't talked with him on this point, but –

Law: He did tell me that once, that he thought that they were pretty neat in appearance. Here's one on page 110.

Sibert: Right there up at the top, there, where it says, "It was bedlam"?

Law: Yes.

Sibert: The next paragraph: "The first Friday a press conference was held shortly after the president's death before the doctors knew about the entrance wounds on Kennedy's back and head and before Perry had spoken with Humes and sorted out the facts." Paragraph 3, line one: "Perry said it was conceivable or possible that the wound on the front of the president's neck could have been an entry wound." So, I think – I don't know – I don't have any way of knowing, but I've always felt like that their first impression, over there at Parkland, was that it might have been an entrance wound.

Law: There is a transcript of a press conference – the first press conference they gave – and [Malcolm Perry] made no bones about it that he felt it was an entrance wound. In later years, he went around saying he didn't really say that. But, he did.

Sibert: Yeah. And another thing: There might have been someone leaning on him.

Law: I've read that there was (chuckles from Sibert). I think the Secret Service came – within a couple of weeks or something?

Sibert: Yeah.

Law: And that's when they began to have doubts about what they saw, from what I've read. I've never –

Sibert: I have no way of knowing. Those were the only things I had made note of in the book.

Law: I just had one more: "Bullet expert analysis and all tests supplied the facts" – talking about the bullet – "the president's garments had holes and tears showing that the missile entered the back in the vicinity of his lower neck, and exited from the front of his shirt immediately behind his tie.

Sibert: If you go back to [the Warren Report] the second paragraph, page 92: examination of the suit jacket" – his coat – "revealed a roughly circular hole approximately a fourteenth of an inch in diameter on the rear of the coat 5¾ inches below the top of the collar. And three quarters of an inch to the right of the center back seam. " So that puts it down there. How could it be in the base of the neck?

Law: Yes. Absolutely.

Sibert: And then the shirt, in the next paragraph: "The shirt worn by the president contained a hole on the back side, 5¾ inches below the top of the collar, 1 1/8 inches to the right of the middle back of the shirt." And so, you've got them both there. And on that face-sheet, roughly, those correspond. The face-sheet that Boswell made, based on Humes measurements and stuff, corresponds with holes in the clothing. So, that pretty well – you've got verification there.

Law: Well, in this book, he certainly goes out of his way to try and defend himself.

Sibert: Well, he's justifying the single-bullet theory. You know that was his –

Law: That was his part in it.

Sibert: Yes.

Law: He's put this case – he's probably the reason we will never know for sure –

Sibert: Yeah. There's another book here, I'm sure your familiar with it, *Accessories After the Fact*, by Sylvia Meagher.[13]

Law: I've heard of it. I've never read it.

Sibert: Oh boy, you ought to get that!

Law: Is it a good one?

Sibert: Yeah. I got it here. I've got the paperback. She is the one who prepared a whole index for this Warren Report.

Law: How about Harrison Livingstone? Have you ever read any of his things? He wrote *High Treason* and *Killing Kennedy*.

Sibert: I've got a lot of books here, *High Treason* by I don't know who –

Law: That's him.

Sibert: Oh, then I've got that, yeah. Livingstone that's who you mentioned and Groden, yeah.

Law: Well, let me ask you a question off the top of my head. It has been claimed that Secret Service Agents Greer and Kellerman were, in some way, part of the plot.

---

13. Sylvia Meagher, *Accessories After the Fact: The Warren Commission, The Authorities, and The Report* (Vintage Books, 1992) (originally published in 1967).

Sibert: Well, let me tell you this – and I don't know whether it's in our 302s or not, maybe it's in one of the interviews – when we interviewed them officially at the White House, the Secret Service agents – that night, I remember this, poor Bill Greer, the driver – you know he's deceased now – said: "If I could have gone faster. But I would try to speed up a little" – now this is going along the parade route – the president would say 'Slow down! Slow down!' "

Law: Did you believe him when he said that? Was he sincere?

Sibert: He certainly appeared to me to be. I think it was really weighing on him.

Law: The problem is this: the people who are really into this want to prove a conspiracy – and I have no problem with that, there well may have been one for all I know – but I believe it's unprovable. So I try not to invest myself in that.

Sibert: No. I feel the same way. You know, if there were a conspiracy, somebody that might have had intimate inside knowledge – maybe when dying of cancer, or something, might say, "Look I've got something on my chest I want to get off." But that has never happened. I say, if it were a conspiracy. And I'm not saying it was. But I always come back and say that I don't buy the single-bullet theory. I'm adamant in that statement.

Law: Have you seen the Zapruder film? Abraham Zapruder's home movie of the assassination?

Sibert: No I haven't. Just pictures that were taken from it.

Law: It appears that it's the first shot that hits him in the throat – there's no sound – but it appears to be the first shot, and he isn't hit in the head until several seconds later.

Sibert: Well, you know one of the Secret Service agents in the car behind swears that he saw that he was hit in the back.

Law: Glen Bennett.

Sibert: I don't recall the agent's name. You asked me about Greer. He gave me every indication – you know, it's tough. You take the Secret Service, and they lost a president. You can imagine how you'd feel. That's like you're after somebody that gets away. You had them trapped or something. Your head's down between your knees.

Law: I always ask this: Is it reasonable to believe that two agents, even if they were involved in a plot, were going to stick themselves into a car knowing it was going to be shot at? How sensible would that be?

Sibert: That's right, yeah.

Law: Because if you are going to be put into that position, nobody's going to know if it's going to hit you or not, are they?

Sibert: No.

Law: So I get confused about it and I like to talk to people who were in some way involved in the events.

Sibert: I've heard that the Secret Service could have been involved in a conspiracy. Gee, I –

Law: Sometimes it seems like it's probable and other times you look at it and it would just be impossible. I've been interested in this since I was a kid, and this is really part of our history, and I would like to put something on the record one way or the other – conspiracy or not conspiracy. I'm interested in it as a historical event.

Sibert: One Sunday afternoon, Anthony Summers called me from London. He had read Lifton's book, and he said, "Is this the Sibert that witnessed the autopsy?" I said that's correct. He said, "Well, I'm reading Lifton's book. Have you read it?" I said, "Yes I have." He said, "What comment would you have on it?" And I said, "Well I would really have no comment," and he kind of laughed and said, "Well, I can understand why" (laughs). I'll tell you another guy that's coming out with a book, the guy that wrote *Helter Skelter?*

Law: Vincent Bugliosi.

Sibert: He called me twice. He's writing a book, I think really trying to justify the Warren Commission.

Law: Well, doesn't that make you a little uncomfortable?

Sibert: (laughs) He called me again – since the deposition in 1997 that I gave. But I took all that stuff up there and they kept the originals and gave me copies of all of it.

Law: Do you think there possibly could have been a conspiracy to kill President Kennedy? Based just on what you know?

Sibert: The books I read make me wonder. You read some of these books, oh, I don't know, some of the interpretations and stuff –

Law: The problem is everybody tries to put their own spin on it. And if you fall in love with a theory, you're doomed.

Sibert: Yeah that's right. Well, you know the thing about Lifton's book, his prime thing was surgery in the head area (photo 21). And we were just repeating what Humes had said that night. Well, he looked at that big 3½-inch wide bone gone out of there – and it would look like surgery, you know?

Law: Do you think that was a bone from the back or the top of the head?

Sibert: I think that was from that big gap in the back part of the head.

Law: You don't think there was a wound in the top of the head? Did you ever see anything like that?

Sibert: Not right in the top of the head.

Law: It was basically towards the back?

Sibert: Towards the rear.

Law: People have told me that there was a flap of scalp that they could move around.

Sibert: Well, there were fragments there. If you take that much bone out, you're going to have the attaching bone where that was blown out – it's going to be movable, you know. It's just like if you take a rubber ball and cut a hole in it and then you put your finger down there, you can move the other rubber parts around because you don't have the tight togetherness that you would have with the bones up there in the top of the skull.

I then asked Sibert if I were to send him a copy of Specter's book would he critique the chapter on Kennedy in his own hand. He agreed. Could I send him a set of Kennedy autopsy pictures to critique?

Sibert: Yeah, if you want to send those to me – up there at that deposition in 1997 they said: "Do you remember ever seeing a picture like this? And I said: "Nothing that neat."

Law: Did it surprise them?

Sibert: I said we never saw any pictures [that night] because they weren't developed. But my recollection of the way that head looked is nothing that would appear as this photograph shows (photo 4). This photograph is too neat.

Law: What was the Review Board's reaction to that?

Sibert: They didn't say, but I'm sure they asked O'Neill the same thing.

Law: How do you think it has affected you over the years? Were you able to go on with your life and just –

Sibert: Oh, you have to. I was so busy, other criminal work – I'm sure O'Neill felt the same way. Bank robberies and stuff. This was another assignment. Of course, it was a great assignment as far as public notice was concerned and effect on the country and everything, but you actually were there, and you just reported what you did – and then you've got other work piling up on you that kept your attention.

Law: Jerrol Custer, the X-ray technician, told me: "I was just there doing my job."

Sibert: That's right, that's how you have to look at it. I've done a lot of investigation where I felt sorry for the person. But you can't let that enter into it. You've got to develop what actually happened and who's responsible – the circumstances and that's it. It's part of your job.

After hanging up, I gathered the autopsy pictures, the lateral and AP X-ray plates, Specter's book, and some skull outlines (just in case he felt like drawing what he recalled of the wounds), and mailed them. And waited.

PASSION
for
TRUTH

**FROM FINDING JFK'S SINGLE BULLET
TO QUESTIONING ANITA HILL
TO IMPEACHING CLINTON**

ARLEN SPECTER
WITH CHARLES ROBBINS

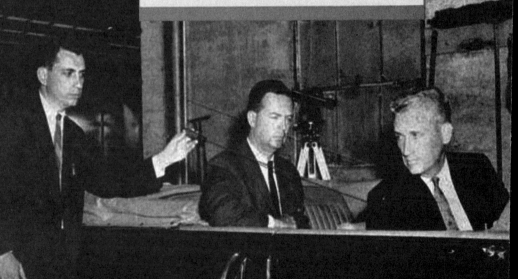

Arlen Spector explains the single bullet theory.

Chapter Ten

James W. Sibert & Francis X. O'Neill

Part Two

A large padded envelope from Mr. Sibert arrived two weeks later. I opened it carefully. Inside was Arlen Specter's book, *Passion for Truth*, and the Kennedy autopsy pictures. For a moment, I felt disappointment. The autopsy pictures had not been critiqued. Then I saw a note – from Jim Sibert. It read: "Bill, there was too much to put in your book, so I did it this way. Best of luck with your research. If you do write a book, give me the title and publisher. Regards, Jim." Did it this way? I looked in Specter's book. On page 49, Sibert had underlined the paragraph where Specter had misspelled Sibert (Siebert) and O'Neill (O'Neal). On page 67, Sibert had underlined this passage: The president's garments were also important, given the controversy over the location of the hole in his body verses the locations of the holes in his clothing. Some critics have seized on the locations of the holes in the suit jacket and shirt to argue that the hole was lower on the president's back than the reports asserted." That was all. I looked in the envelope again. Inside were papers I had missed. There were two sheets of paper with Jim Sibert's handwriting on them labeled, A CRITIQUE OF ARLEN SPECTER'S BOOK "PASSION FOR TRUTH" PART II BY FBI RETIRED SPECIAL AGENT JAMES W. SIBERT. Indeed, point by point, he had gone through the chapter in Specter's book on Kennedy and the Warren Commission showing where he felt the author had gotten things wrong or was in direct contradiction to the known facts of the case. All interesting, but the part of the handwritten document that caught my attention was the last section:
COMMENTARY REGARDING PHOTOGRAPHS AND X-RAYS. "It is to be noted that photographs had not been developed when autopsy completed," Sibert wrote. There followed a listing of the photographs and X-rays I had sent, with brief comments on each:

Autopsy photograph #1. This is my recollection of the tracheotomy incision, (photo 1)

Autopsy photograph #2. Lying on autopsy table with head support, (photo 2)

Autopsy photograph #3. Massive head wound from which part of skull was missing, (photo 3)

Autopsy photograph #4. I can't account for difference between this photo and photo #3 unless it was taken later during restoring the appearance, (photo 4)

Autopsy photograph #5. This has no significance to me. (photo 5)

Autopsy photograph #6. Body was being raised to obtain measurements of back wound, (photo 6)

X-ray #1, lateral. Don't recall seeing this X-ray that night, (photo 8)

X-ray #2, AT Don't recall seeing this X-ray that night, (photo 7)

I called Sibert to thank him and to try to get additional information on the autopsy photographs, since he had not critiqued them to the degree that I had hoped.

Law: If I could just ask a couple of questions on these pictures for clarification?

Sibert: Yeah.

Law: In [photo 6] where they're lifting the president off the table, is that the bullet wound you saw?

Sibert: Yeah. That's the only thing. And of course, they didn't do much there They probed it with a finger and a chrome probe. But I don't remember any other mark on the back than that.

Law: Where they have the president's head in a head-holder? With the phone on the wall. Do you remember a head-holder from that night?

Sibert: The head-holder. Yeah. I think they asked me up there at the deposition. I hadn't recalled it until they showed it. That was just a support thing on the back of the autopsy table supporting the head.

Law: A couple of the autopsy technicians I talked to said they didn't use this kind of head-holder. They used a metal block with differing depths.

Sibert: I didn't remember that type. I don't remember the detail. It could be that [picture] was taken after the morticians and staff were working there till early in the morning you know, that's because we didn't have access. They said they stayed there through midnight – after the autopsy was over and we had departed – until 5:00 AM, reconstructing the head with the morticians. Maybe they could have brought something at that time.

Law: I see. Another question I wanted to ask on the photo where they are lifting him off the table (photo 6): Is this one of the pictures that you think is a cleaner version than what you remember?

Sibert: Where I said was cleaner was the back of the head. That one picture there you know, where the hair's not all matted and everything? That's a much cleaner picture than anything I remembered from that night.

Law: Right. That was my question.

Sibert: There, I think, again, that picture was probably taken, Bill, after the – they were doing all this reconstruction stuff.

Law: The picture that has the president on his back with the little metal table over him? It's number three and it shows a massive wound in the top of the head (photo 3). Do you remember it looking like that?

Sibert: That's the one there where it's neater, where you've got all the matted hair and brain tissue hanging out?

Law reading from Sibert's critique of the picture: "Massive head wound from which part of skull was missing. "

Sibert: I remember a gory picture like that, but I don't remember anything that looked that neat and cleaned up like some of those others are.

I switched the topic to the transcript of the press conference in Dallas held shortly after the doctors had tried in vain to save President Kennedy's life.

Law: I was going back through this book (*Assassination Science* edited by James Fetzer, Catfeet Press, 1998) and in the back pages there is a transcript of the press conference that the Parkland doctors gave. Question: "Where was the entrance wound?" Dr. Malcolm Perry: "There was an entrance wound in the neck. In regards to the one in the head I cannot say." Question: "Which way was the bullet coming on the neck wound? At him?" Perry: "It appeared to be coming at him."

Sibert: Yeah. In other words from the grassy knoll. All I know is what I've read, but over there at Parkland they thought that that was an entrance wound. And you have a lot of corroboration there with nurses who had seen bullet wounds. And the neatness of the puncture there – the anterior throat. In other words it wouldn't be like one coming out, you know, a bullet coming out tears tissue and stuff. I'll tell you, there's a lot of unanswered questions on this thing. I think there was a lot of pressure – just between you and I – I think when the Secret Service went around afterwards they had to make this stuff gel – the single-bullet theory – and this could have been precipitated by Specter. I don't know. But there were some viewpoints that were not only changed, because you had Parkland saying, "Well, then it could have been either an entrance or an exit [wound] in the throat."

Law: The thing that gets confusing is: if the bullet did not go out the throat as claimed, where did the bullet in the throat come from? And so all you have is the testimony of the doctors themselves. When they first did the press conference they said, "It appeared to be coming at him." And now Perry is going around saying he didn't make that statement..

Sibert: I'll tell you – have you been following the Kennedy stuff on the History Channel?

Law: Yes.

Sibert: You remember the last one there, where they had the triangulation and the guy did it said it had to come from that sewer, down by the curb you know? Well, now, if you had it (the head shot) from that, this would be explained if you had an explosive-type bullet. They talked to this guy and they said an explosive- type bullet was used. Well, if you had that curb angle going up, you would have to go up at an angle, you know, to get him in the car, and then would go on up through the throat at an angle to where it would come out the head and exploded. I don't know.

Law: The thing is, when you start looking at some of this stuff, like the copper-jacketed bullet that supposedly hit him in the head. And if you look at those X-rays, the bullet appears to have fragmented.

Sibert: Oh, yeah. Well, that was in our 302, I think – it wasn't in the 302 but the statement was made [it looked] sort of like the milky way, you know, when they threw the X-rays up there showing all this – little spots showed up on the X-rays, white spots in the brain. You had some kind of a bullet that just really fragmentized.

Law: So how does that make sense? I don't know if a copper jacketed bullet can fragmentize or not.

Sibert: I don't know either. I wanted to ask you, did you hear anymore on Specter dueling with Wecht.

Law: I'm going to check into that and see if he actually is going to come to Dallas, because that would be an excellent –

Sibert: That would be worth listening to (laughs).

Law: Well, if he actually does it, it would take a lot of courage on his part I don't think he has because I think deep inside he knows he's wrong.

Sibert: He's been getting a lot of flack on the single-bullet theory, he admits that.

Law: What galls me is he's not even a doctor! He's a lawyer. How do you allow a lawyer to do that?

Sibert: They were grasping at straws the way they handled that. The whole commission. And they pushed a lot of that stuff under the carpet. The grassy knoll witnesses, they didn't want to hear what they had to say. I'll tell you, it was a mess.

After hanging up the phone, I sat for a while, thinking. "They were grasping at straws.... The grassy knoll witnesses, they didn't want to hear what they had to say. I'll tell you, it was a mess."

Some of what Jim Sibert had told me was stunning, e.g., his thoughts on the storm drain in Dealey Plaza and his suggestion that the Secret Service put pressure on the Dallas doctors to change their conclusions as to entry/exit wounds. Not new thoughts to anyone who has studied the case, but – coming from a former FBI agent, half of the Sibert and O'Neill team who had been in the autopsy room and had written in the now infamous FD 302 FBI report, "There has been a tracheotomy performed as well as surgery of the head, namely in the top of the skull," – these comments were mind-blowing.

I decided to send Jim Sibert *Assassination Science and Murder In Dealey Plaza* (also edited by James Fetzer, Catfeet Press, 2000), partly to thank him for what he had done for me, and partly because they describe a wealth of new research on various aspects of the case by highly qualified people, and I was interested in his impressions. Just over a week later, I came home to find that Mr. Sibert had called me twice to say he had received the books and wanted to say thank you. I called him the next day.

"I wasn't expecting anything like that. Goodnight!" Sibert said when I told him I understood he had received the books. "I've read one of them already," he told me chuckling. I was surprised: "Which book did you read?" "*Assassination Science*. They've really done some research in that, haven't they? I'm getting ready to start this other one now, *Murder In Dealey Plaza*. I'm really enjoying these, and of course it's got the up to date stuff in there from the ARRB, you know." I told him, "What I thought you might find interesting was that interview with the Dallas doctors shortly after the president was taken from the hospital, where Perry said 'the bullet appeared to be coming at him.' " Sibert interrupted, "Entry wound. Yeah." I said, "I thought you might like to read the whole thing." "Well," he replied "I had mentioned before about Ford moving that back wound up to the base of the neck, and when I went up for the deposition at the ARRB, I took that article with me, and they said, 'We already have that,' and I said, 'At last I feel vindicated.' Here he's admitting that he moved that [wound]. That bullet wound was where everybody said it was. The Secret Service, the doctors. The clothing [holes] matched it and everything else, you know. Those are things you don't forget when you're an eye witness and you're two feet from it. You're not confused about where the location is. "

I knew Jim Sibert did not give interviews – at least not formal on-the-record interviews – I had tried years before and been told: "I've been asked to give interviews by researchers over the years, but I never have." The conversation was coming to a close. It might have been my final chance to talk to Jim Sibert. I said "I'm going to try to get some other witness interviews for my manuscript and there are a few people down in your area. And if I can manage to get to Florida, would you mind meeting with me?" I held my breath, waiting for his answer. "No," I heard James W. Sibert say. "No, I wouldn't mind."

• • •

Florida's population, according to the 2000 census, is nearly sixteen million. Of all those millions, there was just one I wanted to see: James W. Sibert. I looked out of the window of the Delta flight at the lights below as we descended into Florida International Airport, and wondered what the next day would bring. My day had started at 5:30 AM. Sleep had been almost nonexistent and my nerves were on edge as I checked through my list of things to take to Florida: depositions Sibert had given before the ARRB, a set of Kennedy autopsy pictures, special silver ink pen for Sibert to mark the pictures with. A drawing of the Bethesda morgue as it existed in 1963, a mini tape recorder with tapes, a still camera, and my camcorder. I was aware, of course, that the only formal interview outside of the one he had given to Arlen Specter in 1964 was the one he had given to the ARRB in 1997, and that was under government subpoena. Still, Jim Sibert had agreed to meet with me, and I considered that a miracle in and of itself. I packed the camcorder especially carefully. Now, after a three-hour shuttle ride to the Portland airport, and a seven-hour flight, I was in the land of palm trees, pink (real and plastic) flamingos and retirement homes. The airport was teaming with humanity even at 10:30 at night. I stumbled off the airplane and onto the escalator down to the baggage claim area. Debra Conway of JFK/Lancer Publications and Productions was waiting for me, cell phone held to her right ear. "Here he is," I heard her say. Upon being informed of my interview with Sibert, Debra had asked if she could "come along for backup," and I had agreed. My motive was a selfish one. I figured if Sibert said "no" to my filming the interview, Debra would be there to take notes. She is known throughout the research community as the "document lady" and I was glad to have her along to help prepare me. We were both exhausted by the trip, and decided to wait until morning to go over the documents she had brought along.

Over croissants and coffee, we went over the documents. The Sibert and O'Neill FD 302 report, the airtel that had been sent by the agents or someone else at 2:00 AM on 11/23/63 (photo 12), Kellerman's and Greer's testimony before the Warren Commission, the autopsy face sheet, and other assorted items. I scanned them, mentally making notes of what I wanted to get on record during the interview. I glanced nervously at my watch. Jim Sibert would be arriving to meet us within the hour. I had called him as soon as I was up and ready, to set up our rendezvous, and he had generously offered to take us to pick up our rental car and guide us to his residence.

I took the mini tape recorder from my blue travel bag and handed it to Debra and said in conspiratorial tones, "Right before we start the interview, I'm going to ask Sibert if he minds if I videotape it. If he says no, then I'm going to say, 'But Mr. Sibert, the camcorder is all I brought with me, and I don't think I can write fast enough to get everything down on paper.' If he still says no, then you pull out this recorder and say, 'William, I brought this if that will help.' If he says no to that, then get as much of our conversation as you can." She looked somewhat uncertain and said, "Okay," and put the recorder in her purse. I hadn't clarified ahead of time whether Sibert would be willing to be videotaped as I didn't want to put him off and didn't want to push it, at least not yet. As I was finishing my coffee, I heard what sounded like Jim Sibert's voice. Walking into the lobby, I saw an older gentleman. At eighty-three years of age, Jim Sibert could pass for a man at least a decade younger. Tall, straight backed, with a trim physique, a head of snow-white hair, and chiseled features, he said, "Are you William?" We shook hands. After introducing him to Debra, we gathered our belongings and walked out to the parking lot, where Sibert introduced us to his wife Ester. As we rode along I remarked on how glad I was to have the opportunity to talk to him in person about his recollections of the wounds on President Kennedy's body. Ester Sibert turned round to Debra and me and said, "You know, his brains were blown out of his head." I hope the surprise on my face didn't give too much away. "That was one of the questions I was going to ask," I replied.

James W. Sibert, circa 1963

Chapter Eleven

James W. Sibert & Francis X. O'Neill

Part Three

J im Sibert's office was spacious and comfortably furnished. Framed medals from his service as a fighter pilot were displayed atop a bookcase containing works on World War II, religion, and the murder of President Kennedy Clearly, he was well versed in assassination literature. The moment of truth had come. Debra had her folder of documents, I had my traveling bag with video camera and materials. Sibert sat in his desk chair. "Well, who wants to write? "he said. I took a breath. "Would you mind if I camcorder this?" Ready to go into my spiel, he caught me by surprise with, "No, go right on ahead." I tried to be nonchalant as I took the camcorder out of the bag and set it up. Sibert leaned back in his chair, Debra was in a corner with her folder of documents on her lap, notepad and pen at the ready, and I sat on the couch directly across from our subject. With the camcorder rolling, James W. Sibert took us back in time.

Sibert: Each FBI office had an annual inspection. The inspectors were in the Baltimore office. I was the senior resident agent in the Hyattsville, Maryland, office. O'Neill was my alternate SRA. On November 22, 1963, they had sent one of the inspectors down there to Hyattsville, to conduct our inspection for the resident agency in the morning. In the afternoon, the inspector was then going over to the Silver Spring office to inspect that resident agency before going back to Baltimore. So, we had our inspection and we went out to lunch with the inspectors before they started back over to Silver Spring. We parted downstairs and they got in their car and we came on up to our resident agency office, which was on the third floor. We turned on the standard broadcast and heard that Kennedy had been shot in Dallas. So I went over and picked up the bureau radio and called their car number and said, "You probably haven't heard this, it just came in over the radio, but the president was shot in Dallas and you may want to contact headquarters so you know what is happening." So we followed it then, and we got hold of Major Best who was in charge of security for the Office of Special Investigations at Andrews Air Force Base where the presidential flight unit was based. He said that they'd had word that Air Force One would be coming in at 5:30, with the president's body and President Johnson on board. So I called up to my boss, Ed Tully, and told him what the deal was, and I said that if he wanted to get hold of myself and O'Neill we would be out at Andrews. He could get us through best in the OSI office. So we went out, and then they changed the flight schedule. Instead of coming in at 5:30 they were coming in a little later. I think it was 5:30, but anyway we were there as Air Force One landed at Andrews and Tully called me and said that he'd just got word from the Bureau headquarters there in D.C. with instructions for O'Neill and I to get in the motorcade and go on down to Bethesda and witness the autopsy and carry any bullets that were removed from the body – hand-carry them to the lab to preserve the chain of evidence. So we got hold of Jim Rowley, who was the head of the Secret Service, and I showed him my credentials and told him the instructions we'd had. So he put us in the third car of the motorcade. Of course the president's body was in the ambulance leading the motorcade, and Jackie was with her husband's body. So we got there and they pulled up in front of the National Naval Medical Center in Bethesda, and Jackie and Admiral Burkley, who was the president's personal physician, got out and went upstairs. The ambulance drove out back and we got out and followed it. O'Neill and I helped the Secret Service agents get the casket out of the ambulance and put it on a dolly and rolled it into the autopsy room.

Now, as soon as we got it in there, Humes was there and Boswell and several other military District of Washington personnel from the Navy Medical Center. The casket had been damaged somewhere in transit, whether it was on the loading in Dallas or unloading at Andrews Air Force Base, I don't know. So we opened it up and there was the body. One sheet was around the body and a separate sheet was around the head and this was, of course, blood-soaked because of the extensive wounds. The technicians then took the body out and put it on the autopsy table.

Of course, O'Neill and I were making notes, and I told Frank, "We want to be sure to get the names of everybody in this autopsy room, their rank and affiliation." To my knowledge that was the only record there was. I don't think the Secret Service even had a copy of who was there that night.

So, when they took the wrappings off, Humes saw this big, gaping hole in the back of the head, and he looked at the tracheotomy and he said, "Well, they've done a tracheotomy and apparently a surgery of the head area" (photo 21) because he had a big piece of bone just missing there. And, incidentally, in connection with this, my only regret, since then, is that I didn't have the presence of mind when they brought the piece of bone in later on during the autopsy that I didn't ask him – Dr. Humes – "Would this account for what you first said was surgery of the head area?" because that was the basis of David Lifton's book about the surgery of the head.

Now then, the thing I'd like to point out here is they cleared out the autopsy room because they said they wanted to take X-rays and also wanted to take photographs. So everybody was cleared out. Of course, they had lead-lined vests for protection when they were taking the X-rays. After that was done they got us back in there. I think it was 8 o'clock when the surgery actually started.

Conway: 8:15, that's what you have down [in the 302].

Sibert: Yep. But the thing is, looking back, the cardinal rule whenever you would do an autopsy that comes in from another jurisdiction – and I've witnessed a few – you always, if there has been anything done surgically where that body came from, you get in touch with them and you say, "Look we're getting ready to do our autopsy here, what did you do over there surgically?" Because it was evidence – they did a tracheotomy there, but no contact was made [with Parkland Hospital], at least by Humes and Boswell, that night when they started the autopsy. So they went on the assumption this was a straight autopsy, and there had been surgery in the head area.

Conway: A tracheotomy.

Sibert: Tracheotomy yes; in some places it's called a tracheostomy, and I'll tell you the difference. Tracheotomy is where you do this little incision and tracheostomy is when you put the tube in and all that. I looked that up in the dictionary because I had used "tracheotomy" all the time and that was what was used there that night, but "tracheostomy" also is used and I think that is what was used by Parkland because they had inserted a tube and everything, you know, through the incision there.

So, they started the autopsy and they found this back wound, which was down below the shoulders and up through the middle of the back. It was measured at 5½ inches down from the top of the collar. Now that's another thing here. He came in wrapped in sheets and his clothing went to the laboratory so the autopsy physicians didn't have the benefit of seeing where the holes in the clothing were because they were separated. Now if this had been done over in Parkland, they would have had access to everything. So they found this and they started probing it with their rubber-gloved finger. They also used a chrome probe that they pressed in there, and said, "There's no exit." Finck and Humes and Boswell all agreed. So that put me to thinking, and I said, "Well let me go over and call the laboratory and see if there is any kind of an ice bullet or something that would completely disintegrate. " So they put a marine guard on me and we walked down the hall to another room there where there was a telephone – there was probably one in our room but there were so many people and everything, it was no place to talk. So I called over to the lab and I talked to Chuck Killion, and I said, "Chuck we're over here in this autopsy and they've got a wound in the back and they've probed it with a rubber-gloved finger and a chrome probe and there's no exit." And I said, "Is there any kind of an ice bullet, or do you know of any other kind, that we should consider?" He said, "Well have you heard about the bullet they found on this stretcher in Dallas?" I said, "No, I haven't heard anything. I don't know what's going on over there. " He said, "Well, they found a bullet on a stretcher there near the trauma room over there, but they don't know whether it was Kennedy's or Connally's stretcher." He said that they were flying the bullet in to our laboratory – the firearms lab – for identification and inspection.

I went back and told Humes what they had told me. Now there was the second clue, or should have been, to get in touch with Parkland, but they never called. It seems to me like Humes would have wanted to know more and would have called and asked to talk to a doctor there at Parkland, but that was never done. The first time they called Parkland was Saturday morning, after the Friday night when the autopsy was done. Humes said, "Well the pattern is clear. " First of all – the bullet in the back – when they probed that, evidently it didn't go in straight. He said, "It looks like this came at a downward trajectory of forty-five degrees, from above." He said that it was clear that the bullet wound in the back – they did cardiac manipulation and during the process the bullet fell out on the stretcher. This was all supposition, because he hadn't talked to Parkland and didn't know if they had done cardiac manipulation.

During the autopsy they brought in a piece of bone that was about 3½ inches in length and about 2½ inches wide, I think. They said they found it in the presidential limousine down on the floor. They flew it in and Humes measured it and gave out the measurements. He said that death was due to the massive wound in the head.

We signed a receipt. And here's another thing that in books were "missiles" – if you remember that word was used – but this receipt was made by the Navy and we received it from them. A navy corpsman typed it up and we signed it, but if I had typed up a receipt and composed it I would have just said metal fragments because there was no single bullet that we ever saw there that night at Bethesda.

Law: So it was typed by the corpsman and he was the one who put –

Sibert: Yeah, one of the corpsmen. Probably Humes or Boswell said type up a receipt for this little jar we had and we scratched our initials on the top of it, I think JWS. I was presented with it at the ARRB deposition there in College Park.

We left there about midnight that night and, of course, our cars were out at Andrews because we had ridden in the motorcade. So we had to get transportation down to the Bureau – the firearms laboratory – and I turned this over to Bob Frazier, this little jar. Then we got a clerk to drive us from the laboratory out to Andrews Air Force Base where we picked up our Bureau cars. I got home about 4:30 that morning, and the phone started ringing about a half-hour later, from the Bureau and other places. I sent a teletype that night from the Bureau there, stating what the doctors had said and everything, and that the bullet was on the stretcher and all that (photo 12).[1] Dallas was the office of origin. When an investigation occurred in an auxiliary office, like Baltimore or Philadelphia, it became the office of origin and you sent copies to the Bureau and also copies to the "OO," the office of origin, so they've got the complete picture because they are running and sending out leads and everything based on that.

You're probably familiar with articles in JAMA, *Journal of the American Medical Association*, where they interviewed Humes and Boswell years later.[2] They said that they stayed until about five that morning – the funeral home directors – we had their names listed in our FD 302 – to reconstruct the wound and everything and tidy up the hair because it was matted that night. You can imagine, the blood and everything, when you looked down in there into that cavity. I was probably as close as two foot – O'Neill and I. We were able to observe that wound. So they helped him reconstruct the body on the Saturday morning. Then, after that, they called Parkland and that's when they got hold of – I don't remember whether it was Perry or which doctor over there – but they said, "Well you know we made that tracheotomy over a bullet wound." This had never been considered that night. So you can see the predicament that the autopsy surgeons were in: the body is gone, the funeral home already had taken possession of it and they have another bullet wound that wasn't even considered. This is the beginning of the development of the single-bullet theory, because they had to account for that wound. So we never knew – O'Neill and I were never informed – we got calls from the Bureau, supervisors over there would maybe ask about the 302. They said, "Now you say surgery in the head area, was this your wording?" And we said, "No wait a minute, we're not doctors. This is what we copied down. Statements made by Humes or Boswell or Finck." And the measurements and everything we got from them and that kind of inquiry. But we never heard about a second autopsy report – two autopsy reports – other than ours.

We got back and I called my boss, and I said, "Boss, when do you want O'Neill and I to come in and dictate on this?" This was Saturday morning. I said, "Do you want to call in a steno?" Because Monday, if you remember, was a day of mourning, everything was shut down. And he said, "Let me check with the Bureau." He called me back at home and said, "No, sir. Come in Tuesday morning first thing, that will be fine. We will dictate it then and the steno pool – all the girls – will be in. Our chief steno will take the dictation on this too, the head of the steno pool." So we went up Tuesday, and dictated our report.

---

1. Sent at 2 AM on 11/23/63, the teletype (photo 12) included these words: "One bullet hole just below shoulders to right of spinal column and hand probing indicated trajectory at angle of forty-five to sixty degrees downward and hole of short depth with no point of exit. No bullet located in body."
2. *Journal of the American Medical Association*, 27 May 1992, pp. 2791–2807; 7 October 1992, pp. 1736–1738 and 1748–1754; 24/31 March 1993, pp. 1540–1547.

The first I knew about a second autopsy report or my original 302 being in the possession of somebody was when David Lifton called me in 1976.[3] I was on leave down in Georgia visiting my sister, and we had just finished supper and the phone rang. Of course she answered and she said, "Jim, it's for you." I picked up the phone and this person said, "This is David Lifton. I'm a graduate student at the University of California, Berkeley, working under Dr. So-and-so, professor there. I'm doing research work on the Kennedy assassination and I have your FD 302 here in front of me." I thought that went into the archives because we never even went before the Warren Commission. I said, "Well, wait a minute. You say you're so-and-so. I don't know who you are and you call me on the telephone and say you've got this FD." I said, "Answer this question for me. Look down on the bottom there where O'Neill and I signed our initials. Are there other initials typed in there?" And he said, "Yeah, DFR." I said, "Well, this is it, because that was Doris F. Riednick the chief steno that took the dictation." He said, "Your autopsy report, your FD 302 doesn't jibe with the official autopsy report." And I said, "Well, to me this is the official autopsy." He said, "Oh no," but didn't go into detail. He said, "What is your comment on this?" I said, "I can give it to you in two words. I don't have any: no comment." And he said, "Well, that's not helping me any." I gave him the address of the FBI headquarters in D.C. and said to call them. So when I got back from leave I dictated a memorandum for the file about this telephone call. I had made notes, which is one thing you learn even when making a phone call. So when I got back I dictated an airtel over to the headquarters about getting this phone call down in Georgia. Lifton was so thorough, believe it or not – this will be of interest to you – he traced that back and had the file pulled in Baltimore and got that memo that I had dictated and sent over to Washington. He recorded our telephone conversation.

Law: He recorded it?

Sibert: He recorded it. He had his recording and went up there and compared that memo with everything that was in my airtel, and in his book he said that we must have been very meticulous because it was accurate. So, we hear that there was another autopsy report – bits and pieces. But the Bureau never once called us on the phone and said, "Look, here is the official autopsy report that is out now and it doesn't agree with yours, what gives?" And Gunn asked me this up there and said, "You mean to tell me that they didn't call you and O'Neill back and let you know and go over the differences between the official autopsy report and yours that night?" And I said, "No. If they had, the only thing I could have said is, 'Look, this is what happened that night, that's the record of that

3. Actually 1966.

night, and there could be no changes, that's it.' And O'Neill would have said the same thing." We both were in agreement on it. Then, of course, the other autopsy report came out. That's the reason you had all these people calling about this – book writers and everything – about the difference in autopsy reports. You had one autopsy and two autopsy reports and that's what it boiled down to.

Conway: To clarify: you did not realize that the official report written by the autopsy doctors was different from yours until the JAMA articles came out? Or before then?

Sibert: Well, we had heard rumors that there was another, but I never saw any report and they didn't give me a copy of Humes's. Now there was something else I wanted to mention there. Repeat your question, maybe I'll pick it up again.

Conway: I guess I'm asking if Lifton told you that the 302 didn't match the autopsy report.

Sibert: Right. He said, "Your 302 doesn't match the official autopsy report," and I said, "Well, as far as I'm concerned that's it."

Conway: Okay, so when that happened how long was it after that that you actually got to see or read the official autopsy report, was it when JAMA –

Sibert: Oh, it was years later.

Conway: Years later?

Sibert: Yeah, yes. If they would have asked us, "How do you account for this?" – but they never once mentioned this other autopsy report, and our FD 302 was incorporated in Dallas reports after that period. Here's the thing, and Jim Hosty, I think, mentioned this too – things were really tough then, they were tight. We had just come out of the missile situation down there in Cuba, and here you had a guy, Oswald, that they had traced back there to the book depository and that floor and everything. He had been murdered by Ruby. He certainly was never going to testify in a trial, in a subsequent trial, and at the time they wanted to get this Warren Report out. I think Johnson was pushing them on that, to get that out. And the single-bullet theory was developed as a result of that, and that's the way it was left. Of course, you know what kind of pot shots were being taken at the Warren Commission Report and especially at the single-bullet theory. I forget what year it was. We got a call from Baltimore. They said, "O'Neill and you are to go down to Washington and you are to be interviewed by Senator Specter, who was the counselor for the Warren Commission."

Law: Yeah, I was going to ask you to tell me your thoughts on Mr. Specter and the single-bullet theory.

Sibert: Well I – that single-bullet theory – when they had me come up to the ARRB deposition there at College Park, I said, "Well before I come up there, I want you to know one thing. I'm not an advocate of the single-bullet theory."

I said, "I don't believe it because I stood there two foot from where that bullet wound was in the back, the one that they eventually moved up to the base of the neck. I was there when Boswell made his face sheet and located that wound exactly as we described it in the FD 302." And I said, "Furthermore, when they examined the clothing after it got into the Bureau, those bullet holes in the shirt and the coat were down 5 inches there. So there is no way that bullet could have gone that low then rise up and come out the front of the neck, zigzag and hit Connally and then end up pristine on a stretcher over there in Dallas."

Law: You don't believe in the single-bullet theory. Period.

Sibert: There is no way I will swallow that. They can't put enough sugar on it for me to bite it. That bullet was too low in the back.

Law: Where do you remember seeing it, exactly? Your partner, Frank O'Neill, if I remember right, credits you with finding the bullet hole in the back.

Sibert: Well, let me clarify that. When they had the body over at Parkland, they had a shoving match between the fellow who was going to do the autopsy,[4] who said that the autopsy had to be done in Texas – and they were going to do it there – and you had Kellerman telling them that he had orders from the Secret Service and also from Bobby Kennedy that it was going to be done in Washington. At Parkland, they never knew there was a bullet wound in the back. That body left there and they did not know about the bullet wound in the back. Then, Bethesda did not know there was a bullet wound where the tracheotomy was made. So that is a pathetic situation. It could have been handled if they had made a phone call. The smart thing to have done – if there hadn't been such animosity between the partners over there – put one of those Parkland doctors on Air Force One to come right into Bethesda and say, "Here's what we did." And the clothing should have come in with the body. But they held the clothing – they didn't even undo the tie over there at Parkland and there was a nick in the knot – and here you had this entrance or exit wound in the throat where the tracheotomy was.

Conway: Let's go back to your evening with Mr. Specter.

Sibert: Oh well, of course he was conducting the interview and we couldn't make notes. We were answering the questions – but let me get this right here (retrieves documents) – as I say I told Frank we're going in while the words are fresh on our minds and dictate the questions they were asking. So they gave us a steno and the first question – Specter was asking O'Neill and I these questions.

Sibert (reading):

Question: State exactly what you did on the night of November 22, 1963, and what your instructions were in connection with this incident.

4. Dr. Earl Rose

Answer: We met the presidential aircraft, accompanied the body in the motor-cade, and following arrival at the Navy Medical Center witnessed the autopsy We were instructed solely and specifically to obtain any bullets which might have been in the president's body and take them to the FBI laboratory This was our purpose for being present at the autopsy.

Sibert (no longer reading): Now I want to point this out too. Keep in mind there was no federal statute at that time, '63, that gave any governmental agency juris-diction to investigate the attempted assassination or assassination of a president. That bill was passed in '65. So we were there just like we were instructed, to observe the autopsy and obtain anything removed from the body, identify it and hand-carry it to the laboratory for any possible future trial.

Sibert continues reading: We were seated in the third car in the motorcade.

Sibert (no longer reading): Now O'Neill said five, I think, later on. But it was third, because both of us were given this at the time.

Sibert continues reading: What was the time of the preparation of the autopsy at the hospital?

A: 7:17 PM. That was before they started photographs, X-rays and all that stuff, and getting the authority from Jackie of which X-rays to take and all that.

Q: What time did the autopsy begin?

A: 8:15 PM.

Q: What time did it end?

A: We did not recall, but it was right at midnight when we signed that receipt.

Q: When Boswell and Humes were interviewed in those JAMA articles, they said that there was no more autopsy done after midnight, so that corresponds. But from then until 5 AM, reconstruction work was done with the funeral people. Could it have been 12 midnight or 1 AM?

A: Yes.

Q: What time did Lieutenant Colonel Finck arrive?

A: I've got here Finck is an army medical doctor assigned to the Armed Forces Institute of Pathology. We did not recall. However, it was after the autopsy was in progress.

Q: What time did Agent Sibert call Agent Killion at the FBI lab?

A: Sometime between 11 PM and 12 midnight, because they found this back wound and they couldn't account for it. I went over and came back and told Humes.

Q: Did you call Agent Killion prior to or after the wound was discovered in the president's back?

A: After the wound was discovered. That was the reason I called over about an ice bullet.

Q: Did you observe probing done by medical examiners using the finger in the back wound and by whom was the probing done?

A: Yes. Probing done by Commander Humes.

Sibert (no longer reading): Since then I'm almost positive that Finck also probed that with the chrome probe.

Sibert continues reading:

A: Commander Humes stated that this accounted for no bullet being located which had entered the back region, and that it was entirely possible that the bullet had worked its way back out of the point of entry while cardiac massage was being performed at the Dallas hospital.

Q: Prior to SA Sibert calling the FBI laboratory did either Dr. Humes or Dr. Finck express an opinion that the bullet wound in the back was a point of entry or a point of exit?

A: We can recall no such discussion.

Sibert (no longer reading): Because he said it came down at a 45-degree angle, I think he was assuming that that was an entrance wound in the back.

Law: But did they have an opinion that night?

Sibert: We couldn't recall coming out and saying this is an entrance wound and this is an exit wound, none of that.

Sibert continues reading:

Q: What was the size of the autopsy room?

Sibert (no longer reading): I guess he thought I had a 6-foot ruler and went around there and took measurements.

Sibert continues reading:

Q: Was it wider than this room?

A: It would appear to be.

Q: How close were you to the autopsy?

A: As close as necessary to observe the proceedings.

Q: I know that you delivered two pieces of metal to the FBI laboratory removed from the president's body and that the chief pathologist advised that approximately forty particles and smudges were evidenced from X-rays. Were any additional particles removed?

A: Not to our knowledge. Only two were removed in our presence by Dr. Humes and placed in that jar.

Q: Were you present at all times during the autopsy?

A: At all times one or both agents were present in the autopsy room.

Sibert (no longer reading): We'd been without food since noon. When one of us went out to eat, the other one stayed there, so at all times one or both agents were present.

Sibert continues reading:

Q: Did you make any notes during the course of the evening?

A: Yes.

Q: Do you still have them?

A: No.

Q: What happened to them?

A: After dictating and comparing dictation with the notes, the notes were destroyed.

Sibert (no longer reading): And I went into detail with him on that; I told him there was a mimeograph stencil and when it came back we checked it and made corrections. Then, when it came back we proofread the thing again and it jibed with our notes – the procedure then in the Bureau was that you destroyed your notes after you dictated from them, and your top mimeographed copy was initialed as the file copy. But since then they have changed that. I guess they are probably renting big warehouses now to keep all the agents' notes. Well, it wouldn't be now, because it's all on computers.

Law: But that was standard then in the Bureau – that you destroyed your notes?

Sibert: Standard then, and you dictated within 3 days of your case. On major cases we did it that way.

Sibert continues reading:

Q: I noticed on 11-22-63 Mr. Kellerman stated that the president said, "Get me to a hospital." Is anything which is in quotation marks the exact words that Mr. Kellerman used: "Get me to a hospital."

Sibert (no longer reading): Now, later on, maybe it was the following Monday, the Bureau told us to go over and interview Kellerman and Greer, the driver. We also interviewed Gerry Behn, who was in charge of Secret Service agents, because he wanted to talk to us first. So we made a separate interview form for Behn and then O'Neill interviewed Kellerman and I interviewed Greer. So

O'Neill had the notes on that one – of course we were right there together and put the dictation together, so he asked us to answer that.

Sibert continues reading:

> Q: I also noticed that on 11-23-63 Agent Greer of the Secret Service was quoted as stating that he floored the limousine following the police escort to the hospital – was "floored" his exact wording?
>
> A: I interviewed him and it was. He said, "I floored it."

Sibert (no longer reading): I don't know whether he remembered that. Of course this was while we were there doing the autopsy you know, and maybe talking with the Secret Service guys and maybe it was when one of them went out to eat or maybe when I went out to eat with Greer. That wasn't a formal interview, which occurred later on when we went over to the White House – those were cursory remarks.

Law: That was when you were in the morgue? The first time he mentioned that?

Sibert: That was when we were in the Naval Medical Center there.

Law: Okay, in the Center itself.

Sibert: Yes.

Law: And then you went back?

Sibert: We went out to eat at some time. And we had talked with him during the autopsy and I made informal notes. When we went over to interview him, of course it was a lengthy interview.

Law: Who sent you back to interview him again?

Sibert: The Bureau did. The Bureau called Baltimore and told them. My boss called me and told me they wanted us back over there at the White House to interview Kellerman and Greer there, after the autopsy and everything was over.

Law: Because it was a more formal interview instead of the –

Sibert: Yeah, just casual remarks.

Law: Casual remarks that you wrote down while you were there. They wanted a more formal interview and that is why they sent you back?

Sibert: I imagine so. That's the only thing – they never gave us a reason.

Sibert continues reading:

> Q: Did Greer and Kellerman appear to retain their composure on 11/22?
>
> A: Yes.

Sibert (no longer reading): I mean, I don't know how else you would describe it.

Sibert continues reading:

Q: How long had you been with the FBI?

A: Fourteen years, O'Neill approximately ten.

Q: I note that in the interview with Agent Kellerman conducted on 11/27/63 no mention is made of his remark that the president was overheard to say, "Get me to the hospital." Is that because he did not say so on the twenty-seventh?

Sibert (no longer reading): The twenty-seventh was the day when we went over for the formal interview and Specter is saying in that formal interview it doesn't say anything about get me to the hospital, but O'Neill had it in his original notes you know that we dictated.

Law: There is some confusion for me. When you first interviewed Kellerman or Greer, which one was it that said –

Conway: Kellerman.

Law: Okay, it was Kellerman. Kellerman said he heard the president say, "My God I've been hit."

Sibert: Yeah. O'Neill got that from Kellerman. That was that night.

Law: And then later when you went back to interview him formally he had added something else that he thought the president had said. Is that the way it was?

Sibert: No, this was –

Law: The other one. "Get me to the hospital" was the first one?

Sibert: He said that the first time, but in the formal interview with O'Neill that part wasn't mentioned in there, "Get me to the hospital." I can't see what the confusion is on it, but what he said was informal – "Get me to the hospital" – that was when we talked to him that night. He was recalling what happened, you know, right after.

Law: Right.

Sibert: And now here's what O'Neill's answer was:

A: Yes, however, it is to be noted that Mr. Kellerman advised on 11/27/63 – that he had a chance since 11/22/63 to think and try to reconstruct the entire activities of that day. The statement which he furnished on 11/27/63 in the formal interview were his best recollections of the exact wording used.

Sibert (no longer reading): So maybe he said it, but didn't recall saying it, Kellerman.

Law: I got you.

Sibert: That gets it cleared up?

Law: Yes.

Sibert: All right, now here's the last question [from Specter]:

> Q: This was the end of the formal question and answering interrogation. Special Agents Sibert and O'Neill advised that it was not possible under the circumstances to take notes and they have attempted to reconstruct questions and answers from best recollections.

Sibert (no longer reading): Now when we went over there to be interviewed by Mr. Specter – I'll just read this and if I go too fast then stop me and we will slow up and go back over it again.

Conway: Okay. Are you looking at MD154?

Sibert: Yes.

Conway: I've got that and I can follow along.

Sibert, reading:

> Specter: On March 12, 1964, I interviewed Special Agents Francis X. O'Neill –

Sibert (no longer reading): This is from Specter to J. Lee Rankin. Now you know who J. Lee Rankin is. Before we get started on this, do you know the story on Rankin's son when the ARRB interviewed him? When they went to Rankin's son, the ARRB, they said would you by any chance have anything that your father gave you just as a memento of when he was general counsel of the Warren Commission? As general counsel, he had all of the notes made by all seven members of the Warren Commission, by everybody that had been before that commission. So that's where we get 40,000 notes. Then he said to Rankin's son, "Would you by any chance have any that he gave you that we could get because our job is to collect anything printed on this and get it in to the archives?" He said, "I think I can help you more than that," or something to that effect, and pulled out a box with 40,000 notes – all of the notes that his dad had been in charge of there. That is where they caught Ford. They called him out there in Colorado and they said, "Wait a minute. We've gone over all these notes and the consensus was that this bullet wound was farther down in the back, and they said, "Did you change this?" And of course they knew he had. I've got the copy of that thing that was done by the Associated Press on this.

Law: So, he had to come forward with it.

Sibert: And he said, "I moved it up for clarification." And when the guys told me this – Jerry Gunn – doing the deposition – I said, "Yeah, for clarifying the single-bullet theory, because if you didn't get that up to the back of the neck there is no way it could have come out the front of the throat." So that was where that came about.

Sibert continues reading:

Specter: SA O'Neill and SA Sibert advised that the autopsy surgeons made substantial efforts to determine if there was a –

Sibert (no longer reading): This is Specter's wording. He is saying Sibert told him this.

Sibert continues reading:

Specter: – substantial efforts to determine if there was a missile in President Kennedy's body to explain what happened to a bullet which apparently entered the back of his body.

Sibert (no longer reading): He even used "back of the body" there, and then they moved it up to the neck later on.

Sibert continues reading:

Specter: They stated that the opinion was expressed by both Commander Humes and Lt. Col. Finck that the bullet might have been forced out of the back of the president's body upon the application of external heart massage.

Sibert (no longer reading): Now, when he was interviewing us, he had that FD 302 5½-page thing there. He had to have it. So, some of the things he was asking – he had the answers in there.

Sibert continues reading:

Specter: They stated that this story was advanced after SA Sibert called the FBI laboratory to talk to SA Killion, who advised that the bullet had been found on the stretcher at Parkland Hospital. SA Sibert relayed that information to the doctors. SA O'Neill and Sibert advised that they did not recall any discussion of the theory that the bullet might have been forced out of the body by external cardiac massage until SA Sibert reported the findings of the bullet on the stretcher.

Sibert (no longer reading): However, get this:

Sibert continues reading:

Specter: Neither agent could conclusively rule out the possibility that such a hypothesis was advanced prior to that time.

Sibert (no longer reading): See the weasel wording there?

Sibert continues reading:

> **Specter**: But each expressed the opinion that he thought the theory was expressed after information was obtained about the bullet on the stretcher. SA Sibert advised that he made no notes during the autopsy."

Law: And that's not true is it?

Sibert: No. I told him, you know, that I made voluminous notes.

Sibert continues reading:

> **Specter**: SA O'Neill stated that he made only a few notes which he destroyed after his report was dictated.

Sibert (no longer reading): The guy must have thought I was a genius because I had all the names down there of people in attendance at the autopsy, rank and everything. Wouldn't that be a great mind – it would be like beaming, wouldn't it, from one PDA to another.[5]

Sibert continues reading:

> **Specter**: SA O'Neill advised that his notes would not have shown when the doctors expressed the thought that the bullet might have been forced out by external heart massage in relation to the time that they monitored the presence of the bullet on the Parkland Hospital stretcher. I also questioned SA Sibert and O'Neill about their interview of the SAIC Kellerman and Greer on the portions of the FBI report on which Kellerman and Greer have repudiated.

Sibert (no longer reading): The only thing I can figure here is: you've got Specter, who has developed the single-bullet theory, and, of course, he's in contact with the Secret Service and he's saying there that they repudiated that. But I don't know what's in the ARRB[6] when they interviewed Kellerman and Greer, what they told them. But –

Sibert continues reading:

> Specter: SA Sibert and O'Neill stated that they interviewed Kellerman and Greer formally, November 27, and talked to them only informally at the autopsy. O'Neill stated he is certain that he had a verbatim note on Kellerman's statement, "Get me to the hospital," and also Mrs. Kennedy said, "Oh no." SA O'Neill stated he was sure that they were direct quotes from Kellerman, because O'Neill used question marks in his record, which indicated that he had written these precise words in his notes, which notes have since been destroyed after the

---

5. Personal digital assistant: a hand-held computer
6. Presumably he meant: HSCA.

report was dictated. O'Neill noted that Kellerman did not repeat the language in the interview on the twenty-seventh and that, in the latter interview, O'Neill took down that Kellerman said that, without leading or directing him in any way. I also asked the two special agents about the language in their reports that Greer glanced around and noticed that the president had evidently been hit and, thereafter, got on the radio and communicated with the other vehicles stating that they desired to get the president to the hospital immediately. SA O'Neill and Sibert advised that to the best of their recollections Greer told them just that, but they probably did not make any notes of these comments since their conversation with Greer was informal at the time of the autopsy, and they did not have an opportunity to make extensive notes in accordance with their normal interviewing procedures. Dictated 11:45 AM to 12 noon.

Sibert (no longer reading): Took him fifteen minutes but that – here he's got a page and a half and I've got I don't know how many. Four and a quarter pages.

Conway: I can't believe that he put in there that you guys didn't take any notes.

Sibert: Yeah, when I was at the deposition, he said, "Have you ever had the chance to see what you dictated?" I said, "No, because it was dictated at the Bureau and it was a memo and it wasn't in the Baltimore file. " And he handed me a copy, and I've got that too in all this stuff that I just read.

Conway: Yeah, I saw that.

Sibert: And that's the first time I had seen –

Conway: The first time you'd seen the 302! That is unbelievable.

Sibert: Not the FD 302 but the memorandum we dictated after Specter interviewed us.

Conway: Oh, after Specter. Okay. But Specter knew.

Sibert: He had our FD 302s.

Conway: Right. So he was trying to establish in the records that you had written this so long after and hadn't taken notes and that you were wrong, That's what he was trying to get on record.

Sibert: Well, of course he had the date on that FD 302. Let's see here.

Conway: Is it the twenty-seventh? Twenty-fifth.

Sibert: The twenty-fifth, yes. So he had that, and this was, well – when he interviewed us – what date did I say that was? Here. I've got it right here.

Conway: March 12.

Sibert: March 12. See, we are going back from November 23 to March 12 and you know good and well he had plenty – because all this stuff was furnished to the Warren Commission and stuck in the reports and all that.

Conway: He was trying to take the validity from your reports.

Sibert: Here's the predicament they were in: they had given all this to us that Friday night about the bullet wound in the back – that was the magic bullet that ended up coming out the neck and all that, in the single-bullet theory, and then the massive wound, which was the one that was the cause of death. So he had to, in interviewing us, get that moved up. I don't know what all went on. The Bureau didn't fill us in on that. And that's what they couldn't get over on us. It seems to me like they should have – looking back – and I knew that the Bureau supervisor should have called O'Neill and I there at the resident agency, and said, "Do you know what happened on this? We've got a new autopsy report now," and fill us in on it. But I told him, "I have never been contacted by them." I've been asked questions like, "Is this the doctors' wording? Is this the correct measurement that they gave you on this and all? " But that was the way it went.

Conway: If you don't mind while we are right here: during your deposition they asked you about a memo that looked like it was written at two o'clock in the morning and you said that it wasn't you?

Sibert: Oh, oh I know that. That was about the teletype.

Conway: Right.

Sibert: The teletype that I sent to the Bureau and to Dallas (photo 12). Let's see, have you got – ?

Conway: Because what I'm wondering is: could that have been a result of your call to Killion, could he have given that information out?

Sibert: Let me see if I don't have that teletype. I think I do. Here it is: 11/23/63 to the Director and SAC Dallas (photo 12).

Conway: Okay, and who originated that?

Sibert: I did.

Conway: But didn't you tell the review board that you did not send something out in the middle of the night?

Sibert: Let me see what –

Conway: It's after you got called. He's asking you about what time you were home. What we need to get back to here is the sequence – since we went from Specter's discrepancies to your report, 302. So that if you wouldn't have written the 302 –

Sibert: This would be going back to leaving the Naval Medical Center with the little jar, and we went over there to Bob Frazier to the FBI firearms lab and there is where I had to dictate this. It was two o'clock in the morning.

Conway: Okay, well we skipped that. So since I wasn't sure if you had written it and if you got it from Killion, which is what I supposed – let's talk about that.

Sibert: All I got from Killion was this part here about let's see – "Noted that Secret Service Agent Richard Johnsen" – this all came from Killion who was from Dallas – "turned over to the lab one 6.5-mm rifle bullet approximately a 25-caliber copper-alloy full jacket, which he advised was found on a stretcher in the emergency room at Dallas hospital." So I never saw that at all. That came in, but I got it from Killion, because I'm over at Bethesda calling when the autopsy was being done – calling over to the FBI laboratory and Killion tells me that Johnsen is coming, bringing this bullet into the lab, you see, from Dallas.

Conway: Okay.

Sibert: Things were happening that night!

Conway: Okay. But, also, you talk here about that total body X-ray and autopsy review of one bullet entered the back of head and, therefore, emerged through the top of skull.

Sibert: Now wait a minute –

Conway: But a few minutes ago when we were talking –

Sibert: And therefore emerged through the top – ?

Conway: Yeah. Because we were talking a few minutes ago about not knowing the direction, so I'm wondering if those are your words, or if you – see where it says, "total body X-ray on autopsy"?

Sibert: Yes, yes.

Conway: "One bullet entered back of head and – "

Sibert: " – and emerged from the top of the skull." Right, that's from Humes. He was the one saying that. "And a piece of skull, measuring ... later flown in from Dallas hospital the next day ... Bethesda ... the skull ... metal particles. " He X- rayed that and it had metal fragments on it –

Conway: Okay, so go back to your statement to Specter – I'll continue because you said in your notes, in your notes, not his – page 3 – the first question: "Did Humes or Finck express an opinion as to whether the bullet went in the back? Was it the point of entry or the point of exit?" and you said, "We recall no such discussion. "

Sibert: Wait, wait, this was my notes?

Conway: Yes.

Sibert: Yes here: "Prior to SA Sibert's calling the FBI lab, did either Humes or Finck state an opinion that the bullet wound in the back was a point of entry or a point of exit?" That's the bullet wound in the back.

Conway: In the back.

Sibert: "We can recall no such discussion.

Conway: Okay.

Sibert: But there was nothing mentioned about that head wound there.

Conway: Right.

Sibert: In my report right there, but Humes said over here –

Conway: Okay, so what you were saying is: there was no discussion as to the back wound, but there was as to the head wound.

Sibert: Yes.

Conway: Okay.

Sibert: Right there, look at how they say here, "Entered back of head – one bullet entered back of the head and thereafter emerged through the top of the skull."

Conway: And that is from the –

Sibert: It had a hit in the back here and blew this piece out, and that was Humes' assumption that night.

Conway: Okay.

Sibert: And then that's a piece that was flown in that they found in the limousine and they flew that in that night and Humes took it and X-rayed it and found metal fragments on the edges of that, where the projectile had hit. So does that clear it up?

Conway: Yes. Yes it does, because, when I was reading through this not knowing that you had written it for sure, I guessed that –

Sibert: But this was taken from what he said that night and we hadn't even dictated our FD 302 or nothing. This was just material I had to let Dallas, the office of origin, know what transpired there that night. (Note: This topic is revisited on page 381)

Conway: This is real important because it comes before the 302.

Sibert: Oh yes.

Conway: It's really the first thing that you put out into the field.

Sibert: Right, this was Saturday morning at two o'clock and I think the 302 was dictated the following Tuesday, because the day of mourning was Monday.

Conway: I just wanted to get that in there.

Sibert: That's good.

Conway: In the sequence of the reports.

Sibert: No, that's very important to know.

Conway: We needed to revisit that.

Law: At least we have that part cleared up.

Conway: It's frustrating when you read these depositions and you're not there and you think, "Why are they asking this?"

Sibert: Yes. Anything that pertained to me at that deposition is right here. This goes back there to the House Select Committee on Assassinations stuff – [Donald] Purdy and those guys – and anything with questions about, they gave it to me. O'Neill and I had to go correct the stuff because – one funny thing here if you like a laugh – I was dictating a deposition over there and I said something about Arlen Specter, and I got the recording back for corrections and it said, "Our inspector." So I made that correction. But there was a lot of stuff that we had to correct in those things, and when I tried to describe what the stencil process was I know I sound like a babbling idiot –

Law: Tell me what the stenciling process was.

Sibert: Well, you put the stencil sheet into a standard typewriter, and type directly onto it, not through the ribbon. Where the key hits, it punctures the stencil in the shape of the letter, and, after placement onto a drum, blue ink passes through the letter perforations onto paper. The drum is turned by a handle or by an electrical motor and prints as many pages as needed, one page at a time. Then you put another stencil in for the second page, and so forth. And after they get through with it they discard those stencils. But the original copy – you initialed that and it was your file copy.

Law: Was it possible to change anything on the original – ?

Sibert: The gal in the steno pool put correction fluid on there and the typewriter then cuts through that. It was probably special correction fluid.

Law: Take me back now. Let's go back to the beginning, from the time you are told that you and Frank O'Neill are going to stay with the president's body. Give me the sequence as you remember it. From the time that the airplane drew up, what did you see?

Sibert: Well, as I say, it was coming in for final approach, and we got out there and, of course, it had to taxi further on the tarmac. But we got a hold of Rowley and told him what the Bureau had instructed us to do. He put us in the number-two car and we were there when they were taking – I remember seeing them taking the casket off Air Force One. They had floodlights out there, the press was set up and everything, you know. They loaded it into this navy ambulance that was the first car in the motorcade.

Law: So you personally saw them unload that casket and put it into the ambulance?

Sibert: I can't say I saw them put it into the ambulance, because they were getting the motorcade together. O'Neill and I were getting into car number three. The president's valet was in three. Pamela Turner, who was a secretary to Jackie, she was in our car.

Conway: Did they say anything?

Sibert: Pamela Turner sobbed quite heavily. If you've read any books you can understand why (chuckles).

Law: This is the kind of thing that I'm always interested in. In either Frank O'Neill's or your testimony I read that George Thomas – I think that was the valet's name – how was he reacting to all this?

Sibert: Well, he was his valet. He was in the front seat. O'Neill and I and Pamela were in the rear, and then we had the driver up there. I don't know who he was, whether he was White House or navy or what, but the thing that impressed me the most of this deal was that Suitland Parkway runs from Andrews Air Force Base out through Maryland and hooks in on the East Capital Street in D.C. and everything crossing Suitland Parkway is an overpass – a series of them – and every one of those overpasses was lined with people. Of course it was on the radio and television. And all I can remember is, near dusk, people with white handkerchiefs to their eyes, crying. Another thing: the Metropolitan Police Department – of course it's now the State Police – met the motorcade with motorcycles, and once it started from Andrews Air Force Base until it got to Bethesda, it never stopped once. They leapfrogged. They would open up one intersection, then block off another, and we never stopped once.

Law: How fast do you think you were all going?

Sibert: Oh, they were doing probably thirty or forty, something like that.

Law: Do you remember how long it took you to get from –

Sibert: I have no idea.

Law: Were you in sight of the ambulance the whole time?

Sibert: Not the whole time – there were a few hills – but it was never too far and you knew it was ahead of you.

Law: Tell me the sequence after you get into Bethesda itself.

Sibert: Well, we got there in front of the main entrance. They stopped. They let Jackie out, and Admiral Burkley out, the president's personal physician. They went up into the tower – and some of the others – McHugh, the personal airforce aide of the president – they went up with them. They stayed up in the tower, and I think that there was communication between Burkley or someone would come down to the autopsy room telling them how it was going and conversing with them on that. You know, the interesting thing about this – I don't know whether you know this or not – but when Air Force One was within the aerial District of Washington, they hadn't made up their minds yet whether they were going to Walter Reed Hospital for this or to the Naval Medical Center. Were you aware of that?

Law: I had heard that they were deciding that on the way.

Sibert: Yes. They really hadn't decided much until they got there.

Law: Really? Until they got down to the ground?

Sibert: No, no. When they were getting cleared as they were approaching the Washington, D.C., area. Even when Humes and Boswell were interviewed by the JAMA guy they said it should have been done at Walter Reed because you had the Armed Forces Institute of Pathology right there at Walter Reed where Finck was from. They couldn't get over the fact that they were going to have to do the autopsy I think they even mentioned in the JAMA article there that they were ill-prepared. But the reason was Jack was a navy officer – the PT boat accident[7] and everything – Burkley was a navy admiral, and Bethesda is naval and Reed is army – and Jackie made that decision, I understand.

Law: When the ambulance and the rest of the motorcade pulled up, I understand that there was a period of time when the ambulance was just sitting out there and people didn't exactly know what to do. Do you remember that?

Sibert: I don't remember any long period of time. I'll tell you something – I don't know – but I think they ran a decoy ambulance out there. You've probably read that.

Law: I have read something about that.

Sibert: Yes. And maybe that's where this is – we were there in that number-three car, and once that stopped O'Neill and I got out and walked right up to and around the ambulance to the back of the building, to the autopsy room. And I said to Agent Kellerman, "We're with the FBI." I started to show them my credentials and he said, "Rowley's already told me about you." He looked at my credentials and admitted O'Neill and I in.

Law: The first ambulance, with the casket, would almost have to be the decoy ambulance, wouldn't it?

Sibert: Not from Andrews. I know that the ambulance that led the motorcade was the same one that we unloaded the casket from, out there behind the building.

Law: There's been talk of an ambulance chase –

Sibert: They even had a casket team that was supposed to handle all that there, and we never even saw them. They were chasing some ambulance around there and it was, I don't know –

Law: Well now, that brings me to the point where you walked back around –

Sibert: When they pulled up, Jackie and them got out of the ambulance and we got out of the number-three car. We walked on up to the ambulance there, be-

---

7. In August 1943, a Japanese destroyer rammed U.S. Navy patrol torpedo boat 109 skippered by John F. Kennedy.

cause we didn't know where they were going and wanted to find out. It was just a short distance right around the back.

Law: Do you remember any specific conversation from Admiral Burkley or anybody – Bobby Kennedy – who was there?

Sibert: Bobby wasn't there. See, he was in Washington. Oh, wait a minute, he was. I take it back. We're in Washington now, yes. No, we never conversed with – I never saw Bobby Kennedy at all. I think he got out and went up with Jackie. Yes, that's right.

Law: After you got out of the car did you immediately go around back or did you stay with the ambulance for a while?

Sibert: Well, we followed the ambulance.

Law: You followed the ambulance?

Sibert: Yes, right.

Law: When they went around back, you kind of walked back with it.

Sibert: Yes, well, maybe we trotted a little bit, you know? The entrance to the autopsy room was in the rear. It stopped right out in front of the building.

Law: After the ambulance pulled in the back, take me to what happened next.

Sibert: Well, that's when I identified myself to Kellerman. He said, "Rowley's already told me," and he opened the back and we helped get the casket out – O'Neill, Kellerman, Greer and myself – and I don't know whether some other people had come out of the autopsy room. We lifted that casket and put it on – I didn't remember a dolly being there when I was up at the ARRB – but I do remember since then. And they rolled it in, took it off the dolly, set it down and opened it. The body was in sheets – no clothing – and Humes made his statement about apparent tracheotomy and apparent surgery in the head area (photo 21).

Law: Let's go back. There was an honor guard that was supposed to take the casket in.

Sibert: Yes, that's the one I said. I don't know whether they got lost. They must have been somewhere because –

Law: I can't remember the page, I think its 399 of *Death of a President*,[8] where McHugh, I believe, said that he wanted to be –

Sibert: Is that one of these books?

Law: Yes right there, *Death of a President*.

---

8. William Manchester, *The Death of a President: November 1963* (Harper & Row, 1967)

(Sibert takes the copy of *The Death of a President* from his bookshelf and hands it to Law.)

Law: This is why I like to capture this stuff on film because if you pick up a book or something then I'll remember it and I can write it like that – that you went and picked up a book. Where are my glasses? I'm as blind as a potato and I have no night vision.

Sibert: You have eyes like a potato but you can't see, huh? You can tell I'm an old farm boy cutting the eyes out of potatoes to plant 'em.

Law (reading from *The Death of a President*): When an ambulance drew away from the curb they called, 'That's it – we'll guide you to the morgue.' At the morgue, Wehle, Bird, and the six enlisted men debarked and inspected each other's uniforms while awaiting some movement from the ambulance. It was still as still. The lieutenant crept up and peered inside. It was empty. Even the driver had gone. Panicky, they fled back and saw, among the shining cat's eyes, the uneasy face of Godfrey McHugh. Wehle and Bird colored. The Military District of Washington was meticulous about ceremony; for a casket team to lose a Commander-In-Chief's casket was an astounding lapse and after casting about bitterly – and vainly – for the two doctors, they reformed the tiny escort. The morgue was fronted by a concrete jetty approached along the left side by a short flight of cement steps. Since coffins were the most precious burden to pass this way, the stairs should have been designed for them. They weren't. They were too narrow and a steel handrail was an impediment to bearers. The railing thwarted a gesture of McHugh's. "This once," he thought, "it would be appropriate for a general to join hands with the five enlisted men," and he relieved the coast guardsman in the team. But navigating the ponderous (casket) required exceptional dexterity on the left. McHugh was too old. He tried, and kept trying until his eyes filled with frustration. It was no use. He was holding them all up, and motioning to the lanky coastguard youth, he capitulated.

Sibert: You know that's something they asked me up there [at the ARRB], and I don't remember any military unit there, casket team or anything. Now the guy dictated what happened there, but, boy, when we moved that casket in there, there was no one, no one that helped us.

Conway: And you had the Dallas casket, the big ceremonial casket

Sibert: Well, that big bronze casket – we carried it in there and we set it down and I was right there when they opened the lid and there was no mistaking the president. The big hair and everything. His facial features weren't disturbed at all.

Law: But you don't remember the sequence of –

Sibert: I don't remember anything.

Law: Anything like that? There was nothing like that when –

Sibert: First I ever heard of that was when I read something about it.

Law: Did that shock you when you read it?

Sibert: Not after everything that happened, no (chuckles).

Conway: There was something I don't want to forget to give you. Richard Lipsey was assistant to General Wehle, and I've got his testimony, which you will find very interesting, from the House Select Committee investigation. David Lifton got a copy of the tape, and I agreed to transcribe it. It's fascinating and I brought you a copy of it.

But, before that, I have something from Mary Ferrell, I don't know if you know her – she is a long-time researcher in this. She's your age. I will let you take a look at it. I have a little arrow down there – a very interesting statement (handing a funeral-home document to Sibert, photo 18).

Sibert (reading): … Metal shipping casket … [9]

Sibert (no longer reading): Well now, this was not a shipping casket. A shipping casket, like O'Connor or some of those guys have said that – this thing was an expensive bronze casket, and the handle had been damaged. I don't know whether that occurred during unloading at Andrews or loading there back in Dallas. But it was not a shipping – it was a display casket you'd call it, like you'd pick out at the mortuary to have your person laid away in.

Law: But did you remember the handle being damaged on it?

Sibert: Yes.

Conway: Okay. Well that's – I was just –

Sibert: As I say – we were right there. We helped carry this casket in. It came right out of the ambulance. We were with it all the time and were right there when they opened the lid before they put his body on the autopsy table.

Law: There was no wait in the hall? There is another book, *The Day Kennedy was Shot*[10] in which there's a passage that there, I think, four or five people – I don't remember if it mentions you or Mr. O'Neill – but they said there was a wait there for a few minutes when it was just them with the casket.

Sibert: We were never separated from the casket.

Law: Never?

Sibert: No.

Law: So from the time –

---

9. In the middle of the one-page document, under "Remarks," are the words, "Body removed from metal shipping casket at USNH at Bethesda" (photo 18).
10. Jim Bishop, *The Day Kennedy Was Shot* (Funk & Wagnalls, 1968).

Sibert: We took it into the anteroom, like off the autopsy room, where we put it right down on the floor, the casket right down on the floor. I remember that.

Law: And is that where you remember that they took the body out? Were they in the anteroom when they did it?

Sibert: The medical corpsmen came in and took the body out into the adjacent autopsy room and put it on the table in there.

Law: Okay. Did they come in with a conveyance? Some sort of conveyance and then take the body out and then put it on the conveyance?

Sibert: I don't remember. I think it was on that dolly, or that's not the word –

Conway: Gurney.

Sibert: Gurney. That's the word, the gurney. I don't remember whether they took the casket off the gurney out in the hall. I imagine they rolled it all in there and then took –

Law: And took him right out?

Sibert: You know, so much was going on, those are insignificant things.

Law: Sure.

Sibert: Like they asked me at the ARRB, "Was there a telephone in the autopsy room?" I said that was the least of my worries. I remember going down – there was this guard – and we went into another room where I was by myself to call Killion.

Law: Okay, so tell me about the sequence of events from the time we have the casket with the body inside the morgue. What happens at that point?

Sibert: All right. The medical personnel, or corpsmen, put the body up on the autopsy table. That's about the time when they said, "Well, we're going to clear everybody out of here now, and you have to go out into the hall. "

Law: Did this happen as soon as they took the body out and they put it on the table?

Sibert: Well, there was some other stuff going on and I think this was time for communication between Bobby and Jackie, hooked in with Burkley and Humes – and what they were going to do.

Law: Was there a period of time before they decided what was going to happen next?

Sibert: Yes, yes. Well, this was the preparation, about 7:17 or something like that. I think I said that the first incision was made at 8:00 so you had in this intervening time here, conferences between them, all the photographs taken, at that time. We were excluded from the room then.

Law: Okay. We have the body on the table, and then they unwrap the head.

Sibert: No, they unwrapped the head before, this here again is the sequence. My recollection – yes, that's right – because that head was just blood soaked and it wasn't all covered up, his face wasn't all covered up because I remember you could definitely see his face.

Conway: Were they in the anteroom when they unwrapped him, or when they brought him into the main –

Sibert: I couldn't say for sure.

Conway: This is a drawing of the morgue area (photo 11), if that helps you remember.

Sibert: I remember that gallery. Cooler room, I'm wondering if that's what –

Law: Maybe you were in the cooler room?

Sibert: I called it an anteroom, but probably that –

Law: I think other people have called it an anteroom too, the cooler room. But you don't remember whether they took the body out at that point –

Sibert: I would think, I don't know, this is just reasoning, but they had corpsmen that were carrying, you know, lifting him out of the casket onto the autopsy table and I can't – because I was talking with O'Neill. When I saw what we were up against there, I said, "We've got to get the names of everybody in this autopsy room," and I was probably talking with Kellerman or someone else there. But when they got him on – the only thing I remember is he was removed from there, put on the autopsy table and they cleared everybody out.

Law: Now this is after or before they removed the wrapping?

Sibert: I can't say. I don't know whether the wrappings were taken off in the anteroom or on the autopsy table.

Law: Before they started the X-rays, he was unwrapped?

Sibert: Oh they had to. Yes. They were taking photographs then – the head wounds and everything were all unwrapped, tracheotomy and all that.

Law: What do you remember about the wrappings themselves.

Sibert: Well one, as I recall, the body was wrapped in one, but the head area was in a separate sheet and that was just blood soaked as it could be.

Law: Do you remember whether there were any towels involved in the wrapping of the head?

Sibert: I can't remember any towels in connection with the body. There probably was some up on the – maybe around – the autopsy table. I don't remember that.

Law: But he didn't have any towels wrapped? It was just sheets?

Sibert: Sheets. The body was wrapped in sheets. And this business of body bags – I had it out with Lifton on that. I let him know. I said, "Look, I was a combat squadron commander. When I came back I was grounded due to an injury

I picked up over there. I was a base-operations officer and my job was to go out to all the crashes. So, believe me, I know what a body bag is. There were mountains – you'd have to drive the ambulance as close as you could – go up with the body bags and carry the bodies down that you pulled out of the crash scene." So I don't know where that guy got body bag, but they say they wrapped it in sheets over there at Parkland too.

Law: Now we have him unwrapped and on the table; is that when the order was given to have pictures and X-rays done?

Sibert: Yes. They just cleared us – I don't remember who said they were going to take X-rays and photographs and they cleared everybody out.

Law: Do you remember how long that process took?

Sibert: It was a considerable period of time. Probably close to 45 minutes, something like that.

Law: So that's how long you were in the cooler room or the anteroom?

Sibert: Maybe out in the hall.

Law: Out in the hall?

Sibert: Yes. We were excluded from where they were working. We had no idea what was going on – X-rays or nothin'.

Law: And then they brought you back in right after that.

Sibert: Yes. We were allowed to go back in.

Conway: While you were in the hall, was that where you had the conversation with Greer and Kellerman?

Sibert: I don't remember. During that night, we went out to eat together during a break, when we were having a break there in the autopsy. And when we went out, I think O'Neill was with Kellerman and I was with Bill Greer. Both those guys are dead now, you know? But the four of us never were together. We always wanted one agent there in the autopsy room at all times while it was going on.

Law: What were your first impressions, that you can remember now? After the X-rays and photographs had been taken and you returned to the president on the table, tell me about the wounds. What did you see?

Sibert: Well, we were able to look at that tracheotomy and it was very prevalent. Of course we didn't know anything about – the transfer there at Dallas you know, and I don't think the autopsy physicians knew – they hadn't had time – unless they'd talked to someone before the autopsy and, of course, they didn't say anything like that. The thing I remember was this massive head wound. I mean we're talking about something that was 3'/a inches long and about that size.

Law: Can you take your hand and put it back and tell me where –

Sibert: Yes, it was right back in here (indicates right rear area of the head, behind and above the ear).

Law: I think at one point before the Records Review Board you said that the wound was matted together and hard to see. Was it you who said that?

Sibert: No.

"... about that size."

Law: Didn't you say that before the Review Board?

Sibert: The hair was matted, but there was no question – and I'll tell you the statement I made to Frank. We were both standing there looking into this massive hole in the head. I said, "Frank, think of all the top-secret material that is gone through that brain. And now look at it." I remember saying that to Frank.

Law: Was the wound basically all back here? Or did it have anything in the top area?

Sibert: I don't remember anything in the top of the head. Right in here was this big hole.

Law: Just a big hole there?

Sibert: Mmm. Matted hair, just dripped in blood.

Law: Very, very bloody?

Sibert: Oh my.

Law: I've had one person tell me –

Sibert: Well, if the impact was enough to put brain matter on the motorcycle cop riding on the left rear of that thing there, and all over Jackie and everything – then they had to scrub the limousine out that night, which was a stupid move.

Law: Had you ever seen a tracheotomy before that night?

Sibert: Not a tracheotomy, no.

Law: Tracheostomy?

Sibert: I've never seen one performed, no. The purpose of that is to sustain life, to get that tube in there. They had a little pulse although he was DOA when they took him out of the limousine. I mean that was such a wound, they couldn't – they realized that at Parkland too – but they gave it everything they could.

Law: The reason I ask is because at Parkland they said it was about as big as the end of your little finger.

Sibert: They said it had been enlarged. Yes.

Law: Yes.

Sibert: I've read that too, and all I can do is read it and say, "What happened?"

Law: I guess what I'm asking is: do you think it is overly large for a – I know you're not a medical person –

Sibert: Well, it's like – I thought that when I read that, Perry I think was the guy who did that – he said, "Well, give me a break. I've got to have it large enough to get the tube in there" and everything, you know – but there has been so much bartering back and forth from the Secret Service in Parkland, to get them to come round to the single-bullet theory.

Law: After you noticed the wound in the head – what were the procedures that you remember? Do you remember any conversations from the doctors at that point? I know it's all these years later, and it's hard to keep talking about it.

Sibert: Yes. I can't remember anything specific. Humes as I recall was making the face sheet and writing down some things and I – or not Humes, I mean Boswell – made the face sheet.

Law: Did you get a look at that, that night?

Sibert: I didn't get a good look at it that night. The first time I saw it was when it came out in the *National Enquirer*. They had a copy of it.

Law: The face sheet itself?

Sibert: And then, I think Humes was making the measurements and Boswell was making notes of that. Now I've also read that they think Humes made notes too, of course he burnt the stuff in his fireplace (chuckles). You name it and it happened on this one, I'll tell you.

Law: I'll hand you this and, just so that we know which one you are talking about, that's the so-called stare-of-death photograph (photo 1). Is that basically what he looked like as you recall?

Sibert: It was a large – this is about what it looked like when I saw it. Yes.

Conway: So it wasn't a neat surgical cut. It was open?

Sibert: Right. When he made the tracheotomy there at Parkland he made a surgical cut right over – well, he first said it looked like an entrance wound of the bullet – a small entrance wound compared with –

Law: Do you remember anything like that (photo 3)?

Sibert: I definitely remember that. That's just the way it looked – brain matter – and you could see that hair and blood and it's all – they showed me some pictures up there later on, and you've probably got copies, I think you sent them to me to look at. They were neat and I don't remember anything that neat. This is what I remember from that night.

Law: You recall the body looking like that, right after they took him out of the casket?

Sibert: I don't know what the time period was on it.

Law: But you do remember that –

Sibert: I'll tell you, I didn't see it. Keep in mind that these pictures – the first time I saw them was up at the ARRB deposition. These weren't even developed that night.

Law: But you do remember it looking pretty much like that.

Sibert: That's what the view looked like, yes.

Law: Okay, that's important to know. And how about this one? (photo 2) Pretty consistent with what you remember?

Sibert: Yes.

Law: How about the head-holder there?

Sibert: Yes, they asked me that and I can't remember what, either, I mean –

Law: And this one, do you remember a view like this? (photo 4)

Sibert: No. Right back here is where you would have had that massive wound right in here, and you see that's neat. I don't remember anything that neat. My thought was that that was probably taken after reconstruction was done. In other words, after from midnight until five after they got through doing what maybe they did. I notice you had a hand there with a rubber glove and maybe there was –

Law: Do you remember anything like this flap? Can you recall that? On the side here? Do you remember seeing that?

Sibert: No, I don't remember that.

Law: Okay. It's important for –

Sibert: You can see here there's his hairline down here on the neck, and this wound was right in –

Law: Right in that area?

Sibert: And I mean it was visible.

Law: It was very visible? So this does not match your memory then?

Sibert: No.

Law: Have you seen anything like that? (photo 5)

Sibert: I don't know what that is.

Law: Well, supposedly that is a shot of the notch in the bone, where the bullet either came in or went out.

Conway: If you look at the bottom. This is the neck. So this shows the hole.

Sibert: Now wait a minute. You lost me.

Conway: See, this would be his right ear behind this ruler. This is the back of his neck. That's the back of his head. That's the flap extending, and they are saying that that is a notch from a bullet.

Sibert: We did see that on the screen there on the X-rays that night – showing a lot of little fragments that showed up on the X-rays and everything you know, but we didn't see too many.

Law: This next one I'm going to show you is –

Sibert: I'm wondering maybe they did more X-rays after we were through.

Law: This one of course shows the back wound and it looks pretty far down (photo 6). That's the one that Specter or Gerald Ford had moved up to the base of the neck for clarification.

Sibert: For clarification of the single-bullet theory (chuckles).

Law: Now the wound there in the back – is that the one that you remember?

Sibert: Yep. That's the one that they didn't even know about at Parkland, because they never raised him up off the stretcher over there.

Law: Okay. This is a drawing that was made by one of the technicians of the back wound and what he thought might have happened to the bullet (photo 10). I have shown this to two other men who were there – technicians – and they said that they agree with it. The X-ray technician agreed with it, and one of the other –

Sibert: Meaning the bullet is still in there?

Law: They don't know where the bullet or the fragments went to. I wanted to get your opinion.

Sibert: Let's see, bullet entry, ribs – and the intercostal muscles – now this is his back. This is his back here right?

Law: Yes. Paul O'Connor did it, on the basis that they said that the bullet went in and went down and stopped. Jim Jenkins – Paul O'Connor's partner – told me that he thought that it had gone into the back and stopped. And I said that there was talk about bruising on one of the lungs where it had hit the tip of one of the lungs.

Sibert: There was nothing mentioned that night, before midnight, about a bruise, because they said there was no exit – that back wound. When I came back and told them about the bullet on the stretcher, he jumped right on that and said the bullet went in a short distance and the cardiac manipulation on his back and also on his chest, it fell out on the stretcher. Now that was what we left there with that night. The rest of this stuff was all conspired, as I see it, after Saturday morning when they talked with Parkland and realized that there was a bullet wound (in the anterior neck). He said that he realized – the way Humes talked in that one article there by JAMA – that in talking with them, it was easy to understand how that came through and didn't hit any bone and exited out through the throat, you know. Well, it was nothing like that at that time. That was all developed after we left.

Law: You don't think that's possible do you?

Sibert: I wouldn't know, because all I can know is what they, the doctors, thought when we left there at midnight, that there were two shots – the fatal wound and one in the back that worked its way out during cardiac manipulation – it didn't exit through the throat – they didn't know about the throat wound at all. That's the summation of it when we left.

I didn't see anything that looked so neat (photo 4). Not that night I didn't – that had to have been done as a result of cooperation between Humes or Boswell and the morticians in getting the body prepared for display and all. Of course they didn't have an open casket but, at least, for putting in the casket.

Law: For it to look that nice and neat, and the hair all in place, you think it would have to have been after some kind of reconstruction was done?

Sibert: That was done after midnight. As I say, for all intents and purposes the autopsy itself was over at midnight.

Law: Did the doctors hear anything about the direction of the bullet? Was there any information brought in that night from anyone of being shot from a building?

Sibert: Nothing was mentioned about Oswald. Nothing was mentioned about the book depository, or number of shots fired or anything.

Law: So, they had no idea. No information on that part of it at all came into the morgue?

Sibert: No, to my knowledge not. Of course, Burkley had to know. You know that's a thing I couldn't get over – why didn't Burkley – he was over there and I don't know whether he was in the trauma room in Dallas when they did the tracheotomy – but why didn't he – if I were Burkley and I'd been there, the first thing I'd say to Humes is, "This tracheotomy: we want you to know it was made over a bullet entry, or bullet wound. " Oh, there are so many things in here that – just, why? You know? Our hands were tied. I really never thought, I feel like I should have asked Humes, "Have you called Parkland?" before they even started that night. But as I told the ARRB, I said, "If I had done that, all it would have taken was some military guy there, the general or something, call over to the

Bureau and say, 'We've got an agent here trying to run the autopsy,' and I would have been on my way to Butte, Montana with cumulus nimbus clouds with hail coming out of them, on a disciplinary transfer" (laughs). If that happened now I could do it. In other words the FBI is in charge as a result of that new statute. I'd say, "Look before doing that you ought to call Parkland. You've got to find out what they've done."

Conway: You said that the doctors figured that the bullet entered from the rear and exited the top of the head. Let's talk about that, and if you could get out the autopsy photograph that shows the back of the head even though it doesn't show the big wound (photo 4), or maybe the one that is similar to what you said you remember (photo 3).

Sibert: I think the doctors probably figured that this came down from this angle. He could have been looking this way and it turned him this way and blows this piece out right here and just catches it like this and blows it out (from the top of the head). But they definitely thought that the piece had been blown out from the shot from the rear.

Conway: How did you feel about that?

Sibert: I didn't know anything. I would have had to have knowledge about the possible grassy knoll and all that stuff. But I was blank, you know? Here we are in Bethesda, Maryland, and they're in Dallas, Texas – and all that terrain over there – so I didn't have any feelings at all on it. All of this has come about now since I read this – you've probably read about that one sewer, that drain where they could have walked out. Well now, if they would have shot out of that and get this wound through the neck it would be possible from that angle then to blow a piece out of the top of the head. If it was forward from the grassy knoll. There are so many different –

Conway: The reason I want to ask you is that my sister is in law enforcement. She's a crime-scene expert, so in all the years –

Sibert: A what expert?

Conway: She's a crime-scene expert,

Sibert: Crime scene?

Conway: Blood spatter and all that. She's now retired, but she's a consultant. So, because she does work at home and I am at her house, And I see this stuff, and I'll ask her about a case and from her I've learned a lot – just enough to get me in trouble, I guess. But she tells me that when a shot goes through a body, she can tell the direction of the shot by the size of the wound.

Sibert: Sure, yes.

Conway: So my question –

Sibert: It's just a puncture when it goes in.

Conway: So with the huge wound in the back of the head why did they think the shot came from the back?

Sibert: They didn't know anything that night about the shots. The Bethesda doctors didn't know anything about how many shots were fired – I doubt if they knew much about the book depository. I don't have any way of knowing, but, Humes, I imagine, was in such a furor when his superior told him to come in – he was to do an autopsy on the President of the United States – he was planning on either a party or golfing that day, and you can imagine how that hits you. By their own admission, the body should have gone to Walter Reed because they weren't set up for it.

Law: But did they make a decision that night, that you recall, that it was an exit from the top of the head?

Sibert: No. The only thing they said was that that wound there was at a 45- degree angle into the back, which would indicate that the firing was coming from the rear. That's the only way it could be, if you didn't have any exit wound.

Law: But the doctors didn't make a determination as to the bullets coming in from the rear at all? There was no discussion of –

Sibert: Not that I can recall from that night.

Conway: It entered from the back and it pushed the bone out – where did it exit?

Sibert: Well, say I'm bent over, and you've got somebody up there shooting and if I'm over like this then it could hit here (back of the head) I guess, and explode here (top of the head). That's the only thing I can – how they come to arrive at that, I don't know. And they never had any Zapruder film or anything. But just to make the speculation, I think Humes jumped at that business about that bullet falling out in the cardiac manipulation and – boy – that's not based on anything scientific.

Conway: Have you seen the Zapruder film?

Sibert: Only on TV on the History Channel.

Conway: Would you like to look at it? I have it with me.

Sibert: Do you? Oh, I don't know. I think I've probably seen most of it. Of course the pertinent part is that part in Dealey Plaza anyway.

Conway: It only lasts a few seconds.

Law: Well, why don't we stop here, then you can get it ready and I'll put in a new tape.

(break)

Sibert: The only two bullet wounds that were mentioned that night were the massive wound (in the head) and the wound in the back.

Law: But there was absolutely no decision made, that you know of, by those doctors in terms of the direction he may have been hit from, in the head? No decision was made that night.

Sibert: I think that they were under the impression that it was from the rear due to the fact that you had this one bullet in the back.

Law: So you think that may have led them to the conclusion that he was hit in the back of the head?

Sibert: They may have known about the shots coming out of the book depository, but none of that was discussed during the autopsy or anything.

Conway: (viewing the Zapruder film) This is a close-up of –

Sibert: Connally.

Conway: This is of Connally in the front.

Sibert: He's [JFK] grabbing his throat, isn't he?

Conway: I think that is where they were trying to determine where the governor was shot.

Sibert: That's where [JFK] got hit in the throat or something, wasn't it? Yes. That's where the top of his head – there she goes back, and Clint Hill –

Conway: And what does that make you think when he's thrown to the back like that?

Sibert: You know, I don't know enough about the reaction to a bullet hitting him, really to – but some of them try to say that you would do just the opposite – if you get hit in the front you go forward and all that, but – and Connally swears to this day that he wasn't hit by the same bullet. When he died, he was still saying that. I don't know.

Conway: (noting Sibert's reaction to the film.) It's always hard to watch.

Sibert: What?

Conway: No matter how many times you see it, it's always hard to watch it.

Law: Frank O'Neill, when I asked him about this, said, about witnesses, "I have to go back to the witness that was there. He should know what happened." So, talking about Connally and saying that he wasn't hit by the first shot – Connally would know, he was there.

Sibert: Yes, I agree with that. I have always felt that too.

Conway: I'm going to ask you something personal.

Sibert: Something what?

Conway: I'm going to ask you something personal. What did you tell your family when you got home?

Sibert: Well, I'll tell you, I was so beat. I started out that morning, as I said, with the inspection and at 4:30 the next morning I get in, and I get in the bed and the phone starts ringing and everything. My wife didn't even know where I was at that night. If I was that late on something I would tell one of the other agents to call my home and tell her I was going to be late or something, you know. So I didn't have a chance to call. There were no cell phones back then – you're in the motorcade and all this stuff is starting, you can't say I'm going to call home. That's not quite the proper time. So, finally one of my agents, Gene Wimer, called and said, "Is Si home yet?" She said, "No, where is he at?" He said, "Well, when he gets home he's going to have something to tell you." He knew O'Neill and I were at the autopsy. So, when I came in the next day – but this stuff was all hush-hush. You didn't talk about it right after. I went to church Sunday, and the minister there – small congregation – he said, "We're honored this morning. One of our members is going to be in the honor guard at the rotunda for the president." I just shoved my elbow against my wife and just sat there and didn't say nothing, you know? But I thought, "If you only knew, buddy, somebody has been closer to it than that." But you never said anything and so it just wasn't discussed a lot. Not that the Bureau told you not to discuss it, but –

Law: You weren't under any kind of order not to talk about it?

Sibert: No, not like Bethesda – they got the orders that if anybody discussed that then you know, it was their career. Now you wouldn't have had that at Parkland – that's civilian – see that's the difference. But, as I say, what a shame. I mean, if Bobby Kennedy just hadn't ordered them back and – but there was so many things, assassination attempts on Castro and all that stuff. Oh, the whole thing stinks to the high heavens.

Law: We've gone through the procedures that they performed. Do you remember what the atmosphere was like in the morgue that night? What do you remember picking up on?

Sibert: Well, they asked me up there at the ARRB: "Was it rowdy and uncontrollable?" And I said that it wasn't, but it was a busy place because you had all this brass in there, the Military District of Washington, General Wehle – I'm trying to think – yes, he was the head of the Military District of Washington. You had Admiral Burkley, you had the head of the Naval Medical Center, Stover I think was his name, and all these guys that you know – of course, you don't have that happen every day – an autopsy on the president. So it wasn't rowdy or nothing like that, but it was just – I felt sorry for Humes. I felt sorry for him. He had beads of perspiration all over him. You could tell he was under pressure.

Law: He was under a great deal of pressure?

Sibert: Oh, there's no doubt about it. I mean he was doing an autopsy of the president, and probably a lot of his had been administrative work reviewing autopsies that had been done previously. And then there was all that brass in there, that rank, both army and navy –

Law: You remember high-ranking officials?

Sibert: Oh sure, I've got them in my 302 there.

Law: How many people would you say were in the morgue that night?

Sibert: They were off and on, some of them would come in for something, maybe – here again you don't know what was transferred, what kind of messages transferred from the navy, maybe that they had gotten from Parkland or something, to Humes, because you're not privy to that. There not going to come around and tell you all that. I'm not running the autopsy, we don't have any jurisdiction. We were just there to witness it and take the bullets that were removed.

Law: Was it hard to get in and out of the autopsy?

Sibert: Oh brother, they had security there. They had a marine or navy guy about every 15 feet of those halls. As I said, when I went to make that phone call they had a fellow, the sentry there, take me down to the room and he stayed there with me and followed me back.

Law: So, every time you left somewhere, like the time you went to talk or –

Sibert: Well, when we went into the cafeteria – I don't think they had somebody with us then. But when I asked for a phone, I had an escort to the next room to use a phone to call Killion.

Law: Do you remember when they removed the brain? Were you present for that?

Sibert: That is something that's hazy in my mind. I can't – most of it was blown out. I remember that. When you looked in there you just didn't look – you know, you look at a picture, an anatomical picture of a brain and it's all – there was nothing like that. There was just a cavity.

Law: Okay, that's a good point. But go back to – they brought him in and unwrapped the head and you looked at the wound. When you first looked into the cavity what did you see?

Sibert: Just a big hole, and some of that brain there that was in that one picture – brain matter or the cranium, but I don't have recollections of a perfect brain in there that they would have cut away and removed.

Law: Would you say there was like, just brain matter?

Sibert: As I recall it, brain matter, yes that's –

Law: Just pieces of brain? Maybe half a handful? A handful?

Sibert: I don't know, I wouldn't even try to –

Law: Nothing that would be attached and they would have to bring out?

Sibert: No, I don't remember anything that they would have cut in there and bring out the whole brain.

Law: And you saw the head right after they –

Sibert: Yes, right.

Law: So, you were right there.

Sibert: While they did the autopsy, yes.

Law: You were right there able to look right into the head right after they took and –

Sibert: Maybe not all the time, but you could move up there and see it. You know we were right behind, like those pictures with the headrest, we were right behind there.

Law: Back to the atmosphere of the morgue, they were going in and out. There's been talk of either you or Mr. O'Neill being kept out of the room for some length of time.

Sibert: We were never – that was a statement made that we were kept out of the room – we were never barred from that autopsy room with the exception of when everybody got out for the radiology work and the photographs.

Law: And that was the only time?

Sibert: Somewhere I read that they wouldn't give us access. That never happened.

Law: Do you remember the person in this photograph? (photo 13) His name is Dennis David.

Sibert: I don't recall.

Law: He said that at some point, he was asked if he could type and he said that he could, and he had a clearance up to and including secret. So an agent went with him and he typed up a memorandum. After that was done, there were fragments of bullets that supposedly came from JFK's head and he said he poured them out in his hand and was able to look at them and then the agent took the memo that he had typed, took the ribbon out of the typewriter, and took all that stuff. And basically I'm asking: were you or Mr. O'Neill the agent?

Sibert: I don't remember anything like that.

Law: Nothing like that happened.

Sibert: The only thing I remember being taken out were two slivers that were put in that jar, and somebody even – some high-ranking guy – even said a bullet rolled out – you probably remember that.

Law: That was Osborne, Captain David Osborne, who said that. Okay, do you remember this? I talked recently with John Stover about this. An X-ray technician, said that at some point when they lifted the body up a bullet fragment fell out of the back, and he said, "I'm the only person who remembers that, nobody else remembers it." When I had John Stover on the telephone, I asked him about that and I was not expecting to get any kind of answer. But, he said, "Well, there was a bullet," and he said they took that. He said it was either FBI or Secret Service who said, "Well, we want that," and they took it. Do you remember anything like that?

Conway: That was Stover?

Law: That was John Stover (photo 9) who told me that.

Sibert: About the size of the bullet that the Italian rifle would –

Law: Yes.

Sibert: I don't remember a thing. I've read that in books.

Law: Do you remember seeing this X-ray (photo 7) that night?

Sibert: No. I don't remember seeing an X-ray like that.

Law: Nothing like that at all? Do you remember this at all? This is an X-ray (photo 8) from the side view.

Sibert: No. I don't remember seeing an X-ray like that. The only X-rays we saw was what he put up on the screen and as I remember there was just, I don't remember how many there were, but not very many. So these –

Law: Not too many?

Sibert: Other pictures, X-rays and stuff – we weren't exposed to any of that.

Law: Anything similar?

Sibert: No.

Law: So you don't remember anything at all even close to this?

Sibert: No.

Law: This is a –

Conway: A representation, (photo 15)

Law: Yes, a representation – who did these?

Conway: Boswell.

Law: Would you say that was pretty accurate?

Sibert: Now this is from the back is it? I mean it's showing teeth, but I assume it's probably from the back, right? Parietal bone –

Conway: Yes.

Sibert: Yes. We didn't see any of the paperwork that Boswell did.

Law: Well, this is basically just representing the size of the wound.

Sibert: Oh.

Conway: He did that on a model of a skull, and Doug Home, whom you met, copied what was on the skull. So, Boswell did not draw on this paper, that was Doug.

Sibert: Well, here they've got an entry wound and I don't remember anything like that. Now here would be the ear out here and, as I see it, this entry wound would be where this big bone piece that was missing there – I don't remember anything like that.

Law: How about from the side? (photo 16) Would you say that –

Sibert: I don't remember that bone being that far forward on the skull. In other words, they're saying that all this came – missing bone – down here, missing bone – but of course, I've even often wondered if the marksman didn't use an explosive bullet that exploded on impact. "Large defect – missing bone." I don't remember anything down this far on the frontal, the forehead. You're about at the hairline here.

Law: Was there any damage to his forehead that you remember?

Sibert: No. I don't remember any at all.

Law: Now that's a view from the front, (photo 17) Do you remember anything missing – that big, that large?

Sibert: "Margin of large defect – missing bone." Now do they mean this part right in here?

Conway: I think that whole –

Sibert: This up to here?

Conway: That, yes.

Sibert: I don't remember anything like that.

Law: Nothing that large?

Sibert: No.

Law: I know I've asked you this before in phone conversations – but, do you remember a wound in the hairline?

Sibert: None.

Law: To your knowledge there was no wound in the hairline?

Sibert: None that I observed, or none that was mentioned within my hearing.

Law: Do you think if they would have seen it you would have heard them say, "Here's this wound?"

Sibert: Yes, well, if within earshot. If it was being discussed between Boswell and Humes we would certainly have heard it, I think.

Law: So there was no discussion between the two of them?

Sibert: No, not that I can recall.

Law: Anything else?

Conway: The only thing I have left is the Lipsey piece – the man who I told you gave the testimony that I transcribed – he stated he was doing the same thing that you guys were doing. He was there to observe, and to stay with the body.

Sibert: Who was he with?

Conway: Richard Lipsey was General Wehle's assistant or chief of staff.

Sibert: Wehle – that's the one that I think was the head of the Military District of Washington.

Conway: Right, exactly. Now he gives a description of – he also thought he was told that there was a decoy ambulance and –

Sibert: We weren't even told that that night. O'Neill and I weren't even aware of any of that kind of stuff that night.

Conway: (reading from the HSCA deposition): I (Lipsey) can remember in my own mind – they're trying to read something into it that didn't happen. One book came out that he was shot from three different angles. Another report came out he was only shot once. Another said he was shot seven times. Everybody had their own versions of what happened – how many sounds they heard and the angles of fire they came from. I definitely remember the doctors commenting they were convinced the shots came from the same direction and from the same type of weapon – and it was three shots.

> Question: Did the doctors state that three separate bullets had struck?

> Lipsey: This is one other thing, that to the best of my memory, today, and re-membering what I thought about when all these reports came out, absolutely unequivocally yes, they were convinced that he had been shot three times.

Sibert: I don't see how they could say that, because, you know, they say that the third shot hit the curb. It was a miss. And you had one in the single-bullet theory now, and the fatal wound up here and the third shot that hit the curb, but those doctors didn't know anything about the shot hitting the curb that night. They hadn't even –

Conway: He drew – you remember when you drew on the little sketch for the House Select Committee? – well Lipsey did the same thing. He says one wound on the right side of his head, one in the upper part of his neck and one on the lower part of his neck (photos 19 and 19a).

Sibert: Upper part of his neck?

Conway: Lipsey is saying one was on the side of the head, one was in the hair-line, which he calls the upper part of the neck and then the lower part of his neck, which would be the shoulder or back or whatever you want.

Sibert: Scapula, yes.

Conway: He says (reading): One point was just blown away. This point was just blown away.

Sibert: Yes, that's your –

Conway: Lipsey says (reading): I just can't remember whether there was a point of entrance and then the blown away part or whether it – he must have been sitting like this and then hit like this – and it just blew that away or if it ripped the whole section away.

Question: Either of those two possibilities means one bullet to the head, I think.

Lipsey: Right. One bullet to the head. Then one bullet to the lower head.

Question: Where did that bullet exit?

Lipsey: That's the bullet that exited right here.

Question: The throat.

Conway: Lipsey was saying that you had the back of the head and the large wound, and here's the small hole in the hairline. Okay, then, we've got the back wound and then we've got the throat wound in the front. The bullet went in and came out the throat. I believe that's what he's saying.

Sibert: This would be the single-bullet theory, coming out the throat in the front.

Conway: Yes.

Sibert: Now, I don't recall anything about this wound down here in the hairline.

Conway: But I'm going to give you this, since he claims to be in the room observing in the same type of capacity as you guys –

Sibert: What was his name?

Conway: Richard Lipsey.

Sibert: That wasn't on the list of names I had there.

Conway: He was in the gallery.

Sibert: Oh yes.

Conway: Did you know that the FBI deported a French terrorist from Dallas?

Sibert: Reported a what?

Conway: Deported a French terrorist – who was known to be trying to kill De Gaulle – from Dallas –

Sibert: Is that right?

Conway: – on November 22?

Sibert: I haven't heard that.

Conway: I'll send you that. We found –

Sibert: I'll believe anything now.

Conway: Well, he was – you know, I say terrorist. He was an assassin, and they –

Sibert: Professional hit man?

Conway: [Jean] Souetre was his name. And he was tracking the president. He was in Fort Worth that morning and in Dallas that afternoon, and the French were watching him because De Gaulle was going to Mexico, and they were trying to find out everywhere he was going, like our people should do, and they realized that he was in Dallas and they had him deported. That was never – that information was never given to the Warren Commission, and years later we found a document on it – CIA files.

Sibert: I never heard that before. But you take all those reports of people, you know, that were up there on the grassy knoll, and they flashed badges and Secret Service – because they didn't have any agents up there – and, I'll tell you, there was so much –

Conway: You need to come to Dallas. You could have fun at my house – we have so much I could show you.

(Break)

Law: I want to go back to Greer and Kellerman for a moment. I want to know – when you first saw them – what was their demeanor?

Sibert: Well, the first time we saw them was when we helped them unload the casket, and they were business-like, I mean they weren't shook up. I mean not to the point where they were shaky or anything like that. I wouldn't characterize them like that at all. There was a lot of remorse there about what happened – of course, that's only natural. I don't care who you are, you'd feel that way. But, we talked with them casually when we left the autopsy room to eat. I mean they were coherent and logical and everything. Nothing unusual.

Law: Do you think they were shaken by the events or were they –

Sibert: Oh, I'm sure.

Law: – in a stone professional mode of, "Okay, now we're here – "

Sibert: Well, I think they were shaken – I don't know how to characterize it, but –

Law: When I was talking to your partner, Frank O'Neill, he said that when he was at the [ARRB] they handed him a picture that supposedly was of President Kennedy's brain. When they said, "Does this resemble President Kennedy's brain in any way that you remember?" he said, "No, it doesn't." He said possibly if somebody says it is then it is, but he said, "This isn't as I remember it."

391

Sibert: I think maybe they asked me that too, about the brain. I told them that my recollection was that the only thing I knew about the brain was how it was shot up, and had been blown all over her and over the guy on the motorcycle. Brains everywhere. As I mentioned a while ago, I have no recollections of a brain that you could describe like the anatomical picture you see of the brain, as in some of those books, you know? And when I read that there, about the two brains, that's a new one on me, too.

Law: Well, apparently they did two examinations.

Sibert: Two examinations of his brains. That's a new one on me. I don't – wouldn't have anything to add to that. I have no knowledge at all.

Law: What do you think about that? That's where a lot of these people get confused about certain things that have happened, and they point to conspiracy because now we have records that say that kind of thing.

Sibert: Well, I wouldn't even have any thoughts on that because there was nothing – and the first time I heard this was when I read it in the book, you know? And I think, "It certainly had nothing to do with what happened that night. "

Law: Well, we wouldn't have known about it had it not been for Doug Horne's work.

Sibert: Yeah. That's the first I – when I read that – that was a complete surprise to me.

Conway: Have you ever read Kellerman's testimony before the Warren Commission?

Sibert: No.

Conway: Well, I'll give you that. It's very interesting. He talked about during the X-rays – the bullet fragments – and Specter says (reading): Now did you observe during the course of the autopsy, bullet fragments which you might describe as little stars?

> **Kellerman:** Yes, of the numerous X-rays that were taken mainly of the skull, the head, the reason for it was that through all the probing which these gentlemen were trying to pick up little pieces of evidence in the form of shell fragments, they were unable to locate any. From the X-rays, when they placed the X-ray up against the light, the whole head was like a little mass of stars. There must have been thirty, forty lights where these pieces were so minute that they couldn't be reached. However, all through the series of X-rays, this was the one that they found. Through X-ray that was above the right eye and they removed it. How big a piece –

Sibert: Wait a minute now, above the right eye?

Conway: Yes.

Sibert: I remember – I think I heard the term "milky way" used.

Conway: Like the milky way.

Sibert: Yeah. Somewhere that came along, and whether it was spoken that night afterwards or something – or comment on the X-rays – it was like you said, these small, minute particles that could be small little stars there. I'll tell you, that comes back to that statement I made a while ago – I'm wondering if this wasn't an explosive bullet. You know, there are bullets that are made that way and somewhere I was reading about where they interviewed some guy – I think it was on the History Channel – where he said where they had used an explosive bullet. So, when that would explode, you would get all kinds of particles and metals and everything in there, you know?

Law: I'm not a gun expert, but as far as I know – what they are saying was – the bullet that did the damage was a copper-jacketed bullet, not made to fragment.

Sibert: Yeah, well, the magic bullet was one that doesn't fragmentize. The one that went through – the bullet through the back of the neck and came out here and hit Connally and all that stuff – that was a copper-jacketed bullet.

Conway: So, do you remember specifically where the two fragments that you put in the specimen jar came from?

Sibert: He didn't even state that. He got them out of the brain, and he just put them in this bottle and it had a black cap on it. And Frank and I put FXO, JWS, the date, and screwed the cap on it and took it over there. So, up there at the ARRB they said, "Does this bring back any memories? And I said, "Yeah. That's my initials. "

Conway: Isn't that amazing? I read that in the deposition where they said, "Look behind you."

Law: Yeah.

Conway: They just magically appeared.

Law: What did it feel like when you saw that again after all those years?

Sibert: Well, it brought back a lot of memories of 34 years before. But you almost knew that as small, minute, as those fragments were, that you're not going to get any identification like you could with a regular bullet. You can take that one they supposedly found on the stretcher and get the measurements of it and caliber and all that stuff – you can't get any of that stuff off of minute fragments.

Conway: But that X-ray that has that large fragment behind the eye, now Kellerman says – where I was reading – that the fragment that was removed from behind the eye was about as big as the tip of a match head, a little larger. That's what he said.

Sibert: Tip of a match?

Conway: Yes.

Law: And I guess they're talking about this (pointing to the 6.5 mm "slice" in the AP X-ray; photo 7a).

Conway: Well, that's bigger though –

Sibert: Yeah, that's the size of – that's supposed to be about the size of the caliber that was fired out of Oswald's rifle. See – there was nothing ever mentioned about that in there.

Law: They never mentioned that?

Sibert: No, not that. In fact, one of these books right here said they wondered if that wasn't superimposed on the X-rays or inserted in there, you know, how you can do with photography and stuff now. But nothing was mentioned that night about a projectile on the side or something like that being in there.

Law: Do you remember the feeling when they couldn't find the bullet?

Sibert: Yeah – it was frustration. They said, "There's no exit! " This was the words that they used probing that, and that's when I went in and made this call, see? And that's when Humes assumed that was why there was no exit, because this bullet had just gone in a short ways and cardiac manipulation – when they tried to resuscitate the president, which was an impossibility – it fell out on the stretcher, out of his back.

Conway: Do you remember when the Review Board asked you about a statement in a report when the fragment was brought in to the autopsy room?

Sibert: The fragment or the piece of skull?

Conway: I'm sorry, the piece of skull. It had been removed from the president's head? Do you remember them asking about that?

Sibert: Yeah, and I think I picked that up from the Secret Service agent who had brought it in there and gave it to Humes. I think that, of course when you know, and then later on in the report it was said they found it in the floor of the limousine. So it had been blown out when it hit the president's skull. But "removed," that sounds like it might have been surgery.

Conway: I know.

Sibert: But I think that's the only thing I can think of that was –

Conway: Well, I will tell you, in Kellerman's testimony he uses the same word.

Sibert: He does?

Conway: Yeah.

Sibert: Maybe I picked it up from Kellerman that night. I don't know.

Conway (reading from Kellerman's Warren Commission testimony): I would like your understanding and your observations of the four wounds on President Kennedy.

Kellerman: Okay, this all transpired in the morgue of the Naval Hospital in Bethesda. He had a large wound, this size.

Specter: Indicating a circle with your finger of the diameter of 5 inches, would that be approximately correct?

Kellerman: Yes, circular yes, on this part of the head.

Specter: Indicating the rear portion of the head.

Kellerman: Yes.

Specter: More to the right side of the head?

Kellerman: Right. This was removed.

Specter: When you say this was removed, what do you mean by this?

Kellerman: The skull part was removed.

Specter: All right.

Sibert: He meant it was removed from the remainder of the skull, see? But I could have picked that up, because Kellerman was in charge of that detail, and if a Secret Service agent had have been out where the limousine was and got that and brought it in to Dallas there, and then they flew into Bethesda that night, and brought it in, Kellerman would have been the one that might have asked, "Where did this come from?" And they said, "Removed from the president's skull," or something, and that's where I picked it up.

Conway: Right. And after that Ford says, "Above the ear and back?" Like he's never heard that before. And Kellerman says, "To the left of the ear, sir, and a little high, yes, about right in here." And Specter says again, "When you say, 'removed,' did you mean it was absent when you saw him or taken off by the doctor?" And Kellerman says, "It was absent when I saw him." And Specter says, "Fine."

Sibert: It was absent all right. That's the big cavity

Conway. Yeah, so –

Sibert: I outlined it here (produces a piece of paper with the outline of the piece of skull bone). That's the size of it – this outline – that's how big that piece was (photo 20).

Conway: That's huge! I mean, that's the top of your head. And when did you do this?

Sibert: Oh, when I was reading, I mean off of the autopsy report, let's see –

Conway: What book is that?

Sibert: This is *The Second Oswald* by Popkin.[11]

---

11. Richard H. Popkin, The Second Oswald (Yestermorrow, 1966)

Conway: Oh yes, that's the one that had your 302.

Sibert: That's when Lifton called me, here's where he got that originally, I think, because it was published, I don't know how they got it out of – .

Conway: This jumped out at me when I was reading it.

Sibert: (reading): Also, during the latter stages of the autopsy, a piece of skull measuring 10 by 6.5 cm was brought to Dr. Humes who was instructed that this had been removed from the president's skull. Immediately this section of skull was X-rayed at which time it was determined by Humes that one corner of it revealed minute metal particles. Inspection of this area disclosed the chipping off of the area.

Sibert (no longer reading): But, somewhere else I think I read what that other measurement was.

Conway: This would be 3.9 inches by 2.5 inches (photo 20).

Sibert: That's right, 3.9 inches.

Conway: That's how huge that bone was that they brought from Dallas.

Sibert: Yeah. But of course it wasn't that shape because it was more like an oval shape or raggedy, you know. But that's a large piece of skull to be missing. So you can see why, when a doctor sees that much out, he might think that somebody had –

Law: You told us that you had some training in –

Sibert: Well, I had a 5-hour anatomy course.

Law: Did you do any work on cadavers?

Sibert: Yeah, we worked on cadavers and the origin and insertions of muscles but, you trace them and you could tell the skeletons were of old people.

Law: Had you, prior to this, seen gunshot wounds?

Sibert: No. The autopsies that I'd seen before that one included a kid who had been raped and assaulted. The other was a clerk's wife that had a brain hemorrhage and they had to take the cap off. She was about 3 months pregnant and I witnessed that one. But this was the first gunshot autopsy that I had witnessed, yes.

Law: Just based on your observations –

Sibert: Let me say – I don't consider myself a medical expert. I mean, I just had a little introductory knowledge. I'd been around cadavers and seen the cap taken off of the skull and that sort of thing, so my tongue didn't fly open that night.

Law: One of the people that I have interviewed said normally they had to take the skullcap off to remove the brain, but not in Kennedy's case because there was already a large hole in the head.

Sibert: Oh yes, you could look right down in his head.

Law: David Lifton has made much of the surgery issue –

Sibert: Surgery of the head area.

Law: I have to ask you about surgery of the head area.

Sibert: Where he picked that up was in Humes's first statement when that body came in and they unwrapped it. Tracheotomy, surgery in the head area (photo 21). If I had asked Humes later on and pinned him down, of course he might have said, "Well, now that I've got this bone piece here, that was flown – this big gaping hole probably wasn't surgery in the head. It was blown out. But that never happened.

Conway: Was the scalp torn out?

Sibert: It was jagged there, where that bone had been – it wasn't just like you'd take a knife or a scalpel and get it. It was jagged.

Conway: But you know, in the photograph it does look like a straight edge.

Sibert: Well –

Conway: I know it does. To look at the pictures, it does.

Sibert: My recollection was it was just blown out you know, not like a straight line like you would take a scalpel had cut it out. It wasn't a neat cut like that.

Law: I get confused trying to orient these things because in some pictures, it looks like this part of the skull is gone and –

Sibert: Not the top, in the back. Over to the right side (places his right hand behind and above the ear).

Law: If I'm remembering right, in Dallas, there was a nurse Hinchcliff?

Sibert: Yeah, there was a Hinchcliff there.

Law: She said that the only way you could see the wound was if you lifted the head up and looked. Would you say that was true?

Sibert: That statement would be based on if they had a headrest, where they had his head up, then it would really show, see? Maybe the head was raised by towels – headrest – I don't remember there – but there was no problems looking right into it, just like if you lie on two pillows, I mean your head's going to be higher than on one, and there at Bethesda there was no problem at all to see the head wound – I mean if you were looking at it from the rear. But it could have been that his head was down a little bit on the stretcher, or – I don't know, I'm just supposing – maybe that would be her basis for not seeing the wound. But boy, it was prevalent. You couldn't miss that. That was the outstanding thing of the injuries.

Law: Let's see if I can locate the picture. This is an oversized view, of course, but this is the "stare-of-death" photograph (photo 1). There appears to be some damage to the forehead. Do you remember anything like that?

Sibert: Actually, I don't remember anything in the front view – any injury there at all.

Law: So he looked pretty normal then?

Sibert: Yeah. Looked just like this one here (photo 1). I would consider that – nothing wrong with that facial view – of any injuries or anything exhibited here.

Conway: You didn't see that flap –

Sibert: That flap gets me. I don't remember that either. Now it could have been – maybe I just didn't pick that up in looking at it, but I don't remember that. And that one down here, that drawing (photo 19), Lipsey was it? I don't remember that one at all under the hairline.

Law: Well, would it make sense if they saw that, wouldn't they mention it?

Sibert: Oh undoubtedly, yes. Because they were looking for any evidence of additional bullet wounds.

Conway: Now you know that the doctors testified before the Warren Commission and the House Select Committee said that they did see that wound down there. Do you know that? That wound in the hairline.

Sibert: Yeah, I guess they did.

Conway: Humes and Boswell.

Sibert: I didn't get copies of that House Select Committee. But that's what they told the House Select Committee on Assassinations, right?

Conway: Yeah.

Sibert: But they've changed their stories so many times.

Conway: Yeah, well they –

Sibert: I don't know what to believe.

Conway: The House Select Committee wanted them to move the wound up to the cowlick, but they wouldn't. They said, "No, it was down here in the hairline."

Sibert: Are you talking about a small entrance wound there or was it –

Conway: Small puncture-type wound. That's what they called it.

Sibert: They asked me up there at the ARRB.

Law: That right there, supposedly (photo 4).

Conway: Yeah, that right there. It looks like a little piece of tissue (photo 4a, arrow).

Law: I've had other people tell me that it was a piece of brain matter.

Sibert: Could have been. There was plenty of it around.

Conway: This is from a part of Doug Horne's talk that he gave at the conference a few years back. He was chosen to go to Rochester – the Kodak people I believe?

Sibert: Yeah, I remember reading that.

Conway: Okay. They took the autopsy photos from the archive and digitized them on the computer so that the clarity and focus and – because the ones we have are copies of copies of copies and they've lost their depth – and he made some drawings from what he could see on the computer. He said that the bootleg versions, the ones we typically see, are very dark at the bottom and that's the left superior view of the head (photo 2). He said that the actual image is much better, and shows that the entire back of the head that's lacking in structure. That's the one that he's got his head in the stirrups. It kind of sags there as though it were caved in, where it sits in the stirrup. That is something we had asked about for years, and he said that it is very evident in the good copy of the picture. He says he showed the photograph of the damage to the top of the head and the flap of bone sticking out – damage that was not noticed in Dallas except by Drs. Clark and [Robert] Grossman. Dr. Jones repeatedly said he did not see that at Parkland. He never saw any flap sticking out of the right side nor any damage to the top of the head. Another photograph showed like a V-shaped cut from the forehead. It is indeed a cut made by a knife, according to Dr. Peters. Peters saw this for the first time in 1988 on a Nova show, and the photo shows pieces of skull bone or scalp reflected back. The interior is painted red in some photographs that we see, but it is actually yellow. He said perhaps it was some kind of fat that lies right under your hair?

Sibert: Yeah, there is a layer under there I guess.

Conway: "On the interior of the skull, autopsy photograph 3, shows this V-like cut. " He said, "Boswell did not see the so-called entrance wound in a photograph of the back of the head. The HSCA gave Boswell and Humes a choice for the entrance: the top of the head or tiny speck of something at the bottom near the hairline – they chose the bottom one. Boswell says to the ARRB that he couldn't see it at all. He wouldn't pick either one of the spots offered by the HSCA, but he chose a spot about where the Dallas doctors have said there was an exit wound. The black space seemingly intact with the hair – "

Sibert: Now this exit wound would be on the back of the head, would it?

Conway: Yes, Like what you saw. "A black space seemingly intact with hair and everything looks fine there (see photo 4). The spot previously chosen, which looked like a speck of fat or brain tissue or something (photo 4a, arrow), is indeed a hole, shown more clearly in the Rochester photos. A puncture into the head, whether caused by a bullet or some kind of tampering or what, is unknown." So he refers to it as "tunneling." "Also, there is evidence of a puncture right where Humes and Boswell placed an entrance wound, Horne said it is hard to tell as the hair is thick, but there is a suggestion of it – a puncture here – with blood splatter all around it. Horne called it confusing and intriguing in a distorted photo. With regard to this photograph, Robert Groden said it is a soft-edge matte insertion. Horne did not see evidence of that, but he did say it is extremely strange, the hair is very odd. It's almost as though someone gave JFK a bowl-shaped haircut, put a bowl on his head and cut a Chinese 1890s-style haircut." That's how distorted the picture is, and they're holding the scalp funny, it makes him look like he has an Amish haircut. He says, "But you do have Boswell saying that all the bone underneath there is gone and it is his hand shown pulling up the scalp."

Sibert: Now, that's what I think. You had some bone – you had the one piece that was brought in – the piece that I had the diagram on there. They probably placed that – now this is not during the autopsy, this is after midnight, after they'd given it over to the funeral director attendants there, and Humes and Boswell both helped reconstruct that – that's when they must have done some stretching of tissue or maybe a flap here that they were able to pull over, but you didn't have any bone under it. No skull under it –

Conway: But they are representing that as being pre-autopsy and that's wrong.

Sibert: Yeah. None of that work was done in our presence, see? And, as I say, I didn't realize that they had stayed until five the next morning until I read this JAMA thing, where they were interviewed by that guy and they said they stayed until five, working with the men from Gawler's funeral home in preparing the body and tidying it up. Probably they combed it and got all that blood out and everything there, and combed it down with a comb. Those neat pictures that I said I'd never seen anything look like before. They probably took pictures after they had done that. That wasn't part of the first pictures that were taken, see? It would almost have to be that way.

Conway: Do you think it is possible that what we consider evidence of conspiracy is really because Bobby Kennedy did not want those photos for anyone to see him, but the medical evidence that's missing –

Sibert: You've got that restriction on them in there for that – they couldn't – oh, what I've read about Bobby Kennedy – how he was involved with those attempts on Castro and all that, and he had the adrenal gland problem that they never examined at all, I really think Bobby – I'm just supposing here – probably had a feeling, well, this was a boomerang. It came back to – "maybe I was the cause of my brother being killed." If Castro had anything to do with it, but, now this is the way I've – in thinking of all this stuff – what I've seen on television and books I've read and everything – that I think on this it was like the Warren Commission on the grassy knoll. When somebody said something about the grassy knoll, it didn't get the treatment that it should have got. This one guy had been in the military and had been trained to fall down when there was firing over his head. He said, "You can't tell me anything but that those bullets were coming from behind. " He said, "I've been through this too many times." But you had a patsy. He was dead. He couldn't testify. They were trying to get this Warren Commission Report out. Johnson was putting the heat on Warren and, I think it's pathetic, but I think this: you have to put this whole pattern together to get the true picture.

Conway: That's a good observation.

Law: Jim Jenkins, one of the technicians that was in the room that night – I asked him his feelings about the autopsy and what went on, and he said, "I came out of that autopsy expecting to read that there were at least two shooters."

Sibert: That was the Bethesda autopsy?

Law: The Bethesda autopsy. And he said, "What we saw in that autopsy room bore no relation to the report that was issued. "

Sibert: The official autopsy report. See that's what I say, you had one autopsy and two autopsy reports. You had this business of Secret Service reinterviewing the people in Dallas: "Are you sure now? You say this was an entrance wound, but couldn't this have been either an exit or an entrance wound?" They had to get them to say that if you're going to put the single-bullet theory together.

Law: And if the single bullet theory doesn't work, then it seems that there has to have been conspiracy. And so that's where people keep pushing on this thing. And Lifton comes along and writes *Best Evidence*. What do you think about his theory?

Sibert: Well, he lost me when he zeroed in on this "surgery in the head area" (photo 21) and that had to be done either on the plane in Dallas or en route from Dallas into Andrews Air Force Base. As I recall his book, that was the summation of it, and I just couldn't go along with that. With the Secret Service on board there – you know, you had Secret Service agents during swearing in Johnson and you've got these other loyal Kennedy people who were right there with the casket – don't tell me that. Where would they have gotten the surgical instruments to do surgery on that body on the way back?

Law: That's certainly part of the question, isn't it? Where he says that there would have been time to do it, a limited time, would have been when all the people, including Jacqueline Kennedy, were in the front of plane when Johnson was sworn in.

Sibert: The swearing in. But I don't think all of them would have been there.

Conway: I'll tell you why I don't believe that any more because a really good friend of mine is an Air Force One fanatic, and he has been on it. He has pictures. I have copies of the pictures.

Sibert: Yeah, I've been on it.

Conway: And he said that there is no way in the world there was room in that tiny space to open the casket up, because the way the plane was shaped, just to get it in there they had to cut into the bulkhead – it's still like that, you can still see it – and he said you couldn't have opened the coffin all the way to get him out. You couldn't have opened the coffin.

Law: Part of Lifton's theory is that he was put into some kind of body bag. We have Paul O'Connor who says there was a body bag, which feeds into Lifton's theory that, at some point, they took the body out and stowed it in the baggage compartment. Was it Lipsey who said one of his shoulders was up higher than the other? – which may account for when they put the body in the bottom of the plane – perhaps he was lying on his side – people come up with all kinds of theories.

Sibert: Yeah.

Law: But that's what I'm trying to get to the bottom of. That's why I talk to people who were there so that you can just say, "Well, it's possible" or "No, this is totally not possible, and it's not provable."

Conway: He also thought that they took the body to Walter Reed Hospital and that's where they did the so-called surgery and then they –

Sibert: Took the body to where?

Conway: Walter Reed.

Law: I think that's where he ties the ambulance that got lost, supposedly, in the big supposed chase – there was enough time to – while the official casket is out front, the other ambulance that really has the body, did get lost for a while. Do I have that right, Debra?

Conway: Yes.

Law: Then, that's where they took the body. And they do a quick job, this is Lifton's theory, not mine. I don't have theories. But that's where he's getting this and he uses the phrase "this piece of scalp was removed" in correlation with the surgery, supposed surgery of the body.

Sibert: I don't know. You've talked with Lifton after I have. He was after me – he said for history in the schools – but with O'Connor and them talking about body bags and cheap caskets and all that stuff, I wasn't going to get into that kind of wrangle. Later, I got a call from a Philadelphia TV station. They wanted me to go on with Lifton, you know, and I wouldn't.

Law: He wanted you to be part of it?

Sibert: I wasn't going to get into that kind of a dogfight either.

Law: Don't blame you.

Sibert: He called me several times, and I tried to answer his questions, and told him that the regret I had was that I could have asked Humes if that piece – from the limousine – if that changed his mind on surgery in the head area. Now I don't know whether it would have, but at least it would have shut out this business about head surgery, if he would have said "Well, it wasn't head surgery. I just thought it was, but when the piece came in I realized it was blown out," or something. That would have killed that surgery-of-the-head thesis that Lifton proceeded to use through his whole book.

Law: And basically you don't believe there was surgery on the head?

Sibert: I don't have any way of knowing, but – being there, and Secret Service coming in saying they found this piece in the limousine on the floor between the front and back seat, or wherever it was found there.... You'd have had to have a lot of people tied in on this end to be able – you figure that you'd have to have surgeons, Secret Service and all, to pull off this kind of shenanigan, and I don't think that happened.

I've read that the Mafia was involved in it someway, in the actual shooting. I don't have any proof of it, but there was certainly enough reason for them to be involved – with the Hoffa deal, and feeling that they were double-crossed.

I was at an organized crime conference up in New York, when I was working with the Bureau, and Bobby Kennedy came in and he had a tape of wiretaps and was playing it. And he said, "Can't we get better equipment for us to hear this?" Then he gets up after that and he said he wasn't aware that the FBI had wiretaps. I don't know where he thought we got that from, out of the ether or where, so you know what I thought then.

Law: I can just imagine. I've been told that there was a casket brought in – and we're not talking shipping casket, another nice casket that supposedly had the body of an air force major or colonel.

Sibert: Never heard anything about it. You mean about the same time?

Law: About an hour before the president's body was brought in. It was in the anteroom or the cooler room, and I just wondered if you knew anything or heard anything mentioned –

Sibert: Never anything about a second ambulance, or any of that stuff, until after it was all over and I read it in books or something. But I did tell you about not contacting the honor guard.

Law: There was a supposed ambulance chase.

Sibert: Yeah, and we never came into contact with this group at all to help unload the casket that was supposed to do it. So, I don't know –

Law: So you have no memory of any kind of honor guard or anything?

Sibert: No.

Law: Let's go back over it again. There was just you and Frank O'Neill, Kellerman, Greer –

Sibert: And some other people came out there that were probably medical personnel because that casket was heavy. That was a big bronze casket. Four men couldn't carry it, so they helped get it out and put it on the gurney and it was wheeled on in.

Law: When the ambulance first pulled up, do you remember the length of time that the ambulance may have been out front before it went around back?

Sibert: It wasn't too long. As I say, they let Bobby and Jackie out, who were in the ambulance and it wasn't too long a time before it started moving on around the back. May have been looking for somebody to give directions back around to where the autopsy room – I don't know how experienced the driver of that navy ambulance was.

Law: There's been some talk that the reason that you were sent back to go to the White House for the second interview was that they were basically, in your eyes, suspects.

Sibert: It was what?

Law: You were questioning them as suspects.

Sibert: No. Bureau headquarters called over and said, "Have the agents who conducted these interviews, and were there at the autopsy that night, go back and do formal interviews with these fellows. " I got a full description of Bill Greer, whereas Frank didn't get a full description of Kellerman. They asked if I thought Greer was a suspect because I'd included his description, age, place of birth, and all that stuff there. Greer is sort of a common name, so later on you could have another Bill Greer, but you could compare his description so you could tell which Bill Greer it was. We never had any sense at all like that, when we went over there for those interviews. We had talked to them just off the cuff when we were getting their remarks at the autopsy that night. They wanted a continued interview done and that's why we were sent back over there to the White House.

One of the Parkland doctors contacted me – name escapes me – and I asked him what was his first impression of the neck wound. Was it an entrance wound or an exit wound? And he said it was more or less considered an entrance wound. I don't know who he got that from, but I said that I always wondered about that because they changed it around to be an exit wound with the single bullet theory and all.

Law: Well, in the press conference that was given some hours after the event –

Sibert: Yeah, they said entrance.

Law: And now Dr. Perry's going around saying, "Yeah, but I qualified it with this next statement and they never – "

Sibert: Arm-twisting.

Conway: Well, Kilduff said it was a simple matter of a gunshot right through the head. He said that he was shot in the temple and it came out the back, and then there was the entrance wound in the throat – and then the next day everything was different.

Law: I think the book that I sent to you has Malcolm Kilduff saying that it was a simple matter and they have him frozen right there, pointing to the temple.

Conway: Yeah, but that's what he was told at Parkland – it went in the temple and came out the back, and then boom.

Sibert: Something that was brought out on the History Channel: if they did fire from that drain cover, where they had the cap on, a man could stand and could walk in there. It was a big drainage channel in concrete I guess – he could have gotten in there and stood up and fired out. Now if a guy was firing from there and [Kennedy] was sitting up in that presidential limousine and you hit him here (in the throat) and the bullet is coming up instead of coming down at forty-five degrees from the depository building, I can see where that bullet would blow the top out back here –

Law: Deb and I have talked about that. Earlier you saw the Zapruder film – as he's going behind the sign it seems his arm is dropping and when he comes out from behind the sign he's grabbing at his throat. So he's already been hit in the throat –

Conway: Or the back.

Law: Or the back. And the head shot comes –

Conway: If you think about it, if somebody pounds you on the back, you might do that.

Law: That's possible. The thing that drives me crazy about this is that nothing is cut and dried in it. If that sign had not been there that day, we would maybe know exactly what happened but –

Sibert: They paved that street a lot there and repaired that curb –

Law: Oh, I wish you would go to Dallas. You could go up on the overpass and there's a place to the left where there is a drain. There's a drain and it's still open, but there's also a drain on the other side that they have since paved over.

Sibert: I've always thought – you know we had no jurisdiction there – what would have happened if O'Neill and I would have just gone there and not made any notes or anything. Did you ever see any list of people at that autopsy other than what was in our FD 302? I think that's the only one. I don't think the Secret Service had a listing, I think they got it from us.

Law: The only reason that we know who exactly was there is because you took notes.

Sibert: Yeah. We may have missed a couple, because they could have darted in there and out again and just left a message or something.

Conway: Yeah. I think they found a few more names, but no one substantial. You know you got the bases covered.

Sibert: Even the guys from Gawler's funeral home that were there.

Law: This brings up a question. When you decided to take the names in the morgue, did you pass around paper or did you go around personally and ask each person?

Sibert: We went around. But if someone was busy or got away, we asked. Most of it was eye-to-eye contact.

Law: So you were right there and said what's your name?

Sibert: Yeah. Now we missed on some spelling, because we didn't take time. I misspelled Admiral Burkley.

Law: It was still Burkley but you just spelled it with a different letter or something.

Conway: Burley. You spelled it "Burley."

Sibert: Yeah. He was the only admiral there, and he was the president's personal physician. You know, you were pressed for time, didn't want to miss anything going on and wanted to get all this information too.

Law: How do you think these higher-ranking officials were acting? Did they seem kind of nonchalant and cool, or did they seem like this was a great tragedy and – ?

Sibert: Well, I think that an air of tragedy permeated the whole room. The thing that got me the worst was the drive down Suitland Parkway with all those people down there with handkerchiefs flying. That was something I will never forget. That stood out just as much – almost – as looking at that hole in Kennedy's head, it really did. The impact it had. You think of the sorrow of the people, how they turned out there – and those handkerchiefs, those white handkerchiefs were just everywhere. It was about this time of the evening you know, starting to get dark, but you could make out people's profiles and stuff, and they were at every one of those overpasses.

Law: How did you maintain your composure through all that? I can remember the sadness of my own family, as young as I was.

Sibert: Well, you learn to do it. You learn to be in a lot of tough situations.

Law: I usually end my interviews with this question: do you have anything for the historical record that you would like to add about this case?

Sibert: The only thing I would like to say is that it got off on the wrong foot right there at Parkland. They didn't let things take their normal course, didn't follow the Texas State Law of having the autopsy done there, where you would have had nurses, doctors, everything there. You would have had the clothing there, you would have had Dr. [Earl] Rose who did the autopsy on Ruby. He did it on Oswald. He did it on Tippit and he would have done it on the president. He was a known gunshot pathologist. He had handled a lot of autopsies involving gunshot wounds and you wouldn't have had all this turmoil and everything that resulted from that. If you want my analysis right from the start, that's where it got off on the wrong foot.

Law: Some people would say it got off on the wrong foot like that on purpose, and that they had to get the body out.

Sibert: What?

Law: Where they could control all that.

Sibert: Bobby Kennedy was the one that, as I understand it, gave the Secret Service orders that we were going to do it back here. So Kellerman had the Attorney General [Robert Kennedy], number-one law enforcement officer in the United States, telling him, giving him an order – and he's going to follow it out.

Law: Well, I thank you for your time Mr. Sibert.

Sibert: You're welcome, I've enjoyed it. Gave me a refresher too, and I'll go over a lot of the stuff you've given me that I don't have, Deb. I appreciate it. Listen thanks for those books. I really enjoy them.

Law: Oh, it was my pleasure.

* * *

It is standard procedure for law-enforcement officials to interview witnesses to a crime separately, in order to get untainted views of the event. Thus, the witnesses do not adjust their recollections, consciously or unconsciously. Sibert and O'Neill used this technique when they interviewed Secret Service Agents Roy Kellerman and William Greer, the driver and front-seat passenger of the presidential limousine. "I stayed with Kellerman. And Jim stayed with Greer," Frank O'Neill told me. In turn, I did the same thing with FBI agents, letting each know that I had talked to the other – without giving away a great deal of information – for the express purpose of comparing their stories.

They agree on how the president's body was wrapped: in sheets, with a separate blood-soaked sheet wrapped around the head. Both believe the bullet wound in the back was too low for the single-bullet theory to hold water. Neither remembers a wound in the back of the head at the hairline, as indicated by a spot in photo 4a. Neither remembers the metal head-holder plainly seen in photos 2 and 3. As for the large head wound, Sibert recalled it as being in the right rear, and O'Neill said it was in the "right rear side." According to both, there was no damage to the forehead, although such damage is apparent in photo 1.

When I questioned O'Neill on this, he replied, "Absolutely none. There was no damage to the face or forehead. Absolutely none." When I told him there did seem to be damage to the forehead in some of the autopsy photos, he replied, "None that I saw." It's clear that if the body had no damage to the forehead, but pictures show it, then there is a problem with the autopsy photographs, or the memories of all the Bethesda personnel I have talked to are faulty. It is hard to believe that they all are mistaken on this point.

Concerning the AP X-ray, neither Sibert nor O'Neill had any recollection of the large object that is reportedly a bullet fragment. "I don't recall any. If there was such a thing as that, it certainly wasn't pointed out to me," Frank O'Neill said. When I sent Jim Sibert a copy of the AP X-ray with the object circled, he wrote back saying he had not seen it. Remember: the body was X-rayed to find bullets or bullet fragments, for the FBI agents to collect for laboratory analysis. If the so-called fragment had been in the head the night the X-rays were taken, logically, it should have been seen and taken from the head and given to the FBI agents. But the only bullet fragments from the head, given to them, were too small to have been the large object seen in the X-rays.

The former FBI agents' recollections of the night of November 22, 1963, mesh with each others for the most part (which is significant, because, over lunch, Sibert told me that they have not kept in close touch through the years: "We send Christmas cards to each other, but that's about it."). However, their stories do not mesh in terms of how the casket got into the morgue. Mr. O'Neill claims that he and Mr. Sibert observed an honor guard carry in the heavy Brittania casket. In stark contrast, when I read from page 399 of William Manchester's book *The Death Of a President* – describing the honor guard carrying the casket up the steps to the loading dock – Sibert said: "I don't remember any military unit there – casket team or anything ... when we moved that casket in there, there was no one, no one that helped us."

I find it troubling that the former FBI agents have such differing memories. If an honor guard did the job, surely Jim Sibert would remember it and have no recollection of carrying the casket into the building. The honor guard was made up of military personnel from all of the branches of the armed services, army, navy, air force, coast guard, and marines – each in his respective uniform. It would be hard to forget such a sight. When I said to Jim Sibert, "Let's go back through the sequence again: there was you and Frank O'Neill, Kellerman, Greer – " He responded, "And some other people that came out of the naval thing there that were probably medical personnel 'cause that casket was heavy. That was a big bronze casket. Four men couldn't carry it."

The official version of the casket entry is that it was escorted by an honor guard. James Felder, a member of the detail, did not recall FBI agents being present or helping to carry the casket. The only time he remembered Sibert and O'Neill helping with the casket was at Andrews Air Force Base (*Best Evidence*, Dell edition, page 515). Another of the casket team, Hubert Clark told author David Lifton he did not note any [FBI agents]. "No one but us." Clark did recall the incident where Godfrey McHugh took the position of "the lanky Coast Guard youth" as described by William Manchester in *The Death of a President*. In contrast, Jim Sibert recalled nothing like that.

Frank O'Neill, however, told the Assassination Records Review Board on September 12, 1997: "So we went around. The ambulance stopped. We got out of our car. We went over to the ambulance. I saw Kellerman coming on out. And I went over to him, and I said: 'My name is Frank O'Neill, FBI agent.' He says 'I know. I've already got a call from [James] Rowley that you're going to be here.' He and I and Jim and Greer opened the back of the ambulance. At about this time, the honor guard came. We took the casket out and put it on a conveyance; and wheeled it on in, with the honor guard, up to the steps; and took it on up the step, because I think there was one step there – no, I don't know whether there was a step, or whether it was an incline – but up to the doors here. Pushed the doors open. And inside, after about – oh, ten or fifteen steps, or something like that – there's a door on the left-hand side. We pushed it in there, which is a small anteroom. And in the anteroom were some slots. It was a sort of morgue. It was a morgue that they used for the hospital. I do recall specifically being told that there was a child in one of the slots there that had died that day. We then moved the – for want of a better word – dolly with the casket on it into the autopsy room through the swinging doors, and on over to a group of individuals who were in surgical garb standing right next to an autopsy table."

Q: Could we stop right there?

O'Neill: Sure.

Q: There are some questions I have. Who physically lifted the casket up to the loading dock or the platform? Was that the honor guard, or did you do that?

O'Neill: I believe it was the honor guard, Jim and I and Kellerman and Greer assisted in it and it was the same way pushing it in, and the same way when we got it on – over to the – to the autopsy table.

Q: Do you know approximately what time you arrived at the back of Bethesda Hospital?

O'Neill: It was after 7:00. I believe it was 7:05, something like that.

Q: Okay. And you're quite sure –

O'Neill: Generally speaking.

Q: And you're quite certain that there was an honor guard?

O'Neill: Yes.

Q: Do you know which military branch the honor guard came from?

O'Neill: No. I'd be – I'd be guessing. I think army, but I'm just guessing on that. The easiest thing would be to say navy, because it was a naval installation. But I don't recall exactly who it was.

You cannot have it both ways. The honor guard was either there while the FBI agents were present, or it was not. If Jim Sibert's version of the casket entry is correct, this would point to a shell game with the casket, and, therefore, opportunity to tamper with Kennedy's remains. I believe the Records Review Board had their suspicions about O'Neill's veracity concerning the honor guard being present during the casket entry – at least the one he and Sibert were present for – and that is why they questioned him about the presence of an honor guard and if he knew what branch of the military they came from. Sibert gave his deposition before the Records Review Board on September 11, 1997, and O'Neill was questioned the following day. Jim Sibert, of course, had told the Board that no honor guard was present during the casket entry, raising a red flag. If Frank O'Neill was present at the same time as the honor guard, why didn't he remember that all branches of the military were represented, all in different uniforms? A small point, perhaps, but the question looms large in the tangled skein of events.

There is another reason why the Records Review Board may have had doubts about the honor guard being present for the casket entry attended by the FBI agents. O'Neill was interviewed for the HSCA in 1978 by their representative, Andrew Purdy, who wrote: "Upon arrival at Bethesda, O'Neill stated that the ambulance stopped at the front entrance where Jackie and RFK disembarked to proceed to the 17lh floor. The ambulance then traveled to the rear where O'Neill, Sibert, Greer (Secret Service), and Kellerman (Secret Service) placed the casket on a roller and transported it into the autopsy room." No mention of an honor guard, matching Sibert's recollection of the event. Of course, that was in 1978, before the publication of *Best Evidence*. It is my opinion that Frank O'Neill, after reading the literature and becoming aware of the significance of the fact that no honor guard was present at the FBI agents' casket entry, realized that he'd been had. He had put two and two together and got five – or three: one entry with a shipping casket, one entry without an honor guard, and one entry with an honor guard. This, I believe, would be unacceptable to the former FBI agent who then decided to toe the company line and say that he and Jim Sibert were with the honor guard when the ornate casket was brought into the morgue.

Let me be clear on this point: I have nothing but the highest regard for former FBI agents James W. Sibert and Francis X. O'Neill. Both fought in World War II – members of The Greatest Generation, as the veterans of that era have become known – Sibert as a squadron leader, O'Neill as a paratrooper. Indeed, we can be grateful that Sibert and O'Neill were in the autopsy room taking notes, for, without them, the "official" version of the events given by Humes, Boswell, and Fink, might have passed into history unchallenged. And yet, I'm conflicted about Mr. O'Neill, despite my personal gratitude to him for taking time to respond to my questions and for his comments about the president's body not looking the same in the autopsy pictures versus his memory (although three years later, he told me: "Oh, yes. It looked the same."). When questioned by Jeremy Gunn of the Review Board: "Can you identify that [picture] in any reasonable way as appearing to be the – what the brain looked like of President Kennedy?" he responded, "No." And when I asked O'Neill about the pictures that he was shown by the Records Review Board, he said: "They showed me several pictures, I don't know if it was all of the pictures that were in the archives or not, but they showed me what they thought – several pictures. *And they thought and I thought and Sibert thought it was not as we recalled it whatsoever.*" [emphasis mine] Clearly, O'Neill has to know there is a big problem here. Is he, like Humes, trying to say something and not say it at the same time?[12] His recollection of the casket going into the morgue with an honor guard, when his partner has no memory of that honor guard, leads me to believe that he has changed his story of events, at least where the casket entry is concerned, to avoid contributing to speculation about a shell-game with the casket.

Jim Sibert took a very large step when he agreed to see me in June of 2002. I think he had come to believe that it was time to tell what he knows.

I believe Mr. Sibert when he says there was no honor guard for the casket entry he witnessed. He is very much aware of the controversy concerning the arrival of a cheap metal shipping casket versus the entry of the ornate display casket accompanied by the honor guard. And he knows full well the implication of the casket entering Bethesda Naval Hospital without that honor guard. James W. Sibert is a man in conflict, trying to reconcile what he experienced on that awful evening with what he has since learned from books and the board of inquiry on the assassination. Take, for instance, the question of the brain. Long will I remember riding in the back seat of the Siberts' car before Deb Conway and I conducted the interview, to have Mrs. Sibert turn around and say: "You know, his brains were blown out of his head!" – information that had, obviously, come from her husband. Sibert

12. See Rydberg chapter, page 421.

knows the implications of there being no brain in the cranium. He under-stands the impact of his words when he tells us that no honor guard was present at the entry of the casket, or there was no brain in the head when he first saw Kennedy's body, or that the autopsy pictures don't match his mem-ories of how the body looked. The reader may also recall that when I told him in a telephone conversation that Frank O'Neill had said the picture of the brain he had been shown by the ARRB did not look like the brain he had seen that night and that O'Neill said that he (Sibert) said it didn't look the same either," he replied, "Oh, yes. Yeah, well. . ." and then he chuckled. There was also what I believe was the defining moment in the interview where Si-bert looked at Debra and me and said: "I've often wondered, whoever that marksman was, if he used an exploding bullet. " Sibert knows some kind of ruse was played out that night, forty years ago, in which he was an unwitting participant. He may not be sure of what happened or who set the wheels in motion, but, in his own way – like those of us who search for answers to the complex puzzle of John F. Kennedy's murder – he is trying to put the pieces together.

After I returned home from Florida, I sent Mr. Sibert a copy of Noel Twyman's book *Bloody Treason* (Laurel, 1997) (which, for me is the new cornerstone of the literature on the assassination) as a token of thanks for granting us the opportunity to interview him. Twyman's book brings to the fore questions concerning the shipping casket versus the ornate display cas-ket, body alteration, the forged X-ray and autopsy pictures, etc.

Weeks later, I called Jim, or Si as I now think of him, to see how he liked the book: "You tell Noel Twyman for me that his book is the best thing I've ever read on the assassination."

James W. Sibert, it seems, is a True Believer.

Chapter Twelve

HAROLD A. RYDBERG

I interviewed Harold "Skip" Rydberg (photo 9) by telephone in February, 2003.

Law: Harold, tell me how you managed to be at the National Naval Medical Center, Bethesda.

Rydberg: When I joined the navy in '58, I used to draw a lot in the medical department, and there was a nurse there who told me about a medical illustration school at Bethesda, Maryland. And part of my reenlistment agreement was that I would get that school, since, originally, I had not known that you could combine medicine and art. So, I ended up reenlisting and was sent to Bethesda, Maryland.

Law: So you wanted to do art at that point?

Rydberg: Yes. In medicine. I was already a hospital corpsman, which is a medic in the military.

Law: Were you at Bethesda on November 22, 1963?

Rydberg: Oh, yes. I was there from '62.

Law: Tell me what you remember of the events of that evening.

A young Rydberg

Rydberg: I had become the senior instructor and department head after graduation from medical illustration school, and I was teaching my class. I heard on the radio in the department that President Kennedy had been shot. I stopped the class, stating that, "It's going to be a long day, and we can't possibly concentrate on learning anything with this going on." It was kind of like a blow to your own family member – Kennedy was very popular. I dismissed the class and went back to quarters and saw on television the announcement that he was dead. At the point when I had dismissed the class, he had been sent to Parkland and I knew that he had to be gravely injured because Connally went into the operating room and Kennedy did not, and by the hierarchy, he would have gone first if they had a chance to save him. So, after that was announced, they then announced that we [were] to get in our dress blues – it was in November – and form an honor guard, completely encircling the circle driveway in front of the National Naval Medical Center. We waited until around six-thirty, seven o'clock, when the motorcade

413

came in with Kennedy's body and Jacqueline in the ambulance with him. I saw her holding the side of the flag-draped coffin as they drove up to the front of the hospital, she got out – Captain Stover (photo 9), Admiral Galloway and some other high-ranking officials from the army were also there.

Law: Did you see Bobby Kennedy?

Rydberg: I did not see Bobby Kennedy.

Law: So, you were there for the official ambulance that pulled up out front. You were in the driveway.

Rydberg: Yes.

Law: Tell me what happened after the ambulance pulled up.

Rydberg: It stopped in front, she got out, she was greeted. After a 15-minute period at the maximum, the ambulance then pulled around to the back.

Law: To the best of your recollection, the ambulance was out front for about fifteen minutes?

Rydberg: Yes. It was a gray navy ambulance. It was the protocol for getting her out [of the ambulance] everybody meeting everybody, and her being escorted up to the 17th floor of the tower, which was the presidential suite at that time.

Law: What happened after she got out and went into the building?

Rydberg: After they turned their backs on the ambulance and started walking up the steps, the ambulance left and proceeded around to the back. At that point, I lost sight of it because I was on the other end.

Law: Did the ambulance wait some slight period of time before it went around, even after they had gone into the building?

Rydberg: No.

Law: I've read somewhere – this is according to Manchester – it waited some minutes out front.

Rydberg: No. It left as soon as she started up the steps.

Law: What did you do at that point?

Rydberg: We stayed as the honor guard until the ambulance had left. They had taken the body out and brought it in the morgue and then we were released about thirty-five minutes later.

Law: Were you involved in anything else that evening?

Rydberg: I was not involved with anything with the autopsy on President Kennedy that night. We were more in crowd control. An honor guard. Two cars were totally demolished (chuckles) by people standing on them.

Law: Really?

Rydberg: Yes. It's an open base. It's a hospital. And they locked off the back gate but left the front open.

Law: Is this the one that would be used coming up from Jones Bridge Road?

Rydberg: Yes. There was only one gate that was locked.

Law: That was the one in the back?

Rydberg: Yes.

Law: Do you remember when that happened?

Rydberg: As soon as we knew he was coming in then we got word to start lining the honor guard up.

Law: This is the honor guard for Bethesda, correct?

Rydberg: It's the navy honor guard. The reason the president was brought to the naval school is because he was navy. Eisenhower was army so he went to Walter Reed. And after Kennedy had been sent there, it just became the president's hospital. Period. Everybody.

Law: You were there as part of the honor guard for the navy, just to guard the building, correct?

Rydberg: Crowd control also.

Law: Did you hear any kind of scuttlebutt that night? Anything about they're bringing in another ambulance, a decoy ambulance or –

Rydberg: There was a decoy.

Law: Was this something that you heard, was general knowledge or –

Rydberg: Yeah. It was general knowledge that a decoy was put out to keep anybody, mainly photographers, from knowing when the real one came in – it was orbiting a good ten minutes before he even arrived.

Law: Orbiting. Does that mean on the ground or perhaps –

Rydberg: They were driving around. In the back. They were never in the front.

Law: Now is this to your knowledge – I mean through scuttlebutt – did this ambulance contain the body? Or did the official ambulance contain the body?

Rydberg: The body was in where Jacqueline was. That one went immediately to the morgue. The back entrance. I've never heard anything contrary to that. But I did know about the decoy.

Law: Anything else that you remember from that night? Anything special?

Rydberg: No, not that night. Some friends of mine and I changed into civilian clothes at the quarters and walked into Bethesda – only three blocks – and ate at the International House of Pancakes. Then we came back to the quarters and just kind of talked about it all night long.

Law: Did you hear of any strange activities later? Were you in a position to talk to anybody that would know?

Rydberg: No. Nothing strange. A friend of mine, [Floyd] Riebe, he had medical photography that night, along with [John] Stringer.

Law: Did you talk to Riebe about this later?

Rydberg: Not until I was put under orders and did the drawings.

Law: Let's go to that, then.

Rydberg: A hundred days later.

Law: Tell me how that came about, step by step.

Rydberg: I was teaching class, it was on a Friday and the Master-at-Arms, which is just a title for whoever the chief petty officer was who was controlling the grounds for the day, sent someone – another sailor – to my class and stated that the commanding officer wanted to see me. So, of course, I went. Captain Stover talked with me, with Dr. Humes and Dr. Boswell, and explained to me that I was going to be making drawings for Dr. Humes and Dr. Boswell, to present to the Warren Commission on the assassination of President Kennedy. Dr. Humes, with Stover there and Boswell, told me that that they had no photographs, no X-rays, that I was going to have to do this one verbally: "We'll tell you what to draw."

Law: And at that point, did they do that?

Rydberg: At that point, they told me to get my things, the drawing equipment, the water colors, the boards, stuff like that, in the small room – you know where the presidential suite is now? Well, it's on the third floor by the heliport – anyway, there's a small room on the first floor, a small office that was empty with a desk in it, a flat desk, and that's where I was sequestered (chuckles). With a marine guard on the door.

Law: So, you weren't given any advance notice of this, you were just told to –

Rydberg: No. Zam! It just came in. Boom.

Law: Very quickly.

Rydberg: Very. I had to cancel a date that night. Which was fine.

Law: How did that make you feel?

Rydberg: Caught up in the enormity of it, and at the age – I kind of went on auto pilot. You do what you're told in the military. And I felt somewhat flustered they'd asked me. In retrospect, I wonder why they didn't use a medical illustrator who was far more qualified then I was at that time.

Law: Did they have, for lack of better words, more qualified people at that point?

Rydberg: Not in the navy, no. Walter Reed was loaded with medical illustrators. The University of Maryland was teaching medical illustration. So, all these people were available, but none of them would have done those drawings verbally.

Law: How old were you at this point?

Rydberg: Twenty-two.

Law: And how long had you been studying art at that point?

Rydberg: I had been studying medical art for almost a year.

Law: So you were basically a new student?

Rydberg: Yes. Plus running the [art] school, plus redesigning the syllabus (laughs) –

Law: So, at that age you had quite a bit of responsibility?

Rydberg: – and art director. Yeah. I was the director of medical illustration as well.

Law: So, tell me of the experience. You're now sitting in the room with your drawing equipment and you have these two doctors in there –

Rydberg: Mainly Dr. Humes. Boswell was always mousy. He was quiet.

Law: Try to give me a little bit of the atmosphere of the whole thing when you're sitting there in that room.

Rydberg: He was giving me anatomical landmarks, like the head wound – so many centimeters towards the right side. There was an oval entrance to the gunshot wound, and it exited in the parietal and the temporal lobe area. And there was this much of a space in centimeters. And the neck wound was explained the same way. It was down at C-6, C-7 on the cervical vertebrae, and it was angled down bruising the pleural area of the right lung – the superior portion of it and exiting out by the knot on the tie.

Law: That's what Humes told you?

Rydberg: Yes.

Law: As he was giving the instructions?

Rydberg: And he was kind of conferring with Boswell: "This is right. This would be about right here," and Boswell would do his "Yes."

Law: Did they have notes with them?

Rydberg: No.

Law: They just did this off the tops of their heads?

Rydberg: Yes. They wanted no paper trail.

Law: So you just continued to draw –

Rydberg: I continued to draw, nothing to go by. Couldn't even bring a picture of Kennedy in, so I could draw it to look like him. This was done over two days – a Saturday and a Sunday. On Monday morning they were taken out of the safe and brought up to Admiral Galloway's office, who is the commanding officer of the whole ball of wax, and we looked at all the drawings, then all three concurred that they were what they needed to go before the Commission. These were all good representation of what they had seen.

Law: But you had no access to any kind of pictures?

Rydberg: None. None at all.

Law: Had you ever heard of this being done before, having to draw from someone's description?

Rydberg: No. Not on something this important.

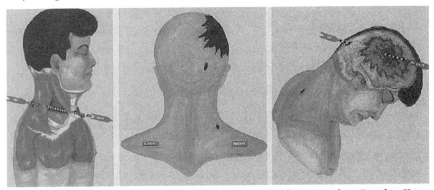

Harold Rydberg made these drawings depicting the entrance and exit wounds on President Kennedy's head and throat from descriptions given to him by Drs. Humes & Boswell on the Friday before the Warren Commission was to meet the following Monday.

Law: Have you ever heard of it since then?

Rydberg: Only when Colonel Finck shows up (laughs). Any time Finck shows up there's trouble.

Law: What does that mean? Tell me about Colonel Finck.

Rydberg: You remember Calley? The lieutenant who was hung out for wiping out a village?

Law: Yes.

Rydberg: Colonel Finck was involved in that. Colonel Finck was involved in the assassination. Colonel Fink was involved in the Pitzer case.

Law: I want to ask you about their personalities. Apparently you knew all of them.

Rydberg: Yeah. I knew Captain Stover (photo 9) very well. He called me "Skip." Which was usually not the protocol in the military, but since the commanding officers called me "Skip," Dr. Humes would call me "Skip" or Harold. Dr. Humes, Captain Stover, who was also a doctor, Lieutenant Commander Pitzer (photo 9), and Boswell all came to my wedding. So they all knew me. They wouldn't just drop into an enlisted man's wedding.

Law: Let's go back to the drawings now for a moment because I want to make sure this is totally covered. So this was right before the Commission hearing –

Rydberg: Right before the Commission hearing.

Law: And they came to you three days before –

Rydberg: Friday afternoon.

Law: And they went before the Commission that Monday?

Rydberg: You got it. Water color. Life size. On a flat desk. Now you see why they were so lousy!

Law: Well, I don't know anything about art, but they don't look lousy to me.

Rydberg: They're awful to me, that's why I redrew it for the cover of my book I – so that you can see I can draw!

Law: At the end of this, after you drew them and they were satisfied, did anything happen after that?

Rydberg: At that point, they realized I wasn't under secret orders (chuckles). Then I was put under secret orders. And they gave me a cover story. The cover story was the Thresher, the submarine that went down. I was actually doing some work for the Thresher if any reporters ever caught on who was doing the drawings. That was my answer.

Law: Did you go before the Commission at all?

Rydberg: No.

Law: Has anyone from an official body ever contacted you?

Rydberg: Oh, boy! After I got out of the navy, I became the art director first at Alabama University School of Medicine, and, four years later, art director at the University of North Carolina, Chapel Hill. That's when I released an article stating that I had done the drawings. The Pentagon called. They told me that I was not to say anything about the assassination until the committee had finished their reviews.

Law: This took place while the House Select Committee was in session?

Rydberg: Yes.

Law: And the Pentagon called you and asked you not to –

Rydberg: They didn't ask me, they told me! Name was Marmelstein. I remember the name because it's just a weird name. I also got a registered letter.

Law: So what happened after that? Were you contacted by The House Select Committee?

Rydberg: Never.

Law: Did anyone else of an official nature contact you?

Rydberg: No one.

Law: That was the sum extent?

Rydberg: That's it. It was quoted to me: "You played such a small and insignificant role. "

Law: Was that by Marmelstein?

Rydberg: Yes.

Law: Was this in 1977, 1978?

Rydberg: The Select Committee – when it was on, yeah.

Law: How were the doctors acting when you were alone with them? What was their manner?

Rydberg: They were quite comfortable. Boswell's always been like a cat in a room full of rocking chairs with its tail on the floor. Boswell's always been jumpy and quiet. Doesn't want to talk about anything. And Captain Humes saw me at Chapel Hill, because I had released another article. I looked up from my desk and here's Captain Humes. He's a civilian at this time, wanting to go to dinner. So, we went to dinner, and I had made some mention in another article about doing the drawings verbally, and that he had burned the notes and retyped them because he didn't want blood on the autopsy report.

Law: Did you believe that story?

Rydberg: I know Dr. Humes, and yes, I do. I believe Dr. Humes did retype them and his rationale was because they were messy. And if you've been in an autopsy, you know that it is quite messy. But I really think Colonel Finck was definitely – he was the forensic ballistics expert. He was the only forensics expert who was there at the autopsy, wanted to make sure that that was an exit and an entrance wound [on the head]. And not like I drew later.

Law: You know Dr. Finck a little?

Rydberg: Oh, yeah.

Law: Okay. Let's go down the line here. Since you know these people and I don't–

Rydberg: Finck was not at my wedding (laughs).

Law: Give me a little personal profile on Dr. Boswell as you knew him.

Rydberg: Dr. Boswell was a very good pathologist, a very good doctor. But not one who wanted the limelight, or any confrontation.

Law: He wanted to stay out of everything?

Rydberg: Very quiet, yes. I was not as friendly with him, but I knew him. Dr. Humes was very laughing, joking, jovial. I had to go through Humes so I could teach anatomy in the autopsy room in the morgue. I've seen many autopsies. At least three hundred. And he was the head of the department, so, of course he gave me permission to bring my class into the autopsies. All the autopsies. Except that one.

Law: It's been stated before that Dr. Boswell and Dr. Humes were basically pencil pushers.

Rydberg: Well, Dr. Humes was the head of pathology and would be the one who would do the autopsy on Kennedy, because he was the department head. He was basically in the administrative part, but he was a doctor. Boswell was head of the labs, but also assisted Humes. They were the heads of the departments, and then there was the head of medical illustration. They didn't want just the – they wanted the heads – literally (laughs).

Law: Do you feel that these fellows knew very well where those head wounds were?

Rydberg: Yes.

Law: Because, even before the Records Review Board, they seemed confused as to where the wounds on the head were.

Rydberg: So was Dr. Perry at Parkland.

Law: Is it credible in your estimation, knowing these people the way you did, that, even all these years later, they were so uncertain as to where bullets either entered or exited [Kennedy's body]?

Rydberg: I really believe honestly that if you go to where the Warren Commission started, LBJ started the Warren Commission, Hoover fed the Warren Commission every bit of information, and Dr. Humes and Dr. Boswell, Dr. Perry – all the rest of them who might know what really happened – know that the evidence that was saved could not be backed up by anybody. And Dr. Humes and Dr. Boswell were facing retirement. They didn't want to lose their retirement. They both gained another rank, too.

Law: Do you think they were the type of people who would just go with the flow?

Rydberg: I think it was a chess game and they were checkmated. I think that always sat wrong with Dr. Humes, that he had to knuckle under.

Law: In essence, there was no choice?

Rydberg: No choice.

Law: So take me back to the dinner that you had with Dr. Humes.

Rydberg: We ate at the Carolina Inn. The UNC owned it. The UNC owns all of Chapel Hill, or did at the time. He wanted to make sure that I knew, from his viewpoint, that those autopsy reports were accurate. He burned them because there was too much of a mess on them. Too much blood. He was trying to back up without causing more clouds over him than I had caused in the article.

Law: So, you wrote this article basically giving the story of him burning the notes, and at some point after that, he looked you up?

Rydberg: (amused) He just showed up and just came right in the office.

Law: So how was the atmosphere at the dinner?

Rydberg: Oh, it was fine. We laughed and joked, had a drink and had dinner, in fact we had roast beef. He picked up the tab.

Law: Did he seem sincere?

Rydberg: I knew Dr. Humes well, and we laughed and joked a lot. We didn't go out drinking together, we just didn't do that, but on a professional level he was very open, very warm, very real. But playing a game of chess, sometimes, one gets checkmated. The better part of valor is to do what he did.

Law: In a best-selling book on this case, twenty something years ago it was stated that Dr. Humes would try to get information to people through subtle use of the language. You had to read the language carefully to understand what doctor Humes was saying. Would he be that kind of person?

Rydberg: Yes. And he'd know you knew if he was using that kind of language.

Law: So you knew him as a person who would do this?

Rydberg: Yes.

Law: That's interesting because he made that curious statement – when he was asked by the House Select Committee to describe where the bullets entered and exited [the head], he said: "It is impossible for the bullet to either have entered or exited from other than behind. " And that's a strange statement to make hearing that it couldn't have done anything but go in the back of the head or come out the back of the head.

Rydberg: Exactly.

Law: So, this would be a tip-off to you in essence, that Dr. Humes was implying something without coming out and saying it?

Rydberg: Yes. He was saving his name and face for the people he knew would know what he was [doing]. If you knew Dr. Humes, you'd know that he could speak that way. And you'd know what he was saying. I talked with him that night at dinner. There was nothing in that cerebral vault or the brain cavity to turn that bullet if it came in from the back and came out the right side. Brain matter has the consistency of scrambled eggs. There's nothing to turn the bullet. Why would it have come out the right side?

Law: Did you discuss this with Humes?

Rydberg: Yes.

Law: What was his reasoning?

Rydberg: That the findings were that the entrance was at the rear and the exit was at the front.

Law: Have you read either of the doctors' testimony before the Records Review Board?

Rydberg: Yes.

Law: Do you find it strange that both had trouble finding the entrance wounds?

Rydberg: No. I don't find that. If you know Colonel Finck – we'll have to plan on his factoring in on this one – usually, an exit wound is the larger of the two. But when you've got a bullet coming in from the right, and you've seen that on the Zapruder film – where Kennedy flies back, his head flies back – it really fragments. The bullet – it was like a dumdum bullet.

Law: Well, according to history, Lee Harvey Oswald used a 6.5 millimeter –

Rydberg: Lee Harvey Oswald didn't hit him from the front.

Law: According to history, the shot didn't come from the front and it wasn't a fragmenting bullet.

Rydberg: Read my book (*Head Of The Dog*). I've placed everything where it belongs. First of all, that quote-unquote "pristine" bullet they found from the neck wound that went through Connally – I'll put it that way – was not a bullet fired at the time. It was part of Oswald's but it was Ruby who put the bullet on the gurney, which was even the wrong gurney.

Law: That would seem to be how it is to me. Give me a little bit of the feeling for the personalities of these doctors.

Rydberg: Humes was an honorable man. Boswell was also honorable, but he was very – if you want the weak link, that would have been Boswell. He would have buckled.

Law: He would have caved in to the pressure, in essence?

Rydberg: He would have. But Humes would not.

Law: As you've read the testimony before the Records Review Board the doctors had trouble pinpointing the entrance wounds in the head –

Rydberg: And that's another way of speaking. They're saying the same thing – "It really wasn't there, it was really in the back, but I'm not going to say that, so I'll have to say it this way." And read between the lines.

Law: These were qualified doctors in your opinion.

Rydberg: All the doctors – any doctor that goes through medical school has about a month of forensics.

Law: So, basically, this double-speak is just that. Trying to tell you something without telling it to you?

Rydberg: Exactly. And I know exactly what Dr. Humes was doing. I've read that testimony, and I know exactly what he was saying. You get a bunch of confused old men on the Warren Commission, which they all were, plus the other assistants they had – Jerry Ford – that would be enough to confuse anybody. And they're going to come out by not saying it.

Law: So, you feel that when Humes was testifying before the Warren Commission he was trying to leave the true record without coming out and hitting them in the face with it.

Rydberg: Exactly. Because he couldn't jeopardize his retirement, he couldn't jeopardize knowing full well that Hoover was the one feeding the Warren Commission, and Johnson was watching. They only got the information that Hoover wanted them to have. And they also knew, by the time the Select Committee started, that half of all the evidence was missing, including the brain. Humes would say: "Let me review the evidence." And they would have stated, "We no longer know where it is. " In other words, you're on a floating boat on thin ice. So they had to go in just about like I did. Verbally reconstruct it.

Law: When you were having the dinner, did he say anything about the autopsy?

Rydberg: We touched lightly on the autopsy, and it was just a typical Y autopsy. An incision from the shoulder down to the sternum, straight down to the pubic area. A lot of minutiae, so to speak. They did a full autopsy on Kennedy, not a partial – it says in some of the books I've read that it was a partial. Jacqueline only wanted a partial. But it was a full autopsy, or they never would have found out about his adrenal glands, which had nothing to do with the assassination. But the more rhetoric they could throw into the report the less likely you are to single out the important parts. Now, I've seen that "death face" ["stare of death"] (photo 1) on Kennedy in the morgue in Lifton's book, which is another funny thing how he got all that information and I was never allowed to see it. But Humes was an honorable man and he was not going to go down quiet. He was going to leave messages for other people to see what he wanted to say but couldn't.

Law: Let's go to Finck.

Rydberg: The only thing I know about Colonel Finck – I did meet him, and he also reviewed these drawings – but I don't remember him being up there with Galloway and Captain Stover and Boswell and myself and Humes. But he was a very strong-armed do-it-my-way-or-no-way type colonel in the army. Special Forces and all the rest of this garbage. Intelligence, you know. That's an oxymoron (laughing). He was the one that they called to do the covers.

Law: The covers?

Rydberg: Well, look at him. He's in Calley. He's in Kennedy. He's in Pitzer.

Law: It does seem rather strange.

Rydberg: The denominator weaves a pretty strong cloth.

Law: He does seem to pop up in –

Rydberg: Any time you want it covered or you want somebody to blame, call Finck. Aptly named. He was a very deadly man, I'll put it that way. I've seen other officers like him, people in Special Forces. Like [Gordon] Liddy, that Nixon had put in his hand in a flame and burn it? That's about like him. He was one you wouldn't turn your back on. I wouldn't.

Law: Well, that sounds ominous.

Rydberg: I'll probably hear from him. If I do, I'll e-mail you (laughing).

Law: He's in Switzerland. I don't think we have too much to fear from Finck.

Rydberg: Is he living there?

Law: He's been there for many years now.

Rydberg: Yeah. I wonder why? It's where his money's at (laughs).

Law: Let's touch on Stover.

Rydberg: Stover was really a warm, caring doctor. Looked after his command. Would send flowers to someone who had lost a loved one – enlisted, or officer. He was a great guy. There's nothing negative I could say about Captain Stover. He's now suffering from Parkinson's, I believe.

Law: I have talked to him a couple of times. The interesting thing about Captain Stover is he seems to be echoed in every little part of this.

Rydberg: Well, he was a commanding officer.

Law: They asked at the Records Review Board when Riebe and Stringer gave their depositions – the pictures that were taken and the holders that the film would have been in were different. The numbers of film plates versus holders were different – and they knew this. And they said, when they were before the ARRB, that they signed receipts for an inventory list stating that all was clear and accurate. And they said that Stover basically said, "Sign it," even though they knew it wasn't accurate.

Rydberg: Well, Stringer was a GS 11 or 12. You think he's going to compromise that? He was also a medical illustrator and did beautiful work.

Law: The point I'm trying to make is that it seems that Captain Stover did know the autopsy pictures were not an accurate inventory, and yet he made these guys, or asked these guys, to sign the statement saying that the inventory was accurate.

Rydberg: Yes, and that would also go back to the same as Humes or Boswell. He had his retirement, and he had to think about himself.

Law: Given what you know of his personality, do you think this would be something he would do?

Rydberg: He would not do that unless it was under orders.

Law: Do you think that Stover was given orders from higher up?

Rydberg: Oh, yes. And higher up was the Commander-in-Chief, better known as LBJ.

Law: I guess any American would probably do what their president wanted at that point.

Rydberg: Well, no. I've got an idiot in office right now that wouldn't, but I'm not going to vote for him (laughter all round). But that's true when you're in the military, the president says something, that's what you do.

Law: Did you know [John T.] Stringer at all?

Rydberg: Yes. Mr. Stringer was an aloof department head. He ran the medical photography department. He was the head of it and the medical photographers did their photographing unless it was a big case. That's why Stringer was brought in as the head of the department.

Law: Have you seen any of Stringer's pictures?

Rydberg: Yes, I have.

Law: Now, I'm not talking of the Kennedy assassination now, I'm –

Rydberg: Medical art. I've seen that.

Law: He's been called one of the best [medical photographers] in the world. So, given that, what's your opinion on the fact that the autopsy pictures [of President Kennedy] have been called some of the sloppiest work ever done?

Rydberg: If you put a pound of manure in a five-pound bag – there was no room to work. There were so many officials in that autopsy room, according to Riebe – because we were buddies – and they had to chase some of them out, there was hardly room to do anything. You've also got to remember, Riebe told me all the photographs taken, all the film used, all the cassettes, the 4x5 negatives immediately were taken by the FBI and CIA and Secret Service. They didn't develop them, but they were developed by one of the labs in Washington under Hoover's control, so, if they were sloppy – Hoover. You can print a photograph out of focus or you can change it.

Law: But he would have, ordinarily – being the kind of person he was – he would probably try to do his best work, don't you think?

Rydberg: Oh, I think he would have tried to do his best work, but his best work is missing.

Law: Have you talked to him about this?

Rydberg: No. I rarely talked to Stringer. We weren't that close.

Law: I'm trying to get a grasp on the fellow's personality.

Rydberg: He played politics, office politics, very well.

Law: I'm just trying to get a grasp of why – other than the fact that there's such great controversy about the photographs – are they of another body, are they of Kennedy –

Rydberg: I don't think I see in the autopsy pictures – Dr. Humes told me, "make sure that right eye is blackened" because that orbital socket was fractured, and that right eye was blackened. Now even in lividity, where the blood settles to the bottom, the bruises will still show. And there is no bruise on that right eye. On that face [in the autopsy photographs].

Law: You're talking about when you had to do the drawings, correct?

Rydberg: Yes. That was one request: "Make sure that right eye is blackened. Bruised. Like you've got a black eye."

Law: Are you familiar with Stringer's style?

Rydberg: Yes.

Law: Just looking at the [autopsy] pictures, do you think that those are his work?

Rydberg: No, I do not think those pictures are the originals he took.

Law: Talk to me about Floyd Riebe and your relationship with him.

Rydberg: Riebe and I always got along. He lived in the same dorm I did. We laughed a lot and went out drinking beer at the men's club on base. He was genial – an all around good guy. And all of a sudden, I'm hearing that he's frozen up. He's not talking to anybody anymore.

Law: Did he talk to you at all? Did you ever have an opportunity to –

Rydberg: I got to ask him – we were at a bar one night – and I said: "You're under secret orders and so am I, so since we're both under the same secret orders about the same secret thing, did those drawings come close to what those wounds were?" And all he said was, "Yes."

Law: The drawings that you did?

Rydberg: Yes. I didn't ask him about the directions [of the shots]. I only asked him about the wounds.

Law: But you never did get an opportunity to discuss anything having to do with the autopsy?

Rydberg: No. He still wouldn't talk. I think the navy had one testicle and somebody else had the other one. And they were going in different directions.

Law: Well, he did come forward later. And talked about the [autopsy] pictures and that he didn't think they were the pictures that he'd taken.

Rydberg: I would not be surprised. None of us want to go down in history as the fools who unwittingly helped pull this thing off.

Law: Is there anything for the historical record that you would like people to know?

Rydberg: For the historical record – it was one of the biggest cover-ups to enhance two people's futures: Johnson and Hoover.

Chapter Thirteen

SAUNDRA K. SPENCER

D
epositions were soon to be released by the Assassination Records Review Board. Most of the listed names were familiar, but neither Debra Conway nor I had heard of Saundra Kay Spencer. So, we did what most researchers of the Kennedy assassination did in like circumstances: we contacted Mary Ferrell.[1] True to form, Mrs. Ferrell found the name in her file and a number. I called in August 1998 and explained who I was and what I was doing. It was, indeed, the Saundra Spencer.

I told her that I had never heard of her before. (I had not yet read her ARRB deposition.) She chuckled: "Well I think they were just going through papers and came upon my name." I asked if I could videotape her for an oral history. "No, I don't want to do that. I work behind the camera, not in front of it." However, she was happy to answer my immediate questions, for which I was grateful.

In November, 1963, she was petty officer in charge of the White House Laboratory at the Naval Photographic Center in Anacostia, Washington, D.C. (photo 14). Within a day or two of the assassination, a Secret-Service agent arrived, carrying films in four holders – exposures of President Kennedy's corpse.

Law: Did someone call and tell you he was coming?

Spencer: Yep. Chief [Robert L.] Knudsen had called saying that an agent would have film negatives to be developed. We were not to pay too much attention to what was on them.

Law: Did you look at the negatives?

Spencer: Yes, I had to. I had to get the color balance right.

Spencer said the agent's name was [James K.] Fox. He stayed with her while she developed the films, even in the darkroom.

---

1. Mrs. Ferrell's death, February 20, 2004, was an inestimable loss to the JFK-research community.

Spencer: They were basic shots of the president's head. He was on his back. They weren't like autopsy pictures. They did not have the incisions, you know, or the cutting of the head.

Law: Did the body have the classic Y-incision denoting the autopsy had been performed?

Spencer: I didn't see any Y-incision. The chest wasn't showing (see photo lc; the chest was "draped"). I don't know when these pictures were taken. They could have been shot in Dallas when [the Dallas doctors] started their work, or it could have been after everything was finished. There is no way to tell. I was not informed.

Law: Can you describe the wounds on the body?

Spencer: The two that I remember were at the back of his head and at his throat. The throat wound was small and slightly off to the right, about thumbnail size.

This was a startling revelation. If Spencer had developed a photograph showing a thumbnail-sized throat wound, the picture had to have been taken before the official autopsy at Bethesda. Those I had spoken to from the Bethesda autopsy had confirmed that the throat wound was an open gash as seen in the "stare-of- death" photograph (photo 1). There is no record of photographs of the corpse taken in Dallas

Spencer: The wound in the back of the head was about two and a quarter [inches] around, slightly off to the right.

Law: Was there massive damage to the head?

Spencer: No. Have you viewed the photos in the National Archives?

Law: Yes, I have (e.g. photo 3).

Spencer: There was none of the massive head trauma that is shown in those photos.

Law: Can you offer an opinion on the wound in the back of the head – was it an entrance wound or an exit?

Spencer: I don't know how it hit. There was no large wound on the face, so I think that it would have to be an exit wound. But that's just my opinion.

Law: I understand. Would you say the top and front of the head were intact.

Spencer: Yes. His face looked normal and relaxed. It didn't have the grimace that is on the other photos.

The negatives she developed were in color and of good quality.

Law: From what angles where the photographs taken?

430

Spencer: Well, I remember a three-quarter length view of the body, a profile, back of the head, and the throat. There was one of the brain next to him –

I almost screamed "WHAT?" in her ear, but somehow I maintained composure. I tried to sound nonchalant: "Was the brain whole?"

Spencer: Yes – the more I think of it – it's almost like they reconstructed his head for the photos so, if they had to show the public something, that's what they would show.

Law: Did the brain have damage to it?

Spencer: No, which surprised me and I doubt that it was his because I didn't see any cutting on [the head]. I didn't see how they could get it out.

Law: It was just beside him?

Spencer: Yes. It was next to the body (photo 5b). The head had no opening big enough to take the brain out. This set of pictures differed from those that are in the National Archives. This was a more respectful set of poses – almost like the body was posed for these pictures. But like I said, after looking at the other (National Archives) photos, I almost think these were shot in case some had to be shown. So the family and everybody could see them. I know they closed the casket, and I never could understand that from the pictures I'd seen.

She went on to say the president's body and hair were clean and free of blood. I asked about the bullet wound in the president's back: none of the photographs that she developed showed the rear of the torso.[2]

She developed and dried the negatives and then ran some test prints; in all, it took an hour or so. Agent Fox then gathered up the negatives and prints and the papers that Spencer had signed, and told her to forget that he had been there.

The ARRB seemed disappointed that she could not identify the autopsy pictures in the National Archives as the one she developed. In her opinion, they were trying to obtain as much information as possible.

If she is not mistaken about what she saw in the photographs that she printed on November 23 or 24, 1963, then Saundra Spencer is a witness to a previously unknown part of the JFK assassination. "I processed the pictures, but nobody can find them, so I don't know. They could be a figment of my imagination," she said, laughing. Turning serious, she added, "I just wish they would surface. It would end a lot of speculation about things."

---

2. If the purpose of this series of photographs was to document the wounds, it is surprising that the back wound was not included.

At Dallas's Parkland Hospital, Dr. Malcolm Perry made a tracheotomy incision over a throat wound about the size of the end of a pencil – enlarging it by a quarter of an inch to insert the endotracheal tube. In Dallas, the president's head wound was about two inches in diameter, which, again, is consistent with what she saw. On the other hand, the location/size/shape aspects of these wounds are in striking contrast with those in the extant autopsy photographs (photos 1-4 and 6).

The intact brain photographed next to Kennedy's body raises more questions. Dallas physician Dr. Robert McClelland, who had a good view of the head wound in the trauma room at Parkland said in his Warren Commission testimony, ". . . probably a third or so at least of the brain tissue, and some of the cerebellar tissue had been blasted out."

I called Saundra several more times with questions. She was always willing to help if she could. I also called her with requests from film-makers working on documentaries on Kennedy who sought her participation. She turned them down, as she did me: "I'd rather not. I developed the negatives – I wasn't [at the autopsy]

She did agree, however, to provide comments on some of the autopsy photographs. I sent an oversized set to provide space for comments and sketches. Three weeks later, they arrived back, along with a hand-written note: "William Law, I hope this helps – it does not add much to what is already known, but maybe you can see something that I didn't – Sandy Spencer." Reading her ARRB testimony about the negatives that she had developed in her Anacostia laboratory was one thing, but seeing the Kennedy autopsy photos with her hand-written annotations and sketches had a power and an immediacy that were as startling as their potential significance is profound:

Photo 1c

- No similar view was included in her "series" of photographs; instead, an oblique shot was taken from the left side.
- The towel underneath the head and shoulders was plain, without stripes.
- The eyes and mouth were closed.
- No cut was visible at the trachea, but slightly below that location was a circular "indent" of three-eighths to a half an inch in diameter.
- The chest and below were "draped."

Photo 2a

- The head was supported by a block positioned under the upper neck.

432

- There was no metal head support.

- Again, there was no neck cut and the mouth and eyes were closed.

- The fabric covering the table had no stripe.

Photo 3b

- In her series, no shot showed the direct top of the head.

Photo 4b

- The back-of-head photograph in her series was taken from the left side.

- There was no open "flap" about the right ear.

- The defect at the back of the head was circular, approximately IV2 to 2 inches in diameter, with a ragged edge.

Photo 5b

- Spencer did not see a photograph of the open skull.

- She provided a rough sketch of the upper torso and head ("skull closed"). On the left side of the head (right side of the sketch) was a ruler, then a pointer and a brain, "fairly intact. "

Photo 6b

- She saw "no shot showing bullet wounds to the back of [the] upper torso."

The presidential military honor guard guarding one of the morgue doors.

AFTERWORD-2005

Perception can be mercurial and I am well aware of the frailty of memory. Nevertheless, the human consciousness can be stamped with impressions that are indelible. Memories of seminal events can last a lifetime, and I believe this to be true for those present in the autopsy room at the Bethesda Naval Hospital on the evening of 11/22/63.

The passage of years has blurred recollection of details, and the individuals involved have, naturally, spoken with each other. They are aware of inconsistencies. Still, each continues to tell the version of events that memory dictates. It was, after all, their perceptions and feelings that I wanted to explore. I neither expected nor hoped that their stories would dovetail neatly. In fact, I would have been suspicious of collusion if that had turned out to be the case. Each had specific tasks according to his training, and each has a unique set of recollections that only partially overlaps with those of the others. And those observations and feelings, when combined with those of the witnesses in Dealey Plaza and the testimony of the doctors and nurses in attendance in Trauma Room One at Parkland Hospital, form the mosaic of conspiracy.

The Bethesda witnesses are the cornerstone of the cold-blooded conspiracy that removed the chief executive of the United States. These young men – the best and the brightest of their generation, foot soldiers on the field of history – had their idealism and innocence shattered on that long-ago November night. If the Warren Report is the official history of the Kennedy assassination, then the Dealey Plaza witnesses, the Parkland physicians and nurses and the Bethesda enlisted men are the counterbalance to that history.

Albert Einstein once said, "I do not believe God plays dice with the cosmos." And I do not believe that the life of John Fitzgerald Kennedy was ended by the lone action of a malcontent. There was order. There was planning. And there was control in the chaos of Dallas and Bethesda.

Jim Jenkins asked me, "What do you hope to gain from this? Another investigation like the one in the '70s? The whitewash of the Warren Commission? No one besides people like you and I really care." In my heart of hearts I am hoping that people do care, that the general public will not shrink in fear from the exhortation of the thirty-fifth President of the United States – "Ask not what your country can do for you, ask what you can do for your country" – and will force the powers that be into full disclosure. However, time is not on our side. I was 6 years old when John Kennedy lost his life. At this writing, I am in my mid-forties. Paul O'Connor, Jim Jenkins, and Dennis David, all in their early to late twenties in 1963, are now in their early to late sixties. Jerrol Custer passed away in July 2000, his destiny, his rendezvous with death, complete.

In the chapters on former FBI Agents Sibert and O'Neill, I stated that I believe that prosectors Humes and Boswell were aware of shenanigans with the president's remains before they received them on the night of November 22, 1963. Harold "Skip" Rydberg provides some background on how the doctors were willing to go along with being manipulated and, in turn, manipulated others. I had the pleasure of meeting Skip in Fort Myers, Florida, in 2003 when I was offered a position as a consultant to film director Brian McKenna for his documentary *Killing Kennedy*. I was brought into the project mainly due to my relationship with James Sibert, whom McKenna wanted to interview for the documentary. The long-suffering Sibert once again bowed to my request and agreed to let Brian, his cameraman Stefan, a locally hired soundman, and me invade his home for yet another interview. I had put Associate Producer John Murray in touch with Rydberg, and he had convinced the former Warren Commission artist to share his recollections on film.

Harold Rydberg is tall and lanky, with a deep baritone voice made all the deeper and somewhat raspy by years of chain-smoking. Like Paul O'Connor, Rydberg exuded warmth. He was totally relaxed, had an air of self-confidence and expressed very strong opinions about the assassination. His recollections of what he experienced at the hands of Humes and Boswell, and how his sketches were used by the Warren Commission, give us a better understanding of how all those connected to the aftermath of the assassination were compartmentalized and controlled.

The strange tale of photography technician Saundra Spencer provides another twist in this dark saga. A few days after the assassination, Spencer developed negatives – given to her by Secret Service photographer James K. Fox – which showed that the president's wounds were similar to those seen at Parkland Memorial Hospital. The wound at the back of the head was described by Spencer as about two inches in diameter, jagged, and slightly to the right of center. No damage was seen by her to the top-right area of the head or to the forehead. The throat wound she saw was "thumb-nail size," consistent with the three-quarters inch incision that Dr. Perry made across the wound to accommodate a tracheostomy tube. If Ms. Spencer is telling the truth, her testimony is some of the most explosive to come to light.

Given all that has been discovered in the intervening decades, I believe that Spencer's testimony points to a scenario that – for whatever reason – was discarded by the conspirators. She told me, "They weren't like autopsy pictures. They were more like pre-autopsy pictures. It was a more respectful set of pictures than I saw at the Archives." It seems she saw negatives exposed before the official autopsy at

Bethesda Naval Hospital, before the opening of the cranium to remove the brain, before the expansion of the throat wound either in an attempt to obscure a frontal entry or as a result of a hasty search for a bullet. Saundra Spencer is a credible witness. She worked at the Naval Photographic Center in Anacostia, where the White House had a great deal of photography work done. Her claim of being contacted by Secret Service photographer Fox and told to develop the negatives and of being asked to sign documents after which the agent collected all of the evidentiary material and told her to "forget I was here" echoes the account of Dennis David. My conversations with Saundra Spencer left me with impression that she is without guile and does not grasp why her testimony is vitally important. She did her job, did as she was told to do and went on with her life, not realizing that her memory holds pieces of the puzzle to the greatest murder mystery of our time.

Saundra's recollections give us a clearer picture of the conspiracy that took the president's life. She has not sought the limelight, turning me down for a personal interview, and rejecting requests I made on behalf of producer-director Nigel Turner and film director Brian McKenna. She did, however, agree to critique a set of National Archive Kennedy autopsy photographs, pointing out significant differences between them and the negatives she developed.

Perception, as defined by Webster's Dictionary is, "Act, process, or faculty of discernment, i.e., clearness of mental sight." No fewer than fifty-one witnesses to the event in Dealey Plaza, had the clearness of mental sight to believe that shot(s) were fired from places other than the Texas School Book Depository.

The motivations and actions of Lee Harvey Oswald are beyond the scope of this book, but it is clear from much information gathered over the years that he was more than the "lone nut" portrayed by the Warren Commission, as was Jack Ruby.

It is also clear from patterns found in documents now available to the public, and indeed noted in the interviews in this book, that even official investigations were willing to ignore conflicting evidence in the medical aspect of the assassination, for example, the Assassination Records Review Board.

None of the Review Board members believed there was a conspiracy to kill President Kennedy and stated that no evidence of conspiracy was found during their records review.[1] However, not one Board member attended any medical witness's deposition or read the transcript of any medical deposition during the lifespan of the ARRB.[2]

Inexplicably, the Warren Commission chose not to introduce the autopsy photographs and X-rays as evidence. The HSCA, although aware of major discrepancies between the head wound described by the treating physicians and the head wound described and imaged at the president's autopsy approximately 6.5 hours after the shooting, also failed to show the autopsy photographs to any of the Dallas doctors. And in a final insult to history, the National Archives refused to allow the ARRB to bring the autopsy photos to Dallas for the Dallas physician's interviews in 1998, resulting in a woefully incomplete record where no Dallas doctors have officially been shown the autopsy photos. Consequently, the ARRB's considerable focus upon events at the autopsy has done nothing to illuminate or resolve the apparent Dallas-Bethesda conflict.

Here are some interesting findings from the ARRB's work

• A review of HSCA records has revealed that two brains may have been examined subsequent to the completion of the autopsy on the body of John F. Kennedy.[3]

• In deposition under oath, Dr. Humes, one of the three autopsy prosecutors, finally acknowledged under persistent questioning – in testimony that differs from what he told the Warren Commission – that he had destroyed both his notes taken at the autopsy and the first draft of the autopsy report.[4]

• The autopsy photos were digitized pro bono by the Eastman Kodak Company on the most advanced digital scanner in the world for preservation. The digitizing should also provide assistance to those who wish to pursue the question of whether the autopsy photographs were altered.[5]

1. ARRB Final Re port, Septembe r 9, 1998.
2. The Culture of the ARRB, A Behind the Scenes Look," by former Senior Staff Member Doug Horne, Kennedy Assassination Chronicles Vol. 5, Issue 1, 1999.
3. Says Assassinations Board Report; Staff Member Concludes 2 Different Specimens Were Examined," *Washington Post*, November 10, 1998.
4. ARRB Final Report, September 9, 1998.
5. Ibid.

- There is also evidence that a variety of materials seem to have simply disappeared. Even the camera listed as the one used at the autopsy now in evidence could not be verified as the actual camera in use at the time for comparison purposes.[6]

- In a letter to the HSCA, the lawyer for the president's personal physician offered to present evidence that individuals other than Lee Oswald were involved in the murder of the president. No evidence has been found that the HSCA responded to the offer.[7]

Those still on this mortal coil – writers, researchers, and witnesses to history – continue to cry out against the indifference of the government. In the guise of national security, the bureaucracy continues to keep information we seek behind closed doors, locked and tightly guarded. From this time and place, at the beginning of the new century, we must strive to be brave. To be bold. John Kennedy often said, "It is better to light the candle than curse the darkness." If the darkness of the Kennedy assassination is ever to be exposed to light, then the members of the Kennedy family must stand with those who care deeply about the memory of their father, brother, uncle and cousin. The records that have been under their protection and control since the assassination must be released for public scrutiny. And as painful as it will be, President Kennedy's remains must be exhumed to be examined this time by the top pathologists in the nation. These actions will, hopefully, allow determination of the direction of the gunfire, and then, armed with this information, the decision of whether a new investigation is warranted can be made. Only by taking these steps will this country be able to come to grips with the nagging questions that have plagued it since Friday November 22, 1963. Until then, there can be expectation neither of truth for the living nor justice for the dead. And the indignant spirit of John Fitzgerald Kennedy will continue to call out to us across the abyss of time.

* * *

I am alone at night in Dealey Plaza. Forty years have now passed since John Kennedy took that dark ride into history. Six years have passed since my first encounter with Jerrol Custer, the X-ray technician at Bethesda. He has passed on. Were his memories accurate? I'd never know. Paul O'Connor's health had continued to decline, and there were days he could hardly

---

6. Ibid.

7. Richard A. Sprague HSCA memo, Re: William F. Illig, attorney, Dr. George G. Burkley, Vice Admiral, U.S. Navy, March 18, 1977,

walk, but still his cheerful spirit came through when we would call each other, sometimes talking about the assassination when some new theory cropped up or a new documentary had appeared on TV More often than not, we would just talk about what was going on in our lives, how the book was coming along or how Paul's beloved Florida "Gators" football team was doing. I continued to stay in touch with Jim Jenkins as well, and felt that I had gotten to know him better and gained his trust over the ensuing years, such that when I asked him and the rest of the "boys" to come to Florida for a gathering to discuss the Kennedy autopsy pictures, he brought his wife Jackie. "Don't forget about me, now," he had said in our last phone conversation. "Come to Alabama and see Jackie and me sometime. " Dennis David was now fully retired and he and his wife Dorothy planned to "travel and see some of the country." They were waiting for me back at the hotel after a joint presentation at the latest Lancer conference. The last time I had been in touch with 85-year-old Jim "Si" Sibert, he was working out three days a week; it was heartening to know that he was still so active. As for Frank O'Neill, we had not talked since the year before when I had asked him to make drawings of Kennedy's wounds for this book. "I'll do them and shoot them out to you." But, he never did.

I took one last look around the plaza. I had gotten what I had originally wanted here. I was closer to whatever "truth" there is to be found concerning Kennedy's assassination, yet still had more questions than answers. I looked toward the triple underpass."How pleasant the cool tunnel will be … " the evening breeze seemed to whisper. I turned, bowed my head against the night and walked up the incline of the grassy knoll, behind the picket fence and into the parking lot.

INTERVIEW WITH ALLAN EAGLESHAM, APRIL 2001

Law: How long have you been researching the circumstances of the death of Lieutenant Commander William B. Pitzer (photo 9)?

Eaglesham: I've been interested in the Kennedy Assassination for over 20 years and visited Dealey Plaza in 1979. I read books over the years, but it didn't become an all-consuming interest until the early 90s after I wrote a letter to the local newspaper. They had run a long article with illustrations in support of the single-bullet theory to mark the thirtieth anniversary of the assassination. So, I responded to that. Robin Palmer, who lives here in town [Ithaca, NY], saw the letter and invited me to participate on his TV show: *For The Duration*. It was a local cable-access program that from time to time covered aspects of the 1960s assassinations. I didn't have television and had never seen the show. Through Robin I met [ex-Special Forces Lieutenant Colonel] Daniel Marvin several months later. Dan had told Robin of his Pitzer connection – that the CIA had asked him to assassinate William Pitzer. So, it rolled from there. The Pitzer case has been a chief interest since mid-1994.

Law: So, basically you first got into the Pitzer story through Dan Marvin.

Eaglesham: Yes, as a logical consequence of knowing Robin, who had been working with Marvin on other things for a couple of years before Dan had told him his Pitzer story. Of course, then I was anxious to meet Dan. At that point I had published a short article in the *Fourth Decade* on the "sniper's nest," and felt it was very important that Dan tell his story for the benefit of the JFK research community in general, via the pages of the *Fourth Decade*. His article ("Bits & Pieces, A Green Beret on the Periphery of the JFK Assassination") appeared in the May 1995 issue, as a result of my encouragement, and I helped by editing and structuring it. Around that time, he was invited to be on *The Men Who Killed*

441

Kennedy television program, and again that would probably not have happened if Robin and I hadn't strongly encouraged him to participate.

Law: Now, as a consequence of all this, you were working on a book together as I understand it?

Eaglesham: Yes, that was an idea that was being tossed around. If one accepts Dan's story, that the CIA asked him to kill Pitzer, it really is potentially pivotal, assuming that the reason the CIA had a contract on his life was linked to Dennis David's story that Pitzer had a film of the Kennedy autopsy. This was obviously of critical importance, matched only by the fact that, if William Pitzer was murdered, it was covered up by the U.S. Navy and the FBI. So the implications were profound, and if they could be brought to the light of day it would be very important as a key aspect of the Kennedy assassination cover-up.

Law: So tell me, what is your opinion, now that you worked with him for a while on this, what are the circumstances now?

Eaglesham: With Dan Marvin?

Law: With Dan Marvin.

Eaglesham: An essential component of Dan's story was that he had walked out to see the CIA man at Fort Bragg with one Captain David Vanek. Dan then approached the CIA man alone, and Vanek waited out of earshot. Dan was offered the contract on Pitzer's life, he declined that contract, walked away, then the CIA man walked towards David Vanek, and if you read Dan's article and see him on *The Men Who Killed Kennedy* it can be interpreted that David Vanek may have assassinated William Pitzer. Recently, however, Marvin has stated that it was never his intention to implicate Vanek. On *The Men Who Killed Kennedy*, he mentioned his efforts to trace Vanek, whereas when the ARRB found Vanek and sent an affidavit from him refuting all of Marvin's claims, Marvin then played down the potential importance of how Vanek could support Marvin's story that they had, indeed, met a CIA man that day at Fort Bragg – which seemed strange to Robin Palmer and me.

Of course, we don't know what the CIA man said to Vanek, but at least Vanek could have supported the story that they did meet the CIA man, which would be consistent with Dan's contention that he was asked to kill William Pitzer. But Marvin showed no immediate interest in contacting Vanek himself. As I said, this seemed peculiar to Robin and me, and when he wrote back to the ARRB [in response to the letter from Timothy Wray, of the ARRB, informing Marvin of Vanek's existence – Marvin had told Palmer and me that he'd been told anonymously that Vanek had died], he was suddenly vague in his recollections of the events of the day on which he said he was solicited by the CIA agent. In *The Men Who Killed Kennedy* and in his *Fourth Decade* article, he says that he walked out with Vanek, and they chatted as they walked along, and he is one hundred percent certain that the man who was with him was David Vanek. And yet in his letter back to Timothy Wray of the ARRB, his words were along the lines of: the man I think was Vanek – the man I believe was Vanek.

Therefore, Palmer and I asked him at that point, "What is it Dan? Are you certain or are you uncertain? How close were you to Vanek that day? And, he said, "Well, Vanek was standing maybe about 40 feet away in the shade of the trees – that was as close as I came to him that day. So I really can't be absolutely certain that it was Vanek." And again, William, if you go back and check the story, he said that he had walked out with Vanek to meet the CIA agent. This may seem to you or to anybody else like a qualitative difference, but for Palmer and me it was a concrete difference that was underpinned by how very evasive Dan became and how uncomfortable he seemed with the conversation, how he cut it short and exited just as soon as he possibly could.

Robin and I very, very reluctantly were forced to the conclusion that Marvin was hiding something. We had stuck our necks out in supporting his various controversial claims, therefore we felt a moral obligation to bring this development to the attention of the JFK research community, and we attempted to do that by writing to Jerry Rose, editor of the *Fourth Decade*. We asked Jerry to publish a letter telling the community of our misgivings, and asked him to send a copy to Marvin, to get his response, and let the readership of the *Fourth Decade* be the judge. But, Jerry chose not to do so. Instead, I posted the letter on the Internet.

And so, we came to doubt Marvin's story relating to David Vanek. And that's the thin edge of the wedge. If he's less than certain of that aspect of the story, and becomes evasive, we feel you have to regard everything else that he says with circumspection.

Law: This caused you to walk away from the project you were working on with Marvin, but you did carry on your research on Bill Pitzer by yourself?

Eaglesham: I continued my interest in William Pitzer. I did have a couple of contacts with Marvin. He called me about something – he clearly was uncomfortable about the breakdown in the relationship with Robin and me, and, on two or three occasions, he tried to patch things up. But I felt it was impossible to maintain a working relationship.

This all happened in February and March of 1997. For many, many weeks there was no contact between us. Suddenly the phone rang one evening and it was Dan saying that his FOIA request for FBI files on the Pitzer investigation had come through. He said they were dynamite: Pitzer's fingerprints weren't on the gun, and other factors were consistent with Pitzer having been murdered. Did I want to come over and look at the documents? I said, "Well, let me think about it, let me sleep on it." Next day we spoke again on the telephone: "I'd like to see the documents, but can I copy them?" He said, "No, I don't want you to copy them." So I said, "If I can't copy them, then the information is of no use to me; if I tell people there's evidence that Pitzer was murdered, but I can't produce any support for that evidence, no one will believe me. So, I'm not interested in seeing the documents unless I can copy them." That is where it lay for a couple of weeks; then he called again, early on a Sunday evening, saying that he had just been on the phone with Robin, who had a video of Dan's that he wanted back. Robin had said, "Well, Dan, if you give us a copy of the FBI documents, I will give you your video back! " And, surprisingly, Marvin agreed. He said to me, "I have a copy here. Robin is busy, so can you come over and collect it now?" Which I did.

I started reading the documents immediately, of course, and, my goodness, they were very confusing. There were about a hundred and fifty pages, which I arranged in chronological order and after two or three readings I began to see how strongly the new information was consistent with murder and inconsistent with suicide. At that point again I felt an obligation to bring this potentially important information to the attention of the JFK research community.

Law: So, tell me, you've read the report – you've written an in-depth article on it, touch on some of the points that you feel why Bill Pitzer was murdered.

Eaglesham: The wounds. The fatal wound was to the right temple, entering at the right temple, exiting above and slightly behind the left ear. There's been a lot of talk in the literature that Bill Pitzer was left-handed, and would not have shot himself in the right temple. Mrs. Pitzer is on record as saying he was not left-handed, he was right-handed. So that's not part of this thinking. However, the information in the FBI documents is very specific. There were no powder bums on the skin; if the muzzle had not been in contact with the skin, but he did kill himself, there would have been powder burns around the wound. And in their interviews with the FBI, the autopsy doctors stated that there was no muzzle mark. As a result, the FBI did tests to see how far away that gun would have been held, so that, when it was discharged, there would be no powder bums. The results of that test are in the FBI report and they state that the gun would have to be held three feet or more away. Try aiming a gun to your head from a distance of three feet – not easy to do. Lieutenant Commander Steyn, U.S. Navy medical examiner, saw the body – he was the official who was called in to declare death. He saw the body approximately ten minutes after it was discovered. He described a wound in the left temple. The body was lying on its right side with the right side of the head towards the floor. The left side of the head was exposed. The navy medical examiner described a wound to the left temple. The autopsy report, where it covered the overall appearance of the body, described an entry wound in the right temple and the exit wound behind the left ear; it made no reference to the visible wound in the left temple that was described by the navy medical examiner as he saw the body lying on the floor. However, the autopsy report described a third hole in the skull at the left temple, which was visible only after removal of the brain. Now, you might say, "Okay, it's possible that there would be a third hole in the skull if the bullet fragmented as it passed through and a fragment spun off and hit the skull on the inside. However, the autopsy report is specific in terms of the path of the bullet through the brain; there's no evidence in the description of that path that there was any fragmentation of the bullet. In other words, William, they described a hole in the left temple of the skull bone, that apparently had no counterpart in terms of a lesion in the brain or in the skin.

Law: Just a hole in the skull itself?

Eaglesham: Just in the skull bone itself. Interestingly however, the hole in the skull bone itself was in the left temple at the same general location as the wound that is described by the navy medical examiner. Now, there's another complicating component to the wounds aspect. For reasons that I'm still not quite certain of, the Montgomery County medical examiner was called in. He arrived around 9:15, and made a cursory viewing of the body soon after he arrived. But didn't make a detailed examination of the body until 11:30. I don't know why there was such a time delay there. However, this civilian medical examiner, Dr. Ball, was specific in saying that he inquired as to whether the body had been moved or the crime scene had been changed in any way, and he was told, "No." The crime scene and the body were as when found. Dr. Ball described a wound that had a muzzle mark and powder burns, in complete contrast with the entry wound described in the autopsy report. Unfortunately, Ball did not specify the location of that head wound. Again I have to ask you to visualize this: that the body is lying with the right side of the head to the floor, and the left side of the head exposed. Dr. Ball said he examined the body untouched. I think it's not too much of a stretch to deduce that Dr. Ball was describing the wound in the left temple that was described also by Lieutenant Commander Steyn, the navy medical examiner. In other words, there was a wound, a bullet wound, in the left temple that had muzzle marks and powder burns, which was not described in the autopsy report.

Law: So what does this point to, to you?

Eaglesham: This indicates to me that the autopsy report had to be consistent with suicide. And two entry wounds, one on one side of the head and one on the other are not consistent with suicide. Maybe that is too much of a conspiracy theorist view of things, but I would like to hear it if someone can provide a more plausible explanation. You have four men who are experts in terms of seeing and working with dead bodies, two medical examiners and two autopsy doctors. Two of these people are saying one thing and two are saying another. I don't think there's any way in which you can reconcile this without part of the explanation being that two of the people, i.e., the autopsy doctors, were not giving all of the information in the autopsy report. Or, the autopsy report that is currently available is not the full report, because the full report would have been more indicative of homicide rather than suicide. I think the obvious explanation is there's a component of a cover-up. The physical evidence is much more indicative of a homicide then a suicide, and personally I believe that Bill Pitzer was murdered. The other side of that coin, of course, is that two Navy inquiries and one FBI inquiry all came to the conclusion that Lieutenant Commander Pitzer committed suicide. That conclusion, however, is not based on the physical evidence. The opinion of suicide is based on people saying that Pitzer was over-worked and depressed. On the other hand, the interviews by the FBI show that no one thought he was so depressed that he was likely to commit suicide. Now some of the things that Bill Pitzer said in his last few days of his life can be construed as indicative of someone contemplating suicide, such as after two friends died within a few days, he said, "I wonder who the third one will be?" Okay, one can take that as indicative of suicide if, in fact, it's underpinned by physical evidence that also indicates suicide. But the ruling of suicide was based on third-party opinion, completely ignoring the physical evidence.

Law: I'm a little confused about the ballistic tests and what they showed. Reading from the article: "The same bullet in the cylinder had been discharged in that weapon. Neither the cartridge or the live round in the revolver were Special ammunition and must have been loaded with extreme difficulty, according to the FBI lab report."

Eaglesham: Yes, the gun that was found on the floor beside the body was a .38 Special. That information can be gleaned only by looking carefully at the hand-written lab notes of the ballistics expert. The FOIA release included the FBI report on their investigation, as well as ancillary documents that were generated as part of the preparation for that report. The ballistics expert, in his hand-written notes, states that this revolver was a Special, whereas everywhere else it was referred to only as a ".38 S&W." I believe there's not necessarily a discrepancy there, because the non-Special type of revolver was essentially obsolete at that time. It's likely that just in saying .38 it could be assumed that it was a .38 Special. However, the slug found on the floor near the body was not from a Special bullet. It was from an old non-Special type of bullet. I hope I'm not getting completely confusing at this point. The Special is a longer bullet that packs more punch. The non-Special bullet is shorter and is actually a little fatter then the Special. It is difficult, and can be impossible, to load a non-Special bullet into a Special revolver. Whoever fired that revolver that day, therefore, apparently went to some effort to get that non-Special bullet into it. Does that make any sense?

Law: Yes, it does, and that's what I wanted to try and understand. I wasn't quite grasping the significance of the regular .38 versus the Special. Tell me about the blackboard in Pitzer's office with the indentation.

Eaglesham: There was a blackboard at the scene that had an indentation. That indentation was cut out and processed by the FBI for metal deposits. It did have metal deposits and the indications are that the indentation resulted from a bullet strike. However, when one considers the position of the blackboard, the position of the body, and the position of the spent slug, the investigators believed that there had to have been a point of ricochet. It was impossible for Bill Pitzer to have killed himself where he had been standing or sitting, for that bullet to then hit that blackboard and end up about six feet from the body. The angles just weren't right. So the investigators from the FBI and Naval Investigative Service tried to find that point of ricochet in the studio, but were unable to do so.

Law: So, we have an indentation on the blackboard that doesn't really fit with any of the trajectories.

Eaglesham: Exactly. There were bone particles on the spent slug that was found on the floor, however, no bone particles were reported to be associated with the indentation in the blackboard. If that bullet passed through Bill Pitzer's brain and picked up bone particles, and then hit the hard surface of a blackboard, it seems to me highly likely that some of those bone particles would be left behind on the indentation of the blackboard, but that didn't seem to happen.

Law: The blackboard was completely clear of bone particles?

Eaglesham: Apparently.

Law: No bone or brain matter?

Eaglesham: Nothing mentioned at all in the report.

Law: Did William Pitzer have any family?

Eaglesham: Yes, he was a family man, with a wife and two sons.

Law: Now as I understand it, Bill's wife has never been comfortable with the thinking that her husband committed suicide.

Eaglesham: That's correct.

Law: Have you talked to Mrs. Pitzer at all?

Eaglesham: I haven't talked to her, no. Dan Marvin called her on two occasions that I know of, and I have the tape recordings of those conversations. And it's clear to me that on both occasions she was uncomfortable with Dan raising this whole issue again. She believes – now this is my interpretation – that Bill was murdered and that nothing positive can be gained by unearthing the whole thing.

If it turns out that it was murder, it is important to keep in mind the possibility that it had nothing to do with the JFK autopsy. In that case, it's important to understand that it does not preclude the validity of Dennis David's story. In other words, a film of the JFK autopsy may yet exist. William Pitzer's expertise was in closed-circuit television, which was a new and evolving field at that time. According to Dennis David, he had in his possession a copy of a film of the autopsy on President Kennedy's body, and pictures and slides made from it, early in the week after the assassination. However, the FBI record of who was present at the autopsy does not include the name of William Pitzer. People who were there have stated that Pitzer was not present. Jerrol Custer is a notable exception. At one time Mr. Custer said that Pitzer was taking photographs and later in his interview with you he claimed that Pitzer took movie film of the activities there. However, John Stringer told me that Bill Pitzer was definitely not in the autopsy room that evening – but I'm getting a little ahead of myself. I put two and two together here. Accepting that Bill Pitzer was not in the autopsy room that evening, is it possible that he could have obtained a movie film by some other means? I asked various researchers whether they had any evidence at all that the autopsy room was wired for closed-circuit television, and none had. I'd been in touch with Denis Morissette, a researcher in Canada, about various things over a period of time, and at that stage he had written some questions to Commanders Humes and Boswell, which gave me the idea of doing the same to inquire about closed-circuit television in the autopsy room. By one of those funny quirks of fate, just two or three days after I got a letter off to Jim Humes, I received an e-mail from Denis saying he had been in touch with Barb Junkkarinen, an old e-mail JFK friend of mine, who had shared with Denis that she had evidence of closed-circuit television in the autopsy room from Commander Humes himself, in his testimony to the ARRB.

Law: He let it be known that there was closed-circuit television in the room.

Eaglesham: He let it slip. My interpretation of how the question and answer session went is that he let it slip that the autopsy room was wired for closed- circuit television. He divulged that the autopsy room was wired for closed-circuit television, but said that the system wasn't switched on that evening. Anyway, I had the information that I had been looking for, for two or three years. Then probably a week or two later, the phone rings and I pick it up and there's an unfamiliar voice saying, "This is Jim Humes." And I thought he said "Jung" as in Carl Jung, "This is Jim Jung"; suddenly I realized James Humes was calling me! He said that he didn't remember whether the autopsy room was wired for closed- circuit television at that time, which contrasts with what he said to the ARRB when he was reminiscing about activities in the autopsy room, but it's interesting that, again, he was quite certain that the autopsy wasn't recorded on closed-circuit television. So, I'm saying that the hardware was there, the expertise was there, and Dr. Humes shared the information that he had worked closely with Bill Pitzer in producing movie films for medical training purposes: those movies were produced on video and then were transferred to movie film.

Law: What I find extremely interesting is that Humes or Boswell, any of the doctors are not known for divulging any information and hardly speak to or write to researchers as a rule (laughter from Eaglesham) and here you have Dr. Humes calling you!

Eaglesham: I know, William, and I don't blame you if you find it hard to believe. I can only tell you that it's the truth.

Law: No, I believe you – I'm just astounded – you struck a nerve somewhere.

Eaglesham: Yes, I may have struck a nerve. He said he'd read the article – I'd enclosed the first article published in JFK/Deep Politics Quarterly – and I now wonder if that was the wrong thing to do. Anyway, he said he'd read it and he said he believed that Pitzer committed suicide and that I was barking up the wrong tree. But – he called. A couple of other things: Last year I had a conversation with someone who is close to the Pitzer family, which produced two interesting underpinnings. Bill Pitzer went into work on the evening of the Kennedy assassination. He went into work – he thought he might be needed. Another member of the Pitzer family has also assured me that he was called into work that evening for special duty.

Law: So he was there.

Eaglesham: Apparently, he was there. Secondly, after he died, the Pitzer residence was searched by the navy.

Law: Is that standard procedure that you know of?

Eaglesham: I've tried to find out and different folks say different things.

Law: Is there a general consensus among the people you've asked?

Eaglesham: I don't know enough people to ask. Dennis David, for instance, found it highly significant. Other people have said it might be routine because William Pitzer had top-secret clearance. But it's such an unusual circumstance that very few people have had experience of it.

* * *

As a result of Allan Eaglesham's continued research into the death of William B. Pitzer, the Cold Case Squad of the Naval Criminal Investigative Service has reviewed the U.S. Navy files, and those of the FBI, on the Pitzer case. In July, 2000, Allan was informed by the NCIS that, without photographs from the autopsy on William Pitzer's body, it is impossible to justify reopening the investigation. The Pitzer case is closed, again.

Note added in proof by Allan Eaglesham:
  I made contact with William Pitzer's son, Robert, in June of 2000, and suggested that he attempt to obtain possession of a photograph taken at the scene by means of a FOIA request. Eventually, Mr. Pitzer obtained a copy of the photograph, and on 14 July 2001, I received a copy of it from him. I took

449

it to Herbert L. MacDonell, Professor of Criminalistics and Director of the Laboratory of Forensic Science, Corning, NY. Professor MacDonell examined the photograph and an enlargement I had made of the head area. He was not surprised when I told him that the subject had been found to have committed suicide. However, he was surprised when I said that, officially, he had committed suicide by shooting himself in the right temple. Without prompting from me, Professor MacDonell had concluded from his viewing of the photograph and the enlargement that there was a bullet wound in the left temple, indicating homicide.

In August 2002 – with my help – Mr. Pitzer obtained copies of photographs taken at the autopsy on his father's body He refused to share copies with me, but allowed researcher Kenneth Hersh to see them. It was clear to Mr. Hersh that there was no bullet wound in the left temple. Therefore, the strongest evidence for homicide is no longer applicable. However, a critical component is whether the wound in the right temple bears characteristics of a contact shot – consistent with suicide – or characteristics of a shot from more than three feet – indicative of homicide. At Mr. Pitzer's request, Mr. Hersh arranged for forensic experts to view the photographs; however, at the last moment, Mr. Pitzer declined to cooperate.

In March 2004, I saw some of the autopsy photographs and confirmed the absence of a wound in the left temple. The right-temple wound had the characteristics of a tight-contact shot, consistent with, but not probative of, suicide. I was not given any copies. Efforts continue to obtain these photographs by FOIA in order to have them examined by forensics experts and the results made public. More information and updates may be obtained at http://www.manuscriptservice.com/Pitzer.html.

PHOTO SECTION

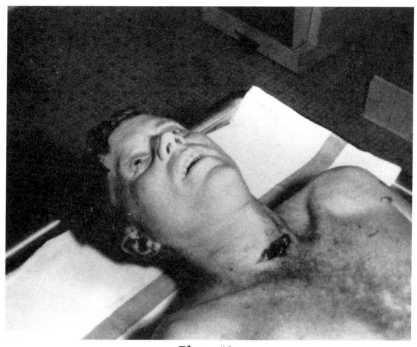

Photo #1.
The 'stare of death."

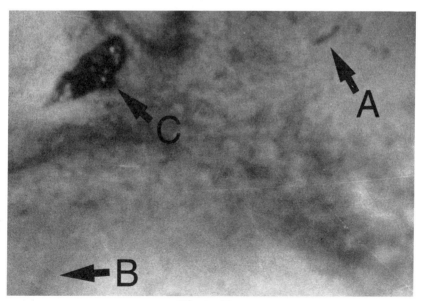

Photo #1a.
A and B indicate cuts made at Parkland hospital;
C indicates the margin of the bullet wound in the throat.

Photo #1b.
Wooden object or X-ray machine?"

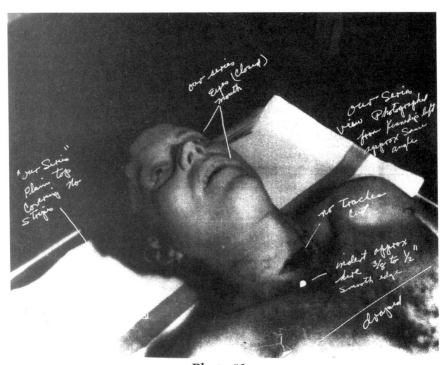

Photo #1c.
Saundra Spencer's rendering of the so-called stare of death photograph.

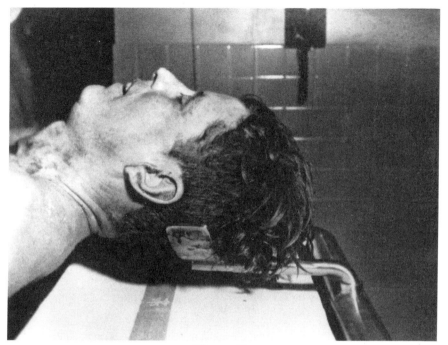

Photo #2.

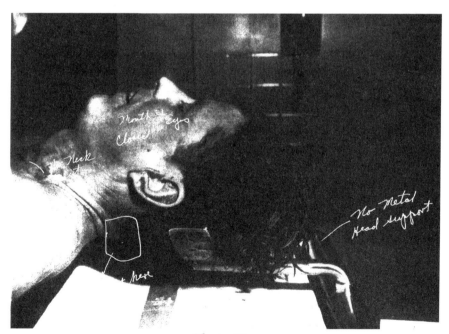

Photo #2a.

Note where Ms. Spencer has drawn in a chalk block under Kennedy's neck with the annotation: no metal head support.

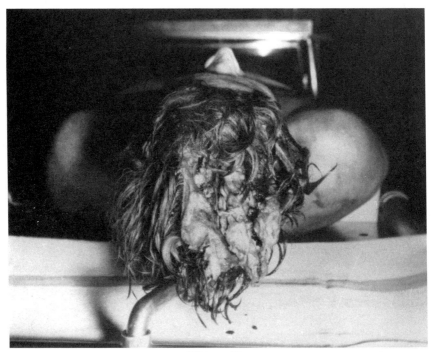

Photo #3.

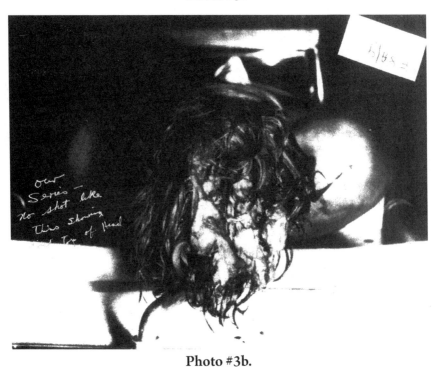

Photo #3b.
Annotations by Saundra Spencer.

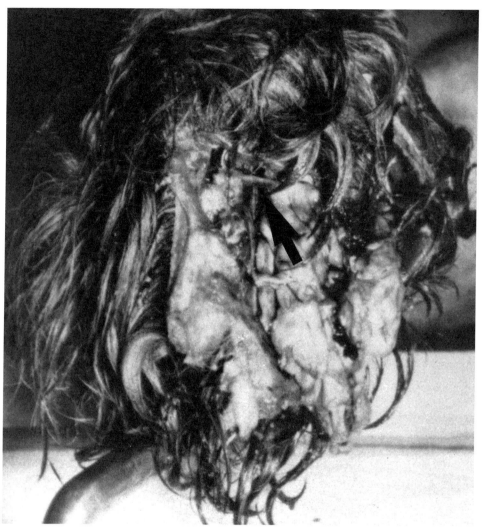

Photo #3a.
Indicating the "clip."

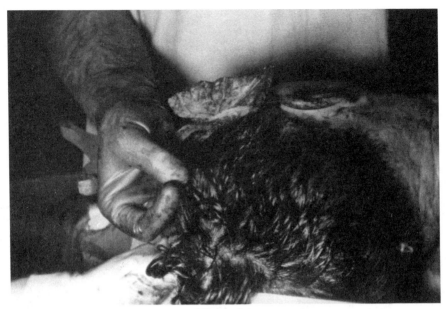

Photo #4.

Note the so-called "bat wing" flap of bone above Kennedy's right ear. This later fell off during the examination of the head?

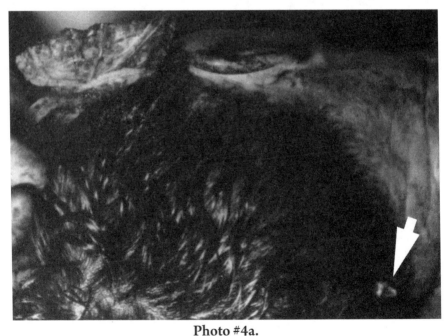

Photo #4a.

Brain Matter or bullet wound?

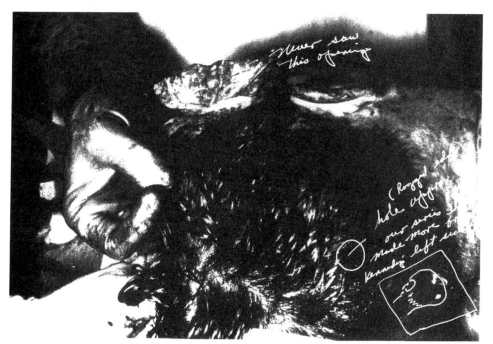

Photo #4b.
Annotations by Saundra Spencer.

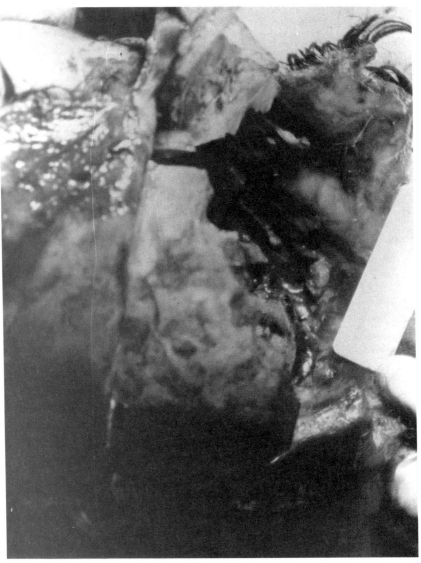

Photo #5.

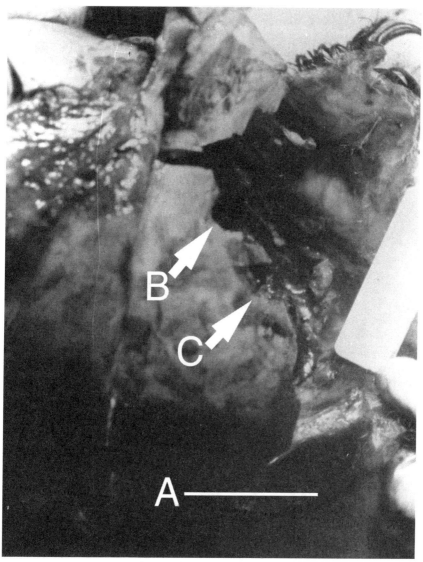

Photo #5a.
A indicates the nuchal line; B and C indicate notches in the skull bone.

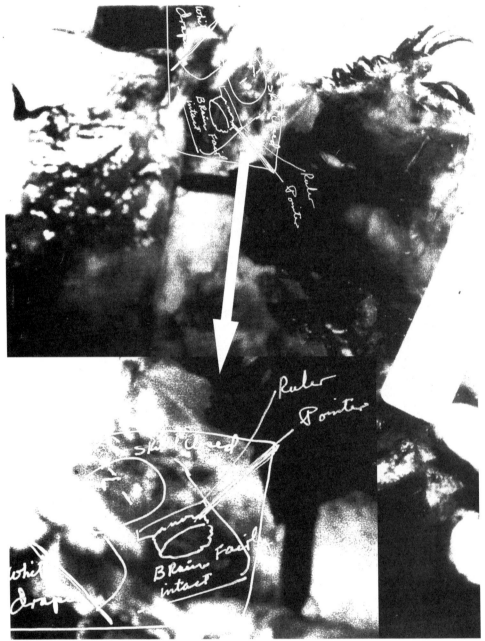

Photo #5b.
Annotations by Saundra Spencer.

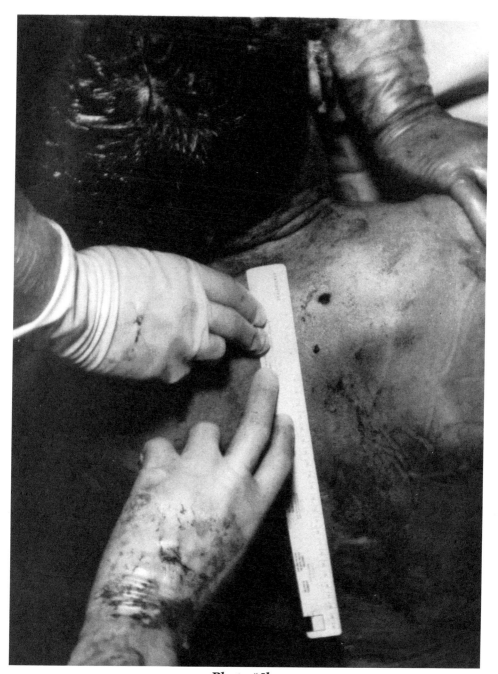

Photo #5b.
This bullet wound to Kennedy's back was not seen at Parkland Hospital due to failure of the doctors and nurses to turn the President over, at any point during their examination.

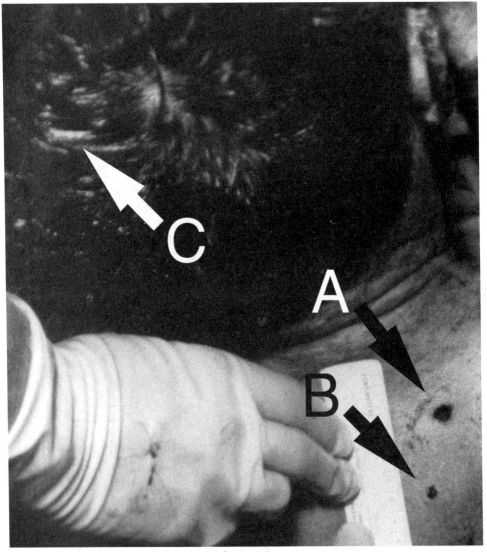

Photo #6a
A indicates a probable entry wound and B a spot of dried blood;
C indicates possibly a suture needle; D is the cowlick.

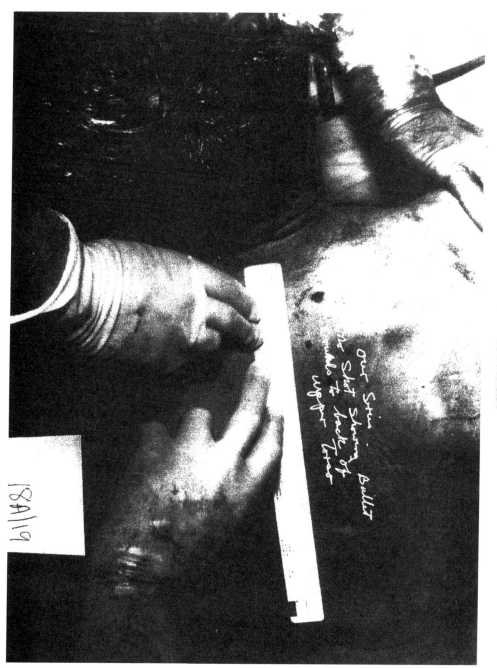

Photo #6b
Annotations by Saundra Spencer.

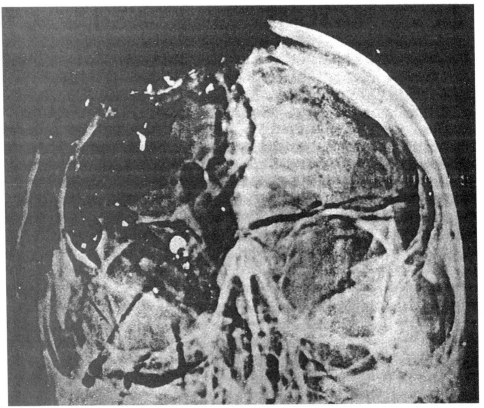

Photo #7

Anterior-posterior (AP) X-ray. Note large bullet fragment on right side of Kennedy's skull. This was not seen at any point on the night of November 22, 1963 by anyone present in the Bethesda morgue. It was only seen years later, in 1968 during the so-called Clark panel hearings.

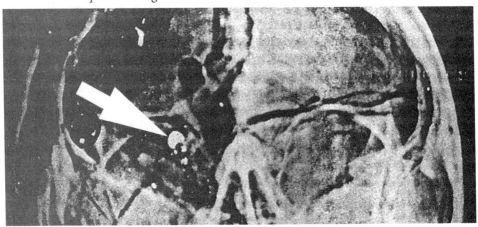

Photo #7a.
Indicating a 6.5-mm diameter metal fragment.

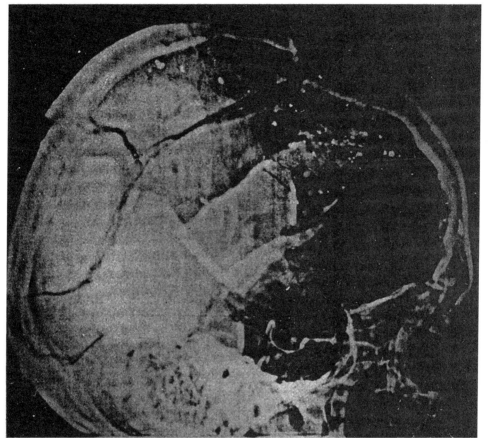

Photo #8
Right lateral X-ray.

Note regarding photos 1-8: On November 23, 1963, James K. Fox, the Secret Service photographic expert, was given the autopsy film holders by JFK's personal physician, Admiral George Burkley, and told to develop them. At that time he made three sets of black and white autopsy photo prints at the Secret Service lab. On November 27, 1963, additional official copies were made at the Naval Processing Center. Copies of these photos were later given to JFK assassination researcher Mark Crouch who then made them available to JFK researchers. In 1992, the autopsy photos were specifically exempted from the JFK Records Act. ARRB Senior Staffer Doug Horne stated at the JFK Lancer 1998 Conference that these unofficial photos are cropped differently and are not as clear or precise as the originals in the National Archives. Viewing the "Fox Set" is the only way this evidence is available to the public.

The X-rays are exhibits from the HSCA hearings and were obtained from the National Archives.

Photo #9

(L–R) John Stover, unknown, unknown, Harold Rydberg and William Pitzer.
(courtesy of Harold Rydberg).

Right Upper Back of JFK

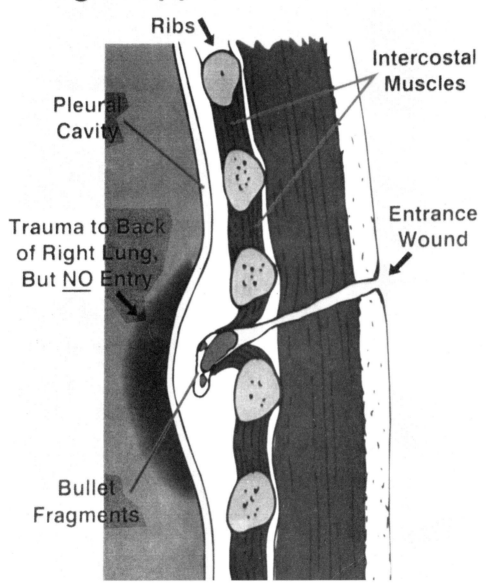

Photo #10

Paul O'Connor's sketch of the back wound. This drawing was done at the direction of Paul O'Connor. The bullet fragments drawn here have added some confusion over the years. There was never any bullet fragments found in the back wound, O'Connor added these in the drawing to show what should have been there

(courtesy of Paul O'Connor).

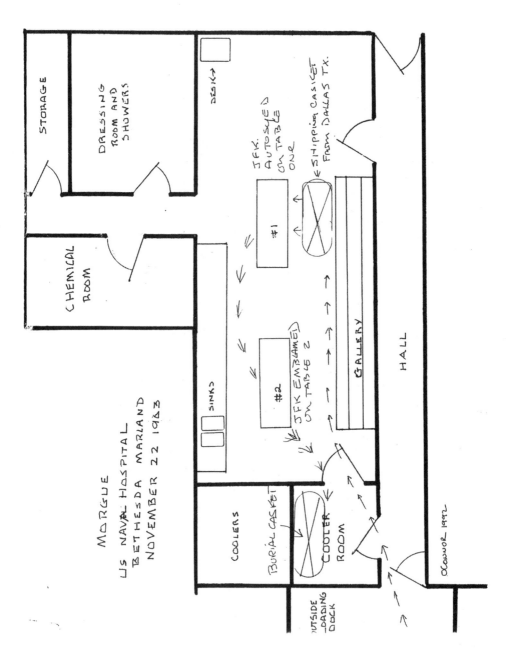

Photo #11
Paul O'Connor's sketch of the morgue.
(*courtesy of Paul O'Connor*).

URGENT 11-23-53   2-00   AM TRC

TO DIRECTOR AND SAC, DALLAS

FROM SAC, BALTIMORE

ASSASSINATION OF PRESIDENT JOHN F. KENNEDY.

BUAGENTS MET PRESIDENTIAL PLANE ON LANDING AT ANDREWS AFB, MD.
AND ACCOMPANIED MOTORCADE IN WHITE HOUSE CAR TO NATIONAL NAVAL
MEDICAL CENTER, BETHESDA WHERE AUTOPSY PERFORMED. AUTOPSY
WITNESSED BY THREE SECRET SERVICE AGENTS, TWO BUAGENTS AND
ATTENDING PHYSICIANS AT CENTER.

TOTAL BODY XRAY AND AUTOPSY REVEALED ONE BULLET ENTERED
BACK OF HEAD AND THEREAFTER EMERGED THROUGH TOP OF SKULL. PIECE
OF SKULL MEASURING TEN BY SIX POINT FIVE CENTIMETERS LATER FLOWN
IN FROM DALLAS HOSPITAL AND XRAYS BETHESDA DISCLOSED MINUTE
METAL FRAGMENTS IN THIS PIECE WHERE BULLET EMERGED FROM SKULL.
TWO METAL FRAGMENTS REMOVED FROM BRAIN AREA, ONE IS SEVEN BY TWO
MILLIMETERS AND THE OTHER IS THREE BY ONE MILLIMETERS. THESE
TWO METAL FRAGMENTS HAND CARRIED BY BU AGENTS TO FBI. LAB.

ONE BULLET HOLE LOCATED JUST BELOW SHOULDERS TO RIGHT OF
SPINAL COLUMN AND HAND PROBING INDICATED TRAJECTORY AT ANGLE
OF FORTY FIVE TO SIXTY DEGREES DOWNWARD AND HOLE OF SHORT
DEPTH WITH NO POINT OF EXIT. NO BULLET LOCATED IN BODY.

END PAGE ONE

MR. BELMONT FOR THE DIRECTOR

SEVEN

PATHOLIGIST OF OPINION BULLET WORKED WAY OUT OF BACK
DURING CARDIAC MASSAGE PERFORMED AT DALLAS. IT IS NOTED
THAT SECRET SERVICE AGENT RICHARD JOHNSON TURNED OVER TO BULAB
ONE SIX POINT FIVE MILLIMETER RIFLE BULLET, PAREN APPROX
TWENTY FIVE CAL PAREN, COPPER ALLOY, FULL JACKET, WHICH HE ADVISED WA
FOUND ON STRETCHER IN EMERGENCY ROOM AT DALLAS HOSPITAL. AT TIME
IT WAS NOT KNOWN IF STRETCHER WAS THAT WHICH HAD BEEN USED FOR PRESI-
LENT.

SECRET SERVICE HAS FULLY COOPERATED WITH BUAGENTS AND ADVISED
WOULD MAKE PHOTOS TAKEN OF AUTOPSY AND XRAYS AVAILABLE AT BU
REQUEST.

Photo #12

Teletype dictated by FBI SA James Sibert at 2 AM, 11/23/63

Photo #13

Dennis David gave orders to unload a plain metal shipping casket at the back of the Bethesda Naval Hospital morgue some twenty minutes before the official ambulance containing the Dallas gasket arrived. *(Picture courtesy of Dennis David).*

Photo #14

Saundra Kay Spencer was petty officer in charge of the White House laboratory at the Naval photographic Center in Anacostia Washington DC. Within a day or two of the Kennedy assassination Spencer was brought negatives in 4x5 holders by James K. Fox, the Secret Service photographer and told to develop the negatives. Spencer told the author that they were a set of negatives that showed President Kennedy's body in a more respectful pose than the autopsy photographs we have today in the National Archives. These negatives and test prints made by Spencer have never been seen and are not in the existing collection at the National Archives. *(Picture courtesy of Saundra Spencer).*

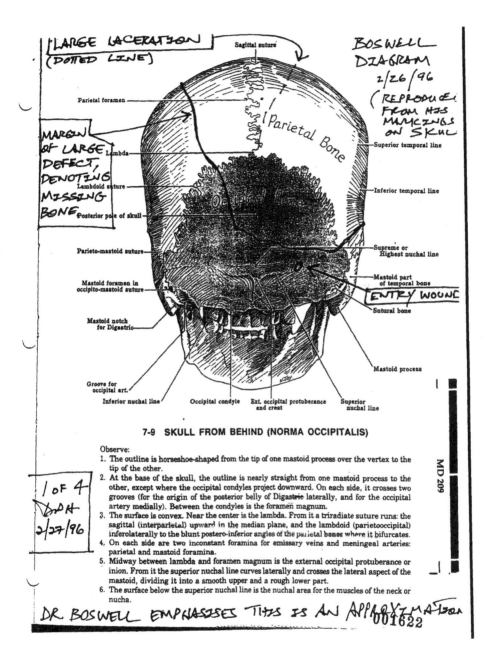

7-9 SKULL FROM BEHIND (NORMA OCCIPITALIS)

Observe:
1. The outline is horseshoe-shaped from the tip of one mastoid process over the vertex to the tip of the other.
2. At the base of the skull, the outline is nearly straight from one mastoid process to the other, except where the occipital condyles project downward. On each side there are two grooves (for the origin of the posterior belly of Digastric laterally, and for the occipital artery medially). Between the condyles is the foramen magnum.
3. The surface is convex. Near the center is the lambda. From it a triradiate suture runs: the sagittal (interparietal) upward in the median plane, and the lambdoid (parietooccipital) inferolaterally to the blunt postero-inferior angles of the parietal bones where it bifurcates.
4. On each side are two inconstant foramina for emissary veins and meningeal arteries: parietal and mastoid foramina.
5. Midway between lambda and foramen magnum is the external occipital protuberance or inion. From it the superior nuchal line curves laterally and crosses the lateral aspect of the mastoid, dividing it into a smooth upper and a rough lower part.
6. The surface below the superior nuchal line is the nuchal area for the muscles of the neck or nucha.

DR. BOSWELL EMPHASISES THIS IS AN APPROXIMATION

001622

Photo #15

Representation by Doug Horne (ARRB) of J. Thornton Boswell's description of the head.

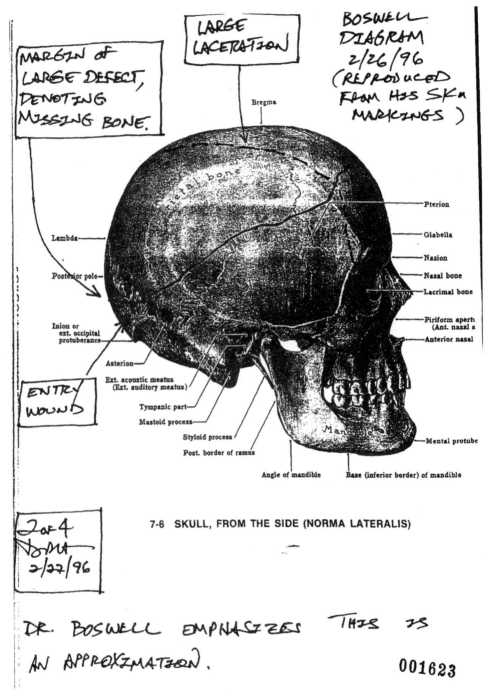

Photo #16

Representation by Doug Horne (ARRB) of J. Thornton Boswell's description of the head.

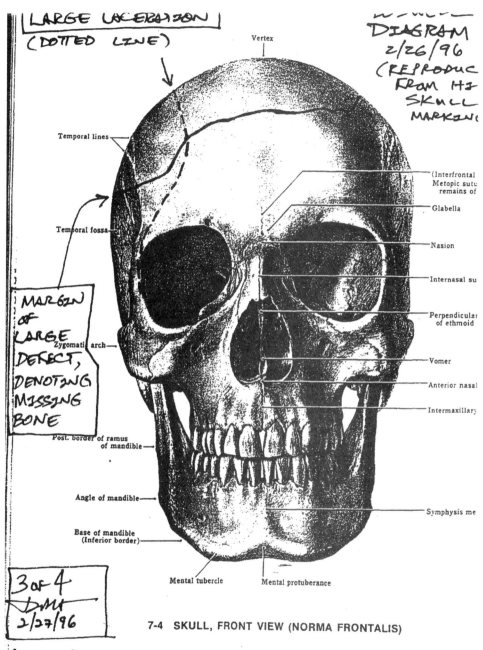

LARGE LACERATION
(DOTTED LINE)

DIAGRAM
2/26/96
(REPRODUC
FROM H?
SKULL
MARKIN(

Vertex

Temporal lines

Temporal fossa

(Interfrontal
Metopic sutu
remains of

Glabella

Nasion

Internasal su

Perpendicular
of ethmoid

Vomer

Anterior nasal

Intermaxillary

MARGIN
OF
LARGE
DEFECT,
DENOTING
MISSING
BONE

Zygomatic arch

Post. border of ramus
of mandible

Angle of mandible

Base of mandible
(Inferior border)

Symphysis me

Mental tubercle

Mental protuberance

3 OF 4
DWM
2/27/96

7-4 SKULL, FRONT VIEW (NORMA FRONTALIS)

DR. BOSWELL EMPHASIZES THIS IS
AN APPROXIMATION.

001624

Photo #17
Representation by Doug Horne (ARRB) of J. Thornton Boswell's description of the head.

475

Name ..... *John F. Kennedy* ..... Age .....

Place of Death ..... *Dallas Texas* ..... Phone .....

Res. Address ..... WHITE HOUSE ..... Res. Phone .....

Sent by ..... *Col. Miller* ..... Date ..... 11/22/62 ..... Time ..... 4:35 P.M. ..... Received by ..... B

Remove to ..... WHITE HOUSE FROM USNH ..... By ..... U.S. GOVT. AMBULANCE

Physician ..... Address ..... Phone .....

Autopsy ..... YES — USNH (BETHESDA, MD) ..... Cause of Death .....

Conveyance No. U.S. ..... Embalmer ..... JOHN VAN HOESEN — ED STROBLE — TOM ROBINSON ..... Autopsy Chart by .....
NAVY AMBULANCE ..... (UNDER SUPERVISION- JOSEPH E. HAGAN)

Flowers ..... Florist ..... Price .....

Arrangements:—When ..... 11 P.M. ..... Where ..... S.R. ..... Certificate Data ..... by USG

Car to Call:—Address ..... US GOVT - OK ..... Time ..... Ordered by .....

Suit ..... own - OK - JEH ..... Dress .....

Other garments ..... 11 - OK JEH.

Dressing: When ..... soon as embalmed ..... Lady Attendant .....

Hair Instructions .....

Length ..... Width ..... Depth .....

Remarks:

All preparation, dressing, casketing done at Bethesda - USNH.

CASKET ORDER ..... EIREH

Style No. ..... MARSELLUS 710 ..... Stock No. 3737

Size ..... 6/6 ..... Color ..... MAHOG. ..... Plate ..... NO ..... Crucifix ..... NO

Urn No.

Remarks: *Body removed from metal shipping casket at USNH at Beth*

CASKET DELIVERY DETAILS

Date ..... 11-23-1963 ..... Time ..... 2 A.M. ..... Place ..... U.S. NAVAL HOSPITAL

Catafalque & Pedestal ..... BY U.S.GOVT. ..... Catholic Equipment: ALL BY WHITE HOU
JEH OK ..... OK JE
..... OK

Flower Racks ..... Lady Attendant ..... Metal lining Keys ..... Dressing Case ..... Flag ..... Kits .....

..... doz Chairs ..... doz. Fans ..... Date ..... Time .....

Remarks: .....

Case or Vault ..... Style No. ..... Wilbert-Triune ..... Size ..... 30 x 86 ..... Color ..... Bronze

Cemetery ..... Shipping ..... Handles ..... Plate ..... Delivered to ..... Arl. Cemetery

Date ..... Time ..... Vault ordered by ..... J.F. Edison ..... Case delivered by .....

MD 129

Photo #18

Funeral-home document stating, "Body removed from metal shipping casket…"

476

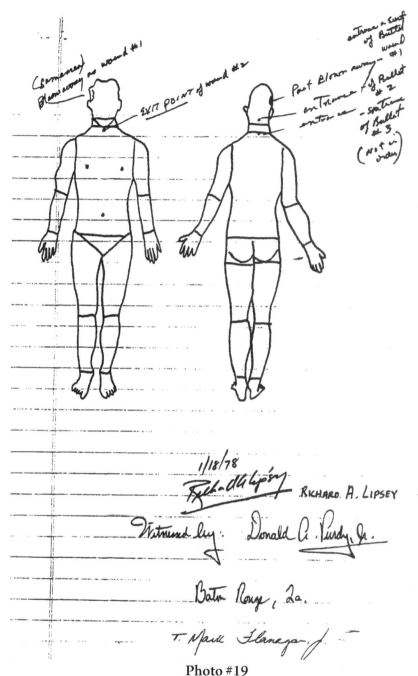

Photo #19
Richard Lipsey's sketch for the HSCA.

Entrance or exit of bullet

Part blown away - wound #1

Entrance of bullet #2

Entrance of bullet #3

(Not in order)

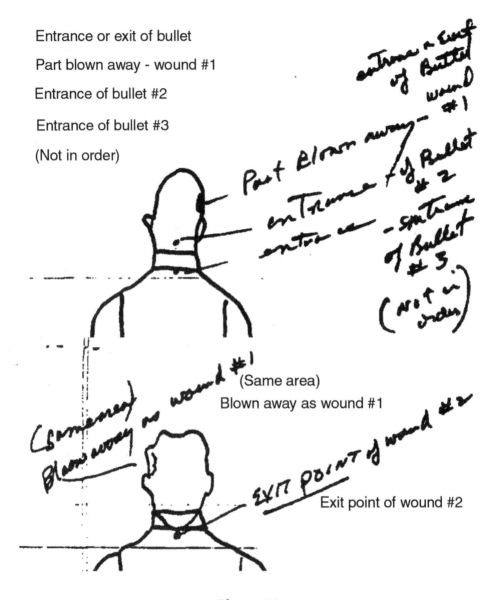

(Same area)

Blown away as wound #1

Exit point of wound #2

Photo #19a

Richard Lipsey's annotations indicating an entry wound at the hairline at the back of the head and an exit wound over the right ear.

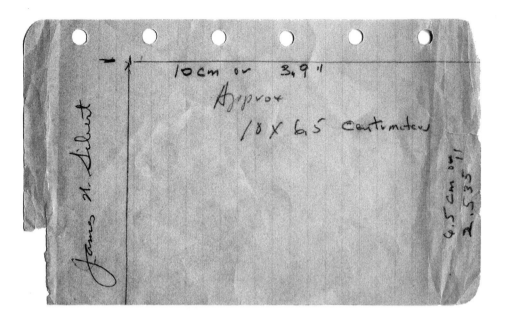

Handwritten notes on image:
10 cm or 3.9"
Approx
10 X 6.5 Centimeters

Photo #20

3.9 x 2.5 inches (10 x 6.5 cm), approximating the area of a skull fragment delivered to the autopsy room.

Sibert pulled out small paperback book titled The Two Oswald's *and took out this small yellowed piece of paper. Sibert had years before tried to figure out the size of John F. Kennedy's head wound from his own memory and drew the measurements himself. When I asked Sibert if he would draw me a duplicate copy in his own hand, he handed me the original. "Here, you can have this one," he said..*

The President's body was removed from the casket in which it had been transported and was placed on the autopsy table, at which time the complete body was wrapped in a sheet and the head area contained an additional wrapping which was saturated with blood. Following the removal of the wrapping, it was ascertained that the President's clothing had been removed and it was also apparent that <u>a tracheotomy had been performed, as well as surgery of the head area, namely, in the top of the skull</u>. All personnel with the exception of medical officers needed in the taking of photographs and X-Rays were requested to leave the autopsy room and remain in an adjacent room.

Photo #21

Paragraph from the report of FBI Special Agents Sibert and O'Neill stating that surgery had been performed on the head.

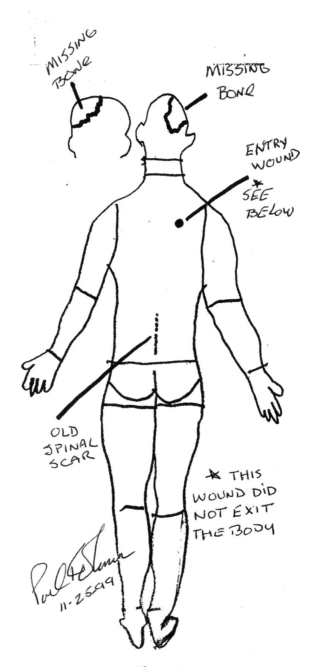

Photo #22

Paul O'Connor's sketch indicating his recollection of the extent of the head wound and location of the back wound. (*courtesy of Paul O'Connor*)

Index